You've a meeting in Katowice, a convention in Tashkent, in fact, there's a chance for business opportunities all over Eastern Europe.

Don't leave the airline to chance.

Next time you find yourself travelling to Eastern Europe, there's only one name you need to know, Lufthansa. We fly to 22 destinations over 290 times a week from Germany and offer nearly 300 flights a week to Germany from the United Kingdom.
In fact, when it comes to Eastern Europe, Lufthansa is the airline you know you can trust to get you there.
For reservations and information please contact your travel agent or call Lufthansa on 0345 252 252.

Lufthansa offers the following number of weekly flights:

Almaty	4	Odessa	2
Baku	2	Prague	43
Belgrade	6	Riga	10
Bucharest	14	Sofia	14
Budapest	36	St Petersburg	12
Ekaterinburg	2	Tallinn	4
Katowice	4	Tashkent	2
Kiev	7	Tirana	2
Ljubljana	13	Vilnius	7
Minsk	8	Warsaw	45
Moscow	47	Zagreb	12
Novosibirsk	2		

 Lufthansa

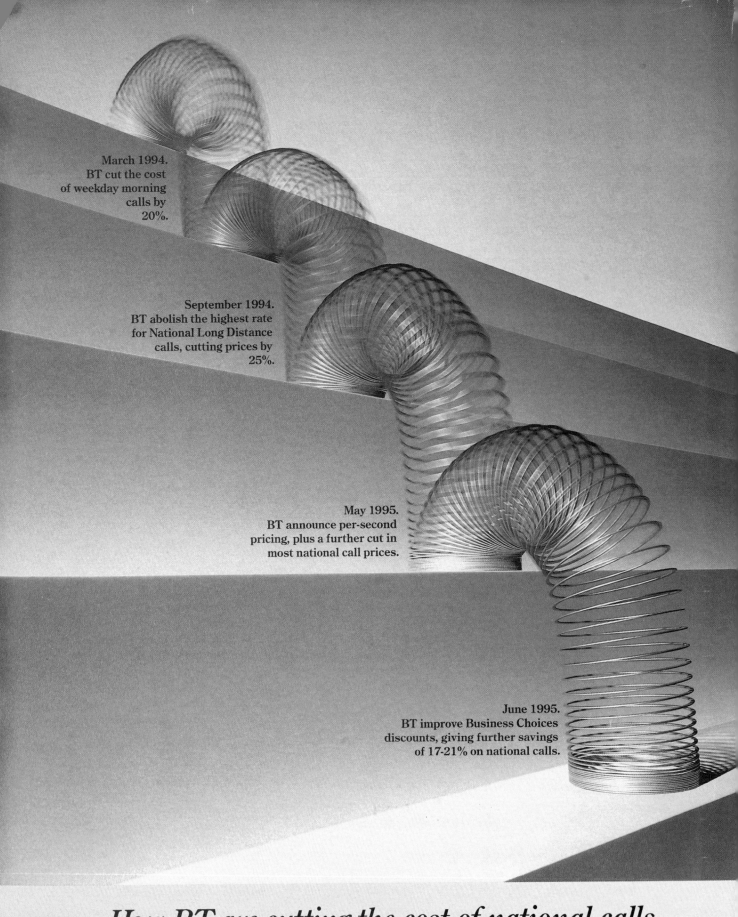

March 1994.
BT cut the cost
of weekday morning
calls by
20%.

September 1994.
BT abolish the highest rate
for National Long Distance
calls, cutting prices by
25%.

May 1995.
BT announce per-second
pricing, plus a further cut in
most national call prices.

June 1995.
BT improve Business Choices
discounts, giving further savings
of 17-21% on national calls.

How BT are cutting the cost of national calls.
A step-by-step guide.

As you can see, BT are constantly taking steps to cut the cost of doing business by phone and fax.

Our national call prices, in particular, have been steadily tumbling.

18 months ago, a 3-minute national daytime call made in the morning cost 50p. The same call now costs less than 30p.

And with our Business Choices discount scheme, you could mak additional savings of 17-21%.

To find out more about BT's commitment to cutting business ca prices, call **Free**fone *0800* **800 890** now.

It'll cost you 0p a minute.

You're better off with **BT**

CBI

EUROPEAN BUSINESS HANDBOOK

1996

General Editor
ADAM JOLLY

Foreword by
SIR BRYAN NICHOLSON
President, Confederation of British Industry

ZYGMUNT TYSZKIEWICZ
Secretary General, UNICE

Endorsed by
UNICE

KOGAN
PAGE

First edition published in 1993

This (third) edition published in 1996

This handbook was compiled based on information correct in June 1995.

Apart from any fair dealing for the purposes of research or
private study, or criticism or review, as permitted under the
Copyright, Designs and Patents Act, 1988, this publication may
only be reproduced, stored or transmitted, in any form, or by
any means, with the prior permission in writing of the
publishers, or in the case of reprographic reproduction in
accordance with the terms of licences issued by the Copyright
Licensing Agency. Enquiries concerning reproduction outside
those terms should be sent to the publishers at the
undermentioned address:

Kogan Page Ltd
120 Pentonville Road
London N1 9JN

© Kogan Page 1996

British Library Cataloguing in Publication Data

A CIP record for this book is available from the British Library.

ISBN 0 7494 1798 6

Typeset by DP Photosetting, Aylesbury, Bucks
Printed and bound in Great Britain by
Unwin Brothers Ltd, The Gresham Press, Old Woking, Surrey

Management Buy-Out of
Red Star Parcels Limited
from
British Railways Board

Equity provided by:
BZW Private Equity Limited

Debt provided by:
TSB Commercial Finance Limited

The undersigned advised the purchaser

_____

September 1995

**This announcement appears as a
matter of record only.**

KPMG Corporate Finance

Banco do Brasil

1. The Brazilian Market – A great opportunity

The implementation of the stabilization program, in July 1994, was a milestone for the Brazilian economy. Consumer and business confidence grew in response to the dramatic fall in inflation. Increase in both output level and employment rate have been reported. Policies have provided dramatic economic improvements like the reduction of trade barriers and the change in economic policy regime, which allows for more clear and far-reaching information. The excellent results of such a stabilization plan are represented in the rise of 5.7% of GDP, reaching US$ 531 billion in 1994.

2. The Real Trade Partner

Banco do Brasil sees its foreign trade financing operations as an important strategy for its positioning in the international and domestic markets. As such, it can offer you a wide range of traditional and tailor-made banking products and also effective consulting & advisory services on the Brazilian market.

3. International Capital Market

Banco do Brasil established a unique international securities house – BB-Securities – incorporating and centralizing the extensive resources and trading operations of the Bank. Using an extensive client and investor base worldwide, it actively participated in numerous Eurobond issues, having managed or co-managed eleven of them. These particular issues helped borrowers raise over US$ 1 billion.

In addition to its dedication to the primary market, BB-Securities has also been very active in the secondary market, effecting a large number of trades in Eurobonds, Brady Bonds, Medium Term Notes, Commercial Papers and other securities in the international market. For further information, please contact us at:

BB Amsterdam
Tel. (3120) 625-5942
Fax. (3120) 625 3241

BB Barcelona
Tel. (343) 487-2772
Fax. (343) 487 1949

BB Hamburg
Tel. (49) 40-361340
Fax. (49) 40-365866

BB London
Tel. (171) 606-7101
Fax. (171) 606-2877

BB Milan
Tel. (392) 805-2801
Fax. (392) 890-0265

BB Zurich
Tel. (411) 221-3183
Fax. (411) 211 9053

BB Brussels
Tel. (322) 289-5200
Fax. (322) 502-8244

BB Lisbon
Tel. (3511) 315-8406
Fax. (3511) 523-3180

BB Madrid
Tel. (341) 431-1872
Fax. (341) 575-2607

BB Paris
Tel. (331) 405-35530
Fax. (331) 405-35500

BB Rome
Tel. (396) 488-0707
Fax. (396) 488-2984

BB Vienna
Tel. (431) 512-66630
Fax. (431) 512-1042

The business is foreign trade.

The right partner is Banco do Brasil.

The new foreign trade practices are changing the attractive Brazilian market. Banco do Brasil maintains the tradition in innovating and leads the process. Here is why:

• 45 units in 32 countries, linked via BB Worldnet, allow you to identify foreign trade opportunities with Brazil.

• 905 correspondent banks in 145 countries.

• Almost 5,000 domestic branches, strategically located over the country.

• 5,500 outlets at Mercosur can be reached

through a mutual cooperation agreement with the major Latin American banks.

• Specific credit lines plus all traditional products, which keeps the bank ready to achieve the Continent integration.

To take advantages of all that, Banco do Brasil offers you its subsidiaries: BB Leasing Company, in New York; BB Securities, in London; BB Europe, in Brussels, which operates in the financial market with the guarantee of an European Union bank; Banco do Brasil AG,

in Vienna - the business gateway for Eastern Europe emergent markets. As you can see, Banco do Brasil keeps your convenience in mind, assisting you from the identification of business opportunities up to its final foreign exchange transactions. So, think it over: if foreign trade is your business, Banco do Brasil is your right partner.

 **BANCO DO BRASIL**

LONDON 34 King Street, P.O. Box 131 London ECV2-8ES England Phone: (4471)6067101 - Fax (4471)6062877 **NEW YORK** 550 Fifth Avenue - P.O. Box 4449 New York - NY 10036-USA Phone: (1212)6267000 - Fax (1212)6267045 **TOKYO** New Kokusai Building, 4-1 Marunouchi 3 - Chome, Chiyoda-Ku - P.O. Box 1726 Tokyo 100-Japan Phone: (813)32136511 - Fax (813)32841923

HELP PROTECT SOCIETY
AGAINST DRUG SMUGGLING

If you know or just suspect somebody of involvement in DRUG SMUGGLING - DON'T JUST IGNORE IT-REPORT IT.

All information will be treated IN CONFIDENCE so call our 24 HOUR ACTION LINE.

You need not give your name.

INFORMATION LEADING TO AN ARREST WILL BE ELIGIBLE FOR A CASH REWARD.

DRUG SMUGGLING ACTION LINE
0800 59 5000
(ALL CALLS FREE)

Can your business help?

It is not only private individuals who can help us fight drugs trafficking. Through our UK Anti-Drugs Alliance initiative, we have already signed Memoranda of Understanding with 90 companies, establishing an Alliance business membership of over 10,000 individuals.

The Alliance recognises the value of the specialist knowledge people have in their own work area. In particular, the ability to distinguish unusual activity or events outside the norm, even a small detail that is not quite right - it could indicate a drugs consignment.

With information gained from the trade, Customs can effectively target "high risk" consignments while facilitating the movement of legitimate goods and traffic as we all operate in a more liberalised trade environment.

For more information, please contact: Gill Castle, Customs Directorate, HM Customs and Excise, New King's Beam House, 22 Upper Ground, London SE1 9PJ. Tel: 0171- 865 4761.

RING THE HOTLINE: 0800 59 5000 IF YOU THINK YOU HAVE INFORMATION THAT CAN HELP US.

H M CUSTOMS & EXCISE

Contents

Contents

Contents

Contents

Contents

Contents

Foreword

UNICE warmly welcomes the 1996 edition of the *CBI European Business Handbook*.

This is now well established as a most valuable tool for companies wishing to do business in our continent.

1996 will see the start of yet another inter-governmental conference (IGC), whose aim will be to revise the Treaty on European Union so that it can function with 25 or 30 Member States. Business, through its national and European organizations, must help to steer the IGC negotiations in the right direction. The background to its message could be as follows:

Economic crises do not have only negative effects. The deep recession Europe suffered from 1992–94, provoked very healthy self-examination. It led to careful diagnosis of our ills and to prescription of remedies to make our economies more competi-tive, more dynamic and more job-creating.

However, the medicine is bitter and unpleasant to take. Deep structural reforms are essential before unemployment can be brought down to tolerable levels. That will require considerable political cour-age and determination.

Yet there is no alternative. To succeed in a global economy, Europe must compete with the best. Capital is highly mobile and will flow to where pro-spects are most attractive. To draw in its rightful share of inward investment, Europe, therefore, needs to compete not only on the quality and price of the goods and services that it sells, but also on the 'investor-friendliness' of its regulatory and fiscal frameworks.

Now that the economic crisis is receding, will our political and business leaders have the courage to apply the necessary remedies? Will they take the politically unpopular measures essential to bring about fundamental reforms? Above all, are they prepared:

- to go the whole way in implementing the Single Market?
- strictly to apply competition rules, including reduction, then abolition of, State aids?
- to stick to the EMU convergence criteria and move resolutely towards the single currency?
- to open-up the European market – in strict accordance with multilateral trading rules – especially to Eastern and Central Europe?
- to make all markets, but especially the labour market, far more flexible?
- to reduce and simplify national and European Union regulations?
- to reduce the size and role of the State in our economies, in particular, though not exclu-sively, through reform of the social protection systems?
- to encourage entrepreneurship and facilitate creation and development of SMEs?
- to reform the education and training systems, so they meet the needs of the twenty-first century?

Of course, competitiveness is not an end in itself, but it is the indispensable means for achieving growth, job creation and prosperity. As such, the 1996 Intergovernmental Conference must put it at the forefront of all policy-making at European level. The cost of failure to do this will be very great. The prize for success is the preservation of Europe as a place in which it is good to live, work, invest and do business.

Zygmunt Tyszkiewicz
Secretary General, UNICE
the Union of Industrial and Employers'
Confederation of Europe

Foreword

Welcome to the 1996 edition of the *CBI European Business Handbook*.

1996 will be a milestone in the development of the European Union, with the Ingergovernmental Conference raising fundamental questions about the future of the Union.

This handbook opens with a look at the developing constitutional background against which you will be doing business in Europe. What might be the implications of a single currency? What will social Europe mean for you? Who will be members of the Union in the next century? These are questions we cannot avoid.

But, as always, the focus is on practical information to help you do business in the European market. The advent of the Single Market has been the biggest single change to the business landscape in my career. No longer are we British or French or German companies trading in British or French or German markets. For more and more of us, Europe is our market. In business, at least, it is true to say that we are all Europeans now!

I must thank all our member companies and our sister federations across Europe who have provided invaluable sketches of the lie of the land in each country and sector. Without them we would not be able to identify the progress we have made in developing the right conditions for business in Europe and more importantly, the areas where we need to push still harder.

I am confident our efforts will come to fruition in the business opportunities described in the *CBI European Business Handbook*.

Sir Bryan Nicholson
President, Confederation of British Industry

The Contributors

Howard Archer is Research Manager of Market Intelligence, the Natwest Group.

David Atkins is Publications Manager at The Monks Partnership.

Rob Bailey is an analyst in the Greene Belfield-Smith division of Touche Ross Management Consultants, and recently authored *The Continental European Visitor Attractions Survey*, published by Touche Ross.

Bruce Ballantine is Chairman of Business Decisions Ltd and editor of UNICE Competitiveness Reports and the UNICE Regulatory Report.

Nick Barnes is European Property Researcher at DTZ Debenham Thorpe, London.

Mia Bartonova is Deputy Managing Director at Research International World Service, a worldwide research consultancy with special focus on Eastern Europe, the Middle East, Asia and Africa.

David Blacklock is Director of Siddall & Company.

Ben Brittain is the General Manager of the London office of Bank Austria.

Richard Brooks is the Founding Partner of Wavehill Consultants, established in 1992 to provide economic and strategy consultancy to local government, the European Commission and the private sector.

Andrew Brown is Director General of the Advertising Association.

Daniel Byk is Head of Division A2, Eurostat.

Lynn Campbell is Managing Director of Lloyd's Registrar Quality Assurance.

Peter Cotterell is Secretary General of the National Exhibitors Association. He is also author of *Conferences – An Organiser's Guide* and *Exhibitions – An Exhibitor's Guide*.

Philip Daubeney is Chief Executive of the Electricity Association.

Dr Ross Davies is Director of the Oxford Institute of Retail Management, Templeton College, Oxford.

Mark Ebert is Global Coordinator of UBS's M & A efforts. UBS is Switzerland's biggest bank in terms of assets, shareholders' equity and market capitalization, and is a global provider of a wide range of financing, trading, asset management and advisory services.

Robert Edwards is a Tax Partner at Arthur Andersen.

Niall Fitzgerald is Vice-Chairman of Unilever and Chairman of the CBI Europe Committee.

James Flynn is a Partner with Linklaters & Paines in Brussels.

Paul Forrest is Senior Economist at Moscow Narodny Bank Ltd.

Mike Grabner is Director of BT Europe.

Faye Gregory is Sales and Marketing Director at LinguaTel.

Philip Hanson is an Industrial Consultant for IBM UK Ltd.

Rachel Hoey is Manager of Thomas Cook Commercial Foreign Exchange.

Carl Hopkins is a Partner with Nabarro Nathanson.

David M Howell is Business Development Director – Europe, at WS Atkins International Ltd.

Adam Jolly is projects editor of *CBI News* and has worked on a series of CBI guides on doing business in Europe. He writes regularly on emerging markets across the world.

Helen Jones is Tax Manager at Arthur Andersen.

Dr Alexander H G Rinnooy Kan is President of the Confederation of Netherlands Industry and Employers.

David Kern is Chief Economist and Head of Market Intelligence at the Natwest Group.

Kirk Kleine is Research Assistant at the University of St Gallen, Switzerland.

Georg von Krogh is Professor for Business Administration at the University of St Gallen, Switzerland.

Ralph Land is Chairman of UNICE East and Central Europe Relations Working Group.

Jonathan Langston is Director of BDO Hospitality Consulting, the UK member firm of BDO International, one of the largest accounting and business organizations in the world.

Tony Lucking is an Air Transport Consultant.

Neil Martin is Manager of the Centre for Construction Market Information.

Colin Maud of Achilles Information is Chairman of the CBI Public Procurement Contact Group.

Kip Meek is Director of Spectrum Strategy Consultants Ltd.

Les Middleditch is Director of Sales and Marketing for Business Travel International, which is a joint venture company comprising of the world's leading business travel agents. Its founding partner is Hogg Robinson BTI.

Paul Morgan is Head of Marketing and Regulatory Affairs at Telia International Ltd.

Denis Mortier is Chairman of the European Venture Capital Association.

Liz Mortlock is Media Relations Manager at British Gas.

David Murray is a Management Consultant at Maine Consulting Services and chairs the Professional and Technical Board at the Institute of Quality Insurance.

Gerry O'Brien is an Associate for Wavehill Consultants.

Lynn Oxborrow is a Research Fellow at the Nottinghamshire European Textiles and Clothing Observatory at Nottingham Trent University.

Chris J Pickles is the Director of the European Association of Securities Dealers.

Dr Heinrich von Pierer is President and Chief Executive Officer of Siemens AG.

Renato Pieri is Professor of Agricultural Economics at the Catholic University of the Sacred Heart, Piacenza, Italy.

Vicky Pryce is a Partner of KPMG, responsible for corporate strategy. She has wide-ranging experience of strategy issues on a pan-European basis, with particular reference to former COMECON states.

Daniele Rama is Assistant Professor of Agricultural Marketing at the Catholic University of the Sacred Heart, Piacenza, Italy.

Sylvia Riot is Senior HR Consultant at Towers Perrin.

Johan Roos is Professor of Strategy at the Institute for Management Development, University of St Gallen, Switzerland.

Kate Seekings is a Consultant in the Greene Belfield-Smith division of Touche Ross Management Consultants and has previously worked for the World Travel and Tourism Council. She wrote *The Politics of Tourism*.

Graham Shuttleworth is Associate Director of the National Economic Research Associates. He helped to set up the Electricity Pool for England and Wales and also advised the European Commission on the cost of transmission access. He co-authored a study of the French Single Buyer proposal.

John Siraut works for Ernst & Young's European Location Advisory Service. Ernst & Young have undertaken a wide range of location studies for companies establishing or relocating European HQs.

Derek Smith is UK Coordinator at ESST, Innovation in European Businesses, Ecole Polytechnique Fédérale de Lausanne.

G J Squires is a member of the National Fraud and Investment Group at Coopers & Lybrand and is based at their London Forensic Accounting Offices. He was formerly Head of the City of London Fraud Squad.

Lee Tate is Vice-Chairman of the EDI Association, which aims to encourage improvements in the efficiency of industry, commerce and government by taking a lead in promoting the widespread use of electronic commerce. He is currently Director of ICL Sorbus, the customer service arm of ICL.

Charles Thoma is a Consultant in KPMG's London office, specializing in corporate strategy and location issues.

Stephen Tromans is Partner and Head of the Environmental Law Department at Simmons & Simmons.

Simon M Trappes-Lomax is Agent and Market Analyst for Jones Lang Wooton in Warsaw.

Gry Ulverud is a representative of the Confederation of Norwegian Business and Industry in Brussels.

Chris Voss is BT Professor of Total Quality Management at the London Business School.

Professor Norbert Walter is Chief Economist of the Deutsche Bank Group.

Richard Warren is Course Director of the Euro-Managers Programme at South Thames College.

Graham Watson is a Partner in the Greene Belfield-Smith division of Touche Ross Management Consultants and has over 25 years' experience in the tourism and leisure industries.

James Wilson is Senior Vice President, Europe Region for TNT Express Worldwide, Europe's leading express distribution company.

Tim Wood is Managing Director of Corporate Development Partners.

Peter Young is International Director of the Adam Smith Institute.

PART

1

The Constitution of Europe

Creating a Europe that Works

Niall FitzGerald, Vice-Chairman of Unilever & Chairman of CBI Europe Committee

British business is firmly committed to being at the heart of Europe. As a statement, this should be unremarkable. Access to European markets is central to the UK's business prosperity, helping us create wealth and jobs, providing a stable basis for trade in a fiercely competitive world. Countries to the east are clamouring for entry, eager to enjoy the obvious benefits.

The views currently expressed by some politicians from all sides, however, make me want to shout it from the rooftops. If we are to improve Europe's global competitiveness, create a successful Single Market, provide a climate for more jobs to be created and secured, then we must be fully involved in the process. Of course, there are areas that need improving, and criticisms that rightly should be made, but we must be positive. We cannot afford to be less than 100 per cent committed – it is in all of our interests. We all need a Europe that works.

I see this clearly from within a £30 billion business, which competes effectively around the world but derives its strength from £16 billion turnover generated across Europe. We are greatly indebted to our founding fathers who had the vision to see what could be achieved by working together within Europe. We have at times been fierce critics of the inefficiencies and unwieldy bureaucracy of the European Union (EU), but always with constructive intent. We want it to work.

But business can only do so much; government

has an equally important role to play. I know, through my dealings with colleagues in other member states, that the UK is losing credibility as a negotiating partner in the EU. Political divisions over Europe and the hyperbolic statements which result have often been misguided and are deeply damaging. The splits make it harder to do business and harm our economic interests. Unity is not just an issue for the political parties, but for us all.

The government must reestablish its credibility as a negotiating partner and demonstrate that it can be a constructive force within the EU. As we approach the 1996 Inter-Governmental Conference (IGC), and with it the chance to mould the future shape of the EU, we cannot afford to be marginalized. Many UK-inspired ideas – notably on competitiveness and deregulation – are gaining ground within both the Commission and other member states. To be truly effective in realizing these goals, the UK has to work from within and to participate fully in the EU's political and economic decision making.

The IGC is an ideal time for such a commitment to be made. Discussion over what should be on the agenda when the 15 states finally meet has triggered debate across the Union as to the purposes and effectiveness of the EU. The CBI's most recent contribution to the debate is 'Shaping the future: a Europe that works', which sets out the fundamental principles and policies on which a successful Europe can be built.

1

For business in Europe to flourish it must build on its two major strengths: a Single Market containing some of the most sophisticated consumers and producers in the world, and a real diversity of skills and resources fuelled by a long history of inventiveness and entrepreneurship. To do this, the Union must above all be competitive. It is an oft-repeated word, but a crucial one. The focus of all thinking must be President Santer's excellent maxim, which he repeated at the CBI Annual Dinner in May 1995, that the EU must take 'less action, but better action'.

Europe is burdened by declining competitiveness and growing unemployment, and faces a major threat from the 'Asian Tiger' economies of the East. Unilever competes on a global scale and encounters the determination and skill of developing and emerging economies and their people on every continent. Europe's problems are not cyclical but structural and require structural solutions. Business people or politicians who do not face up to these facts are ignoring the hard realities of leadership.

The Single Market, the bedrock of the Union, must be the focus of most attention. The benefits are obvious: trade with other member states now accounts for over half the UK's total exports, and the Single Market is vital in attracting inward investment that brings with it much-needed jobs. The removal of barriers means increased competition and lower costs, which in turn means more choice, lower prices and better quality products for consumers. The rewards are obvious – failure to make the most of Europe is an expensive business.

But the Single Market is still incomplete, and those barriers to trade and competition that remain are preventing firms from all nations from taking full advantage. State aid, like that currently propping up Iberian Airways, needs to be strictly controlled. Some markets, such as transport, energy and tele-communications, are a priority for liberalization. The EU also needs to be zealous in ensuring that existing Single Market legislation is properly implemented and enforced. The level playing-field must become a reality, not remain a hard-working cliché.

What about a single currency? Many CBI members think that a successful single currency would support the Single Market, bringing long-term economic stability and benefits to business. In my view this is sensible thinking, but the issue needs to be debated in a *balanced* way. It is very clear that for a single currency to become a workable proposition there must be rigorous application of the economic criteria set down at Maastricht, and a full and realistic assessment of both the costs and benefits involved. This should happen across the EU and we must be part of it.

A single currency certainly should not be rejected as an option for the UK, and is a prime example of where involvement in the debate, fully and constructively, is vital to our future. I want the UK to be an active participant, able to influence decisions and the direction that the EU takes as we head into a new millennium. The European debate must not be left to the politicians or bureaucrats: the future of Europe is far too important for that. Nor must we allow decisions which will have a profound impact on British business to be taken without our engagement, involvement and leadership. We must all work within Europe, if we want a Europe that works.

FLANDERS

STAR REGION IN EUROPE

F landers. Star Region in Europe. This is a bold claim, yet one which is made with quiet confidence and backed by an enviable track record.

Flanders has for centuries been a hub of trade and culture, and its patronage of the arts and learning has always been a direct consequence of the wealth generated through commerce and trade with Europe and the world.

A proud past is not enough to survive and continue to prosper in a world of fierce commercial competition, however. Not content to rest on past achievements, the Government of Flanders has introduced a number of financial incentives to encourage more international investment.

Twelve good reasons to invest in Flanders

★ Flanders is located in the **heart** of the main Western **European markets** and the EC decision-making centre

★ **Excellent infrastructure facilities:** Brussels International Airport - Three major, modern seaports - Superb illuminated, toll-free motorways

★ **Highest per capita exports** in the world

★ At the crossroads of Latin and Germanic cultures, and hence an **ideal test market** for Europe.

★ **Highly diversified industrial base** with unlimited sub-contracting opportunities

★ Highly qualified, motivated and productive **work force**

★ Highest number of **quadrilingual speakers** in the world

★ One of the **lowest inflation rates** in Europe and the industrialised world

★ Readily available **real-estate** at competitive prices

★ **Tailor-made incentives** offered by the government

★ **Ideal research and development environment** thanks to exemplary cooperation between the universities and industry.

★ **Quality of life**

Flanders has all the advantages to pave the way to prosperity in the Europe of tomorrow. A star region for astute investors in search of that extra edge that makes for sustained and competitive growth. A proud commercial and cultural past together with an innate ability to adapt and innovate make Flanders the region of choice for sound and profitable business opportunities.

FIOC-Headquarters
Jean-Pierre Vandeloo
Managing Director
Markiesstraat, 1
1000 Brussels,Belgium
Tel.32-2-507 38 52
Fax 32-2-507 38 51

FIOC-Asia
Ben De Smit
Arcadia Argos
Bloc A 01-05
235 Arcadia Road
Singapore 1128
Republic of Singapore
Tel. 65-467 64 21
Fax 65-467 70 57

FIOC-USA East
70,walnut Street
Wellesney,
MA 02181-USA
Tel.1-617-239 82 25
Fax 1-617-239 82 96

FIOC-USA West
Filip Vandenbussche
2471, E. Bayshore Road,
Suite 510
Palo Alto,
CA 94303 - USA
Tel. 1-415-354 81 50
Fax 1-415-424 95 16

FIOC-Scandinavia
Maurits Baesen
World Trade Center
Box 70396
10724 Stockholm
Sweden
Tel. 46-8-700 62 05
Fax 46-8-700 62 07

2 EMU:
Economic Considerations

David Kern, Chief Economist and Head of Market Intelligence, NatWest Group
Howard Archer, Research Manager, Market Intelligence, NatWest Group

Introduction

In this paper, we examine three issues: the general arguments for and against economic and monetary union (EMU); how EMU will evolve over the medium and long term; and the more specific arguments for and against the UK joining if EMU proceeds.

Background to Single Currency Areas

The strength of the economic case for EMU, and for UK participation, depends crucially on the degree to which the member countries form an 'optimal currency area'. This describes conditions under which the benefits of a single currency are most likely to outweigh the costs. The benefits include: saving on transaction costs; reduced uncertainty and greater market transparency leading to increased trade and capital movements; and, perhaps most importantly in the case of EMU, increased monetary credibility leading to greater price stability and lower interest rates. Notable costs are: erosion of national monetary sovereignty; and the loss of the exchange rate as a key adjustment mechanism for the national economy.

The following conditions must generally be satisfied for a single currency area to be successful:

- a high degree of labour and capital mobility;
- substantial interdependence between the countries;

- similar, open, and ideally diversified economies, so that any economic shocks will have broadly the same impact on all member countries, thus requiring common policy responses;
- flexible wages and prices.

Is EMU an optimal Single Currency Area?

Trade flows show that a high degree of interdependence already exists among EU countries (see

	Exports	Imports
EU	64.0	62.0
Austria	65.6	69.3
Belgium/Luxembourg	75.1	76.0
Denmark	62.7	65.0
Finland	59.1	57.8
France	62.4	61.6
Germany	58.6	56.1
Greece	62.6	66.0
Ireland	73.8	61.0
Italy	60.7	63.5
Netherlands	78.9	65.7
Portugal	80.2	74.5
Spain	73.0	67.4
Sweden	65.2	70.2
UK	54.6	52.5

* EU comprising 15 countries.

Source: OECD, Monthly Statistics of Foreign Trade, April 1995

Table 2.1 Share of trade going to other EU* countries in 1993 (% of total export, imports)

Table 2.1). Indeed, EU policy has long attempted to improve the EU's position as a single currency area, by developing the single market and encouraging greater coordination of monetary, economic and fiscal policy. Furthermore, to participate in EMU, a country must meet nominal economic convergence criteria relating to exchange rate and price stability, government deficit and public spending levels, and long-term interest rates (see Table 2.2).

However, for a single currency area to be successful, there must also be convergence of real economic factors – such as productivity, unemployment and labour costs. Given present current widespread disparities within the EU, there is a firm belief that major progress needs to be made among potential EMU participants – particularly non-core potential entrants such as Spain and Portugal – in these areas. Furthermore, given factors such as language and cultural differences, and different pension structures, it is questionable whether labour mobility across participant EMU countries can be improved significantly in the 1990s.

EMU's prospects will be significantly influenced by which countries initially participate; and by the state and structure of the economies that join subsequently. The Bundesbank and the Bank of England have both stressed the importance of achieving proper convergence rather than trying to meet specific EMU timetable goals. If real convergence is not achieved, the probable outcome for countries with high wages and low productivity growth would

be long-term stagnation, unemployment and migration. The adverse effects could only be alleviated through larger fiscal transfers to the affected regions; but trying to increase significantly the scale of transfers between countries and payment contributions could be very divisive.

How will EMU evolve?

In spite of many uncertainties and rapidly changing economic situations and political pressures, we believe that the balance of probabilities is that a number of core Western European countries will start EMU in 1999. The most likely initial participants will be Germany, France, the Benelux countries and Austria. Ireland, Finland and Denmark (although the latter has announced it will use its opt-out clause) are also probable early participants. Depending on how rigorously the qualifying criteria are applied, only Greece appears to be definitely ruled out of EMU by 1999. However, Italy faces serious problems that may not enable it to meet the EMU qualifying criteria by 1999. Portugal, Spain and Sweden also seem currently unlikely to be among the initial participants, given expected continuing German insistence on strict application of the qualifying criteria.

On balance, it is likely that the EMU process will evolve broadly along the lines set out in a recent European Commission Green Paper which favours a gradualist approach to the introduction of a single currency rather than a 'big bang'. The decision as to which countries will participate will probably be

	Consumer price inflation	Government deficits	Public debt	Long-term interest rates	Exchange rate
Belgium	yes	no	no	yes	yes
Denmark	yes	yes	no	yes	yes
France	yes	no	yes	yes	yes
Germany	yes	yes	yes	yes	yes
Greece	no	no	no	no	no
Ireland	yes	yes	no*	yes	yes
Italy	no	no	no	no	no
Luxembourg	yes	yes	yes	yes	yes
Netherlands	yes	yes	no	yes	yes
Portugal	no	no	no	no	yes
Spain	no	no	no	no	yes
UK	yes	yes	yes	yes	no
Austria	yes	no	no	yes	yes
Finland	yes	no	no	yes	yes
Sweden	yes	no	no	yes	yes

* Ireland has not been identified by the European Commission as failing this criterion.

Table 2.2 EMU forecast qualifying positions in 1996

taken at the EU Heads of Government meeting in December 1997, or at the very latest in the first half of 1998.

EMU is most likely to start on 1 January 1999 with a total fixing of the participant countries' exchange rates and a common monetary policy with a single central bank (the European Central Bank) and uniform interest rates. The new single currency (whatever it is called) will become a currency in its own right and will no longer be defined as a basket of currencies as is the ECU currently.

Over a period of some three years, banks and financial institutions will convert their activities to the single currency, with the European Commission hoping rapidly to establish a 'critical mass' to boost credibility. Although new single currency notes and coins would not be introduced during this period, public administrations and private enterprises would have to formulate, and would be encouraged to start to implement, changeover plans, eg in accounting and administrative practices. However, businesses will almost certainly prefer to avoid implementing changeover arrangements until the actual introduction of single currency notes and coins. This will probably occur in the year 2002 or 2003 and, ideally after a short period, participant countries' national currencies would be withdrawn and cease to become legal tender.

Clearly, this is an idealized picture, because it leaves out of the assessment possible political pressures for abandoning the whole project if serious recessionary circumstances were to occur in the various EU countries in this transitional period. It also disregards serious potential tensions between the core participants and the outsiders.

The economic case for UK participation in EMU

1. The UK is likely to enjoy greater anti-inflation credibility and lower and less volatile interest rates, assuming that the European Central Bank (ECB) has similar goals to the Bundesbank and achieves a comparable reputation for price stability. The greater coordination of monetary policy should reduce both interest rate differentials across the EU and the average overall rate. The European Commission estimates that this could increase EU output by up to 2.0 per cent.

2. A boost to UK trade and investment resulting from reduced uncertainty in doing business in the various EMU markets and the greater trans-

parency of economic links.

3. Lower transaction costs for UK trade, tourism and international business in general. However, the gains from this source would probably be fairly small. The European Commission has calculated that foreign exchange transaction cost savings would amount to 0.4 per cent of total EU gross domestic product (GDP) per annum, but UK gains are likely to be below average due to our trade patterns and financial market sophistication.

4. The UK's attraction as a source for inward investment could be boosted by EMU's enhancement of the European Single Market. In contrast, if EMU goes ahead without the UK, our attraction for foreign investment may suffer as we could be perceived to be a 'second-tier' country which is becoming more isolated within the EU.

5. The City of London's position as a major financial centre could be undermined if the UK is outside EMU. Admittedly, some observers believe that London could actually benefit if EMU was inward looking and restrictive. However if, as seems more likely, global pressures force the EU to adopt outward-looking and liberal practices, London would face serious risks.

6. Loss of political influence and credibility, both globally and within Europe, could be the result of the UK staying outside EMU. There is a clear risk of the UK being marginalized if EMU proves successful and its members are perceived as 'core' EU economies.

7. The single currency will develop into a major international currency, which will carry significant commercial and financial advantages; and the ECB will be able to pursue exchange rate stability between the single currency, the dollar and the yen.

The economic case against UK participation in EMU

1. The UK will lose the exchange rate as a key adjustment mechanism. The current UK recovery, for example, has been aided significantly by the boost to competitiveness arising from a weaker exchange rate against both EU and non-EU currencies.

2. There could be serious long-term risks to the UK in joining EMU if we do not match other members' performances in key areas such as pro-

ductivity, unit labour costs, current account performance, etc. An inability to sustain competitiveness could have serious adverse repercussions, resulting in reduced growth, higher unemployment and, in the extreme case, economic decline.

3. Short-term interest rates have a comparatively greater impact on the UK economy than other EU countries. Over time, this differing impact should be gradually reduced as the UK moves to greater usage of longer-term lending. However, as long as greater UK reliance on short-term rates persists, a common monetary policy under EMU could result in inappropriate interest rate movements for the UK economy.

4. EMU could lead to higher taxation in the UK if wealthy participants have to subsidize poorer ones.

5. Movements in the single currency against the dollar could have more impact on the UK than other EMU countries because of our greater proportion of dollar-denominated exports. If the single currency has similar characteristics to the DM, which has generally been stronger than sterling against the dollar, UK competitiveness could suffer.

6. There will be substantial costs – even if primarily of a 'one-off' nature – for banks, in particular, and businesses in adjusting to the single currency. This is a minor consideration if EMU proves to be permanent, but the costs would be very high if it collapsed.

7. Member countries' banking systems may have to adopt German-style rules for doing business with the ECB, eg the UK would have to introduce minimum reserve requirements. The City of London is concerned that increased regulation would damage its attraction as a financial centre.

Summary

The UK is very likely to meet the economic criteria for joining EMU by 1999, but the issue is highly controversial and divisive internally. Whatever the outcome of the next General Election, it seems increasingly likely that the issue of whether or not the UK joins EMU will have to be decided in a referendum.

The economic cases for and against EMU are finely balanced and there will continue to be scope for legitimate differences of view. The matter is complicated by the extreme difficulty of forming meaningful, quantifiable estimates of the claimed advantages and disadvantages.

However, it is clear that the economic case for EMU will be stronger, and the grounds for UK membership greater, the more the convergence that is achieved by the participant countries in terms of both nominal and real criteria. If one believes that the UK can maintain its competitiveness, there are, on balance, potential benefits in joining EMU and serious risks in staying out. However, if we genuinely believe that we cannot compete, it would be in this country's best economic interest to stay out of EMU.

3 Deregulation in Europe

Dr A H G Rinooy Kan, President, Confederation of Netherlands Industry VNO-NCW

Action programme for deregulation

The European Regulatory Framework should meet the challenge of employment growth and competitiveness, while taking into account the political commitment to achieving high standards in working conditions and environmental and consumer protection. To achieve these goals, the benefits of the Single Market for business, workers and consumers must be maximized. It is therefore essential to assess the effectiveness of European Union (EU) employment and competitiveness policies to ensure that they do not impose unnecessary costs or obstacles to innovation. Individuals and firms need to be certain that laws are introduced only when they are required, and that such laws minimize compliance costs. Transparency, proportionality and coherence in legislation are keys to enhancing wealth creation and employment opportunities. Legislative simplification can also help to bring the EU closer to its citizens.

This is one of the main considerations in the *Molitor Committee Report*. The Molitor Committee was established in September 1994 by the European Commission as a group of independent experts to examine the impact of Community and national legislation on employment and competitiveness. The UK member of the Molitor Committee was Sir Michael Angus, who played an important role in the meetings. I represented the Netherlands. Through-

out the work of the Molitor Committee we worked in close cooperation with the CBI. In June 1995 the Molitor Committee presented its report to the European Commission.

The Committee concluded that a comprehensive action programme on simplification is required. This action programme should be based on the following principles:

- Wealth creation and sustained employment growth must be recognized as essential conditions to enable further improvement in the quality of life; this can only be achieved if the European economy is world class.
- Standards to be achieved must be 'affordable', given the competitiveness challenge, and must be based on objective need (founded where appropriate on scientific evidence).
- Businesses, workers and consumers should be consulted and actively involved both in helping to establish appropriate standards and in evaluating the most effective means to achieve them. We need to make the best use of available market instruments and commitments undertaken voluntarily, rather than by means of direct regulation, where appropriate.
- The impact of direct regulation (both individually and collectively) on competitiveness and employment must be explicitly considered in the design and review of legislation.

▓ Simplification and even deregulation must be actively pursued as an integral part of policies to enhance competitiveness.

The Committee intended that its report should be a contribution to creating a culture of simplification leading, where necessary, to deregulation – deeply embedded at EU and national level – stimulating competitiveness and employment.

The work of the Molitor Committee is an important step forward in the direction of improving the regulatory framework in Europe. Overregulation is stifling growth, reducing competitiveness and costing Europe jobs. Regulations are imposing costs and inflexibilities which frustrate enterprise, hamper innovation and deter investment.

European business does not need more regulation, we need fewer, better quality and less burdensome regulations. Deregulation means a reduction in the overwhelming number of overprescriptive, overcomplicated and frequently contradictory European regulations. The cumulative effect of too many regulations damages growth and competitiveness.

A culture of simplification is needed

Action is needed at the European level. The ideal regulatory regime which would result from these actions would enhance competitiveness and employment, while maintaining appropriate standards of protection and behaviour. The 'ideal' regime would have the following characteristics:

▓ Fewer, better quality and less burdensome regulations.

▓ Regulations which support the overriding requirement for growth, international competitiveness and employment.

▓ Regulations, both at the European and national levels, based on objective need.

▓ Single Market regulations limited to those areas in which Single Market benefits are significant; harmonization should not be pursued for its own sake.

▓ Principles of proportionality and subsidiarity rigorously adhered to.

▓ Even-handed implementation and enforcement of EU Directives vigorously pursued across all member states.

The Molitor Committee suggested a common strategy for improving the quality of Community legislation. Proposals for new legislation should be thoroughly tested for need and scope. If the Council and Parliament are to make informed decisions, each proposal for legislation needs to be accompanied by an objective analysis of the relevant facts, providing a proper basis on which political judgement can be made. These facts include the scientific evidence (where appropriate), international comparisons, the results of consultation with firms and other interested groups, the evaluation of appropriate instruments, and an objective 'cost–benefit' appraisal, taking into account all quantitative and qualitative factors.

A greater degree of transparency for and consultation with those most concerned is necessary during the preparation of Community legislation. Consultation with business should be effective, systematic, and carried out in due time.

Government and business must work together to find more sensible approaches to meeting the public interest, while keeping costs as low as possible. The efficiency of regulation has to be improved to ensure that industries are not hampered in creating jobs and providing economic growth.

The momentum for deregulation should be increased

Regulation is both the responsibility of the EC and of national authorities at all levels. The cumulative impact on competitiveness and employment results first from the scope and character of EC legislation, then from the rigour and evenness with which this legislation is transposed and applied in member states (this second level is often neglected, but is of great importance). Finally, additional burdens result from regulations imposed by national governments acting in their own areas of national competence. If the competitiveness challenge is to be met and the cumulative burden of regulation reduced, each of these levels must be tackled vigorously. There will be little purpose in the Union simplifying its legislation, if under the cover of subsidiarity or transposition member states take an opposite course. Such counter-action would make their own economies less competitive and undermine the effectiveness of Union policy as a whole. The Molitor Committee's recommendations for action at the Community level need to be mirrored by each member state. Some national initiatives have been taken. These experiments have yielded useful results and lessons, but in each case it is clear that the task has only just begun. We should therefore increase the momentum for deregulation, both on a national and European level.

Simplification and deregulation require a change in the culture of policy making. This challenge cannot be avoided by either national governments or the institutions of the EU, if the competitiveness of European business is to be improved and higher employment levels sustained.

Our aim should be to release European industry from the shackles of unnecessary rules and regulations. European industry must not be tied down by unnecessary bureaucracy and its governments should do all they can to relieve this burden.

Social Dialogue

James Flynn, Partner, Linklaters & Paines, Brussels

For the uninitiated, social dialogue might sound like a guide to conversation in polite society, perhaps the sort of book Elizabeth Bennet was brought up on. In the EU context it is the name given to the process by which consensus is sought by representatives of those engaged in the world of work, particularly but not exclusively, in the context of the Maastricht Treaty arrangements on social policy.

This is a complex, evolving and rather intangible area. This article seeks to answer some fundamental questions concerning the Social Dialogue: What is the legal framework for the Social Dialogue? Who are the participants? What is the effect of the British opt-out? What has been achieved so far and what next?

Legal framework

The Member States at Maastricht failed to agree amendments to the EC Treaty social policy provisions as they then stood. They compromised by shunting a text acceptable to 11 states into an Agreement on Social Policy annexed to a Protocol attached to the EC Treaty, authorizing the 11 to use the EC institutions for the purposes of the Agreement and sanctioning the UK opt-out. The three new Member States sought no opt-outs.

Thus the unamended social provisions of the pre-Maastricht EC Treaty are applicable in all 15 Member States. Where possible, social policy measures are adopted under the EC Treaty, so that they apply in the UK. This has sometimes been done on

arguably spurious legal bases: the adoption of rules on working time as health and safety measures are under challenge by the UK before the European Court.

Articles 3 and 4 of the Social Policy Agreement require the Commission to consult management and labour on the possible direction of Community action and the content of any envisaged proposal. Management and labour may decide to enter into contractual relations, including agreements, concerning the matters on which the Commission consults them. Such agreements may either be implemented locally or by Council decision following a Commission proposal.

Who are the social partners?

The Commission has specified criteria concerning the bodies to be consulted. They must:

- ▨ be either cross-industry or sectoral and be organized at European level;
- ▨ consist of organizations which are 'an integral and recognized part of Member State social partner structures', have the capacity to negotiate agreements and be representative of all Member States as far as possible;
- ▨ have adequate structures to ensure effective participation in consultation.

That Commission communication lists organizations which may be consulted, broadly as follows:

- ▨ **Cross-industry organizations** Union of Industrial and Employers' Confederation of Europe (UNICE). European Centre of Enterprises with Public Participation (CEEP) and European Trade Union Confederation (ETUC);

■ **Cross-industry organizations representing categories of workers or undertakings** European Association of Craft, Small- and Medium-sized Enterprises (UEAPME), EUROPMI, CEC and Eurocadres;

■ **Specific organizations** EUROCHAMBRES;

■ **Sectoral organizations** Those with no cross-industry affiliation may be consulted where appropriate.

UNICE, CEEP and ETUC are the major players and were engaged in 'Euro-negotiations' before the Agreement elevated the significance of social dialogue. Indeed, Articles 3 and 4 of the Agreement are based on a 1991 agreement between them on the role of the social partners. Certain organizations, in particular European Confederation of Independent Trade Unions (CESI) and UEAPME, have been seeking actively to be more involved in the social dialogue.

At a meeting between Jacques Santer, Padraig Flynn, UNICE, CEEP and ETUC in May 1995, the Commission restated its position that social partners should decide for themselves with whom they can negotiate. There is an understanding between the three main players that to allow others in would fragment the dialogue. In some cases, however, there is dialogue at sectoral level on issues peculiar to those sectors. The Commission offers funding for such meetings.

Effect of British opt-out

As the UK is not party to the Agreement, it is not bound by legislative measures or negotiated agreements adopted under it. However, in the real world of industrial relations, UK employers and employees may find themselves affected by such measures. The European Works Councils (EWC) Directive (see below) brought this squarely into public view. Many British companies are caught by virtue of the scale of their operations in the Eleven; many groups in the Eleven have extensive British operations. They have found it difficult to leave their British employees out of the Works Councils arrangements and most would not want to: over a dozen British groups have set up EWC structures already. From the government perspective, it could be said that they at least have done so voluntarily rather than under compulsion.

It is sometimes said that the opt-out gives Britain the worst of both worlds in that it is affected by the measures agreed but has no place at the negotiating table. This is not the whole truth as, both at Council (of Ministers) and social partner level, the UK has at least 'observer' status and perhaps more in practice. Under UNICE's statutes, consensus has to be reached among all members affected by any agreement negotiated within the social dialogue framework. While CBI members are clearly not directly affected by such agreements, they are likely to be indirectly affected (whatever view is taken on the probability of the ending of the opt-out). The CBI plays a full part in the preparation of UNICE's negotiating positions even if it cannot vote on the outcome. The TUC's role within ETUC is similar.

Achievements so far
European Works Councils
In February 1994, following a UK veto of an earlier proposal, Social Commissioner Flynn proposed a legal framework for agreement at company or group level between central management and employee representatives. Under the Social Policy Agreement, the Commission decided to consult the social partners. However, they failed to reach agreement. The Commission, therefore, progressed its legislative proposal, which was adopted in somewhat altered form by the Council in September 1994.

Current proposals under negotiation
Atypical work
In December 1994, the UK vetoed a draft directive to give part-time workers the same rights as full-time workers with regard to pay and benefits. Early in 1995, the Council reached stalemate on a compromise draft. The Commission consulted the social partners on the direction the EU should take for part-time, fixed-term and temporary agency workers. At the time of writing, the outcome of this consultation was not known.

Burden of proof in sex discrimination cases
The Commission has asked the social partners whether the EU should act to ensure that employers bear the burden of proof in sex discrimination cases.

Parental leave
In September 1994, the Commission accepted that UK opposition to the draft directive on parental leave ruled out the possibility of its adoption under the EC

Treaty. Social Agreement discussions under the first phase of consultation on the Commission's proposals for the reconciliation of professional and family life started in February 1995, and the second phase in June 1995, leading to the conclusion of a proposed agreement in November 1995. At the time of writing, this agreement was awaiting ratification by the decision-making bodies of ETUC, UNICE and CEEP. If ratified, the social partners look set to achieve, for the first time, an agreement capable of implementation at community level in accordance with Articles 3 and 4 of the Social Policy Agreement.

What next?

Discussions continue on the content and timing of the Inter-Governmental Conference (IGC) to begin in 1996 as required by the Maastricht Treaty. The Commission has made it plain that it would like to see an end to the UK opt-out and the reintegration of all social policy into the EC Treaty framework. The Westendorp reflection group cannot resolve the issue because the present British government clearly will not opt in. However, the IGC will probably not wind up until after the British election which must take place by the first half of 1997. An incoming Labour government would be committed to ending the opt-out.

The social partners will be involved in the IGC debate. UNICE's position has not yet emerged; the ETUC has already called for the Social Charter to be incorporated into the EC Treaty.

Interesting times lie ahead but for British business, the uncertainty and frustration looks set to continue for a while.

5 Integrating Eastern and Central Europe into the EU

Ralph Land, Chairman, UNICE East and Central Europe Relations Working Group

A number of the former communist countries of Eastern and Central Europe have negotiated or are in the final stages of negotiating association agreements with the EU. All of them have made it abundantly clear that association represents only a stage towards their ultimate objective of becoming fully fledged members of the EU, at what most of them hope will be an early date.

The countries concerned are Bulgaria, the Czech Republic, Hungary, Poland, Romania, Slovakia, Slovenia and the three Baltic Republics, Estonia, Latvia and Lithuania. Other countries from the former Soviet Union may later also want to join, but the more probable candidates would be Croatia and in due course other states of former Yugoslavia.

The EU has embarked on a strategy to help the associated countries to become full members, recognizing the importance to Europe and the World of these countries making a successful transition to political pluralism and market economies. It is recognized that the failure to achieve these objectives could have catastrophic effects on the rest of the world.

Background

At present the transition process is beset with difficulties. Trade and output in all countries have been substantially reduced. At the same time unemployment in most of the countries has increased, combined with considerable social dislocation.

Investment has been insufficient to modernize industry, to make it competitive with that in the West, despite international and EU financial aid and support. A number of countries, led by the Czech Republic, Poland, Hungary, Slovenia, Estonia and to a lesser extent Slovakia, are beginning to show growth. The remainder are showing signs of stabilization and it is not unreasonable to expect some growth next year.

Despite their economic problems a number of the states have valuable resources and skilled low-cost labour forces. The EU has not helped by making it difficult for them to sell the products that represent their main strength in the EU, in industries such as textiles, steel and agriculture. On the other hand, the EU and Britain in particular have provided invaluable know-how help in developing a new generation of managers and in helping to set up the legal and financial infrastructure required by modern market economies.

The pre-accession strategy

In 1994 the European Commission was asked to prepare a pre-accession strategy designed to help the countries prepare themselves for eventual full membership. It was recognized that it would be premature at this time to establish a detailed timetable for negotiations and also that, as opposed to the EFTA countries which acceded to the EU in one block, the Eastern European countries would become

CeeNet – The City Network for East West Trade

Sponsored by:
The Corporation of London

Aim:
To assist Central and East European entrepreneurs to use the business facilities of the City of London

Method:
To provide sound advice through introductions to a broad network of City professionals covering banking, brokerage, inward investment or general business guidance.

City Network for East West Trade
Warnford Court
Throgmorton Street
London EC2N 2AT
Tel: 0171 638 9299 Fax: 0171 588 8555

CeeNet

The Lord Mayor of London announced in April 1995 the launch of a new commercial centre to promote the City of London and the great range of services available within it to traders, bankers and businessmen from Central and Eastern Europe. Kester George CBE, formerly the British Department of Trade and Industry's leading expert on the area, was appointed Director.

CeeNet, as the organization is known, has the financial backing of the Corporation of London and is overseen by a steering group of experienced businessmen.

CeeNet has already begun to find contacts for mutually profitable business with Central and Eastern Europe, to arrange training seminars on City procedures and to advise on particular projects for setting up new business in the City of London.

CeeNet is a non-profit making organization.

members on individual timetables related to their progress on convergence. In any case, the EU is in no position to consider timetables before the Inter-Governmental Conference in 1996 in which key decisions, concerning issues such as further deepening versus widening, have to be taken.

Irrespective of the timetable of accession, the pre-accession strategy will apply to all the aspirant countries. Its chief features are the creation of a structured relationship with each country to develop action plans for the convergence of legal and financial structures and detailed provisions for the adjustment and reduction of tariffs and quotas, including the harmonization of rules of origin. In those areas where the EU has placed major hurdles in the way of Eastern and Central European exports, there will be specific improvements. At this time there remains a significant problem over agriculture and there can be little doubt that the accession of the Eastern and Central European countries could not occur without a substantial modification of Common Agricultural Policy. The Commission has been charged with preparing an analysis and proposals before the end of 1995. This promises to be one of the

more controversial issues. As yet, the budgetary impact on the EU of such a major expansion has not been evaluated, nor have the full effects on other EU strategies been evaluated, such as regional support policies, including the Mediterranean development policies and the accession plans of other countries such as Turkey.

The agreement by the member states to the pre-accession strategy was followed by a 300-page white paper detailing the steps that would need to be taken by the aspirant countries to enable them to meet all the conditions of the internal market. The EU plans to expand the PHARE programme (the programme used to channel aid to Eastern and Central Europe) to provide finance and expertise to help in achieving the pre-accession strategy and the aims of the white paper.

In general the Eastern and Central European countries hope for full membership at an early date. Poland and the Czech Republic, the two most advanced countries, would expect to become full members by the year 2000, despite the probable continued divergence of their economies with those of the more prosperous EU countries. However, they

5

rightly point out that the Greek economy was further behind when it was allowed to accede. A number of Western economists believe that too early an accession could place an intolerable strain on fragile economies and political systems. My own view is that the most probable timetable starts around 2005 and would stretch to 2015 for some of the less developed countries. However, it is probable that ultimately the key decisions will be taken on political rather than on economic grounds.

The effects on the business community and the role of UNICE

The business community is on the whole insufficiently aware of the opportunities and perhaps the competition that will follow the implementation of the pre-accession strategy. In the first place, the strategy will be put into effect in all of the countries listed above, irrespective of their eventual accession dates or indeed if they accede at all. Secondly, issues such as rules of origin policy, tariff and quota policies, and anti-dumping procedures are going to have profound effects on trade and will in some cases prove to be controversial. Different points of view between Southern and Northern European countries, especially those with a particular interest in Eastern and Central Europe, are already becoming apparent. In addition, there are issues around the future trade relations between the EU and the rest of the former communist bloc, in particular countries like Ukraine, which may well have aspirations to join the EU.

UNICE (Union of Industrial and Employers Confederations of Europe) has an important role to play to ensure that the voice of European industry is properly heard before strategies become policies. Already, a number of issues have been raised. In addition, UNICE will play a part in helping to shape future PHARE strategies and in monitoring their effectiveness. It is important that an open dialogue is established with the officials of the Commission. The record of important contributions made by UNICE on other issues gives them a strong platform to be heard on issues concerning Eastern and Central Europe.

PART

2

Europe's Economic Performance

European Prospects

Professor Norbert Walter, Chief Economist, Deutsche Bank Group

False starts into the 1990s

At the end of the 1980s, Europe looked set for integration, deepening and widening its relationships. It also appeared to be at the core of defeating communism in a peaceful way. Europe seemed poised to become the star of the 1990s. This perspective has proved to be false. Europe is no longer in the limelight (in the positive sense). Instead of pulling ahead with integration, Europe is beginning to disintegrate – and not just in former Yugoslavia.

German unification has factually derailed European integration. This partly has to do with (mostly unwarranted) envy and distrust by Germany's partners of its commitment to Western Europe. Partly, it is a consequence of gross misguidance of the German unification process, which has made it much more expensive than necessary. An ill-designed wage and fiscal-policy response in Germany, provoking excessive monetary restriction, was the cause of macro-policy misalignment in Europe. Over-regulated and interventionist policies were extended to the new Länder, making it difficult to enhance work incentives, or precluding them altogether. As a result, Europe's growth remains subdued and unemployment has stayed high or has even risen. There is a mounting aversion to risk, and investment thus remains low.

Such policies would have been unwelcome in themselves. But the fall-out was particularly severe under the prevailing circumstances, ie those of ever-

more intense global competition. After successful restructuring over the past decade, the US economy has sharpened its competitive edge considerably, helped in part by the depreciation of the US dollar. The competition facing Europe has increased at the same time through the emergence of a number of East European, South East Asian and Latin American economies.

Viewed from abroad, Europe seems both inward-looking – always threatening to become a fortress – and attractive, as the pillar in the triad which is developing the greatest momentum towards institutional integration, more than in either the Americas or the Asian region. In a sense, the EU is envied for its institutional progress.

Deepening and widening of the EU – indispensable but not yet assured

More recently, especially after the Maastricht Treaty was signed, the momentum stalled and doubts emerged concerning the speed of integration. On occasion there were even doubts about the direction. Widening the EU was questioned by those who feared dilution and those who felt they would be deprived by having to share structural funds with new members in Central and Eastern Europe. Others –perhaps less vocal, but at least as important in blocking the integration of Eastern Europe – feared additional difficulties for structurally weak sectors in their own economies.

But not only the widening of the EU is questioned. Deepening has run into massive counter-attacks by academics, politicians and citizens. National identities remain strong if not central; misconceptions about the necessary superstructure of the EU are mushrooming and evoke national, if not nationalist, attitudes.

In the post-World War II period, Europe never moved forward smoothly. There is no difference today. The 1989 revolution, coming so unexpectedly, necessitates reflections, adaptations and therefore a stretching of the timetable envisaged in the second half of the 1980s. But experience shows that after a pause, or even setbacks, Europe was always ready for further progress. It will be no different this time. After the setback of the first half of the 1990s, the second half will bring progress again.

The Inter-Governmental Conference (IGC) beginning in 1996 should set the ball rolling. Hopefully the enlargement to the North and fresh thinking in the UK will overcome the present situation where the Paris/Bonn axis is the sole motor of European integration. Many of the divisions in Europe are based on misconceptions and misunderstanding. Europe obviously cannot and should not eradicate the nation state. Equally obvious, however, is a need to treat truly European issues at the appropriate level. The principle of subsidiarity, if properly communicated and adequately translated into a concrete hierarchy of tasks and responsibilities for the different (at least three, if not four) levels of government, will help greatly. Majority voting on issues of practical importance, qualified majority voting for essential issues and a unanimous vote on existential questions should be the rule for European policies.

The process of deepening Europe is, however, not confined to the IGC. The Single Market is anything but complete and the major task of forming EMU is not yet successfully accomplished. Europe's reality is a far cry from the aim of truly establishing the 'four freedoms' (free movement of goods and services, capital and labour). EMU is still confronted with doubts of many citizens, business people, academics and politicians. The divide runs across nations and political parties. Obviously, either an external crisis to unite Europeans or a grand effort by the supporters of monetary union is necessary if EMU is to be achieved successfully by 1999.

At this juncture the probability of EMU by 1999 is

about 55–60 per cent. The countries with the best chances for initial membership are France, Germany, Benelux and Austria. The key question is whether France will be able to fulfil the convergence criteria despite current budgetary problems. Three to four other countries are in the running: most of them should have no difficulty in achieving the Maastricht convergence criteria, but might opt out for political reasons.

The widening of the EU to the East has made initial progress. Association arrangements have been concluded with a number of Central and East European states. However, no firm commitment for membership has been granted to these countries, despite their clear request. This mainly has to do with fears of old EU members that enlarging the EU would dilute structural funds, thus reducing their own access. Others fear that new members would threaten weak industries in Western Europe, particularly because of low wages in the East. These industries include textiles, steel, shipyards, coal-mining and agriculture in particular.

If Western Europe does not want to obstruct European integration, there will have to be a complete overhaul of the common agricultural policy (CAP), amounting to no less than the dismantling of the system. A new division of labour needs to be accepted, if the present EU members do not want to obfuscate the historic trends. In any case, the results of the Uruguay Round necessitate steps in this direction. The question of winners and losers in this process is certainly not easy. The best abstract answer, however, was given a good 200 years ago by the Scottish economist Adam Smith in his *Wealth of Nations*. Applying it to the present situation, Europe can only successfully compete in an open and integrating world economy if it allows its own Koreas and Vietnams (ie, countries like the Czech Republic or Hungary) to be integrated into its division of labour. If Western Europe seeks to protect itself by closing out Central and East European countries, this will produce losers all over Europe: Eastern Europe will be frustrated in its effort to link up to democracy and the market economy (and may be threatened with a relapse) while Western Europe will fail to improve its competitiveness as a consequence of subsidising sunset industries and old jobs, and will thus fall victim in truly global markets.

Trading opportunities

The Arab British Chamber of Commerce is uniquely qualified to give you the expert and reliable guidance you'll need to trade successfully with the Arab Countries. Each country has its own cultures, traditions and etiquette. The markets are highly competitive.

Our board of directors consist of 40 leading Arab and British businessmen. And we have been promoting Arab-British trade and economic cooperation for the past twenty years. Arab Chambers of Commerce are large and powerful organisations and in almost all Arab countries membership is compulsory. So joining the Chamber can put you into contact with an important business network.

In addition to the services listed, we are always on hand to give prompt answers to individual problems and help your company stay ahead.

mines of information

Certify all commercial documents.

Arrange for commercial documents to be legalised by the Arab embassy concerned.

Arrange visas for business visits to Arab countries.

Business information & membership services.

Arabic language and other training courses.

Resolve commercial disputes.

Library with a comprehensive collection of business directories & reference books.

Translate commercial, legal, and technical documents.

Exhibitions, workshops, conferences & meetings on economic and commercial developments.

Multilingual publications & business bulletins with circulation of around 55,000.

THE ARAB-BRITISH
CHAMBER OF COMMERCE

**6 BELGRAVE SQUARE
LONDON SW1X 8PH**
TEL: 0171 235 4363
FAX: 0171 245 6688
CABLES: ARABRI LONDON
TELEX: 22171 ARABRI G

ARAB-BRITISH
CHAMBER OF COMMERCE 299484 ARABIS G

Please send me membership details about the
Arab British Chamber of Commerce

Name: .... Position: ....

Company name: ....

Company address: ....

.... Post code: ....

Tel: ....

Fax: ....

The Arab-British Chamber of Commerce

The Arab-British Chamber of Commerce has its primary purpose the promotion of two-way trade and economic co-operation between the Arab countries and the United Kingdom. First established in 1975, the Chamber occupies a unique position in Arab-British relations because it is a Joint Chamber operating at an international level and connected through its board membership to the powerful and influential network of Arab Chambers of Commerce and Industry.

The Chamber provides first class services to its members and to the Arab and British business communities in general.

Over its lifetime the Chamber has created an extensive network of contact with Arab and British governments and businesses. It works in close co-operation with the League of Arab States and its specialised agencies, Arab diplomatic missions in London, the General Union of Chambers of Commercial Industry and Agriculture for the Arab countries with the Department of Trade and Industry in the United Kingdom, and the Committee for Middle East Trade (COMET).

In the European Union the Chamber has been asked by the Commission in Brussels to promote its joint venture programme ECIP (European Communities Invest-ment Partners), and to act as European organiser for the European Union – Gulf Co-operation Council Third Industrial Conference in Muscat, Oman, in October 1995. This key appointment arises out of the role the Chamber plays in the structure of the Euro-Arab Chambers of Commerce which play a similar role to itself in the E.U. states, where it is the acknowledged leader.

The Chamber is governed by a Joint Board of Directors, drawn equally from the Arab and British business communities. The Chairman, *Sir Richard Beaumont*, is a former British Ambassador to several Arab states. The Secretary-General, *Mr. Abdul Karim Al-Mudfaris,* is an Arab diplomat with long experience in commercial relations.

The Chamber is well qualified to give British and Arab companies the expert and reliable guidance they need to trade successfully with each other. The services offered are structured to meet real needs of business people which are: to receive reliable analysis and information of particular markets, to be properly informed of when cultural factors are crucial to setting up business relations, and what those factors are; to enjoy the opportunity of making valuable contracts; and have a system on hand which smoothes the passage of goods and services once deals have been struck and orders made.

Here is brief description of the service provided by the chamber:

Business Information Department

Manned by experienced graduates, this department operates with the benefit of the largest Arab companies database to be found anywhere in Europe. It is has an extensive database of British companies to satisfy the needs of Arab company enquiries for trade contacts.

The department has a number of publications. There is a *"Weekly Business Bulletin"* produced exclusively for members, which provides information on tenders and business opportunities in the Arab countries. A monthly bilingual magazine "Arab-British Trade", has a 15,000 circulation in the Arab states and a 15,000 circulation in Britain. This magazine seeks to provide company strategies with analysis and commentary on economic and trade development, and related issues, in both the United Kingdom and the Arab world.

Of particular benefit to Arab members, but with spin-off benefits for British companies and institutions, is the department's *"Science & Technology Now"* magazine. This seeks to aid the transfer of technology from British and Europe to Arab business and education. The magazine is aimed at a top Arab readership. It is bilingual, with a circulation of 15,000 to Arab readers, and carries articles on technological developments emanating from British universities and commercial companies which, through licence, or joint venture, can have a practical application in Arab economics.

Public Affairs Department

The Chamber's Public Affairs Department carries responsibility for organising exhibitions for Arab states in London. In creating these exhibitions the Chamber demonstrates to a British business audience that the Arab industrial sector is growing, and growing fast, and that it represents a new and competitive source of goods for British importers, and is also a source of joint venture for British manufacturers anxious to gain a foothold in the ever burgeoning export markets in the Middle East.

The Public Affairs Department also takes part in British exhibitions in the

Arab world; and has the responsibility of organising seminars and workshops.

Certification & Documentation Department

A vital function in international trade is the efficient handling of documentation. All products that leave British bound for Arab customers require a "passport" which signifies to the recipient country that they are genuine, not fakes, and the information about the source of their manufacture and their specifications are true and not fraudulent. That "passport" takes the form of certificates of origin.

The certificates of origin are dealt with by the Certification & Documentation Department which thus provides a "one door" entry for British companies certification in relation to export documentation. The department prides itself on its policy of never allowing a backlog to gather. All documentation is turned over and completed within 24 hours, which includes advising companies of any clerical or administrative errors, they may have made, or new changes in Arab states' commercial laws affecting imports.

As can be seen from this brief description the Chamber is an international organisation linked into the Arab world of government and business at the highest levels, using those contacts to stimulate activity between Arab and British business and promulgate valuable information to keep keep trade flowing in both directions.

In a long and enduring relationship between the Arab people and the British, the Chamber is proud to be playing a role as an organisation offering a helping hand to both in their pursuit of trade and a higher standard of living for all of the people concerned.

For a brochure on Membership benefits write to:
The Arab-British Chamber of Commerce
6 Belgrave Square, London SW1X 8PH
Tel: 0171-235 4363
Fax: 0171-245 6688/0171-396 4499

SAME MEETING

DIFFERENT CITY

ShareVision PC 3000

INTRODUCING SHAREVISION PC3000.

The desktop, video tele-conferencing system that will revolutionise the way you do your daily business, giving you the power to work together with your colleague even though you may be thousands of miles apart. This affordable system will dramatically reduce your travel expenses, and because it works over a normal telephone line, it is cheaper to run than other systems that use digital (ISDN) lines. ShareVision is cheaper than a fax and faster than a flight.

ShareVision PC3000 was designed for your PC and it gives you the capability to see and hear your colleague whilst collaboratively working with any Windows application, demonstrate and explain your ideas to a customer and see their reaction immediately, or you can display a design concept and work together on the corrections.

ShareVision PC3000 comes complete with a camera, discreet handsfree microphone, Video capture card and high-speed modem so you can

also enjoy fast file transfer, automatic fax send and retrieval and convenient access to the net and remote email users.

In the world today there are already many businesses which are employing the ShareVision system to improve productivity and gain a competitive advantage. At Creative Labs we believe that ShareVision PC3000 will completely change the way you do business in the future. But don't just take our word for it, visit an authorised ShareVision dealer and see it for yourself.

Call 01245 265 265 for your free demonstration CD-ROM and the location of your nearest ShareVision dealer.

CREATIVE LABS - CHANGING THE WAY YOU DO BUSINESS.

CREATIVE

CREATIVE LABS

Europe in the 21st century: greying and stagnating?

Europe's outlook into the 21st century is not described fully by discussing the deepening and widening of the EU. Demographic trends are going to pose a major challenge. They will create particularly acute problems because of the inappropriate pension schemes in most countries. Despite an obvious trend to ageing populations – especially pronounced in countries like Germany, Denmark and Italy – pay-as-you-go schemes predominate. The benefits under such schemes are still being expanded and contribution rates are skyrocketing. Instruments to alleviate the burden, such as funded or partly-funded systems on a private basis, are politically unacceptable in many places. So the pension timebomb is ticking.

One solution – at least for a period of time – would be to allow (selective) immigration into Europe. This will tend to come about anyhow after the turn of the century, because Europe's population is ageing and shrinking whereas those of Africa and the Middle East will be rising but will remain poor.

There would be every reason to start immediately to prepare future emigrants in the countries concerned. Language skills are required to reduce the social costs of later integration. Curricula should therefore be adjusted today in Egypt, Morocco and Turkey to facilitate integration in three to ten years' time. That would help defuse timebombs in those countries and the pension timebomb in greying Europe. Such migration is essential not only to fill many of the service jobs demanding low or medium skills; it is also obvious that the rapid introduction of modern technology will be held up in Europe if the shortage of young people is not alleviated. Bringing capital from the EU to these people is certainly a partial alternative. However, quite a few of the problems mentioned can only be helped by immigration into Europe. A major obstacle, though, is the mounting xenophobia in much of Europe. It is partly a relapse into medieval attitudes, partly a reaction to rising unemployment among the low-skilled. Only a far-sighted approach, indicating the temporary nature of the present problems, can help set Europe en route to a prosperous future. If we fail to move in this direction, or even if it only takes too long to make the U-turn, Europe's future will be bleak and definitely very bumpy.

European Competitiveness

Bruce Ballantine, Business Decisions Ltd

There is no single measure of European competitiveness. However, two of the key measures indicate that European competitiveness has declined over time: the rate of growth in real gross domestic product (GDP) per head (the standard of living) and the level of unemployment.

In the 1970s, Europe grew faster than the rest of the OECD countries in terms of real GDP per head. In the 1980s, it grew marginally more slowly, but in the 1990s Europe has grown much more slowly (Figure. 7.1). This is linked closely to the slower than average rate of export growth during the past 25 years (Figure 7.2).

Unemployment in Europe was close to the OECD average until 1975, but European unemployment has grown much faster since then (Figure 7.3).

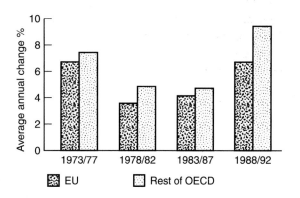

Source: OECD & Eurostat

Figure 7.2 Export growth

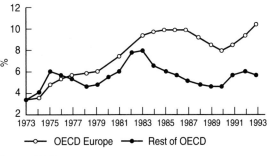

Source: OECD

Figure 7.3 Unemployment

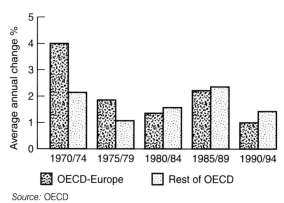

Source: OECD

Figure 7.1 GDP per head

This is linked closely to the poor rate of job creation in the private sector in Europe. Job growth in the private sector in Europe has averaged 0.3 per cent per annum over the last 25 years, compared with 1.0 per cent per annum in Japan and 1.8 per cent per annum in the USA (Figure 7.4).

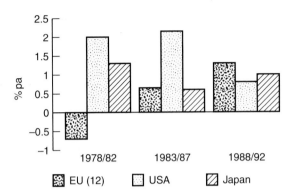

Source: OECD

Figure 7.4 Job growth in the private sector

The causes

Just as there is no single measure of this relative decline, there is no single cause. However, the principal causes can be divided into three main groups:

- costs are too high;
- productivity is too low; and
- the macro-environment is not sufficiently stable and predictable.

Costs

The three principal areas of costs where European companies are disadvantaged are the costs of labour, the costs of capital and the costs of energy.

The average hourly pay of a production worker in Europe was similar to the average pay of production workers in the rest of the OECD, over the five-year period 1989–93. Taxes on employers (such as social security taxes and payroll taxes) were, however, significantly higher in Europe. Hence the total cost of employing a production worker in Europe was some 20 per cent higher than in the rest of the OECD.

Moreover, taxes on employees were also higher in Europe, so that the average take-home pay of a production worker in Europe was 20 per cent less than their counterpart in the rest of the OECD (Figure 7.5).

The cost of capital is also higher in Europe than in Japan or in the USA, according to a recent survey by Coopers and Lybrand for the European Commission. The real cost of capital before tax, expressed as the weighted average cost of debt and equity, in the European Union in 1990 was over 18 per cent

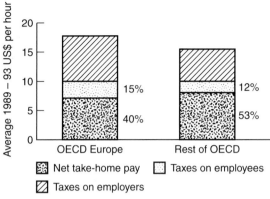

Source: ERT estimate

Figure 7.5 Average take-home pay

compared with less than 15 per cent in Japan and the USA (Figure 7.6). There are no similar data over time, but long-term interest rates have been consistently higher in Europe than in Japan or the USA.

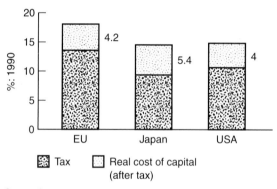

Source: Coopers & Lybrand

Figure 7.6 Cost of capital

Energy costs have risen too fast in Europe and are now too high compared with the USA. For example, industrial electricity costs have risen much faster in Europe than in the USA in the last decade

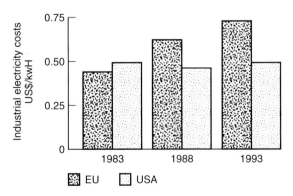

Source: IEA

Figure 7.7 Electricity costs

and are now some 50 per cent higher. A part of the difference is the result of the devaluation of the dollar relative to the ECU during this period. But the principal explanations are extra taxation on electricity in many European countries and little competition among suppliers in Europe (Figure 7.7).

Productivity

It is difficult to measure productivity accurately, but indications are that European productivity lags behind Japan and the USA, both in absolute terms and in terms of its rate of growth over time.

The rate of growth of industrial productivity in Europe has been some 10 per cent less than in Japan and the USA during the last 15 years (Figure 7.8). Moreover, according to a recent study by McKinsey, European industrial productivity in six key sectors of the economy lags behind Japan by some 10 per cent and the USA by some 30 per cent.

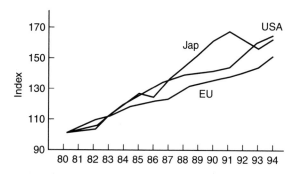

Source: European Commission

Figure 7.8 Productivity in manufacturing, 1980 = 100
(gross value added at 1985 prices per person employed)

The principal reasons for this are:

- labour flexibility has been less. This has been caused, for example, by a lower capacity utilization because of limits on the number of hours worked (Table 7.1);

Hours per annum	1980	1985	1990
EU	1760	1710	1705
Japan	2140	2148	2103
USA	1941	1995	1981

Source: US Department of Labor

Table 7.1 Average hours worked in manufacturing industry

- R&D expenditure has been lower (Figure 7.9);
- the pace of industrial restructuring has been slower. This is reflected in the slower growth of 'high-tech' industries (Figure 7.9), a slower growth rate in sectors of strong demand (Figure 7.11), and a slower growth rate in fast-growing markets (Figure 7.12);
- management performance has been poorer.

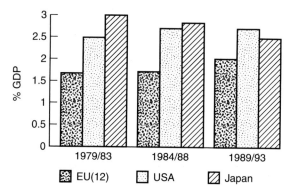

Source: OECD

Figure 7.9 R & D expenditure

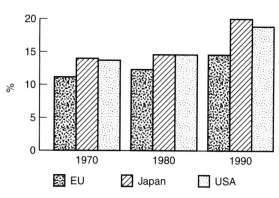

Source: Elquist & McKelvey

Figure 7.10 Growth in high-tech industries

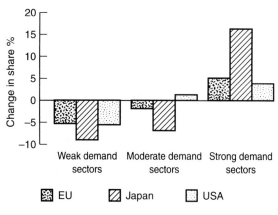

Source: European Commission (DGIII)

Figure 7.11 Gross value added in manufacturing: 1980–90

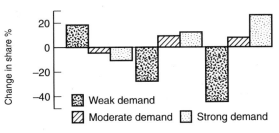

Source: European Commission (DGIII)

Figure 7.12 Sectoral distribution of manufacturing exports 1992

The macroenvironment

There are a number of indicators of the extent to which the macroenvironment in Europe is less stable and predictable than that in Japan or the USA. An outstanding example of this is the rate at which currencies fluctuate.

There is only one US dollar for the 260 million inhabitants of the USA. There is only one Japanese yen for the 125 million inhabitants of Japan. However, there are 14 different currencies for the 350 million inhabitants of the European Union. In addition, there have been major fluctuations, over time, in the relative value of the European currencies against each other.

The value of the strongest currency has fluctuated against the weakest currency by some 15 per cent per annum (on the basis of the EU 12) and even by some 5 per cent per annum (on the basis of the four major EU economies) during the last 15 years.

The tax burden in Europe is higher than in the rest of the OECD, and the rate of increase is also faster. From 37 per cent in the early 1970s, taxes in Europe as a share of GDP have now risen to 44 per cent. During the same period, the tax burden in the rest of the OECD has risen from 28 per cent to only 31 per cent (Figure 7.13).

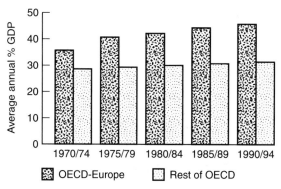

Source: OECD

Figure 7.13 Tax burden

Another important feature of the European macroenvironment is that the level of savings (and hence the amount available for investment) is low. The level of savings in the European Union has declined by almost one-sixth over the past 20 years to a rate of 19 per cent of GDP. At the same time, the level of savings in the rest of the OECD has declined by less than one-tenth to 22 per cent (Figure 7.14). The principal reason for this is the high level of public sector deficits in Europe.

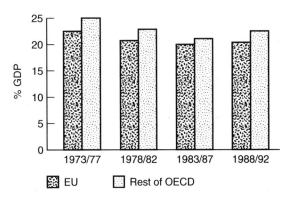

Figure 7.14 Level of savings

Another key element of the macroenvironment is the regulatory framework under which firms based in Europe compete. According to a survey of 2100 companies undertaken by Business Decisions Limited on behalf of UNICE, companies consider that:

- regulations impose a major constraint on their competitiveness because they make it more difficult to innovate, to improve their operating efficiency and to respond to changes in the business environment;
- the three regulatory areas that create most problems for them are tax and other administrative regulations, employment regulations and environmental regulations;
- the principal shortcomings of regulations are that there are too many, that they are too complex, and that the standards set for regulations vary between countries.

Summary

One of the consequences of this triple squeeze is that company profitability has been significantly lower in Europe than in the rest of the OECD, most particularly Japan and the USA. Over the past 25 years, the rate of return on capital employed of companies based in Europe has averaged 12.5 per cent, com-

LILLE - BRUSSELS
ECONOMIC AXIS

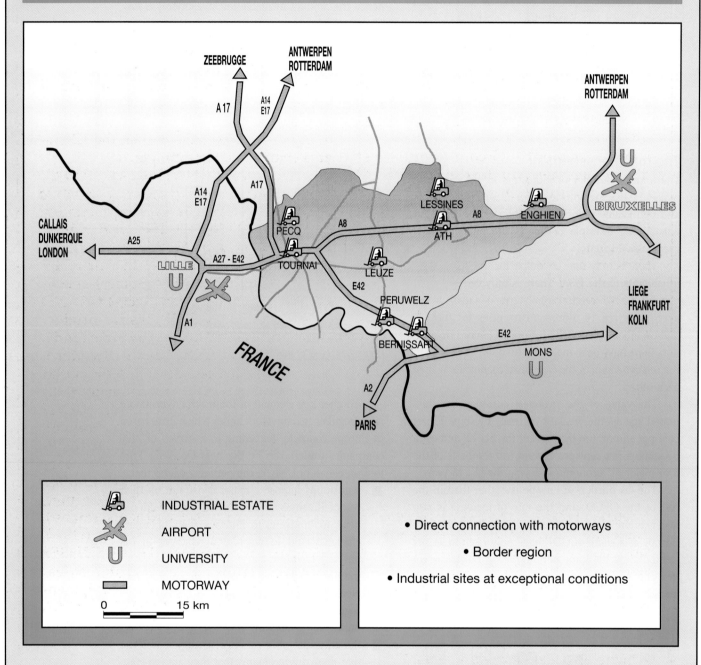

Legend:

 INDUSTRIAL ESTATE

AIRPORT

U UNIVERSITY

MOTORWAY

0   15 km

- Direct connection with motorways
- Border region
- Industrial sites at exceptional conditions

Your Development Partner

IDETA

IDETA : Inter-community Agency for Economic Development
11, Rue Saint Jacques   Tél. + 32.69.23.47.01
7500 Tournai - Belgium   Fax + 32.69.23.47.00

For any information please contact HENRI DEHARENG and his team

Supported by the Walloon Region and FEDER.

BELGIUM AT THE HEART OF EUROPE
THE IDETA REGION

Your investments will benefit from a particularly attractive aid system and environment

THE IDETA region, an outstanding region for investors, at the heart of the European golden triangle, lies on the London-Lille-Brussels axis, in one of the most promising economic areas in Europe.

These are the location possibilities offered by the Intecommunale de Developpement Economique et d'Amenagement du Territoire (IDETA) (Intercommunal Organisation for the Economic Development and Land-Use Planning). The zone of action of this intercommunal organisation covers the territory of 20 municipalities, with a total population of some 250,000 inhabitants.

The region has an excellent communications system:
• Direct connection with the motorway network
• Brussels International Airport is less than 1 hour
• Lille-Lesquin European Airport can be reached in under 25 minutes
• French Super High Speed Train "TGV" links TODAY our region to PARIS in 80 minutes.

A region of parks, mountains and castles:
The quiet beauty of the region's countryside, its rivers and its forests provide a series of pleasures to the newcomer, as do the old city streets and the architectural splendours of the "Chateau de Beloeil" and the "Cathedrale de Tournai".

A favourable economic environment:
The region has a long tradition in textiles, mining, quarrying, printing, publishing, the cement industry, construction and agriculture and food. In recent years the region has diversified into leading technologies such as chemicals and para-medical equipment.

IDETA, your partner for your establishment:
• creation and development of industrial sites
• welcoming of investors, providing information and logistic back-up for small and medium enterprises,
• creation and development of natural parks

Many companies have chosen the IDETA area before you. For example:
BAXTER INTERNATIONAL (USA), medico-surgical equipment BAYER (Germany), parachemicals-pharmacy BTR/DUNLOP (UK), PVC and rubber conveyor belts CASTERMAN (Belgium), printing and publishing (Tintin) ELF AQUITAINE/ATOCHEM (France), chemicals-parachemicals (fertilizers) GRAND METROPOLITAN (U.K), biscuit production HOLDERBANK (Switzerland), cement works HOGANAS (Sweden), chemicals (metal powders) HUPPE FORM (Germany), movable and acoustic partitions in metal and wood ITALCEMENTI (Italy), cement works KIABI (France), clothing (distribution centre) KRUPP-POLYSIUS (Germany), large boiler construction PSA (France), automobiles (distribution centre) SALUC (Belgium), snooker balls SUDZUCKER (Germany), sugar refinery SUN CHEMICAL (USA), energy curing products TROIS SUISSES (France), clothing (mail order sales) VALEO (France), automobile equipment headlamps VAN DEN BROEKE-LUTOSA (Belgium), potato-based deep-frozen products.

How to join them?
Send a fax with your name and address to receive more information to **IDETA Henri Dehareng 11, rue St Jacques B-7 500 Tournai Tel: 32/69/23.47.01   Fax: 32/69/23.47.00**

pared with 16 per cent in Japan and the USA (Figure 7.15).

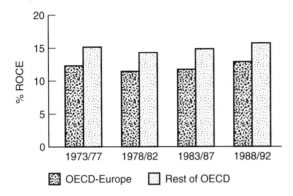

Source: OECD

Figure 7.15 Return on capital employed

Conclusion

There is no single solution that will reverse the decline in the competitiveness of Europe. Nonetheless, there is general agreement that it is the responsibility of the managements (and the shareholders) of individual firms to improve the competitiveness of their firms. Action must, however, also be taken by the European Union and the individual member states to create an environment within which firms based in Europe can improve their competitiveness.

Japanese companies have improved their competitiveness almost continuously since the end of the Second World War. There has also been a significant turnround in the competitive performance of American companies during the past decade.

Moreover, there are a number of sectors in which European performance is world class and there are a few European companies that are world class in almost all other sectors.

In addition, companies based in Europe have a number of important advantages:

- the size of the European market, as the Single Market becomes a reality;
- the quality of the education system;
- the scientific and technological tradition;
- the European social model, which balances the needs of governments, shareholders, employees and consumers;
- the consensus style of political decision making;
- the low level of corporate debt.

However, taken overall, the competitiveness of Europe has declined during the past 25 years, most notably in the last decade.

This decline has neither a single cause nor a single solution. No single individual or group has been responsible for causing the decline, nor is responsible for solving it. Europe needs to make a number of policy changes at the levels of the European Union and the member states, and to encourage changes in the behaviour of the social partners, firms and individuals throughout the Union.

There are some differences between the policy proposals in the various reports summarized above; but most are differences of degree, not of kind. Moreover, all are agreed that, to improve competitiveness, to increase growth and to create employment, action must be taken now by all institutions and by all individuals throughout the European Union.

References

- The UNICE Competitiveness Reports entitled *Making Europe more competitive: Towards world class performance.*
- The White Paper from the European Commission entitled *Growth, Competitiveness and Employment.*
- The Communication from the European Commission on *An Industrial Competitiveness Policy.*
- The Report by the European Round Table entitled *Competitiveness: The Way towards Growth and Jobs.*
- The UNICE Regulatory Report entitled *Releasing Europe's Potential: Through Targeted Regulatory Reform.*
- *The First Report of the Competitiveness Advisory Group* to the President of the European Commission, Prime Ministers and Heads of State.

The Industrial Challenge for Europe

Dr Heinrich von Pierer, President & Chief Executive Officer, Siemens AG

Western European commerce and industry are facing unprecedented competition from abroad: from the United States, the emerging free-market economies of eastern Europe, but most of all from the countries of South-east Asia. The competition from the Pacific region in particular poses an ever-increasing challenge to the European Union's economic well-being, and radical measures are needed to redress a deteriorating situation. But to do this it is necessary to be aware of the boundary conditions that prevail. Essentially there are six factors that have most influenced or are still influencing the situation.

Market liberalization

The era of national champions is coming to an end. Margaret Thatcher and John Major have shown an alternative way. Continental Europe has learnt a lesson from Great Britain in this respect. Airlines, telecommunications companies, energy and water utilities and many other public services have been privatized and 'exposed to the rigors of the market'. Railways will soon be added to this impressive list of 'liberalized' activities. The net effect of all this is that procurement policies will change. Large international concerns such as Siemens are particularly pleased about these developments, although there are many in Germany who still have reservations about such developments when applied within the Federal Republic. Whatever one's view, liberalization does mean increasing competition with a vengeance,

lower prices and inevitably reducing margins for suppliers.

The good news is that as a direct consequence of the opening of markets, particularly those of the 'public sector', companies other than a chosen few are now able to bid for contracts. The liberalized electricity supply industry is a case in point. Prior to liberalization only a few, mostly national companies were allowed to bid for contracts. Privatization changed all this and as a result Siemens, for example, has built and is building a number of high-efficiency combined-cycle power stations in England.

The first factor that is changing the conditions of international trade is thus that national companies can no longer be protected by the shield of public sector spending policy. The prevailing attitude is now 'value for money' and those companies – largely irrespective of national origin – that can meet this basic criterion are in with a chance. Those who do not will fail.

Market globalization

The United Kingdom has always had an advantage in terms of globalization because every child grows up as a potential global player by learning what amounts to the world's *lingua franca*, English. Moreover, the Commonwealth, and with it the British merchant navy, set the standards for world trade. This also made British banks and merchants the leaders in world financial commerce.

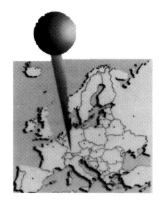

The entrepreneuralism that was so prevalent in early Victorian Britain represented a global state of mind and an attitude that went beyond national boundaries. Obviously, the days of empire and imperial preferences have gone, but nonetheless the wider vision is still essential if the Europeans are to succeed in the global market. In essence, globalization boils down to having the same competitors, the same products and the same prices in all major markets.

'The same prices' mean those that are settling at lower and lower levels, which is good news for the consumer and bad news for the supplier. Typically in telecommunications, prices are eroding at a rate of 10 per cent annually and in computers price attrition is even more dramatic. Clearly the lesson here is that Europe has to adjust to and learn to live with this economic entropy if it is to remain relatively prosperous.

Eastern Europe

The decline and fall of the Soviet system liberated economic forces that are still to be fully appreciated. It released a pent-up demand for goods and services, but unfortunately without the concomitant ability to pay. One of the net effects of this is an 'open' and relatively low-cost labour market. This is felt particularly strongly in the higher wage economies such as Germany, where skilled labour costs DM44 an hour while across the border in the Czech Republic it is only some DM3–5 per hour – or about one-tenth of that in Germany. To a lessening degree this differential is reflected throughout Western Europe. Furthermore, and in Germany particularly, the already adverse cost situation is worsening: the recent round of wage agreements between trade unions and employers in Germany has made employment costs rise by half as much again when compared with Czech labour costs.

South-east Asia

In South-east Asia people work longer hours at relatively lower cost, and into the bargain have a notable flair for innovation – they are not, as many believe in the West, just copiers of Western technology. The large and growing markets are in this part of the world and will remain there for some years to come. High-tech innovation plus low manufacturing costs is the success formula that has turned South-east Asian suppliers into fierce tiger-like competitors of European (and, of course, American) industry.

Why is this? The answer is simple: the region has high growth rates both in terms of population and, therefore, market potential. To illustrate this, look at the basic statistics:

- By the end of the twentieth century the population will have grown by 200 million, from 2.8 to 3.0 billion people.
- The electrical and electronics market has a growth rate of about 12 per cent/annum in China and the ASEAN (Association of South East Asian Nations) countries, whereas it is just above 4 per cent in the European Union.
- The backlog in demand for telephone lines in China alone is almost as large as the total number of telephone lines worldwide – which is currently about 800 million. The mind almost boggles at such statistics, but it gives an indication as to the scale of business opportunity in the region!

Clearly the demand for goods and services in South-east Asia is going to be one of the driving forces of the world's economy for a long time to come. European business has to meet the challenges head on if it is to maintain its position into the third millennium. Failure to do so will have dire consequences for Europe's standard of living.

Technological change

Ever since the industrial revolution, technology has been one of the main spurs to bringing about change. This will continue to be the case into the distant future. The important consideration, however, is how to harness technological change for the general good. This, of course, is an omnibus question and cannot be answered by industry or commerce alone. It involves all aspects of society and the future direction the world will take.

Having recognized this, it is nonetheless important to appreciate what technologies are driving economic endeavour in order to harness them for the general good. For example, in the electrical industry microelectronics and software are currently key determinants of business. Typically:

- microelectronic devices are becoming smaller and smaller;
- they are becoming more and more powerful;
- and prices continue to tumble.

For example, 20 years ago a one megabit of electronic memory, which is about 60 A4 pages of text, cost

Market meets Science:
Fraunhofer-
Institut für Integrierte Schaltungen

Fraunhofer Institut
Integrierte Schaltungen

Fraunhofer-Gesellschaft
The Fraunhofer-Gesellschaft was founded as a non profit organisation and today employs a staff of 7,700 men and women. It operates 47 research institutes in 14 German Länder, and maintains a resource centre in the United States. The success of the Fraunhofer-Gesellschaft lies in its decentralized organizational structure. The total volume of research is valued at DM 941 million. Whilst the administrative headquarters are in Munich, the 47 institutes operate from 31 different locations, where they carry out their respective work as independant "profit centres" in close partnership with local industry. Contact research for and with industry represents the main area of activity reaching a total value of DM 596 million in 1992.

Research at the Fraunhofer-Gesellschaft concentrates on the engineering and natural sciences. Of key importance amongst the research fields are microelectronics and microsystem technologies, production and manufacturing technologies, data processing and communications technology, factory organisation and company management, the development of new materials, environmental protection and preventative health care, and processing technologies particularly those concerned with biological processes.

Fraunhofer-Group for Microelectronics and Microsystems
A number of 6 institutes are working in the fields of microelectronics and microsystems. Among these the Fraunhofer-Institut für Integrierte Schaltungen (FhG-IIS) dedicates its work to the development of microelectronic systems and devices as well as Integrated Circuits for various applications. The institute was established to practice technology transfer from university research into industrial applications in the fields of microelectronic systems and Application Specific Integrated Circuits (ASICs). Small and medium sized companies are addressed as well as large industries. Research and development projects are carried out in close cooperation with industrial customers. This tight contact to various market segments enables the scientific staff to react flexibly to changing market needs and conditions.

Research and Development
Research fields include development of microcontrollers, intelligent sensors and actuators, analog and digital integrated circuits, analog/digital converters, and high speed circuits. These sophisticated technologies are employed to further develop system applications in the telecommunication sector such as digital audio broadcasting (DAB) and in the field of industrial electronics such as image processing systems for quality control in industrial processes. A major contribution lies in the audio coding scheme for the world standard known as ISO-MPEG-Standard IS 11172-3 (MPEG1), Layer 3.

Technology Transfer
Through national and international technology transfer programmes the Fraunhofer-Institut für Integrierte Schaltungen concentrates on providing access to microelectronics for small and medium sized industries (SMIs). In cooperation with numerous European technology transfer institutions a network is operated aiming at removing the obstacles against using modern microelectronics. Within the consortium, a number of measures was developed to make cost-sharing among several companies possible: the multi project wafer (MPW)-service can bring several designs on one single mask set so that prototypes and small volume can be offered at low prices. In addition, agreements were reached with CAD vendors on software tools. Furthermore, development cost can be reduced by developing one single ASIC, for instance a bus controller, within so-called working groups serving several clients, who would then share the cost. 57 of these working groups have operated successfully so far.

Practical technology transfer ranges from information transfer through PR activities, over seminars and training courses to contract research and development projects. New concepts for product development are employed as well as the latest technologies. Independence from any technology vendor is a precondition for picking the optimum solution in order to solve a given problem. The customers are supported from conceptual studies over the various project phases up to the functional prototype. Technology transfer is furtheron practiced by means of consultation, provision of CAD-equipment, and support at any step in the design cycle. As a very efficient way in getting SMIs in touch with ASICs "training on the project" is offered. Staff members of the customer are trained at the FhG-IIS. The training is not based on any academic subject, but on the specific customers project. The next ASIC project can then be carried out by the customer himself.

The FhG-IIS offers a variety of seminars dedicated to information and education of industry staff members. The majority of seminars is tailored to the needs of small and medium sized industries. More than 30 events are organized each year.

Example product innovation

Electrocardiographic ECG devices for patient monitoring are widely used in medical diagnostics. Conventional ECG eqipment is used for stationary application. Manufacturer are continuously forced to improve product features and to reduce selling price in order to survive as a company. This has motivated a medium sized German company to apply for assistance at the Fraunhofer-Institut für Integrierte Schaltungen.

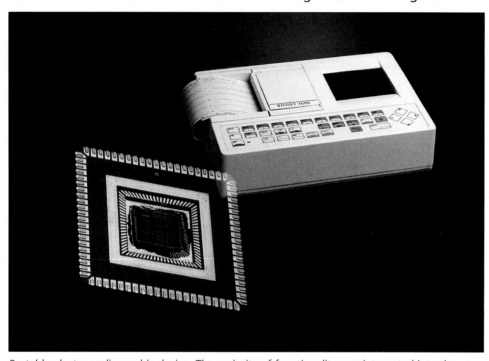

Portable electrocardiographic device. The majority of functionality was integrated into the application specific integrated circuit (ASIC).

The question was: would it be possible to integrate the majority of funcionality in one single microchip (ASIC) and what would be the development costs for this innovation? After extensive consultations a feasibility study was carried out. The results were encouraging for the customer resulting in a turn key development.

The project at the FhG-IIS was carried out in two major steps. First, the most critical analog and mixed analog/digital functions were integrated on a test chip which was fabricated via the MPW-service. A minimum of prototype costs could thus be achieved. After a second prototype run the complete functional ASIC was fabricated in 2µm CMOS technology including 9 input channels with low noise pre-amplifiers, switched capacitor low pass filters, sample and hold circuitry, a 13 bit analog/digital converter, and a microcontroller with 2 seriell interfaces.

This successful ASIC development project led to a significant reduction in product size, power dissipation, and last but not least system costs. This new (see figure) product is now being sold as a portable electrocardiograph. By the introduction of modern ASIC technology the system costs could be cut by half of the preceeding costs.

Fraunhofer-Institut für Integrierte Schaltungen
Am Weichselgarten 3
D-91058 Erlangen
Tel: ++49 9131 776 0
Fax: ++49 9131 776 999

"Well researched, comprehensive and useful" Sir Leon Brittan

KOGAN PAGE

Second Edition

Doing Business with South Africa

Consultant Editor: Jonathan Reuvid

"An outstanding publication"
Johannesburg Stock Exchange

Fully researched, up-to-date and including contributions from leading investment and industrial development companies, this is the essential, practical guide to doing business in South Africa.

With publication timed to coincide with the new government's first budget, it offers sound advice on trade and investment opportunities and analyses the corporate, governmental and legal strategies that lie at the heart of economic considerations

Order your copy from your bookseller today – or call our credit card hotline on 071 278 0433

£35.00 250 pages Order ref: KS347

Kogan Page, 120 Pentonville Road, London N1 9JN

KOGAN PAGE

about DM150,000. At the time, this was about the price of a terraced house in Germany. Today the same amount of memory can be had for the price of a glass of beer.

Increasing subminiaturization also means that production content is declining as much as labour content. Production jobs in the conventional meaning of the phrase are being lost at almost an exponential rate, whereas employment involving engineering, software and services in general is increasing. Unfortunately, the losses of the former do not equal the gains of the latter, and this is one of the dilemmas of increasingly innovative technology.

Currency turbulence

Money is the lubricant of trade, for without it we all would be back in the age of barter. The problem is that the 'quality' of the lubricant is not the same throughout the world, and consequently trade flows more easily in some places than in others. The effect of this is that money itself becomes a commodity and introduces friction into the mechanism of trade.

Evidence of this is the kind of monetary volatility experienced over the past few months, which raises a number of fundamental questions. In the short term all appears to be safe, but such currency movements will have considerable long-term consequences and, therefore, have to be addressed.

Frequent and wide fluctuation in monetary values demonstrates the importance of greater monetary stability for world trade and is the principal *raison d'être* for a uniform European currency. It would have to be a stable currency, of course, and this implies meeting the strict conditions agreed at Maastricht.

These are the six most important factors that currently affect world trade in general and the competitive position of the European Union in particular. The message is clear: competitive pressure is increasing and we all have to adjust. Europe can adjust, but it must be prepared to be more proactive and less reactive. The saying 'Act or you will be acted upon' is relevant to the European condition; or as a well-known American entrepreneur succinctly put it: 'Control your destiny before somebody else does.'

9 Privatization in Europe

Peter Young, International Director, Adam Smith Institute

In Europe privatization used to be an enthusiasm confined largely to Britain. Today this is no longer so. Privatization is a significant economic policy in almost all countries of both West and East Europe.

The most important development is of course the very substantial privatization programmes that are being implemented in post-communist European countries. In former East Germany alone some 13,600 enterprises have been privatized, a figure which does not include the 25,000 small retail businesses that have also been privatized there. In Poland, Hungary and the Czech Republic, very large numbers of enterprises, large and small, have also been privatized. Privatization in the post-communist countries is a *sine qua non* of the creation of market economies; a virtually universal goal of those countries.

In Western Europe the potential for privatization was of course much less, in that nationalization never extended very far. Britain nationalized to a much greater extent than most West European countries. Nevertheless, significant numbers of major companies in Western Europe are state-owned, particularly in the utility sectors. Previous West European attempts to privatize have been rather tentative. It is only in the last few years, under the pressure of European-wide liberalization, that privatization has begun to gather pace.

The extent of privatization in post-communist European countries has been influenced strongly by whether they initially chose a case-by-case or mass

privatization approach. Several of the first post-communist countries to embark upon privatization programmes, most notably Hungary and Poland, chose to deal with each company individually in the context of privatization.

However, all post-communist countries have found that the company-by-company approach to privatization takes too long and have introduced, or are considering the introduction of, some form of mass privatization, in which buying power is injected into the domestic population, through vouchers or other means, and a more uniform approach is taken to the privatization of a large number of companies.

All East European countries, however, have continued with some privatization on a company-by-company basis, in particular involving those companies sold to foreign investors, and some large companies especially important for the economy. These privatizations have been carried out in a number of ways, sometimes involving tenders, other times direct negotiation with one purchaser or joint ventures. In most countries, with the exception of Hungary, privatization to foreign purchasers has not constituted a particularly large part of the privatization process.

During 1990–91, around 80 per cent of Hungarian privatization sales were to foreign investors; this proportion fell to 55 per cent in 1992 and 33 per cent in 1993, as the most attractive Hungarian companies had already been sold and more opportunities became available in other central and eastern European countries. By the end of 1992, there were over 17,000 Hungarian companies with foreign investors, with foreigners holding an average 54 per cent stake; these figures can be contrasted with 1989, when there were only 1,350 firms with foreign investors, with an average stake of 24 per cent. A total of US$7.2 bn was invested in Hungary by the end of 1993, 90 per cent of which was accounted for by the fifty largest investors.

In the Czech Republic, the government's primary strategy has been to encourage foreign investment into companies after they have been privatized, although there have been a number of significant privatizations and joint ventures involving foreign firms, such as the Skoda–Volkswagen deal. The Czech government concentrated on rapid mass privatization through a voucher scheme in which Czech citizens used vouchers to bid for shares in state companies. 1,491 Czech and Slovak companies were privatized in the first wave of voucher privatization in 1992, and these represented some 50 per cent of GDP in the former Czechoslovakia. In subsequent voucher privatization waves in the Czech Republic, most of the rest of the state sector has been sold off. By the end of 1994 almost 60 per cent of GNP in the Czech Republic was generated by the private sector, a change that was largely due to privatization.

Czech enterprises have had to undergo significant restructuring. In the past, 70 per cent of exports went to COMECON markets: in 1995, 70 per cent were sold to western markets. The total volume of exports has increased by 14.6 per cent compared with 1991, despite a 22.5 per cent drop in trade with Slovakia.

Poland, which first adopted a case-by-case approach, has privatized more slowly. However, small retail enterprises were sold very quickly and many smaller enterprises were sold through a type of employee buyout. By the end of 1994, 764 firms had been privatized in Poland by means of a type of leveraged buyout, in which the enterprise management and employees, plus sometimes outside entrepreneurs, acquired the assets and liabilities of state enterprises, at first by lease, then freehold once all payments by instalment had been made. Now Poland has adopted a form of mass privatization, in which shares in some 400 large enterprises will be allocated to around 15 investment funds, ownership of which will later be given to Polish citizens.

Privatization in the advanced East European countries – Poland, Hungary and the Czech Republic – is now extending to the utility sectors, such as electricity, gas and telecommunications. Soon, some of those countries will have privatized to a greater extent than their West European neighbours.

In Western Europe, European Union directives are forcing the pace of liberalization. For example, a directive requiring countries to open all international and domestic telephone calls to full competition by 1 January 1998 has pressured many West European countries into liberalizing and privatizing their telecommunications sectors.

In Germany, Deutsche Telekom, the state monopoly telecommunications operator, is now slated for privatization in 1996. It needs privatization not just to comply with European Union directives but also to raise cash to reduce its over DM100 bn debt and continue its DM60 bn investment programme in Eastern Germany.

Privatization in France, which was suspended by the previous socialist government, picked up again under the centre-right governments of Balladur and Juppe. Banque Nationale de Paris, Rhone Poulenc, Pechiney, Usinor Sacilor and Union des Assurances de Paris have already been sold. Others on the list of around 20 companies include Air France, Renault and Thomson. Unlike most other countries, however, the French are still holding back from privatizing their major monopoly utilities, most notably France Telecom and Electricité de France. They will not be able to hold out against the tide for very much longer, however. The companies themselves are being held back in the world market because of their public sector status.

In other parts of Western Europe the nominal political colour of the government is not much of a guide to the speed of privatization. The socialists have just regained power in Portugal, for example, and are committed not just to continuing the privatization programme, but to speeding it up. The new socialist Finance Minister, Antonio Sousa Franco, has promised to present a programme of 'rapid and intensive' privatizations. This is expected to include electricity distribution companies, gas companies, remaining state shares in Portugal Telecom, airports, Air Portugal, and mining, cement, steel and shipyard companies, amongst others.

In Spain, which has had a socialist government for some time, commitment to privatization has recently increased, with the acceptance that the 'crown jewels' of the state sector, such as the state phone company Telefonica, the banking group Argentaria and the state airline Iberia, should be fully privatized. If, as is likely, the conservative opposition party Partido Popular wins power in 1996, the speed of the programme will increase further.

In Italy, recent governments have been committed to privatization of the major state assets, such as Telecom Italia, the oil and gas company ENI, and the electricity company ENEL, and the process looks as if it is finally about to happen.

The prospects for continued privatization in Western and Eastern Europe look good. As experience is built up, countries have been able to gain confidence and learn from each other. Pressure on the laggards is building up. Five years ago one couldn't have been sure, but today it is certain that the future of Europe is private.

PART

3

European Markets in Flux

The Russian Federation in 1996

Paul Forrest, Senior Economist, Moscow Narodny Bank Ltd

Given that the Russian Federation has undergone such dramatic change over the past few years, and that political economic developments there have regularly been described as either unique, seminal or epic, the most reassuring feature of 1996 may be that it will ultimately come to be described as a year of consolidation. With a new Russian Duma due to be convened in January, following the elections scheduled for December 1995, and a Presidential election programmed for July next year, political events during 1996 should provide the basis for the normalization of political and economic life in the Federation.

While the successful completion of the transition period may still be some years away, with recent history in Central and Eastern Europe a useful pointer, stabilization, consolidation and recovery will be the chief characteristics not only of government policy but of general economic developments. Even assuming an electoral swing, in either the Duma or Presidential elections, to the political parties opposed to reform, it is difficult to envisage how the market reform process can be reversed. With over 60 per cent of Russia's measured GDP originating in the private sector, a greater proportion than that produced in Italy, the decentralization of economic decision making and the extension of private ownership would seem to make the market reform process irreversible. Indeed, events over the last few months, most notably the ill health of President Yeltsin, the

Chechen emergency and August's inter-bank crisis, all serve to highlight the resilience of the economy, and the increasing distance that is emerging between political events and economic developments.

Following a period in which the introduction of market mechanisms has been largely unrestrained, and the authorities have encountered considerable difficulties recording economic activity, let alone attempting to regulate it, a period of consolidation will inevitably involve some shake-outs. As a result, the August inter-bank crisis may provide a useful illustration of the impact that a sustained period of government-sponsored macroeconomic stabilization may have on the wider economy.

Of the almost 3000 banks estimated to be operating in Russia (prior to August 1995), well over half are new institutions, established since 1991, with relatively small funding resources. These banks had been able to enjoy relatively easy profits from financing hard currency trade, benefiting from the sustained erosion of rouble-denominated debt as a result of surging inflation, and from speculating against the rouble on foreign exchanges and on the appreciation of rouble-denominated assets on the commodity exchanges and in property markets. However, the prevailing economic conditions that favoured these banks began to be transformed earlier in the year, when the Central Bank of Russia adopted a more disciplined policy approach. In particular, the tightening of monetary and credit policies by the authorities, particularly the higher reserve requirements imposed by the Central Bank and the establishment of the rouble foreign exchange corridor, greatly curtailed the profit-making potential of these Russian institutions. Indeed, the announcement that the exchange rate corridor policy will be sustained at least until the end of 1995, when some banks were perhaps speculating that the policy would only last until 1 October, as originally proposed, may have been a factor in the crisis. Under this policy, the Central Bank aims to keep the rouble trading in a corridor of between R4300 to R4900 against the US$.

With currency arbitrage increasingly limited by the effective stabilization of the rouble, and severely constraining profit making, Russian banks became reluctant to extend rouble credits on the inter-bank market, precipitating the liquidity crisis. The Central Bank, by only extending short-relief credits to the more established institutions, in effect used the crisis to force through a consolidation of the banking system, not only improving its financial soundness, but improving it in terms of commercial and economic viability. As the banks themselves are forced as a result of commercial logic to adopt more prudent lending operations, the wider economy will be forced to adopt more commercially oriented development programmes, with the less viable enterprises forced to adapt or liquidate.

Nevertheless, the economic rationalizations and restructuring that will probably take place during 1996 are only likely to have a limited impact on overall economic output. This is largely the result of the fact that after the massive GDP decline recorded over the previous three years, economic indicators suggest that the Russian economy may bottom out in 1995, and some limited recovery in output may be sustained during 1996. Industrial output figures for the first half of 1995 suggest that some stabilization of production is occurring. In addition, it is possible that the economic deterioration experienced since the demise of communism may have been greatly overstated by official statistics unable to measure the rapid expansion of the private sector. Indirect measures of economic activity, such as electricity consumption and unemployment levels, suggest a less dramatic, although still considerable contraction in economic activity. The apparent size of the private sector, and in particular its increasing absorption into the formal economy as the taxation net expands, should permit some recovery in economic performance, despite the fact that authorities are tightening

fiscal discipline. Indeed, the government's stabilization programme, with its 1995 targeted budget deficit equivalent to 5.6 per cent of GDP and the support of the International Monetary Fund (IMF), should enable significant gains to be made against inflation, which is expected to fall to a monthly rate of 1–2 per cent by the year-end. While political resistance to the authorities' attempts to tighten fiscal discipline is likely to be intense from a variety of quarters, the need to meet the conditionality of the IMF stand-by facility, and the increasing popular disquiet over hyperinflation, should enable the authorities to sustain the tight fiscal strategy. With the easing of inflationary pressures and the establishment of the rouble foreign exchange corridor, speculative pressure against the rouble has eased considerably. As a result, and notwithstanding the scale of capital flight sustained during 1994 and the limited recovery in 1995, 1996 should see a significant recovery in hard-currency capital inflows, both Russian-offshore and foreign, after the Presidential election.

Russian reforms are therefore progressing and the first benefits are beginning to accrue. Banks are becoming more involved in the productive side of the economy, especially following a decree allowing commercial banks to manage federally owned stakes in some of Russia's leading companies. However, the requirements of a banking system capable of funding corporate working capital in a market economy – where banks provide a clearing system for funds – represent a considerable departure from the traditional role of Russian banks. One of the largest difficulties is the lack of finance available to companies; if financing can be made available to Russian entities, not only raw materials but also high value products can be obtained. However, the traditional approaches to credit assessment are of minimal value in such an economy, and close contacts with Russian partners are essential to guarantee performance. Often difficulties can also be overcome using countertrade deals, although this requires an imaginative business approach. For large-scale projects, the overlapping of various authorities creates additional problems and uncertainties.

As the stabilization of the economy proceeds and the influence of political considerations begins to mirror the experience in established market economies, more and more business opportunities arise. Many uncertainties now stem from the political process, particularly the speculation over the likely outcome of the forthcoming elections. Nevertheless, reforms have progressed so far that a complete reversal of the process is unlikely to occur. Business opportunities with Russia should be treated cau- tiously, although recent developments suggest that an optimistic approach is not unwarranted.

11 Austria

Bank Austria

Three key events have had a major impact on the political and economic framework of Austria in the last decade. The opening up of the East, participation in the European Economic Area and finally entry into the EU on 1 January 1995 shifted Austria from its peripheral position to the centre of a new and very potent economic area. Austria has therefore become even more attractive as an important economic location in Europe and as a link to Eastern Europe.

Austria has always enjoyed relatively close links with Eastern Europe and therefore followed a 'double-edged strategy'. Austrian economic policy had its centre of gravity in Western Europe but, at the same time, economic ties were also nurtured with the states of Eastern Europe. The proportion of trade with Eastern Europe in Austria's balance of trade was higher than in any other European country even before the opening up of the East – with the exception of Finland. This special position for Austria was already exploited by a series of multinational companies, which established themselves in Austria even before the collapse of communism in the East. The opening up of Eastern Europe and membership of the EU have increased the importance of Austria as a location and springboard for Eastern Europe.

What advantages are there now for international companies which want to operate in Eastern Europe from a base in Austria? The main arguments in favour of Austria are certainly the high Western standard of production, excellent Eastern European

know-how, the stable economic and political environment and also the high standard of living. An important factor is the favourable cost base, which results from supporting Eastern European markets from Austria. The high transaction costs which generally arise when developing new markets in Eastern Europe can be minimized by selecting Austria as a site, since foreign companies can profit from the existing sales channels, from valuable contacts established over many years and from the decades of experience possessed by Austrian companies. Another factor not to be underestimated is the special understanding, for historical reasons, of the mentality of partners in neighbouring states to the east of Austria.

At the top of the list for companies in selecting their site is the immediate cost aspect. Supporting Eastern European markets from an Austrian base can be many times more cost effective than the activities of international companies on site. The rents alone are higher in many Eastern European capitals than in Austria. At the same time, the transport costs can be kept low as the result of the optimum geographical position of Austria, in particular Vienna, and in light of the well-developed infrastructure network. Another factor in favour of Austria is that in many cases it is still easier to find there qualified staff with the necessary skills. A final factor to stress is the considerable amount of information for companies which want to locate in Austria. Banks, public bodies

The Austrian For Banking.

© Spanish Riding School

"As changes in Europe gather pace, the unique qualities of Austrian banking are being rediscovered. Austria's largest bank - Bank Austria - enjoys the highest 'Triple A' ratings and offers the most comprehensive international network. Bank Austria London provides a gateway to the New Europe for U.K. companies, financial institutions and private bindividuals."

For further information on how you can benefit from The Austrian For Banking - and all in plain English, contact Ben Brittain the General Manager at Bank Austria London on 0171 588 4085. Member of the Securities and Futures Authority.

Bank Austria
LONDON

11

and research institutes are important partners who give valuable practical and national economic information.

A balance sheet of the development of business with the countries of Eastern Europe shows that Austria seems to have managed by and large to have made optimum use of the opportunities resulting from the opening up of the East. The high increases in exports to these countries show that Austrian companies have secured a firm place with customers in Eastern Europe. Those Austrian companies which operate in the field of mechanical engineering and motor vehicle production and the production of processed goods and consumer goods have profited particularly strongly from the dynamic growth in exports to the East.

Austria was able almost to double its exports to the East overall between 1989 and 1994 following the fall of the Iron Curtain. If a comparison is made based on the direct Eastern neighbours alone, there has been a tripling of exports. After the EU, Eastern Europe is therefore the second most important market for Austrian products.

Additional competitors have also arisen, however, alongside the rise of new and certainly active markets in the East. These altered framework conditions have set in motion far-reaching structural changes in the Austrian economy. These restructuring processes are extremely painful in some areas, but lead overall to the development of higher value product sectors. Some examples of negatively affected sectors are the Austrian cement, fertilizer, and textile and clothing industries. The production of agricultural machinery and timber processing are also affected by competition from the East.

Numerous companies have already reacted successfully to the altered framework conditions, however, through active counter-strategies and relocation of parts of their production to the East. Exploitation of the relatively low standard of living improves the international competitiveness of the Austrian companies. This process costs jobs on the one hand, but on the other hand new jobs are created in Austria through improved trade links. The net effect of this development has been a clear plus for employment statistics.

The entry of Austria into the EU also had positive effects for these branches of the economy. The handicaps in trade were therefore eliminated, which had had a negative effect on competitiveness until the end of 1994. Until then, differential customs duty was

levied on Austrian goods which were exported to the EU and contained proportions of Eastern European added value. The end of this practice noticeably eased matters for domestic industry, in particular textile, clothing and leather processing.

The fact that Austrian companies have taken their opportunities for active internationalization can also be seen very well in the high proportion of Austrian direct investment in Eastern Europe, in international terms. As of the end of 1994, approximately 13,700 projects with Austrian participation had been registered and invested Austrian capital was running at around US$2.7 billion. Measured against overall international foreign investment in Eastern Europe, Austria's share in projects was 8 per cent and around 10 per cent of invested capital.

Austrian economic policy reacted very quickly in supporting the states of Eastern Europe in their process of transformation. For example, Austria began earlier than other Western countries to eliminate barriers to trade. Meanwhile around 700 foreign companies are operating via Austrian branches in Eastern European markets. The entry of Austria into the EU therefore triggered an additional, principally positive impetus for the economy with regard to activities directed towards Central and Eastern Europe. The planned expansion of the EU eastwards will lend still greater weight to Austria as a catalyst in the process of bringing these countries closer to the EU.

Membership of the EU sets new challenges for Austria's economy, however, in other areas. The OECD in its latest country report, for example, emphasized above all the additional burdens for the budget which a consistent consolidation of national finances necessitates. With the precondition that the finance situation is solved, the OECD nevertheless anticipates solid economic growth for Austria, in the coming years, with lower unemployment and moderate inflation. Significant structural problems resulting from the entry into the EU and the integration of Eastern Europe remain to be solved. In the opinion of OECD experts, in addition to the labour market situation, these relate to overregulation, market entry barriers and inadequate competition in the service sector.

The test of Austria's capability to adjust quickly to the new environment will be the 1996 budget. This must be the first in a series of budgets with the aim of guaranteeing that through the appropriate savings and massive changes in the structure of the budget,

Austria joins that group of countries which meet the Maastricht criteria. The particular challenge consists of ensuring that budgetary consolidation has the smallest possible negative effect on economic growth and unemployment and inflation rates.

As regards the elimination of market entry barriers and the low level of competition in a series of sectors in comparison with other European countries, there have already been considerable successes in recent years. The banking sector is an example in the service sector of deregulation in recent years.

In other areas where a monopoly exists at pre-sent, such as in telecommunications, a gradual opening up of the market is imminent, beginning in 1996.

Great progress was made, in 1995 in particular, in privatizing state-owned companies. The stock market flotation of Böhler Uddeholm and VOEST-ALPINE Stahl saw two nationalized companies placed on the Vienna Stock Exchange and attracted great interest among domestic and foreign investors. Other large privatization projects are scheduled for the years ahead.

12 Norway

Gry Ulverud, NHO Brussels Office

On 28 November 1994, 52 per cent of the Norwegian population said 'no' to the EU. Twenty-two years after the first referendum, the population has not changed its point of view: Norway refused, once again, to participate in the construction of a European Union.

There are various reasons for the Norwegian 'no', mainly linked to historical and economical factors. Norway is a very young country, gaining independence only in 1905. After the glorious Viking period, it became a Danish, then a Swedish colony, 'exploited by its colonial masters, and deprived of human and natural resources' – as seen by some Norwegians. This awareness of being 'the European Belgian Congo' has resulted in a very strong desire to protect Norwegian independence and sovereignty, at any cost. Thus, asking the Norwegian population to join a European *Union* goes beyond a rational economic or political choice. The economic arguments for joining the EU are also difficult to explain to citizens of one of the world's richest countries. Oil and gas have given Norway wealth and welfare, and the 'man in the street' sees no reason for this to change. One of the lessons Norwegian business and industry learnt from the last referendum was that, although the voters believe that EU membership would be better for business and industry, political reasons were more important.

A year after the 'no', the Norwegian economy is still one of the strongest in the world, and BNP growth is higher than that in the EU. The Norwegian population believes this is the 'reward' for saying 'no' to the EU. Norwegian business and industry know that this is not so, but that the continued strong Norwegian economy is partly due to the EEA Agreement.

As plans for the internal market developed, Norway and the other EFTA countries recognized the need to enter into an agreement which would ensure their participation in the process. The EEA negotiations were initiated in 1990, and the EEA Agreement was signed two years later. Iceland, Liechtenstein, Norway and the 15 EU countries participate in the agreement.

Through the Agreement on the European Economic Area (EEA) Norway is a part of the EU's internal market, and in addition has incorporated EU legislation on other sociopolitical issues such as environmental protection, working life and consumer protection.

Under the EEA Agreement the participating countries have both rights and obligations. In order to ensure the fulfilment of the agreement, it is essential that all parties follow the same rules. Joint legislation requires a system of cooperation for approving and amending provisions and settling disputes. The EFTA Surveillance Authority (ESA) and the European Commission both have the duty to ensure that all the EEA countries comply equally with the common rules. The Commission and ESA have the authority to intervene if undertakings or authorities break the rules.

Although the EEA Agreement does not include joint agricultural or fisheries policies, it provides greater opportunities for trade in these sectors than did previous free-trade agreements between the EU and Norway.

Free movement of goods, capital, services and persons
Goods

A large part of the EEA Agreement concerns common rules for trade in goods, a field where EU legislation to a large extent has been introduced throughout the EEA. Common rules apply to areas such as competition, guidelines for state aid, public procurement, new arrangements for trade in fishery and agricultural products, and elimination of technical barriers to trade.

The EU is a customs union while EFTA is a free-trade area. Therefore the EEA Agreement embodies common rules of origin specifying which commodities are exempted from duties and can be sold freely within the EEA. The products must be either manufactured with materials from EEA countries or, if materials originate from countries outside the EEA, they must be processed in accordance with the rules of origin.

Trade between countries is impeded not only by customs duties, but also by 'hidden' barriers to trade, such as product specifications, different control routines, environmental standards, packaging regulations, etc. Product specifications are harmonized inside the EEA, approximately the same way as inside the EU.

The EEA Agreement includes legislation in the field of public procurement. The agreement gives EU companies the possibility of delivering to the Norwegian public sector, and likewise Norwegian companies access to EU's public markets.

Capital

The EEA Agreement includes regulation for the movement of capital between all 18 EEA countries. As a guiding principle national regulations, for instance regarding investments, cannot discriminate between national and foreign investors and no restrictions are to be made on capital transactions across national boundaries within the EEA. Even though Norway participates in the Single Market regarding free movement of capital, the EEA Agreement does not open up Norwegian participation in economic and monetary union.

Services

Through the EEA Agreement, much of the EU legislation on trade in services across national borders has been adopted by the EEA countries. The most important service sectors in which the agreement has special rules are transport (road, rail, air and shipping), financial services (including banking, insurance and securities trading), telecommunications and television.

Persons

The principle of the free movement of persons means that nationals of EEA countries may travel freely, apply for jobs and establish themselves as self-employed in the whole area. All nationals of the EU enjoy these rights in Norway.

Other spheres of cooperation

The EEA Agreement is not only concerned with trade and common access to the internal market. The agreement has expanded the organized cooperation of Iceland, Liechtenstein, Norway and the EU countries to include many areas of common interest. These areas include environmental protection, working environment, matters relating to equal rights and labour laws, consumer protection, research and development, education, culture, company law, measures for small and medium-sized enterprises, tourism, statistics, information services and disaster preparedness. Norwegian companies can apply for EU funding in these fields, and participate in cooperation with EU companies.

Under the EEA Agreement Norway has full participation rights in the fourth EU framework research programme. The country pays a fee to the EU for this participation, which gives Norwegian participants the same rights and obligations as participants from the EU.

The EEA Agreement – challenges for the business community

The EEA Agreement ensures Norwegian participation in the European internal market. Since the agreement came into effect, the Confederation of Norwegian Business and Industry (NHO) has, however, discovered some weak points that must not be overlooked.

12

Important trading parties do not know of the EAA

This is a most important challenge for Norwegian business and industry in their relations with the rest of Europe. Undoubtedly Norway has a good trade agreement with the EU. But without important efforts to make the agreement known, it will not work as efficiently and smoothly as was intended. Norwegian authorities and various organisations (eg NHO) are determined to counter this lack of knowledged.

Limitation in free trade between the EU, Iceland, Liechtenstein and Norway

Inside the EEA, companies still meet obstacles in their daily relations with European counterparts. The NHO has recently conducted a survey of its members, trying to discover the technical barriers companies meet in spite of the EEA Agreement.

The majority of companies surveyed recognized that standards, product specifications and recognition of tests and certificates were the main obstacles to free trade. Many companies also mention duties, taxes, costs due to border-crossing formalities and environmental standards as constituting barriers inside the internal market created by the EEA Agreement. Unfortunately, the common EEA rules meant to solve these practical barriers to trade are insufficiently known to the users.

In order to circulate freely in the EEA, a product must prove that it originated inside the area. The rules of origin regulating the right to free circulation are complicated, and a source of problems for the free trade. Contrary to other trade agreements the EEA allows full cumulation, which means that value added in different EEA countries can be added together.

The rules of origin create some problems for Norwegian industry, in particular the textile sector. Because of EU agreements with the Central and Eastern European Countries (CEEC), producers from the EU can make use of cheap labour in these countries, and reintroduce processed products into the EU market without losing the right to free circulation inside the EU. The European agreements allow cumulation between the EU and the CEEC. This possibility of cumulation does not exist between the EEA and the CEEC. Thus, if a Norwegian producer manufactures a product in Poland, they will not be able to sell it freely inside the EEA afterwards. The difference between the rules of origin of the EU and the EEA is quite damaging for some industries, and the contracting parties are negotiating to find a solution to the problem.

Other limitations to trade between Norway and the EU stem from the fact that the EEA Agreement does not cover the following:

- *duty-free quotas on fish and processed fish;*
- *tariff duties on processed fish and processed agricultural products:* duties are particularly damaging to exports of processed fish;
- *anti-dumping and import surveillance:* the EEA Agreement does not guarantee that the EU will refrain from applying anti-dumping measures to Norwegian fish exports.

Lack of political influence

Better knowledge about the EEA Agreement within the EEA business community may reduce some of its weaknesses, but in the long term the lack of political influence will be felt. Norwegian authorities have only limited powers in the process leading to new legislation relevant to the Single Market. The EEA Agreement gives them some formal rights at the preparatory level, but Norway has no decisional powers when new legislation is adopted by the Council.

In fact, one could say that the EEA Agreement opens up markets and obliges Norwegian business and industry to follow EU legislation, without giving political power to influence the development of the rules that affect the country directly. This might be economically satisfactory in the short term. In the long run, however, it may be politically and economically damaging to Norway. Therefore the Confederation of Norwegian Business and Industry still puts EU membership on the top of the agenda.

Turkey

The Office of the Prime Minister, Turkey

Which is Europe's fastest-growing large economy? Which is the one looking forward to growth in its Gross National Product of 8.8 per cent in 1996? With a population of over 60 million and one of the highest growth rates of the OECD area in the last thirty years, the answer is plainly Turkey. Yet relatively few businessmen know this in Britain.

Elsewhere, awareness of Turkey's business potential is growing. Turkey already ranks among the US's top ten 'Big Emerging Markets' across the globe. According to analysts and local businessmen, within a few years it will have become Europe's nearest equivalent to the dynamic economies of South East Asia. Turkey's rapidly industrializing economy has become a force to be reckoned with in South Eastern Europe and the Middle East.

For nearly 30 years Turkey has been one of the fastest developing economies in the entire OECD. It crossed the threshold from an agrarian economy to an industrial one in the late 1970s. Around the same time, reforms to the economy and a shift toward trade liberalization, helped produce an upsurge of private sector business activity. Income per capita is now around $2,750, still behind the economies of Spain, Portugal, and Greece, but the gap is closing.

'I think this country is extraordinarily under-rated', says the manager of one large British company in Turkey. 'Its achievements deserve to be much more widely known and appreciated.' Like most international businessmen who know the country

well, he believes Turkey offers remarkable opportunities. Despite some market turbulence in 1994, business in Turkey had a very strong year in 1995. 'Order books have been full. We are bursting at the seams,' reports one international accountancy company in Istanbul.

Set against the long-term perspective, this picture is not surprising. For many years businessmen and economists have noted that Turkey has many comparative advantages to help create a dynamic economy. These include a very favourable geographical location for international trade; a youthful and well-educated workforce; a well-established private sector; a sophisticated financial infrastructure; and above all, a remarkable entrepreneurial spirit. These factors help explain why Turkey's GNP has averaged growth of over 5 per cent a year for the last quarter of a century, helping propel *per capita* income steadily closer to levels in the rest of Europe. Turkey in the mid-1990s is a predominantly industrial and urban society.

Manufacturing accounted for about a fifth of Gross Domestic Product in 1994 and services represented just under 60 per cent. By contrast, agriculture contributed only 16 per cent, though it still employs about 42 per cent of the workforce, ahead of services and industry.

Several Turkish industries have now shown themselves highly competitive in the international markets. These include textiles, private sector steel and ceramics. Turkey's exports are largely supplied by industry. Agricultural exports, including staple products such as tobacco, cotton, and mohair, now make up just a fifth of total exports of $18.5 bn in 1994. At the start of the 1980s these traditional exports made up nearly four fifths of exports.

However the short-term picture has not always been so favourable. Successive Turkish governments have had to weigh economic priorities against the requirement to provide high levels of employment and keep wages as high as possible. These conflicting constraints have produced both chronic budget deficits and periodic squeezes on the current account and balance of payments. At several points in the last quarter of a century, payment deficits have brought the economy into severe temporary difficulties.

One of these moments of stress occurred early in 1994 when Turkey had a miniature version of the crisis which overwhelmed Mexico later that year. Alarmed by growing deficits on foreign trade and on the government budget, short-term investors took fright when ratings agencies downgraded Turkish risk. The result was a temporary market collapse when the local currency, the Turkish Lira, slumped from TL17,000 to the dollar, to TL50,000 to the dollar. The currency later stabilized at around TL35,000 to the dollar.

The government responded on 5 April 1994, by pushing through a series of reform measures intended to cut spending, boost revenues, and tighten up fiscal procedures. One-off taxes were charged on many luxury items. Computerization of Turkey's tax system has been speeded up. This package opened the way for a stand-by agreement with the IMF, and a rapid recovery in both foreign payments and the Public Sector Borrowing Requirement (PBSR).

Within a few months, the main economic indicators showed a strong improvement. There was a budget surplus by the summer months of 1994. Exports responded rapidly to the devaluation. By the end of the year, though there was no overall growth, the Turkish economy was back in equilibrium and the stage was set for 1995's strong business performance.

During 1995, external payments have remained under control. There was a small surplus on the current account in the first six months and Turkey has had no difficulties servicing its $65.5 billion foreign debt. Market confidence, shaken in 1994, has gradually returned, as demonstrated by a series of syndicated loans.

Other aspects of economic management by the government are also showing progress. The April 5 Programme made a clear promise for a withdrawal by the state from the management of the economy and a cut back on perks such as cars and houses for state sector employees. Changes of this sort are being pushed through, despite entrenched opposition from parts of the public sector.

The most important part of the government's programme, however, is the sell-off of state industries to the private sector. Since the state has traditionally owned more than half of industrial output, this represents a major economic and cultural change. It will also ease the burden on the Treasury and reduce the public sector borrowing requirement. In 1994 transfers from the Treasury to loss-making state economic enterprises amounted to just under 15 per cent of the borrowing requirement. Around $1 billion has been raised from sell-offs during 1995. The pace of the privatization programme will pick up rapidly in 1995.

Meanwhile the outlook for international companies in 1996 remains very encouraging. Two things are likely to shape the markets during the year. One is the customs union between Turkey and the European Union which is due to come into force on 1 January 1996. Many Turkish observers already believe that the customs union will mean significant change in management of the Turkish economy. There will have to be more concern for currency stability and tougher anti-inflationary policies. It may take some time before these needs are seen as inescapable priorities, but it looks as if the days of 60–80 per cent inflation in Turkey are numbered.

In addition, the fact that general elections are due in late 1995 means that the period of political instability is likely to be relatively short-lived. In the past, general elections in Turkey have been periods when politics have been temporarily placed above economic priorities for quite long periods. Prime Minister Tansu Çiller, an ex-university economics professor is well-aware of the need to avoid what she calls 'an election economy'.

Mrs Çiller's True Path Party (TPP) goes into the general elections with considerable advantages. The TPP has provided Turkey with four years of political stability and economic growth, while consistently working to democratize the political system. It is therefore the party most frequently tipped to lead the country again after the elections.

Now you can invest in Asia, the Middle East, the Mediterranean, the Balkans and the Black Sea... without ever leaving Europe.

Now, as in the past, Turkey is right at the center of the world's greatest trade routes. At the junction of Europe and Asia. At the hub of the Mediterranean and the Black Sea. At the threshold of the world's newest and most exciting markets.

But Turkey has more than geographical access to offer. A nation of plenty, Turkey is home to industry and agriculture, commerce and services. The skilled workforce is highly entrepreneurial in spirit. Sophisticated telecommunications networks ensure instantaneous connections with the rest of the world. New motorways traverse the country and air links to 84 domestic and international destinations make travelling a snap.

Many of the best known corporate names in the world discovered Turkey's long-term advantages years ago. As a technically-sound partner capable of producing top quality goods and services. As a profitable market of considerable potential. As a center for regional expansion. And as a modern and rewarding place to do business.

So if you are keen to expand your business without leaving Europe, isn't it time you found out what so many already know: Turkey is the <u>key</u> place to be.

TURKEY
THE KEY

Undersecretariat of Treasury General Directorate of Foreign Investment Tel: (+90-312) 212 58 79-212 58 80 Fax: (+90-312) 212 89 16

13

In Turkey's main business and financial centres, there is strong confidence about the future as 1996 approaches. The feeling in Istanbul is that Turkey's private sector has now reached the point of steady self-sustained growth and is much less dependent on government management of the economy than it was a decade ago. The customs union is expected to lead to a rapid expansion of business between Turkey and the rest of Europe and, hopefully, to much greater flows of direct private investment from Western Europe and beyond. 'Within a few years, Europe really will see its own equivalent of an "Asian Tiger" here on its doorstep,' says the chairman of one leading Istanbul merchant bank.

PART

4

Trends in European Costs

Cost of Living in Western Europe

European Consortium of Management Consultants, Eurocost

The European Consortium of Management Consultants (ECMC) is a network of experienced management consultancies spanning the European Union. Collinson Grant Consultants is the UK member. The ECMC works with clients throughout Europe and the rest of the world. Together, the members have produced a guide to the *Cost of Living in Western Europe.*

Eurocost is a Luxembourg-based organization which has a unique method for calculating worldwide cost of living comparisons. These data are most frequently used to adjust the salaries of expatriate workers.

Prices in Europe

ECMC collected the prices for goods and services during August 1995 in most of the countries of the EU. They are reproduced in local currency in the appendix to this chapter.

The information is designed as a general guideline to Western European prices. While every effort has been made to confirm data, no responsibility for accuracy is accepted by ECMC. As background information, rates of inflation from 1991 in each country are reported in Table 14.1.

The data are general. Prices alter with location and it is difficult to obtain true figures. People's opinions on quality vary. Conversion into sterling may mislead because of fluctuations in exchange

rates. With these reservations, this chapter compares costs.

Comparative costs of living

Since 1990, rates of inflation in Western Europe have fallen, quite markedly in Greece, Portugal and the UK. This is shown in Table 14.1.

Table 14.2 was prepared from the data in the Appendix and provides comparative data on elements of cost of living which allow some general observations to be made. The conversion to sterling was made on 4 September 1995 using cross-exchange rates.

Accommodation

The price of houses is sensitive to location within each country and at a great premium in capitals. Bonn and Paris are particularly expensive, while Dublin and Stockholm offer relatively cheap residences.

The cost of office accommodation is even more affected by its position. Good premises in the capitals can command rents over £300 per square metre per year. Provincial rates may be much less. Lisbon, Paris and, to a lesser extent, London are in the higher range. Copenhagen and Dublin have moderate costs.

Communications

There are differing philosophies on the price of telephone calls. Ireland has a particularly wide dis-

	1990	1991	1992	1993	1994	12 months change to June 1995
Austria	3.7	3.2	3.9	3.5	3.3	2.6
Belgium	4.0	3.1	2.3	2.7	2.6	1.3
Denmark	2.9	2.3	2.1	1.2	2.1	2.1
Finland	5.5	4.1	2.9	2.1	1.2	0.4
France	3.4	3.1	2.4	2.0	1.8	1.6
Germany	2.7	3.3	3.8	4.0	3.4	2.3
Greece	22.0	16.3	13.7	12.6	17.2	9.7
Ireland	2.7	3.1	3.0	1.4	3.7	2.8
Italy	6.0	5.9	4.9	4.3	4.6	5.8
Luxembourg	–	3.0	3.0	3.5	2.4	2.3
Netherlands	2.4	3.5	3.1	2.5	3.0	2.1
Norway	4.6	3.3	2.3	2.2	1.2	2.7
Portugal	14.0	10.2	8.2	6.1	6.7	3.8
Spain	6.7	5.6	5.6	4.4	5.6	5.1
Sweden	7.5	5.2	4.0	4.1	2.6	2.7
Switzerland	5.4	5.5	3.9	3.1	1.0	2.1
UK	9.5	5.6	3.7	1.7	2.8	3.5

Source: OECD Main Economic Indicators

Table 14.1 Inflation rates: consumer prices (%)

parity between local and long-distance, whereas in Portugal this is minimal. The Netherlands, Portugal, Sweden and the UK offer long-distance calls at less than 10 pence per minute; Germany, Italy and Ireland are in the range from 30 to 75 pence. Post, much more consistent, is around 30 to 40 pence for a domestic letter across the countries surveyed.

Clothes and personal care
The ranges of prices for men's clothing are wide but overlap. Men's suits are available in the £200 to £300 bracket almost everywhere, but there are opportunities to pay significantly more in Portugal, Sweden and France. Shoes, however, are less expensive in Ireland, The Netherlands and Portugal. Germany, Italy and Sweden offer men's footwear at a little over £100, but in France it is possible to pay over £200. Shirts are fairly uniformly around £30, though the UK remains inexpensive while Sweden once more has high prices. The era of the £10 haircut has passed other than in Ireland and Spain, the consistent average elsewhere being around £15.

Women's off-the-peg suits retail at less than £200 in Ireland and the UK and are available at up to £250 almost everywhere, although there are premium prices in Belgium, France and Sweden. Tights in Germany and Portugal are significantly more expensive than elsewhere. Hairdressing is more varied for women than for men, ranging from £12.80

in Ireland to four times that amount in Belgium and Germany.

Consumer durables
In the white goods sector the most expensive fridge–freezers are found in Germany, Spain and Sweden, with the cheapest in Italy and prices otherwise in the £400 to £600 range. Washing machines tend to be similar in price to fridge–freezers, although they are considerably less expensive in Ireland and Sweden and significantly more in France and The Netherlands. Gas cookers are cheaper than electric, other than in Sweden and the UK, where they are relatively expensive. Television sets are quite cheap in France, The Netherlands and, interestingly, Portugal, where electrical goods are otherwise in the upper ranges of price.

Entertainment
Scotch whisky is cheapest in Belgium, Greece and Spain, and available at between £12 and £13 in Italy, Ireland, Portugal and the UK, but is around £16 to £18 in France, Germany and The Netherlands and double that in Sweden, where wine is also exceptionally costly. Predictably, wine is cheaper in Portugal, Italy and France than in the UK, The Netherlands and Ireland. A glass of lager is still available for less than £1 in Italy, The Netherlands, Spain and the UK, but is two and three times that in

	Belgium	Denmark	France	Germany	Italy	Ireland	Greece	Netherlands	Portugal	Spain	Sweden	UK
Accommodation												
House 3/4 beds, good area (£'000)	295	225	382	440	237	97	181	177	270	410	99	209
Business												
Annual rent per m² office, including tax	172.00	104.00	318.00	157.00	120.00	114.00	83.00	137.00	338.00	102.00	176.00	225.00
Clothes and personal care												
Men: lounge suit	259.00	301.00	382.00	264.00	263.00	265.00	242.00	275.00	337.00	282.00	528.00	210.00
haircut	12.95	17.60	15.30	17.60	15.84	10.00	10.60	11.80	14.80	7.70	15.00	16.00
Women: off-the-peg suit	431.00	199.00	319.00	220.00	251.00	153.00	242.00	236.00	253.00	359.00	509.00	170.00
haircut/blow dry	54.00	26.40	25.00	44.00	27.70	12.80	15.14	19.60	15.00	38.00	28.00	22.00
Consumer goods												
Fridge/freezer	548.00	589.00	433.00	616.00	347.00	490.00	605.00	393.00	549.00	667.00	666.00	462.00
Washing machine	561.00	589.00	510.00	606.00	307.00	409.00	393.00	471.00	507.00	385.00	528.00	455.00
Television 34 cm	215.00	294.00	217.00	220.00	267.00	204.00	242.00	157.00	211.00	144.00	217.00	257.00
Entertainment												
Scotch	10.79	29.44	16.57	16.70	12.68	12.27	9.08	17.67	12.70	7.70	36.70	13.00
Litre wine	2.15	3.55	1.78	2.64	0.79	4.08	2.42	3.33	0.63	1.28	4.58	2.70
20 cigarettes	1.84	3.50	2.16	2.13	1.19	2.87	1.15	1.96	1.48	1.03	2.73	2.76
Theatre ticket	14.00	8.05	19.12	26.40	34.66	8.20	6.05	23.56	2.53	10.26	24.70	16.50
Evening meal for 4	162.00	237.00	191.00	220.00	188.00	225.00	182.00	177.00	169.00	133.00	352.00	183.00
Food												
1 kg rump steak	7.73	12.67	16.57	15.40	7.13	7.97	6.66	11.78	10.98	7.44	7.04	10.10
6 eggs	0.77	1.02	0.89	0.79	0.79	1.11	0.51	0.48	0.63	0.64	0.93	0.77
Litre milk	0.65	0.79	0.38	0.48	0.79	0.60	0.78	0.41	0.57	0.49	0.53	0.60
1 kg apples	1.08	1.81	1.40	1.54	1.11	1.25	0.91	0.78	1.35	1.10	1.67	1.18
100 g instant coffee	1.51	5.54	2.17	2.64	1.66	2.46	1.85	2.59	1.35	2.20	3.61	1.65
Transport												
Mondeo GLX 2.0 petrol	15868.00	23090.00	13386.00	17475.00	13866.00	20470.00	230470.00	18957.00	28867.00	17091.00	17048.00	15975.00
Litre unleaded petrol	0.58	0.62	0.75	0.69	0.67	0.59	0.58	0.74	0.61	0.56	0.66	0.54
Minimum taxi fare	2.59	2.31	3.19	1.72	2.38	2.56	0.91	2.20	1.05	1.95	2.03	1.80

Note: Data in local currencies for August 1995 were converted to £ sterling at the cross-exchange rates shown in the *Financial Times* of 4 September 1995

Table 14.2 *Comparative costs of living in Western Europe*

14

Germany and Sweden respectively, while the price in Portugal must encourage the sale of wine. Cigarettes sell at around the £2 mark, but are notably cheaper in Italy, Portugal and Spain and nearer to £3 in Ireland, Sweden and the UK.

Seats at the theatre cost three and four times as much as at the cinema other than in Portugal, where both are, comparatively, a bargain. Germany, Italy, The Netherlands and Sweden are the most costly.

Less than £100 will still cover a business lunch for four in Italy, Ireland, Portugal and the UK, but restaurants in Germany and Sweden charge more than double that. Lunch is almost invariably around half the price of dinner. An evening meal for four is around the £200 mark almost everywhere, with the exception of Sweden, where £352 is quoted.

Food

The cost of a kilogram of rump steak varies from around £8 in Belgium, Ireland, Italy and Spain to £15 and £16 in Germany and France. The Netherlands, Portugal and the UK have intermediate prices.

The price of six fresh eggs varies from less than 50p in The Netherlands to over £1 in Ireland. A litre of milk remains inexpensive throughout Europe, prices ranging from a modest 79p in Italy to an almost self-effacing 38p in France. Olive oil costs from £3 to £4 on average, except in Italy, Greece and, unexpectedly, Ireland, but is more expensive in Germany and, once again, Sweden. Fruit and vegetables are markedly good value in The Netherlands and Portugal, while German prices are consistent with those for other foods – high. Coffee is cheapest in Portugal, dearest in Sweden, and from £1.60 to £2.60 elsewhere.

Transport

The price of a litre of petrol ranges from 54p in the UK to 75p in France. Car prices vary more. The compact Renault Clio is as little as £6735 in Italy, as much as £10,917 in the Netherlands. Variances are even greater for medium-sized cars, the Ford Mondeo being quoted at £13,386 in France and more than double that in Portugal. The price of the 'executive' BMW 520i is lowest in France and Italy at just below £20,000 but over £30,000 in Ireland and The Netherlands and recorded as £36,686 in Portugal.

There appears to be little correlation between the cost of cars and the price of car hire. Rented cars and taxis are expensive in France, where car prices are

low, and cheaper in The Netherlands, where the reverse obtains. Taxis are little over £1 in Portugal, despite the prohibitive cost of cars, and elsewhere around £2.

Summary

The ECMC snapshot of prices in Europe reflects some of the effects of the distinction between the countries with strong currencies, particularly Germany, France and Belgium – the 'core' bloc – and those with weaker currencies – the 'peripheral' group – such as Italy, Spain, Sweden and the UK. Since the beginning of 1992, the lira, peseta and sterling have fallen against the Deutschmark and franc, thus increasing their competitiveness. Variable currencies create imbalances in a single market, as the information gathered by the ECMC shows.

Cost of living differences (Eurocost)

Table 14.3 demonstrates the cost of living differences within the European Union. The data were collected in April 1995 and calculated using London as base 100. All indices exclude rent.

Eurocost calculates three types of cost of living comparison indices. The difference is based on the assumption that as a person spends a period of time abroad, their spending habits will change to suit local circumstances. Thus, Eurocost conducts family budget surveys among expatriates to create weighting patterns that put raw price data into context. Prices

City	Home-based index	Adapted expenditure index	Host-based index
Amsterdam	120.03	116.10	112.29
Athens	114.06	105.97	98.45
Bonn	128.99	122.66	116.64
Brussels	130.40	124.20	118.29
Copenhagen	160.21	154.88	149.73
Dublin	117.64	115.75	113.90
Helsinki	165.83	150.39	136.39
Lisbon	110.39	94.56	81.00
Luxembourg	132.76	123.37	114.64
Madrid	108.09	102.87	97.91
Paris	125.43	121.57	117.82
Rome	99.12	94.45	90.00
Stockholm	142.43	128.68	116.25
Vienna	173.92	159.47	146.22

Table 14.3 Cost of living

are collected using a global network of independent consultants and surveyors.

The home-based index assumes that expatriates will continue to buy exactly the same quantity and type of goods as at home. As the expatriate becomes used to local surroundings after a few months, the adapted expenditure index is the most accurate measure of cost of living comparisons. The host-based index is calculated using the consumption patterns of long-term expatriates.

15 Living Costs in Central and Eastern Europe

Mia M Bartonova, Deputy Managing Director, RI World Service

Central and, to a lesser degree, Eastern European countries are now considered by many manufacturers to be part of Western Europe; a large number of Western products and services are being actively marketed to their local populations. Many more companies are considering entry into these markets.While there is general information available about individual countries, many information sources which are taken for granted in the more developed markets are not yet available across the entire region. Living costs can provide a useful guide to the spending power of consumers in the region.

The countries covered here are the Czech Republic, Hungary, Poland, Bulgaria and Romania. The prices and related information presented in this chapter were collected by our associates in each country during July 1995. Although we have tried to ensure that the information collected was standardized, individual perceptions and judgements regarding income/items of expenditure might have influenced some of the data. The figures quoted were obtained in the capital city of each country and

represent the average income and costs of items/services. In all countries the costs of many items of expenditure vary between the capital city and other areas of the country, with costs in the capital being higher. In some countries there was also a variation recorded between different areas within the capital.

Inflation rates differ across the region.The Czech Republic has the lowest inflation rate (10 per cent), the other Central European countries and Bulgaria and Romania have had an inflation rate of between 20 and 30 per cent in the past year. In order to provide easily comparable data the figures quoted are in US$, not in the local currencies. The prevailing exchange rates on 30 July are shown in Table 15.1.

In the last four years, most local consumers have embraced the new economic situation. The majority have learnt to differentiate between Western brands, and the old perception 'all from the West is the best' has been abandoned. 'Value for money', an almost unknown concept four years ago, has percolated into everyday vocabulary. Advertising, initially almost universally welcome and accepted, now needs to be

Czech Republic (koruna)	Hungary (forint)	Poland (new zloty)	Bulgaria (lev)	Romania (lei)
KC 27	FL 125	NZL 2.45	LV 68	Lei 2064

Table 15.1 Exchange rates at end of July 1995 against 1 US$

more closely targeted and convey more than just the brand name. Consumers want to be told not only the product benefits, but also supporting evidence to substantiate the claims made about the product. In each country there is a rising proportion of consumers who reject Western advertising; many prefer to buy local, cheaper brands.

The price of the newly found political and economic freedom has been an increase in the cost of living. While a minority of the population in each market has considerably increased their income and standard of living, the majority have found it more difficult to manage on their income. Many feel their overall standard of living has declined. Under the old system many items of food, transport, housing and energy costs were subsidized by the state. Now the new governments are phasing out the subsidies, and the consumers are having to pay the full costs. The degree of subsidies and the items where subsidies still apply vary across the region and are changing constantly. The cost of living data presented in this chapter cover:

- income
- taxation/other deductions;
- VAT and costs of accommodation;
- energy;
- selected food items;
- entertainment;
- clothes;
- consumer goods;
- motor cars;
- fuel and transport.

The information should be considered as a snapshot of the local situation at one particular time (July 1995) and not as an authoritative statement regarding current living costs in the region. We are grateful to our associates who have collected the information in individual countries:

Czech Republic	AISA and Opinion Window, Prague
Hungary	Median Opinion and Marketing Research, Budapest
Poland	PENTOR Institute for Opinion Research, Warsaw
Bulgaria	BBSS British Balkan Social Surveys, Sofia
Romania	MIA Marketing Institute, Bucharest

Exchange rates

The exchange rate in the Czech Republic has been stable against the main Western currencies, and the koruna has strengthened by around 5 per cent in the past year. However, in Poland, Hungary, Bulgaria and Romania the local currencies have been depreciating against Western currencies every year.

In Poland and Romania the depreciation has been around 10 per cent, while in Hungary and Bulgaria the local currencies have depreciated by 25 per cent against the US dollar. In Bulgaria and Romania further marked depreciation is projected by local economists.

Salaries

The salaries quoted in Table 15.2 are the mid range for each occupation type for staff working in medium to large privatized/joint venture companies. There are large variations (+/−50 per cent) in salaries for senior positions and smaller variations (+/−30 per cent) in salaries for other positions.

In state-controlled nationalized companies the salaries/wages paid are significantly lower. Most of the countries in the region have an official minimum wage; however, this is not always adhered to, particularly among agricultural and casual labour workers.

	Czech Republic	Hungary	Poland	Bulgaria	Romania
Managing director	30,000	24,000	30,000	9,000	8,500
Sales manager	15,000	10,000	12,000	6,000	5,500
Computer specialist	10,000	8,000	12,000	3,500	3,600
Bilingual secretary (25–35 yrs)	7,500	5,500	8,000	2,500	3,600
Manual worker	3,600	3,000	3,000	850	800
Non-manual worker	4,400	4,500	4,500	850	800

Table 15.2 Gross annual salaries, medium-sized privatized companies and joint ventures (all figures in US$)

15

	Czech Republic	Hungary	Poland	Bulgaria	Romania
Single person's allowance	900	880	70	450	
Lowest rate	15%	20%	21%	20%	23%
Starts	900/yr	880/yr	71/yr	450/yr	2,000/yr
Highest rate	43%	44%	45%	50%	37%
Starts	40,000/yr	5,000/yr	10,000/yr	2,000/yr	3,000/yr
Social security, pension, healthcare	13%	10%	0%	0%	0%

Table 15.3 Income tax/social security/pension paid by employees (all figures in US$)

In the past year there has been a significant rise in the salaries paid to senior managers in the Czech Republic, Poland and Hungary.

Tax

The income tax figures provided are the official figures. All countries have several tax bands, the lowest and highest of which are shown in Table 15.3. In all countries employers pay social security/pension/healthcare contributions to the State; the rate is based on a percentage of the total salary/wage bill of the company and varies from 5 per cent in Hungary to 35 per cent and 27 per cent in Bulgaria and Romania respectively.

The following comments are not based on official information, but on our experience in the region. Many adults have more than one job, particularly if their main employer is the State. The usual form of payment for second and subsequent jobs is cash. Frequently many of the transactions/payments will be in Western rather than local currency and thus can not be easily traced by the authorities. The local governments, particularly in the Eastern European countries, currently do not have the resources and facilities to collect all the income tax due. In Hungary the government estimates that 40 per cent of all income avoids taxation.

VAT rates are shown in Table 15.4.

Accommodation

The prices quoted in Table 15.5 are for rentals in the private sector. There are very few properties available for rent in good, central areas of each capital city, thus the cost can vary up to 50 per cent from the figures shown above.

In Central European countries the vast majority of the local population do not pay rents as high as those quoted below; locals would pay around half. In Eastern European countries the local population would pay 10–20 per cent of the quoted figures.

Czech Republic	Hungary	Poland	Bulgaria	Romania
22% other goods 5% food/services	25% 10% basics	22% 7% basics 0% food	18%	18%

Table 15.4 Level of VAT on goods and services

	Czech Republic	Hungary	Poland	Bulgaria	Romania
3 bedrooms + living room with private kitchen and bathroom facilities	500	650	450	300	250
2 bedrooms + living room with private kitchen and bathroom facilities	380	500	300	200	175

Table 15.5 Accommodation – monthly rental for an unfurnished flat in a good area (usually fairly central), with central heating (including taxes and services) (all figures in US$)

	Czech Republic	Hungary	Poland	Bulgaria	Romania
Electricity					
Standing charge/month	Free	Free	2	0.15	Free
1 unit charge (kW hour)	0.04	0.06	0.07	0.02	0.03
Gas					
Standing charge/month	Free	Free	4	Free	Free
1 unit charge (m³)	0.13	Free up to 11,000	0.18	0.03	0.03

Table 15.6 Energy, domestic charges (all figures in US$)

Most of the local population live in State-owned (or what was State-owned) property which is not accessible to non-nationals. In most countries houses outside the centres of big cities are privately owned.

Energy

The cost of energy has increased in the region over the last three years. Further significant increases are expected as currently the governments still provide some subsidies to this industry sector, thus keeping consumer prices lower.

Food and entertainment

The prices quoted in Tables 15.7 and 15.8 are for either top quality local products which are occasionally not available, or for the cheaper Western brands which are freely available, although the distribution might be uneven/patchy in each market.

	Czech Republic	Hungary	Poland	Bulgaria	Romania
1 kg rumpsteak	5.5	6	4.3	4.5	4
1 kg chicken	1.7	3	2.5	1.6	2.5
6 fresh eggs	0.35	0.6	0.7	0.5	0.4
1 kg flour	0.4	0.3	0.6	0.3	0.8
1 kg sugar	0.8	0.7	0.8	0.6	0.7
0.25 kg butter	0.8	0.5	0.8	0.6	0.7
1 lt milk	0.4	0.5	0.5	0.4	0.5
1 kg apples	1.0	0.6	0.6	1.0	0.5
1 kg potatoes	1.0	0.8	0.9	0.5	0.4
100 g instant coffee	2.3	4.0	0.9	2.0	2.5
100 g tea	1.3	2.0	1.5	2.0	1.5

Table 15.7 Food (all figures in US$)

	Czech Republic	Hungary	Poland	Bulgaria	Romania
1 bottle imported whisky	20	25	31	12	15
0.5 lt beer (in bar/café)	0.7	1.1	1.4	0.5	0.5
1 pack cigarettes (20)	1.5	1.0	1.1	1.0	0.8
Cinema ticket	1.3	1.5	2.4	1.0	0.5
Theatre ticket	8	8	8	1	0.7
Dinner for 4 (fashionable restaurant) including apéritif, 3 course meal, 2 bottles wine & coffee	120	120	190	160	190

Table 15.8 Entertainment (all figures in US$)

15

The vast majority of consumers in the area will have little or no experience of fashionable restaurants; the high prices make visits to such establishments unaffordable and an unnecessary luxury. The prices quoted can be used as guideline costs for business entertainment in the region.

Clothes

The prices quoted in Table 15.9 are for either top quality local products which are frequently not available, or for the cheaper Western brands which are freely available, although the distribution might be uneven/patchy in each market.

Consumer goods

The prices quoted in Table 15.10 are for the main, middle of the range Western brands which are freely available (although the distribution might be uneven/patchy) in each market, or for top quality local products, which are either frequently not available or the country does not have the facilities to manufacture products locally.

	Czech Republic	Hungary	Poland	Bulgaria	Romania
Men					
2 piece suit	250	200	190	150	80
Leather shoes	80	60	50	60	60
Poly/cotton shirt	15	20	20	10	10
Women					
2 piece suit	220	200	150	150	60
Leather shoes	70	50	50	60	30
Summer dress	60	60	50	80	60
Tights (1 pr)	2	1.5	1.2	2	2

Table 15.9 Clothes (all figures in US$)

	Czech Republic	Hungary	Poland	Bulgaria	Romania
Fridge/freezer	650	400	400	400	400
Cooker	300	300	350	400	300
Washing machine	550	500	400	400	450
Vacuum cleaner	180	200	150	200	200
Portable colour TV	450	300	450	400	250
Video cassette recorder	500	300	350	300	450
Hairdryer	30	20	25	25	30

Table 15.10 Consumer goods (all figures in US$)

Transport

	Czech Republic	Hungary	Poland	Bulgaria	Romania
Fiat Cinquecento	8,000	8,000	8,000	7,500	–
Fiat Uno	–	11,000	9,100	9,900	7,000
Ford Mondeo	22,200	24,000	19,000	18,500	–
Ford Escort	16,500	–	16,000	59,000	19,000
1 lt petrol	0.8	0.8	0.9	0.5	0.3
Bus/underground journey	0.2	0.3	0.3	0.1	0.1

Table 15.11 Motor cars/petrol/transport costs (all figures in US$)

The European Directors' Pay League

David Atkins, Monks Partnership

In July, the report by Sir Richard Greenbury's Study Group into directors' remuneration stated in the introduction that 'For the most part, remuneration levels for Directors in the UK lie within the range of European practice and well below American levels'. The Group recognized the difficulty of finding reliable data on which to base cross-border comparisons of senior management remuneration, and obtained advice from more than one firm of specialist consultants.

Even if reliable data are available, evaluating them can be difficult. When grappling with the remuneration of directors and chief executives of UK privatized utilities the House of Commons Employment Committee commented in its report, 'What relation these sums bear to salary levels for comparable jobs in other countries is an even more complex question, as differences in culture, tax regimes and definitions heavily influence amounts of pay and the way pay is structured.' In other words, how can one be sure that one is not comparing chalk with cheese or, indeed, apples with pears?

For a start, it is important to ensure that comparisons are made between the same type of organization. This is not just a question of avoiding comparison of, say, a chain of retail shops with an aircraft manufacturer, but ensuring, for example, that parent companies are compared with parent companies and not with subsidiaries of an equivalent turnover.

It is important to distinguish between the two types of organization. For, it could be argued, international comparisons between the pay levels of directors of parent companies may be largely irrelevant since the company is owned by the shareholders, whether private or institutional, and pay in each country will settle at a level which is acceptable to the shareholders and is sufficient to attract and motivate the appropriate calibre of senior manager. On the other hand, pay levels in subsidiary companies in different countries may well display some degree of cross-border parity, particularly if the subsidiaries are of the same international or multinational parent.

Pay Comparisons for parent companies

Until the publication of the Cadbury Committee's report on the Financial Aspects of Corporate Governance in December 1992, the only requirements regarding the public disclosure of the remuneration of UK directors of parent companies was that laid out in the Companies Act. Essentially, all that was required (and still is) was that the company's annual report and accounts should disclose:

▦ an aggregate of the emoluments of all directors;
▦ the emoluments of the chairman separately stated;
▦ the emoluments of the highest paid director if greater than the chairman;

◼ the emoluments of the directors analysed by £5000 emolument bands.

Directors working wholly or mainly outside the UK are excluded from this latter requirement.

Since the implementation of the Cadbury Code of Best Practice, a series of statements and guidelines on disclosure practice have been issued by, among others, the Association of British Insurers, the Accounting Standards Board and, most recently, Sir Richard Greenbury's Study Group. The result has been that the level of disclosure of main board pay and remuneration practices in UK annual reports has undergone a radical change. For instance, a survey by Monks Partnership in December 1994 of FT-SE 100 company annual reports showed that only two itemized the elements of remuneration of named executive directors. By June 1995 the number had risen to 48 – of these, a quarter met the Greenbury Code requirement of itemizing the emoluments of both executive and non-executive directors.

In the USA, levels of disclosure similar to the UK are available in company proxy statements – but only for the five highest paid officers. In Europe, disclosure practice in most countries has yet to reach even the levels required by company law in the UK. In general, the best that can be expected is a mention of total board emoluments. In some countries, even though a legal requirement, companies may 'omit' this piece of information. It should be stressed that, as always, there are notable exceptions.

The consequence is that in continental Europe there is relatively little reliable information in the public domain about the pay levels of parent company directors. Information must come from other sources, such as surveys, pay clubs and, of course, hearsay, which inevitably gives an incomplete picture.

Pay comparisons for subsidiary companies

Information on senior management pay levels in subsidiary companies is more readily available from surveys because international and multinational organizations want to ensure that pay levels in different countries are in line with national norms. To do this they need access to data and so are more willing to take part in remuneration surveys than are national parent companies.

Even if data are available, as the Employment Committee pointed out, cross-border comparisons require careful evaluation. Most obviously, changes

in exchange rates can distort the data – anyone who took a holiday in France in summer 1995 will vouch for the fact that their pounds bought considerably fewer francs than a year before. Add to this distortions created by different taxation systems, social security costs, lifestyles and cost of living, it becomes clear why comparisons should be viewed with a measure of scepticism.

Each year, Monks Partnership researches senior management remuneration in, predominantly, the subsidiaries of multinationals across Europe. Figure 16.1 provides a comparison of the total earnings (basic salary and any annual bonus) for a board director of a subsidiary company in 14 European countries. It is assumed the subsidiary in each of the countries has an annual turnover broadly equivalent to £50 million.

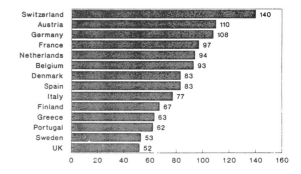

Figure 16.1 Gross earnings before tax (£'000) – subsidiary company director, company with £50 million turnover

As in previous years, Switzerland heads the European Directors' Pay League of 14 countries with gross earnings equivalent to £140,000, followed some way behind by Austria and Germany. UK directors, together with Swedish colleagues, bring up the rear at around £52,000. A similar comparison in 1994 ranked the UK directors' position at 11. Elsewhere the gross earnings rankings remain broadly similar to 1994.

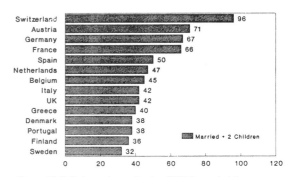

Figure 16.2 Net earnings after tax (£'000) – subsidiary company director, company with £50 million turnover

Figure 16.2 shows the effect of tax and social security costs on gross earnings. For tax purposes the assumption is that the executive is married and has two children. No allowance has been made for other tax deductions such as church tax in Switzerland and Germany. The biggest change in position is with the UK, rising from bottom to 9th position. The other major position changes affected by tax are those of Denmark, down from 8th to 11th and Finland, down from 10th to 13th.

Figure 16.3 provides a comparison of spending power once cost of living is taken into account. Switzerland remains at the top of the table, followed by Germany and Austria which have swapped places. Spain is in 4th position, closely followed by France and Italy. The UK's position remains unchanged at 9th equal with Greece. Three Nordic nations occupy the bottom positions.

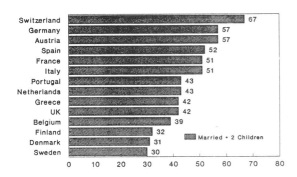

Figure 16.3 Earnings after tax and cost of living (£'000) – subsidiary company director, company with £50 million turnover

These figures show that, depending on the criteria, a UK director could be considered the worst paid in Europe, or towards the bottom of a league table of 14 countries.

Pay increases

One of the factors that will affect the year-to-year position in the league table is pay increases during the year. Figure 16.4 shows how directors' salaries have moved over the 12 months to July 1995. It shows the median increase in subsidiary company directors' basic salary and the same increases adjusted for inflation. It should be noted that increases in Belgium during the period were restricted by a partial wage 'freeze'. It is noteworthy that overall pay increases were, with the exception of Italy and Belgium, in a narrow band of 4–6 per cent and after adjustment for inflation between 1 and 3 per cent.

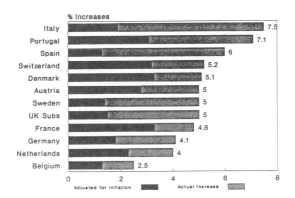

Figure 16.4 Base salary increases – subsidiary company director, July 1994 to July 1995

Other aspects of remuneration

Most directors will be eligible for a range of benefits in addition to cash. The range will vary from country to country. Three elements of an executive remuneration package are examined below.

Share options

Most UK directors will be eligible to participate in a share option scheme. As Figure 16.5 shows, only in four other countries are more than 50 per cent of director posts eligible to take part in a share option scheme. In general, the value of options granted is likely to be lower than in the UK, where the total value is typically of the order of three times salary. Following the publication of the Greenbury Report and the loss of the tax concession for Inland Revenue approved schemes announced by the Chancellor of the Exchequer on 17 July, it is possible that UK companies may review their share option practice.

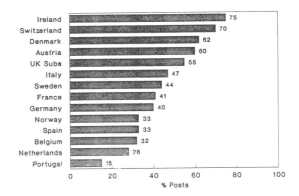

Figure 16.5 Share options (posts eligible)

Company cars

At director level most organizations make a company car available (see Figure 16.6). Only in Switzerland,

Sweden and Norway does the percentage of posts provided with company cars fall below 80 per cent. Below board level the provision of company cars drops dramatically. Germany, Austria and the UK are the only countries where 80 per cent or more of senior management posts – those reporting to a director – benefit from the provision of a company car. In France, for example, only 40 per cent of senior management posts in the study were provided with a company car.

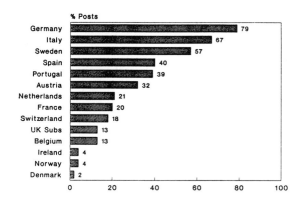

Figure 16.7 Holidays – subsidiary company director

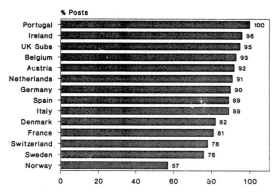

Figure 16.6 Company car provision – subsidiary company director

Holidays

Holiday entitlement is one of the few benefits which is relatively independent of status. Entitlement to holidays shows a wide variation across Europe (see Figure 16.7). In Germany 79 per cent of director posts are eligible for 30 or more days' holiday, while in Denmark the percentage drops to 2 per cent. The figures are for holiday entitlement in addition to national and bank holidays. The percentages in the UK, France, The Netherlands and Belgium may be influenced by the high percentage of subsidiaries of

US organizations in the sample. A survey of national companies in these countries would probably produce a higher percentage of posts with 30 days' holiday or more.

Where stands the UK director?

In terms of gross cash pay, directors of a UK subsidiary appear to be less well paid than colleagues in Continental Europe. Once tax, social security and cost of living are taken into account the actual spending power available would appear to position an executive's earnings around the middle of a European League Table – supporting the statement about international comparisons made by Sir Richard Greenbury's Group in its report.

Once other aspects of the remuneration package are taken into account – such as share options – the position of UK directors' earnings in the league table may rise. On the other hand, in terms of individual benefits such as cars and holidays, directors in some other European countries may be better placed.

The Salary Jungle in Eastern Europe

Sylvie Riot, Senior HR Consultant, Towers Perrin

Since the early 1990s, the search for accurate and meaningful information on pay levels and remuneration trends in Eastern Europe has been greatly complicated by the fragility of a labour market conditioned by very different principles. The privatization process that started in 1990 has triggered a liberalization of former state-owned enterprises and has generated fluctuations in pay at all hierarchical levels: management, professional, technical, manual and administration.

The influence of foreign capital and changes in ownership have provoked a sectoral division of pay markets, which has taken the following shape:

- public sector;
- local private sector;
- foreign private sector (whether partly or wholly owned).

In addition to the privatization process, radical changes in skill requirements in the 'new' private sector have led to different pay practices that seek to reward for:

- proficiency in foreign languages;
- computer or other systems knowledge;
- forecasting and planning abilities linked to business strategy;
- leadership qualities (including performance management).

These changes have occurred throughout the Eastern European region to a greater or lesser extent depending on whether labour markets were in the capitals or the provinces.

The complexity of pay and labour markets is best illustrated with an example. Table 17.1 shows variations in pay for a managing director in Poland, depending on the type of company and the location.

Private sector/location	Average total cash (gross) pa (new zloty)
Former state enterprise in southern Poland	63,360
New foreign company in southern Poland	132,000
Former state enterprise in Warsaw	92,700
New foreign company in Warsaw	210,000

Note: £1 = new zloty 3.85

Source: Towers Perrin, September 1995

Table 17.1 Managing director, Poland (manufacturing company, 500 to 1000 employees)

The differences in average pay can be as high as three and a half times more pay between the lowest (former state enterprise in southern Poland) and the highest (new foreign company in Warsaw). Even differences between a new foreign company in southern Poland and Warsaw show substantial disparity in pay levels (new zloty 132,000 to 210,000).

Looking back four to five years, everyone involved in that region would probably have said that the more settled Eastern European countries could progressively bring very low pay levels for executives to 'decent' European standards. At that time, it was not expected that Eastern European pay would equal that of Western European countries, only that it would progress steadily over the years.

The reality has definitely surpassed that initial conservative expectation. Countries such as Poland and Hungary have witnessed a veritable pay explosion, especially with regard to managerial jobs. This phenomenon was caused by a combination of factors, particularly:

- management skill shortage/scarcity and fierce competition;
- lack of historical remuneration data especially at executive level;
- foreign employers' minimal understanding and appreciation of pay markets;
- more *ad hoc* individually negotiated pay packages;
- foreign personnel assignments on expatriate conditions.

Some of the remuneration issues brought about as a result of this pay explosion have not necessarily been addressed immediately since more urgent business pressures, ranging from firming up a privatization deal to starting up a sales company, were primary concerns. Attracting or retaining good-calibre people had its price and most companies, although sometimes reluctantly, accepted that cost as part of their initial business investment strategy.

What has come to light, however, is the development of stronger demands from managers to benefit from:

- enhanced packages – rather similar to expatriate package benefits but not quite as extensive (ie housing allowance, children's education assistance, rest and relaxation breaks or company paid foreign holidays);
- typical Western benefit provisions, such as eligibility for healthcare and retirement programmes, although country tax and legislation may not always be ready for the introduction of such programmes;
- large, regular pay increases to protect their employment income against galloping inflation independently from merit increases;
- parity with other (neighbouring) country operations' pay policies and programmes.

It is clear that these demands reflect a certain element of impatience on the part of Eastern European managers (who would welcome immediate recognition of their 'worth') but also a disassociation from the reality of reward principles. In the West, these principles may introduce the concept of:

- *result orientation;* ie performance-related pay versus potential-related pay;
- *applied skills:* skill enhancement/acquisition may not suffice, but the gain of experience in the use of acquired skills enhances earnings;
- *equity:* parity within the country or capital where the job is based, therefore within a well-defined pay market environment;
- *pay movement:* progression through pay ranges is pursuant to the achievement of agreed goals often determined at corporate, operational and personal level.

Unfortunately, these principles are challenged by the volatility of the labour market. Studying the resumé of young managerial talent provides an interesting insight into what could represent a recruitment manager's nightmare. The average stay in a given job is 10–12 months and job changes provide quick access to a supervisory or management role within a couple of years for university graduates, although real experience in a given job might be very thin.

Another complication from a reward standpoint originates from the great number of young Eastern European managers returning to that region after spending most of their lives in the West. Their Western remuneration packages set an example for their bilingual contemporaries working locally. The disparity in pay causes tensions within companies predominantly employing young talent (ie most of the newly established foreign sales and marketing companies).

Reward management within that context represents a true challenge, especially for the regional or headquarters human resource departments where examples of pay disparity and discrimination between employees justly raise questions from a practical, as well as philosophical, standpoint. The answers vary according to each country and, probably, according to the development stage of the local operation.

This 'salary jungle' will not disappear of its own accord. It should, however, succumb to a well-thought-out strategy. Solutions that involve better and regular market comparisons, enhanced communication of pay packages, guided skill acquisition programmes and the introduction of retention devices are being implemented successfully. This must be a good sign for employers in such an unpredictable environment.

Real Estate Costs in Western Europe

Nick Barnes, European Property Researcher, DTZ Debenham Thorpe, London

In the cost-conscious post-recessionary mid-1990s, the issue of effective cost management has assumed a far greater importance than was the case in the heady days of the mid and late 1980s. Part of this change has involved the way in which companies view their property commitments. For long almost overlooked by many occupiers, there is now a growing realization of the significance of property in respect of the operational costs of a business. In practical terms this means not simply comparing the differences in occupational costs between locations, but also ensuring optimum efficiency in terms of building occupancy; in other words, ensuring accommodation works in harmony with the operational requirements of the business. So often the locational dimension and building characteristics, both physical and legal, have acted as constraints on the efficiency of core businesses.

This chapter examines the key costs associated with the occupation of office and industrial premises in Western Europe and considers related issues which will have an impact on the occupier's total real estate bill.

What are the key real estate costs?

An important question facing a would-be occupier is whether to rent or buy accommodation. The answer to this question will depend on the particular circumstances of the company involved and, to a cer-

tain degree, on prevailing property market conditions. Generally, however, a new venture in a foreign country will seek, at least initially, to lease, so this article focuses on costs associated with the renting, rather than the buying, of commercial premises.

Lease agreements between landlords and tenants will vary the obligations of the respective parties involved. Broadly speaking, however, the most important cost items associated with rented accommodation are rent, service charges and local real estate taxes. Differing levels of cost between countries across Europe are apparent in all three categories – indeed, variations between locations within the same country or even the same city can be substantial. Differences between the supply/demand cycles of national, regional and local markets will inevitably result in price differentials, as will the size, quality, age and specific location of the building concerned.

Top rents for prime new office accommodation in capital city central business district locations in Western Europe currently range from ECU 455 per square metre per annum in London (City) and Paris down to around ECU 195 per square metre per annum in Amsterdam and Brussels (see Figure 18.1). These figures reflect 'headline rents', which may be substantially reduced when occupier incentives are taken into account, a factor which is considered in more detail later. Current rental levels for the best industrial/warehouse accommodation stand at

18

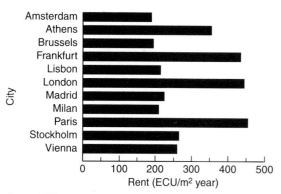

Source: DTZ

Figure 18.1 Prime office rents

around ECU 40 per square metre per annum in Athens and Milan, up to ECU 90–95 in Lisbon and London (see Figure 18.2).

Service charge levels may vary between buildings in the same location depending on the quality of the building concerned and the range of amenities offered, eg reception facilities, air conditioning and 24-hour operations. Service charges can range from ECU 85 per square metre per annum for a prime multitenanted office building in the City of London to around ECU 20 per square metre for a building of similar specification in the best location in Madrid and Lisbon.

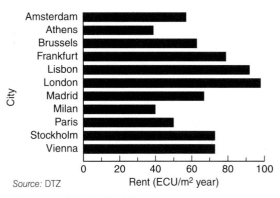

Source: DTZ

Figure 18.2 Prime industrial/warehouse rents

Local real estate taxes show the greatest variation: in the City of London they can be as high as ECU 340 per square metre per annum, while in Madrid and Amsterdam they are very small. This variation is largely explained by the different approaches to calculating the base applicable in each country and by the scope of the taxes themselves. In Spain, local real estate taxes are calculated on the basis of the cadastral value of the property, to which each local authority will apply its own multiplier. In

the Netherlands, the tax base is the capital value (assessed annually) of a building, which varies by district according to the multiplier used by each local authority. In the UK, the tax base, effectively, is the rental value of the building as at a given date to which a nationally fixed multiplier is applied.

In addition, the occupier will need to consider legal fees and estate agent fees, which can vary significantly. The handling of VAT is also not uniform across Europe – both in terms of the rate applicable and whether or not it is chargeable. VAT on property transactions currently ranges from 19 per cent in Italy to 15 per cent in Germany where the application of VAT can be optional, according to the wishes of the parties involved.

Factors affecting occupier accommodation costs

Having established that the key real estate costs will vary according to a range of factors, the occupier must bear in mind that there are other issues, not so immediately apparent, which can affect the relative cost of accommodation.

First, quoted rental levels may be subject either to some form of discount – eg a rent-free period – or premium, depending on the strength of the market. In the City of London, for example, at the low point of the market in 1992, office occupiers could negotiate rent-free periods of three years or more, plus substantial contributions towards fitting-out costs and, in some cases, agreements to take back their existing space. As the market has improved and the availability of, in particular, high quality office space has reduced, the level of incentives on offer has reduced. This trend will continue as the market returns to balance. Similar patterns have occurred across Western Europe's main property markets: in Frankfurt, tenants can currently obtain up to six months rent free compared to 12–18 months at the bottom of the market.

Second, despite the existence of the Single European Market, substantial differences remain in real estate practice between countries. So far as the occupier is concerned, these differences are particularly marked in the area of lease structure and landlord and tenant obligations. Typical lease lengths can range from as little as one year in Portugal (with annually indexed rents linked to the cost of living index) up to 25 years in the UK (with five-yearly, upwards only rent reviews to open market value).

The responsibilities of the tenant will also vary

	Typical lease length	Rent review (frequency)	Rent indexation basis (frequency)	Landlord responsible	Tenant responsible
UK	up to 25 years	5 yearly	–	minimal	structural and internal repairs
ITALY	6 years	–	75% of cost of living (annual)	structural repairs	normal maintenance costs
FRANCE	9 years	3 yearly	cost of building (3 yearly or annual)	structural repairs and land tax	normal maintenance costs
PORTUGAL	1 year	–	cost of living (annual)	structural repairs	internal repairs

Source: DTZ

Table 18.1 Examples of Lease Obligations in Western Europe

according to the terms of the lease (see Table 18.1). The UK pattern, where leases are typically drafted on a full repairing and insuring (FRI) basis under which the tenant is obliged to carry out all repairs and insurance items, is atypical of practices throughout mainland Europe. There the usual arrangement is for internal repairing leases with the tenant only responsible for internal repairs and normal maintenance. While the variations in tenant responsibilities for repairs will affect total annual property costs, the marked differences in lease length can materially affect the occupiers' flexibility and indeed financial position if their accounting procedures require them to capitalize lease obligations.

Even if the rent and associated costs for a similar building in two countries appear comparable, this may not mean that the real cost to the occupier will be truly comparable since lettable areas can vary significantly between countries. This variation arises because local measuring practice in each country can include different components of a standard office floorplate within the total floor area assessed for rent; for example, toilet space is excluded from lettable areas in the UK, while non-structural walls are excluded in France. To illustrate the point, recent survey evidence gathered by the DTZ network indicates that in Belgium the lettable area is almost 100 per cent of the gross floorspace, whereas in Austria the figure is closer to 70 per cent. This means that the occupier will effectively be paying quite different amounts for each square metre of usable space in the two cities – even if rents are fixed at the same level.

Another important consideration for the pro-

spective occupier of office space in Western Europe is the difference which exists between space allocation standards per employee. In London and Paris, for example, around 15 square metres is typically allocated per office employee in a bank/financial services sector environment, which can compare with as much as 30 square metres for similar functions in

Amsterdam. Clearly, this will affect the occupier's total accommodation costs and makes the simple comparison of real estate costs on a square metre basis potentially misleading.

Conclusions

It is clear that real estate costs and practices are not uniform across Europe. This is, in part, a reflection of the strength of the different markets at any given time, but also demonstrates the underlying differences in structure between markets. Provided occupiers are aware of these variations they can make the necessary calculations which will enable a like-for-like comparison between locations.

Having carried out this process, however, there remain further factors which require careful consideration. It is very important for occupiers to match their accommodation to their business operational requirements in terms of specification and location. This requires not just an assessment of the current circumstances of the business, but also an appreciation of anticipated changes to corporate policies which will affect accommodation requirements. The impact of technology and changing workplace practice will also affect working environments. This is particularly noticeable in the office sector where 'hotdesking' and 'homeworking' are changing the long-term requirement for office space. Finally, every occupier should recognize the financial importance of accommodation. This requires premises to be treated not merely as a location for carrying out a business operation, but also as a workable asset with an appropriately important position in the corporate balance sheet. This principle, of course, applies regardless of the country in which an occupier locates.

The Property Path of Eastern Europe

Simon M Trappes-Lomax, Jones Lang Wootton, Warsaw

Since the break-up of the Soviet Union, Poland, Hungary and the Czech Republic have each embarked on a series of privatization processes that have initiated Central Europe's gradual alignment with the free market forces of Western Europe. This has prompted a steady flow of foreign investment targeted towards the region, which in turn is stimulating and developing property markets.

The property markets of Central and Eastern Europe are characterized by a marked imbalance between overall supply of prime quality commercial premises, and current and anticipated future demand. This has resulted in occupancy costs in the capitals of the region rivalling those of the most sophisticated cities in the world.

While the sophisticated markets of the West slowly emerge from the effects of recent recession, and appear ever more crowded, the sights of property developers and investment funds are increasingly focused on the comparatively lucrative markets of Central Europe. However, this added awareness and involvement in the region on the part of developers largely have to date been countered by difficulties in raising finance for much needed development activity.

Despite the increased activity of US and Western European manufacturers, retail and distribution firms, and their need for Western-quality premises, Western financial institutions have proved consistently sluggish in their approach to releasing finance for new developments. The reasons for this are many, but mainly revolve around various factors, including the perceived political task associated with new emerging markets; untried new legislation governing property ownership and usage; and the fact that traditional institutional investors have an intrinsic need for detailed information, including a good insight into a property market track record over a significant period, which as yet cannot be served effectively. All of these factors provoke a cautious approach on the part of potential investors. This has remained a consistently frustrating obstacle, especially considering the widely held view that potential yields on prudent developments are comparatively high in comparison with those of similar developments in most Western European capitals.

Poland

Poland has travelled a long way since it became the first Warsaw Pact state to embark on fast-track economic reforms. The political climate is stabilizing as political leaders increasingly recognize the importance of maintaining the economic course and reforms that have been initiated; momentum is increasing and is to a large degree dictated by the new breed of entrepreneur. Economic growth was put at 4.5 per cent during 1994 and the estimated rate is 5.9 per cent for 1995; unofficially, however, economic growth is recognized as being a couple of percentage points higher. Inflation, still high at approximately 30 per cent, is maintaining a falling trend.

Prospects for the real-estate market look good. The service sector continues to expand rapidly. Vacancy rates have not risen above 0 per cent over the last two years and our estimated figure on demand is 80,000 square metres per annum and rising. Total office stock is well below that of other European capitals, with only approximately 5 per cent of current stock representing 'Western standards'. We envisage a continued undersupply into the next millennium. Rents as a result continue to be high, with no let-up expected for the foreseeable future.

The Investment Market

We believe that property investment in Poland will increasingly be seen as a credible investment portfolio component. However, the market will have to mature further before it begins to attract the type of institutional investors traditionally associated with property investment in more developed countries. Prime yields are currently quoted at between 12 and 15 per cent, which we anticipate will harden as the market matures.

Letting Market

Offices

The Warsaw office market is seriously undersupplied in relation to comparable cities. Despite a few new developments, stock remains limited. New additions to stock, such as the recently completed initial phase of the Atrium Business Centre, a modern office development comprising nearly 9000 square metres of prime quality office space, often prove prohibitive to companies at the initial stages of setting up operations in Poland. This is because of the difficulty in foreseeing future corporate requirements, and the high rents commanded by the few modern office facilities which remain in the region of $50 per square metre per month.

Retail

There is a keen interest on the part of international retail chains in the potential that Warsaw holds. This is resulting in the retail market enjoying continued expansion. The LIM Galleria and the Atrium Business Centre are both considered significant new additions to retail stock. Rents typically reflect a rate of $80 per square metre per month.

Retail trends reflect those of more developed Western centres and serve as an incentive to Western retailers. We anticipate growing international retail activity, and perhaps the extension of established German distribution networks into Poland.

Hungary

Lack of confidence in the current political climate is the single major influence stalling economic growth in Hungary. The coalition government witnessed a 22.5 per cent devaluation of the florint in its first year of office, and it is expected that further devaluations in the order of 16–17 per cent will have to be implemented by the end of 1995. These measures have been taken to counter a rising debt/GDP ratio and a very heavy budget deficit reaching 7 per cent of GDP. The government has also cut its social spending programme and raised import taxes by 8 per cent.

These measures do not seem to have prevented companies with commitments in Hungary from pursuing their plans. However, it remains to be seen whether the current financial strategy will affect the flow of inward investment. The property market has remained active but constrained owing to the limited supply of available stock.

Investment Market

The investment market is quiet with no prime quality buildings having been traded for a considerable period. Despite the creation of various funds for investment in the purchase of property, few appear to have been active.

A settling in the economic climate will be required to stimulate more activity, and until then we expect to see the increased involvement of entrepreneurial individuals who are less risk conscious, and smaller funds anticipating future stability and likely future returns. Yields remain above 10 per cent.

Letting Market

Offices

Inadequate stock remains the main constraint. With little development activity expected in the immediate future, the availability of prime stock has fallen to virtually nil.

Buildings considered to be prime include Bank Center, a Canadian/Hungarian development comprising 30,000 square metres of usable space, and Hold Utca 27, a Belgian development providing 2800 square metres. Rents for prime office accommodation are generally quoted in the region of DM45–50 per square metre per month. Demand remains at a level of between 50,000 and 60,000 square metres.

Retail

There has been a healthy increase in the number, quality and size of supermarkets throughout Hungary. There is also a definite increase in the number of high quality retailers examining the market with a view to commencing business activities. However, despite plans for modern shopping centres, Budapest still lacks an established retail market. Rents for prominent retail locations stand at approximately DM130 per square metre per month.

Czech Republic

The completion of the most successful privatization process undertaken anywhere underlines the degree of commitment and energy which has resulted in the dramatic economic turnaround of what was one of the most orthodox and centrally planned economies in Europe.

After four years of recession the economy grew by 2.6 per cent in 1994, and further growth of 4.8 per cent is expected during 1995. A strong service sector is in place, construction and industrial output is growing, and unemployment is a tolerable 3.3 per cent.

Inflation remains a problem and will probably demand a higher degree of foreign investment to tackle. There is a swelling trade deficit, although this is largely hidden by revenue from tourism which yielded over $2 billion in 1994.

Investment Market

The lack of investment-grade product remains the main hindrance to the development of an investment market, despite the interest shown by various institutional investors. A number of properties have been sold for refurbishment to developers, or owner-occupiers. Prices, however, vary widely owing to the uncertain market. Yields for prime quality space are quoted in the order of 10–12 per cent.

Letting Market
Offices

The complete lack of available international-quality office accommodation has resulted in a total lack of choice and minimal transactions. However, 18,000 square metres of quality space will become available in October 1995 on completion of Praha City Centre. This will be followed in early 1996 by the completion of the Darex project comprising 5,000 square metres and Myslbek with 17,500 square metres. Prime rents for quality space currently fetch DM44–55 per square metre per month.

Retail

Both urban and out-of-town retail development is attracting growing interest; several international operators are currently seeking good locations to establish their outlets. Fast food chains have proved very active, and demand for greenfield sites to construct high turnover food or DIY outlets is growing. Retail rents are quoted at approximately DM130 per square metre per month and above.

Conclusion

Lack of financing remains the main factor holding back the further development of international-standard commercial property throughout the region, so maintaining high occupancy rates. This bottleneck in supply may in part be relieved by the added awareness of Western financial institutions, but the long-term solution must lie in the eventual understanding and involvement in the concept of property as an investment on the part of financial institutions based in the individual countries of the region. The degree to which either happens will rest in the political and economic courses chartered over the coming years, directly influencing that all-important business stimulant, confidence.

PART

5

A Competitive Infrastructure for Business

The Development of Europe's Fibre-Optic Network

20

Richard Warren, Course Director, Euro-Managers Programme,
South Thames College

Rumpelstiltskin managed to weave straw into gold. European cable companies are trying to do the same with fibre-optic cable. Judging by the amount of multicoloured lines drawn on the pavement of our cities, they must be expanding their cable networks at a phenomenal rate. According to a recent DTI report, local UK cable companies are connecting up well over a million homes a year to their networks, and the growth rate is increasing. Almost any business in a UK city is now within linking distance of a fibre-optic cable. The UK government's target of supplying cable links to 80–85 per cent of the population looks like being reached well before the end of the millennium. Much of mainland Europe is speeding ahead with linking its business and consumers to the fibre-optic network, mainly through the efforts of their national telecommunication companies.

The cables themselves are merely bundles of thin glass strands, but each strand is capable of carrying as much data as 150,000 copper wire telephone lines! It is not only telephone conversations that can be transmitted. Television programmes, computer data and programmes, videoconferences, virtually anything that can be reduced to electronic signals can pass down the 'cable' at the speed of light. It is this enormous potential that makes the cable companies invest so heavily in laying down the infrastructure often referred to as 'the superhighway'. The technology of cramming so much information into one single channel is called broad-band communications;

normal telephone wires can only handle narrow-band communications which do not allow transferring voice, data and pictures all at once.

In the UK private companies have exclusive area franchises, usually lasting for seven years. They are, however, likely to remain monopoly providers of cable-borne services to their customers beyond this exclusive period, unless new legislation is implemented to make them share their network infrastructure. It is not surprising, therefore, that the first areas to be covered by companies are those most commercially attractive, with high population or business densities. Technology, however, is helping out in less populated areas where the volume of traffic does not make it viable to lay cables. Radio and infrared signalling systems are capable of handling data at almost the same speed as fibre-optic cable. Fortunately rural areas are less populated than urban areas, so there is less chance of clogging the airwaves in the way that London mobile telephones do.

Throughout the rest of Europe the national telecommunication companies are mainly responsible for providing the fibre-optic infrastructure. Political will therefore tends to dictate the speed and spread of the network. The debate over the benefits of public or private provision of cable networks is the same as that over the provision of other services such as water, electricity, gas, etc. The resulting disparities in customer charges and service quality are also the same. For example, it costs 20 times as much to make a connection between Brighton and Calais as it does between Brighton and Glasgow. Unlike EuroStar trains, which have to slow down when they cross from France to the UK, data services have to slow down dramatically when they cross in the other direction (unless the customer wants to pay a very high premium).

In the less developed regions of Europe, where the immediate financial benefit of providing networks is not apparent, Brussels steps in to help out. The European Structure Fund is helping establish fibre-optic networks in many European regions. Greece, Spain and the new German *Länder* are being provided with infrastructures as technically advanced as any in the world. DG13, the European Commission Directorate responsible for telecommunications, has a large research and development budget to help expand and improve access to Europe's broad-band telecommunication services.

As the UK is leading Europe in building a comprehensive fibre-optic network, it is also leading the debate in which services to provide. Having laid their cables to the consumers' front door the companies now need to provide services for which those consumers will pay. Herein lies today's problem for cable companies: what to provide, and at what price.

For domestic customers the most obvious service is mass entertainment in the form of live television and videofilms. Unfortunately, consumers who have already purchased satellite dishes are unlikely to want even more television programmes unless there is some form of added value. Interaction between the consumer and the television provider is possible via fibre-optics, as are locally produced programmes with a high local content. These forms of entertainment may be cheaper to produce but by definition they can only cater for a limited market. It is more profitable to relay a popular soap opera to a large audience than to produce and dispatch a local programme to a very small audience. Added to the commercial aspects are the political considerations. The media regulators in Berlin recently instructed the main cable company to drop CNN (Cable News Network) in preference to a local German-language rock music station, VIVA. Other states in Germany are considering the same steps. Even in the UK regulators have some say over the content of cable transmissions. The most obvious area is pornography, for which different member states have different standards. Any Briton wishing to view certain Dutch channels has to invest in a satellite dish;

having done so they are unlikely to subscribe to a cable service providing a less intense service. Another threat to cable companies comes in the form of a British Telecom (BT) experiment in East Anglia. Although BT is not allowed to transmit television on a wide scale at present, it is running an 'experiment' transmitting selected videofilms over its standard telephone lines to a small East Anglian community. The quality is good and bound to improve greatly between now and the time that government allows BT full access to the media market. When consumers can dial up and request any film they want, when they want to see it, what use will they have for a hundred television channels?

The three million European users of on-line services such as the Internet will also need a strong incentive to switch from their current service provider. Domestic Internet users already manage to obtain a reasonable speed of service by using data-compression technology and forgoing some of the pretty pictures that take so long to transmit. In order to provide that extra incentive for the consumer, the American media tycoon Will Hearst is combining Internet services with home shopping, television and telephone all in one service. He believes that by so doing he can attract customers and generate multiple revenue streams (consumers and suppliers). He plans to offer his complete service to cable companies who would be able to keep about £14 of the £20 monthly subscription fee from each consumer. This is a lot less than the cable companies had planned for when setting up their networks. The original business plans assumed that they would recoup the setting up costs by controlling the content of their networks and charging premium rates. Allowing Mr Hearst free access to their networks would destroy that policy, leaving only a few select niche markets for the cable companies to exploit. The fact that some mature American cable companies are taking his offer seriously must worry the younger European companies.

The business market is a little brighter. For business users fibre-optic technology provides a range of services which make considerable savings in overheads, improve company efficiency and competitiveness. Most companies network their computers within an office already, to allow easy transfer of information between workers. Cable offers the chance to network computers beyond the local area with the same effect. The banks' automated teller machines demonstrate how effective this can be. As well as machines, teams of people can also work together on projects without having to meet physically. Individuals can share a computer program to develop an idea, and can hear and see each other, while they are working. Managers need not travel to conferences etc, they can sit in on board meetings while remaining in their own offices. 'Back offices' can be located wherever accommodation and quality labour are cheapest. Information can be accessed from around the world in a user-friendly form, with graphs, pictures and even video, to help explain complex data or provide training. The European Commission has invested heavily in the development of these tools in an effort to help European businesses achieve a competitive edge over their world rivals.

Perhaps the service offering the greatest general potential for imaginative companies is the ability to allow workers to work from, or near, home using the high quality telecommunications medium to keep in touch with their base office (thus the term 'teleworkers'). Many workers can manage their workload from home, or properly equipped centres near their home. Apart from being environmentally friendly (reducing commuter traffic) and beneficial to the worker (greater flexibility), teleworking reduces company overheads. A typical arrangement for workers is to work four days 'at home' and one day in the office. Thus five workers can share one desk! Few companies object to a reduction of 80 per cent in accommodation costs. Teleworking also provides a community benefit. Without the need to travel daily into the city centre, workers are happy to remain living in rural areas, or even move back into the countryside. The restoration of rural life opens more employment possibilities within those communities, even if it is just servicing teleworkers and their families. There are already networks of 'telecentres' in Britain, and parts of mainland Europe, that provide the basic services required by teleworkers. Here again the European Commission is providing encouragement. Teleworking is viewed by the Commission as a major plank in its employment initiatives.

Perhaps the cable companies should accept Will Hearst's offer to provide for their domestic customers, and concentrate their efforts on encouraging businesses to scatter their employees to the remote corners of Europe.

Fraunhofer-Institut fuer Angewandte Festkoerperphysik (Applied Solid State Physics) Freiburg/Germany

The Fraunhofer-Institut fuer Angewandte Festkoerperphysik (IAF) is a research institute of the Fraunhofer-Gesellschaft (FhG) for Applied Research. FhG is named after Joseph-von Fraunhofer, also famous for his discovery of the Fraunhofer lines in the solar spectrum. Fraunhofer was a self-made scientist and entrepreneur with an extraordinary talent of directly linking science and business, a philosophy adopted by the FhG since its foundation in 1949.

Objectives of the institute with a total of 200 employees are research and development to realise components for systems in the information and communication areas as well as in the laser area. R&D projects focus on materials with acknowledged or potential importance for electronics, optoelectronics, microwave and millimeterwave technology and infrared technology as well. Activities span a bow from basic material research over optimization of manufacturing processes in an advanced clean room to prototype integrated circuits (ICs) for customers' applications.

IAF's R&D is focused on the technology of microelectronic and optoelectronic devices and ICs based on III-V compound semiconductors such as GaAs/AlGaAs/InGaAs/GaInP/InP, group III nitrides and antimonides. Such devices and ICs are key components for advanced high-tech systems in high-frequency telecommunication, high-bit-rate optical communication, high-speed signal and data processing and laser technology based on power diode lasers.

The rapid development of wireless terrestrial and satellite-based communication, mobile radio, traffic guidance and environmental control calls for an extension of the radio frequency spectrum into the microwave and millimeter wave range. Frequencies up to 100 GHz are on demand in the long-term. To capitalise on the enormous market potential of wireless communication the cost-effective production of monolithic microwave and millimeterwave Integrated circuits (MMICs) is the most important prerequisite.

In the framework of the strategic joint programme "III-V Electronics" founded by the German government IAF has developed numerous high-yield MMICs for low-noise satellite receivers, for radar systems and traffic guidance, all based on their GaAs/AlGaAs/InGaAs HEMT technology. A characteristic feature of these MMICs are coplanar waveguides for interconnects and passive devices. Compared to microstrip waveguides mostly utilized today, they offer a technically simpler and hence much more cost-effective IC production. Fundamental properties of coplanar waveguides have been thoroughly investigated for the first time. Many important passive coplanar devices have been developed and characterized which are now included in a database for MMICs. This database is now available for MMIC prototyping.

In advanced information systems found in computing, consumer electronics, telecommunication, multimedia, and automated manufacturing electrons alone can no longer handle transmission and processing of voice, data and video. Increasingly, photons are utilized as information carriers. Optical transmission has already

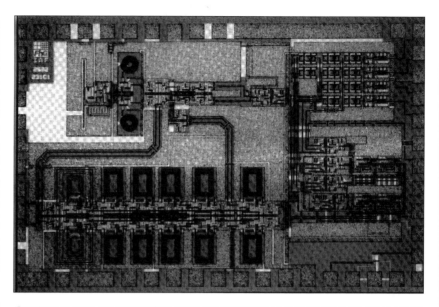

Optoelectronic single chip receiver IC for optical data transmission up to 10 billions of bits per second (10 Gbits). This allows simultaneous reception of 150000 phone calls or 5000 image phone calls or 70 high-definition TV programmes via one single optical fibre (chip size 2 x 3 mm².

seen a breakthrough in various areas of communication and has proven economical performance especially in telecommunication. This development was rendered possible through the excellent properties and the availability of optoelectronic devices such as laser diodes or photodiodes mainly based on the III-V compound semiconductors GaAs and InP, which are compatible with microelectronic ICs. Not only in telecommunication are photons profitable but also in all situations which require large streams of information, e.g. in high-performance computers and distributed processor systems.

In the framework of an other government funded joint effort "Photonics" IAF have developed optoelectronic Integrated circuits (OEICs) to demonstrate a high-bit-rate optical transmission system for up to 20 Gbit/s. A system for a data rate of 40 Gbit/s is under development. Two options are pursued, one being serial optical transmission with time division multiplexing, the other being optical parallel links. Based on IAF's GaAs/AlGaAs/InGaAs-technology diode lasers of high direct modulation frequency (>30 GHz) and broad-band photodiodes are being developed together with the necessary electronic circuitry. Objective is the monolithic integration of electronic and optoelectronic devices, a real challenge for III-V heterostructure technology due to the different vertical device structures. A monolithic driver-laserdiode-OEIC and a complete monolithic receiver OEIC made from photo diode, trans impedance amplifier, main amplifier, data regenerator, clock recovery, and demultiplexer have been successfully demonstrated. This receiver OEIC (see figure) has a complexity not yet achieved elsewhere. For parallel transmission, monolithic optoelectronic transmitter and receiver arrays have been developed.

Semiconductor diode lasers usually come as stripes a few micrometers wide and some 100 micrometers long. Coherent light leaves these edge emitters through one of the front facets of

the stripe – an ideal geometry for light coupling into an optical fibre. Hence, laser diodes have found their first mainstream application in optical telecommunication. Here, high modulation frequency, narrow spectral linewidth and small optical output power are required.

Recently, the development of laser diodes also aims at increasing optical output power. Laser diodes not only serve to transmit optical information but also to transmit optical power. High power densities turn laser diodes to high power diode lasers. In many respects, these have technical and economic advantages over other types of lasers. First of all is the superior efficiency in transforming electrical power into optical power peaking at 30–40 per cent and even beyond 50 per cent in the near future. In comparison, with other lasers only 10–20 per cent are achieved. The microelectronics-related cost effective manufacturing technology offers volume production of high power diode lasers.

IAF is also active in this promising field of III-V technology. Optical output powers beyond 30 Watts from MOPAs (master oscillator power amplifier) power diode lasers are targeted. Even higher values seem feasible if the heat dissipated during laser action is removed through diamond heat spreaders. Heat dissipating submounts containing diamond are also developed at the IAF which belongs to the internationally leading research institutes in the area of CVD (chemically vapour deposited) diamond.

New research directions started recently at the IAF are the development of blue emitters based on gallium nitride (GaN) as well as high temperature electronics up to 600°C based on silicon carbide (SiC).

Fraunhofer Institut fuer Angewandte Festkoerperphysik
Tullastrasse 72, D-79108, Freiburg, Germany
Tel +49(0) 7 61/51 59-0
Fax +49(0) 7 61/51 59-4 00

Progress and Trends in Financial Services

Gerry O'Brien, Associate, Wavehill Consultants

The European Commission (EC) has sought from the inception of the European Union (EU) in 1958 to foster open competition and create a single internal market in a range of sectors including banking, insurance and security markets. Although the initial thrust was in agriculture and industry, the EC has in recent years turned its attention to financial services. In 1977 the first banking directive sought to establish the conditions for a genuine common market in banking. In 1989 the second directive sought to coordinate laws, regulations and administrative provisions relating to credit institutions. Within the overall aims of harmonization and mutual recognition of national supervisory authorities, a bank is supervised by the authorities in the country in which it has its registered office.

On 1 July 1987 the Single European Act came into force and aimed to create a market totally without frontiers in goods and services by 1 January 1993. As a result of the Maastricht Treaty, exchange controls were effectively abolished within most of the EU from 1 January 1994 (there are still exceptions in the cases of Greece, Ireland, Portugal and Spain). Additionally, differential exchange rates were abolished, with the exceptions of Belgium and Luxembourg. As a company you will eventually want to repatriate profits to the UK. Whilst normally this should not be a problem, you should always check

that there are no local rules affecting capital transfers, especially in Greece.

Thus we have a position where the EC has effectively created a single market in financial services and has abolished exchange controls. This is good news, but for whom? The thrust of the EC's actions seems to have been primarily to allow competition between European financial institutions and allow them to grow in size and strength to compete against US and Japanese giants. Of course some would think that these two aims could be mutually incompatible. Big, strong banks might be too big and strong for the good of their customers.

In many ways the marketplace is having more effect than EC or national regulations. After all, these are often running fast just to keep up with the dishonest and/or incompetent (Barlow Clowes, BCCI, Barings, etc.). In the meantime the major players are consolidating their position. Solid, dull but rich German banks are buying up old-established, exciting but undercapitalized London institutions (Deutsche Bank and Morgan Grenfell in 1989, Dresdner Bank and Kleinworts in 1995). Equally London clearing banks are buying German private banks (Lloyds & SMH of Frankfurt in 1984). However, this is all investment in niche markets. The nearest any European bank has to a national presence in another EU country is a nationalized French bank, Crédit

Lyonnais, which in the 1980s bought everything in sight including, unintentionally, Cannon Cinemas. Needless to say, this attempt to nurture national prestige has ended in spectacular failure, with the French government trying to persuade the EC to allow them to bail out Crédit Lyonnais to the tune of FF45 billion ($9.4 billion) in addition to the FF23 billion that they had in 1994. The EC is wisely resisting, but will eventually give in.

So where does this leave a UK enterprise which wants to expand into continental Europe? Probably still in the hands of the London and Scottish clearers. In London or Edinburgh you may find a continental bank that will offer you services. Additionally, quasi-banks such as ex-building societies are around but do not have a tradition of commercial banking, especially with overseas connections.

An enterprise thinking of expanding into the EU needs first to consider what it wants to do, and the type of banking facilities that this will require (see Table 21.1).

Your UK bank will be able to recommend a local bank and provide you with references. Almost without exception for day-to-day banking you will get a better service from a local retail bank than from an overseas branch of a British bank. This is not because the UK banks give a bad service but because they specialize in large corporates. However, you will not be aware of local conditions such as credit terms or whether factoring exists. Additionally, charges can vary significantly from the UK norm. For instance, whereas in the UK there is a maximum commission for money transfer, in Germany there is not and this can make a dramatic difference to the total charges involved. Make sure you fully understand the structure of local bank charges.

When choosing a bank steer clear of second-tier banks. Bank collapses are rare, but they do happen. Also many banks have a specialism (eg the Dutch Bank ING specializes in emerging markets such as Eastern Europe). If appropriate try and find a bank that has a specialism that is relevant to you.

	Joint venture	Sub-contracting	Agent	Subsidiary/branch office
Type of enterprise				
Manufacturing	✓	✓		✓
Research & development	✓	✓		✓
Exporting	✓		✓	✓
Importing	✓		✓	✓
Banking requirements				
Foreign exchange	✓	✓	✓	✓
Local facilities	✓			✓

Table 21.1 Types of enterprise and banking requirements

All of these types of enterprise, either singly or in any combination, will bring different banking requirements, which will be mirrored by management and control issues. These should not be considered in isolation. The UK company will not only be dealing with new rules but also foreign conditions and customs. Especially, bearing in mind that Europe does not end with the EU, it also includes the new market-oriented democracies of Central and Eastern Europe.

A UK bank can deal with money transfer and foreign exchange, and payment can be made easily and speedily anywhere within the EU. They will have correspondent banks in all major cities. The problems start to arise when you have an overseas subsidiary which has its own banking requirements.

Do not forget that in most countries you can use your UK cashpoint card in local cash dispensers; this is a very convenient and cheap way of getting local currency on business trips.

In most countries there is a British Chamber of Commerce, and London, Edinburgh and other major cities may have a chamber of commerce for the country concerned. You can get advice from these as well as from your own bank's overseas division. The Department of Trade and Industry (DTI) will provide a lot of support and advice to UK enterprises wishing to extend their businesses abroad. It is well worth trying as many sources of advice as possible, especially if it is free!

It is essential to have good legal and accounting advice from a specialist who knows the country concerned. The Law Society and Institute of Chartered Accountants can help here. It is often compulsory to join the local Chamber of Commerce in the country concerned; these can be very useful with local advice and contacts.

Another solution is to form a joint venture with a local partner, who will have all the local knowledge needed. However, the possibility always exists that they will put their interests before yours. Sometimes you will have built up a relationship with a potential partner over a period of time, but even here there are possible problems. There is a process in banking and accountancy called due diligence, which is intended to investigate thoroughly the financial standing of a partner. This can be expensive but, like a house survey, often saves trouble in the long run.

The EC seeks to offer consumers a wider range of competing financial products, irrespective of nationality of customer and provider. This, taken in conjunction with the ending of exchange controls, means that an enterprise or an individual can borrow capital in any EU country, in any currency, against any collateral and repaid from any source. This can

seem very attractive if you can find interest rates significantly lower than in your domestic market. However, it is a path fraught with danger. Many years ago the J. Lyons Company borrowed heavily in US dollars and Swiss francs because of the attractive loan terms. Unfortunately sterling sank against both currencies. Lyons only had sterling assets and earnings with which to service the loans, which got ever larger in sterling terms, and was eventually sunk to become part of Allied Lyons (and their name has now disappeared altogether). More recently ECU-denominated mortgages were fashionable in Italy. Again, the collapse of the lira has led to a crisis, with the value of the mortgage increasing in a way that makes UK negative equity look like child's play. Only take on foreign currency liabilities if you can service them from assets and cash flow denominated in the same currency. Currency speculation can be unsuccessful and you need to take care in this respect.

Although this advice is intended to cover the European Union and associated states it is, of course, relevant to all overseas markets.

22 Winning Access to European Energy Markets

Graham Shuttleworth, Associate Director, National Economic Research Associates

Philip Daubeney, Chief Executive, Electricity Association

The liberalization of European energy markets
Graham Shuttleworth

The debate over liberalization of the European energy industry rumbles on, within both European institutions and member states. During 1995, one question rose to the top of the pile: which customers can choose their supplier of energy? Finding a compromise will keep European institutions busy for some time; meanwhile, events within member states are running ahead of the European timetable.

Until recently, most European energy industries were characterized by a high degree of vertical integration and monopoly. The assumption that monopoly was the natural order in energy was called into question during the 1980s and 1990s by major reforms in the US, the UK and Scandinavia. In these countries, generation was separated from transmission and allowed to sell direct to distribution companies or even to final consumers. These developments triggered interest in a single European energy market.

In 1992, the Commission produced first draft Directives on 'third-party access' (TPA) for the gas and electricity sectors. The drafts drew heavily on British experience and effectively required each member state to set up competitive energy markets with separate grid companies offering mandatory transmission access to all producers, distribution companies and large industrial customers. This

approach provoked outrage from a number of member states, where neither the governments nor the utilities were ready for such thoroughgoing reform. The period since 1993 has therefore been spent trying to find a compromise consistent with the traditions of the 15 member states.

The first attempt at compromise in December 1993 reduced 'unbundling' to a matter of accounting and replaced 'mandatory' rights of access with provisions for 'negotiated' access. No one knows what this means in practice, as the debate then took off in another direction.

In October 1994, the French government produced a counter-proposal for the electricity sector, suggesting that only major utilities should have the right to choose their supplier. This 'single buyer model' followed closely the US Public Utilities Regulation and Policy Act (1978). It would maintain each utility's sales monopoly over distribution companies and large industrial customers.

The European Council considered the single buyer model long and hard. Given a preference for TPA in some member states, the Council was keen to establish whether the two systems could coexist within a single energy market. To test this, the Institute of Energy Economics at the University of Cologne was asked whether the two systems would produce similar outcomes within a single energy market. Unfortunately for the Council, the Institute concluded what was obvious to most casual observers – that the two systems differed in many respects and would in fact produce different outcomes.

The Commission responded with a modified single buyer proposal which was more compatible with TPA. The single buyer was to 'respect the principles of objectivity, transparency and non-discrimination'. In addition, the Commission insisted that 'eligible customers' should be allowed to choose their own supplier (except possibly in 'small systems'). Such freedom of choice rather undermines the French concept of a 'single' buyer.

The Spanish Presidency of 1995 now has to find a compromise. The current sticking point is the definition of 'eligible customers'; large industrial customers are included in the proposal, but distribution companies are not. We can only wait and see whether the solution brokered at the European level narrows or broadens customer choice.

In the meantime, member states are taking matters into their own hands. In the electricity sector, Britain, Sweden and Finland have established separate transmission companies. The Portuguese government and the German Federal Cartel Office favour choice without unbundling. The new Spanish electricity law envisages an 'independent sector' for independent generators and some large customers. Even the Italian government (sometimes) proposes breaking up ENEL prior to privatization.

In the gas sector, things are moving more slowly. There are fewer producers clamouring for access to transmission networks and, consequently, fewer proposals for reform. However, 'gas bubbles' in the North Sea and Eastern Europe could disturb this relative calm. Once Europe's industrial customers spot cheap gas opportunities, we can expect a stormy debate over third-party access for gas.

So, while the need for compromise slows up European debate on liberalization, national governments are devising their own reforms. They are responding to local conditions with only half an eye on Brussels. Eventually, both energy producers and energy consumers will start to respond with their feet, by choosing the system they prefer. This will prove a stricter test of reform proposals than any continuing debate at the European level.

National Power, the UK's leading electricity generator, is now operating internationally.

We are building a global business by long-term investment in and the management of private power generation assets.

We offer the resources and expertise that have brought us acknowledged success in our competitive home market.

National Power works by developing partnerships to work with customers, suppliers, utilities, governments and plant and fuel suppliers. We invest in new, profitable project developments – but we also acquire existing power stations.

A WORLD FORCE IN POWER GENERATION.

We've already made a powerful start – in the USA, Pakistan, Spain and Portugal.

These projects represent a wide range of coal, oil and gas-fired assets. We are also part of a consortium developing 'clean burn' coal technology.

Wherever you find us, now and in the future, we will manage and operate the plant in which we hold a substantial stake.

While each project is different, our standards will be the same. World class.

For further information, please contact:

Australia Office: Sydney. Tel: + 61 2 238 2131. Fax: + 61 2 238 2179. (Contact: David Keeling)

China Office: Beijing. Tel: + 86 1 0466 3110. Fax: + 86 1 0466 4149. (Contact: Andrew Holt)

India Office: New Delhi. Tel: + 91 11 464 6126/7. Fax: + 91 11 461 0557. (Contact: Tom Scott-Morey)

Indonesia Office: Jakarta. Tel: + 62 21 5735654/ 5735655. Fax: + 62 21 573 5657. (Contact: Iain McMorrine)

Pakistan Office: Karachi. Tel: + 92 21 570922. Fax: + 92 321 335971. (Contact: Tom Mackay)

Portugal Office: Lisbon. Tel: + 351 1417 2621. Fax: + 351 1417 2622. (Contact: Robert Robinson)

Singapore Office: Singapore. Tel: + 65 299 6300. Fax: + 65 299 3121. (Contact: Bob Chew)

Thailand Office: Bangkok. Tel: + 66 2 718 1443. Fax: + 66 2 718 1441. (Contact: Robert Mann)

UK Office: Windmill Hill Business Park, Whitehill Way, Swindon, SN5 6PB. Tel: + 44 1793 892 992. Fax: + 44 1793 892921. (Contact: Peter Windsor)

US Office: Houston. Tel: + 713 613 4300. Fax: + 713 613 4301. (Contact: James Moore)

National Power

INTERNATIONAL

Enter 59 on Enquiry Card

Case Study I:
National Power's approach to Europe

When it was created in the privatization of the British electricity industry some five years ago, National Power was a big fish in a medium-sized pond. It was the biggest power generator with some 32,000 MW and the market leader in the new, competitive electricity market in England and Wales.

Today, in response to the substantial amount of new plant brought into the system by new entrants, National Power has significantly less capacity in the UK; but it is now active in power projects around the world. National Power is well on its way to becoming an international power company rather than a UK utility.

The company will invest substantial sums in overseas power projects by the end of the century, provided the right projects can be developed. Already it is recognized as one of the leading participants in the fast-growing global independent power-generation market; and the company expects to become a big fish in a very big pond.

Underlying the decision to develop internationally was the recognition that opportunities were opening up around the world for independent power generation and that the company's skills, experience and resources could give it a competitive edge in what is a difficult, embryonic but fast-growing market.

Across the world governments have come to recognize the benefits of liberalizing their economies. Many need to expand their power systems and acknowledge that, given the costs involved, this can best be done by introducing private sector management, by privatizing existing assets or encouraging competition. It has been estimated that by the end of the twentieth century US$800 billion worth of investment in new power plant will be required and it has been suggested that perhaps a fifth of that will be provided by independent power producers.

Despite the scale of the potential opportunities, developing international power projects is a difficult process and many or most of the companies seeking to participate in the market are likely to fail. The companies which survive and succeed will be those which have strong competitive advantages. Apart from its project development and financing skills National Power has four great strengths:

▨ *Power plant experience:* the company has first-hand experience in developing, constructing, operating and maintaining a diverse range of power plant. It is among the world's biggest owner/operators of coal-fired capacity and also has interests as owner/operator or joint venture investor/operator in oil-fired plant, CCGTs and open cycle gas turbines, combined heat and power plant, hydro stations and wind farms.

▨ *Privatization experience:* the UK electricity privatization gave the company invaluable experience of organizational and cultural change and the problems that can arise with the introduction of competition into generation and supply. Its key expertise includes market design and development, power purchase agreement negotiation, settlements systems, energy trading and change management.

▨ *International experience:* at privatization National Power inherited British Electricity International, the overseas consultancy arm of the UK electricity supply industry, which had worked in more than 70 different countries from Australia to Zimbabwe.

▨ *Finance:* the company is one of the world's biggest investor-owned generators. It has a strong balance sheet and expects to be cash positive in its UK business.

National Power originally identified seven markets (Europe, North America, Australasia, China, India, Pakistan and South-East Asia) as its primary areas of interest and is seeking to establish long-term businesses in these areas, each potentially involving several projects. In addition, the company is now considering projects elsewhere in the world. First steps have been taken through major investments in the USA, Pakistan and, not least, Europe, where National Power is the lead investor and joint operator in the 600 MW Pego power station in Porgugal.

In the continental market National Power's vision is to secure a pan-European power generation business over the next decade, meeting the needs of a wide range of customers via investments in a balanced portfolio of projects covering:

▨ new build independent power plants;
▨ combined heat and power;
▨ acquisition of existing assets.

The four big determinants in realizing the vision are energy market liberalization, the availability of large volumes of gas, the geographical and sector diversity of the markets and lastly increasing environmental pressures.

Beyond stating forcefully the case for the break-up of existing entrenched power utility monopolies in Europe, National Power's scope of action in influencing the first determinant is limited. However, the approach to the other determinants will influence the first by creating commercial realities which will eventually be reflected in governmental and European Union level policy.

Turning to the second determinant, National Power believes that a coherent gas strategy is essential to unlock investment in the new build independent power plants, particularly in Southern Europe, namely Portugal, Spain, Italy, Greece and Turkey. Gas will predominate as the most important new power plant fuel in these markets pushed by new supplies from the North Sea, the Maghreb and Russia and pulled by increasing environmental and cost pressures. National Power is positioning itself as a player in the continental European gas market, building on its strength as a gas purchaser and trader in the UK. Needless to say, the black fossil fuels (coal, oil, orimulsion) will not be neglected as they will be significant in specific locations, notably Central Europe, and provide a hedge against gas supply uncertainty and monopoly gas interests.

The geographical and product diversity of the European market presents a challenge to National Power and others, starting from a predominantly national base with offices established so far only in Portugal and Poland. The aim is to expand that presence in the next few years with a view to substantial operations in perhaps four major markets. The difficulty is that the targets themselves can and do move according to local political and regulatory development. With regard to market sectors, combining heat and power will enable National Power to circumvent hostile infrastructure barriers by selling power and heat to large energy users, as well as providing a low-risk entry strategy to countries where large independent power plant is still blocked. National Power is a partner with the Irish state utility,

---

Case Study I: *(continued)*

ESB, in the jointly owned company Transpower in developing the European combined heat and power market outside the UK.

Environmental pressures were touched on in regard to gas and Southern Europe, but it is in the countries of Central Europe, who aspire to membership of the European Union, that these pressures come most clearly into focus. Here the major market opportunity is the refurbishment or conversion to gas of old polluting coal-fired plant. A good example is Poland, where National Power is closely involved with the managers of individual power stations in formulating their strategies to meet the impact of environmental legislation. National Power's approach to environmental issues embraces not only emissions but noise, visual impact and local nature considerations.

National Power believes that tackling the three determinants of gas, geographical product diversity and environment can help to bring about in a practical way the ultimate goal of a liberalized energy market in Europe. National Power's strengths, as outlined above, will combine to make it a significant player in the emerging pan-European power market.

This article was prepared in September 1995 and takes no account of any subsequent changes.

Case Study II:
Developments in the European Gas Markets
British Gas plc

Privatization, liberalization and changing attitudes, not to say markets, have all contributed to a rapid change in the way the natural gas market has altered in Britain over the past 10–15 years. With new markets opening up and technology advancing to facilitate the movement of gas further afield, Europe has become a key area of interest for British Gas, both for upstream and downstream business opportunities. Added to this, the European Energy Charter Treaty signed in December 1994 is expected to encourage the development of links between Europe and the countries of the former Soviet Union, as well as cooperation in the development of energy production and distribution.

Germany has the largest European gas market, and privatizations in the East have provided a unique opportunity to enter the new unified Germany. British Gas, in its first participation in an overseas privatization, was allocated shares in a number of East German energy companies. In 1992 BG obtained a 25 per cent share in two regional distribution companies, GSA and EWS, with a combined turnover of £175 million in 1994. The company also owns 5 per cent of the Eastern transmission company VNG, with a turnover of £1 billion in 1994 and a 30 per cent share in DBI, a small energy services company.

For British Gas, exploration and production activities currently extend into continental Europe and equity is held in Italy, The Netherlands and Poland. In recent years, the company has been proactively working with the relevant ministries and industry members in the Czech and Slovak Republics, Hungary, Poland and Romania to help them understand the key issues to be considered in the privatization of the gas industries, including those of operating in a market economy, regulation, industry structure and the interests of foreign investors. Except for the former East Germany, privatization of the gas industry in the region has not yet begun, although British Gas is well positioned and committed to participate, when the opportunities arise in these countries. The diverse nature of continental gas requirements in relation to dependence on gas imports and the development of gas supplies from large-scale distant sources has, until now, emphasized the isolation of the gas market in the UK.

To emphasize its commitment to Europe, British Gas is actively involved in the planned Europe 'Interconnector' which will connect the UK gas grid with the European grid at Zeebrugge, opening up further opportunities for future developments. The company has a 40 per cent share in the Interconnector pipeline project which will provide 20 billion cubic metres per year of capacity for transporting gas between Britain's mainland and continental Europe. Other partners in the project are Amerada Hess, British Petroleum, Conoco, Distrigas, Elf, National Power, Gazprom and Ruhrgas. Detailed design is now being completed and, subject to planning permissions, work is scheduled to begin on construction of the pipeline in 1996. First gas is expected to be transported towards the end of 1998. British Gas will be looking to continental Europe for new markets. Gas will be supplied from British Gas's extensive UKCS reserves, thus Interconnector will be a new premium source of reliable gas for the region.

Environmental concerns throughout Europe have resulted in the changing trend towards gas as a fuel for power generation. The advantages of natural gas are not confined to reducing sulphur emissions. The debate about global warming and the role of carbon dioxide emissions in a possible greenhouse effect has also become a major political issue – with combustion resulting in at least 25–30 per cent less carbon dioxide than for oil and at least 40–50 per cent less than for coal, gas is a clear choice of fuel for power generation into the next century.

British Gas is developing projects with partners in Italy to build, run and operate up to 500MW of cogeneration plant in various sites and is also working in Eastern and Central Europe. In Hungary and Poland it is investigating opportunities to develop further cogeneration plants.

The markets for gas in Europe are expanding, and demand is likely to increase, thus developments in the European energy market are seen as opportunities for British Gas. The UK is an integral part of Europe and, looking to the future, UKCS gas reserves and infrastructure will become a significant part of a pan-European gas network.

Electricity liberalization in the EU

Neil Williams

Since February 1992, the EU Council of Ministers has been discussing a proposed directive aimed at creating a single electricity market. The initial Commission draft envisaged mandatory third-party access (TPA) together with unbundling of accounts and management, and as such was welcomed by the UK electricity industry. However, opposition at the time from most EU governments and the European Parliament led to a watered down version of the Directive, which nevertheless retained some competitive elements, eg:

■ Large customers (those consuming more than 100 GWh/year) and distributors would be able to negotiate access to the grid.

■ Member states could choose between either a licensing system for new plant or a tendering procedure.

Furthermore, vertically integrated companies would be required to unbundle their accounts for generation, transmission and distribution, although there was no requirement for management unbundling; the transmission system however had to be operated by an 'administratively independent' transmission system operator (TSO).

The Council of Ministers was, however, still unable to achieve agreement with most of the opposition coming from France, Belgium, Italy and Greece, especially in regard to provision for negotiating third-party access.

The single buyer model

In autumn 1994, the debate took a new twist when the French government proposed that member states should be allowed to choose between a system of negotiated third-party access (NTPA) and a so-called single buyer system. In this system, some competition would be introduced in electricity generation through competitive bidding for new plant, but a single organization would have a monopoly of buying and selling electricity within a given member state or region. The French government claimed that this approach was necessary in order to be able to plan the system properly and to maintain uniform tariffs. One small exception would be allowed: some energy-intensive users would be able to import directly from another member state, although these imports too would have to be sold back to the single buyer.

From a competitive viewpoint, the shortcomings of the single buyer system are fairly clear. The single buyer essentially decides which competitors should enter the market, and when. The single buyer system lends itself to discrimination in favour of national generators and equipment suppliers, and as such runs counter to the principles of the Single European Market. Moreover, where a single buyer system in one member state trades with a more open electricity market in another the benefits of trade tend not to be shared but to go to the single buyer, thereby strengthening the position of monopoly utilities while damaging those companies which operate in a more competitive system. There is also considerable doubt about whether the single buyer system is compatible with the European Treaties.

November 1994 Energy Council

The Energy Council meeting in November 1994 was able to reach agreement in principle on four key areas; the Directive's provisions for competition in generation; unbundling of accounts; a reduction in the detailed provisions concerning the network operator; and an agreement that public service obligations must be clearly defined, transparent, non-discriminatory and capable of being monitored.

However, no agreement was reached on the crucial question of NTPA and the single buyer system. Instead, the Council asked the Commission to look at whether the single buyer model could result in equivalent levels of competition with those member states opting for NTPA, and whether the concept complied with the provisions of the EU Treaty.

Following a detailed analysis by the University of Cologne, the Commission published in March 1995 a Working Paper on the issue of reciprocity between the single buyer and NTPA systems. The paper concluded that the two systems did not provide an equivalent degree of market opening, but that the single buyer system could be made acceptable if modified in certain ways. The Commission specified six criteria which should be met.

■ Electricity distributors and large customers must have the freedom to contract with producers both inside and outside their member state.

■ The single buyer must purchase imports on the basis of transparent transmission tariffs and can only refuse to do so for technical reasons, eg a lack of transmission capacity.

■ When the single buyer is part of an integrated

company, management structures must be unbundled to prevent the in-house generating business obtaining an unfair advantage.

■ Tendering procedures for new plant ('competitive bidding') should be organized by the public authorities or an independent body.

■ Independent producers must be authorized to build power stations outside the tendering procedure.

■ Large customers must be able to build a direct line to an external or independent producer.

June 1995 Energy Council

The Council of Ministers in June 1995 again failed to reach agreement on the text of a draft directive, although it did reaffirm that European electricity systems must progressively take market mechanisms into account and allow for the coexistence of both the single buyer and negotiated TPA systems, subject to conditions of reciprocity and equivalent effects being achieved.

Spanish Presidency text

In the light of Council decisions the incoming Spanish Presidency of the European Union issued a new text of the Electricity Directive, intended to serve as a basis for negotiation in the run-up to the Energy Council meeting of December 1995.

The main effect of the redraft is to incorporate the concept of the single buyer into the Directive, accepting the coexistence of the SB and negotiated TPA models. The main changes from the earlier Commission draft are as follows:

■ Member states can decide to exclude distributors from network access if they so wish. This marks a retreat from the Commission's Working Paper issued in March 1995.

■ Independent power producers will be able to operate in single buyer countries, but authorization can be refused if the total amount of independent generation exceeds a certain percentage of total generation on the system. This percentage is to be agreed by negotiation in the Council.

■ There are various references to long-term planning, which will strengthen the ability of single buyer type systems to limit competition.

■ The single buyer will be required to operate

separately from generation and distribution activities in an integrated company (management unbundling) and will have to purchase electricity on the basis of published transmission tariffs. In the negotiated TPA system, there is no requirement for management unbundling or publication of transmission tariffs.

■ Integrated utilities will have to unbundle their accounts for the benefit of their national regulator, but will no longer be required to publish them.

■ Provisions allowing independents to construct transmission lines have been removed.

■ Member states will be able to reserve 15 per cent of their market for indigenous fuels (a concession to Ireland and Spain).

■ The timetable has slipped by about four years: implementation of the Directive is now set for January 1998 and review for 1 January 2003.

DG XVII and the Presidency are clearly hoping for an agreement by the end of 1995 and to this end have introduced elements of compromise. However, the balance of the text may now have shifted too far for the increasing number of pro-liberalization member states to accept: there are frequent references to long-term planning and other restraints on competition, but little emphasis on reciprocity. Indeed, the characteristics of the single buyer and NTPA are so different that it is questionable whether a *single* energy market can emerge from them. The UK electricity industry is looking for in particular fair and reciprocal trading rights between different member states; freedom for large industrial customers and distribution companies to have direct access to networks; right of establishment anywhere in the EU without restriction on size; and unbundling of management and accounts in vertically integrated companies.

It is doubtful whether the latest Presidency text could achieve an effective electricity market. There are two fundamental alternatives: a Commission Directive using Article 90.3 of the Treaty, as was used to liberalize the telecom sector; or a series of test cases in the Court of Justice. However, the first option does not appear to be politically feasible at a time when the Commission is under attack from some governments for having too much power. The legal route, on the other hand, will be both time consuming and unpredictable in outcome.

Tele-communications

Mike Grabiner, Director, BT Europe

The critical commodity

Information will be the critical commodity of the twenty-first century. Access to information will be of fundamental importance to business and social life. Information networks will be as important to the economies of the twenty-first century as the internal combustion engine has been to the twentieth century or as railways were to the nineteenth.

As society evolves, fair and equitable access to information becomes an important social goal. Provided that customer requirements are at the centre of industry thinking and planning, then the vision so eloquently promoted by US Vice President Al Gore of an information superhighway that passes every business, every school, every home, every library and every hospital is achievable.

This is all the more important since telecommunications, unlike textiles or machine tools, is not a distinct trade sector – it is integral to trade itself. As Sir Leon Brittan said recently: 'Trade in telecommunications is a facilitator of trade in other sectors. In fact, trade and telecommunications are mutually dependent.' Companies that have access to the best priced, best quality and most innovative telecommunications are more likely to become competitive globally, creating sustainable wealth and jobs. More than this, telephone and communications technology generally are at the point of lift-off, poised for exponential growth.

True, there are still obstacles to be overcome.

Many consumers still perceive the telephone as a high-cost luxury. Customers in the UK, for example, spend less than £5 a week on telephone calls – less than they spend on alcohol and tobacco.

However, recent experience in the cellular telephone market proves that the potential for explosive growth exists. In just a few years the mobile phone has gone from being almost exclusively a business tool to an everyday piece of equipment. By mid-1995 there were about 4 million users in the UK and predictions are that this figure could reach 13 million by the year 2000, with more than 250 million users worldwide.

What customers want

Among the business community, the demand already exists for the services and savings that the new technology will bring. A 1994 survey of European business leaders, commissioned by BT, showed that 93 per cent considered that an open telecommunications market will play an important role in developing a stronger Europe. Respondents are clear that monopolistic telecommunications providers and a lack of common technical standards are significantly inhibiting progress.

They know that without a single market for telecommunications, they cannot have a true single market for trade. Just 7 per cent of them are satisfied that local telecommunications technology is keeping pace with that available elsewhere. By contrast, 37 per cent of their American counterparts were very satisfied with the introduction of new telecommunications technology.

At the moment, businesses in the vast majority of European countries that do not enjoy liberalized telecommunications services can only look enviously at the open markets of the UK and the US. The technology is there, as is the customer demand, but there is a delay in developing a regulatory regime appropriate to the needs of the market. This delay poses a serious threat to the long-term development of global markets and those businesses that wish to compete in those markets.

Business worldwide wants to see governments setting clear and consistent rules, allowing open access to markets – with a minimum of interference. The private sector must be allowed to set the pace.

The information society

The possibilities are endless. One can imagine a world in which you can be in touch, whenever you want, wherever you are, in which you can work from home and at the hours that suit you, in which every child has on-line access to every museum in the world, in which you can shop and bank from home, in which you can have on-line access to the best medical expertise, wherever you happen to be, or can be treated at the scene of an accident by a doctor hundreds of miles away.

All these things are possible now, but the cost of providing them will be high and there is so much about this market that is currently unknown, not least the services that customers will take to, wish to use and be willing to pay for. Consequently, in the summer of 1995 BT launched one of the world's major trials of interactive multimedia services. Some 2500 customers in the Colchester and Ipswich region will be given access – using the standard television and telephone – to a range of interactive services, from video on demand to local information and interactive advertising services, home shopping and home banking. By the time the trial is over, we should have the closest glimpse yet of the information society of the twenty-first century.

Competition and regulation

The telecommunications industry is a peculiarly political one and becoming more so. Consequently, government has a key role to play in its development. In the UK we have the paradox of the most liberal and open telecommunications market in the world and one of the most interventionist regulatory regimes.

Oftel – the Office of Telecommunications – was established to protect the consumer from any abuse of market dominance by BT, privatized more than 10 years ago. Its key objective was to ensure that customers got the best possible service on the best possible terms, and this meant protecting and promoting emerging competition.

There can be no doubt that competition has been very good news for customers. They have benefited from more choice, innovation, lower prices and a better service, that is the same in the depths of rural areas as in the centres of our cities.

Good news on prices

A recent OECD survey stated that telephone prices in the UK are among the lowest in the world. The case for privatization and liberalization could scarcely be made more emphatically.

Between privatization in 1984 and July 1995 BT reduced prices by 46 per cent in real terms. The cost of national calls fell by 64 per cent in real terms and the cost of local calls by 34 per cent. Between December 1993 and July 1995 there were price cuts totalling more than £1 billion. That customers see this as good value for money is clearly reflected in the dramatic increase in the number of homes that have a phone. In March 1984 75 per cent of UK households had a line; but by March 1994 this had increased to 91 per cent.

In addition, the UK experience shows that the inevitable pain – caused by the need to reduce the size of traditional telecommunications workforces – can be borne responsibly. In the five years to 1995, BT reduced its workforce by around 100,000 on an entirely voluntary basis and without significant industrial relations problems.

But the world is changing. The new entrants to the telecommunications market – many of which are backed by American companies with home market monopolies – are increasingly well established and the convergence of technologies has created opportunities that were unimaginable a few years ago. Unfortunately, the UK regulatory system is now past its sell-by date. Market entry support should be just that; once competitors have established themselves, they should be encouraged to fend for themselves.

A clear vision

What operators need from regulators – around the

world as well as in the UK – is a clear vision of the future, a precise and stable regulatory framework that gives them the scope to realize their potential. Although regulation aims at protecting the consumer, it can have the opposite effect and work against what customers want. For example, in the case of the freedom to package services – to bundle together lines and calls – some consumers would prefer to pay a higher fixed charge in exchange for lower call prices; others would be prepared to pay more for the calls they make. Consumers ought to be able to choose the package that best suits their individual needs; suppliers ought to have the scope to rebalance their prices in a way that reflects the underlying costs and enables them to meet those needs. At present, that freedom does not exist.

The European perspective

Changing the perspective from the UK to Europe as a whole, we are at a defining point in the sometimes slow progress towards a single market in the communications sector. The moment is critical because the 1998 accord – all telecommunications will be liberalized within the EU by 1 January 1998 – has elevated telecommunications to the status of a key external relations and trade issue for the Union. Bringing this sector fully into the World Trade Organization (WTO) multilateral trading system would be of enormous benefit to global trade.

In Europe, the situation might currently be described as 'poised', ready for take-off. Even before a single market in telecommunications has been established, policy makers are beginning to wrestle with extending that single market to embrace the convergent electronic publishing and broadcasting sectors. At the same time, and in parallel, the European Commission has launched studies into the feasibility of a pan-European sectoral regulator to cater for the new cross-border freedoms.

Momentum not moratorium

These are key issues for European trade and competitiveness, but the expectation that on 1 January 1998 European telecommunications will – at a stroke – be free looks excessively optimistic in the light of member states' reluctance to implement previous Directives. Already there is much special pleading from the incumbent State-owned telecommunications monopolies throughout the EU and in too many places the 1 January 1998 date is regarded as a

reason to do nothing until then. Unfortunately, the failure to liberalize quickly and effectively could have a hugely deleterious effect on European trade. It is essential to keep the momentum going, but how is this to be done?

First, there is competition policy. The consistent application of Treaty of Rome rules in the telecommunications industry is essential. This will also help to boost the liberalization process itself, by ensuring that global alliances involving European companies are predicated on all participants having open domestic markets. Rigorous conditions should be applied to proposed alliances, and where these conditions are not met, such alliances should be blocked.

Secondly, 1996 offers something of a trial run because that is the date for liberalizing the cable TV and mobile markets. We must stick to this legislative timetable.

Thirdly, liberalization and competition decisions are worthless without adequate enforcement and implementation. Without a firmer commitment from those agreeing the political accord, the 1998 deadline for the liberalization of public voice services and infrastructure will be nothing more than a formality.

The 1996 Inter-governmental Conference (IGC) has a major role to play in consolidating the single market. In particular, it can debate the mechanisms for achieving adequate enforcement – there are advantages in a pan-EU regulatory institution for the converging communications sectors. The 1996 conference should take steps to improve powers of appropriate enforcement so that a single market will exist in reality as well as in practice.

Fourthly, there is regulatory policy. It is one thing to open up markets but – in a sector as complex as telecommunications – it is quite another to create and maintain regulatory conditions that enable sustainable competition. Among other things, this will require harmonized rules across Europe on universal service funding, network interconnection, licensing, accounting transparency and cross-subsidization of services.

The heart of the matter

A single market in telecommunications and the sectors with which it is converging is not a European policy sideshow. It is right at the heart of the prospects for the EU generally. And, in just the same way, the creation of a free and open *global* market is critical to the development of world trade.

Telecommunications is at the heart of modern business and social life; it helps to create trade and has enormous social and political impact. The industry faces two key challenges – to offer global communications solutions to a business community that is increasingly operating globally, and to develop the information society. We have the technology and the customer demand exists, but the missing ingredient is free and fair competition. Regulators in the UK, Europe and around the world need a clear vision of the future of the industry, and need to act in a way that promotes genuine competitiveness, from which a wealth of customer benefits will flow.

A Competitive Transport Infrastructure for Europe

James Wilson, Senior Vice President, Europe Region, TNT Express Worldwide

Europe is expanding. Since the fruition of the Single Market in 1993 we have seen accelerated growth of trade between member states within the European Union. Some of the legislation designed to liberalize and harmonize EU transport infrastructures is now in place and the focus lies on how best to encourage and facilitate inter-European trade.

Increased trade in the region is putting unprecedented pressure on existing transport networks and the introduction of legislation to control the inevitable problems caused by expansion is vital. Already, some time-consuming processes have been cut out; however, there is still a need for greater harmonization, particularly in the area of customs, taxes and transport policies. Further infrastructure developments are also required in roads and airports, particularly in Eastern Europe, and there is an increasing need for centralized production and warehousing.

The introduction of the European White Paper on transport in December 1994 allowed for several changes in the way in which transportation systems operate throughout the European Union. 'Sustainable mobility' guarantees the implementation of Single Market rules and the establishment of a truly integrated transport system by the year 2000. It looks at the huge projected growth of road transportation, multimodal transport and the environmental issues affecting transport policies.

The Commission advised that by the target date of the year 2000, the proposed trans-European network of road, rail, inland waterways and air links will require investment of ECU220 billion. While the European Union could mobilize ECU90 billion of that total, says the Commission, it is 'inconceivable' that the remainder could be financed through the budget.

Some of the 26 projects listed as necessary by the Commission to create an overall trans-European network have been progressed. However, the fruition of a competitive transport infrastructure for Europe relies on more than government funding. It relies on private investment.

One industry in particular understands that integrated transport systems are of paramount importance to the effective transportation of goods across Europe. The express distribution industry is playing a vital role in highlighting trans-European transport network requirements and smoothing the way for other international traders. A united Europe is bringing unprecedented opportunities. The introduction of the Single Market and the breakdown of barriers means that small and medium-sized businesses are able to trade more easily within Europe. This is creating a more competitive trading environment, bringing with it better service for customers.

The industry is at the forefront of developing the communications networks solutions needed for transporting goods across the world. Tailoring transport logistics solutions to customer needs has certainly been made easier by the accelerated

Total Freight Solutions

As industries begin to regard Europe as a domestic market, freight haulage problems multiply. To keep freight moving efficiently you need flexibility and expertise.

Mainline Freight offers you both.

We are a new company, yet we draw on more than a century of practical railway experience to solve the most complex freight transport problems. Every year we shift 30 million tonnes of heavy materials. That's only the visible result of a total solution. We also negotiate track access, plan rail schedules, control train movements and manage infrastructure services. Many of Britain's largest companies regard us as part of their production cycle, and we work closely with them to create innovative transport solutions.

If freight haulage is important to your industry, we understand your business. We own the depots, locomotives and wagons. And we have the professional traincrews and specialists. Let them help you develop a comprehensive freight haulage strategy. For information, contact:

Bill Reeve, Business Development Manager, McBeath House,

310 Goswell Road, London EC1V 7LL, Tel. 0171 713 2440

Moving Mountains, All the Way Down the Line

Mainline

Mainline Freight Ltd

A major force

Mainline Freight Ltd works with many of the nation's largest industrial companies transporting materials to or from their customers throughout the country over some of the most intensively used railway in the world.

It is a major force in the UK freight haulage market, moving 30 million tonnes of material every year.

Mainline Freight is still a relatively new name in the heavy haul business but, as one of the new companies created n April 1994 in response to the government's proposals to privatise British Rail, it has a well-established pedigree. The companies are successor bodies of Trainload Freight, BR's most consistently profitable business.

Mainline's predecessors established a reputation as innovators in the rail industry. They played a part in the development of such innovations as merry-go-round trains, self-discharging trains – which enable customers to forego the high capital costs of installing underground discharge systems, fuel-efficient locomotives and automatic vehicle identification systems.

Skills and Resources

In a new competitive environment, Mainline Freight is intent on making a name for itself in its own right as an expert rail freight haulier of proven substance. It is building on years of experience and skills to provide a service to its customers that meets their needs and changing market requirements.

Mainline's resource base of over 200 heavy locomotives and some 6000 wagons means it is a company that can handle the current needs of its customers and gives it the capability to tackle the major projects of the future.

Mainline's managing director, Kim Jordan is clear about company direction: "Our immediate aims as a new company are to maintain the strength of our existing business, and expand into new markets and above all, to meet the needs of our customers as comprehensively, efficiently and flexibly as possible".

A Comprehensive Service

Mainline's core business is to transport heavy materials by rail. To qualify as bulk freight with potential for sustained profitable operation the traffic on offer should ideally have five basic characteristics:

    i) significant volumes – normally in excess of 100,000 tonnes a year

    ii) trains running direct from source to destination with no intermediate marshalling

    iii) customers loading and unloading trains in their own private sidings

    iv) regular movements – daily or even several times a day

    v) makes full use of the pulling power of the locomotives – in other words, big, heavy trains.

Trainload Freight's success in maintaining profit levels was due to adherence to these principles. While they remain central to its philosophy, Mainline Freight is keen to explore the prospects for less regular train load operations where this can be undertaken competitively.

Traditionally, the largest market segments for the railway's bulk freight businesses have been coal for electricity generation and materials for the construction industry.

Mainline moves coal from ports and collieries to power stations for the generators and is active in the industrial coal market as well. It also transports materials for the construction industry, primarily aggregates such as limestone from the Mendips, granite from Leicestershire, sand and gravel from East Anglia and marine-dredged and imported aggregate from the south coast and the Thames.

In addition to these larger markets, Mainline hauls oil and petroleum to and from refineries, industrial and domestic waste for disposal at landfill sites, chemicals, scrap and finished metals.

The environment certainly benefits from Mainline's business – its trains typically carry anything between 1000 and 4000 tonnes of material and move the equivalent of at least 4,000 lorry loads every day.

Re-structuring and a new business

A new business for Mainline Freight is the very complex provision of train services for railway infrastructure engineering contractors. This business came to the bulk freight companies as British Rail was re-organised in preparation for privatisation and is very difficult to traditional trainload traffic.

Mainline carries materials such as stone ballast, rails and track equipment which are used for the essential maintenance and renewal of the railway network, and works with the infrastructure engineers and with Railtrack, the owner of most of Britain's railway infrastructure.

Major project work is another aspect to this new business. Large-scale engineering projects such as the proposed high-speed Channel Tunnel rail link will use vast quantities of materials – quantities usually associated with rail, rather than good, haulage.

Mainline has already been involved with a number of high-profile projects, including the Heathrow Express link and significant railway resignalling schemes and appears well placed to benefit from being based in the south-east of Britain, an area of strategic economic importance.

Forecasts for the south-east suggest that it will provide the main focus for renewed economic growth in the UK as we approach the new millennium.

A complete transport package

The punctual and safe delivery of materials from one point to another is Mainline Freight's primary task, but it can offer a range of services much more extensive than that. It provides a complete product design and execution service which includes train service planning, terminal design, the supply of wagons and the procurement and management of track access to the rail network.

Mainline's expertise extends to advising its customers on the availability of Government grants for track access and capital facilities and helps them through the application process.

Barry Graham, Mainline's commercial director recognises that customers have high expectations of the newly competitive freight market: "Our objective at all times is to help our customers find the most cost-effective solution to their transport requirements through a reliable plan which deploys both our own and our customer's assets to the highest attainable levels of efficiency. We then aim to translate this into a dependable service in practice.

"We strive to offer a well-managed, efficient and comprehensive service together with the ability to understand and executive the most complex requirements."

Valued Customers

Mainline has an impressive client list. They work with national companies such as National Power, PowerGen, Coal Investments, Bolsover Coalite, ARC, Foster Yeoman, Redland Aggregates, Castle Cement, Bardon Roadstone, Camas Aggregates, Tarmac Roadstone, Tarmac Topmix, Esso and Shanks & McEwan.

Innovation

The railway industry of the future will be very different from the railway industry of the past and the new players will need to develop new skills and services to suit the needs of the time.

Mainline Freight's managers have a proven track record of freight transport professionalism. That professionalism has gone beyond the traditional bulk freight and now is looking to Europe.

It is a member of the Piggyback Consortium, a group of businesses, local authorities and other organisations which is exploring the potential of developing railway wagons to carry lorry trailers from the Channel Tunnel, ports and terminals across the UK rail network.

Mainline has joined forces with one of Europe's leading wagon designers and builders – Finland's Oy Transtech to develop prototype wagons and will contribute to service and technical planning.

Not only is this development environmentally desirable with the potential to take thousands of lorry journeys from Britain's road, it also creates rail transport opportunities in new general merchandise markets.

Competition and sale

The bulk freight market is more competitive and complex than ever before.

Government is encouraging new operators to enter the market through its policy of open access. There are two similar bulk freight companies to Mainline Freight and some customers of those companies are investing in locomotives and wagons. All track access, station facility and depot access contracts must be approved by the industry regulator.

Sale of Mainline Freight and other bulk freight companies, due to take place early in 1996, adds another significant dimension to the whole market.

Mainline's managers have seen many changes in recent years and understand that change, even for the better, cannot be achieved without some pain.

They believe, however, that the skills and experience they have accumulated over many years of providing their customers with services they need will enable them to meet these challenges and maintain customer confidence.

Mainline Freight Limited
McBeath House, 310 Goswell Road, London EC1V 7LL
Tel. 0171-713 2422

24

developments in pan-European transport infrastructure.

The most significant of all the recent developments came in January 1993, when the boundaries between European Union countries were relaxed and many customs regulations removed. Prior to January 1993, many countries within the European Community had detailed customs formalities which meant it could take up to three hours to process inbound clearances on arrival. For example, in France or Italy, although an aircraft may have arrived at 6 am, the goods would not be released from customs until late morning.

Although next-day delivery service within the European Union was achievable, deliveries could not normally be made until the afternoon. Changes in customs procedures have made the transportation of goods within Europe much easier, and have given express delivery companies the ability to offer guaranteed morning deliveries – by 9 am in major cities.

A number of key industries have benefited from the easier transportation of goods across Europe. Industries including technology, electronics, telecommunications and automotive parts are accounting for an increasing amount of the express distribution industry's business in Europe.

With improved communications systems, transportation of goods by road and air is easier. The new customs regulations which have abolished customs clearance charges, mean that companies have been able to reduce their prices and offer a competitive deal to customers.

The opening of the much awaited Channel Tunnel, one of the 26 projects outlined by the EC, has had a significant effect on pan-European trade. The speed and frequency of the Eurotunnel service allows express distribution companies to offer further improved delivery and collection times to customers. TNT Express Worldwide has over 150 trailers using the tunnel route into Europe each week and is currently moving over 130 tonnes of consignments per night via the tunnel. More than 95 per cent of the company's road system traffic now uses the Channel Tunnel to distribute goods throughout the continent – a huge increase on the company's original prediction of approximately 30 per cent of its total UK export business.

The express distribution industry has recognized that computer technology and the creation of a worldwide information system network is a clear way to provide customers with an enhanced service.

Many express distribution companies are already on the Internet. Competing aggressively in the marketplace means that companies must constantly strive for the most efficient operating systems available.

Express distribution industry operations in Europe have an exciting future ahead. The industry is growing rapidly, yet there remains huge potential for product development and expansion into other European countries.

Eastern Europe, in particular, represents an enormous level of potential to expanding trade networks. The estimated total paid in investment in the region for the five years 1990 to 1995 runs at over US$18 million, with the association with the European Union more important than ever. Historically, trade links of former Eastern bloc countries with the USSR were much stronger than with the European Union. Lack of trade demand from the West meant that road networks and the quality of the roads remained poor. With only basic investment from Eastern bloc powers, heavily bureaucratic administrative systems and centrally run communist economies, combined with poor communications, resulted in a serious lack of interest in investing in the region by Western-based industry.

The industry needs to help customers to adjust to the changes occurring in the region, offering expert advice on the best method of shipping and overland distribution in each country. As a service industry, it has a responsibility to lead the way in creating an environment in which other businesses can operate. For this reason, TNT Express Worldwide is committed to the Eastern European market and believes the region holds great business opportunities. It has invested heavily in the area – over US$4 million – establishing the infrastructure to service both current business and the expected growth.

PART

6

Trends in Consumer Markets

Retailing Within Europe in the Middle of the Decade

25

Ross Davies, Oxford Institute of Retail Management, Templeton College, Oxford

Retailing has always been a major barometer of change, not just of the condition of national economies but of society's attitudes and mores as well. During the fast-track growth circumstances of the late 1980s when the appetite of consumers to spend was whetted, retail companies throughout Western Europe, but especially in the UK and the Mediterranean countries, expanded at a blistering pace. In the East in the early 1990s once the Wall had come down, the same might be said of companies developing in the Czech Republic, Hungary and Poland. By 1995, however, we have witnessed a sea-change in the growth experiences and aspirations of companies in the West. Companies will limp rather than run into the second half of the decade, mainly because of the chastened feelings of consumers and a more cautious approach to development on the part of the retailers themselves. In the East more development can be expected to take place, but the second half of the decade will be noted mainly as a period of consolidation.

The shift from consumer-driven growth in the economies of Western European countries, through recession in the early 1990s, to the fairly uniform export-led recoveries and the concomitant change in consumer predilections, from wayward spending to careful discrimination, are now background trends that are well known. In retailing, the responses have been almost immediate. The number of companies in Western Europe facing difficulties in 1995 has been numerous: Kingfisher, WH Smith and Etam in the UK, with significantly reduced profits for the year; Galerias Preciados of Spain, Konsum Osterreich of Austria and the T Group of Finland, which collapsed financially; and Karstadt and Kaufhof, two of the stalwarts of the German department store industry, running up substantial debts after acquiring Hertie and Horten companies respectively.

In Eastern Europe, at least in the most developed states, consolidation is manifesting itself in the change from a previous dash for growth for presence, largely by Western German but also Dutch and Belgian companies, to a conversion of temporary structures into more permanent buildings. The apocryphal stories of stores being built as aluminium tents, of generators being used to support lighting and telecommunications systems, and workers and managers being hugely unreliable on when they would or would not work, are fast becoming a part of history.

Public policy constraints

Certain retailers, particularly those that have developed 'out of town', have also found their potential business growth constrained by new planning approaches and regulations. In the last two years, Belgium and France have introduced tougher new laws to curb the further building of hypermarkets, while in Portugal, a temporary moratorium on such development has frozen the construction of stores and also shopping centres, even those which have planning permission. Greece has recently imposed some new controls and Spain is likely to follow suit in late 1995 or early 1996. At the root of these impositions is government concern at the impact of large stores on small ones and the further contribution this might make to unemployment. A supplementary concern are the adverse effects which too much out-of-town development can have on traditional town centres.

Better protection of town centres and their improvement over the next decade is at the heart of the Department of the Environment's revision of PPG6 (Planning Policy Guidance Note 6) in late 1995. This exhorts local authorities to identify sites in their plans for new retail development which preferably should be within, or on the edge of, town centres and not out of town. Such strictures will not curb the decentralization process immediately, however, for there remains so much more development already in the pipeline. In the medium to long term, nevertheless, we should see a considerable slowing of the opening of food superstores, retail warehouses and the new American concepts of warehouse clubs, factory outlet malls and regional shopping centres.

Responses to saturation

While the tougher planning policies in the UK and elsewhere have frustrated some retailers, others have welcomed the new attention being given to town centres. In the UK and also probably in Belgium and France, it is likely that even food retailers and DIY traders will not be averse to the changes at this time. This is because, within these two sectors, especially, there are now high levels of store saturation which make it difficult for companies to find sufficient sites to maintain the number of store openings that have been seen in recent years. Further development would also mean the invasion of each other's local monopolistic territories.

Saturation, particularly within food retailing, has also forced many of the biggest companies to rethink their growth strategies at mid-decade. Sainsbury signalled in 1995, through the acquisition of Texas Homecare, that it was going to diversify. Tesco, with its new concepts of Tesco Metro and Tesco Express, its acquisition of Catteau in France and investment in Hungary, suggests it is going to both innovate and internationalize. Internationalization, especially through the acquisition of companies in the USA, has been the preferred route of other companies, such as

Albert Heijn, Delhaize le Lion and Tengelmann (in The Netherlands, Belgium and Germany respectively) when faced with growing saturation in their home markets. The entry of French companies into the Mediterranean countries and German companies into the more developed countries of Eastern Europe has shown little sign of abating in 1995, although some of the largest cities are now beginning to experience a surfeit of floorspace.

Competition and discounting

A distinctive feature of the internationalization process at mid-decade has been the accelerating growth of deep discounting operations in nearly all countries of Europe. It has been particularly marked in food retailing and within the UK. Aldi from Germany and Netto from Denmark have recently been joined by Lidl and Schwarz in developing 'no frills' stores in the UK, although Penny Market, the German Rewe brand, and ED, the French Carrefour concept, fared less well in 1995. Club warehousing also seems to have struggled in the UK, perhaps because the pack sizes are too big for UK consumers who mainly lack the basements and more spacious garages of their American counterparts. Nurdin and Peacock, with a British response to the Price Costco warehouses, sold their three Cargo Club outlets to Sainsbury in 1995.

Elsewhere within Europe, the growth of discounting has been particularly conspicuous in the Scandinavian countries. Denmark has the second highest market share after Germany of food retailing commanded by deep discounters, and its chains such as Netto and Fakta have been able to take advantage of the recent relaxation of Sunday trading hours. The Norwegian chain Rimi is developing rapidly, not only within its home market but in Sweden too. The mighty German food discounters have also been expanding into Eastern Europe, of course. Outside food retailing, Europe can expect to see an expansion of discounting activity in the fashion and textile trades in the second half of the decade. This has already been heralded in the UK and France by the opening of factory outlet centres, selling out-of-season stock or slightly blemished products at substantially reduced prices.

New technological preoccupations

The hype surrounding the information superhighway concept has whipped up a new round of teleshopping projects across the world. Several companies within Europe are offering retail services on the Internet, especially the food and mail order companies. Sainsbury launched a Wine Direct service in April 1995 and joined in a virtual reality shopping mall scheme developed by Barclays Merchant Services. Tesco is offering a wine service through Compuserve's shopping centre, and Safeway is doing the same in BT's recent launch of a series of teleshopping schemes in East Anglia. Other contributors to the BT scheme are WH Smith, Littlewoods, Sears (Adams and Olympus), Past Times and Thomas Cook.

Customer loyalty programmes are also an area that has commanded much attention. Relatively few of these are sophisticated, however, in the sense of using smart cards or even swipe cards. Delhaize le Lion in Belgium, Albert Heijn in The Netherlands and Tesco in the UK are among the leading innovators in the food trade. Other emerging areas of interest concern experiments in self-scanning, led by Albert Heijn and Safeway; new electronic tagging systems, which combine security measures with stock control, being evaluated by Delhaize le Lion and Dixons; and store-based marketing activity using interactive television sets and kiosks, promoted mostly by the leisure and entertainment-based retail chains. The concept of ECR (Efficient Customer Response), linking store-based marketing activity with supply chain management, has also become a 'flavour of the year', but it is only the largest, mostly food retailers across Europe which are seeking to embrace it.

Prospects for 1996 and Beyond

As virtually all the Western European economies continue to improve in 1996 and beyond and the political shifts of the more advanced states in the East become entrenched, retailers can expect to see some improvement in the marketplace across the continent over the next few years. Individual companies, however, will find the marketplace an even tougher one than it has been in the first half of the 1990s, for all the reasons reviewed above: increased competition, growing saturation, greater public planning controls, and the need for IT investment and development. Above all, companies will have to win back the trust and confidence of consumers which the recessionary years set back to a very marked degree (Figure 25.1).

Those companies which will find the challenges hardest will be those dependent on single sectors of trade in discretionary spending areas: white and brown goods, electrical goods, DIY, and some aspects of leisure and entertainment. Those that will be most insulated and best prepared to face the challenges will be those conglomerates with a mixed set of trades pursuing alternative growth strategies to the end of the decade. The biggest companies (listed in Table 25.1), with some exceptions, look set to continue to become even bigger, with the enormous German groups reaping greater rewards from their investments in the East and the French giants profiting from further growth in the South. The UK's

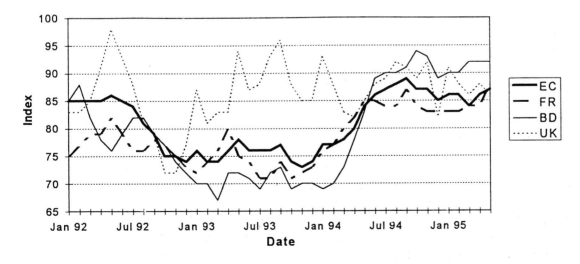

Source: 'European Economic Issues for Retailers', *European Retail Digest*, Summer 1995, Oxford Institute of Retail Management

Figure 25.1 Consumer confidence

biggest companies, Sainsbury, Tesco and Marks and Spencer, can also be expected to benefit significantly from their international activity as well as from improved conditions in the home market.

Retail group	Country of origin	Main sector(s) covered	Group sales (ECU million)
Metro Group	Germany/Switzerland	Food; non-food; wholesale	50,000 [e]
Edeka	Germany	Wholesale-based buying group/food; non-food	27,350 *
Tengelmann	Germany	Grocery; hypermarkets; DIY; clothing; drugstores	25,529
Rewe	Germany	Buying group/food; non-food	24,000 *
Carrefour	France	Hypermarkets; food; DIY	23,610 *
Aldi	Germany	Discount food	22,200 [e]
Leclerc	France	Retailer association/food; non-food	19,110 *
Intermarché	France	Retailer association/food; non-food	18,515
Promodès	France	Hypermarkets; supermarkets; discount food	14,690
Sainsbury	UK	Supermarkets; hypermarkets; DIY	14,650
Karstadt	Germany	Department stores; mail order; non-food	14,125 *
Ahold	Netherlands	Supermarkets; off-licences	13,560
Auchan	France	Hypermarkets; DIY; other non-food	13,310
Tesco	UK	Supermarkets	13,030
Casino	France	Hypermarkets; supermarkets	10,100
Otto Versand	Germany	Mail order; non-food	10,030
Delhaize 'Le Lion'	Belgium	Supermarkets; discount food	9,550
Marks & Spencer	UK	Mixed goods	8,780
Quelle	Germany	Mail order	7,635
SHV Makro	Netherlands	Cash and carry; supermarkets; hypermarkets	7,550

* Including VAT   [e] Estimated

Source: Corporate Intelligence on Retailing, 1995.

Table 25.1 Leading European retail organizations, 1994

Consumer Trends in the European Travel Industry

Rob Bailey, Kate Seekings and Graham Wason, Touche Ross Management Consultants, Greene Belfield-Smith Division

Travel and tourism is the world's largest industry, accounting for 11.4 per cent of global GDP – US$3.4 trillion according to the World Travel and Tourism Council (WTTC). Although tourism plays an important role in many developing world countries, Europe is the dominant player in world tourism, both in terms of international arrivals and international tourism receipts. In 1994, for example, Europe accounted for some 50 per cent of all international tourist receipt and over 60 per cent of tourist arrivals. From modest numbers of travellers leaving and coming to Europe in the immediate post-war period, Europe has escalated to its present leading position. The role of tourism within the region's economy should not be underestimated, accounting (according to the WTTC) for 13.4 per cent of GDP (US$1.1 trillion), one in eight jobs, 15.5 per cent of capital investment and 15.1 per cent of taxes.

European countries are among the world's leading tourism destinations with France, as the world's top destination country, Spain, Italy, Hungary, the UK, Austria and Germany. Furthermore, Europeans are among the world's leading travellers and spenders. As a result, trends in consumer behaviour among European travellers have a highly significant impact, not just on Europe but also on far-flung developed and fledgling destinations.

However, Europe's share of international tourism arrivals is decreasing. Although Europeans have a relatively high propensity to holiday within

their own continent as opposed to travelling outside their region's boundaries, as Figure 26.1 illustrates, this is being increasingly challenged by the attraction of exotic destinations in Asia, Latin America and Africa. While the World Tourism Organisation (WTO) forecasts international tourist arrivals in the region to grow by just over 2.7 per cent between 1990 and 2000 and 2.5 per cent between 2000 and 2010, it also forecasts a decline in Europe's share of international tourism from 62 per cent in 1990 to 51 per cent in 2010.

For the purposes of this chapter, tourism is defined as the movement of people away from their home for a period of more than one night, therefore including travel for leisure, business, education and visiting friends and relatives. Rising levels of personal disposable income, increasing personal mobility, relatively cheap air flights, improved transport infrastructure, greater car ownership and more availability of free time are among the factors which are influencing the key emerging consumer trends in the market. These have been compounded by demographic, technological and political factors. In this chapter, we address a number of key sectors of the European tourism market and examine how consumer trends are developing, and how they are likely to develop up to the millennium.

Any review of consumer trends must take into account the varying levels of maturity within the different European countries. The initial immature

26

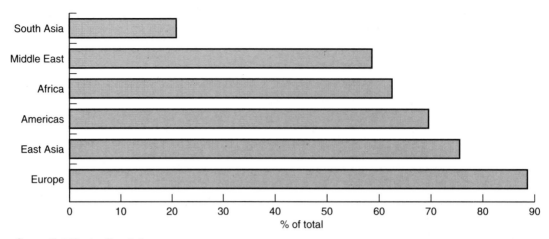

Source: World Tourism Organisation

Figure 26.1 Tourists who holiday in their own region, 1994

market (for example Albania today), characterized by little travel with only wealthy individuals having the resources to travel, offers limited economies of scale which limit the scope for packages. This typically develops into a more mature stage where the masses exhibit a greater propensity and ability to travel, and hence packaging by the industry develops (countries which fall into this category would include Italy and Spain). Stage three is the most mature stage, where the masses as well as wealthier sections of the population have become experienced travellers and are therefore more sophisticated in their demands in terms of greater quality and flexibility, typical in such countries as the UK and Germany, both of which went through stage two during the 1960s and 1970s.

In addition to segmentation by market maturity, significant markets are developing from demographic changes, notably the senior and youth travel markets. According to recent research conducted for the International Hotel Association and the European Travel Council, senior travel should no longer be treated as a fringe market. Two major factors are influencing its size. One factor is the actual increase in the size of the 55+ age bracket – the Economist Intelligence Unit believes that by the year 2000, one in four Europeans will be over the age of 55, ie over 200 million people. The second factor is the growing propensity among this age group to travel. Combined, these factors make the 55+ segment one of the most interesting for the tourism industry, especially as the segment is non-seasonally confined and enjoys relatively high levels of personal disposable income.

The travel behaviour of this age group is often misunderstood. Clearly, the older segment of the group requires specialist attention due to a lack of personal mobility. However, for many – and an increasing amount – this sector is more active than ever before. Travel patterns have been established at an earlier age: those who were in their thirties in the 1960s, when mass travel was born, are now in their sixties and are the first senior group of people who have grown up with travel as an essential part of their lifestyle. They do not want to be 'ghetto-ized', and interestingly, the German tour operator Neckerman has now dropped all use of the word 'senior' or any reference to this special market.

These reasons provide a major opportunity for the travel industry if approached subtly and with an appreciation of the different segments within the age group. The group is characterized by travelling to the continent's warmer climates and cultural destinations, often out of season, and in many cases purchasing second homes, apartments and timeshare properties in these locations. A further common characteristic is seeking to undertake learning in combination with leisure, and we are seeing a growth in special interest, often learning holidays, such as the Elderhostel concept in the US whereby guests stay in university or student hostels and follow courses.

Commonly held perceptions of backpack laden students struggling across Europe have also been shattered by recent research by Aviation and Tourism International (ATI) which has proven this sector to be increasingly significant. Europe has experienced an explosion in youth educated at tertiary level (higher education); for example, in Germany two-thirds of all young people have a tertiary qualification either at university or post-school technical training. In the UK this is just under half and in Europe around one-third. This expanding sector has a greater propensity to travel and the supply side has responded by providing a sophisticated network of student discounts on air flights, rail travel and entrance to visitor attractions. However, the ATI research suggests that contrary to these commonly held views, youth travel patterns are remarkably similar to those of their parents, with the majority of travel undertaken by car and staying in hotels.

Sixteen per cent of all arrivals in Europe are for business purposes; in the UK this percentage rises to 25 per cent. Business travel within Europe has grown in spite of the recession of the early 1990s, although there has been a distinct trend, especially from the UK and Germany, of business travel focusing on Brussels at the expense of travel to other European destinations.

The late 1980s and early 1990s have seen some significant changes in consumer trends in business travel. Belt tightening among companies all around Europe has resulted in a trading down of all aspects of travel. Deals on hotels, air flights and car hire have become characteristic of the 1990s. Companies are increasingly developing corporate policies with more restricted travel budgets – although there remains considerable diversity across Europe, with German companies most likely to have a detailed policy.

Business travel management is scrutinized, and frequent flyer programmes which tend to benefit employees rather than companies are controversial. As a result, the relationship between companies and their travel agents is changing, with the former increasingly demanding that agents earn their commission on the basis of what they save their clients. Recently there has been an increase, especially in the UK, of companies having specialized business travel agent 'branches' in house.

Technology is clearly having a dramatic effect on all travel, including business-motivated travel, especially through increasingly sophisticated reservation systems. What is interesting, however, is that the forecast drop in business travel through the growth of videoconferencing has not occurred. While in time videoconferencing may reduce the amount of marginal business such as follow-up meetings, it seems unlikely that it will replace the demand for core business travel.

The relaxation of inbound and outbound travel restrictions brought about by political and economic change in Central and Eastern Europe has changed the face of European travel markets. Central and Eastern Europe's historic cities are now easily accessible. Table 26.1 clearly shows how important Hungary, Poland and the Czech Republic have become as destinations.

Rank		Country	Arrivals ('000s)	% change 1993/1994
1994	1985			
1	1	France	60,639	0.90
2	2	Spain	43,232	7.85
3	3	Italy	27,276	3.40
4	8	Hungary	21,425	–6.05
5	5	United Kingdom	19,705	1.11
6	4	Austria	17,894	–1.99
7	16	Poland	17,595	3.50
8	12*	Czech Republic	17,000	47.83
9	6	Germany	14,494	1.02
10	7	Switzerland	12,561	1.30

* includes the Slovak Republic

Source: World Tourism Organisation, 1995

Table 26.1 Top ten tourism destinations in Europe, international tourist arrivals (excluding same-day visitors), 1994

Even more significant to European tourism, Central and Eastern Europeans are now travelling throughout the continent until so recently restricted. A small but increasingly significant travel industry is emerging often providing the means of travel, usually by coach. As with travel among Europeans in general, the other catalyst for the masses has been the motor car, often doubling as accommodation.

One of the fastest growth sectors of the European tourism market has been the short-break sector. This was particularly rapid during the late 1980s, with the first signs of the growth waning during the economic recession of 1992. Short breaks involve either a domestic or international trip of between a one- and three-night stay, and on the back of the growth in short-break holiday taking there has been a growth in city-based cultural tourism.

The development of short breaks has been made possible by three trends. First is the increasing propensity among Europeans to take shorter, more frequent holidays throughout the year. The second trend has been the response by the industry to package weekends to fill otherwise underutilized accommodation. The third trend has been the shrinkage of travel times with major new transportation links. The trip between London and Paris now only takes around three and a half hours and, interestingly, some 15 per cent of British Channel Tunnel passengers are visiting France for the first time. Other examples of improved transportation links include the proposed US$3 billion Øresund link between Denmark and Sweden and the extension of the bullet train network from France to Italy.

Visitor attractions are becoming an increasingly important element of destination tourism resources; they add character to an area and, in a small number of examples such as the largest theme parks, generate tourism traffic in their own right. Some (such as Disneyland Paris) even boast overnight stays in on-site accommodation. In a recent survey undertaken by Touche Ross Management Consultants which examined performance trends at over 130 continental European visitor attractions, the increasing popularity of visitor attractions was clear. From Touche Ross's sample of attractions, Figure 26.2 illustrates the growth in attendances in Western Europe since 1990, largely due to higher levels of income and greater mobility, while Central and Eastern Europe has experienced a significant downturn in the performance of its attractions. A major reason for this has been the collapse of the Russian outbound market, which has historically been a major generator of tourism to the countries of Central and Eastern Europe. Patterns of intra-European travel are in transition, with Central and Eastern European tourists exhibiting a higher propensity to visit the previously restricted Western destinations rather

than those of their own region. As such, the majority of international visits are limited to either a day trip to a neighbouring country (eg Poles travelling to Germany), or an overnight stay in whatever mode of transport available.

During the 1980s concern for the environment grew rapidly both among consumers and industry. While these issues are currently less fashionable, it is clear that consumers are more educated as to the potentially negative impacts of tourism. As a result, developments such as Benidorm and Torremolinos have undergone major facelifts. The sprawling, unplanned growth of beach resorts during the 1960s and 1970s has been surpassed by a generally more considerate approach, with governments realizing that restrictions on tourism-related construction are crucial. As the demand for this type of holiday is diminishing in number in parallel to the reduction in the unskilled workforce across Europe, these resorts have been forced either to develop new markets (for example charter flights from Moscow), or to upgrade their product by developing improved tourist infrastructures, hotels and restaurants.

The term 'ecotourism' has become overhyped and misused. However, there has been a clear trend, since the late 1980s, towards more activity and nature-related holidays. One notable example of this has been the growth of agrotourism, especially in Italy and France. One recent demonstration of industry response to consumer demands has been the launch earlier this year of *The Green Hotelier* magazine by the International Hotel Environment

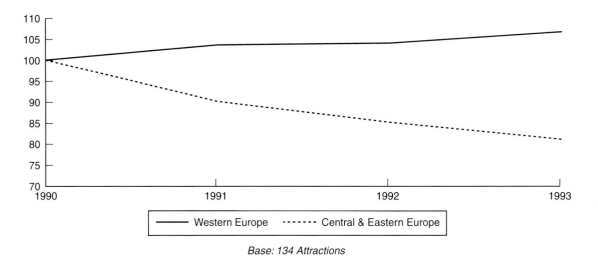

Base: 134 Attractions

Source: Touche Ross Management Consultants

Figure 26.2 Indexed trends in attendances at continental European visitor attractions, 1990 to 1993

Initiative of leading hotel chains, which focuses on ways hotels can become more environmentally focused.

Further consumer trends involve increasingly sophisticated travel-related technology. These developments are already changing the procedure of organizing and purchasing travel and by the turn of the millennium are likely to have transformed the face of European travel.

Recent developments include the continual developments in airline Central Reservations Systems (CRS), whereby hotel rooms as well as airline tickets can be purchased, the use of the Internet as a direct sales distribution channel, interactive CD, smart-card systems which enable cashless purchasing, and the use of Ceefax and similar systems. Developments such as these will make it easier for consumers to book their travel directly and are likely further to encourage the developing trend of independent travel.

Forecasts of future trends make for an exciting profession, given the rapidly changing political and economic nature of Europe. Looking at the relative strengths of the trends which have developed over the past 10 years, we surmise that the following demand-side characteristics are likely to be experienced over the next five years:

- an increasingly differentiated composition of the market;
- increased demand for quality and an understanding of host destinations' environmental and social issues;
- increasing movements of people from Central and Eastern Europe to the West and vice versa;
- growth in short-break markets and additional holidays in the West, which will mirror corresponding levels of personal income and free-time allocation, including city-based tourism made easier by transport infrastructure developments such as the Channel Tunnel;
- growth of independently organized holidays assisted by the flexibility offered by travel-related technology.

27 An Advertising Single Market:
Theory or Practice?

Andrew Brown, Director General, Advertising Association

While advertising is a very diverse and hetero-geneous business, it is also a helpful barometer of economic performance in individual member states. It is indicative of economic recovery, or the reverse, and its key indicators are company profitability, consumer spending and unemployment – the latter being particularly important in classified advertising. In addition, as a generalization, the wealthier the country, the higher advertising's share of GNP.

However, there is also a political dimension. Advertising is a key tool of competition that enables market penetration and product distribution to be achieved with the consequent benefits of consumer choice, competitive pricing and product innovation. However, this can mean that there is a political price to be paid. It is not therefore surprising that sub-stantial national legislation exists which is restrictive or protectionist in nature and which impedes the development of a true single market. The advertising business, as with all media-related sectors, has a high political profile, and the combination of cultural and social viewpoints ensures that there are considerable variations between member states about what is either allowable or acceptable. Thus in any view about the future both economic and political dimensions must be considered.

Advertising expenditure in Europe grew impressively in most countries in 1994 and, for the first time, reached 50 billion ECU with a growth rate of 6.7 per cent. The four countries that showed the largest real growth were Greece, Sweden, Portugal and the UK – which showed an 8.3 per cent increase. Only Spain, Belgium and Italy showed minor decreases.

The vibrant economic health of most European advertising markets is illustrated by the fact that, despite the continued growth of commercial televi-sion, press advertising also grew strongly, having borne the brunt of the recession. In 1994 Denmark, Finland, Greece, Sweden and the UK all experienced press advertising expenditure growth in excess of 5 per cent.

Television continued its rapid development. In 1993 it became the largest display advertising medium, overtaking newspapers for the first time, and in 1994 registered a pan-European growth rate of 10.5 per cent.

The economic outlook for 1995 and beyond is very promising. The GDP of the European Union as a whole is forecast to grow by approximately 3 per cent in both 1995 and 1996. Consequently the relationship between economic performance and advertising expenditure means the latter is also expected to grow, and at a faster rate, and build on its recovery from the recession which lingered in some countries into 1993.

The outlook for television is brighter still. Deregulation should provide advertisers with more television capacity in terrestrial television, coupled with the increase from cable and satellite broadcasters.

An Advertising Single Market: Theory or Practice?   CHAPTER

27

In line with this optimistic outlook the Advertising Association forecasts that every country will achieve real advertising expenditure growth in 1995, resulting in an overall EU figure of 4 per cent and total advertising revenue reaching another record figure.

The political outlook is, however, more variable and less predictable. Certain advertising sectors continue to be threatened by the possibility of severe statutory restrictions at European level, and political debates over proposals for revised European rules for the broadcast media will be central to developments in 1996. There is pressure to include new media services – still at an embryonic and fragile stage – in these deliberations, which could seriously curtail their development.

Sectoral areas under threat of bans or restrictions, from a variety of sources, include alcohol, toys, confectionery and soft drinks, pharmaceuticals and cars, as well as the perennial issue of tobacco advertising.

Proposals are also under discussion concerning advertising and the media that have social engineering dimensions. These include the portrayal of women and the use of stereotypes; the formation of healthier dietary patterns, particularly for children; and the use of models with suntans which may be deemed to be encouraging an unhealthy practice! Anxieties exist about teleshopping, pornography on the Internet, and definitions of what is broadcasting and what is a one-to-one subscription service.

In cross-border advertising the debate between country of origin and country of destination as the source of the regulatory regime continues. The European Commission – and the Advertising Association – favours the former, as only this way will national barriers to trade be properly removed.

However, particularly in areas of taste and decency, this will raise cultural and perhaps legal problems; what is perfectly acceptable in one member state will generate consumer complaints in another. For example, nudity is unexceptional in French advertising but raises many eyebrows in the UK where, by and large, it is not allowed for national advertisers. Will this generate a two-tier regulatory system? This has happened in Germany where comparative advertising is against the law: here an advertisement placed in France, which appeared in Germany, featured comparative prices and became the subject of a court case. The judgment was in favour of the advertiser on a country-of-origin basis, but the result still means that there is discrimination against national German advertisers who are forbidden to use the practice.

A recent feature of proposed legislation affecting advertising will be a greater emphasis on the protection of children from the influence of commercial communications. The Scandinavian member states will be seeking to protect and preserve their tough anti-advertising legislation by proposing the introduction of similar measures throughout the European Union. In November 1993 Greece instituted a ban on all TV advertising of toys before 10 pm (this was a protectionist measure and is currently being investigated by the European Commission) and severe restrictions exist in parts of Belgium. However, a recent judgment in the EFTA Court against Norway's attempt to ban toy advertising via satellite provided some reassurance.

And at the heart of this issue is the difference between member states' attitudes to restrictions and control and, perhaps even more importantly, to their implementation: some want to legislate for everything, while others believe in effective self-regulation, under the effective legal framework provided by the Directive on Misleading Advertising (1984); this is the stance taken by both UK industry and government.

The European Commission's green paper on commercial communications, expected at the end of 1995, should set the parameters of Commission policy both towards advertising and other marketing communications and the important issue of self-regulation. This may act as a restraining influence in respect of particular legislative proposals. UK advertising stands to gain from a more open and less nationally regulated single market, and the European Commission's welcome assessment of advertising as a vital element of market access and competitiveness will be of great significance in future legislative proposals. But political uncertainty will continue through 1996, as several member states hold national elections, and the inter-governmental conference generates caution in the European legislative process.

Thus the prospects are fair but the threats are real. Social and sectoral policies, and sometimes protectionist trading policies masquerading as social ones, can restrict the competitive economic development that all want to see from a true single market and for which we must continue to press.

28 The Prospects for European Media

Kip Meek, Director, Spectrum Strategy Consultants Ltd

Ten years ago the European media environment was stable and somewhat dull. Television was delivered mainly via terrestrial transmitters (the main exceptions being the Netherlands and Belgium) and this limited the number of channels available. Commercial radio was reasonably well developed in some countries – with black spots such as the UK where BBC dominance had restricted the growth of a commercial sector. Print's production technology had been recently revolutionized, but the product had not been radically changed. Overall, the European media environment was characterized by national – not European – markets and by a regulated, traditional structure.

All this has changed. The last decade has seen a media revolution, the key trends of which are as follows:

- **The emergence of pay TV** Pioneered by Canal Plus in France, pay TV has also emerged as a powerful force in the UK and is developing elsewhere – notably Spain, Scandinavia, Belgium, the Netherlands and, to a lesser extent, Germany;

- **The development of new delivery media** In each market, this takes a different form: Germany has experienced rapid growth of both cable and direct-to-home (DTH) satellite services; the UK has experienced much more rapid DTH than cable growth; other markets remain less affected by new transmission media –

notably Italy, Spain and France. No one doubts, however, their time will come particularly with the stimulus of digital technology;

- **The emergence of players with Europe-wide aspirations** A decade ago, CLT was one of the few companies with media interests in several European countries. Now companies and individuals such as Canal Plus, Leo Kirch, Silvio Berlusconi, Richemont/Nethold and several others all aspire to build European or global businesses;

- **The introduction of foreign (particularly American) capital** American phone and cable companies in particular have shown an appetite to invest in the infrastructure of European media. U S West, the Denver-based phone company, now has British, Dutch and Spanish cable properties and is active in Italy, Poland and other European countries. Other companies, Nynex, TCI, Comcast, Time Warner to name but a few, are also heavily involved. The foreign company that casts the longest shadow is, however, Rupert Murdoch – the main shareholder in BSkyB, the owner of much of the British press, a 50 per cent shareholder in Vox, as well as an established player in the US and Asia.

The emergence of these trends has made it difficult to forecast the prospects for European media, particularly the audio-visual part of it. Predicting the future is made even more difficult by the prospect of the

Canon

A Revolution in the Office

Filing has been a key element of office management for centuries, but despite the dramatic increase in the amount of filing carried out and the numbers of people involved, methods have changed very little. Increasingly, many businesses find themselves in a dilemma. On the one hand, the need to store, retrieve and archive information can be of paramount importance. Yet, the time it takes employees to organise filing, and the space archived information occupies, normally incurs tremendous costs.

The need for organisations to adopt document management strategies and solutions is confirmed by the findings of recent surveys. According to industry reports, conducted by KPMG Peat Marwick and others, no fewer than 10,000 filing cabinets are delivered each month to businesses in the UK alone – and at least one four-drawer cabinet exists for each of the UK's 13.5 million office workers. Perhaps even more concerning than this epidemic of filing cabinets, is the fact that half of all paper-based information searches fail to produce the correct document!

Happily, the necessity for a solution – to the global growth of paperwork and impending chaos – has resulted in the creation and development of a number of computer-based document image processing systems. Now, just as the PC superseded the typewriter and the fax machine replaced the telex, electronic filing has begun to take over from manual systems in the computerised office.

What is Electronic Filing?

Electronic filing is a development made possible by computer technology and, in the case of Canon's Canofile system, the hardware looks very similar to a PC. Just like other computers, Canofile has a monitor and keyboard – but integrated with these is a document scanner and an internal disk drive.

The filing process itself is designed to be as simple and straightforward as possible. The operator slides the item to be filed into the scanner, chooses where in the system to file the document and Canofile does the rest. Anything from a business card to an A3 sales leaflet can be stored, and photographs and other graphics scan just as easily as text. Original documents can then be returned, recycled or thrown away.

The process is also very speedy. Canofile is capable of processing paperwork at rates of up to 50 pages per minute and both sides of the document can be scanned simultaneously. Once scanned, files are stored either on magneto-optical discs (MODs) or later onto compact discs. This means that there is no physical limit to the amount of information that can be stored at any time – new discs can be added as files accumulate. Staggeringly, a single compact disc can hold 13,000 pages of fully indexed filing. That's the equivalent of three whole filing cabinets of information – on one pocket-sized, wafer thin disk.

Retrieving documents from Canofile is just as simple as storing them. Files can be quickly and easily called up on

Canon ISD – Canofile 510B

screen and then printed at the touch of a button.

An added bonus of switching to Canofile is that, unlike manual filing, it's virtually impossible to lose electronically filed information. For example, it's all too easy to place a manually-filed document in the wrong folder. However, using the powerful Canofile 'wild card' search facility, it is possible to seek out an electronically filed item speedily – even if it isn't stored where you expect it to be.

With Canofile, it is possible to resolve a customer's query in seconds, or quickly perform tasks that could take hours with a manual filing system. As well as the phenomenal time savings compared with traditional filing methods, adopting a document management system frees staff up to perform other tasks and releases expensive office space for more important and efficient uses.

Also, since the information is stored in a form easily recognised by computer systems – with the aid of Canon's own software – data can be electronically transferred onto a standard personal computer or PC network. From there it can be linked and made part of a powerful workflow or groupware solution.

The Canofile Range

Enhancements in office management and the working environment continue at breathtaking speed. Although it is only five years since Canon introduced

Canofile to the marketplace, in that short time it has become the most popular desktop electronic filing system in the world. There are now over 20,000 systems in operation in offices across the globe, with 30% of the companies listed in 'The Times Top 100' already benefiting from Canofile technology.

Launched in 1990, the Canofile range of electronic filing solutions has a 70 per cent share of the electronic imaging market and comprises the recently launched Canofile 510B which automatically reads barcodes; the flagship Canofile 510; the entry level Canofile 250; the Canofile 250 Alpha; as well as a range of standalone and networkable software which run in conjunction with the latest PC operating environments – including Windows 95. Canofile is a proven technology with an established upgrade path and, with the document image processing market set for massive growth in the next 18 months, Canon is ready to meet future demand.

Delivering the Goods for Securicor Network Europe

With more than 150,000 shipments to deliver throughout Europe each year, Securicor Network Europe relies upon careful planning and control to keep its service operating smoothly. Securicor's employees need to be able to react quickly to customer requirements, and access information instantly. The old manual filing system used to be adequate, but the business grew so much that the strain was beginning to show. It was decided that something had to be done to speed up information handling and reduce the amount of space used for paperwork storage.

Canon ISD – CF-file+ V4.0 Software

The problem was quickly solved when Canofile came on the scene. Now, a year's paperwork that used to be stored in 60 four-drawer cabinets is held on just 20 Canon discs. Information can be accessed instantly, extra warehouse space has been created, and the service is going from strength to strength. The next step is to install barcode scanning equipment for proof of deliveries, so the service can become even more streamlined.

Powering London Electricity's Customer Communications

Although its first Canofile was only installed in July 1994 – to replace the manual correspondence filing system at the company's Stratford office – London Electricity now has 12 Canofile systems in operation. The speed of the transition from manual filing to Canofile, however, belies the care taken in selecting the best solution. The eventual decision to concentrate exclusively on Canofile was only made after thorough evaluation of the system and comparison with alternative filing methods.

Canon came through with flying colours for a number of reasons. These included the high level of support and training offered by Canon, and the product's networking flexibility. Alan Beales of London Electricity believes that Canofile is the most reliable system that the company has ever purchased, and he is currently working very closely with Canon and other technology suppliers towards his next objective – a totally electronic office!

Hunting for Paperwork – A Thing of the Past

Working from its base near the historic old Croydon Airport in Surrey, Hunting Airmotive specialises in the repair and maintenance of aircraft engines. Although aero engines have many similarities to automotive engines, the overhaul and repair process is much more complex.

Paperwork dominates every job at Hunting Airmotive, because the stringent safety regulations of the Civil Aviation Authority (CAA) demand that each repair, modification or replacement of a part is carefully checked and recorded. This process generates an enormous amount of paper. In fact, a typical overhaul job on a single aircraft engine may require as many as 500 separate documents, checklists and labels to be recorded and retained on file.

Before Hunting Airmotive took delivery of a Canofile 250, data was stored on microfilm – a slow and laborious process. Now, the documents from each job are rapidly scanned and recorded onto optical disc. As a safeguard, duplicate back-up discs are kept.

The CAA has also given its seal of approval to the system. After the Canofile passed reliability checks during an audit of recording and safety procedures, Hunting Airmotive are now able to confidently shred the original documents, saving valuable storage space and improving efficiency.

Canon (UK) Ltd.,
Canon House, Manor Road, Wallington, Surrey
Tel: 0181 773 6000, Fax: 0181 773 6060

development of interactive media products and services, and of a digital revolution, either of which could give telephone companies an important new role in media.

France

Canal Plus pioneered pay TV in Europe and became very profitable and powerful as a result. Because of this success and its medium being single channel terrestrial television, no multi-channel medium has succeeded in France – Plan Cable failed and no appreciable DTH service has established itself. Canal Plus and TFI (the dominant free-to-air broadcaster) remain the major players. However, several media players have committed to launch digital pay TV and pay-per-view packages into France within the next year. These include Canal Plus (advantaged by its established consumer base and strong rights position), plus CLT (with an international partner, possibly News International), France Television and Arté/TFI.

Germany

German media is dominated by large power blocks: Bertelsmann, mainly in print media but with important audio visual interests; Leo Kirch (and Axel Springer), the dominant player in content rights; and the commercial operating companies, particularly Sat I and RTL+. The wild card in this environment is Deutsche Telekom, which owns the cable that has quickly become the dominant delivery medium with 50 per cent penetration of homes. In the anticipated shift to digital transmission, Deutsche Telekom will work with content players to feed the huge increment in channel capacity that digital delivers. However, Deutsche Telekom has to overcome the strong heritage of free television in Germany, with Première the only pay channel still struggling to break even.

Italy

The highly competitive television broadcasting market in Italy is poised for dramatic change. The market is still dominated by the terrestrial broadcasters – RAI, Mediaset and producer Cecchi Gori (who recently acquired two existing channels), plus approximately 800 local stations. The only pay TV available has been supplied by Telepiu, now owned by Kirch, Nethold and Fininvest. However, as Tele-

piu migrates to digital satellite broadcasting and the government prepares to licence cable franchises in 1996, consortia of potential satellite and cable service providers are forming to exploit the largest remaining untapped pay TV market in Europe. Exact details of the regulation are still unsettled, but the key players are likely to be service providers RAI (partnered with Warner, RCS and Sony), Telepiu (with its investors Kirch and Nethold) and Cecchi Gori, and potential infrastructure/service players Olivetti (with US West) and Telecom Italia.

Spain

The Spanish pay TV market is dominated by Canal Plus Espana, the very successful terrestrially delivered channel. Through its alliance with Telefonica, Canal Plus is set to retain its position even in the face of the long-awaited cable legislation that is due to be passed by early 1997. The legislation will allow the practically non-existent cable market to take shape and begin to grow. As presently drafted, the legislation will create a duopoly in each region, with Telefonica and one other allowed to offer telecoms and television services. It will be interesting to see if foreign or local investors will be able to take on Canal Plus/Telefonica and reap the rewards of this potentially profitable market.

UK

ITV, the BBC and Channel 4 remain the dominant players in terms of audiences in the UK. However, BSkyB, through its pay TV revenues, has proved itself capable of wielding immense resources. This has allowed it to purchase key sports and film rights and prospectively begin to eat into the heartland of the terrestrial players – their dominance of British-made original programming. However, new players may also play an important part. A fifth terrestrial channel, owned by Pearson and MAI, is due to be launched in early 1997 and digital terrestrial could also give both the traditional British broadcasters and new ones a chance to upset the equilibrium further.

Overall, expect European media to become more dynamic, not less. The fertile combination of increased leisure time across all European societies, technology change, re-regulation and investment capital from outside the sector presages a volatile decade to come.

BT Mobile

Whether in Milan, Madrid or Malmo, the international business traveller need never be out of touch or unable to send or receive information when on the move. BT Mobile, the UK's leading cellular service provider, innovative solutions for those in need of dynamic communications.

GSM – Global System for Mobile Communication - is the fast developing global standard for digital cellular telephony. Just the one mobile phone connected through BT Mobile will work on 31 networks in 22 countries, mostly in Europe – such as Greece up to Sweden and across to Portugal, but also including Australia, South Africa and Hong Kong. During the course of the next year, overseas coverage will grow even more, extending into Eastern Europe and most other parts of the continent as well as the Far East.

In addition to the ability to use your mobile phone abroad, GSM provides many other enhancements. In simple terms, the transition to this second generation mobile network can be likened to the move from a record player (analogue technology) to a compact disc player (digital sound reproduction). As a result, therefore, the digital network offers better call clarity, and enhanced security: a key benefit for executives who need to talk confidentially away from the office.

It is conservatively predicted that by the year 2000, 10 million – or one in six people – will have a mobile phone and GSM gives service providers such as BT Mobile the capacity to meet these market demands in this decade and beyond.

It is also important to note that GSM and its demanding specifications effectively keep the door open for future technological bene-

fits, providing a platform for a range of advanced services of particular interest to business people who travel internationally. For example, GSM supports sophisticated communication technology such as Mobile Data, which enables the access or transmission of data over a cellular network via a cellphone, portable PC, and a cellular interface.

BT Mobile has, for example, teamed up with Apple to allow its customers to send and receive data, fax, e-mail and verbal information over GSM networks with data capability. This means that the international traveller can remotely access information from their desktop computer back in the office, or from the company's local area network. In short, everything that can be done from the desktop back at base can be done on the move.

This means that if a customer wants the price tonight but you've only just left a meeting; a colleague needs you to check a proposal but you're a three-hour train journey away; or you've a meeting to schedule and need to check colleagues' diaries: you can now do all of this straight away.

Gone are the days when a trip overseas meant being cut off from the office. In an age when barriers to the movement of goods and services continue to fall and access is opened up to new markets, BT Mobile offers solutions on the GSM network which signal the way forward for executives operating abroad.

Using IT to In

Information Technology is now a firm part of most businesses and the PC is a standard feature on many employee's desks, so the infrastructure exists to enable data residing on many organisation's systems to be used proactively to drive the business.

Whilst the majority of organisations have computerised areas such as accounts, many have still not seen the benefits of applying IT to sales and marketing. Yet these core business functions – everyone has to sell to survive – are the ones which can potentially reap the most rewards from computerisation.

It is a fact that in many organisations, up to 80% of stored data is never accessed which is a waste of resources in that not only did it cost money to actually capture the data in the first place, but this asset is now lying unused and is progressively becoming out of date therefore dimishing its value.

By effectively utilising IT to not only capture but also profitably use this data, the sales and marketing processes in particular can be radically transformed. Some of the major benefits that can be derived are:

Capturing the right data.
There is no point gathering data for the sake of it and a sales and marketing system will help to ensure the right information is gathered. With a carefully thought out structure business managers can specify which data they want the sales force to capture ensuring that the right information on clients and prospects is recorded for them to use.

Availability of information.
Important information about clients comes into a company from many sources, but principally ffrom the people dealing directly with the customer, be they office based telesales or a field sales force. In an organisation where sales people do not use a computerised system, this vital information is either locked away in their heads, or on various pieces of paper buried in a filing cabinet. By having the sales force use such a system, the data is made accessible for others to profitably use such as sales managers or the marketing department.

Increasingly departments in companies do not work in isolation but need to share such information for mutual benefit. For example the information held in your accounts system can be used elsewhere. Your sales ledger which records who has bought what and when, is tremendously useful marketing data which if linked to a sales and marketing system will give the managers in these areas a good picture of the buying habits of customers.

Increasing productivity.
A computerised sales system gives the sales person the ability to automate many tasks therefore increasing productivity. If all prospects and clients are recorded on a database, the sales personcan ensure leads are followed up by setting recall dates with alarms, automatically record what correspondence has been sent and when, and organise their time by scheduling meetings and telephone calls. Asystem with group scheduling will also allow teams to work together more effectively.

For the sales manager the advantages are many. Because the information is on the database they will be able to monitor sales performance, track leads accurately and use the data to produce sales forecasts and monitor sales cycles allowing the sales process to be as productive as possible.

Increased productivity would also come from the marketing department using the data gathered by sales (or from the accounts system) to profile the client base thereby getting a picture of who the clients are and where they come from. Prospects can then be targeted more effectively reducing the waste associated with poorly executed mailshots.

prove Sales.

The effectiveness of marketing campaigns can be evaluated directly against sales ensuring that marketing directs its efforts where it is most effective.

Imroved customer service.
Everyone knows the importance of keeping your customers happy and the positive effect this can have on the long term profitability of a company.

With a networked sales system you can ensure that common errors such as two sales people talking to the same prospect or customers being sent inappropriate mailshots are minimised, whilst the sales people can make sure they remember to return calls and keep promises by using the automated recall facilities.

The database can also be used to administer customer satisfaction surveys to monitor the quality of your service and therefore spot any potential problems at an early stage.

These are a few of the most obvious and direct benefits of computerising the sales and marketing functions which are achieved by capturing information and then disseminating it and using it to better understand your business and customers.

So how do I go about getting some of these benefits?
Come and talk to us! FMI Limited is a software services company which has over 12 years' experience of providing abroad range of clients with practical and easy to use PC based systems that deliver real business benefits.

Over the years we have installed many computerised sales and marketing systems for a wide variety of clients and specialise in the **TeleMagic** system from Sage Plc. We are in fact the largest TleMagic dealer in the UK, a position we achieved through the implementation of many successful systems.

FMI can not only supply the software, but also a full range of services from initial consultancy, to bespoke tailoring, networking, training and after sales support to ensure the long term success of the system.

More than just a technical company.
We believe that in order to ensure the appropriate use of IT within an organisation, both technical skill and a thorough understanding of how the system will work in its environment are needed.

We appreciate that a computer systems is a tool which is subservient to an organisation's needs, and exists solely to help achieve given business goals such as greater efficiency or a reduction in costs. A testament of the validity of our practical approach is the amount of repeat business we have from clients, and the fact that systems developed by~FMI many years ago are still successfully in use today.

To discuss the benefits of computerised sales and marketing systems contact us on 0171-432-3281 and we would be more than happy to evaluate your specific needs.

But don't take our word for it, here's are what some users of TeleMagic have to say:

"TeleMagic has improved my productivity by at least 30%"
Scott Robertson-Bridges Corporation.

"...the number of calls made and generally handled has risen by over 50%. Revenue creation has also reisen considerably..."
Frank Pottle – Euromoney.

"TeleMagic is an outstanding program ... it has increased my income and confidence in dealing with prospective clients"
Interwest Financial Advisers.

FAX 5000P

&

CONNECT 5000 SOFTWARE

WHAT YOU SEE IS WHAT YOU FAX

Whether in a large office or on the desk at home, the **Brother Fax 5000P** provides the perfect communications link especially when installed with **Connect 5000** PC–compatible software†. This opens a whole new dimension in faxing as well as offering printing and scanning capabilities.

FOR MORE INFORMATION RING
KAREN HASKINS NOW ON

0161-931 2302

brother ®

BROTHER BUSINESS MACHINES DIVISION,
SHEPLEY STREET, AUDENSHAW, MANCHESTER M34 5JD

†Requirements: Windows™ 3.1+, 10 Mb Hard Disk Space, 4 Mb RAM.

BRITISH FACSIMILE INDUSTRY
CONSULTATIVE COMMITTEE

What to Buy *for business* **BEST BUY**
FAX 5000P
July 1995 issue

With Connect 5000 – what you see is what you fax!

Together the Fax 5000P and Connect 5000 software offer multi-functionality to a singularly high standard, with features such as:

- Laser quality plain paper printing
- Broadcasting
- Ultra low cost per copy
- Enlarging/reducing copy mode
- 30 page automatic document feed
- Receives faxes straight onto screen
- A4 scanning facility (200 x 200 dpi resolution)
- Fax forwarding
- 500 name address book
- 15 page upgradeable memory

brother®

Increased fax performance from Brother
Adds two new models to fax portfolio

Brother is adding two new feature rich plain paper models to its award winning facsimile range. The new **Fax 1700P** cost effectively combines fax, phone, answering machine and paging facilities. The **Fax 1200P** replaces the highly successful Fax 1000P – the machine that brought plain paper faxes within reach of even the most cost-conscious businesses.

Phil Jones, Brother's fax product manager says: "We're constantly upgrading our products as we strive to deliver the best possible solutions at the most competitive price. Our Fax 1000P was the lowest cost plain paper fax ever produced and now with the Fax 1200P we're offering an even better model at practically the same price. It's perfect for companies that need to watch the expenses but still demand the highest quality and performance."

The Fax 1200P and Fax 1700P are ideal machines for people concerned at the increasing costs involved in running a business. Unlike the runaway cost associated with inkjet printing, Brother's thermal transfer printing technology on both products means that the costs per copy are fixed.

Fax 1700P

Based on acclaimed Message Manager technology, the 1700P is a plain paper version of Brother's Fax 490DT. It has an increased modem speed of 14,400 bps so faxes can be sent in as little as nine seconds. Faxes can also be remotely retrieved from any fax worldwide as well as automatically stored or redirected.

"The 1700P is the perfect tool for anyone in danger of missing vital information while they're away from home or the office," says Phil Jones. "The cost of the machine, compared to the potential loss in business caused by an unattended office is comparatively small."

Equipped with a revolutionary chip which gives unprecedented voice clarity amongst digital-based telephone/ansamachine faxes, the 1700P represents the ultimate in plain paper fax machine specification.

Its 1024kb memory facility gives the machine storage for 50 pages of fax or 14 minutes audio – or a combination of both. It can also identify incoming voice or fax and automatically respond accordingly, on a single telephone line.

Furthermore, the advanced memory capability provides a broadcast facility allowing one document to be faxed to 130 destinations sequentially.

The new machine has an increased grey scale of 64 levels to improve picture reproduction and a 20 sheet automatic document feeder.

Fax 1200P

The Fax 1200P offers all the facilities of the Fax 1000P it supersedes, but is lighter and more compact.

Multi Resolution Transmission (also a feature of the 1700P) allows the user to send – in one transmission – up to 20 pages containing a variety of presentation formats. Text, drawings and photographs can be sent with a different resolution setting for each different page: fine, super fine or photo.

Also, the machine automatically generates half page cover sheets in advance which can include a customised message.

The Fax 1200P has a 'smoothing' feature to smooth jagged lines that can distort text or images, regardless of the resolution quality of the machine that sent them.

Despite the audio and visual messages given out by the machine itself, the Fax 1200P will still receive ten pages of fax and print them when the paper is replenished. Like the 1700P, it also offers a broadcast facility.

With other features including a 200 sheet cassette tray, 70 fast dial numbers, 64 shade grey scale for photographs, onscreen user prompts and convenient copying for SOHO and inter departmental use, the 1200P will provide businesses with all the latest features and technology at an astoundingly low price.

Both models offer PC connectability via Brother's Connect 5000 interface adding PC-based fax, scan and printing capability.

---

brother®

Brother breaks the mould with MFC 6000

The ultimate piece of space and cost saving technology comes from Brother in the shape of the MFC 6000 which provides plain paper fax, laser printer, copier, scanner and fax modem facilities all in one neat desktop unit, at little more than the cost of a plain paper laser fax.

Perfect for a corporate department or small businesses, the MFC 6000 combines the technology of two of Brother's most innovative products: the HL630 printer (UK printer of the year 1994) and the Fax 5000P. The new machine offers superb performance, low running costs and an initial outlay of only £1299 (RRP).

Corporate customers will undoubtedly benefit from the printing facilities offered by the MFC 6000. By incorporating the HL630 printer engine, the MFC 6000 will function as a stand alone six page per minute machine, but all for the cost of a laser plain paper fax.

Brother's network card option for the MFC 6000 facilitates network-wide printing. Wordcraft Lasercraft network PC software is also available for those corporate users looking for a network fax option.

Says Phil Jones, Brother's fax product manager; "The MFC 6000 is a great innovation.

"Having all five products in one unit obviously saves space making it much more cost effective. It's perfect for use in a departmentalised organisation where each group needs its own facilities.

"Brother is renowned for employing the very latest technology in its printer and fax products," he continues. "The result of merging these technologies is more than just the sum of the parts and at significantly less cost. It's a vital component to any office where time, money and quality are prime motivators."

The MCF 6000's use of ground-breaking technology quashes the criticisms traditionally aimed at multi function fax machines: that they are slow, have low resolution and allow only one function to be used at a time. As well as offering <u>five</u> products in one the MFC 6000 gives fast print speeds, high resolution and simultaneous operation, allowing background printing as faxes are sent and received.

The MPC6000 offers full inbound and outbound traffic from a personal computer. Its PC interface allows users to fax directly from any Windows application and receive incoming faxes directly into their machine and view them on screen.

The MFC 6000 offers plain paper laser fax output. It has a 15 page memory (upgradeable to 75), remote fax retrieval and fax forwarding. Low priced consumables and high product performance make it a cost effective option.

Award winning printing

The award winning printing technology of the MFC 6000 offers two major benefits; speed and enhanced memory capacity. With enhanced memory management, for example, a machine with just 512k memory can print files that similar machines can't do without memory expansion.

With Brother's use of advanced data compression technology, the MFC6000 operates at an impressive 6ppm. Furthermore, the straight paper path reduces the time it takes for the paper to go through and eliminates paper jams and curling. The speed on the first page makes printing appear to be instantaneous.

Other features of the MFC 6000 include a built-in reduce/enlarge copying mode, eradicating the need to buy a separate photo copier. Additionally it can scan in text, logos, line arts and images for use in other documents.

This latest addition to the Brother portfolio extends the company's environmentally friendly product range. It offers sleep mode, economy printing and low ozone emissions.

brother®

Brother launches flagship printer

Brother has launched its most advanced printer to date, so strengthening its position in the laser market.

The HL-1260 is a 12 page per minute (ppm) laser printer which uses Brother's own true 600dpi laser engine. The combination of Brother's High Resolution Control technology (HRC) and micro fine toner delivers superb 1200 dpi equivalent class print quality, but at a speed and price most network managers wouldn't believe.

The HL-1260 is ideal for single user and LAN printing needs. By incorporating a fast 20 MHz 32 bit-RISC based controller, 2MB of memory with advanced memory management, a bi-directional high speed parallel interface and serial interface, a standard MIO port and High Speed Driver, the HL-1260 can run as close to optimum engine speed as possible.

While the added benefit of being fully networkable in both Ethernet and Token Ring 'ready-to-run' configurations, makes the HL-1260 an ideal choice for LAN users. Further more, Brother's Printset programme enables windows and network LAN managers not only to monitor network printer status, but also to re-configure remotely.

In addition to providing PCL5e, BR-script Level 2 (Brother's own Postcript Language emulation), Epson FX850 and IBM Proprinter XL emulations as standard, the HL-1260 automatically switches emulation based on the incoming data, as well as retaining PCL emulation resources – such as soft fonts and macros – ready for the next print job.

With up to 20Mb of Flash RAM or 40Mb of Hard disk online storage available through PCMCIA type I/III support, the HL-1260 gives network users the ultimate in printing flexibility.

Designed with a 500 sheet input tray capacity and an additional 500 page option – as well as an extra 150 manual feed flip down tray – the innovative HL-1260's massive 1,150 total input capacity, more than meets the volume printing challenge thrown down by today's network needs.

Other features include straight paper path printing – which cuts down the time it takes paper to go through and reduces both paper jams and curling – 75 scalable fonts and 12 bit map fonts and an auto duplex option – allowing printing on both side of the paper – the HL-1260 gives network users the ultimate in printing flexibility.

David York Brother's Printer Sales Manager said, "The HL-1260 is a machine that will have our competitors running for cover! It has the speed and high volume capacity that is so vital for any network environment, while maintaining the highest standards in print quality.

"The HL-1260 cements Brother's long term commitment to the laser printer market by strengthening our already highly successful range and with a list price of £1,249 it's an extremely attractive proposition for consumers."

B B C *W O R L D   S E R V I C E*

THE BUSINESS OF GLOBAL BUSINESS NEWS

By Martin Webber, Editor, World Business Report, BBC World Service

Does business news make boring radio? I don't believes it does. Nor does The BBC World Service, broadcasting from the fringes of the City of London. The World Service has recently embarked on a significant expansion of its business and economics coverage. *World Business Report* its flagship financial affairs programme, is now broadcast five times daily and the entire team of financial journalists has been brought in-house leading to a greatly enhanced global business news service. Our business news programmes now offer more benefits; from the latest international share prices to key interviews and expert analysis.

Since the collapse of the Communist bloc in Eastern Europe the world news agenda has been re-defined. The relative significant of domestic politics in the United States and what was the Soviet Union has faded. At the same time, developing countries that were, for decades, stable but poor command economies, are now embracing free markets and all the moral and practical dilemmas they entail.

Of course, the BBC World Service isn't the only media organisation to recognise the interest in financial affairs. In the past few years both the Financial Times and The Economist have invested huge sums in distribution outside Britain – and they've repeated significant rewards in both readership and profit.

Radio and newspapers are very different animals though. From a wealth of information on a page, readers can pick out the few pieces that interest them. Radio is different. For *World Business Report* this means some difficult decisions need to be taken about how to balance programme content.

We need to provide the most important currency rates and share indices for those that import and export or who follow the investment trends. And these must be precise and predictable, and yes, perhaps a little boring for those whose lives aren't affected directly by the markets' daily ebb and flow. But the numbers are just one element of a business programme.

On-line home computers are becoming cheaper, and will increasingly provide a more appropriate and flexible method of delivering raw data for those that really need it.

As financial journalists our most important role is to deliver perspective and analysis. Raw company announcements and economics statistics are indeed dull. But if you choose the key issues, get to the real players and right experts, the subject is simply fascinating. From Singapore

BBC *W O R L D   S E R V I C E*

WORLD *Business* REPORT   **FOR EUROPE**
also for North Africa, Middle East and Former Soviet Union

Frequencies

GMT Edition	0905	1205	1325	1730	1925	2105	0305
Short Wave	17.705 17.64 15.575 15.07 12.095 11.76 9.41 7.325 6.195	17.705 17.64 15.575 15.07 12.09 11.76 9.41	21.47 17.705 17.64 15.575 15.07 12.095 11.76 9.41	15.07 12.095 9.41 6.195 6.18 3.955	15.07 12.095 9.41 6.195 6.18 3.955	11.835 9.41 7.325 6.195 6.18 3.955	Not broadcast to the region, but Americas frequencies 7.325 6.175 5.975
Medium Wave For SE England, NW Germany, NE France & Benelux		648 kHz (463m)	648 kHz (463m)	648 kHz (463m)	648 kHz (463m)		
Medium wave to East Mediterranean	1323 kHz (227m)	1323 kHz (227m)	1323 kHz (227m)	1323 kHz (227m)	1323 kHz (227m)	1323 kHz (227m)	
Medium Wave in Moscow and St Petersberg		1260 kHz (238m)					
Medium Wave from Gibralter Broadcasting Corp.				1458 kHz (206m)	1458 kHz (206m)	1458 kHz (206m)	
FM Berlin		90.2 MHz	90.2 MHz	90.2 MHz	90.2 MHz	90.2 MHz	
FM Prague*	101.1 MHz	101.1 MHz	101.1 MHz	101.1 MHz		101.1 MHz	
FM Sofia, Bulgaria	91.0 MHz	91.0 MHz	91.0 MHz	91.0 MHz	91.0 MHz	91.0 MHz	
FM Geneva region (from Radio 74)	88.8 MHz (at 1030 CET)			88.8 MHz			

By satellite 24 hours a day on Astra 19.2degE 11.553 GHz (UK Gold) audio 7.38 MHz or Eutelsat 13degE 11.620 Ghz audio 7.38 MHz

*The FM service for Prague is also available in Banska Bystrica on 105.4FM, Bratislava 93.8, Brno 101.7, Ceske Budejovice 89.9, Kosice 103.2, Pardubice 99.1, Plzen 98.6 and Usti Nad Labem 105.8. Listeners in parts of Vienna may also be able to hear the 93.8 and 101.7 frequencies.

share scandals to multi-million dollar megamergers, from commodity market chaos to dollar disasters, they all fit into a complex web of related developments, each raising difficult dilemmas and where there are never easy answers.

But with other broadcasters, particularly television, entering the market, what special element can can international radio station offer?

Radio can react faster and more flexibly than any other medium, and that's crucial when it comes to reflecting today's volatile financial markets. Radio can take you live to the hubbub of the dealing floors of the foreign exchange markets at a minute's notice.

On *World Business Report* over the past few months, we've asked the Chicago fund manager, David Herro, why he forced the Saatchi Brothers out of Saatchi and Saatchi, and we've asked the President of the BJP, India's Hindu nationalist party, the BJP, why it cancelled a major foreign investment project.

Naturally, there are some inherent dangers in trying to please both the specialists and the generalists. It is easy to think that the only answer is to turn business into entertainment. In doing so, the substance may be lost, and since business news can never be as entertaining as genuine entertainment, what's left can easily fail to either inform or entertain.

In my view, the golden rules are "don't patronise", don't over-estimate what the audience has in the way of background knowledge, but don't under-estimate either their enthusiasm for learning more. Another golden rule is cut out the jargon. We avoid "rafts" of economics statistics floating around on our programme.

Any tabloid journalist worth his salt will tell you that what sells papers are the "human interest" stories. As business reports, we are lucky in that the humans that interest us aren't the fanatics who bomb and murder. We're not obsessed either with that other strange breed – the politician.

Instead, we follow the ordinary and the extraordinary. Even the apparently dry economic forecasts are really just a branch of psychology. The way an economy behaves is simply the result of adding up the unpredictable reactions of millions of ordinary people to events – falling house prices, losing a World Cup soccer match, or job insecurity. No equation can predict the spending and employment decisions of millions of ordinary people.

Coverage of such events is all in a day's work for the busy reporters of *World Business Report* from Bush House. Our daily raw material is usually fascinating, often entertaining, and certainly never boring.

For further information about BBC World Service business programmes write to:

Martin Webber, Business Unit
BBC World Service, Bush House, PO Box 76
Strand, London WC2B 4PH, U.K.

PART

7

Competitive Manufacturing

PATENT AND SCIENTIFIC INFORMATION

In increasingly competitive markets, and with global operations, companies only succeed by staying ahead of the competition.

The decision to enter new markets and create new products is critical to the prosperity of business. Top quality information, at the right time, is essential for decision-making by senior management and for innovative R&D. It can help organisations identify real opportunities and reduce unnecessary risks.

From devising strategy and developing new product concepts, to taking a technical invention right through to the marketplace, information from scientific and patent sources is critical. Fortune 500 companies have long recognised the value of patent and scientific information as a key business tool.

Patents – a key information source

The nature of patents and patent law makes these documents a unique data source within company's innovation process.

Under patent law the details of an invention must be kept secret until the patent has been filed. In addition, patents have to contain enough detail for an expert specialising in the field to recreate the invention. Therefore they give a detailed description of the manufacturing process, the composition of a new drug or the design of components of machinery. Studies have shown that 70-90% of inventions are only ever disclosed in patents. Monitoring patents therefore provides much earlier, and often additional, information than other sources.

Patent information also provides a unique source for identifying organisations working in the area of interest. Analysis of patent information can help in arranging a technology transfer, or in negotiating a license for a product for manufacturing, importing or marketing.

Despite the critical advantage that this information can provide it is not fully exploited by many companies in their strategic planning or R&D. For example, it has been estimated that around 30% of all R&D funding in Europe could be saved if the information available from searching patents was used more astutely.

Derwent Information Limited

For over 40 years, Derwent's information solutions have met the needs of Fortune 500 corporations, and equally important, fulfilled the information demands of smaller more specialised organisations – ultimately the large organisations of the future.

Derwent collates information from 40 patent-issuing authorities, and more than 1,200 scientific journals and conference proceedings worldwide. Each document goes through a rigorous screening, classification, abstracting, indexing, coding and quality assessment process to extract the essential information. Comprehensive subject coding and English-language abstracts ensure that even obscure information is accessible.

Customers are able to access this information in a variety of ways. Formats and media include online, CD-ROM, diskette, Internet and print.

Derwent is part of the Thomson Business Information Group, within the Thomson Corporation. It's headquarters are in London, with operations in North America (Washington DC) and Japan (Tokyo).

Derwent World Patents Index

Derwent's flagship product – Derwent World Patents Index (DWPI) is a comprehensive database of patents published worldwide and made available in a single language. It describes more than 7 million separate inventions from over 40 patent-issuing authorities around the world. It provides bibliographic information, English-language abstracts, comprehensive indexing, and the world's largest collection of patent drawings online.

For further information contact Miriam McColgan: Email eurinfo@derwent.co.uk Fax +44 171 344 2821

The European Textiles and Clothing Sector

29

Lynn Oxborrow, Nottingham Trent University

The European textiles and clothing industry covers a range of products from carpets to technical textiles; high fashion to premature baby wear. Employing some 2.5 million people in over 100 thousand businesses, the industry is often regarded as one in permanent decline, unable to survive competition from imports. However, this apparent overall trend masks a wide disparity of performance, depending on region and product type.

Industry performance

In the European textile and clothing sector, overall performance demonstrates a limited recovery, after declining sales from the mid-1980s until 1993. Exports have increased and although imports rose during the early part of 1994, by the second half of the year this increase had slowed. In spite of increases in production, 14,000 jobs were shed in the sector during 1994, representing a loss of 5 per cent.

The textile sector has shown the earliest and most consistent growth, with production increasing by 4 per cent and turnover by 1 per cent during 1994. The highest rates of growth are in technical textiles, especially in Germany and Italy, although specialist production in other regions has performed well. The clothing sector has shown slower growth, the best performing areas being Italian production for the export market and manufacture in Denmark, fuelled by increases in domestic demand for high value-added, branded goods.

Employment in textiles and clothing has shrunk by 10 per cent in Germany, while in Norway jobs have been created in the sector. In Spain and in Nottinghamshire, UK, reports indicate that, while redundancies have occurred in large companies, there is evidence of job creation in small firms. In spite of job losses, investment rates in Ireland and Spain show that companies are updating machinery, while producers in France, Portugal and Italy have invested in improved information links with customers and suppliers, increasing responsiveness to market demand.

Although profitability has increased in textiles and clothing, rates are lower than in other sectors. Attempts to reduce costs have resulted in outsourcing to countries with lower labour costs, particularly affecting low value, domestic garment manufacturing in Germany, Denmark and Norway. However, as the use of fabrics of EU origin avoids tariffs on reimported goods, the domestic textile sector has to some extent been supported by this tendency. At the same time, the low waged economies of Southern Europe have seen the cost of labour increase relatively quickly, eroding the cost advantage of firms in Portugal and Greece. Increased raw material costs have largely been absorbed by textile and clothing manufacturers and are only filtering into the market gradually. Pressure on margins has therefore increased, while the economy has been unable to support consumer price increases.

Regulatory pressures

The gradual phasing out of the Multi Fibre Agreement (MFA) will have a significant effect on the textiles and clothing sector. Imports of low value products will increase over the next few years, emphasizing the need for European businesses to increase competitiveness in high value-added, quick response production, flexible to market demand for design, performance and value.

Environmental regulation is likely to increase with concern regarding raw material supply and textile finishing, although this is not seen as a threat to the domestic finishing sector. Some countries, such as Germany, have strict regulations concerning the packaging of products, and in the UK major retailers are reducing the use of packaging, primarily to reduce preretailing delay, but with environmental advantages. A system of eco-labelling is under development and will map the environmental impact of garments from raw material to final consumption.

Industry structure

The structure of the industry and the markets which it serves vary considerably between regions. One common element is the large number of small firms. In Portugal, 70 per cent of firms have fewer than 10 employees and in the UK three-quarters of businesses employ less than 20 people. In some regions, textiles and clothing remain dominated by family businesses, particularly in the Mediterranean economies. In spite of high unemployment, the industry suffers from labour shortages and is characterized by low skill levels and relatively large numbers employed in the informal economy and as home workers, issues which have been prioritized in regional and national support to the industry.

The structure of the marketplace affects the organizational structure of the sector. In the UK, the market is dominated by large chain stores, which have, throughout the 1980s, encouraged the development of large vertically integrated manufacturing corporations, linked into monopolistic supply-chain relationships. In Italy and France, manufacturers supply highly responsive and flexible specialized chains, such as Benetton, through information-intensive subcontracting networks. In Sweden, manufacturers are benefiting from the increased market share of independent stores, at the expense of chain stores which import larger proportions of stock. Although in Spain some manufacturers, for example

Zara, have turned to retailing in order to secure their market position, in Portugal the majority of production is made on a cut, make and trim basis for Northern European retailers.

Global competitiveness

Although the EU trade balance for textile products is negative, the industry's competitiveness is boosted by the export orientation of some sectors. In Portugal and Belgium, exports to other countries in the European Union represent a high proportion of turnover, but are threatened by recession and low priced competition. In Italy, however, the textile and clothing sector has seen a 30 per cent increase in exports outside the EU during the past year. This has secured an early increase in apparel sales and in textiles, both for direct export and for the manufacture of goods for export markets. Recent instability of European currencies has created cost advantages for exporters in some countries, such as the UK, and has been damaging to others.

Future prospects

Most European countries have not experienced a sustained increase in domestic demand for textile and clothing products, and growth areas such as technical textiles are forecast to stabilize throughout 1995. However, after years of decline and restructuring the sector has emerged with improved efficiency and potential for strategic development. There are tentative indications for some retailers that policy towards domestic supply has changed favourably in order to satisfy demand for rapid response and flexibility.

However, while domestic markets remain depressed and companies seek further cost cutting through outsourcing, export markets outside the EU offer better prospects. Statistics from the British Knitwear and Clothing Export Council indicate that the top 15 markets for clothing include not only the USA, Japan and Saudi Arabia, but also Russia and Morocco. Anecdotal evidence suggests that demand for branded Western goods in the Far East is high, and manufacturers can capitalize on the reputation of European design in other new markets.

In addition, efforts to increase the level of integration throughout the supply chain and improve exchange of market intelligence using information technology will help maintain the market advantage of domestic suppliers. Nottinghamshire companies interviewed in 1995 indicate that export sales are

TOULOUSE MIDI-PYRENEES
HAS A LOT GOING FOR IT

Toulouse Midi-Pyrénées in Europe.

ELECTRONICS

Motorola.

HEALTH CARE INDUSTRY

Laboratoires Fabre   (Photo : G. Bouquillon)

AEROSPACE

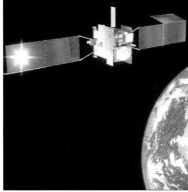

Satellite STENTOR   (Photo : D. Ducros)

BIOTECHNOLOGY

Sanofi Recherches.

The selected location of major firms

Aerospatiale • Airbus Industrie • Alcan • Alcatel Espace • A.T.R. • Bosch • Fuji • Grand Metropolitan • Honeywell • Kodak • Matra Marconi Space • Motorola • Rockwell Collins • Rohr Europe • Siemens Automotive • Storagetek • Thomson…

And among them, 306 international companies

A full range of international and French sub-contractors
• mechanical, electrical, electronic.

Europe's most prestigious R & D environment
• The largest in France after Paris
• 10,500 researchers, 400 laboratories and 6 joint labs
• Over 1,000 industry/research contracts signed each year.

France's N°2 education centre
• 108,000 students of which 12 % are foreigners.
• 1,500 engineers, 5,000 technicians and 5,000 PhD's graduate annually.

And also the quality of life.

N°1 European Space Centre
N°1 European Aeronautics Centre
N°1 French Electronics Centre
(active components; robotics; automatic systems)
N°1 French Data-Processing Centre outside Paris
One of the top three Bio-Technology Centres in France
One of the top Agri-Business Centres in France.

For professional help and advice on your business development project in Toulouse Midi-Pyrénées, please contact:
Tim Wood, 36 Earls Court Square, London SW59DQ
Tel: 071 370 6939 - Fax: 071 835 2081

growing; half of the companies indicate that turnover has increased and few firms have reduced employment. A growing number of those companies are trading on design and leadtime as competitive strengths and decreasing reliance on price as a selling factor. Indications suggest that the textile and clothing industry is addressing the issues which will maintain the competitiveness of European manufacturing in the face of increased world competition.

Note

The Nottinghamshire European Textile and Clothing Observatory was established in 1994 by Nottinghamshire County Council with support from the European Union, to provide strategic and market intelligence for the textile and clothing sector. The Observatory conducts a rolling survey of local companies and produces an annual Register of Capacity and State of the Industry Report. For further information contact Lynn Oxborrow, The Nottingham Trent University, Burton St, Nottingham, tel: 0115 948 6040.

Sources

Central Statistical Office (1993) *Size Analysis of UK Businesses.*

Crewe, L., May, C. and Oxborrow, L. (1994) *The Nottinghamshire Textile and Clothing Sector: A State of the Industry Report*, Nottingham.

The British Knitwear and Clothing Export Council (1994) *Fifteen Top Export Markets: The British Apparel Export Awards.*

'Economic Situation and Prospects in the Main Industrialised Countries' (1995) *Comitextil*, Bulletin 95/1–2.

Scheffer, M. (1994) *The Changing Map of European Textiles: Production Strategies of Textiles and Clothing Firms*, OETH.

British Apparel and Textiles Confederation (1995) *Trendata.*

European Construction Prospects

30

Neil Martin, Manager, Centre for Construction Market Information (CCMI)

With the UK construction industry still in the doldrums after a sustained recession beginning in 1991, many UK companies are looking to Europe for their salvation. Although 1994 did finally see positive growth of 3.2 per cent for the UK, most forecasting agencies are predicting a dismal end to 1995 with a fall of 2 per cent on the previous year.

European prospects for construction, according to the recent Euroconstruct conference held in London in June, look healthy with growth expected in 1995 and 1996. The general economic recovery in Europe will be reflected in increased construction activity. Scandinavia is emerging from a deep recession and countries from this region are among the strongest predicted performers for 1996. Finland heads the league table as Europe's fastest growing construction market with +11 per cent, Norway at +5.9 per cent and Denmark at +4.5 per cent.

The German construction industry dominates the European scene, representing over 30 per cent of total output at ECU218 billion (1994 prices). France is the second largest construction industry with ECU98 billion. The UK represents ECU64 billion output and is the fourth largest construction industry in Europe, below Italy at ECU85 billion.

Most countries' construction economies have suffered some degree of recession over the last five years, with only Germany, Austria and Portugal experiencing positive growth during this period.

Germany

Since reunification in 1990 Germany has enjoyed stable growth in all sectors of construction: housing, industrial and commercial building. This growth is, however, slowing down as output will reduce from 7.5 per cent growth in 1994 to 5.0 per cent in 1995 and 2.0 per cent in 1996. Housing particularly represents a large percentage of total output, 34 per cent as compared to that in the UK at 15 per cent. This large proportion of total output reflects the end of eight years of unprecedented growth for the housing sector, fuelled largely by reunification. The immigration of one million people into the former West Germany from East Germany and other adjacent countries in 1990 created a demand for 400–500,000 new housing units. By the year 2000 western Germany is expected to have four million more households than assessed in the 1987 census. Housing output in 1990 hit its lowest level since 1957 with only 62,000 units, due mainly to the dismantling of the former East German administration and financing in 1989. It is expected that housing output will slow down considerably into 1996 and beyond, particularly in western Germany, as the mortgage interest depreciation programme expired at the end of 1994 and other factors mitigate against growth.

In the former East Germany upgrading and new building of suitable housing will continue beyond 1996. Housing growth is forecast up to the end of the century, fuelled by the regional promotion law for rental housing that remains in effect until 1996. However, the dampening factors of the expiration of the mortgage interest depreciation programme, the high cost of land and high building costs will signal patchy growth in the years 1996–2000, after a sustained period of growth since 1993.

Many of the UK's major construction firms have been active in Germany for some years, together with specialist subcontractors and other skilled workers.

France

Europe's second largest market, France should recover in 1995 after three years of recession, 1993 being the nadir of construction output. Growth of 1.3 per cent in 1995 is expected to be followed by an increase of 2.4 per cent in 1996.

New residential construction worth ECU20.2 billion performed well in 1994, with a 5.7 per cent growth followed by a predicted 5.3 per cent increase in 1995. Factors for this growth include budget measures to encourage growth in the government-subsidized rental sector and in subsidized owner occupation. Mortgage rate reductions in 1993 and 1994 stimulated demand, as did the general increase in consumer credit. Although 1995 is predicted to achieve over 5 per cent increase in housing output, housing starts will fall compared to 1994 as budget measures are geared to reducing governmental deficits and interest rates have crept up by 2.2 per cent during 1994, further eroding confidence. This will result in housing output falling by 2.2 per cent in 1996 compared with the previous year.

Private non-residential building will be the star performer in 1996, with a predicted increase of 10.7 per cent after four years of negative growth. All sectors, agricultural, industrial and the office market, should enjoy growth. Industrial production is expected to rise in 1995 by 4.2 per cent and by 3.9 per cent in 1996. Excess production capacity in 1993 and 1994 has largely disappeared in 1995 and new capacity is required. Investment in production will increase growth in starts during 1995 by 12 per cent, followed by strong growth in 1996 of 18 per cent.

Office building has suffered a downturn since 1991, with 1993 seeing a 21 per cent reduction in output on the previous year. As with the UK, over-capacity has had a drastic effect on the sector; however, this reduction in output is slowing down and 1996 will see a 2 per cent increase in activity. The service sector in France should see between 275,000

and 300,000 jobs created each year in 1995 and 1996 and existing office space is perceived as being inadequate for this growth.

Civil engineering, worth ECU21 billion in 1994, can expect growth in 1996 following a period of decline since 1991. The large state-owned enterprises will significantly increase investment in the electricity network, the gas distribution system and the railway system.

Italy

The other significant construction economy in Europe is Italy, where political scandals have held up work in the last two years particularly in the sector of publicly funded infrastructure work. Construction output will finally recover in 1995, with growth of 2.1 per cent predicted for 1996. Civil engineering will recover in 1995 and 1996. In June 1995 a new law on public works was passed which freed up the bureaucratic hold-ups and achieved consensus among the contracting participants. This helped stimulate private investment in projects.

The high-speed rail link between Milan and Turin will continue work in 1995 and 1996. Roadwork investment will increase in 1995 by 30 per cent and by 15 per cent in 1996, with major schemes planned for Messina–Palermo, Turin–Savona, Rome and Perugia.

Central and Eastern Europe

Construction economies in Central and Eastern Europe are of great attraction for other European countries' contractors and material suppliers. Poland, the Czech and Slovak Republics, Hungary and Slovenia are the only former Eastern bloc countries to have successfully made the transition to viable economies. In 1995 and 1996 these construction markets will be attractive sources of work. Poland is forecast for 4.0 per cent growth in 1995 and 5.5 per cent in 1996. The Czech Republic is the most lucrative market, with 6.5 per cent in 1995 and 8.2 per cent predicted for 1996. Its neighbour, the Slovak Republic, is forecast for 2.0 per cent growth in 1995 and 8.0 per cent in 1996. Hungary, beset by rising inflation, will see budgetary deficits restricting public spending and reducing growth to a respectable 2.0 per cent in 1995 and the same in 1996. Although UK contractors and material suppliers are involved in these markets, German and US companies have been entrenched in construction work there for some years. Funding from international programmes has financed much of the new work in these countries. The World Bank through the International Bank for Reconstruction and Development (IRBD), the European Investment Bank (EIB), the European Bank for Reconstruction and Development (EBRD) and the PHARE programme have all contributed to funding of projects in these countries.

Retail development, the reconstruction of outdated industrial stock and tourism-related projects are areas of growth. Infrastructure projects relating to rail, road and air travel are also areas of expansion. Projects relating to environmental works, water, sewerage and power will be sources of work far into the future, as disregard for the environment in the past has left the Czech Republic and Poland in particular with serious pollution problems.

Europe's top construction companies

The performance of construction companies in Europe is examined in a recent report, *Europe's Top 500 Construction Companies*. Europe's top companies, the 300 largest contractors and 200 largest building materials producers, constitute 35–40 per cent of the European building and construction market. This market equals approximately £580 billion, of which £245 billion is building materials and £335 billion is labour. Cross-border activities have seen these companies doubling their foreign-earned turnover since 1988. Building materials producers have outstripped contractors in profits earned through foreign activity. On average Europe's 50 largest building materials producers do more than half their business abroad.

Expansion into Western European markets, and increasingly Central and Eastern Europe, has been by acquisitions, particularly by the basic heavy-side materials producers of concrete, cement and tiles. The Eastern European markets have been targeted mainly by German companies who have not traditionally been export led. The largest exports among European companies have been achieved by Saint Gobain and Alcatel Calile (both French), followed by the UK's RMC Group, Pilkington, Redland and Wolseley.

The future trend is likely to see greater integration of activity across Europe. The larger material producers are likely to continue to expand through the purchase of weaker competitors. Contractors will need to be of sufficient size to bid for European contracts. UK subcontractors will continue to benefit from linking up with major project contractors, both British and German, to enter the lucrative Central and Eastern European markets.

Sources

Euroconstruct, June 1995 – available from Construction Forecasting and Research Ltd, Tel: 0171 379 5339

BMP Forecasts, July 1995 – available from National Council of Building Materials Producers, Tel: 0171 323 3770

Europe's Top 500 Construction Companies
Construction and Property in Poland
Construction and Property in Czech Republic
Construction and Property in Slovakia
Construction and Property in Hungary
Construction and Property in Germany
– available from Centre for Construction Market Information, Tel: 0171 580 4949

31 Europe's Sun Belt

Tim Wood, Corporate Development Partners

'Most of the activity in electronics manufacturing in Europe is happening around the periphery,' says Charles Lovatt, Managing Director of L.I. Components, based in Dumfermline, Scotland. L.I. Components finds and supplies components for manufacturers of electronic circuit boards when they have unexpectedly run out of a part.

What he says highlights the effect that generous government incentives have had over the past 25 years in influencing the location of the newer manufacturing plant towards the periphery of Europe.

As many regions vie with each other to attract manufacturing industry, it may be worth looking at the evolution of such investment. Originally, factories were built close to the raw materials or energy sources on which they relied. Towards the end of the nineteenth century, as the transport infrastructure and sources of energy improved, factories tended to be built closer to the markets that they served.

In today's world-scale economy, a product's overall cost to the point of sale has become a prime consideration. For many industries the Pacific Rim countries have become the lowest cost producers and in order to compete the old industrialized world has been forced to compensate for their higher manufacturing costs by means of grants and incentives.

Of course, some manufacturing industry is more mobile than others; for example, shoe manufacturing appears to be more so than food processing, where hygiene and market proximity are still important.

Electronics manufacturing has also been particularly affected, whereas aerospace, which relies on a vast supporting manufacturing base, has not yet succumbed. However, even this is likely to change as joint ventures are established in the Far East, and aerospace may well follow what has happened in the automobile industry.

Today, we observe another effect which is becoming increasingly visible in Europe – and particularly in technology-based companies which rely on highly trained personnel and whose business supplies a significant service element. These so-called soft companies are generally young, first generation and have to have access to a reservoir of talented young graduates. Two facts rapidly emerge: these people like to live and work where there are other like-minded people, and they tend to favour an academic environment, preferably in pleasant surroundings.

Well-served regional airports and today's fantastic telecommunications have allowed what would formerly have been only a dream to become a reality.

In the USA, California's Silicon Valley and Boston's Route 128 are early examples of successful colonies of technology-based companies. Cambridge in England produced a similar effect in the 1970s and early 1980s centred around the university and its financial support – which was enthusiastically supplemented by the venture capital industry. Even today, the pull of Cambridge is still generally considered to be outperforming its European rivals.

This trend has not gone unnoticed in France where intellectual and scientific eminence has long been prized. The policy-makers of the 1970s concluded that the draw of the Mediterranean climate and lifestyle could match anything elsewhere and sought to replicate the environment which many of the newer high-tech US companies had grown accustomed to at home. Sophia Antipolis was created close to Nice and soon Digital Equipment and Dow Chemical moved in.

However, the key to real success appears to require the existence of a strong university scientific base to feed the new generation of companies. IBM thus chose Montpellier, Motorola is expanding its European headquarters in Toulouse and Hewlett-Packard saw the attractions of the mountains and set up its operations in Grenoble.

We are now seeing a second generation of smaller companies springing up in this 'sun belt'. Some were people who have left the major employers, some are university start-ups, and an increasing number are from Northern Europe, attracted by the perceived good lifestyle.

These soft companies generate very high added value and provide a spectacular springboard for future industrial growth in a region. So far, the importance of these small, often start-up companies with less than 10 people (not 'employees', for their structure remains equally fluid) appears to have been largely overlooked by the planners, in spite of what has happened elsewhere.

Such enterprises do not need much encouragement, but experience in the USA suggests that the venture capital industry plays a major role as a catalyst. At present in this respect France has to some extent trailed the rest of Europe –with the exception of the ever-present, government-funded ANVAR. Those US and UK venture capital firms that adventured into France once firmly remained in Paris, but today this has started to change, and it bodes well for Europe's Sun Belt. For example, L.I. Components is opening a sales office far from the madding crowds in Pamiers, between Toulouse and the Pyrénées.

32 The Logic of Knowledge Alliances in the Pharmaceutical Industry

Johan Roos, Professor of Strategy, Institute for Management Development (IMD), Lausanne

Georg von Krogh, Professor for Business Administration, University of St Gallen

Dirk Kleine, Research Assistant, University of St Gallen

This chapter deals with knowledge development through strategic alliances in the pharmaceutical industry. Our objective is twofold:

- to help managers by shedding more light on this important managerial issue; and
- by doing this, to illustrate a practical management tool for understanding and shaping argumentation.

Most pharmaceutical managers agree that in order to meet the increasing scale and pace of change across markets, products and technologies, the development and transfer of knowledge have become even more critical, both to the survival and further advancement of pharmaceutical companies. Many pharmaceutical companies have used alliances as alternatives to internal knowledge generation, even in collaboration with competitors. Some companies derive knowledge from their alliance partners, internalize it, and use it to improve their own competitive base. For example, a pharmaceutical company may form an alliance with a biotechnology company as a means of developing biotechnology-derived products. Other companies jointly develop knowledge in new fields to improve each partner's respective competitive advantage. This is the case when two pharmaceutical companies set up codevelopment deals for a compound. The pharmaceutical industry is full of many other examples of such alliances and many pharmaceutical managers subscribe to these kinds of cooperative strategies, as illustrated by the following statements:

- *CEO of Swiss pharmaceutical firm:* 'Creating strategic alliances is essential because it is dangerous for us to think that we know everything.'
- *President of US pharmaceutical firm:* 'Tearing down our corporate walls and exposing our organizational knowledge will be the key to surviving in this knowledge-driven business environment.'
- *Director of Strategic Planning, Norwegian pharmaceutical firm:* 'We are shifting to what I call the "Collaborative Organization" where former competitors develop strategic partnerships and unite knowledge and capabilities, not assets. We want to use ability for the purpose of mutual benefit, not control.'

Having analysed interview notes, reports, articles from trade magazines and company statements, a typical claim surfaces that is made by many pharmaceutical companies today:

It is critical to our future success to make use of alliances to increase the speed and efficiency of our knowledge development.

Look at this claim. Is it well reasoned and logical? Why? Why not? What are the building blocks supporting this claim? What are the unarticulated assumptions underlying this claim? These are the questions we will address in this chapter. To understand better the underlying logic of the claim stated above, we use the tool of argument mapping.

Argument mapping

Arguments can typically be broken down into three major components:

- the claim, which is the conclusion of an argument;
- the ground(s), which is the 'raw data' offered to support the claim;
- the warrant(s), that show how the ground(s) support the claim.

We have uncovered a simple chain of arguments that forms the overall claim of knowledge development through alliances. Most claims are the product of a series of preceding claims and can be the potential ground for still more claims in the future. This is a natural way to develop knowledge in companies; managers connect arguments over time in different discussions and in different written material. A group of pharmaceutical researchers, for instance, may hit on ways of developing a new drug by connecting and reacting to each other's arguments.

At times, we are so confident in a claim that we take it for granted and quickly think forward to its next implication. In one case a pharmaceutical manager stated that, 'The era of comfort and continuity in the pharmaceutical industry is gone.' As this claim is commonly accepted in the pharmaceutical industry, managers are quickly moving forward to its implications – discovering ways of exploring and identifying opportunities offered by the new marketplace. At other times, we may have serious doubts about a claim and want to review its foundations: the grounds and warrants on which it was built. For example, if a manager puts forward the claim that his

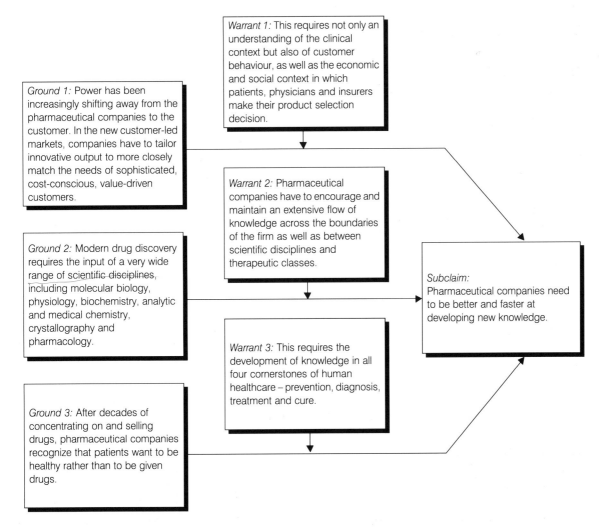

Figure 32.1 Partial argument

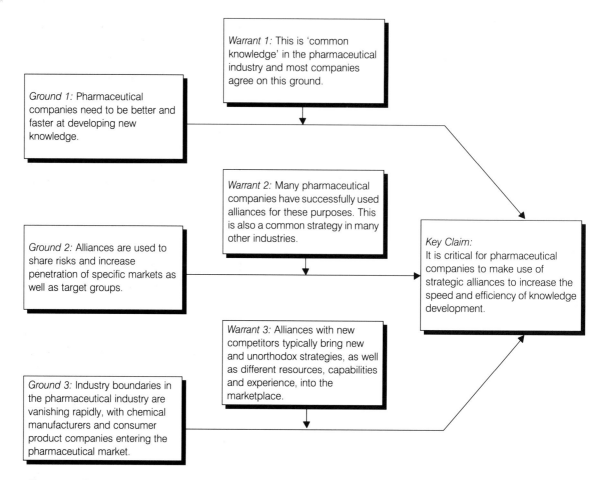

Figure 32.2 Full argument

very successful pharmaceutical company has drastically to change its current strategies to survive in the future, other employees will typically question and thereby retrace this claim to find out more about its underlying grounds.

Figures 32.1 and 32.2 serve as examples of how a chain of arguments can be traced back, using as an example the importance of knowledge development through strategic alliances in the pharmaceutical industry. Figure 32.1 provides an analysis of some grounds, linked through warrants, to the claim that pharmaceutical companies need to be better and faster at developing new knowledge. Figure 32.2 adopts this claim as ground in developing the full argument that 'It is critical for pharmaceutical companies to make use of strategic alliances to increase the speed and efficiency of knowledge development'.

The three grounds were selected on the basis of the frequency with which they are cited in consultancy reports and expert statements on the pharmaceutical industry. We next consider how these grounds might be linked to claim 1, by examining the hidden assumptions behind each statement. The above warrants illustrate the inferences which allow the grounds to act as rational support for claim 1.

Figure 32.2 puts the pieces together and demonstrates the effectiveness of the argument-mapping process. The subclaim becomes ground 1, and is linked by a warrant to the key claim of this article, that 'it is critical for pharmaceutical companies to make use of strategic alliances to increase the speed and efficiency of knowledge development'.

Examine the grounds listed in Figure 32.2 carefully. Do they establish the truth, correctness, or soundness of the key claim? If so, explore the warrants and check whether they connect the grounds and key claim in a relevant way.

Of course, there are many other grounds and warrants that can be used to support these claims regarding knowledge development and alliances. The ones we have selected are only examples. Thus we urge you to think about them and add any other grounds and warrants you believe to be relevant.

Implications

Our study points to three key implications for managers in the pharmaceutical industry

Knowledge development through alliances *is* an important managerial issue in pharmaceutical companies.

The focus of this chapter represents an increasingly important managerial issue in the pharmaceutical industry. We have presented some of the arguments that reveal the logic behind managers' use of alliances as a means to development knowledge and, therefore, to enhance long-term competitiveness of their companies. Each manager in the pharmaceutical industry needs to ensure that he or she fully understands how to develop, sustain and exit alliances. Hence, it is useful to consider questions such as the following:

- What are the conditions necessary to realize the development and transfer of knowledge in our alliances?
- How can firms adopt a faster and more active approach to managing knowledge transfer and development processes?
- What are the methods and procedures for managing our own knowledge?

Argument mapping *is* a managerial tool

Arguments are parts of conversations which, in turn, are the manifestation of knowledge development. From this perspective, management is a forum where language is used for the purposes of reasoning and deciding. It is natural that we should attempt to understand this particular use of language. Knowledge and language go hand in hand.

However, arguments are not always clear, nor logical. By looking behind claims and reflecting on what is seen as 'obvious', we can better understand what is or is not meant, and why some claims *can* be made. Each pharmaceutical manager needs to reflect on this individually, and study his or her own and others' argumentation on various organizational and strategic issues. By mapping a chain of arguments, you can follow a sequence of reasoning either forward or backward. You may discover the consequences and implications of an initial argument, or the concealed grounds on which the first argument relied. Either way, new insights may surface and previously unquestioned, yet unjustified, grounds may be detected!

There is also a need to reflect on arguments in group discussions, for example within project teams. A number of people engaged in a discussion may, in collaboration, pursue chains of arguments further than any one of them could have done while thinking alone. Typically, group discussions in an alliance setting provide the possibility of making new discoveries by pooling ideas and constructing arguments. Therefore, discussing and uncovering arguments in groups both within the organization and with external partners is a powerful means for developing new knowledge.

Argument mapping *can* be a strategic issue

By uncovering strategic arguments managers can be able to explore and develop effective arguments at various levels – be it industry, company, business unit, management team or individual level. It can be very insightful to reflect on questions like, 'What arguments exist on an industry level that have not yet been taken up by our company? How does the process of argument development occur within our top management team, ie what chains of arguments does a new claim create? Comparing your own argumentation processes with those of the competitors – what are the differences?.'

Furthermore, analysing the structure of arguments can also be applied to many other organizational and strategic issues. For example, we can think about the arguments used in consideration of organizational change, strategy development or core competencies in pharmaceutical companies. Exploring the logic behind these issues will also increase our understanding and knowledge. Following the advice of the philosopher Stephen Toulmin, we should reflect more on 'what sorts of arguments could be produced for the things we claim to know?'

Further reading

Huff, A. (1990) *Mapping Strategic Thought*, John Wiley.

Lorange, P. and Roos, J. (1992) *Strategic Alliances: Formation, Implementation and Evolution*, Blackwell.

von Krogh, G. and Roos, J. (1996) *Managing Knowledge in Cooperation and Competition*, Sage (forthcoming).

von Krogh, G. and Roos, J. (1995) *Organizational Epistemology*, Macmillan.

von Krogh, G. and Roos, J. (eds) (1994) 'Knowledge in Organizations, Knowledge Transfer and Cooperative Strategies', *International Business Review*, Special Issue, Vol. 3, No. 4.

Roos, J. and von Krogh, G. (1995) 'What you see depends on who you are', *IMD Perspectives*, No. 7.

33 Food Processing

Renato Pieri, Professor of Agricultural Economics, and

Daniele Rama, Assistant Professor of Agricultural Marketing, both at the Catholic University of the Sacred Heart, Piacenza, Italy

In all developed countries the agri-food system is characterized by major changes that are deeply modifying the nature of competition, the success factors and all types of vertical relationships between different sectors. All this implies an impact on the strategies and performances of companies and the welfare of consumers.

The new consumer

Socioeconomic and demographic changes, the increased revenue per capita, the evolution of taste, preferences and lifestyles are bringing about a growing demand for variety and better quality. In addition, the new consumer is more selective and has a clearer understanding of the product's features and their influence on health.

In North America, and more recently in some European countries, the widespread environmental consciousness and concern tend to influence food consumption. The reasons underlying this new perception are similar to the nutritional and dietary concerns. This new sensibility favours a demand for more natural products and simple packaging, and encourages consumers to pay more attention to technical processes and to stock-breeding methods.

The evolution of taste and preferences has caused a general decrease or slowing down of the demand for fats (above all animal), red meat (particularly beef), coffee and alcohol. For several market categories, consumption has shifted towards pro-

ducts having a higher fibre and carbohydrate content or those perceived as light and fresh, for example yoghurt and soft cheese. Much more attention is paid to the residues of pesticides in vegetable product and of hormones and antibiotics left by stock-farming.

The economy of safe food has become an interesting research area, with models and approaches aiming at monitoring the impact on food demand of the degree of risk perception in the mind of consumers or of varying the information consumers are given. Another theme of study is the relationship between sociodemographic variables, namely income and education level, and the capability of the consumer to collect and use this information. The results of this literature are important, both for the public authorities entitled to define rules, and for companies which are offered new opportunities for product differentiation, relying on the information regarding nutritional content and safety of food products.[1]

Empirical analysis has highlighted that food habits change according to current trends, although with different intensity, in all advanced countries.[2] This implies a much greater globalization of taste and preferences. However, this globalization does not bring about standardization and levelling out of food habits; on the contrary, among the strongest trends in the process of globalization is an increased demand for variety. More global consumers are able to express

Packaging problems?

Our first question: **Are you solving the right problem?**

Our first suggestion: **We help you formulate your packaging problem.**

Our second suggestion: **We offer you the solution of your packaging problem.**

Based on our knowledge of every stage in the packaging eco cycle, we offer research, consulting, testing and education in the packaging field.

Our speeialist areas: • Strategy & management • Packaging design • Packaging materials •
Packaging production • Testing & analysis •
The roles of packaging in the ecological system, the distribution systems and the society in general.

SWEDISH PACKAGING RESEARCH
INSTITUTE

Box 9, S-164 93 Kista, Sweden.
Tel: +46 8 752 57 00 Fax: +46 8 751 38 89

PACKFORSK– Swedish Packaging Research Institute

The main objective of Packforsk is to be an attractive partner to all levels within the packaging field, be it in research, consulting, testing or education.

Based on detailed knowledge of all elements of the packaging ecocycle - from raw materials to the packaging in use - Packforsk can offer a high level of expertise.

The fundamental research activities are financed partly by the Swedish government, partly by the Packforsk Foundation. The Foundation represents about 250 companies and organisations, mainly in the Nordic countries.

Special research projects are supported by various industrial and commercial groups within the Foundation. The Institute is also funded by the EU Commission and other funds.

Packforsk also offers consultancy services, covering the entire packaging field. Training and educational courses up to doctor's degree are other activities of importance to raise the competitive edge of the packaging industry and its customers.

A research institute of Packforsks size (50 persons) will, however, not be able to compete with the research sources multinational companies have to put up within their specific segment to secure competitiveness. The specific competence of Packforsk is instead to be the important "bridge" in border areas between different stages in the packaging ecocycle.

All research and technical people at Packforsk are specialized in at least one of six areas of expertise:

Strategy and management
Packaging is playing an increasingly important strategic role for companies in more and more branches of the industry. The concept is to integrate packaging in the overall activities of the companies to support the business development of the companies.

The Business Intelligence unit is able to find all kinds of international information related to packaging materials and packaging via databases of its own or other international databases. And as a member of such international organizations as IAPRI (The International Association of Packaging Research Institutes) Packforsk is part in strong international networks and strategic alliances with other institutes.

Packaging design
A high overall utilization of resources requires that all kinds of products reach the end-users fit for use. This will make optimum use of resources available and minimize the costs involved.

Packforsk is able to provide appropriate knowledge about the overall requirements related to the total packaging chain in order to achieve attractive, efficient packages with a minimum use of resources.

Packaging materials
The mechanical, physical and chemical characteristics of the packaging materials used are of major importance to the protective functions of packagings. Today's demand for increased recycling adds another important dimensions when selected materials.

The activities in this area aim at assessing the protective function of selected packaging materials and their suitability for different applications. Special attention is given packagings for food and medical products.

Packaging production
Knowledge of product properties in terms of resistance is vital when selecting packagings and deciding on their design.

The studies of the requirements to be used by the packaging materials in packaging production, packing and end use are devoted partly to studies of productivity, partly to the quality of the converted material and the filled packaging.

Testing and analysis
Testing to establish the ability of packagings to withstand various transportation and environmental conditions are two major areas of activity at Packforsk.

By investigating in laboratory how well products and packagings withstand transportation, handling and storage under different conditions and how well the products then function in their end user environments customers are offered cheaper and much easier testing with a high reliability than testing in real environments.

The roles of packaging
Packagings are often seen as being a decisive factor in the economics of distribution. Any study of the different roles packagings play should take on overall view in which both internal and external environmental aspects are given full consideration.

It is therefore important to establish between on one hand distribution requirements, environmental considerations and the demands of society as a whole and on the other hand packaging structural design, dimensions and choice of materials.

The advantages of membership
The consulting and educational activities are of course open to all companies. A membership in the Packforsk Foundation offers, however, many advantages, these being to most important:

The chance to influence and actively participate in research projects.

First-hand information about the results of the research and the possibility of fast implementation of new findings at the own company.

Access to the "future vision" which Packforsk's strategic committee draws up every year.

Continuous information about technological and market developments through the Business Intelligence Service.

The opportunity to make use of customised service, via your own contact person at Packforsk. Top priority and discounted fees for consultancy, testing, training courses, and much more.

To get detailed information about our activities and membership etc, please contact us:

Packforsk, tel +46 8 752 57 00, fax +46 8 751 38 89

Institute for Animal Health

Infectious diseases of farm animals cost the farming community around 17% of turnover even in a good year. Thus the cost to the UK is around £1.5 bilion per year. If there were to be an outbreak of foot-and-mouth disease in the European Union then the costs would at least double in the affected areas.

The Institute for Animal Health is the largest research organisation in the UK carrying out research on the infectious diseases of farm animals. The Institute is sponsored by the Biotechnology and Biological Sciences Research Council. It employs around 550 staff. The diseases in its portfolio include not only those normally found in the UK but also several of major economic importance that could spread to the country such as foot-and-mouth disease and African swine fever.

At the IAH disease is fought through strategic research aimed at creating new control methods. Only through a thorough understanding of the pathogen and its interaction with the host can new, accurate diagnostic tests and control methods be developed. Necessarily the facilities and resources are considerable, as one would expect of an internationally renowned institute:

- Laboratory and animal accommodation for containing dangerous (statutory) infections
- animals of known genetic and health status
- gnotobiotic facilities
- production facilities for transgenic mice and embryo manipulation
- surgical facilities
- a wide range of strains of pathogens
- specialist biological databases
- world reference laboratories for major infections of major economic importance
- advanced biomathematical modelling capabilities

The research has two, interlinked thrusts –

- understanding **immunological mechanisms** in order to improve vaccines and immune therapies
- developing **non-immune strategies,** such as utilising disease resistance genes, inhibiting the replication of viral pathogens and exploiting biomathematics and epidemiology.

The Institute is structured to offer an *integrated, multidisciplinary* and *flexible* approach to disease research, ranging from the molecule to the gene, the cell to the whole organism and on to populations of animals.

Despite the unpredictability of disease change, the Institute's *flexibility* has allowed an immediate, taking up

---

The IAH portfolio

African horse sickness
African swine fever
Avian infectious bronchitis
Bluetongue
Bovine spongiform encephalopathy
Bovine virus diarrhoea
Coccidiosis
Encephalomyocarditis
Foot-and-mouth disease
Fowl pox
Infectious bursal disease
Lumpy skin disease
Marek's disease
Mastitis
Peste des petits ruminants
Respiratory syncytial virus infection
Rinderpest
Salmonella
Scrapie
Swine vesicular disease
Theileriosis
Transmissible gastroenteritis
Turkey rhinotracheitis

---

of new problems such as BSE or salmonellas in eggs.

IAH seeks to maximise the value of its resources through **collaborations** which build on the complementarity of the partners. IAH has on-going collaborations with 18 universities in the UK, the most numerous being with Oxford, Reading, Bristol and Edinburgh. The Institute is also collaborating with over 30 other countries.

It is host to two major pharmaceutical companies and to the Edward Jenner Institute for Vaccine Research.

Current IAH collaborations		
UK Universities	Europe	Beyond Europe
Aberdeen	Austria	Argentina
Belfast	Belgium	Australia
Bristol	Commonwealth of	Brazil
Cambridge	Independent States	Canada
Dundee	Denmark	Chile
Edinburgh	Finland	French Guinea
Glasgow	France	India
Kent	Germany	Israel
Leicester	Greece	Ivory Coast
Liverpool	Netherlands	Japan
London	Poland	Kenya
Nottingham	Portugal	Mexico
Oxford	Spain	Morocco
Reading	Serbia	Saudi Arabia
St Andrews	Sweden	United States of
Stratyclyde	Switzerland	America
Warwick		Zimbabwe
York		

Its **training programmes** equip people from around the world to respond to the ever-present scourge of disease. It has a vigorous **PhD programme.** Advertisements giving details of PhD opportunities are published early in the New Year. Many members of staff hold honorary university appointments and contribute by lecturing or examining. The Institute is an *Associated Institution* of the Universities of Reading and Bristol.

The IAH is a **major international centre for the diagnosis and control of disease.** It is responsible not only to MAFF but also to the EU, OIE and FAO for diagnosing and maintaining surveillance for the major diseases that threaten the EU, including foot-and-mouth disease.

The Institute maintains a **Contracts Group** which has an international reputation for its commercial research and its service to customers. The Group carries out trials on vaccines, antibiotics, pharmaceutical compounds, disinfectants and nutritional products to test efficacy, safety and tolerance. Batch testing of vaccines for potency and interference of maternal antibodies with vaccine efficacy are also within the Group's competence.

Trials are fully documented at each stage and once completed the client receives a report which can be used as part of the registration documentation for new products. The Group keeps abreast of current biological and pharmaceutical registration requirements to ensure its procedures and protocols are in line with specifications.

Further information is available from the Director, Professor F J Bourne.

INSTITUTE FOR ANIMAL HEALTH
Compton, Newbury,
Berks, RG20 7NN
Tel: +44 (0)1635-578411
Fax: +44 (0)1635-577237

preferences not only concerning their traditional and local products, but also products and diets belonging to other regions or ethnic groups. This process of dispersal of habits and preferences, which in previous decades was characteristic of inter-regional normalization within each country, is currently operating more and more at an international level, because of greater mobility in jobs, study and tourism.

The new consumer is more informed and more conscious about price and the price–quality ratio, and is less reliant on brands. This is partly due to the recent recession and to price competition in the retail sector.

The agri-food system

In all advanced countries, the agri-food system is of a considerable size in terms of production, added value and employment.[3]

Obviously, the system's internal composition in each country changes over time. The relative importance of farming decreases; agricultural firms tend to become like manufacturing industries, receiving input from the market and transforming it into agricultural raw materials, the market for which is now international. In addition farms tend to increase in average size as well as their degree of product specialization. Vertical disintegration choices redefine the boundaries of farms. This implies that farms are completely open to the market and interdependent with other sectors.

On the other hand, the central role of food industries is getting stronger, particularly for those industries producing the most elaborate goods. The size of companies is increasing as well as the concentration in distribution, which tends to play a strategic role in the agri-food system and to influence the strategies adopted by the other parties in the system.

Together with these changes two aspects acquire importance. The first is the growing interdependence of markets and the internationalization of firms, which implies a greater opening up of national systems. This means that greater opportunities for export on one side, and the competitive pressure of imports on the other, contribute to define scenarios that are deeply different from those of more recent years where the agri-food systems were basically

closed. To this extent, policies and purchasing strategies adopted by corporate and voluntary large-scale retailing chains have played a decisive role.

The second aspect deriving from the growing internal complexity of the system and from the evolution of demand concerns the opportunities and requirements of cooperation and vertical coordination among companies belonging to different segments of the system. Vertical relationships, their nature and evolution, are growing in importance in defining competitive environments where agribusiness companies operate.

Forms of vertical coordination are becoming increasingly popular, where arrangements more complex than the simple sale contract have been found to be more effective in providing farmers with the necessary information, while offering the processors greater guarantees of quality in farm products.[4]

Deep changes are also taking place in the vertical relationships between food industries and retailers. As the concentration of retailing is increasing, the size and the purchasing power of the firms in this sector are growing as well. These companies, thanks to modern computer technology, have become the chosen place for collecting crucial information on the choices and behaviour of the end consumer.

The change in vertical relationships at this point in the agri-food chain encourages firms to intensify non-price strategies, launch new products and strengthen their brand policies. The higher fixed costs of applying such strategies and capabilities, mainly in the marketing area, mean there is a requirement to operate in economic environments where this type of competition intensifies, favour the major companies and cause increasing concentration.

Therefore the opportunities for small firms decrease, although the spread of own-brand products bearing the brand name of the retailer could be a counter-trend, in recreating or preserving some space in the market for small- to medium-size firms that produce for large retailers.[5]

Technological changes

Product and process innovations often concern both the entire agri-food industry and each of its stages. The whole system is characterized by greater technological opportunities, which allow any kind of firm to introduce innovations in line with variety and with concerns about health expressed by the new consumer.

In the food industry technological changes have been fostered by a remarkable flow of process and product innovation: ultra-filtering, extrusion, continuous production lines, controlled atmosphere, new packaging, controlled fermentation. These developments make several technical opportunities available to the food industry, which enjoys a situation of technological redundancy. That is to say, the availability of basic knowledge does not constrain product innovation. This is a specific feature of the food industry, and depends both on the relevance of opportunities offered by nutritional science and the incremental nature of product innovation in this industry.

Consumers accept innovation only if it is incremental, as in this way it does not bring about radical changes in their dietary habits. As the amount of basic knowledge needed to accomplish incremental innovation is obviously lower than the knowledge necessary to launch completely new products, a particularly favourable relationship between the availability of technological opportunities and the input of basic knowledge necessary to launch new products is a specific feature of the food industry.[6]

This situation seems destined to continue. In fact, because of the evolution of demand, consumers are more willing to pay for innovative products, while firms are encouraged to react to pressures and to the higher purchasing power of retailers by intensifying their innovation strategies.

The main product and process innovations come from the spread of biotechnology and computer technologies, able fully to meet the demand of the new consumer.

Biotechnology includes all those techniques using living organisms to make new products or to modify existing ones, in order to improve plants or animals or to develop specific micro-organisms. These technologies are used in farming in order to obtain more productive animals and plants more resistant to parasites, therefore healthier for the consumer and with a lower impact on the environment. In other words, biotechnology allows the creation of animal or vegetable products with the desired features: less fat in pork meat, lower cholesterol content in red meat and in eggs, maize adequate for the breeding of certain animal species or for some specific industrial purposes, and so on. This innova-

tion has a remarkable impact on the social and economic situation; in some instances, unfair competition is reported as a consequence of an incorrect manipulation of information.[7]

Electronically controlled production processes cause a reduction in error margins and in production costs by saving energy, with a more effective use of production factors; this gain in effectiveness allows for the reduction of pollution in farming and for reducing the residue content in food.

The need for information is becoming a crucial requirement for those firms operating in the farm and food sector. Therefore, it is easy to understand the importance of market information in deciding the success of companies, of their production plans and of their investments. However, all this depends on the reliability, effectiveness and timeliness of market information.

Internationalization of markets and companies

We have already highlighted the tendency of national farm and food systems to open up to international markets. In farming, internationalization coincides with inputs from international markets – machines, pharmaceutical products, genetic material, biotechnology – and with a greater importance of international trade for local production. This process is favoured by the reduction of the economic distance between different markets, thanks to improvements in preservation techniques and transportation of farming raw materials and food products on one hand, and in information processing on the other.

As a result, also in the primary sector, international markets frequently influence decisions concerning production and the results obtained by firms. Particularly within a framework of growing interdependence of markets, the uncertainties are getting stronger due to heavy North–South imbalances and the impact of social and economic changes taking place in the Eastern and Central European countries and in some Asian countries.

A crucial contribution to the internationalization of the agri-food industry comes from the multi-nationalization of food companies, exemplified by the setting up of free trade areas – European Union, EFTA, NAFTA, MERCOSUR, ASEAN, PBEC, PECC, APEC, AAEC – and by the intense activity in cross-border mergers and acquisitions; by the growing levels of interdependence, both commercial and productive; and by the spread of strategic alliances

33

and partnerships. Food companies have been active for a long time in promoting internationalization strategies. For many countries, sales abroad are explained by overseas investment and, consequently, by the growth of multinationalization processes rather than the export of food products.[8]

The internationalization process, made possible by growing market segmentation and the globalization of taste and preferences, is encouraged by the importance acquired by non-price competitive strategies, reflected by increasing marketing and R&D costs. The globalization of taste and preferences and the process of market segmentation, owing to the demand for variety and the reduction in economic and cultural differences, entail the existence of common market segments in more countries and an even more international demand. Therefore, a growing number of products can be sold in several national markets through the same brand and marketing strategies, or by modifying them slightly in order to adjust to the local taste.

Integration between segmentation and globalization means that, if a firm has a product able successfully to meet the demands of a certain market segment in a given country, it is also able to detect and satisfy the needs of the same segment in other countries. This favours the spread of global brands, offering the same products in more countries, the adjustment of some external features – as for example design and packaging – to the local taste and preferences not carrying any remarkable increase in costs.

The main factor determining internationalization strategies is the possibility for companies to exploit their knowledge and learning in marketing and R&D functions. These intangible assets constitute a competitive advantage in internationalization and geographical diversification of overseas investments. The same factors that favour growth

and diversification determine internationalization strategies.

Internationalization of farm and food systems is also promoted by the adoption of internationalization strategies by firms in the retail sector. These companies' cross-border investments are still less relevant than investments by the food industries, but the main British, French and German chains report an upward trend.

An important consequence of these processes is the even larger spatial horizon of retail companies' purchasing policies – this is a factor which tends to strengthen and make competition even more international.

End notes

1   J A Caswell, *Economics of Food Safety*, Elsevier, New York, 1991.

2   J M Connor, 'North America as a Precursor of Changes in Western European Food-Purchasing Patterns', *European Review of Agricultural Economics*, n. 2, 1994.

3   B Traill, *Prospects for the European Food System*, Elsevier, London, 1991.

4   A Barkema, 'Reaching Consumers in the Twenty-first Century: The Short Way Around the Barn', *American Journal of Agricultural Economics*, n. 5, 1990.

5   D Hugues (ed.), *Breaking with Tradition*, Wye College Press, Wye, Ashford (Kent), 1994.

6   G Galizzi and L Venturini (eds), *Economics of Innovation: The Case of Food Industry*, Physica-Verlag, Heidelberg (forthcoming).

7   G E Gaull and R A Goldberg (eds), *New Technologies and the Future of Food and Nutrition*, John Wiley and Sons Inc., New York, 1991; G Galizzi and D Rama, 'Le biotecnologie in agricoltura', in E Sgreccia and V Mele (eds), *Ingegneria genetica e biotecnologie nel futuro dell'uomo*, Vita e Pensiero, Milano, 1992.

8   R Green, 'Les determinants de la restructuration des grands groupes agro-alimentaires au niveau mondial', in Cahiers de l'ISMEA – Economie et Sociétés, *Les stratégies agro-industrielles*, P.U.G., Grenoble, 1989.

PART

Developing Business in the Single Market

RESEARCH SOLUTIONS CONSULTANCY

Research Solutions Consultancy specialises in bringing an innovative and action-oriented approach to research-based consultancy. Projects are commissioned by clients needing help to tackle planning and decision-making on

- **market entry strategies**
- **product and market strategies**
- **new product development**
- **corporate acquisitions**
- **promotional strategies and marcoms performance testing**
- **image management**
- **customer care and quality initiatives**

We have experience of a wide range of markets from 'hi-tec' to 'no tec', though the majority of our clients sell in the business-to-business arena.

We employ techniques such as focus groups; executive interviewing; telephone interviewing; structured trade-off methodologies; statistical data analysis; and market modelling.

Approximately 80% of our projects are international in scope, with the focus on Western Europe, Eastern Europe and Asia-Pacific countries. We are also able to offer high quality research and consultancy in the North American and South American markets through our close association with the Chicago-based Richmark Group.

For more information, call Angela Fox on 0171-498 1452

RS
Research
• Solutions •
consultancy

Research Solutions Consultancy, 8 Priory House, 8 Battersea Park Road, London SW8 4BH
Tel: 0171-498 1452 Fax: 0171-498 1385 Email: 100640.747@compuserve.com

---

Market knowledge – the key to success

You want to take advantage of opportunities in Europe, but how **exactly** should you set about it? How do you match success in your home market with success elsewhere? You cannot attack all the markets at once, so which should you prioritise?

If you are planning to expand into new markets, or further consolidate existing export performance, you will be asking yourself just these sorts of questions.

To decide whether to enter or expand in a market you need **information**, such as:
- the size and structure of the market
- who the competition are, and where their strengths and weaknesses lie
- how distribution channels are structured
- who the customers are and how to make your product appeal to them

You may have a great product, but that is not enough. Your success in the home market has also been built on your **knowledge** of that market.

You know who the customers are, who your competitors are, and how to distribute your products. You know how competitive the market is, and what price you should be charging. You understand why your product is a success – what your customers like about it, what makes it different from your competitors' products. You know how to promote these benefits to new customers and generate more sales. And you know what aftersales service your customers need to keep them coming back.

All these things will be different in new markets, and market research will tell you how. Really good research from a consultancy will get you the information you need **quickly,** and help you act on it **effectively.**

The cost of not understanding these markets can be great. Your product specification might be a winner at home, but wrong for the export customer. Buyers in the UK might find your advertising witty, but it could be considered insulting in other markets. Your distributors at home might demand large discounts, but lower margins may be acceptable elsewhere.

Even when your company has established itself in Europe, you need information to protect that success. Others may try to enter the market, and the competitive situation may change. Customers may demand new products or better service. Again, market research is the key. Customer satisfaction research and image tracking studies provide the tools to help you see these changes and allow you to respond before your competitors do.

To get more information on how market research can put you ahead and keep you ahead in Europe, call Angela Fox at Research Solutions Consultancy on (+44) 0171 498 1452

Research Solutions Consultancy
8 Priory House,
8 Battersea Park Road
London SW8 4BH
Tel: 0171-498 1452
Fax: 0171-498 1385
Email: 100640.747@compuserve.com

Business Data for European Planning

34

Daniel Byk, Head of Division A2, Eurostat

The arrival of the Single European Market brought greater opportunities for European business people but also required business planning of a different kind. The increase in the number of readily accessible markets means that making the choice of where to operate and where to sell is more important than ever before. This pan-European nature of modern business makes it essential that the structures, expectations and nature of foreign markets are as well understood as one's home market.

While most businesses have a sound knowledge of their own markets, they need to be able to see how alternative possibilities compare. Making correct decisions requires access to information resources that can be quickly understood and easily used to start the planning process. It is essential that the information is relevant to all the pan-European possibilities and can be accurately compared between different countries and even between regions.

Raw information is readily available from the National Statistical Institute of the country, or countries, in question. However, this information has always been produced by different methodologies and based on different assumptions in each country; for examples, the definition of unemployment varies according to the country where the figures are generated. For truly comparable statistical data, the best source is the official European source – Eurostat, the Statistical Office of the European Communities.

Eurostat was not created as a service to busi-

nesses but to provide the European Union with a high quality statistical information service to act as a sound base for the decision-making process. The advantage for industry and business is that this service and its materials are available for general use. Eurostat harmonizes the information that is provided by the various national statistical organizations, meaning that it is one source for 15 countries and that its data are comparable from region to region, from country to country and – as far as possible – from industry to industry.

Data collected by Eurostat are available in a number of formats including publications, electronic products and specific enquiry services. Among the topics covered are:

- economy and finance;
- energy and industry;
- agriculture, forestry and fisheries;
- distributive trades, services and transport;
- population and social conditions;
- external trade;
- environment.

Within each of these categories there is a wealth of information, offered at different levels to suit different types of enquiry. While the use of Eurostat data will rarely be sufficient to make that all-important final business decision, it is usually an excellent starting point for the investigation process.

Demonstrations of the planning power of pan-European data are regularly provided to businesses

EXPORT INTELLIGENCE
PRELINK LIMITED

Right now, somebody, somewhere, has business for you.
...WE KNOW WHO

■ **Export Intelligence** can boost your export sales. We connect UK exporters to overseas buyers and markets.

■ Your latest export sales leads could come from anywhere in the world. They could come at any moment. And when they do, we will know.

■ Export Intelligence catalogues the most recent overseas leads and you can choose to receive bulletins that are specific to your business from over 32 product sectors.

■ Export Intelligence involves a unique network of 600 experts in over 200 countries and territories, working round the clock.

■ Only Export Intelligence delivers the overseas leads that are a precise match for your needs. *Can you afford to be without it?*

Call us now on:

0181 900 1313
(fax: 0181 900 1268)

Or write to us at:

Sales Department, *Prelink Limited*, Export House, Wembley Hill Road, Wembley, Middlesex HA9 8BR.

FREE Export Trade Bulletin to all enquirers

A MERCURY ENTERPRISE

EBH/ANL/96

when Eurostat visits trade exhibitions across Europe. These are typical examples of the enquiries successfully handled by use of the Eurostat CD, a collection from the various databases held by Eurostat:

■ A manufacturer of maintenance equipment for air conditioning units was interested to see what the possibilities might be in the hotel trade; an analysis of hotels of four star rating and more – later followed by analysis of hotels with 200 beds or more – drew a picture across France, Italy, Spain, Portugal and Greece which indicated clearly where the greatest potential was to be found.

■ A manufacturer of mirrors and other decorative glassware was interested in opening a new factory; the Eurostat CD was able to identify, from a number of specified locations, those which offered the best opportunities in terms of labour rates and employment possibilities.

The Eurostat CD is just one collection of data from the major databases held by Eurostat, offering access to European industrial and economic statistics. 'New Cronos' contains over 75 million pieces of data, covering every sector of the economy. The informa-

Export Intelligence in a Changing World

Many exporters will be familiar with Export Intelligence as the DTI service set up over 20 years ago to process export sales leads gathered in British embassies and other overseas posts for the benefit of British companies. Since the wholly owned Mercury subsidiary Prelink Limited took over and then retained the contract for providing Export Intelligence in the late '80s, both the service itself and the way it is marketed have been subject to change with substantial investments in technology and much enhanced information.

Independent research indicates that Export Intelligence generates significant additional business for UK exporters. This was estimated at some £400 million in 1993, including new and ongoing business resulting from Export Intelligence notices and more than doubled last year at £946 million. Export Intelligence customers are exceptionally diverse ranging from small companies that are predominantly exporters to major corporations and companies of all sizes, dipping their toes in the water for the first time.

At the present time Prelink is actively marketing partnership arrangements with Business Links and other organisations with incentives when such bodies encourage their members to become Prelink customers and new facilities for low frequency users. This means that newcomers to exporting and companies that previously used the service at second hand via their membership of trade associations or chambers of commerce can try low-cost entry and/or a much more timely service than was possible before.

The raw information that Prelink processes and distributes is gathered by commercial officers in over 200 British posts around the world. It includes sales leads given by overseas companies keen to buy British, details of overseas agents and distributors wanting to make new contacts, market trends, information about major pro-jects, and long and short dated calls to tender.

Historically the quality of information has varied according to local circumstances and business practices. However Prelink has been phoning in new guidelines on what is required over the last year with the result that the depth and consistency of intelligence received is being steadily upgraded to match current and future needs of exporters.

Customers began to see the benefits of this new quality control earlier in 1995 but it will be another six to nine months before the process is complete and the benefits have filtered through to the entire customer base of nearly 3,000 companies and business organisations.

Prelink receives information about 40,000 export opportunities each year, arriving by fax at a rate of up to 200 per working day. The processing they

undergo is a matter of data inputting and matching against predefined product/service codes. Coding is a highly specialised task carried out by a team of 10 coders using specially developed software. The system include multi-level prioritisation of leads for more sensitive turnround and a unique integrated code search facility to ensure correct and consistent matching of information with customers' requirements.

Each company that joins Export Intelligence has a "profile" prepared which details the products and services offered against the codes and combines this information with the countries of interest and the types of intelligence wanted – for instance sales leads, agents and distributors seeking products to market, aid projects, tenders etc. The annual for fee ranges upwards from £250 plus VAT according to the diversity of products, types of information required and world regions of interest.

The result is that 500,000 Export Intelligence notices are distributed by fax and mail to Prelink's customers each year. As the market research suggests, the leads are extremely productive, however the diligence with which customer companies follow up the leads is as much a key to success as Prelink's ongoing process of upgrading the quality of leads.

Leads generally include information on how to respond whether in English or another language and often they advise a rapid faxed response to register interest and then a follow up with product specifications, price details and so forth.

The feedback received via British posts and from individual customers shows companies use the information to open up new markets and to build business in areas they have identified as being of prime importance.

Recent success stories include a wallpaper distributor delighted with new opportunities in Lithuania and eastern Europe generally, a business stationery company opening up new markets in the Caribbean to replace sales in Africa and numerous examples of engineering companies succeeding everywhere from Western Europe to Japan and the USA.

For further information please contact
Trevor Fromant, General Manager,
Prelink Limited
Tel 0181-900 1313

tion is mainly for the European member states but it also covers Japan, the USA and other Union trade partners. 'Comext' contains the statistics on trade between the member states and on their trade with over 300 non-member countries.

The variety of printed products available offers everything from snapshots of particular areas and country groupings through to full pan-European analysis. 'Portrait of the Regions', for instance, covers the regions of the European Union, providing maps, summaries and social breakdowns among the information. It is an excellent starting point for any business person looking to understand the complexity of the European market.

Socioeconomic trends and data are also covered within the Eurostat remit, offering insights into living conditions, wage scales and relative regional purchasing power. Much of this information is brought together in 'A Social Portrait of Europe' in which the statistical tables are illustrated by coloured graphics and short texts.

Despite the range and scale of this information service, it can be accessed easily through a local contact. A sales agent in each member state can order publications and electronic products – the Eurostat information desks have detail of the local contact. Eurostat also provides a data sales service. This service is available from the Information Office in Luxembourg and from the Data Shop in Brussels, which can be contacted for simple queries about features of Europe such as how many doctors there are in Europe or how much steel was produced in a given period.

The services offered by Eurostat will suit the needs of many business and industry planners in Europe. They offer the ability to make realistic comparisons across Europe and to make informed decisions based on accurate data. The opportunities offered by the Single Market are very real, although lack of information may make them seem distant. Using the right business planning data should bring those opportunities much closer.

Eurostat Information Office	Eurostat Data Shop
Batiment Jean Monnet	130 Rue de la Loi
L-Luxembourg	B-1049 Brussels
Tel: +352 4301 34567	Tel: +32 2 299 66 66
Fax: +352 43 64 04	Fax: +32 2 295 01 25

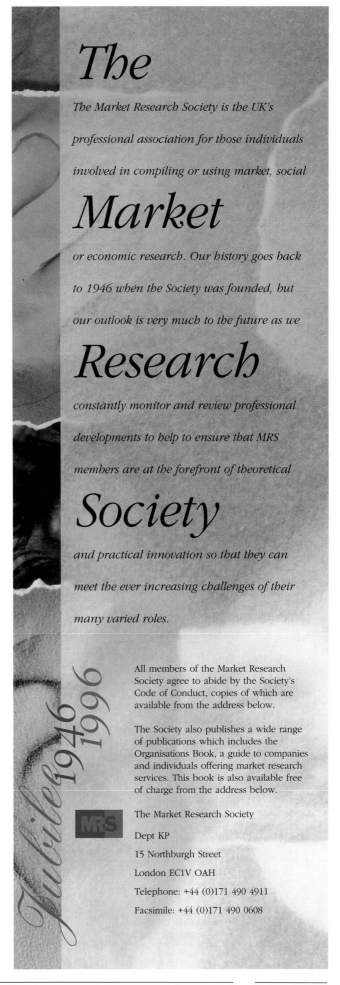

The

The Market Research Society is the UK's

professional association for those individuals

involved in compiling or using market, social

Market

or economic research. Our history goes back

to 1946 when the Society was founded, but

our outlook is very much to the future as we

Research

constantly monitor and review professional

developments to help to ensure that MRS

members are at the forefront of theoretical

Society

and practical innovation so that they can

meet the ever increasing challenges of their

many varied roles.

All members of the Market Research Society agree to abide by the Society's Code of Conduct, copies of which are available from the address below.

The Society also publishes a wide range of publications which includes the Organisations Book, a guide to companies and individuals offering market research services. This book is also available free of charge from the address below.

The Market Research Society

Dept KP

15 Northburgh Street

London EC1V OAH

Telephone: +44 (0)171 490 4911

Facsimile: +44 (0)171 490 0608

europe **INFORMATION** service

The inside track on Europe

Europe Information Service (EIS) is Brussels' leading publisher specialised in European Community affairs.

EIS collects, analyses and publishes key information on the initiatives of the European Union.

EIS newsletters and reports monitor all major issues and developments in European legislation by providing a detailed coverage of projects, decisions and regulations emanating from European Institutions.

flagship bi-weekly: ❑ *european report**

periodical publications:

❑ *europe environment**
❑ *agri service international*
❑ *tech-europe**
❑ *euro-east**
*available online and on CD-ROM

❑ *europe energy**
❑ *agri-industry europe**
❑ *european social policy**
❑ *monthly report on europe*

❑ *transport europe**
❑ *multinational service**
❑ *europe intelligence*
❑ *european insight*

latest reports published:

❑ *Convention on Insolvency Law*
❑ *Eurpean Union activities on the environment - 1995*
❑ *European social policy for business*

For more information, please contact Lucyna Gutman-Grauer, Marketing Manager
Europe Information Service s.a. rue de Genève 6 B-1140 Bruxelles Belgium Phone 32 2 + 242 60 20 Fax 32 2 + 242 95 49

Understand Europe

M ore than ever, Europe continues to occupy centre stage in the news arena. Whether in the negative sense at times: no opportunity is lost to criticise, for example, the inability of the European Union to resolve or intervene positively in the major conflicts taking place both in Europe and in the rest of the world: the former Yugoslavia, Africa, the Middle East, or to show itself closer to the citizen who is often at a loss to understand its action. Or in a positive sense: the European Union has, after all, made it possible for the countries of Europe to live through an unprecedented era of peace for the first time in centuries. It has achieved a true customs union, established a "common market", the culmination of an extensive series of measures to harmonise or simplify rule which had been hitherto national prerogatives (80% of national legislation is today of European Union origin). And, in particular today by the questions it is raising: having just completed the accession of three new Member States all eyes are now on the countries of Central and Eastern Europe and several smaller Mediterranean states, all hoping for relatively rapid membership. The Union is currently considering a root and branch reform of some of its operating procedures during the Intergovernmental Conference in 1996. Finally, it is making progress towards one of the objectives foreseen at the time of its creation: an Economic and Monetary Union with a single currency.

Industrialist, politician, lobbyist, or simple citizen, everyone is concerned by the development of the European movement, and even if progress seems at times to be painfully slow, will continue to be so. If information truly is power, the need to have ready access to extensive and reliable sources concerning the activities of the European Union or other European organisations, has become a strategic necessity: whether to understand a failure, or to be aware of a new Directive in the works.

By Eric Van Puyvedle
Editor in Chief
Europe Information Service

For harmonized statistics which are reliable and comparable...

Our task is to provide the European Union with a high-quality statistical information service

Information Office
Jean Monnet Building B3/89
L- 2920 Luxembourg
Tel. (352) 4301 34567
Fax (352) 43 64 04

Data-Shop
Rue de la Loi 130
B-1049 Brussels
Tel. (32-2) 299 66 66
Fax (32-2) 295 01 25

The shortest distance between you and successful INNOVATION

The European Commission's commitment to research, technology and development is important to you whatever your business. CORDIS can help you access the work being done across Europe and beyond. Whether you're looking for information on what is happening, partners and funding for your own research, or an opportunity to participate in the Europe-wide drive to a bright new future, you should be looking at CORDIS.

CORDIS is the Community Research and Development Information Service. It is both an information source and an electronic meeting place. It is available to you on-line, free of charge, or in CD ROM format.

Contact CORDIS Customer Service for an information pack and discover the shortest route between your business and the innovation that will help secure your future.

CORDIS Customer Service, c/o ECHO, BP 2373, L-2373, Luxembourg.

Tel +352 3498 1240 Fax +352 3498 1248

E-MAIL HELPDESK@cordis.lu

CORDIS

Community R&D Information Service

Proven Experience in Managing Multinational Projects

BPRI's projects are co-ordinated from the UK and run with the help of its network of associates and local contacts, where required. Countries covered include:

- United Kingdom
- Europe: Austria, Belgium, Denmark, Finland, France, Germany, Greece, Ireland, Italy, Luxembourg, Netherlands, Norway, Portugal, Spain, Sweden, Switzerland
- United States
- Far East: Hong Kong, Japan, Malaysia, Singapore, Taiwan, Thailand
- Other: Algeria, Australia, Brazil, Canada, Colombia, Mexico, Nigeria, Saudi Arabia, Turkey, Venezuela

Recent research projects include:

- Corporate & Strategic Planning
- Market Entry Studies
- Identification of Partners and Acquisition Studies
- International Positioning
- International Product Launches
- Decision Making in Multinationals
- Global Account Development
- Multinational Performance Monitoring
- International Communications
- International Human Resource Strategies

For further information about BPRI please contact: Caroline Willcocks, Client Services Director, BPRI, Waterloo Court,

International Research-Based Business and Marketing Consultancy

BPRI has four divisions:

- Corporate & Strategic

  Programmes to enhance corporate image, identity, positioning and communications and facilitate business unit development and organisational change
- Marketing & Market Research

  Planning studies involving demand forests, segmentation, purchasing and usage behaviour and investigation of all elements of the marketing mix. Specialising in the following market sectors:
  - Business, consumer and professional services
  - City and financial markets
  - Industrial and office products
  - Information technology
- Performance Monitoring and Service Improvement

  Programmes to retain and leverage the customer base by determining customer expectations and satisfaction level, developing servicing standards, monitoring performance, benchmarking and measuring employee effectiveness
- Opinion Leader Panels

  BPRI runs a number of panels. The Political Opinion Panel (POP) comprises over 100 British MPS and the City Opinion Panel (COP) is made up of 'leading luminaries' in the City. BPRI is intending to re-launch the European Political Opinion Panel (EPOP) consisting of MEPs in the autumn.

  For further information about BPRI please contact: Caroline Willcocks, Client Services Director, BPRI, Waterloo Court,

Harmonising standards in international public relations

The international public relations community has set itself the task of maintaining the highest possible standards of professional consultancy.

Over the last eleven years the number of consultancies has grown to keep pace with the proliferation of new media channels, and the need for industry, commerce and government to communicate effectively to their audiences.

ICO was created in 1986 and represents public relations consultancies associations in fifteen countries.

It is an organisation dedicated to sharing information on consultancy practice, harmonising operating standards, and increasing the awareness of the value of professional PR advice.

For further information and a directory (price £15) of our member consultancies around Europe, please contact:

ico

ico
Willow House
Willow Place
London
SW1P 1JH
Tel: +44 171 233 6026
Facsimile: +44 171 828 4797

International connections in public relations

The consistency of public relations consultancy practice across borders is a key element for both the quality of service to clients and the sound growth of tne consultancy business. The need to foster professional consistency at the highest quality and efficiency levels is one of the reasons why the International Committee of Public Relations Consultancies Associations was formed in 1986.

The trade associations of PR consultancies in fifteen countries in Europe and the Counselors Academy of the PRSA in North America are associated to ICO, together with observers from other countries. Their members, and their members' clients, benefit from the organisation's work in five major areas:

• **Ethical standards** – establishing a sound relationship between a consultancy and its client, and conforming to national codes of ethics, new based on internationally agreed standards.

• **Quality standards** – ICO supports officially recognised qualifications such as ISO 9000 so that clients can rely on improved levels of service and quality.

• **Harmonising professional practices** – ICO provides access to a wide range of internal management and business development programmes, improving member's performance in business and public relations services and techniques.

• **International market information** – ICO publishes a yearly Directory, as well as surveys of market data, trends and national cost-structure including wages, which helps the development of international PR projects.

• **Representation of professional interests** – ICO has developed links with major organisations, media associations and government bodies, to represent the views of our members, and cooperates on matters pertaining to international training in communications skills.

If you are looking for public relations services that meet the highest standards, ICO can help you find the perfect PR partners via our international referral system. For further information please contact ICO, Willow House, Willow Place, London SW1P 1JH, UK. Tel +44 171 233 6026, fax +44 171 828 4797.

---

35 Turn Tele-communications to Your Financial Advantage

Paul Morgan, Head of Marketing and Regulatory Affairs,
Telia International UK Limited

Organizations throughout Europe are fast realizing the benefits that telecoms liberalization can bring. Often the introduction of a competitor to the existing state monopoly or 'PTT' means cheaper long-distance or international calls. Yet the real benefit of competition comes with the increase in choice of telecoms services, often tailored specifically to a customer's need.

One difficulty in assessing the impact of competition across Europe is that the process of telecoms liberalization is at different stages of development, depending on which country you look at. As a result, we see more competition in some countries than in others and major differences in the choice of service and, most noticeably, pricing.

The first new service that tends to spring from competition is known as 'resale'. A new telecom company, the 'reseller', delivers services through capacity which it has leased from the national PTT, effectively reselling that capacity to the business or domestic customer. Often the new company can provide better and lower cost services than the PTT, even though it is partly using the national operator's network.

There are three reasons for this being possible. First, the new player will target a specific market niche. So it does not have to bear the costs and overheads of being all things to all people. The new service provider is not handicapped by a legacy of old technology and old working practices which

burden many PTTs. Finally, a regulatory environment is put in place which encourages competition and prevents the national operator from using its position to stifle competitors.

For companies which have dealings in more than one country, international resale can mean immediate and often substantial savings on call charges and a wider choice of service options. There are two methods of international resale. The first, known as 'single end resale', involves the customer having a dedicated leased line to the service provider. The call is then routed direct to the distant and public network (known as the PSTN) to its destination by the reseller in the normal way. Single end resale is not attractive to smaller business customers because of the high cost of leased lines.

The second technique, known as international simple resale (ISR), is more affordable to the smaller business as it involves no leased line. The call is automatically routed to the ISR service provider via an access code which has been programmed into the customer's office phone system or PABX. The ISR service provider then passes the call via the public network. Older PABXs which cannot be programmed with the access code can be fitted with an automatic routing box instead. ISR means smaller companies can now make big company savings on international calls.

For most countries in Europe ISR is not permitted. However, if we look at the two most

Telia is today's communications partner of choice for all medium to small-sized businesses. Why? Because quite simply Telia has dedicated itself to meeting their specific needs: • high quality national and international calls • free access to the service • significantly reduced costs • ability to include business calls from home • a simple tariff structure based on UK business needs • itemised billing options providing valuable management control information • services which are easy to implement and operate • 24 hour, 7 days a week support. In addition, Telia provides a variety of value-added, customer driven products and services to meet your changing telecommunications needs. ————— **To find out more, call us now on: 0800 454 899**

Telia International UK Ltd. 114A Cromwell Road London SW7 4ES Tel: +44 171 416 0306 Fax: +44 171 416 0307

‡‡‡ telia

Your competitive edge in Telecommunications

	UK (BT)	Sweden	Italy	France	Germany
Near Europe	£0.91	£0.37	£1.08	£1.20	£1.56
Far Europe	£1.16	£0.90	£1.08	£1.43	£1.75

Note: Near Europe – immediate bordering countries
Far Europe – rest of Europe

Table 35.1 Basic tariffs for a three-minute call

deregulated countries, Sweden and the UK, where ISR is allowed, we can see the real effect of competition on international call charges. Table 35.1 shows the public operators' basic tariffs for a three-minute European call in April 1995.

It is clear that open markets mean lower call charges. It is also significant that the reduction in charges is not at the expense of service quality. Indeed, Sweden and the UK are both recognized for high standards and customer satisfaction.

Although in theory the European telecoms market will be fully open to competition by 1998, there are a number of obstacles to be overcome. National PTTs are understandably less than keen on international simple resale, and as a result the terms under which competitors purchase these services are likely to be punitive. The national operator is also likely to hide behind its obligation to provide a universal service to ensure that the market evolves to suit its own structures rather than meet customer needs. So while it is both technically feasible and commercially desirable, ISR continues to be held back by the vested interest of some PTTs.

If we look in some detail at the example of the UK, we can see how competition, or the threat of competition, has helped drive down international call charges with the result that the UK offers a favourable tariffing regime for business with an international bias. In the UK liberalization started in the early 1980s with the privatization of BT and the introduction of Mercury as an alternative facilities-based supplier. There then followed 10 years of duopoly. The 1990/91 duopoly review further increased competition, with over 150 licences now either granted or pending. The UK government devised the concept of international simple resale as a strand of international competition. This, however, falls far short of full international facility competition which remains in the hands of the duopoly. The aim of introducing ISR was to exert pressure on the

duopoly in the UK in the hope that this would bring down international tariffs.

In the 1990s reports began to appear in the press that international call charges were artificially high due to the accounting rate system. This is the means by which the public network operator at the distant end of a call is paid for the delivery of that call to its destination. By October 1990 the Director General of telecoms regulator Oftel was recommending that ISR of voice telephony should be allowed only to those destinations with market reciprocity. As a result, ISR is only allowed between the UK, Australia, Sweden and the USA.

Michael Heseltine, then Secretary of State for Industry, went on record at the time, saying that lower prices and value-added services which the resale operators plan to offer will create more choice and flexibility for the telecoms customer. This he maintained would attract investment from large international companies who would see Britain as an attractive place to do business. Today we can see that far-sighted 'resellers' are rapidly developing just such value-added services thanks to a deregulated environment. These customer-focused services, combined with the savings that ISR can bring, offer businesses a real and attractive alternative to the duopoly suppliers.

As a result of this liberalization we have seen international call prices drop by about one-third over the past three years. I expect prices to fall by a further third over the next three years. However, this fall in prices for international calls has little to do with ISR directly and more to do with the price cap imposed on BT by Oftel. However, these price points were determined by the existence of real or potential competitors. It is this potential for competition on international calls that has led the duopolists to introduce lower international tariffs, as the government intended.

With the arrival of competition, resale service

providers in the UK now have the option of using an alternative supplier to BT and Mercury for their international traffic. By choosing the most appropriate of the new network providers, the reseller has the opportunity to provide true least cost routing for international calls. The benefits of these additional cost savings can then be passed on to the reseller's customers.

Thanks to a phenomenon known as 'hubbing', the new resale service providers can provide customers with a truly global telephony service. Although ISR is only allowed to certain countries at the moment, the distant end public network or PSTN also includes the international PSTN for the country. This in turn provides the gateway to other countries' PSTNs around the world. As an example, international calls routed through one company are passed over a dedicated leased line to Sweden, which is deregulated for ISR. The Swedish national operator has its own international PSTN which then provides UK callers with low cost access to the rest of the world. Such hubbing means that the reseller is able to provide the most cost effective and best performing routes for international telephony. Operators in countries which do not allow ISR are not able to provide such a service. This means ISR countries such as the UK and Sweden present a distinct advantage to international customers.

So should businesses be looking to change over to a reseller rather than continue with the duopolists? And if so, what are the considerations in choosing the right type of reseller? The answer to the first question should be a resounding 'yes'. Not only will you save money on international calls, but the use of modern switching equipment and an international network platform will mean the same quality of service can be delivered at a lower cost. Indeed, when we look at the improved flexibility in terms of billing and the

presentation of customized, usable management information, that quality can be greatly enhanced.

However, when considering the choice of reseller you should look carefully at the reseller's technical capacity to proved high quality telecommunication links. This may be determined by the extent to which the reseller 'multiplexes' or divides up its international private leased circuits to carry as many calls as necessary to one line. You should also take note of the main geographic focus of the reseller.

Some resellers are in the market to exploit a short-term opportunity to undercut the national operators' prices. Others are there for the longer term, to establish a customer base and a service platform to meet all of the customer's needs for both international and domestic telecoms. If you are planning for the longer term you should be looking to establish a partnership with a reseller who shares your own long-term objectives and values.

Although many resellers may appear relatively small compared to the national PTT, they are often subsidiaries of global organizations with the resources to develop a broad range of services within liberalizing markets. These resellers offer a real alternative to the duopoly suppliers, with both immediate cost benefits and value-added services which will increase over time. By their very nature these smaller operators focus on satisfying niche market needs, usually targeting specific target sectors with a tailormade price-competitive offering. Of necessity these resellers have to provide a better quality of service and customer contact than the national operator. For the serious long-term player the result is that more innovative customer-focused services will be devised at better prices and standards than any incumbent national operator who has to be 'all things to all men'.

36 Sources of EU Funding

Richard Brooks, Partner, Wavehill Consultants, London

'How can I get some money from the European Commission to help fund the development of my company?' This is the first question that almost all business people ask me after I introduce myself as an independent consultant to the European Commission. So it must be an important issue for business leaders and poorly communicated by the various bodies responsible for the marketing of such programmes. The subject of developing successful bids for EC economic assistance often appears to conjure up images of a talented game fisherman landing an oversize fish using skill and experience, or an intricate watchmaker producing instruments of precision and accuracy. Far be it from me to dispel such a myth.

It is true that there are many different programmes and subprogrammes administered by the EC and that each one, almost without exception, is titled by way of a French acronym. I estimate that the EC launches or relaunches a new funding programme for business every three months. Often the name and rules may change a bit, but they usually address the same basic areas. However, there is some basic information and a few ground rules, which will indicate if your business is eligible for any assistance funding.

Basic information and the strategic context

If the EC had a vision statement, it would almost certainly focus on the need to create an identifiable economic area that can compete on an equal basis with any economy in the world, while creating employment and reducing the effects of economic and social inequality.

To help define the effects of inequalities between different economies and regions within Europe and readdress the balance, the EC has developed a method to identify and help finance areas with specific economic problems, using structural funds. These are known as objective priorities and are described in Table 36.1.

Businesses situated in one of the designated regions will find it easier to receive certain funding than those situated outside. A sliding scale of assistance, depending on regional objectives, is made available to projects that will benefit the local economy, such as building a new production facility, improving infrastructure, or training of the workforce.

Often the local council, or a specific government body (for example the local Training & Enterprise Council – TEC) will administer these programmes and will be responsible for selecting suitable proposals for funding assistance.

Companies not in special regions can still receive funding

The EC has undertaken much research into how to maintain and expand the European Union's competitive advantage against other economies around the

Priority	Business access to funding	Description of objective
Objective 1	Excellent	To develop and redevelop regions whose economies are less than 75% of EU GDP average
Objective 2	Very good	To redevelop areas in industrial decline where unemployment is higher than the EU average
Objective 3	Poor	To combat unemployment, especially in the young
Objective 4	N/A	UK has opted out of this objective
Objective 5	Good	To develop rural economies, especially good if your company is linked to food and agriculture

Table 36.1 Objective priorities

world. Hiding among the big political issues, such as the free movement of trade under GATT and the introduction of a single European currency unit, exist some less publicised but equally important issues. The promotion of innovation and technology and business cooperation programmes, as methods of stimulating economic growth, is a high priority. Companies in Europe are financially encouraged to enter into collaborative agreements with organizations from other economic regions such as Central and Eastern Europe, non-EU Mediterranean, Asia and Latin America.

The promotion of the development and adaptation of technology and the access to new markets for smaller and medium-sized enterprises (SMEs) is important to the EC. Important enough for 13 billion ECU to be earmarked for distribution to eligible companies, for the promotion of research and technological development during 1994–8. A further estimated 13 billion ECU has been allocated for cooperation programmes over the same period.

Funding for research and development: the fourth framework

The 13 billion ECU Fourth Framework Programme is the largest and most direct amount of funding assistance ever provided for businesses in Europe by the EC. The areas funded are shown in Table 36.2.

Organizations wishing to apply for funding generally have to apply as part of an international consortium, consisting of at least three members, one of which must be from another country and ideally from an Objective 1 area. Partners from some non-European countries are possible and for small com-

panies, some of the rules of application and administration are relaxed.

The application process can often take at least one man-month of management time and it is advisable to obtain experienced help to steer the project. There are a number of specialized consultancies that provide this service and the NatWest Bank Technology Unit (the only Big Five bank to have such a facility) will be able to suggest some names.

Action 1	R&D Programmes	Amount (ECU millions)
1	Information Technology	1932
2	Telematics	843
3	Advanced Communication Technologies	630
4	Industrial & Materials Technologies	1707
5	Measurement & Testing	288
6	Environment & Climate	852
7	Marine Sciences & Technologies	228
8	Biotechnology	552
9	Biomedicine & Health	336
10	Agriculture & Fisheries	684
11	Clean & Efficient Technologies	1002
12	Nuclear Fission Safety	414
13	Controlled Thermonuclear Fusion	840
14	Transport	240
15	Targeted Socioeconomic Research	138
Action 2	Cooperation with other countries and international organizations	540
Action 3	Dissemination & exploitation of results	330
Action 4	Training & travel for research personnel	744

Table 36.2 Fourth Framework Programme 1994–8

Grants, interest free loans and equity participation

The EC is committed to the assistance of the developing countries. Among the financial packages to combat food shortages and help with natural disasters are several commercial investment promotion schemes that can be very beneficial to businesses looking to invest in such countries.

Arguably the best programme is **The European Community Investment Partners Programme**, or ECIP for short. The scheme covers Latin America, Asia, non-EU Mediterranean countries including Israel, and South Africa from 1996. The scheme helps to finance the stages of overseas capital investment such as sourcing of potential partners in these areas, feasibility studies, business plan development and the adaptation of market specific prototypes. If the proposed scheme is viable, the EC may then finance up to 20 per cent of the capital of the project, if certain targets and requirements are met. Other similar programmes are available for Central and Eastern Europe. It is advisable to seek the counsel of experienced European Commission consultants, who can steer the development of proposals and act as a neutral arbitrator between partners. Such financing significantly reduces the risk of overseas investment.

There are many programmes to assist businesses directly and indirectly with the funding of growth and development. These almost always focus on technology and/or cooperation between companies in different countries and fund only a part of the project costs.

There are some completely free programmes; however, these are usually pilot projects. One such project is 100 per cent paid for by the EC and run by Wavehill Consultants as UK project managers.

The aim is to help a wide range of technology-based businesses in the UK develop collaboration projects with companies in Israel. Companies taking part range from small start-up companies still developing their first product, to several technology stocks listed on the London Stock Exchange. The programme demonstrates clearly the importance of technology development and business cooperation.

If your company invests abroad, especially in manufacturing and production, or is involved in developing or using new technologies and processes, then exploring and exploiting European funding opportunities should be an essential part of any planning decision.

Tendering to the Public Sector in the EU

37

Colin Maund, Achilles Information Ltd
Chairman, CBI Public Procurement Contact Group

EU procurement legislation

The programme of EU public procurement legislation, consisting of six directives, covers public and private organizations. Companies which provide works, supplies and services to the bodies covered are already benefiting from the directives, and can expect improved commercial opportunities as the coverage of the directives increases and the rules become more strongly embedded.

The legislation covers purchases made by the following organizations:

- utilities, ie water, energy (including electricity, gas, coal and upstream oil), transport and telecommunications, whether operating in the public or private sectors;
- central, regional and local government;
- other public authorities, such as health authorities, police forces and schools/universities.

Selling to public purchasers is big business; it makes up about 15 per cent of the EU's gross domestic product (£506 billion at 1990 prices). In the past less than 5 per cent of these public contracts have been awarded to foreign suppliers. It is estimated that up to two-thirds of the £506 billion of purchases can be effectively opened for bids from foreign suppliers. This could result in both significant cost savings to the public purse – equivalent to 0.5 per cent of community GDP, or £17 billion at 1990 prices – and in major commercial opportunities for suppliers.

The EU procurement legislation covers all purchases made by utilities and public sector bodies above certain financial thresholds. The purpose of the directives is to prevent discrimination between suppliers, particularly on grounds of nationality. This is to be achieved by ensuring that public and utility purchasers behave transparently and objectively when awarding contracts.

The main stipulations of the directives are:

- the EU-wide advertising of contracts in the *Official Journal*;
- non-discriminatory technical specifications and standards;
- non-discriminatory selection of bidders, and award of contracts based on objective criteria;
- redress for aggrieved parties when the procedures are not followed.

The directives

Public sector

Supplies Directive

Covers the purchase of products when contracts exceed the following thresholds: 200,000 ECU (£149,728) for regional and local government; 125,576 ECU (£96,403) for central government and other bodies subject to the GATT Government Procurement Agreement.

Works Directive

Covers building and civil engineering contracts exceeding ECU 5 million (£3.74 million).

Services Directive
Covers all services contracts exceeding 200,000 ECU (£149,728).

Compliance Directive
This aims to ensure compliance with the three directives and provides redress to suppliers in cases of infringements of the directives, examples of which are:

■ failure to advertise a contract;
■ failure to observe time limits;
■ discrimination in the award of a contract;
■ the use of criteria not specified in the notice.

Redress is through measures such as the suspension of contract award procedures and damage payments.

Utilities

Utilities Directive
Covers supplies, works and services contracts over the following thresholds: 600,000 ECU (£449,184) for supplies and services contracts in the telecoms sector; 400,000 ECU (£299,456) for supplies and services contracts in other sectors; 5 million ECU (£3.74 million) for works contracts in all sectors.

Remedies Directive
This aims to ensure compliance with the utilities directive and makes available remedies to suppliers, including suspension of contract award procedures and damages.

Opportunities for UK business
Liberalization of the EU procurement market represents a threat to UK suppliers, but also a major opportunity. Competition from abroad for contracts in the UK is likely to intensify, and UK suppliers must take steps to reinforce relations with their public sector customers. However, the opportunities from the opening up of previously restricted EU markets more than compensate for the challenges in the domestic market. Two areas potential suppliers may wish to consider in relation to EU markets are how to access information about contracts, and the tendering process.

Information systems
Within the EU, procurement opportunities can be accessed through the following information sources:

■ the *Official Journal of the European Communities*, in which all contracts above certain thresholds must be advertised;

■ *Tenders Electronic Daily* (TED), an on-line data service, which allows tailormade searches related to a company's specific interests;
■ *Export Intelligence Service*, a database of export opportunities throughout the world;
■ trade journals.

Help and advice about procurement opportunities in the EU can be obtained from trade associations, Euro-Information Centres and the DTI's regional offices.

A recent DTI/CBI survey found that most companies seek procurement opportunities through direct contact with purchasers, rather than through the sources listed above. This may be due to the oft-quoted complaint from UK companies that other EU member states are not advertising contracts and award notices to the same extent as the UK. Companies' preference for face-to-face contacts with purchasers suggests that export promotion schemes are a good means of identifying commercial opportunities. However, in addition to identifying specific contracts, the four information points listed above are useful sources of general market information on specific purchasers and sectors.

Tendering
The regulations and standards surrounding tendering are often difficult for companies who are new to the public procurement market. Entering into joint ventures or other collaborative arrangements can often get around this problem. This is especially the case with smaller firms, who may not have the resources to mount a bid by themselves. Smaller firms should also be aware of opportunities as sub-contractors on larger-scale projects.

Problems with tendering have been identified by suppliers, according to the DTI/CBI survey, in relation to barriers to entry to qualification lists and abuses of the accelerated procedure in bidding for contracts. Companies experiencing these should notify the DTI's Single Market Compliance Unit (SMCU), which can bring cases to the notice of the European Commission.

Companies have the right of legal redress – through the compliance and remedies directives – in cases where a breach of the directives has occurred. The same survey found that this route was rarely taken by suppliers. More common was the lodging of a complaint either with the relevant trade association, or with the government, through the SMCU.

Opportunities to supply purchasers in the EU have, since the conclusion of the Uruguay Round of the GATT negotiations, been extended further in international markets. The Government Procurement Agreement (GPA), signed in 1994, expands the coverage of the procurement rules to a greater number of countries and to the hitherto excluded works and services sectors. The new rules should ensure that UK suppliers are treated no less favourably than suppliers from other countries that have signed the GPA. Suppliers who bid unsuccessfully for a contract will, under the terms of the GPA, be entitled to a debrief.

The rules already apply in full to the European Economic Area states, and will be progressively extended to the associated states of Eastern Europe.

The future

An EU-wide review of the directives is due to begin in 1996, with appropriate modifications and improvements of the directives to be initiated. Business needs to make a strong input to the review, based on practical information on how the legislation is working.

More open European and global procurement markets will be matched by new opportunities in the UK market, where increased liberalization will intensify the competition already emerging from the government's policies, including contracting out, the Private Finance Initiative and the privatization of the utilities.

38 Electronic Commerce and the Internet

Lee Tate, Vice Chairman of the EDI Association (EDIA)

During the last decade electronic data interchange (EDI) has been promoted not only as a new way of doing business, but also as the platform from which it would be possible for business to free itself from operational and organizational constraints resulting from both geography and technology. Changing the way things are done, or business process re-engineering, would give way to a fundamental change in the scope of businesses themselves. The evolutionary would give way to the revolutionary.

In order to operate an EDI service it is necessary for both parties to a transaction to have an agreed electronic form which can be understood by each party's computer system, and preferably by everybody. Standard messages are passed electronically, eliminating the need for paper and opening the door to the 'virtual corporation'.

Inhibitors to growth

While the growth of EDI has been a success story, it has been heavily dependent on a number of factors which are both supportive and restrictive.

In the first place, the development of the standards has been a tortuous process, subject to both its own international political and administrative complexity. This has resulted in a long competition between the pragmatic sectoral and national standards movements, and the 'global standard'. Thankfully, there are only three major standards currently in use globally – rather than the thousands

of potential 'standards' if companies were left to their own devices.

The second factor is that the dynamics of growing electronic communities have only worked in markets in which there is a chain of power which enables the powerful to 'encourage' the not-so-powerful to use EDI. The result is that the major successes are in supply chain communities where buying power is the principal motivational force. In these instances, the process of re-engineering the business is well down the track, with pressure to reduce cost and improve service driving inventory costs back up the supply chain.

In those areas in which trading partners are arranged more democratically – and particularly internationally – confusion or non-availability of standards, coupled with the lack of commercial pressure, has meant that the pace of development in electronic commerce has been determined by the pace of the slowest mover, who is often stationary!

Thus the original dream of a paperless, frontierless, global trading system seems as far away as ever. In many countries, particularly on the Asia Pacific rim, direct government intervention has been seen as the key – this has varied from benevolent patronage in Hong Kong to robust interventionism in Singapore.

In the UK, the government actually financed campaigns to promote the growth of the electronic and telecoms services 'made possible' by deregulation. It is arguable that they would have fuelled more growth in EDI by actually doing it themselves. To date, government has been seen to talk a lot and do little and, if anything, is talking less now than ten years ago.

Electronic commerce beckons

In spite of all this, EDI has become a well-established business practice for a large number of the top UK corporations. The use of a predominantly national set of standards (Tradacoms) has helped enormously. In the large supply chain applications, particularly in retail, many suppliers are still using a primitive form of EDI and have not yet integrated the electronic documents being received and sent by their customers into their own computer systems.

A key dependency is that the software suppliers – whether of bespoke, internal, or package solutions – must address the problem of integrating the electronic outputs and inputs to the system into the end-user applications. This is one of the key drivers required to provide a credible momentum from the methodology of EDI to a broader application of electronic commerce.

The term 'electronic commerce' means many things to many people. Not all communication falls into the 'application-to-application' category – heaven help us, people might actually wish to communicate personally! Electronic mail (E-mail), therefore, clearly fits into the picture.

What's in a name?

So what, then, is electronic commerce, if not simply a rebadging of electronic trade or a new Americanism for EDI + E-mail?

It is clear that neither of the two methodologies, let alone a combination, can ever be the totality of electronic business communications. Nor can it represent the full set of available means of developing a co-operative electronic environment across business and government.

From a supplier's perspective, electronic commerce is an extension of EDI to all aspects of 'doing business electronically'. What this means in practice is that there are now further offerings in the portfolio. These include a range of shared applications and databases to offer the same data to both vendor and customer across the supply chain to drive *out* cost from all areas, not just drive it *along* the supply chain. In theory this should address the issue of distributing the benefits of electronic commerce across all the

participants. Co-managed inventory systems are, in reality, a cultural rather than a technological revolution.

A further interesting extension of electronic commerce is the development of electronic billboards, supporting vendor-driven supply markets, which opens the door to the creation of 'broker' markets. These are particularly appropriate in produce markets, where retailers can order until blue in the face, but can't make strawberries ripen on the day they want. Another perceived opportunity would be in the highly specific print markets where availability of resource is more significant than buying power. Market development will determine the success of this area rather than the technology. The knowledgeable will recognise that electronic broker markets are by no means new in some sectors – container capacity at sea is one which springs to mind.

The Internet, WWW and Bill Gates

And what is to be made of the Information Superhighway, the Internet and the World Wide Web (WWW) in all this? And what about Microsoft with

SWEDISH INSTITUTE FOR SYSTEMS DEVELOPMENT

SISU

www.sisu.se

Swedish Institute for Systems Development

The Swedish Institute for Systems Development, SISU, was established in 1984 jointly by the Swedish National Board for Industrial and Technical Development (NUTEK) and by a number of founding organisations. Today SISU co-operates with 40 affiliated companies and government departments, some examples are Telia, Sweden Post, Swedish Defence Material Administration, Ericsson, Asea-Brown-Boweri, Digital, Skandia, The Swedish State Power Board and Volvo.

SISU's mission is to serve as a bridge between national and international research institutes and universities and networks, and the industrial, business and public sectors in Sweden. Hence, the primary goal of SISU is to provide an infrastructure for the development of improved competence in information systems development and use throughout the public and private sectors of the Swedish national economy. SISU employs about 30 researchers and has an annual budget of 3 MECU. SISU's research is currently divided into the following areas:

Strategic Applications of Internet Technology. This area investigates the application of Internet-related technologies as strategic resources in the IT-infrastructure of organisations. This effort is motivated by the current growth and impact of services and technologies related to the Internet as witnessed during recent years. Together with its member organisations, SISU is exploring the potential of internal applications of Internet technology, improving work flows, document management and customer services.

Business Intelligence and Decision Support. In this research area SISU studies issues concerning the use of information technology to support business intelligence and decision support processes. Together with Swedish industry SISU is exploring new technologies that can be used to keep track of trends, emerging technologies, competitors, market opportunities etc. Projects in this area aim at finding and defining suitable models for business intelligence databases, developing methods for efficient business intelligence, developing easy-to-use information technology support for business intelligence, study best practice in data warehousing.

Legacy Systems. Research in this area investigates methods and strategies for the renewal and replacement of existing information systems in organisations. This requires an understanding of the possibilities given by new architectures for information systems and of the factors affecting decisions to replace or renew an existing information system. In this research, particular emphasis is put on the relationships between the business activity and the supporting information systems, in order to describe the effects of migration processes on the business.

Integrated Product and Service Development with Information Technology. The research aims at finding methods and support for shortening lead time and improve quality in product and service development. A concurrent engineering approach has been adopted and adapted to improve the development process which contain a large portion of software development. A best practice model of concurrent engineering has been developed based on the research in concurrent engineering and on a number of case studies in the Swedish industry.

Collaborative Work and Group Computers. Research in this area aims at finding suitable usage models for computer supported collaborative work. SISU is carrying out experiments with group computers, such as Xerox Liveboard, personal video conferencing and personal digital assistants, to establish efficient ways of using this technology to improve the work processes in an organisation.

SISU is actively participating in European collaborative research and development and has been a key actor in several projects in the CEC research programmes Telematics, Milord and Esprit. Current projects involve development of enabling technologies for multimedia brokers, trial applications of face recognition techniques, data warehousing applications and experiments with European wide collaboration networks integrating personal video conferencing and World Wide Web. SISU is also part of ESPITI – European software process improvement training initiative.

As a complement to the research and development activities SISU offers several information services to Swedish industry. This includes executive technology briefings, conference and technology monitoring, state of-the-art seminars and training courses.

More information about SISU can be found on World Wide Web, "http://www.sisu.se".

Windows 95, and Mr Gates' networking aspirations?

There is a view among 'EDI people' that the Internet is fundamentally insecure and used by ever-increasing numbers of academics, librarians, school-children and a variety of perverts, but not by business people. The fact is that, even today, the majority of people connected to the Internet are broadly speaking employed in business. The growth is well established and to pretend that Internet will not become the *de facto* personal networking standard is to whistle in the wind.

A safe assumption, therefore, is that general commodity E-mail will be handled by the Internet. But simply being interconnected to the Internet will not deliver cost advantages.

Equally, there are cynics about the use of the WWW for commercial purposes. While volumes of business in Web shopping malls are still comparatively low, the growth is dynamic. Early examples of supply chain Web applications are now in position. The banks have already worked out how to beat the 'security problem' and credit card transactions are being processed.

It is important that technologists understand the business drivers. It is not a question of whether supermarket chains sell wine on the WWW or not. The issue is related to commerce. Should the price be the high street price, including mark-up on real estate costs? Why should the personal shopper pay less? When will Web-only retailers leap into competition?

It is rumoured that the world's largest single CD store sells only through Web sites. Closer to home, a UK distributor of video and music to retail outlets is implementing an ordering system on the WWW at 30 per cent of the cost of EDI.

The availability in the newest Microsoft offerings of standard business forms, together with networking, presents an exciting opportunity for the electronic commerce user. Given Microsoft's predominance in the business market, this will go a long way to resolving the problem of small to medium-size enterprises wishing to implement electronic commerce.

There is a spirit of change abroad. The winners will be those who embrace the new opportunities, not those who defend the old. The future is difficult to predict, but the excitement is intense.

39 Cross-border Payments

Rachel Hoey, Manager, Thomas Cook Commercial Foreign Exchange

A by-product of dealing in imports and exports is the need to cope with the seemingly vicarious systems and procedures for moving funds across national borders. Often businesses are experts in their own field, but find the administrative burden of paying or receiving foreign currency payments confusing. These difficulties arise for a number of reasons, but can largely be categorized into two groups – those that relate to the experience of the user/customer, and those that relate to the complexities surrounding domestic banking systems talking to other banks across borders.

Regarding the first group, customers may lack experience in juggling exchange rates, or knowledge of alternative methods of payment and the relative benefits. In respect of the second group, despite the increasingly common standards and communication systems in the banking world, there remains a disparity between the domestic settlement systems of countries around the world and, in particular, their sophistication in dealing with millions of payments that move across borders.

This chapter highlights some practical hints as to how businesses can become more aware of what they can expect in timing of payments being sent and received, the way charges can be levied, and alternatives that may be explored in order to minimize cost – both direct and indirect.

Pitfalls

Firstly, timing. The time it takes for a payment to arrive at the beneficiary's account (ie the supplier being paid) after the instructions are released by a business in the UK will vary between users. There are five key factors in determining the length of time a payment takes to get to its destination:

1. How you communicate with your international payment provider (generally your bank) and the speed of that communication. A common system used is the post, but you are at risk of taking two or more days before it can be actioned. Most other methods, such as telephoning or personal delivery may mean same-day release by your provider. In the event that you have urgent payments or that you have left the payment to the last minute, you should check whether the system you are currently using is meeting your needs.

2. How quickly your provider will respond to your request and the speed of release into the international banking system. There is no guarantee that all payment instructions that you send to your provider are released the same day: you should check with your provider how long it is before the instruction is on its way to the destination bank. There are providers, like Thomas Cook Commercial Foreign Exchange, that release

Does Your Company Need to Make International Payments?

Then we could offer you a better way to do them through one of the world's largest Foreign Exchange specialists - Thomas Cook

- Thomas Cook Commercial Foreign Exchange offers a specialist service designed to provide the best possible international payments programme for small to medium sized companies. So whatever the volume and frequency of your transactions, you will be treated as a valued client.
- You will have a dedicated account executive and corporate dealer working with you on your business needs. All your transactions can be conducted directly by phone and fax.
- We provide our clients with up to the minute information and advice on the factors influencing currency movements.
- We also assist clients with hedging against the risk of foreign exchange fluctuations by offering forward contract facilities.
- <u>And</u> you can choose the most appropriate method of settlement to suit your business.

Nothing could be simpler.

If you would like to find out more, please call us on 01733 502 643 or fill out the coupon below and return to Julie Shaw, Thomas Cook Commercial Foreign Exchange, P.O.Box 36, Thorpe Wood, Peterborough PE3 6SB. We look forward to hearing from you.

Please send me further information on the services of Thomas Cook Commercial Foreign Exchange. ❑
Please call me to discuss my requirements. ❑

Name _____

Position _____

Company _____

Address _____

_____

Tel _____ Fax _____

The Foreign Exchange Specialists

all payments, regardless of size or destination, the same day as long as the deadlines are adhered to.

3. What route and method the payment is released under. Routing of payment through a number of local agent banks before it reaches its destination bank can add extra costs and delay to charges. It can help the process if you liaise with your supplier to ensure correct SWIFT references for the destination bank, as well as rapid movement of electronic transfers through the banking systems.

4. The prioritization given to that payment message by the agent banks responsible for finally getting the payment to your beneficiary's account.

5. The location of your beneficiary's account. Beneficiaries who have accounts in a branch of a bank which is outside the main banking centre in some countries, may mean use of non-electronic message systems to transfer the payment. Some countries are automated in the capital city, but branch communications are by mail. This can add more risk of delay to delivery of payment instructions.

These issues apply to both sending the payment and also receiving international currency payments. When you are on the receiving end, you are experiencing the converse of what beneficiaries in foreign countries experience. It may be worthwhile talking about any difficulties with your suppliers or customers in order to improve terms wherever possible. This would be of practical benefit if you have a relationship with an overseas party whereby you both send and receive payments. The possibility of netting the traffic is a practice that is continuing to grow in the import–export market in the larger end.

Charges

Charges are levied on both outgoing and incoming payments as a result of the following:

■ Your provider levies a commission charge;
■ The agent banks involved in passing the payments levy a handling charge.

Firstly, the most common practice for charging is a sliding commission structure depending on the size of the payment and sometimes the currency or method of transfer. Paper-based methods of transfer are the cheapest and there are even differences in the speed of these. The greatest growth area of payments is in electronic transfers, normally using the worldwide interbank electronic transfer system, SWIFT. Generally charges get allocated to the latter as it

moves through the banking systems internationally.

The way your provider charges you becomes more important as the volume of payments increases. Thomas Cook Commercial Foreign Exchange is one of the few that has a flat charging structure with all bar the most difficult of charges absorbed into the flat fee: no further charges are levied. This is a helpful arrangement for a manager to know in advance the cost of the service, and it assists with the speed of bookkeeping and reconciliations.

The second source of charges are the levies that apply as the payment moves through agent banks. The banks usually charge the sender or receiver for handling the transfer if they are not a customer of their bank. The levels of charges vary both by country and by bank, and uniformity is a long way off. It is possible to send all payments or receive them with the charges being absorbed by the other party. Such arrangements would have to be confirmed with the sending bank prior to departure, although to make the arrangement work users have to have agreed it with the recipient of the charges.

Costs

In addition to the direct costs of charges as described above, there are more hidden indirect costs associated with dealing in international payments. This area is where there is most need for support by the payment provider, particularly in the middle and small corporate market.

The ability to forecast foreign currency requirements is a necessary pre-requisite for a company to take the next step and manage the exposure risk that results from being a sterling-based operator receiving or sending value in currency. The differences in exchange rates between the time of commitment and the value date (date of execution of the payment) may give rise to a foreign exchange loss. It is possible to use exchange management products like forwards and options to mitigate the risk of loss in part or full, depending on the risk appetite or profile the company wishes to adopt.

For example, if a company tenders for a job where they will need to import German parts for the manufacture of equipment, the cost of the job, and therefore the profit margin, may be adversely affected by a change in the price of the imports. By taking out an option or forward, that risk can be limited to different degrees. It is not the intention here to discuss the relative merits of the instruments, as each case may require a different strategy: the key thing to

FTA – Foreign Trade Association

FTA represents the commercial policy interests of importing trade companies in Europe vis-à-vis the European Commission, Council and European Parliament.

Foreign
Trade
Association

FTA lobbies

- for the dismantling of quantitative restrictions, tariffs and other import barriers
- for the implementation of the results of the Uruguay Round
- against anti-dumping duties and the introduction of any type of non-tariff barriers, especially in the environmental and social sector.

FTA provides up-to-date and detailed trade policy information in the consumer goods sector.

FTA solves problems concerning import activities of members.

Our aim is free trade in the world economy.

As importing trade you, too, should become a member of FTA and contribute to increase the political weight of the commerce in Europe and the strive for liberalisation in international trade.

FTA – Foreign Trade Association

Avenue de Janvier 5, Bte. 3	Tel. (32 2) 762 05 51	Mauritiussteinweg 1	Tel. (49 221) 92 18 340
B-1200 Bruxelles	Fax (32 2) 762 75 06	D-50676 Cologne	Fax (49 221) 92 18 346

Trade policy framework conditions for the retail trade sector in the Greater European Area

Access to the European Union is according to the Foreign Trade Association, an organisation representing the trade policy interests of the European retail industry, not as free as the European retail trade and their third country suppliers would like it to be.

The sensitive sector of textiles and clothing regulated in the Multifibre Agreement shall as a result of the Uruguay Round be phased out in four steps over a period of 10 years and subsequently integrated into GATT. In the first phase mainly products that had not been subject to quotas have been notified for liberalisation. Expressing great disappointment about these notifications, FTA is actively lobbying for greater liberalisation effects in the second phase.

The sudden introduction of the China quota systems in February/March 1994 that has lead to considerable trade deliberalisations for traditional liberal countries such as the UK and Germany was heavily criticised by the importing trade. Two different, complex quota systems administered from Brussels have been set up to regulate Chinese textile and non-textile imports.

Economically, many quotas seem to make no sense at all. In the silk sector for example China practically has a monopoly. Certain toys and sporting shoes are no longer being produced in the EU. The latter now have been excluded from the non-textile quotas as well as from an antidumping case concerning shoe imports from China following FTA's objections. With respect to the silk quotas the European Commission also could be persuaded to increase these quotas.

Safeguard measures and anti-dumping cases in the consumer goods sector have increased over the past 15 years, especially with regard to Asian imports. In the period from 1991 to 1994 22 anti-dumping cases had been initiated, 19 measures are currently still in force. It is difficult for parties concerned to

contest an anti-dumping case. FTA tries to intervene on behalf of its retail members by issuing a statement providing relevant contesting information. This is not an easy task as European antidumping legislation in many points is open to wide interpretation and the European Commission often takes a protectionist stance.

There has been a general increase in non-tariff-barriers. EU standardisation and labelling, e.g. CE-certification, shoe-labelling and eco-labels, as well as other EU and national legislation legislation in the environmental and health area for many third country producers signifies major obstacles to trade with the European Union.

Equally, social and environmental clauses to be included in trade agreements without controlling mechanisms, would open up many measures for protectionist actions. These issues have to be treated in specialised multilateral forums such as the ILQ, equipped with the appropriate enforcing mechanism. Nevertheless, FTA agrees, special trade incentives for implementation of favourable social policies within the framework of the WTO, as it also is envisaged in the new GSP, may be positive. In any case the importing trade ought not have to bear the risk of non-observance on the part of the supplier countries or firms if it is acting in good faith.

Delegate-General: Dr. Konrad Neundorfer
avenue de Janvier 5, Bte 3, B-12-- Bruxelles
Télephone: 02/762.05.51 Télefax 02/762.75.06
Banque Bruxelles Lambert: 310-0269763-92

Mauritiussteinweg 1, D-50676 Köln
Telephone: (02 21) 92 18 34-0 Telefax (02 21) 9 21 83 46
Dresdner Bank 3 645 587 (BLZ 370800 40)

---

remember is that there are ways to protect margins with more planning for exchange-rate movements that will leave a company less exposed to risk of loss. The option and forward market is more liquid in the larger size deal end of the market. However, there are ways to cover smaller positions.

The issue of international payment and its processes should be evaluated in light of the overall commercial picture and not looked at just as a means to an end. There are ways to reduce administrative burdens on your company by using a provider who is prepared to work with you to relieve as much hassle and manual paperwork as possible. By improving the administration, reducing delays to payments and enhancing the information on traffic, a provider can make international payments an easier and cheaper experience.

Language Training

'Why Can't the English...?'

Faye Gregory, Sales and Marketing Director, LinguaTel

Thanks to a more determined effort by successive Ministers of Education and a focus of public education policies on basic skills, reflected in primary and secondary school syllabuses and OFSTED inspection requirements, the English (Scots and Welsh too) now teach their children how to speak and write standard English. Bernard Shaw's criticism, echoed by Professor Henry Higgins in *Pygmalion*, of Britons' inability to communicate intelligibly in their own language is no longer valid. The quality of communication in industry and commerce within the UK and with its English-speaking trading partners has greatly improved, although not necessarily in proportion to the increased capability for dialogue which advanced telecommunications methodology has delivered. However, 'Why can't the English teach their business people to speak foreign languages?' has become a more pertinent question.

The DTI takes British business's shortcomings in linguistic capability very seriously. Our complacent reliance on English as the *lingua franca* of world trade is now demonstrably a likely cause of lost trade and business opportunities. In February 1995 LinguaTel, an online interpreting and translation specialist, conducted a survey of the UK's top 100 exporting companies to establish their competence in dealing with foreign language enquiries from overseas callers. As a result of this first survey's alarming findings, and funded partially by the DTI National Language for Export Campaign with assistance from Dun &

Bradstreet, LinguaTel conducted further surveys of 100 leading companies in each of the UK's four major exporting competitors: France, Germany, Italy and Spain. The second survey programme provided a comparison of linguistic capabilities among mainland European companies against UK performance.

The UK survey

In the initial survey of UK exporters, professional LinguaTel interpreters, using French, German or Italian mother tongues exclusively, graded their experience of each company's switchboard and sales or marketing department. A two stage assessment was made of:

- The ability of the switchboard operator to understand the caller, or to put someone on the line who could, efficiently and quickly, without leaving the caller on hold for too long.
- The competence of the sales or marketing executive in dealing with the call.

The results are summarized in Tables 40.1 and 40.2.

	French %	German %	Italian %
Call abandoned	52	60	81
Barely managed	24	20	15
Reasonably	14	20	–
Well	10	–	4

Table 40.1 How UK switchboards cope

40

	French %	German %	Italian %
Call never arrived/ abandoned	71	80	72
Barely managed	–	–	3
Reasonably	10	–	14
Well	19	20	10

Table 40.2 How sales/marketing cope

These poor results emphasize what we know instinctively from our own experience; while overseas companies may be willing to *sell* to UK companies in English, they prefer to *buy* in their own language. However, as LinguaTel concludes in its summary, 'it seems that UK exporting companies still rely to a large extent on English being spoken by their customers, and seem totally unprepared for customers to call them.'

The mainland Europe survey

The methodology of the mainland Europe survey was a little different. Each country sample of 100 was divided into four sets of 25 each at random, and each set was telephoned by a qualified LinguaTel interpreter in one of four 'foreign' languages: French, German, Italian, Spanish or English. All interviews were carried out on 31 March 1995.

Competence of switchboards

Among French, German and Italian companies more than 70 per cent of the foreign language calls were dealt with competently. Only among Spanish companies did more than 40 per cent of calls fail at the switchboard. Essentially, twice as many calls were dealt with competently by mainland European countries than by UK exporters (Figure 40.1).

Past the switchboard

Once past the switchboard performance varied

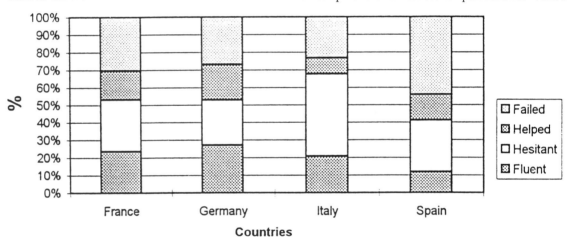

Figure 40.1 Competence of switchboards in handling foreign language calls

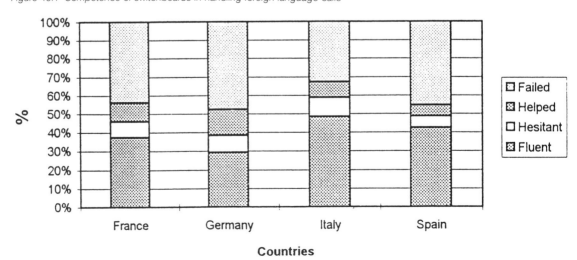

Figure 40.2 What happens when you get past the switchboard

rather more, but in every case there was a much higher standard of ability than among UK exporter companies (Figure 40.2).

The failure rate was lowest among Italian companies (about 32 per cent) and highest among German companies (nearly 50 per cent). More than 40 per cent of French and Spanish companies also registered failures, but in all cases linguistic capability was significantly superior to that of UK companies.

What language would you expect a supplier to use?

Respondents were asked whether they would expect suppliers to deal with them in their own language, or the supplier's. As expected, an overwhelming majority of companies surveyed preferred to buy in their own language (Figure 40.3).

In contrast, the actual experience of written communications revealed that less than 20 per cent of all respondents received faxes and documents in their own language (not much more than 10 per cent in the case of Italian and Spanish companies). Among French and Italian companies 80 per cent or more were used to receiving documents in their supplier's languages. More than 70 per cent of Spanish companies and almost 60 per cent of German companies had the same experience (Figure 40.4).

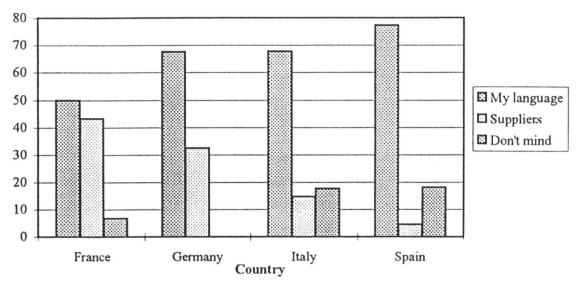

Figure 40.3 What language would you expect a supplier to use?

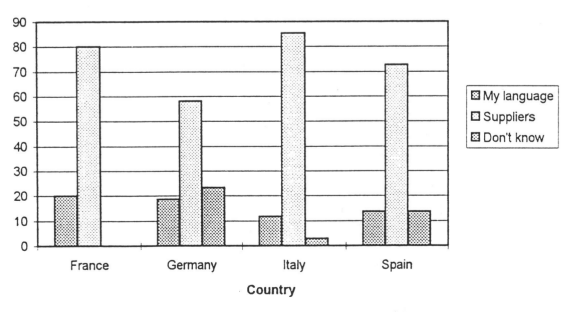

Figure 40.4 What language are faxes and documents received in?

Everyone speaks English

The mainland Europe survey also explored language ability in each of the four country samples and challenged the assumption that everyone speaks English. The results of this investigation are revealing (Table 40.3).

English is the most frequently spoken foreign language by companies in all of the mainland European countries surveyed, except for Italy where German is predominant. However, among German companies the English language is closely challenged by French.

that 70 per cent and more than 60 per cent of companies respectively also provide language training.

When Sir Peter Parker, Chairman of the National Languages for Export Campaign, unveiled the findings of the LinguaTel survey at the 1995 National Language for Export Awards, he commented that 'between 20 and 30 per cent of UK exporting SMEs have reported losing trade for linguistic or cultural reasons'. The converse – that greater competition in Europe and throughout the world for trade requires a greater awareness of customers, their needs and culture and a willingness to operate on their terms, in

	French companies %	German companies %	Italian companies %	Spanish companies %
English	36	38	31	41
French	–	31	17	18
German	20	–	35	18
Italian	17	11	–	23
Spanish	27	20	17	–

Table 40.3 Foreign languages spoken

The survey also revealed an interesting correlation between English language capability and foreign companies' plans to increase trade with the UK in the 12 months following interview (Table 40.4). The correlation may not have statistical significance, but cannot be dismissed as coincidence.

	Planning to increase trade with UK %	English spoken %
French companies	35+	36
German companies	35	38
Italian companies	25+	31
Spanish companies	45	41

Table 40.4 Increasing trade

Foreign language learning

Reflecting the DTI's National Languages for Export Week campaign, the survey also probed the degree of emphasis that companies in mainland Europe put on language training. Among both French and Spanish companies, an impressive 80 per cent said that language training was offered to staff as a matter of course. In Germany and Italy, the survey revealed

their language – is a message that former Trade Minister Richard Needham, one of the UK's most energetic trade ambassadors, proclaimed throughout his period of office.

For British companies wishing to introduce in-house language training courses or to provide access to external language training schools and institutes, there are a number of skilled providers, accredited by the DTI National Languages for Export Campaign, some of which are featured elsewhere in this edition of the *CBI European Business Handbook*. Among these are the Alliance Française, sponsored by the French government, and the Spanish Instituto Cervantes. British universities, including the University of Westminster School of Languages and Birmingham University, provide specialist courses for business people. In addition, there is a range of UK government-sponsored and independent institutes, including NatBlis, International House, Institute of Linguists, Kingston Language Export Centre and Milton Keynes Language Centre.

Many British managers still retain a negative attitude to learning languages, sometimes a reflection of the widespread negative attitudes to the EU. Probably the only way to ensure that British business sharpens up its linguistic skills is to do what many companies in mainland Europe have done successfully and offer financial incentives to employees who undertake language courses voluntarily. For example, financial incentives are usually offered to all senior employees, not only to sales people, in Swiss companies who learn any language relevant to the company's requirements. The inducements are usually offered in stages, with cash bonuses awarded for each improvement in the level of language skill attained. The addition to earnings can be significant for employees gaining proficiency in another language.

Instant foreign languages online

There is no substitute for in-house managers with foreign language competence who can communicate freely with potential and established customers, but there is an effective short cut for those companies who recognize the need but have yet to establish their own capability. LinguaTel provides fully qualified interpreters on-line in all the major European languages who will make outgoing calls, after careful briefing, to designated contacts on behalf of the home company. Caller, interpreter and potential customers are linked online in a three-way conference call and meaningful conversation takes place with both caller and respondent talking through the interpreter to each other. Intonation and telephone

manner give indications of the effectiveness of the call and customer reaction.

Most calls can be made by telephoning Lingua-Tel and being put in contact with a suitable interpreter within 60–90 seconds. Communication in the less used languages or on technical subjects may require pre-booking in order to secure the appropriate interpreter services. LinguaTel's interpreters undergo extensive testing through the UK's first business and commercial evaluation programme designed and administered in conjunction with the Institute of Linguists and City University.

The service described above relates to outgoing calls, but there is also a methodology for those using LinguaTel services to handle incoming foreign language calls competently. LinguaTel provides a language prompt card for telephone receptionists which is simple to use with a phonetic script in key languages. Using the prompt card, a receptionist can direct a foreign language caller to hold the line and can then route the call to an in-house or LinguaTel interpreter. There is no longer any excuse for switchboards failing to answer foreign language calls. LinguaTel is an aproved supplier to the Association of British Chamber of Commerce (BCC), as well as a provider to the DTI and is already playing a significant role in the development of Britain's export trade and overseas commerce.

Instituto Cervantes

Spanish is an important working language within the European Union and fluency in Spanish is a major asset to anyone envisaging working, studying or doing business in Europe. In addition, Spanish is the official language of 19 other countries outside Europe. A glance at some recent statistics gives an idea of the importance of Spanish as a world language and of its fast-growing influence. It is now the fourth language in the world in terms of number of speakers and the second, after English, as the means for international communication. There are 16,429 periodicals, 972 newspapers, 254 TV channels, and 5,112 radio stations currently operating in Spanish.

There are well over 300 million native speakers of Spanish throughout the world, making it the third most widely spoken language after English and Chinese. Because the cultural and economical positions of the countries where Spanish is spoken, encompassing Europe and South America, comprise important areas of influence in terms of culture and trade, Spanish is the second most used working language in the world. This is already generally recognised in international forums, including the United Nations and the European Union. As it now stands Spain is the fastest growing economy in Europe and is undergoing a major process of international expansion, open to foreign market competition. In relation to Britain alone Spain is its third most important trading partner, having seen its trade increased threefold in the last five years. There are more and more British companies already established or intending to do so in Spain in all areas of business (retailing, insurance, building, consulting, engineering, etc.).

Within the common funded programmes of study in the EU, most recently SOCRATES and LEONARDO, of which 10% comprise British students, a knowledge of Spanish is paramount for those wishing to work or complete their studies in Spain on an exchange visit with any university or college. The number of students in secondary education in Europe taking courses in Spanish is well over 1,800,000 supported by approximately 12,000 teachers. There are 132 university departments where Spanish is taught. The highest numbers of students are in France (around 1,500,000 in secondary education and 40,000 in universities) and in Germany (90,000 in secondary education and 16,000 in universities).

In Eastern Europe, Poland has nearly 100 centres of primary and secondary education with around 2,000 students learning Spanish. In Bulgaria, from 640 students in 1985, there are now over 2,000. In both the Slovak and Czech Republics, more than 700 pupils study Spanish at primary level with well over 1,500 in secondary education. The Departments of Spanish in eastern european universities are distributed as follows: CIS: 250; Poland: 5; Czech and Slovak Republics: 5; Hungary: 5; Rumania: 3; Bulgaria: 1; Serbia: 1; Croatia: 1; Slovenia: 1. In these countries, the demand for Spanish has increased over 50% in under two years.

Within the broader context of Spanish outside Europe, in the USA alone, according to the 1990 census there were 22,354,059 people (8.9% of the total population) of Hispanic origin. Future predictions give a much higher figure. Reports from The Department of Education in the same year showed that 62% of all students taking a foreign language course in High School chose Spanish. The number of teachers of Spanish is estimated at around 40,000 with more than 2,000 university departments teaching Spanish. Among them, 193 offer studies at postgraduate level. There are currently 7 national newspapers published in Spanish, 37 TV channels and 97 radio stations. Spanish is a growing language in use within the USA itself and on a par with English within the recent created NAFTA trading area.

In Japan, Spanish is taught in 109 universities with over 5,000 students. Programmes in Spanish from its national TV network show ratings of over half a million viewers. In North Africa and the Middle East Spanish is a subsidiary language in secondary education and in universities.

There is therefore a large quantitative demand for learning Spanish as a foreign language. Unfortunately, the quality with which that demand is being satisfied is currently very variable. The **Instituto Cervantes** was created in 1991 with the intention of raising the international standards with which Spanish is taught. It operates within the framework of its own Charter designed carefully to fulfil the main targets of promoting, teaching and consolidating new areas of specialised learning in Spanish.

The Institute's curriculum has been part of a European programme to regulate and harmonise the teaching and learning of modern languages. This has meant a long process undertaken by the Council of Europe in which a commonly based set of basic communicative skills curricula have been designed at the threshold level for the main european languages. It has been modelled very much along the lines followed by the official centres for the other main languages in Europe, such as the British Council for English, the Alliance Française for French or the Goethe Institute for German, among others, and has a similar international network of centres.

Such international provision for the quality promotion of Spanish language, culture and commerce was long overdue. The increasing demand for Spanish in all areas, cultural, current affairs, commercial *etc.* has contributed greatly to its creation.

The Institute currently has three centres in the UK, in London, Leeds and Manchester. The central provision at all three is the teaching of Spanish at all levels and for a variety of clients. Language is learnt within a cultural framework and special courses are also taught. The Diploma de Español como Lengua Extranjera (DELE) is the qualification of the Spanish Ministry of Education and Science for proficiency in Spanish as a Foreign language at two levels, basic and advanced, and the Instituto Cervantes is the officially recognised body for providing tuition and examination for this award.*

The Instituto Cervantes is a well equipped resource centre with professionally trained language staff and modern teaching materials in place. It has an up to date library equipped with on-line database facilities to which any student, educational institution, industry or business may have access. It exists to provide linguistic training, advice or information at all levels for the support of academic, business, or research interest.

The Institute is very happy to collaborate with other organisations on commercial or academic projects of mutual benefit and to offer advice in areas of its expertise. A particular aim is to foster collaboration at the research level on projects such as the European Union initiative on new techniques for linguistical research (EAGLES). Looking specifically at the provision of language training for business, this forms part of the current curriculum of the Instituto Cervantes in London and is undertaken in close partnership with a variety of professional and other bodies (such as the Spanish Chamber of Commerce, Department of Trade and Industry, and industrial consulting boards) which share a common interest in achieving a wider and deeper understanding of different cultural perspectives and uses of language within business and commerce, so encouraging more productive exchanges.

*Further information on the work of the Instituto Cervantes and available courses may be obtained from the London centre at 22-23 Manchester Square, London W1M 5AP.

Tel: 0171-486 2362   Fax: 0171-935 6167.

The Brunel University Language Centre

The Language Centre, on Brunel University's Uxbridge campus, and easily accessible from Heathrow, is a compact service unit providing an Institution-Wide Language Programme (I.W.L.P.). It exists primarily for Brunel students. However, its enthusiastic staff of experienced qualified teachers, all native speakers of the target language, be it French, German, Spanish or Italian, are available, by arrangement, to offer tuition to local companies at competitive rates.

English as a Foreign Language (EFL) is also a long established service, both to registered overseas students and to commercial customers.

The "extracurricular" language tuition is consumer led. There are no predetermined "businessmen's" courses. Each enquiry leads to a needs analysis and a profile of the prospective client's existing linguistic competence.

Experience shows that no two adult language learners are alike. Nor are their reasons for learning or updating a language at any given moment.

When the learner's aims are determined and his or her previous knowledge and skills assessed, a personal programme of study is drawn up to suit the time available and the agreed frequency of contact. Within these constraints a learning outcome is proposed and the materials chosen to meet it.

There are numerous published courses on the market, many of which are used in language modules for Brunel students. These usually consist of a textbook, audio cassettes and sometimes video recordings. Some are produced with "businessmen" in mind, and may be adapted for group tuition in our two modern language laboratories or for individual tutorials. On the other hand, our teachers are adept at making their own material to suit the agreed requirements of the client. Only then is the programme costed to cover the fees paid to the teacher, any overheads incurred and, naturally, a reasonable profit margin to be re-invested in the Language Centre itself, so that its service to Brunel students enjoys on-going improvement.

While the Centre is very happy to offer its expertise to Industry and Commerce, it cannot ever allow itself to lose sight of its primary aim – the education of Brunel students.

Alan Hersh, Director

Advertisement feature

National Languages for Export Campaign

UK companies face greater language barriers than other countries in Europe. This is largely due to changing trading patterns and the significantly lower baseline of their employees' linguistic competence. UK companies are also planning to undertake less language training than their competitors, although there appears to be greater recognition of the importance of knowing languages than in recent years.

Recent studies show that proportionally more British companies are losing trading opportunities due to language barriers than their counterparts in other EC countries. Smaller companies face the greatest difficulties. Between 20 and 30 per cent of UK exporting SMEs (up to 500 employees) have reported losing trade for linguistic and cultural reasons.

Today, as never before, we are having to search out new markets, often where there is little tradition of speaking English and where we hope to increase our turnover substantially – such as the Pacific Rim and Latin America. The percentage of key non-English speaking markets for UK is likely to carry on rising, and to do business in these markets, companies will need communication strategies. To be successful in the longer term means making a commitment, most companies will need to develop a strategy for their verbal and written communication and cultural awareness needs.

Furthermore, few companies today can expect to avoid some form of international partnership: whether it be from acquisitions, mergers, joint ventures, alliances or international projects. This involves very special talents, communicating with people from the same culture can sometimes be difficult (even when they speak the same language) but, when there is a different language and culture, the possibilities of mis-communication are compounded dramatically.

All international activity involves communication: in global business environment activities involving exchanging information and ideas, decision making, negotiating, motivating, rewarding, managing and leading all require effective translation into other cultures. Every action conveys a message, including even how you shake hands or wave good-bye.

Awareness of where and how the linguistic and cultural element fits in overseas activity varies from company to company.

The DTI-led *National Languages for Export Campaign* is helping companies to address these issues. The Campaign provides an umbrella for a number of individual initiatives to help companies make more informed choices about their language and culture awareness needs.

These include the four "How to do it" guides which provide practical guidance on ways of handling language and culture barriers on *Language Training, Business Culture Training, Translation and Interpreting and Developing Business Language Strategies. Communicado*, an interactive computer disc, has also been produced to help exporters plan a language strategy.

The National Business Language Information Service (NatBLIS) based in CILT (Centre for Information on Language Teaching and Researching) in London can help companies identify appropriate language service providers. The DTI/FCO Overseas Trade Services' Languages in Export Advisory Scheme is also being developed to provide business language advice to UK exporting companies.

Further information on the National Languages for Export Campaign can be obtained from Robert Holkham or Debbie Hardy at the DTI Campaign Office on 0171-215 8146/4857. Fax: 0171-215 8411. For NatBLIS call Penny Rashbrook on 0171-379 5131.

Do you speak business German?

New trends in learning German for business. Ever more businesses in the United Kingdom understand the necessity of foreign languages to be successful in a very competitive European market. Today the need to speak to your customer and potential future partner in his or her native language is beyond dispute. The evidence that by doing so your business will avoid at least unnecessary misunderstandings and at worst loss of valuable contracts is overwhelming.

A number of European languages are prime players in the competition for a direct line to the customer on the continent. Eastern Europe and the new states in the former Soviet Union are a good example of the importance that the German language has acquired since the fall of the Berlin wall. In Prague or Budapest, Warsaw or Moscow, to name but a few capitals where you might want to do business, mastery of the German language guarantees immediate communication and co-operation with your local partners.

Of course, in countries where German is spoken as the native tongue, Germany, Switzerland, and Austria, the advantages are self-evident. These countries, Germany in particular, are of major importance for British business as Germany is the most important trading partner for Great Britain. Even though many people in the German speaking countries may speak good English, your potential clients may prefer to use their own language when it comes down to putting their names on the dotted line. The psychological advantage of starting the business relationship in the language of your customer need not be stressed further.

Within the European Union, French and English are widely used as the official languages of the Brussels bureaucracy. German, however, is used more and more often as a go-between language, especially as there are ever more countries joining the Union where German has been spoken as the first foreign language. The Scandinavian countries are a good example of this trend and the future accession of the Eastern European states to the European Union will doubtless strengthen this trend towards German as the third European language.

In Britain, learning foreign languages has not had the status it certainly deserves in view of the economic developments with its non-English speaking trading partners. Britain at times faces its role within the European Union with hesitation and there may be good psychological and historical reasons for this. However, from an economic point of view, thorough training in the foreign languages that matter makes business sense. Any business that is lost to a European competitor because of the lack of language skills is business lost forever. That this need not be so is shown by the example of many British companies making a sound investment in the language training both of their management and their workforce.

The choice of which language(s) would be best for your business obviously depends on the markets that may be profitable for you. The case for the importance of German in a large number of the European markets and the European Union is very strong. Many companies therefore might consider language training in German for their staff.

Which language provider to choose? By the time you have decided that language training may be essential for your staff you will realise that in most cases a degree course at a universitity will take too much time to be effective for your short and medium term targets. A number of language schools and individual providers offer their services to you without a firm guarantee of success. They often cannot offer internationally recognised diplomas which are essential when you have to consider whether you are receiving value for money.

Within the context of learning a European language, well-established organisations such as the *Institut Français* or the *Goethe-Institut* have long since acquired a reputation for excellence. Recently these institutions have more and more put an emphasis on providing language courses that are tailored to the needs of trade and commerce. For the Goethe-Institut the teaching of German for business has become an integral part of its language teaching philosophy.

The following elements play an essential part in the Goethe-Institut's strategy for teaching business German:

The learner has the choice of several examinations that suit his or her level of language competence. The certificates that are awarded after passing the examination are acknowledged both in the UK and worldwide. Business German Courses are offered for the full range of aptitudes: from beginner's to degree level. The Goethe-Institut courses are accompanied by text books that guarantee solid preparation for these exams. Courses for individual and small groups can be arranged either at the Goethe-Institut or at the location of your business.

The choice of examinations in business German is essential if you want to plan a time schedule for the language training of your staff. You may for example find that some of your employees have already reached a level of competence in German that enables them to take one of the examinations immediately or with just a little time for preparation. Here the Goethe-Institut would help you with a diagnostic test and a short interview to determine the right level. For a more medium term approach enrolment in a business German course at the Institut might offer the best preparation for examinations. In some cases, a short very intensive programme can be arranged; for example in case of staff members to be posted abroad.

Both in Germany and Europe as well as in the United States the Goethe-Institut examinations for business German *Prufung Wirtschaftsdeutsch International and Zertifikat Deutsch fur den Beruf* are well known and universally recognized as they are approved by the *German Chambers of Commerce*. In case your member of staff has to start abroad immediately the Goethe-Instituts in Germany will help you with assessment,

language courses and examinations. This applies equally to the Goethe-Instituts in the other European countries.

Once entered on a business German course with the Goethe-Institut, the participants will receive clear guidance as to their needs for preparing for an examination. Even if they only require a certificate of attendance the goal oriented structure of the courses will guide the participants to a level of success required.

If you prefer the language training to take place at your business premises, for example to minimise the time factor, or to train your staff in those elements of the German language that are essential for your particular business, such tailor-made arrangements are catered for by the Goethe-Institut. For those clients who wish to learn German in an environment that is less oriented towards the day-to-day needs of business, the *Goethe-Instituts in Glasgow, Manchester and London* offer a pleasant learning atmosphere.

The support these learning centres give to the customer is mainly in the area of language learning tools, for example audio-visual, library and information centre, and computer-aided language learning centre. Within a wider context a whole, range of events are on offer at these sites from German films to talks on the German economy, in the which the language learner might participate, both to practice what has been acquired during the course, and the complement the general knowledge of Germany.

Of course, the best results from language training are gained when the course takes place in the country where the language is spoken. 16 *Goethe-Institut* centres in German cities such as *Berlin, Munich, Frankfurt and Dusseldorf* offer the opportunity to make rapid progress in the acquisition of the language.

As the courses and examinations are of an equal standard a smooth transfer from learning German at a Goethe-Institut in the UK is guaranteed as is the continuation on the acquired higher level after returning from Germany.

International Communicators in International Business

As technology continues to overcome distance and time, Europe and the world, we are told, are getting smaller. Paradoxically, at the same time their language requirements become increasingly complex.

Growing internationalisation of business has resulted in greater awareness of Europe's multi-lingual environment. The business communities of all European countries hope to enter this multi-lingual environment, hold their own and compete successfully. As one multi-lingual businessman put it – "I always use the language most likely to clinch the deal" and that, we know, is usually the buyer's language. But even if your company can draw on such language capability, different functions in business require different language skills, technical knowledge and combined language and negotiating skills.

It has often been argued that compared with reading, writing and understanding a language, oral skills are needed more frequently, especially higher up the managerial ladder. However, most business transactions are ultimately based on the written word. In the opening phase, this may encompass technical literature, catalogues, advertising and publicity material, business terms and correspondence. In the closing phase, the terms of the agreement and the order and/or the contract will again be in writing. It follows that whilst social occasions and business meetings require oral skills in the language, they can only be successful if the ground has been prepared. To do this successfully requires specialist skills, the skills of professional translators. Translators are international communicators of the higher order as they transfer not just the words but their meaning in context into a different cultural environment with different terms of reference and different expectations. To do that, translators must be familiar not just with the two languages and the text to be translated; ideally they understand your business intentions and expectations, as well as those of the buyer. They must be given full briefing and access to information. Once briefed, your translator could become a valuable member of your negotiating team.

It is management's job to determine which language skills are required at what stage of the negotiations, to know the limitations of in-house language skills, spoken and written, and how best to augment them as and when required by including in the team outside language specialists, interpreters or translators. It is also management's responsibility to ensure that the entire team, in-house or freelance specialists, are briefed to the optimum level to ensure the team's effectiveness by providing language skills of the required kind at the right level and at the right time. This need not be a million-pound operation. The principle applies equally to the small business just starting out in the Single Market as it applies to any business anywhere in the world conducted in whatever language.

The Institute of Linguists and its Language Services Unit supports the language needs of international business. As a membership body for professional linguists, our freelance interpreter and translator members can provide the required specialist language services in well over 45 languages. The Institute's Diploma in Translation provides quality assurance as it was created to raise standards of translation and put the cowboys out of business. It enjoys increasing popularity and recognition in many European countries. The Institute's Language Services Unit carries out language audits and assists in selection and assessment of linguist personnel. Its oral communication tests cater for the needs for this particular skills. Its certificates enjoy a high reputation for quality.

The Institute of Linguists was created in 1910 to provide the vital language dimension to help British business succeed abroad. Today it pursues the same objectives in Europe and beyond.

Edda Ostarhild,
Chief Executive, Institute of Linguists

National Language Standards

We offer two qualifications based on the National Language Standards: Certificate in Business Language Competence and Language NVQ Units.

Our courses are practical and work-related, developed to improve language performance in the workplace by giving competence and confidence.

We can offer NVQ assessment in companies throughout the UK and train existing language tutors or native speakers to be assessors.

Our specialist language assessor training sessions are run at various locations.

Milton Keynes Language Centre
• NVQ Assessment Centre
• RSA Regional Examining Centre
• D32 / D33 / D34 language assessor training centre

**Exchange House,
494 Midsummer Bld,
Central Milton Keynes
MK9 2EA
Tel: 01908 227555
Fax: 01908 227888**

MILTON KEYNES LANGUAGE CENTRE
National Language Standards

Milton Keynes Language Centre offers two qualifications based on the National Language Standards:
• Certificate in Business Language Competence
• Language NVQ units.

These Standards ensure that language learning is targeted so that people are competent and confident in using foreign languages in practical work-based situations.

Large international companies such as Volkswagen, Audi and Mercedes-Benz have been working with these Standards for some time and are among the first in the country to have employees gaining NVQs in German language.

Milton Keynes Language Centre is a pioneer in the field of vocational assessment in languages and also trains language tutors or native speakers in companies to be qualified assessors. These specialist language assessor training sessions are run at various locations throughout the country.

For more information on language training, qualifications or assessor training, please contact:
Judith McKeon on: 01908-227555

Kingston Language Export Centre

Language Courses for Business

- In company language programmes
- One-to-one & group training
- Intensive language courses
- Open learning language centre

A member of the Association of Language Excellence Centres

**Call 0181 547 7884
Kingston University, Penrhyn Road
Kingston upon Thames
Surrey KT1 2EE
Fax: 0181 547 7392**

KINGSTON
UNIVERSITY

Quality Courses Quality Education

Quality corporate language training in all languages including English.

Winner of the DTI award for best language provider (1994) and accredited as a Language Excellence Centre, RLI is at the leading edge of corporate language training.

- Our **language audits** assist you to plan training strategy throughout all levels of your organisation.
- **Assessment and goal-setting** provide structured, attainable and relevant targets for your personnel.
- **Flexible, skill-targeted courses** designed by experts, and delivered by experienced, professional trainers.
- **Times and venues** to suit your busy schedules.

If your people need to talk business in different languages...talk to us now on 01734 404499

National **Languages for Export**
Award Winner 1994

Full Member of
the Association of
Language Excellence
Centres

Robertson Languages International

In order to do business successfully you have to communicate clearly. This may be on a "one-off" basis with a prospective client, or it may be to establish a long-term working relationship supporting an existing client base or developing trust with suppliers.

Communication may take the form of conversation, formal meeting, social gathering, making presentations, negotiations, exchanging faxes, producing sales literature. All these things and more are needed to build successful bridges between a company or organisation and the other parties involved.

Working in Europe means working within a cohesive structure which binds together many different groups of people. Each member state is proud of its cultural heritage, its national identity, its lifestyle, its status within the Community and above all, its language. A national is defined by its language. As you cross an international border, you move into a totally new linguistic and cultural environment. You may be able to communicate to a certain level in your own language, but you cannot participate fully in a business world in which you do not understand what is being spoken or written at the same table.

At some point, every exporter and organisation communicating across the internal European boundaries finds that they must enhance their language capability if they are to take all the opportunities offered by

membership of the Community.

At Robertson Languages International, we offer a total range of solutions to language problems:

- training in other languages from beginners level to specialist courses for accounts, legal experts and seniors managers;
- updating current skill-levels to be able to make presentations or negotiate in a language which was previously only useful for social conversation;
- cultural briefings, which offer an insight into the way the different member nations do business;
- interpreters for crucial meetings where the participants' language skills may not be sufficiently high;
- translation of documentation by skilled specialist translators who understand your terminology as well as their own craft.

Using one or a combination of these services can smooth the path to better relations and successful business dealings both with your external contacts and internal international teams.

All these services are available and could provide the way forward to a new, exciting and profitable future in Europe.

ROBERTSON LANGUAGES INTERNATIONAL
The Stable Block, Hare Hatch Grange, Bath Road,
Hare Hatch, Reading, Berks RG10 9SA
Tel: 01734 404499   Fax: 01734 404489

Increased potential for customer – focus using language and culture skills

Despite English now being considered by many to be the language of international trade, some 30% of UK companies participating in a recent survey of trade with Europe reported that differences of language and culture are still a significant stumbling block, with the potential to cause loss of business.

One of the best known stories which illustrate this point must be that of the unintended pun made by a motor company which called its new car Nova. Hopefully, they had no intention of selling the car in Spain because *no va* translated into Spanish means *won't go!*

This example is taken from a large organisation. Although language and culture skills are important to a company whatever the size of its operation in foreign markets, financial and staffing restrictions are likely to affect its willingness to look at the issues.

However, a quick review of everyday business procedures – telephone reception, accounts, publicity – from the point of view of the customer who on a day-to-day basis speaks a language other than English, and whose cultural background certainly resonates with different understandings of the way the world works, may inspire companies to make some changes.

Businesses are looking for procedures which facilitate good contact with potential customers and which are neither too costly or too time consuming. Increasingly the languages industry offers a more flexible and business-focused approach to training and other services to give companies a range of solutions.

Business Culture Briefings, for example, are a straightforward way to gain a deeper understanding of the social and business practices of target markets. Or companies may seek help in devising a simple strategy for receptionists and other key personnel to deal with overseas calls. Others might want advice on the recruitment of export and sales staff with suitable levels of language competence, or the employment of interpreters to man exhibition stands at international events and the commissioning of translations for instructions on packaging, product user guide, sales literature and contracts.

All these procedures are easily accessed and can be tailored to the needs of any company. Products and services such as the DTi's Languages in Export Advisory Service (LEXAS), the National Language Standards produced by the Languages Lead Body, and the National Business Language Information Service (NatBLIS) are available to offer independent and objective advice, much of which is free.

There has never been a better time for companies to take a realistic look at the benefits of foreign language and culture skills and to seek advice to find the right level of entry to fit both their company's needs and resources.

Information from the National Business Language Information Service (NatBLIS)

Choosing a Language Training Centre

Selecting a language training provider can be a daunting experience. Open the Yellow Pages and you are bombarded with ads offering Arabic to Zulu screaming for your attention. But how do you know which school offers a professional service? Here are some questions you might like to ask:

• Is the school recognised by the Association of Language Excellence Centres? This is the only professional body in the UK ensuring the highest standards for business language training.

• Who are the teachers? Most schools offer tuition by native-speakers but they are not all qualified teachers. The International House Certificate in Teaching Modern Languages to Adults is among the most highly regarded in language teaching circles – in other words, we train all our own teachers and many of the teachers employed by other schools. So why not come straight to the source?

• How will your individual needs be met? At International House we recognise that everybody has different requirements and budgets. We offer a range of classes from one-to-one tuition to open group courses at all levels during the day, evening or weekend. Our experienced staff will analyse your needs, assess your level, and help you determine the best way forward.

• What teaching approach is used? Good teachers can use a variety of techniques depending on the client. The aim, however, is always the same: to facilitate communication and to build confidence.

• Is there a recognised qualification at the end of the course? The RSA CBLC (Certificate in Business Language Competence) is a practical and nationally recognised examination offered by International House, which is the RSA Regional Examining Centre for London.

• Where will the classes take place? Although we offer in-company courses, many people find it is best to get away from the bustle of work and study in an environment really conducive to learning.

International House is on Piccadilly in the West End, and has purpose-built, air-conditioned classrooms, quiet study rooms, coffee lounges, and an art gallery.

• Are there facilities for self study? It is always important to put some time into self-study between classes. At International House we have a self-access listening centre, library, and video viewing facilities. The School also prides itself on its international atmosphere offering opportunities to practise the language with native-speakers.

International House London is an Educational Trust which has been involved in teaching languages and training teachers since the 1950s. It is part of a world-wide organisation with over 90 schools overseas and, in addition to London, offers language courses in Argentina, Egypt, France, Germany, Italy, Portugal, and Spain.

40

THE UNIVERSITY OF BIRMINGHAM

SCHOOL OF CONTINUING STUDIES

Masters Degree Programmes

**Management of
Learning (M.Ed)** for
• HRM and Training Professionals
• General Managers with
  responsibilities for training

**Counselling Training and
Supervision (M.Ed)** for
• Counsellor setting up in business
• Managers of counselling functions

Counselling at Work (M.Ed/Cert.)
for
• Managers with responsibilities for helping
  people with work-related and personal problems

Modern Languages Unit

Language Services

• Professional advice
• Consultancy

• Language training

• Translations
• Interpreting

Learning Organisations

The University of Birmingham, through the School of Continuing Studies offers a range of courses to middle and senior managers in the public and private sectors. Recent research demonstrates that British industry suffers in comparison with its competitors, partly as a result of deficits in training and skill development and also through a worryingly low level of foreign language skills.

Mindful of these problems and the opportunities which the expanding international European market provides for British companies, the School is offering flexible, part-time or in-house courses to meet these needs. The M.Ed in the Management of Learning concentrates on aspects of learning as they apply to individuals, to enhance their skills within the organisation and to the organisation to enable it to capture and utilise that learning for the overall advantage of the company. The M.Ed in Counselling Training and Supervision takes a specific psychodynamic approach to counselling training and will be of interest to managers for whom staff welfare – closely related to organisational competitiveness – is a major functional concern. The courses in Counselling at Work offer a more general approach to this issue.

The Modern Languages Unit provides tailor-made training, usually on a one-to-one basis, at an appropriate level in all the major world languages. In addition, the Unit offers companies in the Midlands, completely free of charge, an initial analysis of language needs.

To learn more about these services contact:–
University of Birmingham, either School of Continuing Studies Tel: 0121-414 3589 Fax: 0121-414 5619 or Modern Languages Unit Tel: 0121-414 3324 Fax: 0121-414 7250

40

University of Westminster

The School of Languages at the University of Westminster has an international reputation for language teaching and learning. Its staff comprises a high proportion of native speakers in even the rarer languages and is able to respond to a wide variety of student requirements from the general to the highly specific. The premises are equipped with not only excellent library facilities but also a Self Access Language Centre extensive computer provision and satellite television.

Apart from the standard undergraduate and postgraduate day and evening courses in European languages, Russian, Arabic and Chinese, the School also offers through its Short Course Unit one-to-one and small group teaching in any world language tailored to the needs of particular learners. Students on all these courses can gain University of Westminster credits which may lead to further academic qualifications. Above all the School is committed to fitness

for purpose and the achievement of excellence in language learning by means of a combination of traditional methodology and communicative, functional teaching techniques.

At the postgraduate level we offer training in specific language skills notably in translating and interpreting for which the School has an international reputation. The School has a Conference Interpreters Suite designed to simulate 'real-life' experience and students have access to current EU materials.

Students at the School of Languages either full or part-time, day or evening, may expect constant exposure to the culture and language of many countries, not only because they are taught as academic disciplines but because the School has over 70 overseas exchange arrangements which guarantee the mingling of many nationalities in the building.

Learning to speak the language of Business

by Jenny Avery

In the international market place, being able to speak your client's language is not just polite, it makes good business sense. All the marketing and technical know- how in the world won't help if a non-English speaking client can't get past the switchboard or if you can't understand a contract written in a foreign language.

If you don't have the necessary language skills then don't worry, Staffordshire University's Language Excellence Centre can bring them to you. The centre, based at the university's Stoke campus, offers a wide range of services, including in-depth competence training in a variety of languages including French, German, Spanish, Italian, Russian, Japanese, Chinese (Mandarin) and Urdu.

When bosses setting up a new theme park near Barcelona in northern Spain decided to visit Alton Towers, Personnel and Training Manager Lesley Foulkes called Staffordshire University's Language Excellence Centre (LX) for help. The team from Spain wanted to pick up some expertise from the UK's No1 family attraction and so needed help not only with basic conversation, but also with the technical jargon and engineering terms associated with running a theme park.

"There was little English on their side and we had no-one that spoke Spanish so we needed an interpreter," said Lesley. "It was a real godsend and very useful indeed."

As well as providing language training and an interpreting service for overseas visitors, conferences and business negotiations, the Staffordshire LX Centre can also provide translators to help with a variety of foreign correspondence – from commercial letters to technical documents and promotional literature. All translation and interpreting work is carried out by professional language and subject specialists.

Firms can make the most of the up-to-date facilities of the university's Language Centre, including language laboratories, audio, video, and computer facilities, foreign programmes, literature and satellite TV, through the LX centre, which is part of a national network of language centres providing services of a recognised standard to industry. Staff will work on a one to one basis or in larger groups and will tailor training to the needs of individual firms. Alton Towers, GEC, Rolls Royce and Stoke City Council are just a few of the businesses that have made use of the university's language expertise. If you need help with translation, interpreting or language training, contact Anne Clafferty, LX Centre Manager, on (01782) 294639.

Staffordshire
UNIVERSITY

Talk to your customers in a language they can understand

Staffordshire LX Centre can help you to communicate more effectively in overseas markets. We offer a fast and efficient translation service as well as interpreting support. We also provide language training tailored to suit your needs, and to help you develop your skills for business advantage.

To find out how Staffordshire LX Centre can help you, contact:
Anne Clafferty, LX Centre Manager
Staffordshire University
PO Box 661
College Road
Stoke-on-Trent ST4 2XW
Tel 01782 294639
Fax 01782 746113

LANGUAGE - EXCELLENCE
LX
CENTRES

PART

9

European Production

Manufacturing in Europe ... a Home Team Disadvantage?

Philip Hanson, IBM Consulting Group

Chris Voss, BT Professor of Total Quality Management at London Business School

Since late 1992 the IBM Consulting Group and the London Business School have been studying the adoption of best practice and the consequent benefits in operating performance in manufacturing sites across Europe. So far some 800 sites have been individually visited in the UK, Germany, Netherlands, Finland and Switzerland. The results have been interpreted with the close involvement of local IBM teams and university departments in each country.

Implicit in the process has been the establishment of a model of manufacturing best practice and a measure of operating performance. The central hypothesis is that the adoption of this best practice is linked directly to the attainment of high performance. A powerful correlation between practice and performance has consistently been shown in each phase of the project (see Figure 41.1).

▧ *Organisation and culture* With obvious leadership from the chief executive, a clear vision for the business is jointly developed and shared throughout the site. Employees are inspired to follow the direction set and are encouraged and trained to work in teams to take responsibility for its achievement. The measurement of the business is displayed for all to see.

▧ *Logistics* Relationships with suppliers are built on the assumption of lasting partnership. The benefits of joint activity leading to lower total supply chain costs are shared. Outbound logistics are capable of delivery into highly variable

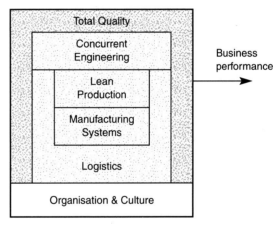

Figure 41.1 Correlation between practice and performance

just-in-time retailers, for example.

▧ *Manufacturing systems* Information technology systems are integrated so that the design process delivers a workable bill of materials to the planning process, for example computer-aided design and manufacturing can realistically be spoken of in the same breath. Materials requirements planning (MRP) schedules are trusted and acted on without need for local modification.

▧ *Lean production* Every aspect of the manufacturing processes that adds cost but not value has been systematically eliminated (eg unnecessary movement, counting, inspection, paperwork, etc).

■ *Concurrent engineering* The design and development process involves suppliers and customers as well as manufacturing and sales teams. The product will not only meet customer requirements but will enable optimum manufacture and distribution.

■ *Total quality* With all business processes sharply focused on meeting and exceeding customer expectations, a spirit of continuous improvement pervades the entire business.

Many factors can be seen to have a bearing on both the adoption of best practice and its consequent effects. The size of manufacturing site, the procurement practice of the supply chain in which it operates, the adoption of various total quality initiatives and the industry sector all have a significant influence on practice and performance.

That the nationality of ownership would similarly be an important influence has been yet a further hypothesis that has been explored. Ownership of manufacturing sites was designated as domestic (e.g. German-owned site operating in Germany); European (eg German-owned site operating in UK); American (USA-owned sites operating in Europe) or Japanese (Japanese-owned sites operating in Europe).

Across Europe foreign-owned sites fare considerably better than those that are domestically owned, suggesting a 'home team disadvantage'. Sites with Japanese parents are particularly outstanding in both practice and performance (see Figure 41.2).

Typically American-owned sites have higher practice and performance than European sites and it is the domestic sites that have the lowest practice and performance overall. The apparent advantage of foreign parents may be for several reasons:

■ They bring new and better practices. The Japanese sites demonstrate significantly better manufacturing practice in almost all areas.

■ The 'greenfield site' effect, allowing latest practice and technology to be adopted without being burdened by obsolete equipment or traditions.

■ Overseas managers can more easily challenge local conventions and manage change more easily.

The Japanese performance is not, however, universally the same across the European countries investigated. When the practice and performance achievements are reduced to a single numeric indicator, it can be seen that while Japanese sites perform best in the UK, American sites perform best in Germany (see Table 41.1).

	Finland	Netherlands	UK	Germany
Domestic	171	172	170	177
European	182	180	174	184
American		190	173	199
Japanese		206	214	188

Table 41.1 Practice and performance index

It is in the area of concurrent engineering practice that domestic sites outperform their overseas-owned counterparts. Many overseas companies do, however, retain significant research and development activity in the home country.

This picture is further complicated by the local effects of inward investment on the first-tier supply base. There is clear evidence that the long-term effects of American inward investment in the UK have encouraged very high levels of best practice in their UK local suppliers, where partnership sourcing strategies over the last 25 years have shared experience in a remarkably open way. With the recent high levels of Japanese inward investment in the UK there is no doubt that the best domestic and European sites in the UK are closing any gap that may have existed

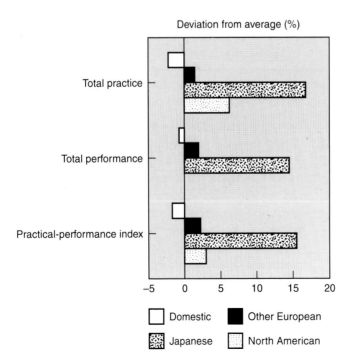

Deviation from average (%)

Figure 41.2 Practice–performance index

Manufacturing in Europe … a Home Team Disadvantage?   CHAPTER

41

between their operation and the American or Japanese practice. This 'pulling' of best practice up the supply chain is very powerful, but takes a great deal longer to show effect than many might expect. Domestic companies trapped in protected markets are meanwhile making rather less obvious progress. In the UK in particular these low practice and performance sites constitute a worrying long tail that will surely not achieve international competitiveness.

Closing the gap and striving to become 'world class' is, of course, not an absolute achievement but is a moving target driven by the best of our international competitors. The steady incremental progress of many Japanese exporting companies has turned to step change in the light of the dramatic variation in the value of the yen. There are increasing examples of 40 per cent and greater reductions in product costs being achieved through a total productive management (TPM) focus on operating efficiencies and systematic value engineering constantly to redesign products for ever lower manufacturing costs.

If TPM is a watchword of Japanese factories operating in Japan, it is not yet to be seen in the same high profile in their European subsidiary plants. Increasingly, however, global manufacturing companies must find it hard to keep their best ideas at home. Many enlightened European companies are to be found exploring the criteria of the Japan Institute of Plant Maintenance awards. What is clear is that we need to constantly be measuring the gap between our practice and performance and that of our competitors wherever they operate.

Note

For details of how to participate in the Made in Europe Programme or copies of the published reports, telephone Matthew Edwards on 0181 575 7700. Manufacturing sites in the UK can participate through the CBI 'PROBE' Programme of the National Manufacturing Council (0171 379 7400).

THE SWEDISH INSTITUTE OF PRODUCTION ENGINEERING RESEARCH

ivf

INSTITUTET FÖR VERKSTADSTEKNISK FORSKNING

150 researchers at IVF perform applied research and development supported by advanced equipment in IVF's workshops in close cooperation with the engineering industry.

IVF's new headquarters in Göteborg.

Spray booth for powder paint.

Advanced experimental industrial painting installation.

IVF-researchers in front of the advanced 200-tonne hydraulic press.

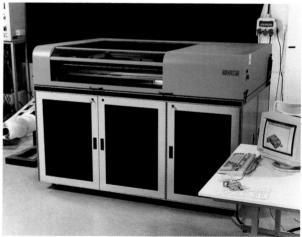

Rapid prototyping machine, LOM-2030.

ABB	Ericsson AB	Luxor AB	SAAB-SCANIA AB
AGA AB	Esab AB	Nobel AB	Siemens-Elema AB
Alfa Laval	FFV	Ovako Steel AB	SSAB Svenskt Stål
Avesta Sheffield AB	Fläkt AB	Plannja AB	3 M Svenska AB
Bahco AB	Hasselblad AB	Pullmax AB	Uddeholm Tooling AB
Bofors AB	HIAB AB	Rank Xerox AB	VME Industries AB
Electrolux AB	Kockums AB	Saab Automobile AB	AB Volvo

Some of the companies with which IVF is collaborating.

IVF, Argongatan 30, S-431 53 MÖLNDAL, SWEDEN Telephone +46 31-706 60 00 Fax +46 31-27 61 30

The Swedish Institute of Production Engineering Research

The Swedish Institute of Production Engineering Research, IVF, works with companies in and suppliers to the engineering industry (e.g. software companies) and conducts applied research and technological development. The objective is to improve the efficiency and competitive strength of engineering companies by developing and disseminating new technological know-how.

IVF, which was founded in 1964, is one of Sweden's largest industrial research institutes. IVF has 200 employees. Over 160 of these are qualified technicians, including five Professors, thirty Doctors or Licentiates of Technology and more than a hundred graduate engineers. IVF's researchers represent both a high level of theoretical expertise and a wide-ranging industrial experience.

IVP's headquarters are located in Göteborg and there are regional offices in Linköping, Stockholm and Luleå.

IVF is a non-profit foundation. Its two principals are NUTEK (the National Board for Industrial and Technical Development) and VI (the Association of Swedish Engineering Industries).

IVF's objectives include:

- monitoring, and evaluating production engineering developments at an international level
- initiating and operating research projects with industry and other national and international research institutions
- development by means by which new technical advances can be utilised by companies
- assisting in the introduction of new technology in individual companies

- disseminating knowledge of new methods of product development and manufacturing technology – not least to smaller and medium-sized companies having only limited resources for their own technology monitoring.

IVF works both with companies on specific projects for them and with research institutes in Sweden and in other countries. Group projects are an efficient way of acquiring and disseminating knowledge. The companies involved act not only as sources of finance, but also participate actively in the work of the project.

IVF has, through the facilities offered by its new headquarters, since the end of 1993, great possibilities to perform applied and production-scale tests of new working methods, equipment and methods of human and organisational aspects of decentralisation.

Through membership in international organisations, participation in joint projects and international standardisation work, IVF has built up a wide-ranging international network of contacts. Among the major European programmes, IVF is participating in for example ESPRIT, BRITE/Euram, COMETT, SPRINT, EUREKA/FAMOS, CRAFT and AIT and in the world-wide IMS-programme.

The Swedish Institute of
Production Engineering Research
Argongatan 30, S-431 53 Mölndal, Sweden

Telephone +46 31-706 60 00
Telefax +46 31-27 61 30
Head of IVF: Director Jan-Crister Persson

42 Dynamic Industrial Clusters

Bruce Ballantine, Business Decisions Ltd

For its Competitiveness Report (1994), UNICE, with support from DG III of the European Commission, commissioned a study from the Centre for Research in Economics and Business Administration in Bergen (SNF). It examines 'the role of dynamic industrial clusters in promoting the competitiveness of firms'. The study was undertaken by Professor Torger Reve and Professor Lars Mathiesen. This chapter summarizes its principal conclusions.

The conceptual basis of the study is the 'industrial diamond model' developed by Professor Michael Porter to analyse the competitive advantage of nations. The model consists of six elements which interact to form the competitiveness of an industry. The four major elements are: demand conditions; factor conditions; related and supporting industries; and the competitive arena. The other two elements included by Porter are the roles of government and chance. Reve extended the model to take into account the dynamic nature of the system in which there is continuous upgrading as a result of the interaction between the different elements.

Some of the key features that are common to dynamic industrial clusters are depicted graphically in Figure 42.1.

Case studies
This model was tested against five broadly based European case studies:

- *natural resource-based clusters*, illustrated by the Finnish forestry industry;
- *technology and market-based clusters*, illustrated by the German auto industry;
- *network-based clusters*, illustrated by the Italian textile and fashion industry;
- *knowledge-based clusters*, illustrated by the Norwegian maritime industry;
- *global hub clusters*, illustrated by financial services in the City of London.

The Finnish forestry industry
Finnish companies remain the market leader in several segments of the forestry value chain, despite the high price of Finnish timber and the emergence of low cost producers of chemical and mechanical pulp in South America and Africa. Their success is the result of a number of factors:

Demand conditions
- The Nordic countries represent more than one-quarter of the global market for printing papers.
- Finnish mills are among the most sophisticated and demanding customers of the fibre-processing industry in the world.
- End-users in Northern Europe are among the most demanding in the world.

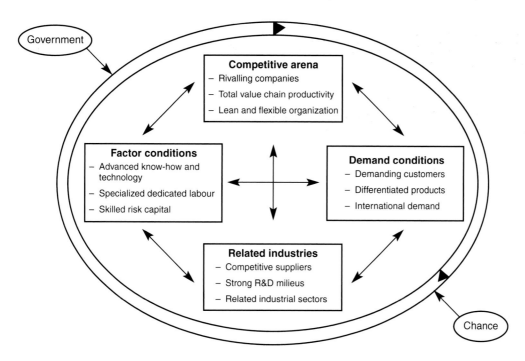

Figure 42.1 Dynamic industrial clusters: factors promoting industrial competitiveness

Factor conditions

- A systematic forest management programme has continually upgraded Finland's basic advantage.
- The large and well-educated labour pool has the specific skills and experience required by companies in the cluster.

Related industries

- Close relations exist between the forestry companies, pulp and paper companies, and companies in the fibre-processing machine sector.
- Engineering and technical consulting companies have also developed.

Competitive arena

- Domestic competition is limited but cooperative strategies, including joint ventures, have been developed to meet global competition.

Government policy

- Government support has focused on the infrastructure needed for the sector, such as R&D, education and transport.

Chance

- After the Second World War, there was a significant increase in demand for forestry products, which the Finnish industry was able quickly to satisfy.

The German auto industry

German companies remain at the forefront of the global automobile industry, particularly in terms of high-performance cars. Their success is based on successful differentiation rather than cost leadership.

Demand conditions

- The German domestic market is the third largest in the world.
- German car buyers are unusually demanding, and have encouraged German car makers to develop more advanced cars.

Factor conditions

- The apprenticeship training system is one source of loyal, skilled employees.
- German universities, including specialized institutes, are a source of mechanical engineering graduates. They are also a source of R&D expertise.
- A selective factor disadvantage is the high level of German wages and the short working week.

Almost 80 years of R&D for the paper industry
The Finnish Pulp and Paper Research Institute

The Finnish pulp and paper industry ranks sixth in the world as a producer, but second as an exporter of pulp and paper products. Annual pulp production is about 8 million tonnes, paper production 7 million tonnes and board production 2 million tonnes. In order to ensure effective long-term R&D, the industry 79 years ago set up a joint research organization, The Finnish Pulp and Paper Research Institute (KCL).

KCL was established in 1916 as a research institute for the Finnish chemical industry. Its first premises were a modest room in connection with the Helsinki University. By the 1920s, however, KCL had become a research institute serving the Finnish pulp and paper industry. With a staff of 320 and a budget of FIM 110 millions, KCL is today the largest research establishment of its kind in the world. Its work encompasses all the unit processes of papermaking, from wood raw material through to the final printed product.

KCL is located in Espoo close to Helsinki University of Technology and the Technical Research Centre of Finland. Its 80,000 cubic metres of building volume include a modern pilot plant. There are also well equipped laboratories, where stages of the papermaking process can be studied on a small scale.

Financing
Some 88% of KCL's budget comes from industry, either in the form of grants or from contract research. Public sector financing accounts for 12% and is allocated on a project-by-project basis. KCL is closely involved in international research work. About 25% of all public sector financing obtained by KCL in 1995 is for international cooperation projects. The research activities of KCL can be classified as follows: 15% consists of jointly financed goal-oriented basic research with a future time span of 5-10 years. 50% consists of jointly financed technical research related to existing products and processes with a time span of 1-5 years. The remaining 35% consists of assignments carried out for individual clients, often dealing with very acute and current problems. Jointly funded research is, of course, for members only. In the area of contract research, however, KCL can also take on work from non-members including foreign companies.

Research
Research themes currently featured in the research programme at KCL include the following subjects:

Efficient utilization of existing fibre raw materials.

Fibre and paper physics, the aim being to improve end-product quality and paper web runnability. Surface treatment technologies with the aim of improving paper printability.

Energy saving and/or improved energy utilization in pulping and papermaking processes. For studies related to mechanical pulping, a new, full-size thermomechanical pulping station was installed in 1991.

Development of non-chlorine based bleaching processes. In this area, investigations related to the use of different oxygen chemicals are of the utmost importance, but work on other methods is also carried out. The MILOX process is an example of a new pulping process developed at the KCL Paper Science Centre. The process is based on peroxyformic acid cooking followed by alkaline peroxide bleaching.

The improvement of process control is a very important area of research in terms of the efficiency of the process and the consistency of product quality. For this purpose KCL has developed its own system called KCL WEDGE. The system is now marketed by KCL Development Oy, a company established for this purpose.

Even though waste paper resources are very limited in Finland, recycled fibre has become an important raw material for the Finnish paper industry. KCL is currently researching the use of recycled fibre in Finnish paper grades.

In recent years, research related to environmental problems has occupied about 15-20% of KCL's total capacity. Considerable resources are being devoted to studying the effects on the environment of effluents and solid wastes from pulp, paper and board mills. To reduce discharges by means of process modifications and effluent treatment methods are also being studied.

KCL Pilot Plant
Process research, evaluation of raw materials and development of industrial products generally require experiments to be carried out under realistic conditions. KCL has a modern and well equipped pilot plant, which can offer the full range of experimental work starting from wood and finishing with a four-colour print.

One of the latest units installed at the pilot plant is a state-of-the-art TMP/CTMP refiner, which can be used for research aimed at energy saving, pulp quality improvement, raw material evaluation and refiner segment trials.

The paper machine offers excellent opportunities for experimental papermaking. Furnishes can be run on the 850 mm wide machine, which includes a headbox, fourdrinier dewatering equipment, 3-nip press section, steam-heated dryer section and machine calender.

Evaluation of base paper, runnability and coating colour is an important part of R&D work at the paper mill. Since mill-scale experiments are expensive, KCL offers pilot-scale coating facilities where clients can conduct their own trials under realistic conditions.

The sheet offset and heatset web offset printing presses at KCL pilot plant are production-scale machines that supplement the pilot trials with controlled test printing under conditions corresponding to those used in commercial practice.

KCL Paper Science Centre
KCL Paper Science Centre (PSC) was founded at KCL in 1989. Its purpose is to promote basic research and the training of scientists and to enhance international cooperation in the pulp and paper industry.

The PSC has established close links with universities and research institutes both in Finland and abroad. University professors participate in its work, either by heading specific projects or by acting as scientific advisers.

Postgraduate and doctoral theses are completed at the PSC, and the research projects also offer study and training opportunities for undergraduate students.

Research focuses on the fundamental physics and chemistry of pulping and papermaking, including the raw materials used and the end products. Although the PSC is concerned principally with research projects, its expertise and scientific equipment are available to outside parties through contract research.

International research cooperation growing
For several years now, KCL has been involved in a variety of joint international projects in the Nordic countries. The Nordpap programme has been launched by the Nordic Industrial Foundation for research by the Nordic pulp and paper industry. KCL played a major role in developing the programme. KCL has taken part in the Nordic Environmental Technology Programme, also supported by the Nordic Industrial Foundation. KCL has also participated in international cooperation at the European level and has been involved in several projects funded by the EU Commission. When Finland now is a full member of EU, the importance of European research cooperation is increasing rapidly.

Oy Keskuslaboratorio-Centrallaboratorium AB
The Finnish Pulp and Paper Research Institute
PO Box 70, FIN-02151 Espoo, Finland

Leader
in pulp and paper research

Founded in 1916, KCL is an independent industrially owned research institute serving the pulp, paper and paperboard industry.

The institute has a staff of 300, of whom approx. 100 are graduates in technology or natural sciences. About 70% of the institute's capacity is devoted to technical research and development for the financing companies. This also includes goal-oriented basic research. The remaining capacity consists of contract research for specific member or non-member clients.

A specific feature of KCL is its pilot plant where all the major unit processes of pulping and paper-making are simulated. This pilot plant also includes a four-colour high-speed heatset offset printing press.

The Finnish Pulp and Paper Research Institute
P.O. Box 70, FIN-02151 Espoo, FINLAND
Tel. +358-0-43 711, Fax +358-0-464-305

Related industries
- German suppliers are competitive and often world-leading companies in their own right.
- The large number of highly competitive suppliers, concentrated in the same areas as the car makers, allow constant interaction between supplier and producer to improve the performance of components and high-performance cars.
- Germany is the home base to world-class manufacturers of production machinery of almost all kinds.

Competitive arena
- Competition between German high-performance car manufacturers has been particularly fierce, forcing competitors constantly to improve product and process technology.
- Competition tends to be based on technical matters rather than price.

Government policy
- The development of high-performance cars was encouraged by the Autobahns which were built during the 1930s.
- Rigorous annual safety inspections were started earlier than in other countries.
- The taxation and environmental policies of the German government have tended to lead policies in other countries.

Chance
- The oil price shock gave fuel-efficient German cars an advantage in the American market.

The Italian textile and clothing industry

The textile and fashion cluster based in Northern Italy offers a wide range of products and services. Italian companies have dominant positions in a number of segments. Supplies of machinery and speciality inputs are dominated by Italian companies.

Demand conditions
- Textile and clothing manufacturers are sophisticated and demanding buyers of tools and machinery.
- The very specialized retailers are extremely knowledgeable and demanding intermediate buyers.

- Italian clothing customers are among the world's most sophisticated and advanced buyers.

Factor conditions
- There are few natural advantages and, in fact, a number of disadvantages such as the high cost of capital. These disadvantages have pressured Italian firms to move into the high-priced segments.
- The family-like organizational structures are particularly well suited to the demands of the textile and clothing sector.

Related industries
- Close vertical relationships between a wide range of specialized firms, throughout the value chain, are of great importance to the textile and clothing cluster.
- The cluster is geographically concentrated in a small area in Northern Italy.

Competitive arena
- Competition is fierce between the large number of family or family-like companies that perform the same type of activities within a concentrated geographic area.
- The separate distribution channels used by the different suppliers also add to the intensity of competition.

Government policy
- National policies (such as labour market regulations) have tended to operate against the best interests of the sector, but local governments have been more supportive.

Chance
- The more or less continuous devaluation of the Italian lira has benefited the sector.

The Norwegian maritime industry

The Norwegian maritime industry has succeeded through a specialization strategy. Shipyards concentrate on the advanced needs of demanding customers, such as offshore constructions for the North Sea oil industry. Shipping companies concentrate on high-value applications such as chemical tankers.

Demand conditions
- Success for Norwegian shipowners is linked principally to the level of world trade.

- A strong home market has been the basis for the success of Norwegian yards and suppliers of maritime equipment and services.

Factor conditions
- Labour of high quality is easily recruited for shipbuilders, service suppliers and shipowners.
- A common pool of knowledge has been developed throughout the Norwegian maritime research milieu.
- Skilled risk capital is also available.

Related industries
- There are close know-how links between customers, manufacturers and suppliers of speciality inputs and related services such as insurance and project management.

Competitive arena
- The Norwegian shipping industry is characterized by intense, often personal rivalry between a number of fierce competitors, most of whom are located in Oslo or Bergen.
- Shipyards and producers of maritime equipment have tended to specialize more, but there are a number of competitors in each speciality.

Government policy
- The Norwegian tax system has benefited shipowners through a favourable system for financing risky shipping projects.
- Subsidies and protective policy have been important factors historically in determining the ability of companies to stay in the global shipping industry.

Chance
- The oil price shocks in the 1970s had a major influence on the development of the maritime sector and the Norwegian shipping industry responded quickly.

Financial services in the City of London

London is the third leg in the global financial market with New York and Tokyo. It has a major share of long-standing services such as international bank lending and investment management, but it also has a large share of newer businesses such as swaps and currency options.

Demand conditions
- The City has developed naturally from serving the needs of the British Empire in the nineteenth century to the needs of multinationals in the late twentieth.
- Customers are sophisticated with a wide range of requirements.

Factor conditions
- The City has been able to draw its talent from a wide range of schools, universities and countries.
- In-house, on-the-job training is of particular importance in this sector, so skills are passed from employee to employee.
- Back-office costs are relatively low.

Related industries
- There is a large number of companies offering a wide range of services within the 'Square Mile' of the City of London.

Competitive arena
- Fierce competition exists between the great number of firms offering similar services not only in London but also in the other two financial centres.

Government policy
- English commercial law is a sound basis for financial contracts.
- The deregulation of the financial services sector provided a major boost to the competitiveness of the sector.

Chance
- Many of the rival centres, particularly in Europe, have suffered from restrictive practices and policies.

Conclusion

SNF conclude that 'Europe needs firms and industries that can win in global competition, not ... industries which require protection from competitive forces to survive.' They argue that the future competitiveness of Europe will depend on the development of cluster industries.

The critical success factors which are common to these five clusters are:
- *Time* is needed to develop the industrial base, such as long-lasting customer relations and brand name positions; to create the necessary

knowledge base, in technology, production and marketing; and to harness the capital and skills needed to exploit the market opportunities.

■ *Critical mass* is important, in specialist niche-oriented industries as well as in industries where economies of scale and scope are present, to undertake each of the stages in the value chain most effectively.

■ Individual *entrepreneurs* play an important role in the early development of clusters because they are willing to take 'unusual' risks.

■ Close relations with international *demanding customers* are probably the single most important factor for international competitiveness, because they encourage innovation and high-quality products.

■ The mixture of *competitive and cooperative relations* between suppliers and customers and even between companies that are competitors in other segments or sectors is another key success factor, because they encourage the development of new products and new processes.

■ The *innovative capabilities of suppliers and sub-suppliers* are critical because they provide new

technology and new production methods, and influence total costs.

■ *Flexible organization and management* is important so that companies can adapt quickly to changing technologies and changing consumer needs.

■ Clusters develop most effectively when there is *continuous investment* by all members of the cluster in knowledge and relationships, so that improvement can be continuous.

■ Cluster industries are subjects of *national pride*, so that they attract the best talent and the best of all the factors of production. Clusters should also attract effective government attention.

References

Michael Porter (1990) *The Competitive Advantage of Nations*, Macmillan Press, Basingstoke.

Torger Reve, Terje Lensberg and Kjell Grønhaug (1992) *A Competitive Norway*, Foundation for Research in Economics and Business Administration, Bergen, Norway.

Torger Reve and Lars Mathiesen (1994) *European Industrial Competitiveness*, Foundation for Research in Economics and Business Administration, Bergen, Norway.

UNICE (1994) *Making Europe More Competitive: Towards World Class Performance*.

European Union R & D:

the Payoff for Industry

43

Mario Bellardinelli, Head of Unit, Dissemination of Scientific and Technical Knowledge, DG XIII, European Commission

It has long been a view of European Union politicians that European industry needs active encouragement to be able to beat its market competitors in terms of technological advancement. This belief has been turned to practice by committing a total of 15 billion ECU to a series of three R & D Framework Programmes. The budget for the Fourth Framework Programme, to cover the years 1994 to 1998, has been fixed at 12.3 billion ECU.

These are substantial sums of money and give a major impetus to European R & D (research and development) operations, yet there are large numbers of European industrialists, particularly in the small and medium-sized enterprise (SME) sector, who have only a sketchy knowledge of the whole process. That is disappointing both for the people concerned with promoting the work and also for the SMEs themselves. Not knowing what is happening means not being part of it – a great potential loss for European industry.

Advancement

So what is being done to help this drive for technological advancement and what exactly can European industry get from it? Put simply, the European Union makes funds available to research establishments and to industry – usually to partnerships of the two – to carry out *precompetitive* research projects. These projects are designed to produce results that can be incorporated by European industry into manu-

facturing or production processes or used in the development of new products.

The essence of the precompetition policy is that the EU is not directly funding a single organization or group to produce a profit-making item. It is accelerating research and development in matters which can then be used by European industry in general, so offering opportunities to manufacturers who cannot afford to carry out their own R & D programmes. The overall aim is to ensure that European industry can compete effectively with the rest of the world.

Finding suitable projects for funding has not been a problem for the EU. Invitations to request funding are oversubscribed and selections have to be made by the organizing departments. Getting the resulting project information to those who can use it has proved less easy, despite the fact that there are specific channels of communication set up and a number of places to begin enquiries.

Knowledge

The main problem among potential users seems to be a basic lack of knowledge that this information is there for them to take. From the moment that a project is agreed by the EU, details are available of the subject, the aims, the participating partners and the main points of contact for further information. Reports are made at agreed intervals on the progress of the projects and the whole process is open to those

43

areas of European industry which can take advantage of the project outcome.

Experience shows that much of European industry simply doesn't know that this information exists, yet there is active promotion via a number of routes. The Community Research and Development Information Service – known by its acronym CORDIS – offers free on-line enquiry and consultation access to a number of databases concerning the R & D activities. These databases cover the research programmes and individual projects, the partners involved, reports and other documentation, plus – for those who easily get lost in European Union jargon – a database of the acronyms used within the administration of the programmes.

News on R & D activities, quoting details of specific projects, is published regularly by CORDIS, both on line, on CD-ROM and in paper format. Directories of the projects and partners are also available in printed form for anyone not equipped for on-line access, and a variety of catalogues offer in-depth guidance to the main areas covered by EU research and development programmes. The on-line access to CORDIS is simply structured and costs only local telephone connection charges.

The CORDIS service is based in Luxembourg, as is the R & D help desk which can be contacted by fax for enquiries, but information is made available locally across the EU via a number of different means. Publications on R & D – indeed, all official EU publications – can be obtained from sales agents in each member country. Many publications are available free of charge on request from the R & D help desks. Assistance of a more personal nature can be found at one of the network of Innovation Relay Centres.

Innovation Relay Centres

As a result of a European Council decision in April 1992 a network of Innovation Relay Centres was established. These relay centres had the remit to promote the EU's R & D activities and to disseminate and exploit the results at local level. The Innovation Relay Centres' aim is to ensure that the EU's R & D programmes are used effectively to make European business more competitive. The centres are hosted by national organizations who already have the skills required to disseminate and exploit research results, bringing better communications and contacts with European business people.

If the sources are not known to those who can use the information, it can soon be corrected. If the lack of access to the information is the result of industry's failure to come to terms with the importance of the R & D drive, that is another matter. For those manufacturers missing out, it is a case of wasted potential.

Even this brief summary shows that there is ample opportunity for European industry to acquaint itself with what is happening in European Union R & D. A more detailed description of the sources would reveal a wealth of information being made available through a variety of easily accessible sources.

Partnerships

The opening up of the Single Market was intended to assist industry by removing barriers and standardizing approaches to trade. In this context, EU research and development encourages and funds partnerships across the European Union. This allows a combination of strengths from different countries and organizations in a way that would have been difficult to achieve beforehand. It is a structured opportunity – especially for smaller organizations – to be involved in pushing back technological frontiers and promoting the growth of European industry at the same time.

It is also an opportunity to benefit from the money paid by member states to the EU. As taxpayers we are ultimately the people who fund the research. As European citizens we should aim to benefit from this research. It would be a shame if that benefit were lacking because European industry failed to take the opportunities offered.

Note

There are areas of European industry fully aware of what is being done by the EU to encourage technological research and development – and there are the others. For those who feel they ought to know more, CORDIS should be the first place they look for information. The Community Research and Development Information Service (CORDIS) provides a repository for all knowledge generated by EU-sponsored research programmes. For further information on EU research and development activities contact:

Innovative Complete Solutions

The Fraunhofer-Institut Informations- und Datenverarbeitung (IITB) in Karlsruhe, Germany

Outsourcing of R&D

Innovative products and cost effective production techniques are vital prerequisites for the market success of industrial companies. Both aspects require constant R&D efforts, often in interdisciplinary co-operation. The complexity of today's technology allows only big enterprises to assemble all necessary expertise in their own organisation. And even big enterprises now observe the „lean" concept, which means lean production, lean management, and also lean R&D. Outsourcing of R&D is therefore constantly gaining in importance. That holds especially true for small and medium enterprises (SME), which in most cases are not able to maintain sufficient R&D capabilities. This deficiency can be compensated by university institutes and contract research organisations. While universities are oriented in principle towards basic research or short term developments, e.g. during the stay of post-graduates, and cannot provide follow-up service, contract research organisations on the other hand offer in most cases applied R&D including development of prototypes and operational systems. They are ready to provide maintenance and re-innovation of products. Taking into account the key function of R&D results as mentioned above outsourcing in this area needs competent and reliable partners.

The Fraunhofer-Gesellschaft

The Fraunhofer-Gesellschaft is Germany's and even Europe's leading non-profit organisation of applied research on a contract basis. As of August 1995 it maintains 46 research establishments at 31 locations and employs staff numbering 8000. Although the Fraunhofer-Gesellschaft was founded in 1949 it is still undergoing dynamic development with the establishment of new institutes and increasing staff levels as a consequence. The mission of the Fraunhofer-Gesellschaft, as explicitly formulated by the German Federal Government, is applied research and technology transfer of basic research results into industrial application. This applies especially, but not only, to supporting SMEs in their R&D needs.

The Fraunhofer-Institut Informations- und Datenverarbeitung

The Fraunhofer-Institut Informations- und Datenverarbeitung (IITB) is one of the 46 establishments. It has a permanent staff of 260, 170 of which are scientists and engineers, and is located at Karlsruhe, one of Germany's leading technology regions with a renowned Technical University, a variety of research centres, and a great number of high tech industrial companies. The Fraunhofer Institute IITB has been devoted since 1956 to applied research and technology transfer in the field of information and data processing, offering customers innovative solutions based on profound expertise in the fields of

• sensor technology and signal processing, • pattern recognition and classification • neural nets and fuzzy techniques • automatic and interactive image interpretation • human-machine interaction • Artificial Intelligence, knowledge-based systems • measurement and control systems, simulation • automation systems • distributed systems and communication • systems engineering • hardware and software development.

This compilation of expertise and methods in combination with the respective process know-how allows the institute to tackle problems from many different application areas. Problems that exceed the competency of the IITB itself can in many cases be solved in co-operation with other Fraunhofer institutes. The scope of services and supply ranges from consulting and preliminary studies through to systems design, development of products and application systems and up to commissioning, system maintenance and re-innovation, and customer training. Examples of application areas dealt with are control and automation systems as well as inspection and diagnosis systems and mechatronics for use in manufacturing and in in-process quality control. These activities are in many cases based on the design of distributed systems and the application of expert systems for improved process guidance. Network management of communication networks as well as management of electricity, water and gas supply systems constitute further important fields of application. A further focal point of efforts are assistance and surveillance systems for traffic control, passenger information, vehicle guidance and environmental situations. Solutions in these areas require special emphasis on the design of user-friendly human-machine interfaces, in which IITB has extensive experience. To improve its own efficiency, but also as an offer to its customers, IITB is developing engineering tools such as software design tools, simulation and evaluation tools for production lines, control systems and user interfaces. In addition, a conformance test laboratory for MAP and various fieldbus protocols as well as an EMC test laboratory for fieldbuses have been established, which offer their services outside the IITB. IITB co-operates with partners from all over Europe either in EEC funded projects or on the basis of bilateral contracts. A selection of examples from recent projects shall highlight the wide spectrum of IITB activities.

Logistics as a rationalisation tool in production

There is a lack of adequate logistics control systems, especially for application in SMEs. They are vital to maintain competitiveness. Simulation systems will gain a major role in this field. They have been long applied for optimising the equipment of manufacturing lines, but the application of on-line simulation systems to optimise the operation of manufacturing lines is not yet common. The central problem is a solution for an optimised real-time scheduling of resources observing the relevant technical restrictions. Based on experience in scheduling in flexible manufacturing lines and in centralised tool management IITB has developed simulation-based systems for logistics control in SMEs.

Evaluation of monospectral and colour images for real-time industrial quality control

In a production line for plywood, large dried veneer-boards have to be cut into strips of certain dimensions and allocated to six different quality classes according to the presence of holes, splits, knots, barks, discoloration and brightness of the veneer. The system developed by IITB classifies the surface of the 3.8m wide veneer moving at a speed of 50 m/min and calculates the optimal cutting positions aiming at maximum yield. Processing of information from colour images is highly important in the inspection of natural goods and also of products in the food and pharmaceutical industries. By use of line scan cameras a high throughput can be achieved with good local resolution. Based on a colour image processing system, which uses sophisticated procedures at a processing speed of 10 Mbyte/s, IITB has developed an application system for the tobacco industry to detect and remove impurities in the tobacco with high reliability.

Automatic image sequence evaluation of crash-test films in the automotive industry

The system developed by IITB automatically extracts the trajectories of special crash marks, which are placed on the dummies representing the passengers, from the image sequence of the high speed crash film. The method used realises an automatic search, automatic positioning and robust tracking of crash marks. It replaces correlation-based methods and enhances them with respect to robustness and accuracy.

Diagnosis of combustion engines by analysis of the rotational uniformity

SERUM (**S**ystem for the **E**valuation of the **R**otational **U**niformity of **M**otors) is a powerful tool for a variety of diagnostic tasks in testing combustion engines, e.g. the cylinder specific detection of misfiring. It is based on a high precision analysis of the angular velocity and acceleration of the crankshaft. SERUM can be used as an individual tool implemented on a portable PC for development and optimisation of motors or as a standard module fully integrated into test beds for quality control and service.

Knowledge-based system for configuration of mixing machines as sales support

COMIX Is a knowledge-based system to assist the distribution department in the configuration of mixing machines. In a first step of the configuration process requirements are analysed. In a second step a mixing machine is constructed which meets these process requirements. The knowledge about physical devices is implemented in objects which represent a model of the mixing machine in a "part-of" hierarchy. The knowledge about the configuration process consists of rules and functions which are implementations of computational laws and industrial standards for mechanical devices. Also heuristic knowledge about the configuration of mixing machines is used. The process of configuration is done stepwise until all parameters of the machine are determined.

Knowledge-based multimedia urban transport and city information system

Public transport is a complex problem that requires information systems able to process a large amount of data by observing additional instructions and experience rules. IITB has developed a knowledge-based method providing decision support using a model of the infrastructure and the transportation process. One application deals with a computer-aided traveller and city information system, which aims to generate optimal routes and connections in complex urban transportation networks with different services (bus, tram, etc.). This system is in operation in the city of Dresden.

Object-oriented production monitoring and control

The continuously increasing requirements on process monitoring and control systems and the increase of the complexity of monitoring and control applications has led to a new concept for process control systems based on the 32-bit generation of computers, standardised communication systems as well as the object-oriented modelling and programming approach. A concrete system implementation PROVIS is available and is installed in a first application at Mercedes-Benz, Bremen.

These examples show that the Fraunhofer-Institute IITB is a competent and reliable partner of European enterprises when outsourcing of R&D is requested.

EMILIA ROMAGNA TECHNOLOGICAL DEVELOPMENT AGENCY

Via Morgagni, 4 - I 40122 Bologna - Italy
Tel 39 51 236242 - Fax 39 51 22780

19, Avenue de L'Yser - B 1040 Bruxelles
Tel 32 2 7327161 - Fax 32 2 7363190

E-mail: NOTICE (VANS): mailbox IT 2026
EUROKOM: M8258@eurokom.ie
INTERNET: aster@ervet.nettuno.it

ASTER PROFILE

ASTER, Emilia Romagna Technological Development Agency, is a non-profit-making organisation which, since 1985, plans, promotes and supports industrial competitiveness improvement, supplying the companies with customised services, with particular emphasis on SMEs needs for innovation, technology transfer, internationalisation, business co-operation, quality improvement and information.

ASTER acts in strict collaboration with companies, research institutes and universities, entrepreneurial associations, Chambers of Commerce and governmental bodies in order to create networks operating at regional, national and international level.

Official expert of the European Parliament, ASTER, with its permanent office in Brussels, provides a connection between the European Commission (CE), the Emilia Romagna Region Government and the companies.

ASTER supplies information services on the bases of both existing national and international data bases and ASTER ad hoc data bases containing information about industrial companies operating in the region, research and technology transfer facilities, innovative enterprises, testing and analysis labs, etc.

ASTER belongs to the ERVET System, created by Emilia Romagna Region for the establishment of enterprises regional policies.

INTERNATIONAL NETWORKS

• **SELEDA**
"Small Enterprises and Local Economic Development Association", constituted by the British Council in order to supply services within integrated initiatives.

• **EURADA**
"European Association of Development Agencies".

• **SCIENCE PARK NETWORK**
Within the framework of CE DG XIII SPRINT programme, project co-ordinated by English Research Society Segal Quince Wicksteed.

• **EDI**
"Electronic Data Interchange", CE DG XIII European network of Awareness Centres for the promotion of EDI in the countries of CE and EFTA.

• **EDITEX EUROPE**
Network of European Research Centres, which, in co-operation with some European textile-clothing association, are testing the EDI for the textile industry.

• **CRAFT Regional Focal Point**
Collaboration with ENEA, one of the National Focal Points appointed by CE DG XII, for the promotion of CRAFT programme, aiming at co-financing research and technological development projects submitted by SMEs. ASTER assists SMEs in obtaining CE funds for their activities.

• **THERMIE OPET NETWORK**
In the framework of CE DG XVII THERMIEprogramme, ASTER was member of OPET, "Organisations for the Promotion of Energy Technology" which organised several meetings and seminars also in East European countries.

• **TII**
"Technology Information Innovation", European association of the innovation support centres and institutions.

• **BC-NET**
"Business Co-operation Network", created by CE DG XXIII in order to encourage industrial co-operation.

• **BRE**
"Bureau de Rapprochement des Entreprises", created CE DG XXIII for the enhancement of industrial co-operation with particular emphasis on Non European countries.

• **COOPECO**
Network for the industrial co-operation with Latin America.

• **FLAIR FLOW**
European Network created in the framework of DG XII FLAIR programme for the diffusion of the results of research and technological development in the agro-industrial sector.

• **BOLIVAR**
International non-governmental organisation whose mission is promoting technological, productive, financial and commercial integration among and with Latin American nations.

MAIN TRANSNATIONAL PROJECTS OF INNOVATION'S DIFFUSION AND TRANSFER

• SPRINT - SPI 072 - Production Planning Software
Within the framework of the CE DG XIII SPRINT Programme, ASTER was leader partner of the specific project SPI 072 "Flexible automation for SMEs". The project faced the problem of Advanced Manufacturing Technology application in SMEs.

• SPRINT - SPI 072 /2 - Quality Assurance Software
Project which aims, starting from the companies' needs, at the customisation and experimentation of software tools supporting the Quality Assurance.

• SPRINT - MINT
ASTER was national leader of the completed MINT project which aimed at promoting the absorption of new technologies by SMEs through the use of consultants with expertise in innovation management.

• SPRINT - SPAC 5/2 - Discovery
CE project aimed at the diffusion, in SMEs, of the results obtained by SPRINT's Specific Projects.

• RACE - WORKNET
ASTER is the co-ordinator of a WORKNET research project, which aims at setting up pilot applications of telework in large, medium and small sized industrial and service enterprises in Italy and France.

• TEDIS - EDI Awareness Centre
Constituted in ASTER in 1993, financed by CE within the TEDIS Programme. Main objective is the promotion of EDI in SMEs and public bodies. ASTER has been working in the field of EDI since 1989.

• TEDIS - ENEIP
Co-ordination of 13 European centres for the analysis of the census of documents, standards, subjects and publications about the EDI in the whole Europe. CE-ASTER project.

• TELEMATIQUE - TEXMOD
Technical co-ordination of the application project of EDI in the textile-clothing pipeline.

• TELEMATICS - TEX AT WORK
Inter-sector EDI and telework application, starting from the textile-clothing pipeline, involving the fields of transports, distribution and banks. Biennial CE-ASTER project.

• CZECH REPUBLIC - PHARE
In co-operation with Nomisma, under CE Phare Programme, project on "Organisational Structure for Administering SMEs Programmes in Czechoslovakia".

• TACIS - KIEV Energy Centre
Evaluation of the energetic efficiency in the industrial and construction sectors for the constitution of an Energy Centre in Kiev. CE project.

• POLAND - BSC
Evaluation study of the Business Support Centre programme in Poland.

• E.DE.T.T. - European Development of Thermal Tourism.
It aims at exchanging experiences among 4 CE partner regions in the field of thermal tourism.

• PARAGUAY - MERCOSUR
Programme of assistance to the Paraguay industrial restructuring in view of the creation of MERCOSUR.
In collaboration with ENEA, National Body for Technology, Energy and Environment.

• URUGUAY - Innovative Energetic Technologies
Consultancy for the Uruguay Ministry of Industry about innovative energetic technologies, know-how transfer, professional training and assistance in the realisation of pilot projects. CE - Paraguay Co-operation Programme project with ASTER's co-ordination.

• ARGENTINA - RUE
Programme for the creation of a Rational Use of Energy Unit in Argentina. CE - ENEA project.

• CHILE - AL INVEST
Organisation of partnership meetings between European and Latin American companies in the telecommunication and software/hardware sectors. CE programme.

• TACIS - MONGOLIA
In collaboration with ERVET, participation to CE project "Reinforcement of Employment Services in Mongolia", which aims at the fostering of the administrative sector and at the management of Labour Exchanges in Mongolia.

• MEDITERRANEAN AREA
Support to Emilia Romagna government for the development of international projects and activities, with specific initiatives in Occupied Territories, Israel, Tunisia and Morocco.

• NOW - NOVA
Support services in the elaboration of entrepreneurial projects for the development of a feminine entrepreneurial class and employment. CE-ASTER project.

ASTER'S PRODUCTS AND SERVICES FOR INNOVATION

A) INNOVATION DIAGNOSIS AND TECHNICAL ASSISTANCE IN THE COMPANIES
• Companies Diagnosis
Analysis of the companies' needs in order to find the best solution in the choice of new technologies in the following fields:
- Information systems
- Industrial automation and new process technologies
- CAD/CAM
- Quality
- EDI
This service uses a common methodology for all productive fields which is composed of a preliminary analysis and a check-up.

B) INTERNATIONAL FUNDING, PARTNERSHIP AND COMPANIES EXCHANGE
• COUNTRY DESK
Global service of information and assistance to the companies in order to set up commercial relations with Non-European countries.
• PARTNERSHIP
In order to encourage the inter-regional exchanges in Europe, ASTER supplies the companies with the opportunity to set up relations with international partners and to be thus introduced in new markets.
• CHANCE
Scheme for the exchange of research, technological and commercial opportunities, industrial co-operation and investment promotion. In collaboration with ERVET.
• ENTER
ASTER has developed a set of services devoted to promote access to European and extra European markets and to foster the use of CE Community funds and tools.
ENTER consists of the following actions.
a) information on EC programmes and calls for tender
b) assistance in EC calls for tender procedures
c) support in the identification of international partners
d) follow up after the approval of the project

C) DATA BASES
• Information from technological international on-line data bases
This information comes from international data bases which ASTER use regularly or "on demand".
ASTER has connections with about 10 international host computers and have access to about 1.000 data bases for the search of information including that of the European Parliament. The subjects are:
* Patents (trends, leaders, competitors, partners)
* Science and Technology (trends, research, solutions)
* Technical norms and standards
* New Products (producers, labels, innovations, strategies)
* Markets and Products (opportunities, risks and trends)
* Import/Export (international exchanges)

• IMPERO: information system on the Emilia Romagna companies. The database contains data related to 90.000 manufacturing companies.
DIRECTORIES
"Research and technology Transfer Facilities"
"Innovative Enterprises"
"Advanced Service Sector"
"Testing and Analysis Laboratories"

SPECIALIST NEWSLETTERS

• ASTERNEWS
Quarterly newsletter with information about technological, scientific, financial, commercial innovations at national and international level, information about how and where to get them and how to exploit them at the best.
• ENTERINFO
Monthly newsletter with information about the calls for proposals relating to the funding of the European Community
• CHANCE
Report about business and technology opportunities distributed every 40 days to the subscriber companies.
• TECH NEWS 44
Five four-monthly newsletter with specialist information about new patents, new products, market information, European legislation for the several sectors.
Ministry of Industry-ASTER project, addressed to new South Italian companies founded under law 44.
• EDI ITALIAN MAGAZINE
It offers a reasoned survey on the most interesting experiences of EDI introduction in Italy and Europe.

CONTACT COUNTRIES

Algeria, Angola, Argentina, Brazil, Bulgaria, Cambodia, Caribbean Countries, Czech Republic, Chile, China, CSI, Egypt, Eritrea, Ethiopia, Philippines, Gambia, Ghana, Japan, Jordan, India, Indonesia, Kenya, Lebanon, Malawi, Morocco, Mexico, Mongolia, Mozambique, Namibia, Nigeria, Baltic Countries, CE Countries, Palestine, Paraguay, Poland, Romania, Syria, Slovene, South Africa, Sudan, Swaziland, Tanzania, Occupied Territories, Tunisia, Ukraine, Uganda, Hungary, Uruguay, USA, Vietnam, Yemen, Zambia, Zimbabwe.

Institute for Surface Chemistry, YKI

Institute for Surface Chemistry, YKI, is an interdisciplinary research institute within applied surface and colloid chemistry, situated close to the Royal Institute of Technology in Stockholm, Sweden. Some seventy companies in the Foundation for Surface Chemistry Research are its principals together with the Swedish National Board for Industrial and Technical Development, NUTEK. YKI has some eighty employees and has been in business over 25 years. It is apart from a newly founded German institute the only surface chemistry institute in Europe. YKI has expanded over the last years and continues to do so as a result of growing industrial interest.

YKI's business concept is to increase the competitiveness of its member companies through surface chemistry. R&D in the form of open projects and confidential contract assignments are carried out by 65 researchers within four sections, oriented towards the following industries: forest products; materials & coatings; the chemical industry; and pharmaceuticals & food. In addition there are two more fundamentally oriented groups: The Surface Force Group KTH/YKI and The Thin Films Group.

Research topics include: environment-friendly surfactants, new cleaning/degreasing systems, coatings, filled plastics, surface modification/characterization, paper-ink-print, deinking, high performance ceramics, friction/wear/lubrication, foam, powder technology, emulsions, fat (lipid) technology and biosurfaces.

YKI helps companies with problem analyses (e.g. 1-2 weeks pre-study); literature surveys; qualified measurements (ESCA, AFM, FT-IR, particle sizing, rheology); improvement of existing and development of new products/processes; training within the fields of surface and colloid chemistry.

Member companies represent a wide range of industries including chemicals producers, forest products, plastics, paint, packaging, pharmaceutical, food and engineering companies. Examples are ABB Corporate Research, Akzo Nobel, Astra, Borealis, Castrol, Dow Europe, DSM Resins, Fuji Photo Film, Hoechst-Perstorp, Kraft Foods, Nalco Chemical, Novo Nordisk, Pharmacia, SCA, SKF, Stora, Tetra Pak and Unilever. Any company or association, regardless of nationality, can become a member.

YKI member companies receive direct access to research findings (open projects); large discounts and priority before non-members on contract research and YKI courses; a visit by YKI scientists during a free consultation day once a year; and many more benefits.

YKI's staff includes three professors, five associate or assistant professors and some 20 PhD students, all affiliated with a university department. This significantly increases the opportunity for active technology transfer to industry, also of results developed at research organizations other than YKI. YKI acts as a bridge between basic research and industrial R&D. Some ten visiting scientists per year also contribute to this. YKI especially encourages member companies to take advantage of the opportunity of placing their own personnel at the Institute for longer or shorter periods.

An important part of the activities of YKI is to organize courses and meetings to promote awareness of surface and colloid chemistry. Annually held events include an introductory course in industrial surface chemistry, a course on surfactants and polymers in aqueous solution and an industrial symposium on surface chemistry. In addition YKI also offers a diverse array of specialized courses and workshops.

Institute for Surface Chemistry, YKI
Drottning Kristinas vag 45, STOCKHOLM
Mailing address:
Box 5607, S-114 86 STOCKHOLM, Sweden

Tel: +46 8 790 99 00
Fax: +46 8 20 89 98
e-mail: info@surfchem.kth.se
No. of employees: ca. 80

ITEC – Instituto Tecnológico para a Europa Comunitária

ITEC – Instituto Tecnológico para a Europa Comunitária is a private non-profit organisation, based in Lisbon, Portugal, having three different lines of action:

- **Research, Development & Technology Transfer: CNT – Centre for New Technologies**

Six technology development and transfer centres are in operation. These are Advanced Production Technologies: Automation Robotics and Instrumentation; Environment (Combustion Processes and Noise Control); Materials (Cellular Materials and Laser Processing); Chemical Analysis; Industrial and Technology Management. CNT has major contracts with the Portuguese and European Industry for R&D and Technology Transfer. We also participate in several European Projects, namely within SPRINT, LIFE, Technology Validation, Craft, among others.

- **Advanced Training: CENFORTEC – Technological Training Centre**

ITEC has a large experience in Vocational Training, being responsible, since 1989, for more than 20,000 hours of training, involving about 1,000 trainees. As an UETP – University Enterprise Training Partnership, we have led several important Cornett contracts and we are now actively participating in Leonardo, Now and Adapt Projects.

- **Entrepreurial Activities: CVE – Centre For Entrepreneurship Support**

As the main promoter of CPIN, the Business and Innovation Centre of Lisbon, we have supported the creation of more than 25 technology based ventures in Portugal. ITEC has developed several other entrepreneurial activities, including a specific program to detect and support new technology based ventures opportunities, called "Programa EIE". We are now creating a Capital Network, with the collaboration of several national and international partners.

ITEC mission is to *"improve the potential of Portuguese industry by supporting companies in the development of technological competencies which allow them to obtain and sustain competitive advantages in international markets"*. Our strength relies in the three dimensions of activity, where technology and training can be integrated and a direct line of work exists to support new ventures based in RTD results.

ITEC also places a strong emphasis on the interface between the university and industry. Originally promoted by Instituto Superior Ténico (Technical University of Lisbon). ITEC keeps strong links with IST, acting as a vehicle of knowledge transfer and valuation as well as a feed-back channel for industry needs and expectations.

In order to respond to industry specific needs, ITEC has devoted a significant effort to the creation of innovative diagnosis methodologies. As a result, ITEC is now operating with RHI, a Human Resources Auditing Tool, that enables CENFORTEC to establish training actions that foresees the actual and future needs of the companies' competencies, providing them with important added value.

ITEC is also establishing TEC+, a programme to audit technology development necessities and innovation opportunities within industrial companies. With TEC+ we are providing an important basis for the work to be carried out by CNT. We are also aiming at a deep understanding of the Portuguese patterns in terms of technology development, fostering the role of ITEC as a policy advisor in terms Science and Technology. The success of TEC+ will make it possible for ITEC to carry out a real industrial oriented research & development.

These innovative methodologies are considered by ITEC as strong enabling mechanisms for our aims of growing penetration in the Portuguese as well as European markets.

Above all, ITEC is an open institution looking forward to have you working with us in research, training or entrepreneurship.

Contact: Eng. José Rui Felizardo – General Manager
Telephone: +351-1-847 68 40   **Fax:** +351 1 847 58 93
E-mail: irf.itec@telepac.pt

Addresses: Advanced Training (CENFORTEC):
R. dos Baldaques, 43 – 1900 Lisboa, Portugal
RD&T (CNT): Azinhaga dos Lameiros à estrada do Paço do Lumlar –
1699 Lisboa Codex, Portugal
Entrepreneurship Support (CVF):
Av. Almirante Reis, 178 r/c – 1000 Lisboa, Portugal

Since 1989

Instituto Tecnológico para a Europa Comunitária

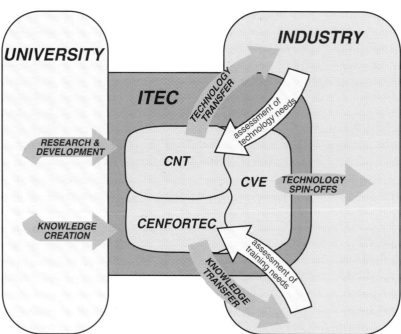

CNT - Centre for New Technologies

- Industrial Oriented R&D
- Demonstration of Advanced Technologies
- Technical Assistance

CVE - Centre for Entrepreneurship Support

- Entrepreneurial Development of Knowledge and Technology

CENFORTEC - Technological Training Centre

- Industrial Valuation of Knowledge
- Knowledge Dissemination
- Training Actions

TECHNOLOGICAL AREAS:

- Advanced Production Technologies
- Materials
- Environment
- Automation, Robotics and Instrumentation
- Industrial and Technology Management
- Chemical

Phone: +351 1 847 68 40   Fax: +351 1 847 58 93   E-mail: jrf.itec@telepac.pt
Address: Estrada do Paço do Lumiar - 1699 Lisboa Codex - Portugal

KOGAN PAGE

Simply the best in business publishing, from personal development to project planning, from Doing Business in Poland to Empowering Your Staff, Kogan Page covers it all. In fact, we have one of the most highly regarded management and business book lists in the world.

If you would like to find out more, call or write today for a free catalogue of publications.

Kogan Page Ltd,
120 Pentonville Road, London N1 9JN
Tel: 0171 278 0433   Fax: 0171 837 6348

43

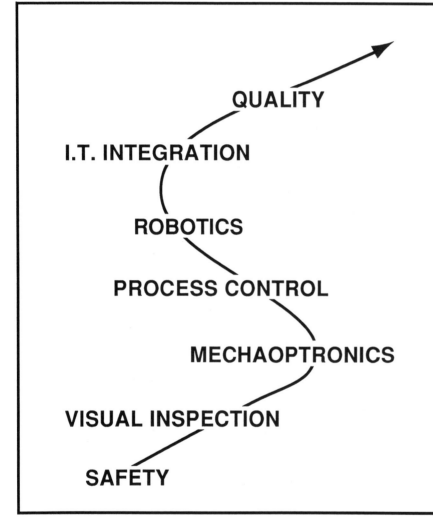

QUALITY

I.T. INTEGRATION

ROBOTICS

PROCESS CONTROL

MECHAOPTRONICS

VISUAL INSPECTION

SAFETY

Ricerca Sviluppo
Documentazione S.p.A.

Address: Via Martignacco, 23
33100 UDINE - ITALY
Phone: +39 432 546980
Fax: +39 432 545973
E-Mail: staff@eidon.it

Quality Management in Europe

44

David Murray, Management Consultant, Maine Consulting Services

Successful companies are devoting ever-increasing attention to the management of quality. In spite of this it is often argued that 'quality management' is about to die out and that the 'quality manager' will become extinct. As with many such over-simplifications there is some truth in this. The traditional quality manager may well be an endangered species. Close attention to the achievement and delivery of quality will, however, be neglected only by organizations with a corporate death-wish.

What are the changes, especially in Europe, sweeping the world of quality management? It is increasingly recognized that products are not merely products: there is a complex combination of product features; timely delivery; advice before purchase and on installation and advice and support during use, among many other components of a product–service mix. In service businesses a still wider variety of quality dimensions come to the fore; human relationships; effective communication; appropriate application of professional skill; listening under-standingly to each individual client. 'Quality' is broadening in other ways. It often incorporates types of managerial work which previously appeared under other headings: business process re-engineering, benchmarking, vision and culture development, to mention but three.

Models of quality management, such as that developed by the European Foundation for Quality Management (EFQM), are also helping to broaden the view of quality within business. This model looks at matters such as customer satisfaction, impact on society and business results. It is concerned with the processes by which these outputs are delivered and the policies, strategies, resource management and leadership which give direction and energy to them.

Companies throughout Europe which have applied the ISO 9000 quality-management system standard to their operations, are now discovering that there are similar standards, either already in existence or about to materialize, covering such topics as environmental impact, health and safety, and even personnel development and training. There is a move toward what some call 'integrated management' but which can be more appropriately, if narrowly, labelled as 'integrated technical administration'.

Quality is moving away from a concentration on sterile uniformity toward managing diversity where every customer wants something different, and toward facilitating continual development where the pace of change is such that to do something the same twice-over is to provide an obsolete service.

Looking forward, the advent of technologies such as robotics, and eventually bioengineering, will remove the emphasis on controlling the variability caused by human involvement in production. This will lead to more attention being given to the quality of intellectual input, as well as to the human rela-tionships surrounding the core productive process.

Kooperationsstelle Hamburg

Research, development and innovation for emission-free industrial cleaning, degreasing and removing

Organic solvents – reduction of the emissions urgently necessary

Replacing of organic solvents is an urgent need of the European Industry. The daily use of volatile organic solvents (VOC) can be hazardous for the user and the environment trough emissions in air, water and soil. Organic solvent emission is a major factor in the build up of atmospheric ozone, a powerful irritant gas, which affects the mucous membrane and respiratory tract and may be carcinogenic. The recent news about summer-smog and the destruction of the upper ozone layer will lead to stricter regulations e.g. the proposed VOC – Directive of the European Commission.

Solutions through product and process innovation

In many cases it is possible to substitute highly volatile organic solvents by cleaning agents that are made of fatty acid esters of vegetable oils (VOFA). In the printing industry, the development of these vegetable cleaning agents has led to a major innovative push in cleaning technology. Initial tests in other industries have shown that fatty acid esters may be suitable for a wide variety of purposes. Emission free, non-toxic and environment friendly cleaning agents are prerequisites for the technology of the future. Fatty acid esters fulfil these requirements.

Fatty acid ester have proved effective in a range of applications. VOFA are produced mainly from renewable resources. They are based on vegetable oils such as soy-bean oil, rape-seed and coconut oils. Fatty acid esters (formed by reacting fatty acids with alcohol) have physical and chemical properties which make them suitable as cleaning agents with a wide range of industrial applications. The most important advantages fatty acid esters have over highly volatile solvents are as follows: • good cleaning effect • low emissions to the air • no toxicity • based on renewable resources.

Benefits to the companies

Benefits gained by successful conversion to vegetable based cleaning products are: • prevention of solvent emissions at the workplace • reduction of the ecological (environmental) pollution especially emissions to the air • as a rule no requirements for explosion-proofing measures • lowering of the fire protection costs • reduction of the consumption of cleaning agents by up to 80% • lowering of the stock-keeping costs

Printing shops that use this new technology now are e.g.: Express Printers, Manchester (UK) Mohndruck, Gutersloh (G), Europe's biggest printing shop Mead-Group, Food Packaging, PLM Houstrup, Houstrup (DK), printing on cans, National Printing Shops (Notes, Stamps).

Further industrial applications

We are just exploring the market of metal degreasing and other applications. New projects will deal with further applications as • mould releases in the construction industry, • graffiti removing, • removing in the paint and ink industry.

An indicator of the increasing prevalence of VOFA is discernible in the European market development of products. In cleaning technology the trend is clearly towards less or non volatile VOFA. The variety of the new products, however, makes it necessary to have criteria for an evaluation of the products.

Kooperationsstelle Hamburg (Cooperation Office)

The "Kooperationsstelle" is a clearing house set up with the objective of improving the exchange of knowledge and information between universities and the workplace. It is supported by the Federal State of Hamburg. In the last years it has carried out research and technology transfer projects.

Kooperationsstelle Hamburg provides research, development and technology transfer. The Kooperationsstelle assists with • a neutral advice, independent from producers and sellers • checklists, • manuals, • help to start projects of all sizes, • experience in national and international project management.

The Kooperationsstelle has in the area of technology developed two bigger projects: **SUBPRINT** for the printing industry and **V**OFA**Pro**, mainly for the metal industry.

European projects: SUBPRINT and VOFAPro.

SUBPRINT is now operating in a total of twelve European countries: Denmark, Germany and Spain, Italy, the Netherlands, the United Kingdom and Luxembourg, Belgium, Austria, Finland, Iceland and Sweden. SUBPRINT has thereby become the largest project within the framework of the SPRINT programme of the EU, GD XIII. The SUB-PRINT project has been extremely successful. In Denmark almost 50% of all Danish printworks now use vegetable based products; both the work and health and the environmental protection agencies have adopted the use of non-volatile solvents into their statutory regulations and are working towards the complete substitution in offset printing.

Overall, great interest in and a good reception for the new technology on the part of the participants from the printing industry have been reported. Practical instruction is the focus of the project work. The clearly established interest in VOFA in all European countries is an effect not only of the increased statutory environmental and work and health demands being made on the printing industry but also of the work of the SUBPRINT project.

In areas of manual application of the cleaning technique it is clear that VOFA have already assumed the pole position of being the newest advance in technology and have been accepted in the industry. In May 1995 at the largest trade fair, DRUPA, in Dusseldorf, the world-wide largest manufacturer of sheet-fed offset printing presses presented a new offset printing press which can be cleaned entirely with VOFA. In addition, the first technical solutions for the recycling of VOFA are now appearing. SUBPRINT has provided such criteria for vegetable cleaning agents. These serve as the basis for and an aid to the selection of alternative products.

On the basis of the SUBPRINT project the Kooperationsstelle extended their work in this sector by another big project, **V**OFA**Pro**.

VOFA**Pro** was established in 1995 as a research project financed by the Agro-Industrial Research Program (AIR), a program of the European Commission jointly conducted by the Directorate General XII (Science, Research and Development) and GD VI (Agriculture and Rural Development). The main goal of the project work is classification and adaptation of vegetable oils and their fatty acid esters in order to widen the fields of application as alternatives to organic solvents. The project is organised as a joint research project with the co-operation of partners in Denmark, Ireland, the Netherlands and Germany. VOFAPro is a initiative of Kooperationsstelle Hamburg and is being carried out in four member countries of the European Union. Kooperationsstelle Hamburg is co-ordinating the project and has the legal responsibility towards the Commission of the European Union.

Lothar Lißner, Kooperationsstelle Hamburg
Besenbinderhof 60, 20097 Hamburg
Tel ++49/40/2858-640, Fax: ++49/40/2858-641

Such a future will demand people with different skills. Indeed, a new generation of people, educated differently and from a broader spectrum of disciplines than could ever have been envisaged by the older generation of quality specialists, is beginning already to shape this future.

The long, hard road – and Europe

One of the most serious failings of quality management on both sides of the Atlantic in recent years has been the habit of following the latest fashions. Companies have drowned under a succession of programmes, all of which made promises of a wonderful future, but were then either abandoned or simply forgotten because the panacea did not deliver a cure; or at least, not within the short timescale allowed, before patience ran out and another fad appeared on the horizon.

Quality management is not about quick and easy answers, nor is it about uni-dimensional techniques and campaigns. It is about a long, hard road toward total excellence that will never be fully achieved because the goal posts will always keep moving. It is about managing a complex combination of technical,

system and human components in a way which is appropriate to the nature, style, stage of development and business aspirations of the individual company, its markets and its customers. The current seriously inadequate ISO 9000 standard is now approaching a substantial revision. Pressure is being exerted, especially from the UK, to ensure that the version to be issued around the year 2000 reflects such understandings.

Within Europe there are specific issues. Competing regions of the world with low costs can now use technologies and managerial methods that enable them to produce both economically and reliably within demanding schedules. Europe, each of its countries, and each individual company, must establish what are to be their competitive roles in the world, focusing the management of quality on the critical success factors for those roles.

What about Central and Eastern Europe? A business magazine in the region recently published a letter complaining that a major Western European manufacturer was selling products manufactured in Eastern Europe without publicizing their source. It was argued that the Western public image of the

Does your boardroom really value ISO 9000?

Lloyd's Register Quality Assurance managing director, Linda Campbell, explains why the boardroom should be using quality management systems as a strategic weapon:

If I were a betting woman I would wager my house on 95 per cent of CEOs not understanding quality management systems, despite their fine words and their signature on their quality policy. The problem as I see it is that most CEOs don't own their quality management system. They see it as something to do with the shop floor. So it's not strategic and consequently has no impact on their thinking. The fact that CEOs have no expectation of ISO 9000 as a strategic tool limits what management systems can do for their business, which in turn reinforces their restricted view of ISO 9000's value.

We in the quality profession haven't helped to dispel this view. In fact, we have done too much to reinforce it by focusing on the shop floor and production control. Too little time has been spent challenging the thinking behind, and commitment to, the quality policy. It is critical to the future of ISO 9000 that we bridge the gap between the CEO's view of ISO 9000 as a production tool and its true value as a strategic weapon.

A good place to start would be to demystify quality by using plain language instead of jargon. Then we may be better able to convince people that quality is everyone's responsibility, including the CEO's, rather than a bolt-on specialist's job.

Unfortunately, new initiatives are coined almost daily which feed on CEOs in their desperate quest for the business panacea. We need to ensure senior managers understand that an effective management system underpins all aspects of business. Otherwise the management system skills and techniques we have developed will be overlooked as companies surf on each new fad. This would, in my opinion, mean we have taken one giant step towards competitiveness only to take two back.

I believe it is the responsibility of every quality manager and assessor to do something about the image and expectations of ISO 9000 if we want to be part of the next stage of business development. To do this it is essential they prove to their CEO that ISO 9000 is about achieving results in all areas of business.

First we need to get senior management to think about what they want to achieve. The nineteenth century philosopher R W Emerson said: 'Thinking is the hardest job in the world. That's why so few of us do it'. I would argue that this is what is missing: it is essential we start the thinking at the top and apply management systems to strategic business processes. We need to get the management system to span from strategy to production, working towards a shared common goal and we need to shift the focus to doing the right things, and not just doing things right.

Another lesson we need to learn concerns targets. Too many companies are allowed to rest on their laurels having achieved ISO 9000. The purpose of management systems is not to be compliant with ISO 9000. The purpose (and value) is to manage a business, managing both improvement and change. We must not let ISO 9000 become the lowest common denominator. If we do, we are selling both ourselves and our CEOs short.

The world at your fingertips

It's all possible when you choose the leading international certification body for your management system. But, don't just take our word for it. New independent research* shows that companies approved to the Quality Management System standard, ISO 9000 by Lloyd's Register Quality Assurance, significantly outperform their competitors in a range of key business indicators – from profitability to sales.

Lloyd's Register Quality Assurance is the leading international certification body – a worldwide force, offering worldwide consistency. From ISO 9000, to the new environmental management system standard BS 7750, EMAS verification, and CE Marking to European Directives, LRQA should be your first choice for boosting business performance.

For more information contact:

Lloyd's Register Quality Assurance

Norfolk House, Wellesley Road, Croydon, UK. CR9 2DT
Telephone: +44 181 688 6883
Fax: +44 181 681 8146

Hiramford, Middlemarch Office Village, Siskin Drive, Coventry, UK. CV3 4FJ
Telephone: +44 1203 882222
Fax: +44 1203 639493

*Fitter Finance, the effects of ISO 9000 on business performance. Phone for your free copy today. Please quote ref: CBI95

LLOYD'S REGISTER QUALITY ASSURANCE

Welcome to the efficient environment

Luxembourg is the southernmost province in Belgium, bordering France and the Grand Duchy of Luxembourg. With 240,000 inhabitants (2 % of Belgium), and as much as 15 % percent of the nation's territory, the "Fair" Province is known to excel in tourism, and for its gracious quality of life. And, along with its natural beauty, it boasts all the assets it takes to satisfy the most demanding of industrial and logistics investors :

The market
The geo-economic centre of the EU is located close to Arlon, the head city. At the centre of Europe's most affluent population areas, 75 million people and the most lucrative markets are within a 300-mile reach.

The connections
This potential can conveniently be reached from non-saturated transportation systems : there is a 4-lane road in any 2-mile radius, two international airports close by (Luxembourg and Brussels) and one of the largest land-based railroad container terminals in the EU. And, of course, direct access to the latest in telecom facilities.

The land and the quality of life
With half of its territory covered in forest, the Luxembourg province is loved for its scenic beauty, pace of life and quality food. Since there is also plenty of competitively priced land available, the environment, to us, is a key element in setting up quality projects.

The people
The available skilled labour pool is young, multi-lingual, productive and ambitious. Moreover, the Province is famous for its low union activism.

The help of friends
Also crucial to the success of the Province have been the close relationships with the authorities at EU and regional levels, especially now on the Ardennes estates.

The references
The Province is praised for its efficiency in terms of incentives, financing and administrative assistance. It is known for the direct access investors have to Province decision makers, from the Governor to I.D.E.Lux, the development agency, who bring their single-contact and continued support before, during and after the investment decision, including in personnel screening, schooling and integration in the local communities.

For over 30 years, the Province's approach to business development has worked wonders. Some of the leading companies of the world, and a lot of small and medium-sized enterprises, have been convinced by this impressive array of assets, such as L'OrÈal, Ferrero, Unilever, Nestle, Mobil Plastics, Champion,...

Welcome in a province which prides itself on its quality of life and determination to move ahead.

UNE ARDEUR D'AVANCE
Province de Luxembourg

idelux

Total Quality Management in Custodial Operations

A guide to understanding and applying the key elements of Total Quality Management

Stephen D Gaudreau, Jacquelyn C Bridge and Eleanor R Fisher

The perfect companion to the Facilities Resource Handbook, *Total Quality Management in Custodial Operations* explores all the aspects of TQM and their relationship to facilities resource management.

This is the first book on Total Quality Management for the building, cleaning and maintenance industry. It provides a comprehensive guide to understanding and applying the key elements of TQM using real custodial teams and step-by-step models addressing the special challenges faced in the building, cleaning, maintenance industry. This valuable reference shows how to motivate employees and customers to help improve the quality of service.

£39.95 Paperback ISBN 1-8844015-25-5
120 pages 279x256mm March 1995

Total Quality in Purchasing and Supplier Management

Rick Fernandez

A 10% reduction in costs for purchasing products and services is equal to a sales increase of 50% for a company with a 10% profit margin. This unique book shows how to achieve it.

It provides a complete systematic approach to implementing purchasing/supplier quality management. Important topics are covered such as:

* *how to define and create a solid customer-supplier relationship*
* *finding suppliers who will best align with the purchaser's organisation, and*
* *how to create win-win relationships that save money and deliver quality goods and services.*

This practical guide shows how to relate the principles of TQM to the tasks of purchasing and supplier management in the everyday work environment.

£25.00 Hardback ISBN 1-884015-00-X
360 pages 235x153mm March 1995

Also Available

The Instant Manager

The 100 Most Important Tasks Facing Managers Today
Cy Charney

Designed for speedy access to the tools needed by effective managers, the topics are arranged alphabetically, from absenteeism to workshops. The book indicates the performance required from managers, while reminding them to watch their own interests and career progression. The author show how to:
* *satisfy customers* • *build a team* • *benchmark performance*
* *empower people* • *communicate*

£9.99 Paperback ISBN 0 7494 1608 4
224 pages 216x135mm May 1995

Fourth Edition
How to be an Even Better Manager

Michael Armstrong

"A practical and straightforward guide to successful management, written with the benefit of over 30 years' experience" BUSINESS EXECUTIVE

The new edition of a bestselling title from one of the UK's most successful management thinkers and writers. A book for both experienced and aspiring managers, this down-to-earth guide covers every aspect of management in a clear and relevant way.

Arranged alphabetically for easy reference, it analyses the aims, skills and functions of 50 specific areas of management in all types of organisation and describes what successful managers need to do to become even more successful.

Also available on cassette
£9.99 Paperback ISBN 0 7494 1383 2 336 pages 216x135mm 1994

The Making of a Manager

How to Launch Your Management Career on the Fast Track

Donald A Wellman

Ideal for any manager wanting to develop and polish their managerial skills to the utmost, this practical guide gives valuable advice and handy tips on everything a manager needs to know in order to operate successfully.

Written in a lively, no-nonsense style this book brings effective management alive by offering tips on:

* *attaining a perfect memory in 30 minutes*
* *measuring and improving employee performance*
* *developing an effective training plan*
* *using meetings to get results*
* *dealing with problem employees*
* *moving up the career ladder.*

Complete with advice on how to assess your success as a manager, this insider guide to getting on in management provides practical insights into every management technique (including the tricks your boss would rather you didn't know).

£18.95 Hardback ISBN 0 7494 1796 X
288 pages 234x153mm January 1996

 KOGAN PAGE

source country was one of low quality; to highlight where the product was made could damage sales. Whatever the facts of that particular case, this situation will not continue for long. In coming years Western Europe will have several serious competitors for productive capacity, in high-value knowledge-based industries as well as in traditional manufacturing, right on the doorstep with rapid road and rail access to its markets. Distinctive quality, constant innovative improvement to retain and attract customers, will be an ever more essential precondition for survival.

Other pressures are emerging. Falling standards of education are causing concern in several countries. In others, the 'greying' of the population is becoming a serious issue, whilst along the southern fringe of the continent is rapidly building demographic pressure from the Middle East and Africa. Before long the implications of such trends will be inescapable aspects of the management of quality.

The European Commission and quality

The Commission is currently developing a 'European Quality Promotion Policy'. Initially it had nineteen areas for action and no indication of how to fund them. It now appears that it will be focused on fewer priority themes, including support for existing programmes such as the European Quality Award and a system for the qualification of quality professionals. Already several of the national member bodies of the European Organisation for Quality (EOQ), including the UK's Institute of Quality Assurance, are working on the development of a pan-European information resource on the Internet, to be launched in late 1995.

The EOQ has also been working on the development of a harmonized scheme for the registration of quality professionals, quality systems managers and quality auditors. An attractive feature of the European scheme, which differs from current UK practice, is that the auditor is seen as being at the pinnacle of the profession with the most rigorous demands for registration. All these developments must take account of the broadening definition of quality and its management.

Quality as vision and values

Finally, there is the growth of what can be labelled 'Management by Conviction'. The recent Royal Society of Arts inquiry into 'Tomorrow's Company' highlighted the need for an inclusive approach to management, which takes into account the valid interests of a wide range of stakeholders, giving less priority to the shareholder. Many companies are devoting time and energy to the creation of a sense of mission and vision throughout the business, identifying the values on which their actions will be based, a shared moral basis (though they may not call it that) for devolved decision-making within decentralized, empowered organizations.

Possibly then, before too long, 'quality' in its broadened sense may be managed in an integrated manner with other functions, not merely in response to a family of administrative standards, but as the means by which to make real a critical aspect of corporate vision – an ethical commitment to the societies which allow business its licence to operate within them. What then will be the qualifications for, the demands upon, and the future of the quality manager?

CE Marking and Standards 45

BSI Standards

However large or small your company, if you are a manufacturer or distributor whose products fall within the scope of the New Approach Directives of the European Community, compliance with the applicable ones will be a vital part of preparing your products for Europe. The New Approach Directives set out essential requirements which must be complied with before your products can be sold anywhere within the European Community – including the UK.

Application of the CE mark is the final step in meeting these requirements. CE marking is an indication to enforcement authorities throughout Europe, eg, Trading Standards Department in the UK, that your product has been legally placed on the market, in accordance with the applicable essential requirements of the relevant directives and with the related conformity assessment procedures. BSI can help you understand your obligations and assist you in fulfilling them.

The marking may only be used on a product which is in the scope of one or more of the directives which currently cover or are proposed to cover:

- electrical equipment;
- simple pressure vessels;
- toy safety;
- construction products;
- electromagnetic compatibility;
- machinery safety;
- personal protective equipment;
- non-automatic weighing machines;

- medical devices;
- telecommunications terminal equipment;
- gas appliances;
- explosives for civil use.

Even if your particular product is not mentioned in the list, it may still have to comply with one or more of the directives. For instance, industrial machinery may have to comply with both the Machinery Safety and the Electromagnetic Compatibility Directives. Remember that misuse of CE marking is a criminal offence. The marking must be applied to products placed on the market (including the country of origin) in all the states of the European Economic Area. This includes the EC and EFTA with the exception of Switzerland.

The directives have varying transition periods and dates by which they come into force. In forthcoming directives there is a transition period during which the manufacturer may choose when to apply the marking. When this transition period ends there is no further concession.

Note that CE marking does not signify conformity with a standard and is not an indication of quality. It is a legal statement for the purpose of the authorities. The CE marking requirements impose new procedures on the manufacturer, which include:

- determining that the product complies with the directive using appropriate measures and, where possible, making use of existing data and test reports;

Selling within Europe?

...when you call BSI on (0181) 996 7111

With all the complexities of CE marking, it's likely you're going to need some expert help in meeting your obligations.

That's where BSI is invaluable.

We'll provide the latest information on EC Directives, standards and approval requirements. Plus, we'll help solve your CE marking problems through our Information Centre enquiry service.

Don't be left behind. Act now, call our Information Centre on (0181) 996 7111 or fax us on (0181) 996 7048. It couldn't be easier.

Helping you build a better business

Information Centre, BSI Standards, 389 Chiswick High Road, London W4 4AL, UK

- where notified bodies are involved, identifying the necessary conformity actions and quality measures to be applied;
- carrying out any necessary staff training;
- appointing a person who is empowered to bind the manufacturer with respect to the directive;
- preparing the Declaration of Conformity;
- maintaining technical files;
- applying the CE marking.

Success depends on a careful assessment of the appropriate directives and requirements. The BSI Standards Information Centre is able to advise on the telephone or provide consultancy with respect to identification and the application to the directives. Other older directives not using the CE marking or national requirement which may apply in addition to the New Approach Directives can also be identified. The advice can include identification of standards and authorities and advice on the administration, documentation and timing of events. Remember – no CE marking, no sale!

BSI Testing and BSI Product Certification are notified bodies which offer services to ensure your goods are placed on the market fully approved. Many of the directive's requirements can also be achieved through registration to ISO 9000. BSI Quality Assurance has a number of programmes to help you prepare for this internationally recognized quality management system standard.

46 Innovation in European Businesses

Derek Smith, UK Coordinator, The European Inter-University Association on Society, Science and Technology (ESST), Ecole Polytechnique Fédérale de Lausanne

The influences shaping innovative business strategies in Europe differ very little from those in the UK. Innovation is driven increasingly by the interfaces of competition (or the anticipation of competition), technology, consumer demand, market conditions and global influences.

While it is relatively straightforward to identify similarities, it is more complex to disentangle historic and contemporary contrasts, but in varying measures they do exist. Business has developed and been shaped by tradition, language, legal systems, financial institutions, and by the regional characteristics of peoples themselves. Using Switzerland as a focus provides an interesting insight.

Quality is part and parcel of the image Switzerland projects to the world and Switzerland is synonymous with quality worldwide. The national and international perception of high-quality craftsmanship which persuaded many of the world's parents to invest in a Swiss watch for important birthdays may be a thing of the past. Nevertheless, Switzerland provides examples of how the drive for quality can act to stimulate innovation.

Competition from Far East manufacturers of low-cost, highly accurate digital and quartz watches captured up to 60 per cent of traditional Swiss markets. At first glance the obvious innovations belong to the Asian producers; after all they captured the major share of the volume market. But Switzerland can offer Europe examples of how Asian competition played a part in stimulating business innovation in at least two identifiable ways.

The initial response was towards a technological solution to the problem. In sharp contrast to the traditional craft-based *horlogerie*, Swatch introduced a watch which was made of plastic, non-repairable and marketed as a fashion accessory. It represented a significant departure from traditional practice and although the new product was not synonymous with conventional watchmaking expertise it was, nevertheless, readily accepted by a market which believed in the quality of the ubiquitous Swiss watch. While such technological developments are impressive, Switzerland highlights another valuable tool in the quest for innovative business success in its blend of science, society and technology.

The Swiss watch industry was largely built upon interdependence and the precision and skills of its workforce; and it is this network of interlocking regional competencies which has been preserved and adapted to new precision industries. Such industries as medical instruments, including pacemakers etc, can permit no margin for error, and consumer confidence can only be absolute.

The notion of innovative businesses linked to a social milieu is by no means new, nor is it confined to the French–Swiss watchmaking region of the Jura Arc. But it is a classic example of how a successful business enterprise can be traced back to hard decisions, built first and foremost upon a long-term

Österreichisches Forschungsinstitut für Chemie und Technik (Austrian Research Institute for Chemistry and Technology) Arsenal, Objekt 213, Franz Grill-Strasse 5, A-1030 Vienna, Austria Tel.: +43 1-798 16 01-0, Fax +43 1-798 16 01-8

Originally established in 1946 as testing and development laboratory of the Austrian Industry, the Institute's activities today include both, materials and products testing conforming to EN 45.001 (accredited by DAP, "Deutsche Akkreditierungssystem Prüfwesen"), and research. An analytical laboratory with the most modern equipment for the determination of special material properties is the basis for efficient research work. A team of 17 university graduates provides the scientific background, and is supported by suitably trained laboratory technicians and other skilled staff.

The Institute is structured into seven different testing and research Institutes which deal with the following research areas:

Austrian Plastics Institute: Fundamental research; analysing methods for the determination of compounds; fire behaviour; possibilities of materials and product testing; processing technology; recycling methods and products; ageing and resistance to weathering; environmental analysis; hygiene.

Austrian Institute for Biomedical Materials Engineering: Use and compatibility of plastics in medical technology; specific test methods for medical devices, in part disposable products (condoms, medical gloves, syringes, etc.) made mainly of plastics and elastomers; implant production; use of dissolved polyurethane under clean-room conditions; assembling of critical medical products under clean-room conditions.

Austrian Institute for Construction: Determination of damages and selection of renovation methods for buildings made of concrete, ceramic building materials, wood, etc.; certificate of suitability for building materials; environmental compatibility (excavated material, soil and ground water samples); noise insulation walls with recycled plastics; drainage methods for masonry; behaviour of and requirements for the sealing of dumps; geotextiles and geomembranes; recycling methods for building rubbish and building site refuse.

Austrian Institute for Sports Technology: Plastics, wood or textile sports floors; lawns; sports areas on a mineral basis; sports- and gymnastics equipment.

Austrian Institute for Paints and Varnishes: Development of paints, varnishes and coatings, new testing methods; analysis of compounds; modifications for special purposes; ageing, weathering and mechanical resistance; analysis of damages and proposals for their repair.

Austrian Packaging Institute for Foodstuffs and Beverages: Mechanical, physico-chemical and microbiological testing; packaging materials and packagings for specific products, for transportation etc.; development of packagings; problems with packaging machinery; environmental problems.

Austrian Institute for Bio-mass Energy: Increasing the efficiency of bio-mass distant heating systems; new opportunities for the use of bio-mass and plant sources of energy; co-firing with other fuels.

---

confidence in the traditional regional skills and competences of its workforce.

There is a confidence in high-quality regional skills which is not only demonstrated by established business, but also by new entrepreneurs. Trust in these regional competencies has also encouraged entrepreneurship from a variety of sources, and here the Swiss example of Delance, a new watchmaking business, is worthy of note. It is a woman's enterprise in which innovation is synonymous with quality, created by women for women. The designer, photographer and all of the skilled assemblers are women. Preserving and investing in traditional regional competences has detonated an energy, fusing a creative employer, a quality product, and an innovative business.

The catalytic effect of Asian markets on European business is being felt not only in precision manufacturing, but also from within the service and financial sectors: in high-wage economies increasing use is being made of outsourcing services in order to reduce costs.

Outsourcing of IT development services from Europe to Egypt, Malaysia, Philippines and Eastern Europe has been growing steadily, but it is India which represents the major market. With over three million engineers, scientists and other technologists (100,000 are employed in the software industry alone), India is the leader in offshore project development. The type of projects which are typically being outsourced for offshore development are the ones requiring either a large number of skilled consultants at one time, or an unfamiliar technology. The Tata Group, for example (US$6 billion annual revenue, and 250,000 employees in 40 countries around the globe), founded Teknosoft in 1985 to promote and develop information technology services.

Because of the increasing globalization of financial markets, Swiss banks felt the need to develop an organization which could complete securities clearing and settlement on an international basis. The outcome was the Indian creation of SECOM, a new on-line–real-time securities settlement system for the Swiss Financial Centre. In simple terms many Swiss securities are settled overnight by qualified Indian staff, and data are returned by telematic link for the next morning's trading.

SECOM was designed to settle everything that a

trader can trade, even the most obscure shares. Apart from following the recommendations of international regulating bodies such as the Fédération Internationale des Bourses de Valeurs, the International Society of Securities Administrators and the European Community, SECOM also guarantees a 100 per cent secure custody service for securities. In the final analysis, the combination of low-cost, real-time, technological and outsourced expert services has made the settlement period in Switzerland one of the shortest in the world.

Like each European country, current business innovation in Switzerland is not only a response to contemporary issues, but is equally a product of its history and the people who shaped it. Switzerland's struggle for survival is characterized by the geographical conditions, its relative preservation during the last two wars, and a concentration on specific industries for which it has acquired a justifiably strong reputation, resulting in one of the highest per capita incomes in the world as it entered the 1990s. But Switzerland, strong as it is, has had and continues to have its crises of adaptation to factors largely outside its control, resulting in a phenomenon

forgotten for decades, unemployment at 5–6 per cent!

Against this background of crisis which is relatively small in comparison with other countries of Europe, the Swiss are endeavouring to re-launch their economy for the twenty-first century. The key features of competitiveness in industry and services, the capacity to innovate in both process and product, job creation and training form the familiar basis of a continuing dialogue.

The 1994 survey by Pierre Rossel at the University of Neuchâtel (Swiss Research on Innovation and Technical Change), summarizes the situation for much of Europe when he states:

All of these issues are closely linked to the capacity of industries and research centres to enter into partnerships which include foreign countries and in particular European ones. All of them are closely linked insofar as the revival (or decline) of the socio-technical and commercial skills are largely tied to the ability, today apparently lacking, to mobilise the various actors in the process coherently.

PART

10

Building European Organizations

Transnational Organization in Europe

David Blacklock, Siddall & Company

Traditionally, European companies have tended to be organized using the country as the building block. The head office was usually an emanation of the original, domestic business and it was rare to find a non-national in it. The management style was 'command and control'. Policy, procedure and targets were passed down. Plentiful and frequent reports were sent up to satisfy the seemingly insatiable demand for information and commentary.

Many firms are still run today with a preponderance of power in the hands of the home base and with national subsidiaries. Yet increasingly transnationals are beginning to break out of this mould and we can see the true European company emerging.

Businesses

The trend today is away from minutely defined businesses each individually managed and coordinated through a matrix. Instead, businesses are to be broad streams with a portfolio of products built around a technology or a market and with the critical mass to be a real (and if necessary divestible) business.

Each business stream may organize itself in the best way for the business. It will probably require a European head. The business stream heads need not be colocated. The support centre for the business head will, in most cases, be very small. It does not need to carry vast amounts of expertise with which to help operating companies. A networking culture within the business will encourage operating managers across the continent to collaborate on problems of mutual concern. Expertise may be dispersed through the business, but must be available and accessible to all.

Functions

Functional expertise is often a core competence of a company. It needs to be available to the chief executive and the business heads from the most able. Expertise in areas such as safety or environmental protection is so important that neglect will lead to the elimination of the company's ability to operate in a country or a community.

Traditionally, responsibility for standards, coordination and functional improvement was assumed by a staff manager in head office. Companies are now trying to achieve functional synergy through proactive networking across business and national structures. This means that cross-business, international, functional teams are charged with the responsibilities previously assumed by headquarters staff. One member of the network will be given a European responsibility for leading on a specific issue or project. It is the network, speaking through the leader, that provides the input to the chief executive and the business heads.

European Foundation for the Improvement of Living and Working Conditions

PROGRAMMES OF THE FOUNDATION

★ Social cohesion

★ Access to employment, innovation and work organisation

★ Human relations within the company, social dialogue and industrial relations

★ Health and safety

★ Socio-economic aspects of sustainable development policies

★ Equal opportunities between women and men

★ Programme of co-ordination, exchange and information/ dissemination

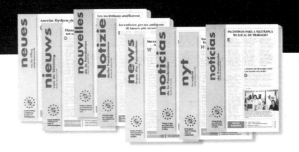

If you wish to be included on the Foundation mailing list or have enquires regarding publications, please contact:
Bríd Nolan, European Foundation for Living & Working Conditions
Loughlinstown House, Shankill, Co. Dublin, Ireland

The country

In each country, there are legal obligations on a company. It is required to lodge accounts, pay tax, provide statistical returns and so forth. Good corporate citizenship and corporate communications often require representation at a national level. Governments and the press like to know 'who is in charge here', so a national chairman or president is often required to act as a sort of constitutional monarch who can appear to the outside world to be 'in charge'.

Rather than make a distinct appointment, the emerging solution is to give the job to one of the business heads within the country or to a senior functional manager who is a national of the country. Depending on the relative respect accorded to breeding, brains, size of business, age, seniority or whatever in a particular country, an appointment is made. The job is not a power base or a channel to head office. The incumbent is there to facilitate the work of the businesses operating in the country.

Within a country an economic case can often be made to combine some administrative services across businesses. Rather than create stand-alone national service centres, one of the businesses agrees to host a service on behalf of the others in exchange for a fee.

Head office and the corporate centre

The parent holding company has to discharge certain statutory and fiduciary duties, so there needs to be some sort of corporate office somewhere. It should be quite small and focused on government, tax and stakeholder issues.

In addition to this statutory head office, there remains the need for a corporate centre to support those activities that are the province of the chief executive. The corporate centre overviews the strategy and allocation of resources. It may set policy in functional areas, but no longer feels obliged to provide 'help' to its businesses.

The location of the corporate centre is a matter of convenience. It is dictated by the needs of the businesses and the political, financial and legal interfaces. Top management do not even have to reside at the corporate centre. If they have multiple responsibilities, combining a business with a functional or

The red pins
indicate the areas of the world
BUPA now covers.

Health Care without frontiers

Health cover in a changing international environment

With increasing globalisation of business, the distribution of a company's workforce is becoming extremely widespread. As companies expand into emerging markets they need to meet this growth with truly international staff, *writes David Boyle, executive director of BUPA International.*

To remain competitive, companies must respond rapidly to developing opportunities. As a result, the last thing they need is for an important link in the chain to break. Such a link is the health and safety of the employee.

Guaranteeing an adequate level of health care for employees across the entire globe is no small task. There is a multitude of national health care facilities and expertise which ranges from the most modern and responsive to the barest minimum stretched to full capacity. Add to this the vast costs which can be accrued in the treatment of illness in many countries where health care is at a premium and the global vision becomes even more fragmented and complex.

Setting up an international health care scheme can seem a somewhat bewildering prospect for the manager of global business. For periods varying from a couple of days to three-to-five years, their employees and their families may find themselves in areas where the local medical facilities are undeveloped, complex and rapidly changing.

Without access to specialist treatment, certain conditions can develop to become fatal, and long and unsophisticated treatment periods can prove dangerous and costly. So even the possibility of falling ill in such cases can bring unwanted stresses.

For the company, such difficult conditions are equally stressful. Employees who move between countries and wish to have access to local medical facilities are subject to the local health care systems.

There is also the question of currency, with local hospitals requiring immediate payment in the relevant currency and refusing to accept certain forms of payment. Administration procedures can be lengthy and bureaucratic, and there can be costly delays in communication.

Developments in European legislation in no way eradicate the different approaches of the member states to national health care provision. In every European country, private insurance has a key role to play in supplementing the level of cover provided by the state.

To ensure an adequate provision for illness and accident, three basic types of private health insurance are needed in Europe, where the costs of sickness absence to industry are immense. In Britain alone, 360 million working days a year are lost, causing a staggering £13 billion. Take a global view of figures like these and one can understand how immense the problem has become.

Employers need to evaluate each national system and take out cover for employees resident in the area to fill the gaps which invariably remain. In countries such as the UK and Spain, they may need duplicate insurance where employers pay independently for rights the State was supposed to guarantee; they may need to take out supplementary or complementary insurance to cover treatment for which the state refuses to pay in countries such as France; in some countries, like Germany, there is the need for the employer to take out 'alternative' insurance where individuals who were able to leave compulsory insurance schemes could expect full coverage to the same standard for employers.

Once can see that Europe, which aims to be unified and aligned, is still subject to a spectrum of different laws and systems. Added to the variations on systems which exist across the globe and one can grasp the complexity of international health insurance.

As employees move across the world, international employers recognise the need to manage their health care globally through a single international expert.

International insurers offers company-focused schemes which span the globe and override the complexities of local systems, affording peace of mind and minimal administrative intervention for the companies and expatriate employees involved. They offer a central point of contact, administration in English and the advice and care of a multi-lingual team.

Developing local schemes and enhancing global schemes requires ongoing awareness of the smallest shifts in the market, concentrating the drivers of change into a small number of companies with a truly international perspective.

Developments in the international corporate market induced the leading insurers to greater levels of responsiveness and customer service. Innovations in managed care to reduce health care costs worldwide, networks of partner medical providers, specially tailored schemes with ancillary benefits and company-specific costs controls demonstrate the continuing growth in sophistication in this expanding market place.

In the future, insurers will increasingly work with international companies as close partners, understanding their specific needs and meeting them locally and globally, providing a balance of security and expertise matched with financial rigor and customer service excellence.

It is for the international companies to understand the importance of this relationship and to use it to their and their employees' best advantage.

For further information on BUPA International schemes for companies and their expatriate workforce, call 01273 208 171 or fax 01273 775 399.

representative role, they may well have their principal place of work dictated by the business rather than corporate need.

The transnational solution

A transnational European organization will appear different to different outsiders. Governments and tax authorities will see 'their' national company with its titular head and its high level of corporate compliance. Journalists will know whom to call. Customers will see coherent business streams supplying products across Europe adapted to the local environment, with consistency of service. Shareholders will see a successful business operating in many countries and with low costs of management and administrative superstructure. Employees will see a loose federation of operating units collaborating within a country, working together in the European marketplace, and collectively solving functional problems.

The corporate ethos will be radically different from that with which many of us grew up. Other businesses, internal suppliers and customers, other functions are colleagues not rivals. This collaborative culture is reinforced when managers are required to wear two or even three hats – business, country,

function – every day of the week. For the manager, the outcome is an enhanced and more rewarding job. For the company, the outcome is superior performance through the harnessing of the abilities and energies of all.

Overcoming the obstacles

The obstacles that arise in implementing this new European company mostly fall under the heading of management culture. The flatter, multiresponsibility management structure imposes a devolved style on top management. But merely telling top managers that they are expected to act as strategists, policy makers and coaches to their team is not enough. Unless they really understand the limitations of their ability to direct, they are likely to revert to type at the first whiff of adversity.

In the face of global competition and accelerating change, most corporations operating in Europe have to face up to these challenges soon. Many of the elements of the transnational organization, such as networking, knowledge sharing and collaborative behaviours, are already being applied successfully by many global companies. Piece by piece, company by company, we can see the future emerging.

Planning and Implementing Projects in Europe

David M Howell, Business Development Director – Europe,
WS Atkins International Ltd

Europe is a complex web of countries drawn together by historic, economic and political influences. While Britain contemplates the relative merits of the 'special relationship' with the USA, the Commonwealth and the European Union, the post 'cold war' Europe is moving forward to greater economic cooperation as a mechanism for reduced cross-border tensions. The immediate effect of this is the expansion of the European Union and the concept of the Single Market, but the rapid development of certain of the Central European countries and the granting of associate membership status is increasing the interest in developing and implementing both infrastructure and industrial and commercial sector projects throughout these regions. Developments in Eastern Europe are naturally slower as the cultural and economic divide is greater, but already there are signs of major infrastructure and private sector developments in Russia and certain of the adjoining countries.

It can therefore be seen that the planning and implementing of projects throughout Europe is a very broad theme. However, it has one common thread – benefit to the promoter either in terms of direct financial reward or economic benefit. Irrespective of culture, therefore, all the countries of Europe recognize the pressures of market forces on public and private sector projects, resulting in the application of procedures well recognized in the more developed countries of Western Europe.

Infrastructure development

The European Union has an ambitious programme of trans-European networks covering road, rail, air and energy links within the community and, in the longer term, Central and Eastern Europe. These projects are perceived as a major catalyst to the development of competitiveness and hence employment growth in the member states. Obstacles to implementation are the problems experienced in preparation, planning, authorization and evaluation of major projects. Funding for such projects frequently involves European Community funds and national funds, but in more and more instances the private sector is expected to make a major contribution. The Channel Tunnel is an example of a major infrastructure link funded entirely by the private sector, and the financial difficulties experienced by the operator clearly demonstrate that a combination of private and public sector finance would have been more appropriate.

The advent of private sector finance to major infrastructure projects is, however, introducing a welcome new discipline – the need to demonstrate an acceptable financial return. The planning of such schemes is therefore a critical task which needs accurately to project not only the usual aspects of capital cost, route options, programme, environmental impact, etc, but a detailed cash flow for construction costs, maintenance costs, revenue collections from users and repayment of debt. Where private sector finance is involved, risk management is a major consideration. The management and allocation of risk were high on the agenda of the consortia bidding for the Channel Tunnel Rail Link.

The British construction industry has seen dramatic changes over the past decade as a result of a government policy of increased competition. While the policy has caused severe damage to parts of the industry, there is no doubt that all the companies who have survived now fully understand their cost structures. This is not the case in many parts of Western Europe, and some of the Southern European countries have a construction sector which does not have a culture of projecting the final project cost or duration. Some of the major infrastructure projects planned as part of the strategic objectives of the EU are in a state of partial completion, with some contracts let under conditions where proper control of time, cost and quality parameters has not received appropriate consideration and where the total financing of the projects has not been fully determined. Even within the EU, there is therefore a need to return to the basics on many projects before successful implementation can take place. More and more there is a need for a marriage between the private and public sectors on the planning and implementation of major infrastructure projects as the pressures on national budgets increase and, in circumstances where projects have been partially completed under different planning, design and construction criteria, risk management is a major priority. The stages for successful projects can be defined as forecast, finance, construct, operate and maintain, but above all, project manage through the complete life cycle!

In Central Europe, the major infrastructure is less well developed and the national governments are generally less able to finance major improvement. They have, therefore, needed to look even more to self-financing projects than their Western neighbours. Hungary has already let certain motorway projects on a 'concession' basis and Poland is currently considering the mechanism for establishment of a major motorway programme. There are many unknowns which must be evaluated in these countries at the planning stage before the projects can be implemented. Key issues include traffic forecasts, land ownership perception to tolling (experience in France suggests that traffic may divert to other routes), tax regimes, inflation and political risk. Evaluating political risk may be very difficult. The

current situation in the Balkans, for example, has a major impact on infrastructure connections between Greece and the remainder of the EU. It is likely that the implementation of many of the major transport projects in Central Europe, particularly in the highway sector, may be delayed as they represent an unacceptable level of risk to the private sector. The aid agencies and the EBRD (via loans) are assisting national governments in these countries in financing the necessary studies to project traffic flows and to establish pilot tolling projects. Further east, the financing of such projects is more difficult and participation by the private sector is less likely. The EBRD has provided loans to certain Eastern European countries for such infrastructure projects, but responsibility for repayment remains with the state.

Industrial and commercial development

Western European countries generally have well-established procedures for the planning and implementation of development projects. Issues of land ownership can still lead to particular difficulties in Greece, as there is currently no nationally based land register (Greece and Albania are the only European Countries without such a register). Land ownership problems arise in some other Western European countries owing to the culture of dividing the land holding between the children on the death of the owner. Reaching agreement between large numbers of relatives who may not be on speaking terms can give rise to great frustration! Those who believe that the British planning system is complex should sample the systems of some of its European neighbours where less of the decision-making process is controlled by trained professionals and more power is vested in local politicians. The planning and implementing of projects requires a good understanding of the local conditions and the discipline to control time, cost and quality. Whilst the planning and construction procedures may vary from country to country in Western Europe, the pattern for each has generally evolved over time and is well understood by the local professionals.

The situation in Central Europe is somewhat different. Land ownership issues are having to be resolved in the post-communist era to take account of pre-war ownerships. Records have, in some instances, been lost and disputes can arise. While many of the sites for possible commercial or industrial development now have clear title, the wise investor will check and double check that the vendor has the right to make the land sale. There are continual examples of Western companies who, after spending substantial fees on planning and design for their future investment, have found that the sale cannot be completed due to problems of land title. *Caveat emptor* is particularly appropriate in these areas.

Environmental considerations have increased in importance in Western Europe, with land contamination becoming a major concern. In Central Europe these concerns are greatly amplified since the demands of the command economy gave little thought to protection of the environment. Contamination from industrial or military activities can be found on city centre and greenfield sites, and careful evaluation of the soils is advisable prior to any purchase. Many Central European countries are concerned at the state of their environment, and legislation is being strengthened to fine those responsible for pollution. Investors need to be aware of the potential long-term risks associated with any potential acquisition. Some Western investors have acquired sites and are systematically cleaning the soil to remove contaminants as development proceeds.

Most Central European professionals and contractors had limited experience of demand-led economies prior to 1990. Efficient use of resources, cost-efficient designs, project management, site planning and quality construction were not criteria which had previously determined success. Planning procedures can be complex, with the new found political freedom effectively halting the decision-making process. Utilities supplies can be a major barrier to development, even for city centre sites. The number of authorities that must be approached can be daunting, and enhancement of supplies can prove extremely difficult. In many instances the authorities have no concept of commercial realism and believe that the purchaser of a site can fund local infrastructure developments.

The past few years have seen a general slump in construction activities taken overall in Central Europe. However, many local contractors are forming links with Western companies, investment in modern equipment is beginning to occur and the quality of construction is improving. Project management and site management skills are still in short supply and these areas need particular attention. The Central European countries are rapidly catching up with their Western neighbours and are presenting very attractive opportunities to business investment.

Investment in industrial or commercial projects in the countries of Eastern Europe represents a higher category of risk. Returns in the development sector can be very high as Western business people continue to explore business opportunities. However, the issues discussed which affect projects in Central Europe are generally more problematic in the countries of the former Soviet Union. Culturally there is no memory of anything but a command economy and the process of change is generally slower. At the other end of the spectrum there are many who operate outside any legal framework, and land ownership, planning, construction and economic and political risk are all issues which must be carefully weighed up against potential benefit.

Conclusions

Infrastructure and building developments share many similar objectives. Each represents a 'shareholder' investment which must produce the appropriate planned return. Many technical skills will be required in the design and implementation of any project, but the key to success is the ability to project manage activities to minimize risk during the planning, design, construction and operation phases. The individual demands will vary from project to project and country to country, but the overall objectives remain unchanged.

J & A Garrigues

1. Introduction

The precedents governing the leasing agreement (financial lease) in Spanish legislation date back to a Decree Law of 1977. This Law provided a special tax system for transactions of this kind when carried out by companies engaging exclusively in this business which were organized and registered pursuant to the provisions of that Law. However, these regulations were very limited, extending only to the formalities relating to finance companies and to the special features of the tax system applicable to transactions of this kind.

From that year, when leasing companies had a turnover of only 15,000,000 million pesetas, until 1989, when this figure rose to 1,700 billion pesetas, few advances were made in the task of completing the legislation governments agreements of this kind; although it is true that Act 26/1988 redefined the leasing agreement, regulating certain partial aspects of it, the basic purpose of this Act was to control the activities of credit institutions.

Under this Act, the following are the elements of the essence of the leasing agreement:

- it was necessary for the lessor to be a duly registered finance company; however, it was generally accepted that failure to comply with this requirement did not entail the nullity of the agreement; at present, Act 3/94 grants to credit institutions authorized in other EEC member countries the possibility of carrying on transactions of this kind in Spain, either through a Spanish branch or under the system of freely rendered services;
- the subject matter of the agreement may be movable or real properties acquired. In accordance with the user's instructions;
- the agreements must have a minimum term of 10 years in the case of real properties, or of two years in the case of movables; the user must allocate the leased properties to a business activity:
- the agreement has to include an option to purchase in the user's favour.

Because of the insufficiency of the legal regulations governing the leasing agreement, the courts will be obliged to classify the agreement in each specific case. This raises the problem of differentiating between the leasing agreement and the purchase and sale agreement. The problem is raised particularly because Act 5/1995 regulating the sale of movables at term, legally extends its effects to all covenants, whatever their legal form may be, purporting to achieve the same economic ends as those of the sale by instalments; and under this Act, entry on the registry of agreements for sale by instalments is a necessary condition to enable to the seller to oppose reservation of ownership or prohibitions against disposal against third parties.

Judgments handed down by the Supreme Court on this matter accept the substance of the leasing agreement except when the circumstances in any specific case permit the existence of a covenant of simulation to be assumed. For this purpose, the decisive factor is the price set for exercise of the option to purchase, understanding that when this price is so low that it is impossible to speak of an independent price, the agreement would not be a leasing agreement but rather a purchase and sale agreement. In some cases, the Supreme Court classified the agreement as a purchase and sale agreement because the user delivered a bill of exchange in payment of the price of the option and the leasing company negotiated the bill, so that the acquisition was already firm.

This problem is raised in different terms in the tax field since the tax consequences provided for the leasing agreement may be denied in cases where, because its circumstances, fraud in law may be understood to exist. Thus we could cite a decision of 1994 in which classification as a leasing agreement was denied to a lease back agreement, because, to secure payment of the rentals, the user delivered promissory notes to the finance company in respect of a pledge, notes which were received by the finance company in payment of the assets it was to acquire for their subsequent lease.

2. Taxation

As the result of the status of owner recognised to the lessor and of user recognized to the lessee, the lessor has to depreciate the assets acquired, deducting the value allocated to the option to purchase during the term of validity stipulated for the option in the respective agreement.

For tax purposes, the lessee treats the rentals as a deductible expense; Act 26/88 limits this deductibility according to the depreciable or non-depreciable nature of the leased properties, and therefore it recognizes the deductibility, in all cases, of the part of the rental corresponding to the financial charge; where the subject matter of the agreement is land, sites or other assets not apt for depreciation, no deductibility is recognized for the part of the rental corresponding to their cost of acquisition.

The former situation was changed upon the publication in Spain of a new General Accountancy Plan in 199 . Under the new rules, where there are no reasonable doubts that the option to purchase will be exercised, the lessee will record the cash value of the property as an intangible asset, showing on the liabilities side of its balance sheet the amount of the total debt, consisting of the rentals agreed plus the price of the option, while the difference (financial charges) will be recorded as expenses to be distributed over various fiscal years according to a financial policy; the rights recorded on the assets side of the balance sheet will be amortized according to the useful life of the leased property. Despite this change, the tax treatment afforded to the leasing agreement remained unchanged.

At present, there is a bill for the Corporate Tax Act which radically changes the tax treatment afforded to the leasing agreement. Where there are no reasonable doubts that the option to purchase is to be exercised (it is assumed that there are no doubts when the price set for the option is less than the difference between the price of acquisition and the sum of maximum funding allocated to depreciation, according to official tables during the period), the user will deduct the amount in respect of annual depreciation that corresponds to the property, attributing the financial component to expenditure. This new system will only be applied to leasing transactions arranged after the system comes into effect, and the Act also provides for an interim period of five years.

Leasing is a complex transaction in which, in legal terms, the lessor retains title to the assets while, from the user's standpoint, the leasing is merely a form of acquisition of assets; this complex nature has been reflected in the vacillating treatment given to the tax credits granted to investments of this kind. At a first stage, emphasising the acquisition by the user, the latter was recognized a tax credit for investments provided *that* it gave an undertaking to the Administration that it would exercise *the* option to purchase (this undertaking was made to the Administration and did not impair the nature of the leasing, the user being able to revoke it at any time). In 1988, this tax credit for the user was eliminated, although this did not mean that the credit was attributed to the lessor. The 1995 Budget Act again grants this tax credit to the lessee provided that two conditions are met; 1) the leasing must relate to movables; a) these movables must be given a ratio of 10% or more in the official depreciation tables. In any case, the amount of the tax credit is reduced in an inverse proportion to the term of the agreement.

No special rules are applicable to Spanish leasing companies in connection with the income they receive from non-residents. Non-residents will be liable for withholding according to domestic limitations in the lessee's country or the limitations applicable under Double Tax Treaties. Lessors will be entitled to deduction of the foreign tax with two limits: 1) the tax actually paid abroad; 2) the tax that they would have had to pay in Spain; since this is the amount resulting from applying the rate of the Spanish tax on the net income originating abroad, it will not be possible to recover this tax.

When the lessee is resident in Spain, for tax purposes the payments it makes are deductible according to the general system. These payments will be subject to withholding in Spain at 25% of their gross amount, unless the reduced rate is applied, established for royalties in the double tax treaties; in exceptional circumstances, no withholdings will be made on payments in respect of the leasing of containers, naval vessels and aircraft on a bareboat basis (understood in administrative practice to include assignment of the use of the aircraft equipped but without a crew) for use in international sea or air navigation.

In Spain, the leasing agreement has become an important instrument for the financing of business concerns, even though the insufficiency of the legislation governing it and the difficulty of classifying it in comparison with the purchase and sale agreement may reduce the lessor's guarantees in comparison with third party lessors of the user. From the tax standpoint, there is a trend towards eliminating the special treatment afforded to this agreement, treatment which largely contributed to its spread.

49 European M&A in Context

Mark Ebert, Global Co-ordinator, Mergers and Acquisitions, UBS

In 1994, the total value of mergers and acquisitions ('M&A') worldwide reached $543 billion, with over 17,500 deals being announced: this was the second highest annual dollar volume and the highest number of transactions ever. The US remains by far the largest M&A market in the world, and 63 per cent of 1994's deal volume, by value, was directed at buying US companies.

1995 has been a bumper year with a record-setting $94.5 billion of deals being announced in Europe as a whole in the first six months. Nevertheless, the picture on a country-by-country basis is still patchy.

In the UK, a record $45 billion of transactions were announced in the first half of this year. Britain's 'hottest' sectors included merchant banks, utilities, building societies and pharmaceuticals. A number of large, high-profile deals ensure the UK retained its position as the leading European target for cross-border acquisitions, surpassing 1994's total deal value just in the first six months.

It had been expected that activity in France would be suppressed by the Presidential elections, but first half deal numbers in 1995 turned out to be roughly consistent with the same period in 1994. Recent highlights included Crown Cork & Seal's purchase of French packaging giant Carnaud-Metalbox, Sodexho buying UK contract caterer Gardner Merchant and the rationalization of the Crédit Lyonnais industrial portfolio, which included the disposals of the MGM cinema chain in the UK

and its banking interests in Brazil.

Germany has risen to second place, behind the US, in the ranking of most active cross-border acquirers in Europe, largely due to the pending £977 million purchase of Kleinwort Benson by Dresdner. Foreign companies attempting German purchases have been known to complain about the country's lack of a formal mechanism for takeover bids. This was addressed in July when the German bourse authorities unveiled a voluntary takeover code requiring predator companies holding 50 per cent of a target company to make an offer to outstanding shareholders. This is the latest in a series of reforms which have included new disclosure and insider trading rules.

These rules accompany the increasing acceptance of M&A in Germany, and many other European countries, as a tool for corporate restructuring. A new regime has just been introduced in the Netherlands to curb measures that many Amsterdam-listed companies had put in place to defend themselves against hostile takeovers. The Swedish government is inviting comments on the proposed abolition of voting restrictions. Switzerland is also on the point of introducing new takeover rules. These were not in place in April 1995 when the country saw its first ever hostile bid, with International Paper making an offer for the non-woven textiles and paper distribution company Holvis.

Elsewhere in Europe, Italy and Spain have

mainly featured as targets, since domestic economic difficulties have continued to dampen the outward acquisition ambitions of local companies.

Bidder country	1st half 1995		Total 1994	
	No.	Value (£m)	No.	Value (£m)
US	208	5,289	430	9,949
Germany	86	3,681	147	5,366
UK	105	2,806	216	6,202
Switzerland	44	2,692	106	1,510
France	81	2,201	190	2,211
Netherlands	77	1,203	113	1,040
Australia	12	1.112	16	409
Multi-Europe	23	1,067	60	2,065
Sweden	52	968	57	152
Norway	16	452	39	207
Hong Kong	7	339	10	87
India	2	302	1	11
Canada	23	294	39	499
Italy	21	200	31	443
Republic of Ireland	16	193	48	1,004
Portugal	2	105	5	47
Others	145	1,069	339	6,293
Total	920	23,973	1847	37,495

Source: Acquisitions Monthly (includes pending transactions)

Table 49.1 Cross-border acquisitions of EU companies: the acquirers

What drives M&A activity?

The main factors which appear to affect the level of M&A activity in a particular country are economics and local culture – the latter category being especially important. The European market remains one of the most difficult because of the variety in local accounting standards, ownership structures, company law, takeover rules, stock exchange rules, tax rules and especially local cultural habits. This causes continuing fragmentation of the market from an M&A point of view, and to a large extent Europe remains a collection of home markets.

To demonstrate the importance of non-economic factors on M&A activity, one need only look at Japan. The country has never come close to achieving the levels of M&A activity that the size of its economy would suggest. To a much greater extent than Germany, many Japanese companies are linked together by complex webs of cross-shareholdings, and hostile bids are virtually unthinkable. Nevertheless, as German attitudes to M&A seem to have been transformed over the last few years, Japan may eventually follow suit.

At the other end of the spectrum, US companies have embraced M&A as their principal tool for building globally competitive, focused businesses. Over the last 15 years or so, the US industrial landscape has been transformed by this kind of corporate activity. Strategy consultancy OC&C conducted an analysis that compared the sales of the top two US and top two European companies operating throughout a selection of aerospace segments. With the exception of landing gear, actuation and helicopters, where European consolidation is well advanced, North American businesses enjoy considerable scale advantages, being over twice as large, on average, as their European competitors.

While scale advantages alone do not guarantee success, being subscale can bring serious penalties. These are exacerbated as large civil aircraft and engine manufacturers narrow their supplier base while encouraging financial risksharing and complete subsystem development.

Planning and execution

Hollywood, and the US leveraged buyout boom in the late 1980s, created the impression that many large M&A transactions were driven by financial engineering. Today, there appears to be a clear motivation shared by companies undertaking successful M&A, and that is to increase competitiveness. The essential first step in planning and executing M&A is to be clear about this fundamental rationale. Any other motivation can be a recipe for disaster.

The much-talked-about trend towards global business has been brought about because growth in the world economy and increasingly free trade give businesses access to wider and wider markets, while opening competition on their home turf. Simply speaking, there are three main ways in which M&A, and other related corporate activity, can help increase competitiveness. Each is interrelated, and consistent with increasing competitiveness through 'globalization'.

■ *Distribution.* The fastest and lowest-risk way to gain access to new markets is to link up with somebody who is already present. The enlarged business would serve customers at a wider range of locations, and may also be able to offer a broader range of complementary products.

■ *Scale.* The ability to build bigger production facilities, or make fuller use of existing capacity, can create cost advantages. Furthermore, larger businesses have a wider base to support expen-

sive or diverse R&D, which is especially important in high-technology areas.

■ *Technology.* Access to technology, or its timely exploitation, has been a key driver of frenetic M&A activity in a number of sectors. Rapidly advancing technology and increasingly open and deregulated markets have greatly shortened the time available to exploit new products. Competitors must be able to marshal the production and distribution capacity to exploit innovations rapidly.

Alongside objective setting comes expectation management. Deals may be judged to 'fail' because original expectations were unrealistic. Companies should also beware of setting narrow internal benchmarks to appraise potential investment opportunities or, rather, not be surprised when no proposals manage to satisfy these criteria.

In a complex cross-border context in particular, it is important to get the appropriate financial and legal advice, both to minimize risk and maximize advantage. Financial advice has evolved considerably since the merger boom of the late 1980s. All of the leading investment banks now recognize that industry expertise is required when competing for transactions, and so have invested heavily in building up sector expertise. However, their clients are not always looking for someone who knows more about the industry than they do: successful M&A sector specialists are not equity analysts but corporate financiers specializing in particular industries. In the European context above all, advisers perform roles which are complex, and which extend to the political and cultural aspects of a transaction as well as the financial ones. The ability to provide broad, integrated services is increasingly important. Furthermore, market conditions also demand flexibility, in the event of a course change by a client or changing market conditions.

Ultimately, the choice of adviser can determine the success or failure of a transaction. What board or CEO can really afford to get it wrong?

50 Tax Avoidance and the 'Controlled Foreign Company'

Robert Edwards, Tax Partner, Arthur Andersen, and

Helen Jones, Tax Manager, Arthur Andersen

As the boundaries continue to come down within Europe and businesses and entrepreneurs are encouraged to expand their activities abroad, more and more jurisdictions are introducing legislation to counteract the use of 'controlled foreign companies' (CFCs). Many countries within Europe now have CFC rules in one form or another – some decidedly more effective than others, but all generally based around the same principles.

Broadly, CFCs are companies in low tax jurisdictions which are used to roll-up profits, keeping them outside the tax net in the investor's home country. The aim of CFC legislation is to counteract this tax avoidance. Without some form of CFC legislation, income or gains arising on these overseas profits would ordinarily only be taxable when remitted back to the home country of the investor, eg in the form of dividends. If the funds can remain outside the country indefinitely they need never be taxed at the investor level.

Historically, many jurisdictions dealt with this problem by restricting the movement of funds or investment abroad through foreign exchange controls. With the lifting of such controls and the removal of trade barriers, most countries now see an effective CFC regime as an essential alternative.

It has been argued that legislation which restricts the free movement of funds is contrary to the principles of the Treaty of Rome. However, most jurisdictions counterclaim that such legislation is

necessary to enable the state to retain fiscal sovereignty and, as this defence has so far been accepted under EU law, more states are expected to implement CFC legislation in the near future.

It is important, therefore, that groups operating within Europe are aware of the various CFC regimes when structuring their international operations. There are important pitfalls to be avoided but, equally, some of the regimes offer tax planning opportunities.

Basic principles of CFC rules

Table 50.1 summarizes the main features of the CFC regimes in a number of European jurisdictions. In general the regimes have certain fundamental principles in common. To fall within a CFC regime the overseas company must be controlled by resident shareholders (which usually requires a more than 50 per cent ownership test to be satisfied, but this can be as low as 10 per cent in the case of France) and the income must be subject to a low rate of tax in the foreign company. The definition of a low rate of tax varies, and in some cases no safe harbour limit is in fact defined in law. Generally, however, tax rates between 0 and 30 per cent are regarded as 'low'.

Tax avoidance is prevented by attributing income from the CFC to the parent where it is taxed on an accruals basis. Most regimes will exempt CFC income generated by an active business, ie only passive income such as interest or dividends arising

Country	Ownership test for determining whether a CFC exists	Minimum tax rate to avoid CFC rules	Type of income attributable to parent	Exemptions from CFC legislation
Finland	At least 50% of capital or voting rights owned by Finnish residents. Attribution only to Finnish taxpayer owning at least 10%.	At least $^3/_5$ of Finnish corporate tax rate.	Share of profits (income and gains).	■ Income derived mainly from industrial or shipping activities.
France	At least 10% ownership of voting or financial rights, or cost of investment in excess of FF150 million.	At least $^1/_3$ of French corporate tax rate.	Share of profits (income and gains).	■ Motive test – must demonstrate that CFC not established primarily to take advantage of privileged tax regime. Assumed if CFC has commercial or industrial activity and carries it out mainly in local market.
Germany	More than 50% of the equity or voting rights in the foreign company owned by German residents.	30%	Passive income and gains which are subject to a low rate of tax.	■ Active income – seven categories of active income include manufacturing/agriculture/banking and insurance/trading/provision of services/renting and licensing activities. There is, however, generally a restriction that these activities may not be undertaken with German connected parties. Raising intragroup finance in overseas markets is also active income if the group companies generate 90% of their income from exempt activities. ■ Intragroup financing – 40% of attributable profits from this activity are exempt from corporate tax and 100% exempt from trade tax. ■ No attribution of portfolio income (ie income from liquid assets) to German residents owning less than 10% of the CFC. ■ *De minimis* limit for portfolio income – DM120,000 if portfolio income is less than 10% of gross CFC income.
Portugal	Either more than 25% of capital controlled by Portuguese residents or more than 30% of capital controlled by Portuguese residents with at least one holding more than 10%.	20%	Share of profits (income and gains).	■ Active income – where at least 75% of the CFC's income is derived from farming, manufacturing or commercial activities with non-Portuguese residents. May not apply if activities comprise banking, insurance, holding shares or intellectual property and leasing.
Spain	50% or more of shares, profits or voting rights owned by Spanish residents.	At least 75% of Spanish corporate income tax rate.	Passive net income and capital gains.	■ If net passive income (excluding connected party financing, insurance and service income) does not exceed 15% of profits and 4% of revenue of CFC and related non-Spanish resident companies.
Sweden	At least 50% of capital or voting rights owned by Swedish residents, and at least 10% held by one Swedish shareholder.	No legal definition. Minimum rate of 10% generally accepted.	Share of profits (income and gains).	■ None
UK	More than 50% of company controlled by UK residents. Attribution only to UK corporate shareholders owning at least 10%.	At least 75% of UK corporate tax rate.	Share of profits – not capital gains.	■ Activity test – CFC has a business establishment and is effectively managed in the overseas territory. ■ Acceptable distribution policy followed – within 18 months of a period end the CFC must distribute to the UK more than 50% of available profits or more than 90% if not a trading company. ■ CFC is at least 35% publicly quoted. ■ Motive test – if no other exemption applies demonstrate that motive for CFC is not avoidance of tax. ■ *De minimis* limit – where attributable profits do not exceed £20,000.

Table 50.1 Summary of CFC rules

in the CFC is attributed and treated as taxable income of the shareholder.

Clearly, any summary of the main principles cannot give the full picture. In a number of cases there is a great deal of subjectivity in determining whether the rules apply (offering both potential opportunities but also uncertainty). This is particularly true when determining whether the rules for claiming exemption apply. For some regimes it is also debatable whether the rules achieve the desired objectives.

France

The French regime was introduced in 1980 and since then has gone through two major revisions, the most recent in April 1993. As with many other countries, only a very limited number of cases have been taken as far as the courts. This may be indicative of the perceived effectiveness of the rules which, more often than not, are used as a deterrent to tax avoidance rather than an active tool.

There is an exemption from the legislation where it can be shown that obtaining the benefit of a favourable tax regime was not the main reason for establishing the CFC. This is automatically assumed if the foreign company has an industrial or commercial activity and carries out its operations mainly in the local market. However, the law does not define 'local market', thereby introducing an element of subjectivity often encountered in CFC rules.

UK

The UK regime was introduced in 1984. In 1993, the definition of a low level of taxation was increased from being less than 50 per cent to less than 75 per cent of the normal UK tax rate. While this amendment has brought a number of previously untaxed companies into the CFC regime, the legislation is still very much seen as a deterrent. This is evidenced by the fact that the legislation must be specifically invoked by order of the Board of the Inland Revenue, rather than applying automatically when the tests are breached.

There are a number of exemptions, including the acceptable distribution test which is used by many groups. This is particularly useful for Dutch 'mixer' structures which are specifically established to enable high-taxed income to be mixed with low-taxed income. Furthermore, unlike most, the UK CFC regime does not encompass capital gains derived at the level of the CFC. This again encourages the use of

low-taxed intermediate holding companies which benefit from participation exemptions such as in The Netherlands and Luxembourg. However, the main opposition party has indicated that this may be one area it will change if it is returned to government in the next few years.

A CFC in a UK group may also, in limited circumstances, be used to advantage to provide financing to an overseas affiliate in countries such as the US. The advantage is obtained by the fact that a CFC established as a look-through for US tax purposes, financed by dollar equity and which lends dollar funds to the US, can avoid having to include foreign exchange movements in its UK tax calculation.

Sweden

Until recently CFCs were typically used by Swedish investors to undertake lease financing activities. This is no longer the case as the schemes relied on an attribution of losses which is no longer available. Now, therefore, rather than seeking to take advantage of the rules, interest is likely to focus on ways of avoiding taxation under the CFC regime. One route may be to hold the CFC through a company in another treaty country. This is very simple avoidance, but relies on the assumption that the interposition of a treaty country does not in itself add a significant tax cost.

Germany

Double tax treaties can often provide opportunities for avoiding the imposition of CFC regimes. For example, under the German/Swiss treaty, income generated at a low tax rate, eg in one of the favourable Swiss cantons, is nevertheless exempt from the German CFC rules under the active trade or business test in the treaty. A similar result may be obtained with Ireland for an Irish manufacturing company able to take advantage of the 10 per cent Irish tax rate.

Other regimes

The CFC regimes in Spain, Portugal and Finland were only introduced in 1995 and, as such, there is currently little experience as to their effect in practice. However, opportunities have already been identified for ways of avoiding the imposition of the regimes.

In Spain, for example, the complex exemption rules have provoked vigorous debate. It should be possible to avoid the rules where the CFC is part of a non-Spanish resident group of companies and provided that the results of the CFC are less than 15 per

We'll make your future less taxing.

For most international companies, the spotlight has fallen on tax affairs as never before.

Increasingly, international links are being forged between governments and revenue collection agencies.

Co-operation at this level will undoubtedly lead to their applying a much sharper focus to your business affairs.

Our skill in developing and implementing tax strategies is renowned the world over.

Our global network of offices works in unison to help you deal with international, multinational and cross border tax issues.

We can offer a complete and comprehensive service to help you maximise all the tax advantages due to you, while at the same time leaving you to concentrate on your business.

One way or another, Arthur Andersen will make your life less taxing. For further information please contact Iain Stitt in Brussels on 32 (2) 510 42 73, or the senior tax partner at your local Arthur Andersen office.

ARTHUR ANDERSEN

ARTHUR ANDERSEN & CO, SC

Arthur Andersen is authorised by the Institute of Chartered Accountants in England and Wales to carry on investment business

cent of the total net profits and 4 per cent of the total revenues of that group.

The Portuguese have taken a slightly different approach and the CFC rules themselves are unlikely to have a far-reaching effect on many groups. However, the authorities have at the same time introduced legislation to restrict payments (eg interest, royalties, service fees, etc) to companies in jurisdictions with more favourable tax regimes. This 'two-pronged' attack on companies in low tax jurisdictions may, in practice, be a much more effective way of discouraging the use of low tax companies within international groups.

Conclusion

As more companies expand internationally and develop more sophisticated tax structures, it is to be expected that further jurisdictions will consider the introduction of a CFC regime as part of their policy to maintain the fiscal base. Even in jurisdictions which have not yet introduced overt CFC legislation, there is already a clear trend towards tightening up perceived tax avoidance through the use of companies in favourable tax regimes, eg by restricting double tax treaty benefits or the application of EC directives, unless it can be demonstrated that tax avoidance is not a motive.

Fraud and Security Risks

G J Squires, Coopers & Lybrand

There are those who see a federal Europe as a desirable goal, readily attainable in this generation or the next: Europe as one huge, supranational geographical area in which its citizens can travel without restriction, buying and selling goods and services at will using a homogeneous currency. They see its peoples conforming to and protected by a common law, and enjoying common democratic rights and privileges. There are others who view a federal Europe as an impossible dream, the vision of romantics who ignore the unbridgeable chasms of language, custom, culture and national pride which crisscross the continent.

A business person seeking to expand into Europe to take advantage of the undoubted opportunities offered by the concept of the Union must make a prosaically practical assessment of the current position. The long-recognized differences in the political and economic priorities of member countries, not to mention differences in policing and juridical practices, make Europe a minefield of conflicting or non-complementary interests, a commercial frontier – land in which pioneering business people must be prepared to use their own resources to protect their interests.

As existing national systems are altered and adapted in the long march towards parity and uniformity, criminals in general and fraudsters in particular are quick to identify and exploit the weaknesses which the changes produce. The existence of a growing number of very intelligent, sophisticated and extraordinarily successful fraudsters must be acknowledged and guarded against. They are often organized, accommodated and equipped in such a way as to make them indistinguishable in appearance from any other successful international business people; indeed, the only real difference is that their deals are a sham. Organized criminal gangs run many a financially secure and apparently respectable corporation, which uses the latest technology and has international representation.

Fraudsters are constantly alert to the possibility of enrolling others into apparently legitimate trading relationships in order to assist in money laundering, or to relieve business people of huge sums of money in advance-fee frauds. Prominent among these is the 'Prime Bank Guarantee' fraud, a spectacularly successful scam in which single corporations have lost millions of dollars in cash, having been duped into believing that they are investing in a 'roll programme' in a purported secret market in which so-called Prime Bank instruments are said by the fraudster to be traded by the world's top banks.

While secrecy is common to many transactions in a highly competitive marketplace, it is also a weapon often used by fraudsters to dissuade their potential victims from seeking proper, independent professional advice. Forgery is another weapon, and corroboration should be sought for all documents of security and letters of comfort, however authentic

Coopers & Lybrand

FORENSIC ACCOUNTING

National Fraud & Investigations Group

➤ Help and advice from specialists with a variety of backgrounds on all aspects of fraud investigation and asset recovery

➤ Independent, Objective and Penetrating

➤ Call one of these contacts for a free initial consultation

London Contacts:

Richard Coleman	0171-212-6278
Ian Trumper	0171-212-8340
Gerry Squires	0171-212-6280

Solutions for Business

The Coopers & Lybrand organisation is one of the world's leading providers of professional services including accounting and auditing, tax and consulting. The organisation comprises national and international practice entities which are members of Coopers & Lybrand International, a limited liability association incorporated in Switzerland, and which serve clients on a globally integrated basis in more than 120 countries

and impressive they may appear. Even genuine documents may have been stolen, or issued by corrupt officials. Similarly, such is the skill of some fraudsters that they persuade reputable bankers, lawyers and accountants to write seemingly innocuous letters which can then be used by the fraudsters to add credibility to a scheme of which the letter writers have no knowledge.

Business people in a 'start-up' situation in a foreign country are vulnerable to the criminal. Offers of financial assistance from little-known entities may later prove to have hidden strings attached. Offers of new and second-hand plant and machinery, computers and office equipment at very attractive prices may seem tempting, and the confidential explanation that tax liability has been evaded may seem reasonable, but any business person who succumbs to such blandishments is courting disaster. Stolen goods, and in particular such things as microchips and antiques, are the new international currency.

The same sort of offences against property and the person can be identified in the criminal codes of each of the countries of Europe, yet the level of protection under the law enjoyed by citizens varies significantly between countries, according to local problems of scarce resources, corruption and political interference. Even well-resourced and well-motivated enforcement agencies can be remarkably uninterested in the activities of criminals based in their own countries, whose illegal operations only affect victims living outside their national boundaries. Even when investigations are begun, the degree of expertise shown – particularly in matters of complex fraud – can be seen to vary enormously between countries. The criminal process cannot be relied on for recovery or recompense.

Perhaps the most traumatic culture shock is experienced by business people seeking to penetrate the markets of Eastern Europe and expecting tó make use of the commercial infrastructure to which they have become accustomed, including credit rating agencies, market regulators and professional advisers operating under a duty of care.

Before extending credit the party at risk must have access to reliable information about the reputation and financial status of the counterparty before the transaction proceeds. In the UK and other European countries where company law is well developed, the corporate entity is a normal and widely accepted trading vehicle, even for people in business in a small way, and credit status information is readily available.

In some of the countries of Eastern Europe with less advanced regulatory systems, strong entrepreneurial individuals play a larger role in business than corporations. While comfort can be drawn from dealing with people who put their fortune and reputation at issue in each business proposition, the fact is that even in Western Europe the information industry is not geared to providing information on individuals.

While some are individuals whose riches have unquestionably been accumulated from perfectly legitimate activities, there is generally great difficulty for a foreigner, in considering a business proposition, to distinguish between legal and illegal sources of funds. One reads much of the burgeoning influence of the 'Russian Mafia', and nothing at all of rags-to-riches success stories of innovative entrepreneurs who have spotted a gap in a rising market. It seems there is a problem of image here.

So, if a federal Europe is unattainable, as some aver, or is at least unachievable in the short term, where might Europe's commercial future lie? How to achieve an environment in which honest European business people may prosper and criminals may be frustrated in their designs? The European dream of free passage of goods and labour over national boundaries is all but realized, but the key to future healthy commercial growth must surely be the free passage of reliable information.

Throughout the world, financial centres generate wealth for those who use them, as well as for the countries in which they are situated. Individually they have shaped and developed rules, practices, controls, ethics and standards. Their individual reputations are linked to the integrity and proficiency of their regulators. Within each financial centre the value of instant access to information about traders and principals, commodities and finance, is well understood. Modern technology is capable of providing that instant access worldwide.

If there is an economic case for the union of Europe, there is a case for the union of its financial centres, and for developing uniformity in regulation, practices and policies. Information could be networked from city to city, making local national controls and bureaucracy irrelevant, as is already the case with international banking. Will the new millennium see the triumph of business over politics?

International Business Solutions
from
INTERNATIONAL BUSINESS SYSTEMS

International

Worldwide availability
Supported in over 30 countries
Multi Language, Multi Currency Systems
International Account Management

Business

Retail & Distribution
Chemical & Pharmaceutical
Production
Field Service
Local Government

Systems

Executive Information
Financial Ledgers
Distribution
Integrated Housing
Integrated Revenues
Manufacturing
Service Management
FMCG

*A*t International Business Systems we supply fully integrated business solutions designed to provide fast, accurate, customer-focussed information across your entire organisation, nationally and internationally.

At International Business Systems we help organisations in both the public and private sectors to gain significant cost and efficiency benefits by having the same software supported by the same high standards, on the same cost-effective platform, with the same terms and conditions.

International Business Systems - putting the business objectives of the customer first.

INVESTOR IN PEOPLE

I.BS
INTERNATIONAL BUSINESS SYSTEMS

INTERNATIONAL BUSINESS SYSTEMS (IBS) AB
Box 3061, s-172 03 Sundyberg, Sweden
Tel +46 8 627 2300

INTERNATIONAL BUSINESS SYSTEMS
2, West Mills, Newbury, Berkshire RG14 5GH
Tel: (01635) 30808 Fax: (01635) 32502

INTERNATIONAL BUSINESS SYSTEMS
Imperial Place, Building 1, Elstree Way, Boreham Wood,
Herts W66 1WE Tel: 0181 207 5655 Fax: 0181 207 6770

PART

11

European Venture Capital

Boosting Europe's Growth Companies

Denis Mortier, CEO, Financière Saint Dominique and Chairman, European Venture Capital Association

Two of the greatest and most urgent challenges facing the whole of Europe are creating sustainable economic growth and reversing endemic unemployment.

The venture capital sector in Europe already confers considerable economic and employment benefits in developing Europe's technological and entrepreneurial potential. Surveys in The Netherlands and France bear this out.

A survey by the Dutch employers' federation VNO found that some 40 per cent of the country's 75 fastest growing companies had been financed by venture capital (less than 2 per cent of all Dutch companies are venture backed). In France, Coopers & Lybrand compared a group of 224 French venture-backed companies with a larger group of non-venture-backed companies. Over four years (1989–93) the first group averaged 34 per cent employment growth, 42 per cent sales growth, 80 per cent export growth and a doubling of investment. All these growth rates were at least three times higher than the non-venture-backed group.

It is no coincidence that venture-backed companies seem consistently to outstrip their non-venture-backed counterparts. Venture capitalists must give high returns to their investors as the sector has an inherently higher risk profile than fixed-interest securities or blue-chip stocks. Venture capitalists identify the best potential performers and not only supply scarce equity resources, but provide advice, contacts and strategic analysis to an otherwise isolated entrepreneur. In short, venture capitalists must be active investors doing everything in their power to help the companies they invest in succeed in providing high returns to *their* investors.

In the past 10 years the venture capital sector in Europe has raised more than ECU46 billion of long-term capital and currently holds investments in an estimated 20,000 privately owned, European growth companies. It has become an economically vital investment sector, and although relatively young, the European sector consists of over 3000 experienced professionals and 500 venture capital firms located in more than 20 European countries. The sector continues to grow and has the potential to be at least three or four times its current size if the present level of activity in the leading countries can be emulated across the continent and the barriers to this happening can be removed.

The European Venture Capital Association (EVCA) has identified a number of institutional, legal and fiscal factors which stand in the way of the realization of the sector reaching its full maturity and believes measures are needed at both the European and national levels.

EVCA's Europe Private Equity White Paper has been written to summarize these factors. It sets out eight key policy challenges which need urgently to be addressed to allow the sector to flourish, which will maximize economic and employment growth potential.

Challenge 1 Encourage dynamic entrepreneurship and management

Europe needs to sow the seeds for more growth-oriented companies by promoting dynamic entrepreneurship at the grass-roots level. Entrepreneurs are the engine of economic growth, and their development deserves attention in Europe's schools and universities. Legislation and fiscal regulation should be systematically scrutinized for their impact on enterprise and revised to favour entrepreneurial, dynamic enterprises. This needs to be complemented with high-quality corporate management and governance structures and practice. The European Single Market must be completed and kept open for international expansion to allow fast-growing companies to exploit wider markets and to compete globally.

Challenge 2 Provide competitive stock markets for smaller and growth companies

There is a need for stock markets to provide Europe's star companies with growth capital at an attractive cost and with high liquidity levels. This will enable these companies to remain independent and avoid acquisition by large corporations before their true potential and contribution to the economy of Europe as independent businesses have been realized. Since such competitive markets are not available to most growth companies in Europe with pan-European ambitions, a new pan-European stock market is needed. The European Single Market for financial and stock market services should be further unified and stimulated.

Challenge 3 Develop and channel sources of long-term capital

Pension funds and other long-term sources of capital need to be developed in all European countries and their investment support to the venture capital sector encouraged. While in Europe banks provide a third of all capital to the sector, their investment horizons are generally shorter, pushing venture capitalists to invest in safer and more mature private companies. In contrast, pension funds provide more than half the

funding for venture capital in the USA, allowing longer-term investment horizons. Furthermore, venture capital needs to be regarded by investors as a distinct asset class with an inherently high risk/reward profile and in-built diversification. The management and investment of long-term sources of capital needs to be liberalized throughout Europe to enable true pan-European investment.

Challenge 4 Provide appropriate fund structures for private equity funds

Investing in venture capital funds should be easy for all investors, yet the reality is different. The structuring of venture capital funds is often highly complex. Some European countries have standard structures for domestic funds, while others have different structures for different purposes, often too restrictive to be practical. Other countries have no appropriate structure, and foreign structures have to be used. Increasingly, funds have investors from several countries and invest across borders. In these cases, the complexities multiply. This has the significant effect of discouraging investors and international investment in the case of smaller funds, as the professional costs involved can be prohibitive and in some cases the problems are insoluble. European countries and the EU should provide legislation to enable efficient fund structures at the local, trans-national, European and international levels.

Challenge 5 Adjust tax rewards for those bearing the highest risks

Tax regimes should allow the highest rewards to be earned by the prime movers of enterprise: the entrepreneur, the key managers and the equity investors or shareholders. Increasing recognition of the value of entrepreneurs to the European economy should be matched by favourable tax treatment, recognizing in part that the risks taken in new enterprises should be matched by the rewards. At present debt financing is treated more favourably by fiscal regimes than equity financing, and the burden of debt on a young company can often prevent its rapid growth. Low or no tax on gains, higher write-offs on losses and private equity (re)investment relief should stimulate all those bearing the great risks in enterprise to invest more.

Challenge 6 Promote investment in innovative start-up ventures

Europe needs to invest more in start-up and innovative businesses. Such investments in particular require the supportive environment advocated in the EVCA White Paper. Government can contribute more directly, especially with tax incentives and by supporting the emergence of international technology-based ventures in Europe. The following measures should be considered at the European level: co-funding by the newly created European Investment Fund of venture capital technology funds and investments; easier implementation of pan-European patents; encouraging the development of spin-offs from the EU's extensive research; and coordination of national technical assistance activities, especially promoting worldwide investment into European businesses in new technology sectors.

Challenge 7 Facilitate the transfer of company ownership to revitalize existing businesses

The easy transfer of ownership is vital for Europe's massive family-owned company sector. More importantly, transfer of company ownership provides an opportunity for further expansion, preferably with the involvement of experienced management, which should be encouraged. It should be ensured that the levy of inheritance or gift tax does not jeopardize the future of a business, and that tax systems should not discriminate, depending on the size of the holding, its term, the tax consolidation thresholds or other factors. This will considerably benefit industrial restructuring in Europe.

Challenge 8 Develop the markets in countries where private equity is emerging

The barriers to the emergence and growth of private equity in some European countries, particularly those in Central and Eastern Europe, need to be removed. As this may not be enough, government needs to take measures to stimulate the markets, utilizing professional profit-seeking and competitive fund managers. Investment incentive and guarantee schemes need to be introduced where there are none, and foreign funding agencies should continue and expand their co-investment activities.

53 EASDAQ:
A European Initiative for High-Growth Companies

Chris J Pickles, Director, European Association of Securities Dealers

In nature, things are either growing or they are dying – they never stand still. The same is true of a nation's economy. The long-term growth of an economy depends very much on how it nurtures the business environment to encourage real industrial growth.

Companies which grow create demand for labour and materials, and this demand feeds back through industry to create more jobs. But that growth can be hindered by the lack of the basic requirements of all companies – capital.

Growing companies often have difficulty in raising capital. In their early days, they do not have a long enough track record to allow them to access many sources of capital – particularly domestic stock markets. And the lack of an adequate number of potential investors in a purely domestic market can mean that even a stock market listing does not provide growing companies with the support which they require.

The reaction of some stock markets has been to develop new initiatives to address the needs of smaller companies. Other stock markets have not yet reacted to these needs. However, new initiatives can often be just the reworking of old approaches, and will bring the same old problems with them.

For the first time, with the launch of the EASDAQ initiatives, market participants – venture capitalists, banks, brokers and professional advisers – from across Europe and the USA have joined together to develop a stock market aimed specifically at high growth, internationally oriented companies. Using the full opportunities offered by the Investment Services Directive, EASDAQ will be a truly pan-European stock market.

One of the greatest success stories in the area of growth markets in recent years has been that of NASDAQ (National Association of Securities Dealers Automated Quotation) in the USA. This market was developed by the market participants themselves to meet the needs of growth companies, investors and intermediaries. Now it is the second largest stock market in North America, close behind the New York Stock Exchange. NASDAQ has helped small companies to succeed and grow in one of the most competitive industrial environments in the world. Some of the companies which lead whole sectors of industry started on NASDAQ, such as Microsoft and Compaq.

EASDAQ (European Association of Securities Dealers Automated Quotation) is based on many of the original principles applied by NASDAQ. Its shareholders are the market participants – NASDAQ itself is a shareholder in EASDAQ. The driving force behind NASDAQ was the NASD (National Association of Securities Dealers). In Europe, the EASD (European Association of Securities Dealers) was created in 1994 by market participants – strongly supported by EVCA (the European Venture Capital Association) – to act as the driving force behind this new European initiative. EASD has now over 60 member organisations from 11 European countries and the USA.

An effective capital market has to provide opportunities to all participants – investors, issuers and intermediaries. Investors need to know that there is an efficient 'exit' from their investment, so that they can realize the true profit potential of their investment. To achieve this, the market needs to be liquid, which means that there has to be an adequate number of potential investors.

A purely domestic market has great difficulties in achieving this critical mass. Part of the success of NASDAQ has been that its North American market has a population of over 250 million inhabitants. EASDAQ, as a pan-European stock market, will be addressing a market with over 300 million inhabitants. And through cross-links with NASDAQ, it will also be able to tap the North American market.

In any economy, the availability of new capital to help small companies to grow is limited. Once initial invested capital has helped to establish the success of a small company, that capital needs to be reinvested into another company offering growth. Only by keeping this initial investment capital moving is economic growth sustainable.

Traditional stock markets have not promoted this recycling of initial investment capital, and therefore have not helped adequately in the growth of their national economies 'from the bottom up'. Although traditional stock exchanges may have hundreds or even thousands of companies listed for trading, some 70 per cent or more of their total trading volume is concentrated in the top 30 or 40 'blue chip' stocks. Just as happens in many other business sectors, national stock exchanges have tended to concentrate on their 'cash cows', earning money from the associated transaction fees. Smaller companies have been left to languish and even die. Little or nothing has been done in the past by many stock exchanges to promote the markets for growing companies.

In the 1960s, the UK media was full of articles about the 'brain drain' – how North American companies were enticing away some of the best minds in the UK to help to develop their industries and make their economies even more competitive. This drain is still there today, but its attraction is not just through better terms and conditions of employment – it is also because other countries offer easier access to adequate capital to meet the needs of growing companies. Recent studies have indicated that, particularly in high-tech industries, where companies have had to go

to North America to meet their capital requirements, too many of those companies have moved their total operations to North America afterwards. This 'corporate emigration' takes with it all of the potential benefits which those new high-growth companies might have brought to their original home economy.

Developing an effective capital market for high growth companies within Europe is therefore of key strategic and economic importance for the nations of Europe. Companies which are learning to 'think global and act local' need a market which thinks and acts that way too.

The Investment Services Directive of the European Commission is breaking down those local barriers to investment and growth opportunities. This is the finance sector's equivalent of the Schengen agreement. UK securities houses will be able to become members of any and all of the stock exchanges within the European Union, without having to have a physical presence in any market outside of their home base. But as the stock exchanges tend to remain separate and competitive, market liquidity is split and spread more thinly across Europe, so that individual national markets for high growth companies can not reach the critical mass necessary for market liquidity and for the success of their market. Although the increasing computerization of stock exchanges makes remote access to those exchanges easier, the costs to securities houses of the necessary computer and communications infrastructure to access the multiplicity of exchanges is enormous. Those costs have to be passed on, to both the investor and then to the issuer – the high growth company which needs to be nurtured.

By having one pan-European stock market for high growth, internationally oriented companies:

- a critical mass of investors and issuers can be achieved more easily;
- costs to investors and intermediaries, and the cost of capital to issuers, can be contained, making the market more attractive to all;
- an efficient market can be created to help high growth companies achieve their true potential, and contribute to the growth of their national industry, the growth of their national economy, and the long-term competitiveness of Europe as a whole.

EASDAQ, which aims to meet the needs of a larger Europe, is more likely to offer greater benefit to individual national economies within the EU, and therefore to the European Union as a whole.

54 Best Practice for Venture Capital

Finding the right structure for a venture capital transaction is rarely straightforward. This chapter features how solutions were fashioned in nine recent transactions, drawing out a wide range of conclusions such as:

- It is often only management teams who have sufficient knowledge to take on the whole business. Trade purchasers may prefer to cherrypick, guarding themselves against possible hidden liabilities;
- It is worth bidders finding out what exactly the vendor is trying to achieve. It is not always the best price, but may include other objectives as well;
- If an approach does not work first time, lines of communication should be kept open. There is often a second chance;
- However complex the equity structure, it has to be balanced with an ability to control the management team;
- A potential MBO team needs to present solid financing, not just expressions of interest. It also needs to have developed contacts with a number of institutions and banks to secure the best terms, as well as building a defensive measure for further ahead in the deal;
- Revolving facilities and invoice discounting

might represent alternatives to the traditional term loan, particularly where flexibility is required;
- The Internet is starting to play a role in moving around large volumes of information within the tight parameters of a deal;
- Completing a venture capital transaction is often a prelude. Restructuring and disposals may then follow to put the company on a footing firm enough for flotation;
- Time spent negotiating with the vendor and institutions in the buy-out process might affect trading, especially where the management team is small and involved in day-to-day operations;
- Once the high drama of a buy-out has been completed, management should then be able to concentrate on running a successful independent business. It will be free of the constraints of a parent company and should have a flexible funding structure in place to overcome bottlenecks and to expand product range;
- Buy-ins provide the opportunity to introduce a new working culture, increasing the level of innovation. Companies coming out of the private sector must learn to become specialists – not all things to all men.

Case Study I
Tricom Automotive:
a classic MBO

In March 1995, as lead advisers to management, Coopers & Lybrand successfully completed the £17 million management buy-out (MBO) of Melfin (UK) Limited, now known as Tricom Automotive Ltd. Tricom, with its headquarters at Eastwood, Nottinghamshire, is a substantial manufacturer of car seats in the UK, concentrating on supplying seats and seating components to the light commercial and off-road 4 × 4 markets. Tricom currently makes all the seats for the Ford Transit, and, among others, seats for the Landrover Discovery and Vauxhall Frontera. Annual turnover is in excess of £60 million.

Tricom was owned by an Italian group, Elcat Spa. Elcat had been in severe financial difficulties for some time, and was in a form of insolvency proceeding in Italy known as Concordato Preventivo. Whilst still controlled by its owner, its affairs were under the keen eye of the Italian Court. Before Christmas last year, the management team believed the time was right to approach Elcat with the proposal for an MBO.

What made Tricom an attractive candidate for an MBO?

Principally, as a business it encapsulated many of the attributes which would satisfy potential funders in a leveraged structure:

- It has a strong management team, comprising individuals with the full breadth of expertise across all the requisite managerial functions.
- The company was well established, having manufactured seats for the Ford Transit for 30 years.
- Tricom brought with it a strong trading record in recent years.
- While, again in line with industry practice, it did not have hard and fast contracts with its OEM customers, as long as it performed well it was virtually assured business for the lifetime of the models for which it supplied. It therefore could project its business forward with a good degree of certainty.
- Several of these features contributed to a sound predictability of future cash flows.
- It had a substantial asset base on which to secure debt.
- It could, it seemed, be acquired for a good price. In summary, Tricom conformed well to the ideal

model for institutions and banks financing a transaction of this nature, representing an acquisition of a sound and mature business with predictable cash flow at a reasonable price.

The MBO process

The financing of an MBO is usually a competitive matter. A well-advised management team will visit a number of institutions and banks in putting together a funding package, not only to ensure they are getting the best terms available for themselves and the ongoing business, but also as a defensive measure to focus the minds of funders as the deal progresses. In Tricom's case, the management were already close to NatWest Bank, and Coopers & Lybrand were introduced by them to act as lead advisers.

Coopers & Lybrand's first task was to assist the management in producing comprehensive financial projections for the business, to price the business and to suggest indicative funding structures. In common with many deals of this nature, the financing structure incorporated an element of institutional equity, mostly comprised of redeemable preference shares, together with a raft of senior debt facilities. The flows of debt repayment and preference share redemptions were modelled in to the company's projected cash flows, and structures formulated accordingly.

The equity package put together by NatWest Ventures implied both a level of cost to the business providing them with a running yield, and also at management's cost a stake in the equity of the company. This stake should provide them with a large proportion of their return on the whole investment, by way of future capital gain on realization.

Given the management's view of the excellent potential for the business over the next few years, a ratchet arrangement was then negotiated, in this case based on exit capitalization; under the ratchet, management's stake in the business is increased proportionately to certain levels of capitalization achieved on exit above a certain threshold.

There are many varieties of ratchet arrangements, for example based around achievement of certain levels of profitability or speed of redemption of shares. The exit-based ratchet both avoids arguments about definitions of 'profits' and incentivizes the team to have an eye for the right exit within a desirable timescale.

Because of the strong possibility of certain developments in the business which could require fairly substantial levels of cash investment in future

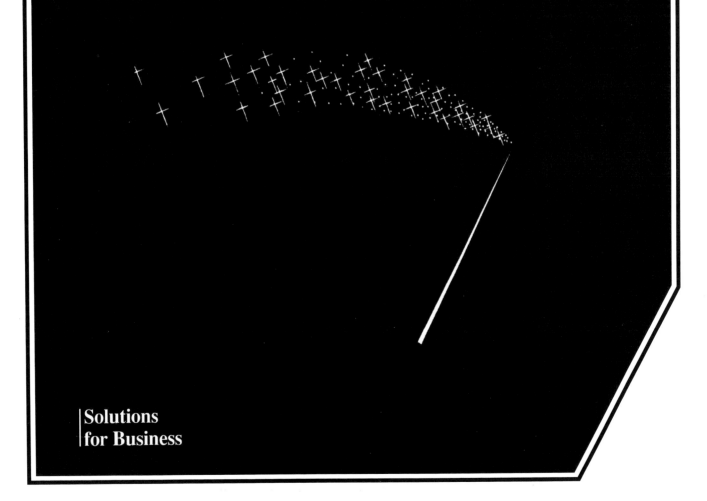

years, it was important to build a sound level of flexibility into the company's banking facilities. A package of revolving facilities together with subsidiary overdraft facilities was structured, protected by covenants negotiated to incorporate the flexible arrangements the business needed. Revolving facilities can represent a good alternative to the traditional term loan, where greater flexibility is required to fund future growth.

The negotiations with Elcat were at times difficult, and involved taking careful account of the needs of the Italian court. They also involved some complex tax issues. Despite this, the deal progressed remarkably smoothly to its completion at the end of March. Paul Southern and Jonathan Wackett, who advised the management team, are both partners in the Northern Corporate Finance Team at Coopers and Lybrand.

Case Study II
ColourCare International:
Snapshot of a buyout

A spree of aggressive acquisition combined with organic growth meant that by the late 1980s ColourCare International had become the leading UK photoprocessor, with a 30 per cent share of the UK market. By 1992 it had an annual turnover of £125 million with operations throughout the UK and in Ireland, France, Belgium, The Netherlands, Spain and Scandinavia. ColourCare provided photoprocessing services to amateur photographers, estate agents, schools and professional photographers and operated from 12 main laboratories in the UK and 235 mini and micro laboratories – located predominantly in branches of Boots the Chemist – and a laboratory in Norway. However, the recession took its toll and pressure to maintain market share in an overcrowded marketplace had made a serious impact on pricing and margins. In the year to 31 March 1993 the ColourCare Group made an operating loss of £3.2 million, which rose to £13.2 million in the following year.

Early in December 1993, ColourCare's UK management team, led by Frank Brenan, were summoned to the board room at their head office in Salisbury and told that ColourCare's parent, London International Group plc (LIG) was shortly to announce a major restructuring and rationalization programme. It became clear that the disposal of ColourCare was essential if LIG was to launch a rescue rights issue.

LIG's original strategy was to sell ColourCare to a trade purchaser. A management buyout was not on the agenda. As the opportunity to acquire a market leader like ColourCare does not often arise, a substantial amount of initial interest was shown by the trade. However, for various reasons trade purchasers decided not to go ahead. By April 1994 Frank Brenan and the other four members of the management team, having spent a number of months biding their time and helping possible buyers with their due diligence, were aware that there were only a small number of interested parties left and made a formal approach to LIG.

The principal advantage of the management team's approach was not the price but the fact that it was the only offer to acquire the entire share capital of the ColourCare group of companies. Other potential purchasers wanted to 'cherry pick' and were not willing to take on the risk of possible hidden liabilities. Only the management team had sufficient knowledge of and confidence in the business to take on everything.

Smith & Williamson Securities was appointed by the management team to provide integrated advice on corporate finance, corporate tax and pensions issues. The period between April 1994 and completion in June two months later was a time of considerable strain and uncertainty for the management team. At no time was LIG prepared to give the MBO team exclusivity and it was only in the last few weeks of negotiations that they had any sense of being in pole position. At that point the team needed to consider a seemingly endless number of commercial and technical issues, including the interests of key suppliers and customers, UK and overseas tax issues (the MBO team had not, historically, dealt with ColourCare's tax position), pensions, property issues, a highly complex working capital adjustment and financial assistance.

ColourCare was eventually sold to the management team for a nominal sum, free of debt, cash and leasing commitments but with trade debtors and creditors. LIG provided a secured loan of £6 million to the buyout vehicle, Nexus Photo Limited, which was interest free for the first year. Equity and mezzanine finance were not required, which saved a further layer of already complex negotiations and also left the management team with complete ownership of the business. NatWest, already bankers to ColourCare, happily provided a working capital facility. One final twist was that the Boots-related business was sold separately to two other parties.

Lessons learnt

Some of the lessons that any prospective management team might learn from this MBO include the following:

- Irrespective of the level of preplanning, the process is often fraught, time consuming and uncertain.
- Dogged persistence will often pay dividends.
- Be realistic about the worth of the business.
- Try to understand what the vendor is trying to achieve. It is often not just the best price but a number of other objectives as well.
- Take advice at the outset.
- It may be easier said than done, but try and keep a certain detachment from the transaction and maintain a sense of humour.

The first year of the management team's new existence has been hectic and challenging. Substantial inroads have been made in reducing the cost base of the business; major new accounts have been won; the continental European mail order business and Irish wholesale business have been sold to an American processor for in excess of £16 million; the Scandinavian business has been sold to a Norwegian processor; and the schools business has been sold to its own management team.

Smith & Williamson provided corporate finance and tax advice for these disposals and assisted the management team on a range of corporate tax planning and compliance issues. The firm provided personal financial planning advice to members of the MBO team and advised on an innovative pension scheme, structured to enable the company to manage future costs, while members benefit from enhanced returns. Smith & Williamson Chartered Accountants has been appointed auditors to the Group.

ColourCare has now started its second year debt free (following repayment of LIG's £6 million loan) and with cash in the business for future investment.

Case Study III
Travers Smith Braithwaite

Travers Smith Braithwaite is one of a dozen firms in the UK most frequently advising on venture capital matters. It has provided advice on the establishment of a variety of limited partnerships and other investment vehicles both in the UK and throughout Europe, and has also advised on numerous management buy-outs and buy-ins, development capital investments and exits. The following case study is illustrative of the complexity of some of the venture capital transactions with which Travers Smith Braithwaite has been involved.

£61 million management buy-out and public takeover of Lee Cooper

Vivat is the parent company of the Lee Cooper group of companies whose principal activity is the manufacture and distribution of Lee Cooper brand jeans and leisurewear. Originally founded in 1890 to manufacture army uniforms, Lee Cooper developed strongly after the Second World War and was floated on the London Stock Exchange in the late 1950s. After suffering financial difficulties in the 1980s a new management team was introduced to help the group refocus on its core clothing manufacturing business and return to profitability. The management team, along with two principal shareholders (which between them held nearly 60 per cent of the shares in roughly equal stakes), agreed on a financing deal with the equity investors (a syndicate comprising NatWest Ventures Ltd and Phoenix Fund Managers Ltd) to enable a public takeover offer of Vivat to be mounted by Chiefco Holdings Plc, the buy-out vehicle. The transaction had to be structured to meet the competing interests of the Chiefco shareholders and comply with the relevant provisions of the City Code on Takeovers and Mergers. In particular:

- One of the major shareholders in Vivat wished to retain its investment in Vivat by exchanging its Vivat shares for Chiefco shares.
- The other Vivat major shareholder wished to realize its investment in cash.
- The possibility of the proposals requiring one of the parties to make a 'Rule 9' mandatory offer under the Takeover Code had to be avoided.
- Another Vivat shareholder who also held a minority stake in Vivat's Tunisian manufacturing subsidiary wished to invest in Chiefco and realize his minority Tunisian shareholding for cash.

Over 12 months of negotiations Travers Smith Braithwaite advised NatWest Markets on the application of the Takeover to a number of proposed bid structures. We assisted NatWest Markets in obtaining formal guidance from the Takeover Panel on such

matters as the composition of the 'concert party' which would be making the takeover offer and the ability of Chiefco to obtain an irrevocable undertaking from the major Vivat shareholder which wished to sell its shares. In all this it was necessary to avoid the possibility of the proposals triggering a requirement on one of the parties to make a mandatory 'Rule 9' offer. The unconditional bid structure eventually adopted met all the above criteria and also ensured that Chiefco would receive firm acceptances of over 50 per cent of Vivat's issued share capital immediately after making the offer. These benefits had to be balanced with the risks associated with unconditional offers, which could have left Chiefco with a large majority stake in Vivat without the ability to acquire the shares of non-accepting shareholders as part of the bid. This risk also had to be reflected in the equity funding documents, such as allowing a variable level of funding of Chiefco.

The other main area of Travers Smith Braithwaite's involvement was advising the investors on Chiefco's proposed equity structure and the ability of the investors to control the actions of Chiefco and the management team. Not only did Chiefco's structure have to ensure that Chiefco would always have sufficient funds to mount the takeover bid, but also it had to reflect the relationship between the three shareholder groups, being the investors, a major Vivat shareholder and the owner of the Tunisian subsidiary interest. Chiefco's articles of association were drafted to provide each shareholder group with distinct share rights, particularly focusing on complex share transfer arrangements which gave some shareholders the right to force through a trade sale of Chiefco and others the right to match any third-party offers for Chiefco.

Other matters governing the relationship between the shareholders were contained in a shareholders' agreement. Since Chiefco was in some ways more akin to a joint venture company, this agreement focused heavily on the relationship between shareholders with further special share transfer provisions, provisions for nominated directors and shareholder consents, and the shareholders' intentions on an eventual realization of their investment through a trade sale or a flotation of Chiefco. As part of the funding was to be provided by way of shareholder loans, we also had to prepare appropriate loan note instruments to reflect the different terms of each shareholder's loan. For example, the repayment terms were, in the case of the investors, to have a variable return based on the internal rate of return achieved by them on a sale or flotation of Chiefco, whereas the returns to other shareholders were linked to prevailing interest rates. The loan notes, in conjunction with banking facilities, had to provide Chiefco with the ability to have a variable level of funding dependent on the level of acceptances received under the offer. This was achieved by agreeing a drawdown schedule which gave Chiefco the right to draw down additional loans as certain defined levels of acceptances were reached. The more usual management controls associated with venture capital transactions were removed to a separate agreement between the management team and the equity investors. Travers Smith Braithwaite advised the investors on an appropriate level of management controls and negotiated them with the management team. This agreement also provided the management team with the investors' commitment to incentivize the management through equity participation in Chiefco. Given the uncertain outcome of the bid, only the basic terms of a scheme were agreed which would provide the management team with varying levels of equity in Chiefco dependent on

Chiefco's value on a flotation or trade sale. This was an alternative to the more usual ratchet arrangements seen in many venture capital transactions. Should the bid have been unsuccessful, an alternative form of management participation in Chiefco could have been negotiated to reflect the different nature of Chiefco's interest in Vivat. Following the acquisition of all the Vivat shares Travers Smith Braithwaite helped structure the management incentive scheme by devising a special new class of share providing a ratchet for the management team. Another complication of this scheme was that any shares obtained by the management were only to dilute certain classes of the equity. This was achieved by giving certain classes of share in Chiefco variable conversion rights to ensure each shareholder group had the correct equity percentage on a flotation or trade sale.

Case Study IV
McBride plc

In late 1992 Ashurst Morris Crisp was asked to act for a consortium of investors supporting a management buy-in bid for the Consumer Products Division of BP

Because you may see things differently tomorrow

Clue:- It's as easy as A.M.C.

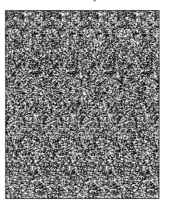

Your lawyers should see the trends and have a commercial understanding of your needs - our clients tell us we do

For further details about the firm contact Karen Hayes on 0171- 638 1111

 ASHURST
MORRIS
CRISP

Nutrition. The MBI team was led by Mike Handley, who had been a Divisional Managing Director of RHM plc. The business being sold was then, and remains, the largest manufacturer of private label household and personal care products in Europe. Its principal customers comprise many of the leading European grocery retailers which sell its products under their own labels or as minor brands, including Asda, Safeway, J Sainsbury and Tesco in the UK, Intermarché, LeClerc and Promodes in France and Esselunga in Italy. Typical products include textile washing powders and liquids, dishwashing products, fabric conditioners, other cleaning products, shampoos, hair sprays, foam baths, deodorants, toothpastes and mouthwashes.

The consortium of financiers[1] backing the buy-in was led by Legal & General Ventures which arranged funding of some £270 million and negotiated the terms of the deal, which was the largest transaction of its type in Europe in 1993. Prior to the final offer Mike Handley was joined by Lord Sheppard of Didgemere, who became non-executive Chairman, and later Terry Monks was recruited as Group Finance Director from the Building Products Division of Caradon plc.

Despite the subdued economic climate at the time, the auction process attracted seven initial bids, resulting in a second round shortlist of four financial syndicates who were requested to submit binding underwritten bids with the minimum of conditions. The vendor set a deadline for the shortlisted bidders to carry out full due diligence on all material issues. Also major points in the draft Acquisition Agreement circulated by the vendor had to be identified and each bidder had to confirm that they had committed funds. This meant that each of the banks and equity investors in the consortium had to obtain internal credit committee or investment committee approvals subject

---

[1] The equity was underwritten by funds managed by Legal & General, Lehman Brothers, Phoenix Fund Managers, BZW Private Equity and by The Ontario Teachers Pension Plan Board. The Mezzanine Debt was underwritten by Mithras Investment Trust and Intermediate Capital Group and the senior debt was led by the Bank of Scotland and underwritten by them and Morgan Grenfell, Barclays Bank and Bank of Tokyo.

only to the final documentation. From the lawyers' perspective this involved not only carrying out preliminary legal due diligence, but also helping to ensure that the outline terms provided by each financier were consistent and there were no conflicting requirements.

The MBI team won the second round and was given an exclusive period of three weeks to complete the transaction. It was made clear that if they failed to complete during that time the second party on the shortlist would be offered the business. Given the intense interest the auction process had generated, this was a credible concern. During those three weeks the corporate structure had to be finalized to take full advantage of the different tax regimes in each country in which the business operated. Legal teams had to be organized in London and each of the relevant jurisdictions in order to manage the process as smoothly as possible. During this period, Loan Agreements had to be drafted and negotiated with both senior and junior lenders, including their security packages across each jurisdiction. The equity documentation had to be prepared and negotiated in a form that was going to be acceptable not only to the original consortium, but also future syndicates. Finally, the detailed terms of the Acquisition Agreement had to be negotiated with the vendor and full legal due diligence completed and reported on to the financiers. In addition, the Group's major customers had to be approached to ensure they were comfortable with the proposals, particularly as the business did not benefit from long-term customer agreements.

The documentation was eventually finalized late at night on 26 May 1993 and was signed by the acquisition vehicle, Templeco Sixteen. The deal was completed on 28 May 1993, and Templeco Sixteen subsequently changed its name to McBride.

Following the transaction Ashurst Morris Crisp was formally appointed by the management team as legal advisers to McBride. During the immediate post-completion period some of the senior debt was refinanced through the new French holding company with a French franc loan. Thereafter discussions continued with the vendor to settle completion accounts and the final price to be paid for the business. In addition, an employee share scheme was put in place to benefit some 150 managers in the business

throughout each country in which the Group operated.

After an initial period of consolidation McBride acquired, using existing resources, Longthorne Laboratories, a small privately owned, private label, personal care business near Leeds. In December 1994 the Group sold its DIY industrial and institutional and contract manufacturing business and its industrial and institutional business in Italy. In April 1995 its textile washing powder activities were significantly expanded by acquiring the private label textile washing powder businesses of Albright & Wilson in the UK and Spain. Shortly afterwards, the Group agreed to sell its interests in its Caribbean joint venture to the joint venture partner and acquired Arco Iris, a small Spanish private label household liquid products manufacturer based near Barcelona. All these transactions required legal input, not least because of the constraints of the original buy-in documentation.

By the end of 1994 plans were being made for a flotation. The Group appointed SBC Warburg to lead a UK and international offer[2]. In order to maximize the value of the Company at the time of the flotation it was decided that the offer should be by way of a book-building exercise rather than a traditional UK underwritten offer. While this is common in the USA, book-building is still a relatively new process in the UK and had never previously been used for an institutionally backed company like McBride. The offer was also made in a number of different jurisdictions, including a Rule 144(A) offer under the US Securities Act. The six months leading up to flotation were spent with the Group's new financial advisers and updating and confirming the due diligence exercises which had been carried out at the time of the buy-in. In addition, four new employee share schemes were established to enable the management and employees throughout the Group to participate in its future. The senior and mezzanine loans taken out at the time of the buy-in became due for repayment on flotation, so new loan agreements had to be negotiated and entered into to take effect from flotation.

McBride's prospectus was published on 21 June 1995 and at the close of business on the first day of public dealings McBride was capitalized at approxi-

---

[2] SBC Warburg, Kleinwort Benson Securities and Lehman Brothers acted as Managers and Underwriters.

mately £350 million. This represented a successful transition of McBride's businesses from being a division of BP through independence as a private company and into the public arena.

Case Study V
Red Star

Despite being one of the UK's leading parcel carriers, indeed it is the only carrier to operate directly on the railway network as well as road, Red Star has made considerable losses in the past few years while the business has seen turnover fall from £71 million in 1991 to below £40 million in 1994. In June 1994, British Railways Board (BRB), instructed its Vendor Unit to commence a sale process for the Red Star business. One of the bidders, a management buy-out team led by John Holmes, who came in as Sales and Marketing Manager following a 13-year career in the parcels sector with DHL and TNT, came to KPMG in late June 1994 for assistance with its bid.

KPMG sees a large number of MBO teams from a variety of business areas, so what was special about this team? Initially the determination and zeal of the team leader was a persuasive influence. However, when this was backed up by a strong business plan and some well thought through strategies to return the business to profitability, KPMG had no hesitation in supporting the MBO.

As with all potential MBOs, KPMG worked closely with the team to develop a well-focused business plan supported by detailed financial projections. In this case the MBO did not have a finance director and consequently more financial input was required from KPMG throughout the buy-out process.

The business plan indicated that the MBO would require funding of around £5 million. KPMG initially took soundings from its high-level contacts within the venture capital industry. The decline in the Red Star business and the links with BR did give rise to scepticism from some quarters. However, as the MBO team approached the deadline for their final bid in November 1994, several indicative offers were being considered, with BZW Private Equity Limited (BZW – formerly Barclay Development Capital Limited) being able to provide the most attractive deal for the management, while also being the most enthusiastic about the opportunity.

In terms of raising debt facilities, KPMG identified invoice discounting as providing the most logical form of working capital funding for this type of business, particularly as there would be an increasing cash requirement as the business grew. With strong asset backing in the form of trade debtors, a number of leading invoice discounters showed interest in the deal. TSB Commercial Finance (TSB) were able to move quickest and, after their initial investigation of the business, provided a formal offer well before the bid deadline set by BRB's Vendor Unit. Both BZW and TSB worked closely with KPMG and the management team in submitting a comprehensive bid to BRB and with three leading names backing the deal there was no doubt that the bid was being taken seriously.

Having spent six months complying with the intricacies of the BR privatization process, KPMG, the MBO team and its backers now waited to find out whether they had been chosen as the preferred bidder. The team were confident that their bid represented the best strategy for rebuilding the Red Star business; the big question was whether the price was high enough to beat the other bidders.

The MBO business plan sets out a strategy aimed at revitalizing the Red Star business by promoting itself as a specialist in the premium parcels market, rather than attempting to be 'all things to all people'. As John Holmes, the leader of the management team, explains, 'Red Star has a number of unique selling points which make it the natural choice and a valued carrier for a wide range of businesses who have urgent or emergency delivery needs. In addition, by going down the franchising route we would aim to expand Red Star's high margin and high revenue products whilst at the same time eliminating currently unavoidable costs.'

The new management team would also take on an external franchise development manager to work closely with FMM, a specialist franchise consultancy. Red Star would then seek to franchise the majority of the parcel points while retaining a core network. The key advantage of this route is that the franchisee becomes responsible for increasing efficiency, productivity and customer service at local level. The parcels delivery industry has been uniquely successful in franchising, with a number of very successful operations within the sector.

The news that the management team had not been chosen as preferred bidder, predominantly based on price, was received in December 1994. This was clearly very bad news for all the parties associated with the MBO and it was difficult to remain optimistic about receiving a second chance, even though it was felt strongly that the final decision was wrong. However, KPMG and the management team continued to keep communications open with the BR Board and its Vendor Unit.

One angle that KPMG had to continue discussions with BRB, was the underwriting of professional fees by the vendor. As Mike Stevens explains, 'On the majority of management buyouts that we are involved with, we insist on an element of the adviser's fees being underwritten by the vendor. This ensures a certain level of commitment is received from a vendor, although clearly this is never a lock-tight guarantee.' Thus, despite coming second in the initial bid process, KPMG, through its fee negotiations with the Vendor Unit, remained in contact with BRB and kept the backers in place. When, in April 1995, BRB felt dissatisfied with progress being made they again approached the management team with a view to completing a transaction as soon as possible.

Negotiations with BR's Vendor Unit were both complex and lengthy, requiring analysis of all the key constituents of the Red Star business in order to finalize a realistic price for the business. In addition to these negotiations KPMG continued to revise the business plan and financial projections to reflect the changing structure of the transaction. This was essential both for the backers and the vendor in order to demonstrate the integrity of the projected cash flows of the business.

It was at this stage of the deal that the legal due diligence commenced. This immediately looked like a one-sided contest as BR's legal representation outnumbered the MBO's by six firms to two. However, over 100 leases and 20 commercial contracts were removed within the agreed timetable and on 2 July, after an all-night vigil checking the format of all the documentation, the conditional sale and purchase contract was signed. Technology also played a part in the process, with both sides using the Internet to facilitate the movement of large volumes of information.

Finally, on 5 September 1995, more than 14 months after KPMG's initial involvement and despite some negative press from the Labour Party's anti-privatization lobby, the Secretary of State gave his approval to the transaction and the sale contract was signed. With its shackles unleashed, a strong business plan and solid financial backing, the MBO team, comprising four senior managers from Red Star and two external appointments including the Finance Director, Steve Dennison, who has joined from

KPMG, intends to awaken what it sees as the 'sleeping giant' which is Red Star and build on its obvious strengths.

Case Study VI
Stoves plc

In late 1988, Sean O'Connor (Chairman) and John Crathorne (Chief Executive) came into Candover with a brief presentation which was more of a proposal than a business plan. They had a vision that it would be possible to build up a UK-owned, UK-based quality British brand in the cooker market. This vision was based on the assumption that they not only understood the consumer, but the product and the market better than anybody else.

Candover was attracted to the idea but said it would prefer them to buy a business rather than set up on a greenfield basis. Some weeks later they came back with a proposal to buy the loss-making Valor Cooker business which at the time had turnover of £17 million and was making losses of around £4 million pa.

Candover thought this proposal had significant potential and put resources into the project to work with the management team to develop the proposal into a business-like form. This was all before there was a company in existence, and the ensuing talks with Yale & Valor which prepared the ground for acquiring the business under terms that would make economic sense in the end took several months.

As lead investor, Candover was responsible for encouraging other investors to put money into the project to not only acquire the business, but provide monies to invest in the development of the company. The other investors were CINVen, Flemings Enterprise Trust and Scottish Eastern Investment Trust.

The buy-in which took place in May 1989 immediately saved 500 jobs and in fact over the past six years Stoves has increased its work force by a further 250. The company has experienced growth to a large extent at the expense of European competitors. John Crathorne and his senior management team, all but one of whom were recruited from outside the company, set about changing the culture of the business: this included establishing cellular forms of working and designing and launching new products which included stand-alone and built-in, both electric and gas. It was also necessary to create relationships with new customers as well as reinforcing the existing main relationship with British Gas, which at the start accounted for over 85 per cent of

Stoves' domestic cooker business and is now down to around 20 per cent.

Six years on, Stoves is a very different business. Investment of £10 million has created what the company believes to be Europe's most flexible cooker-making facility. Over 700 new models have been developed, reaching all sectors of the market. The company which began with virtually one product group, gas free-standing, now manufactures not just gas but also electric, free-standing and built-in products. Five years ago it struggled to launch two or three new models a year: now, when required, it can launch products at the rate of greater or equal to one new model a day. Another progression over the years is stock turn. Six years ago, stock turn was about five times with a very limited product range, and now, at 15 times, Stoves ranks certainly among one of the best in Europe.

In 1995 Stoves floated on the Stock Exchange, one indication of the development the company has made since 1989. The Department of Trade and Industry recently published a booklet on British industry listing 120 model companies, mostly well-known blue chip companies. Stoves ranked among the 20 or 30 smaller companies mentioned.

Case Study VII
Wessex Traincare Limited: a classic buy-out

John Major's government has embarked on the last major privatization – that of British Rail. British Rail is a vast sprawling empire, and the privatization is a huge and complex process. The first major part to be privatized was its passenger and freight train heavy maintenance division. This case study explains briefly the management and employee buyout of the largest of the four heavy maintenance sites, that at Eastleigh, near Southampton.

The Eastleigh site dates back some 80 years, and currently employs over 1000 people. It is very much a traditional heavy engineering site, and this in itself raised a number of issues for the management, their advisers and financiers. Among the first points to be considered were the potential environmental issues which may affect sites of this nature. RPS Clouston were instructed as environment consultants. They produced an excellent report dealing with both health and safety and environmental issues.

Garrett & Co became involved in the buy-out in June 1994, having been introduced to management by the corporate finance advisers, Arthur Andersen.

Given the complexity of privatization, lawyers were introduced to the deal perhaps slightly earlier than is common. However, given that there was a two-stage bidding process, legal input was vital from an early stage. Management are normally newcomers to the buy-out process to an extent, but this was particularly true for a management team who had been brought up in the British Rail culture. In this particular case, the managing director of the MBO team started working for the Eastleigh site in the same year in which the lead partner at Garrett & Co was born! Therefore, the world of due diligence, investment agreements, articles of association and so on were particularly novel to this management team.

Having been introduced to management, the first task, in this particular case, was due diligence and the framing of first round and second round offers. Due diligence was made more difficult than usual as to some extent the blueprint for the maintenance industry after privatization was still being finalized during the due diligence process.

As part of every due diligence process, lawyers look at the suite of contracts available to the target company. Garrett & Co therefore looked at supply agreements and, of course, customer agreements. Again, as part of the privatization, these (previously British Rail 'internal matters') were then being documented and naturally, this posed a number of interesting questions, particularly as some of the suppliers and customers have not been purchased. One needed one eye to the future as well as one eye to the past!

Finance was provided by 3i's Southampton office, and debt finance (in the shape of term loans and performance bonds) was provided by Samuel Montagu. Midland Bank provided an overdraft facility. In a long-running deal of this nature (the sale was eventually concluded in June 1995) it was particularly important that management and their advisers obtained the trust of the financiers, even though to some extent and at some occasions, they were on opposite sides of the table.

Finance was in principle secured at an early stage, as this was vital to give the management buyout bid credibility in the eyes of British Rail. Having got through the first two rounds of competitive tendering, and having been accepted as the primary bidder, matters moved on to completion in the usual way. At this stage, Garrett & Co had to conclude the financing documents with the financiers as well as conclude final negotiations with the

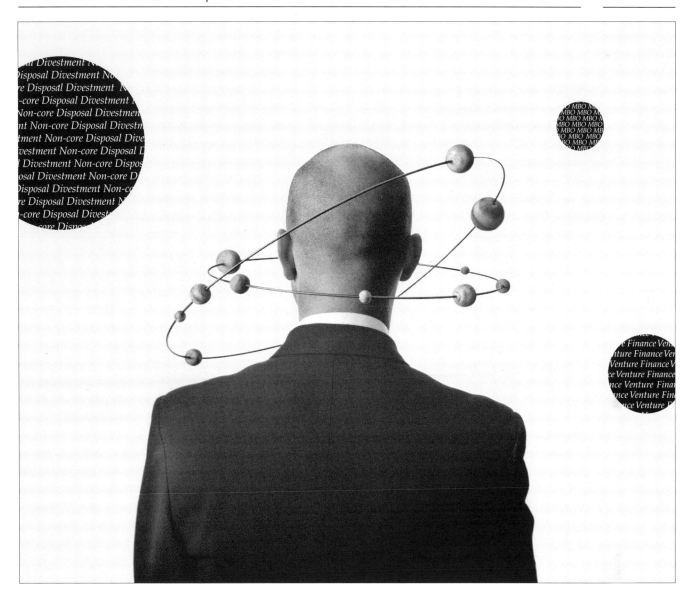

A head for Buy-Outs

Garrett & Co. is a different kind of law firm. With fully integrated offices in 5 major UK locations, we are a truly national firm offering the full range of corporate law services. Our partners have extensive experience in management buy-outs, acting for vendors, management teams or institutions. Our reputation is for getting the deal done.

If you would like more information please call the partner in the office nearest to you:

● Julia Chain (London) 0171 344 0344.

● Stephen Devlin (Manchester) 0161 228 0707.

● Gary Laitner (Birmingham) 0121 698 9000.

● Nick Painter (Leeds) 0113 244 1954.

● Adrian Phillips (Reading) 01734 490 000.

GARRETT & CO

Birmingham, Leeds, London, Manchester, Reading.

Garrett & Co. is associated with the Arthur Andersen international network of law firms and is regulated by The Law Society in the conduct of investment business.

British Rail Vendor Unit. Given that the Vendor Unit's desire was to dispose of all six sites at the same time, the Vendor Unit had a difficult task of shepherding six deals to completion, and in the end all six deals completed, with three purchasing consortia, within one week of each other.

Having completed the buy-out, the next stage is to broaden share ownership to the employees, and the process is currently under way leading to an offer of shares to all employees at Wessex which is hoped to be concluded by the end of 1995.

Eastleigh was in many ways a classic buy-out. Management was stretched by the demands on their times in running the business, negotiating with the vendors and negotiating with their financiers. Their professional advisers were under similar pressure in keeping all aspects of the deal moving forward at the same time and bringing them to a successful conclusion.

Case Study VIII
Inveresk: a buy-out in an uncertain climate

The Inveresk group of companies was founded in the early 1920s when William Harrison brought together a group of mills under the name 'The Inveresk Paper Company'. By the late 1940s the Inveresk group had 18 paper mills in the UK and a total of 32 companies. However, when European trade barriers came down in the mid-1960s many UK mills were affected, including Inveresk which closed or sold many of its operations.

In 1981 Georgia-Pacific Corporation (GP) of the USA acquired the Inveresk group. But, following its US$5 billion acquisition in 1990 of Great Northern Nekoosa Corporation, a pulp paper producer, GP decided to concentrate on its North American activities and to dispose of its 'non-strategic' assets, in order to reduce borrowings and raise cash.

Inveresk was a natural choice for disposal, being a small producer by comparison to GP's other operations and also located outside the USA. Another important factor was that Inveresk's management had expressed a wish to undertake a major investment programme over the following few years.

Stefan Kay, Inveresk's Managing Director, advised of GP's intention to sell Inveresk, obtained the support of his senior management to mount a management buyout bid, prepared a business plan and conducted a 'beauty parade' of six development capital institutions. Morgan Grenfell Development

Capital (MGDC) was appointed as deal leader in May 1990. MGDC was chosen because it had the necessary experience to lead bigger deals, could undertake the complex negotiations with the American vendor, and could successfully provide the funding package.

After arduous negotiations in New York and Scotland with GP and its advisers, MGDC agreed the basis of a deal on 26 June 1990 and obtained a six-week exclusivity period during which GP undertook not to pursue discussions with any other party. MGDC had six weeks to complete its due diligence, obtain the support of a bank and finalize the legal documentation. In the event, the deal took 16 weeks to complete from the agreement date.

The major reasons for the delay were the dramatic changes which took place during the five months of the buy-out discussions. In May 1990, at the start of the buy-out, economic growth was forecast to continue at 2.4 per cent, rising to 2.8 per cent in 1991. By September, most economists recognized that the UK was in recession and previous growth expectations were reduced significantly. The decline in growth had been brought about by the doubling of oil prices following the Iraqi invasion of Kuwait, the appreciation of sterling, high interest rates and entry into the Exchange Rate Mechanism.

A slowdown in the economy has an impact on most industries, but Inveresk was particularly affected. As well as being a capital-intensive industry, paper is a major user of power. Exchange rate fluctuations were very important to Inveresk as 51 per cent of its products were exported and its most important new material, pulp, was imported. During the period while the FT-SE 100 Share Index fell by 5.4 per cent, the paper and packaging sector index fell by 11.8 per cent, despite a premium in the market due to takeover activity in the industry. Senior debt had become much more difficult to obtain and banks applied stricter lending criteria, more conservative gearing, asset security, cash and interest cover ratios and shorter amortization periods.

The implications of the changes in the economy, the paper industry and the financial sector had to be assessed by MGDC and the management team throughout the buy-out period. There were, however, a number of factors that compensated for the adverse changes which occurred during the buy-out discussions. The Inveresk team's knowledge of the industry, their enthusiasm for the buy-out and how they worked together and reacted to adversity during the process, gave MGDC much comfort regard-

Morgan Grenfell Development Capital Limited
Leading Management Buy-Outs

Alexander Drew & Sons Ltd

£20 Million

Management Buy-Out

Morgan Grenfell Development Capital Limited

February 1990

Deutsche Morgan Grenfell

The British School of Motoring Limited

£42 Million

Management Buy-Out

Morgan Grenfell Development Capital Limited

April 1990

Deutsche Morgan Grenfell

Inveresk Limited

£40 Million

Management Buy-Out

Morgan Grenfell Development Capital Limited

October 1990

Deutsche Morgan Grenfell

The Taunton Cider Company Limited

£100 Million

Management Buy-Out

Morgan Grenfell Development Capital Limited

May 1991

Deutsche Morgan Grenfell

Bristow Helicopter Group Limited

£200 Million

Management Buy-Out

Morgan Grenfell Development Capital Limited

November 1991

Deutsche Morgan Grenfell

Maiden Outdoor Advertising Limited

£21 Million

Management Buy-Out

Morgan Grenfell Development Capital Limited

April 1993

Deutsche Morgan Grenfell

Calder Group Limited

£84.5 Million

Management Buy-Out

Morgan Grenfell Development Capital Limited

March 1994

Deutsche Morgan Grenfell

Beni Food Group Limited

£100 Million

Management Buy-Out

Morgan Grenfell Development Capital Limited

10 November 1994

Deutsche Morgan Grenfell

The Sweater Shop Group Limited

£150 Million

Management Buy-Out

Morgan Grenfell Development Capital Limited

27 April 1995

Deutsche Morgan Grenfell

Morgan Grenfell Development Capital Limited
23 Great Winchester Street, London EC2P 2AX
Tel: 0171 588 4545   Fax: 0171 614 5282
Contact: Susan Deacon

Morgan Grenfell Development Capital Limited
35 St Andrew Square, Edinburgh EH2 2AD
Tel: 0131 577 8600   Fax: 0131 557 8306

Deutsche Morgan Grenfell

ing their ability to manage Inveresk following the buy-out.

During the buy-out process management have to spend much of their time involved in negotiating with the vendor and institutions. Accordingly, especially where the management team is small and involved with the day-to-day operations, trading can suffer. Any downturn in current trading during negotiations can jeopardize the buyout, especially in a climate such as that which faced Inveresk. During this period the Inveresk team outperformed all their forecasts and impressed MGDC with the levels of cash generated through cash control and the active management of working capital.

There were times when the deal could have foundered, but on 12 October 1990 MGDC completed the £40 million management buy-out. With the high drama of the buy-out behind them the management team concentrated exclusively on running their independent business successfully. They were no longer constrained from investing in profitable projects by the strategy and cash flow considerations of their parent company. A flexible funding structure had been put in place which allowed them to invest in a number of strategic projects that would release bottlenecks and expand the company's product range. Freedom to manage cash with a better than expected profit performance in the first full year following the buy-out allowed the company to discharge all of its debt by the end of 1991.

In May 1993 Inveresk was successfully floated at a market capitalization of £79 million. In November 1995 the company made its first acquisition since joining the Stock Market, for a consideration of up to £32 million. It now has five speciality paper mills and a wastepaper recycling operation in the UK.

Case Study IX
Olswang, Solicitors

The second-round funding project Advanced Telecommunication Modules Limited (ATML) completed earlier this year had a number of interesting features, both legal and commercial, as are outlined in this case study.

Olswang's Corporate Group undertakes a volume of mainstream venture capital and other equity funding transactions, combined when necessary with our specialist expertise in the 'digital convergence' of the media and communications arena and it was thus with considerable interest that we

came into this project at the recommendation of the Cambridge office of 3i Group plc.

The Cambridge Science and Technology Parks have established a deserved reputation as home to some of the UK's leading-edge technology and development companies and 3i's commitment to this area, not least through its office on one of the Parks, has given it considerable insight into, and many working relationships within, this environment.

The background

ATML was set up in early 1993, originally as a form of joint venture between a skilled team of its founder-management and entrepreneurs, and the Olivetti Group.

At the end of 1993 this crystallized into a corporate relationship, by Olivetti (through its venture capital-style arm) and the other parties investing equity in ATML and by Olivetti's research arm granting ATML a licence of its hardware and software rights for connecting computers and telephony or telecommunications systems using the Asynchronous Transfer Mode (ATM) technology.

In the early 1990s, ATM technology was fast becoming the prevailing choice for high-speed communication in telephony and for computer local area networks – this perception has grown and it can justifiably be regarded as the 'Rolls Royce' of communication system modes.

It takes a digitized stream of data, inserts another stream of digital data out of synchronization with the first, and then 'slices' each stream into segments, allowing them to be transmitted far more quickly than was previously possible. At the point of delivery, the segments are rejoined automatically and deciphered in correct sequence.

This mode of transmission brings considerable benefits – it is extremely fast, highly secure and much more efficient, releasing considerable costs savings for those transmitting high volumes of digital traffic.

However, in 1993–4 it was still relatively new, particularly in its applications in the developing range of ATML products and this posed something of an obstacle. Nonetheless, the company developed within 3i an appreciation of its business and of the market for the technology, and 3i agreed to provide debt funding for further working capital and the acquisition of intellectual property rights, against further equity investment by Olivetti and other private investors. This belies how difficult it had

CLIVE JOHN. DIRECTOR LDC.
ON THE BOARD OF A PRINTING COMPANY AND AN
AEROSPACE COMPONENTS SUPPLIER.

PATRICK SELLERS. DIRECTOR LDC.
ON THE BOARD OF AN EXHIBITION EQUIPMENT COMPANY
AND A TEXTILE MANUFACTURER.

DARRYL EALES. DIRECTOR LDC.
ON THE BOARD OF A FOUNDRY AND ENGINEERING SERVICES
GROUP AND A CHAIN OF NURSING HOMES.

WHAT COULD A VENTURE CAPITAL COMPANY POSSIBLY KNOW ABOUT RUNNING A BUSINESS?

ASK ANY ONE OF THESE BOARD DIRECTORS.

What do these six board directors have in common? They're all investment officers at Lloyds Development Capital. Which means they have practical experience in a variety of markets, from engineering to textile manufacture. You see, at Lloyds Development Capital, we don't just give you money. We go into business with you. If you have a business idea with growth potential, be it for a buy-out, a buy-in, or simply a programme of expansion, we'll provide you with a committed business partnership. One of our investment officers will sit on your board as a non-executive director, so you can benefit from his financial skills. But he'll be far more than a money man.

With energy and enthusiasm that's rare in the financial world, he'll guide you and advise you through every major business move. Our six investment officers here, have spent a total of 65 years in venture capital, sitting on 58 boards. If you'd like to take advantage of this experience, and talk to fellow businessmen with the same resolve to succeed that you have, call Patrick Sellers, in our London office, on 0171 600 3226, Darryl Eales, in Birmingham, on 0121 200 1787, or Stuart Rhodes, in Leeds, on 01132 441 001. You'll be surprised how quickly we respond. One thing we do know is that opportunities don't hang around. So neither do we.

LLOYDS DEVELOPMENT CAPITAL

STUART RHODES. DIRECTOR LDC.
ON THE BOARD OF A PRECISION ENGINEERING COMPANY
AND A TEXTILE MANUFACTURER.

KEITH CARPENTER. DIRECTOR LDC.
ON THE BOARD OF AN INSULATION MANUFACTURER AND
A LADIES CLOTHING COMPANY.

MICHAEL JOSEPH. MANAGING DIRECTOR LDC.
SERVED ON THE BOARD OF A COMPUTER SOFTWARE
AND SERVICES COMPANY AND A BUILDERS MERCHANT.

proved to secure risk capital, whether debt or equity, through typical funding routes in the UK for a business still in relative infancy.

The project

From the end of 1994, ATML had been trying to source more substantial second-round equity funding – particularly needed to fund its business expansion and to penetrate this specialized market sector. The 'early stage' nature of the business and attendant absence of identifiable profitability, combined with the 'new technology–high risk' perception, had continued to dog these efforts to raise typical UK venture capital.

Both to support these efforts and what the shareholders believe to be an appropriate valuation of the business, the company retained ARC Associates, who as a first in Europe, offer an independent specialized investment banking and corporate advisory service focused on the information technology, telecoms and multi-media sectors. They brought to the project deal-structuring and a knowledge of both public and private capital market appetite for this sector.

With ARC leading, the decision was taken to focus on funding sources emanating from the main market place for ATML's business – the West Coast of the US. This proved critical as it gave access to potential venture capital investors already sophisticated in the technology and knowledgeable of the market and its potential.

It also provided access to a financial environment more advanced in its evaluation and valuation, of new technology businesses for future equity fundraisings (as well as more enhanced 'exit' possibilities) through public offerings and/or a NASDAQ or similar listing in the US. This culminated in a draft offer letter in April 1995 for the investment of up to US$11.1 million of new money, from a consortium of predominantly US venture capitalists, but notably including 3i.

Olswang's role was to mesh the differing US and UK venture capital practices and to make the US format of the new equity rights – including 'registration rights' (on a pre-emptive 'cut-back' and 'piggy-back' basis) to demand public offerings of the ATML shares in the US securities markets and 'waited average' anti-dilution protections, unlike their typical UK counterparts – fit with UK company law and, to accommodate that, simultaneously to recast the existing contractual structure between the ATML shareholders, including the IPR licence with Olivetti. With logistics spanning five time zones, completion was achieved in a challenging four weeks.

If this study shows a tendency for European-originated technology to find more receptive and perceptive evaluation and investment in the US, European venture capitalists have to combat this to keep the 'winners'.

PART

12

Location and Development

Location Strategies in the Face of New European Diversity

Charles Thoma, Consultant and **Vicky Pryce,** Partner, KPMG

It doesn't matter where your company is based and where your markets are, the chances are that you have missed business and cost-cutting opportunities, simply because the locations in which your various operations are carried out do not fully capitalize on regional or national competitive advantages. It does not come as a surprise to many that companies write their software in India, manufacture clothing in Hungary, Portugal or Morocco, have their head-quarters in Paris, Brussels or London and locate their service centres in cities like Dublin, Strasbourg or Berlin. But how do you know that your operations are located in the place in which they can be most effectively carried out? Could they better be per-formed elsewhere? And, if so, how do you select which of your functions to relocate and where do you relocate them?

Few would deny that the 1990s have been the witnesses of tremendous change, of which the fall of the Berlin wall, greater European integration, NAFTA, the unprecedented rise of the yen and the South East Asian 'tiger' economies are but a few examples. All of these have had a significant impact on firms' operations and, consequently, on the way in which they design and implement their strategies. How should non-EU companies establish themselves within the confines of the Union? How should European companies restructure their operations in order not to duplicate some of their efforts and what form should this restructuring take? Can customer

service functions be centralized and where should they be centralized? What message can companies send to their suppliers or customers regarding their commitment to a specific market?

All these questions need to flow from the firm's corporate strategy. A vital stage in this process is the detailed analysis of the business's value chain of activities in order to identify the degree of cen-tralization and concentration that can be achieved, the linkages required between these activities and the value and cost drivers associated with them. This then allows management to decide on the location criteria relevant to each set of activities.

Yet, even at this stage, the location decision remains as complex as the range of choices which face the firm. For, although as recently as the late 1980s companies opted for centralization or a 'multi-local' presence, now internal structures have reached a new level of complexity. Many would agree that a company's manufacturing operations do not need to be located with its headquarters. But what about the back-office function, the financial processing, the R&D efforts, the service departments or the dis-tribution centres? Where are their optimal locations? Can some of them be grouped together or should they all be separate? Do some cities or regions have characteristics that satisfy the needs of several or all of these activities?

Given that centralization of operations in pan-European companies is becoming more virtual than

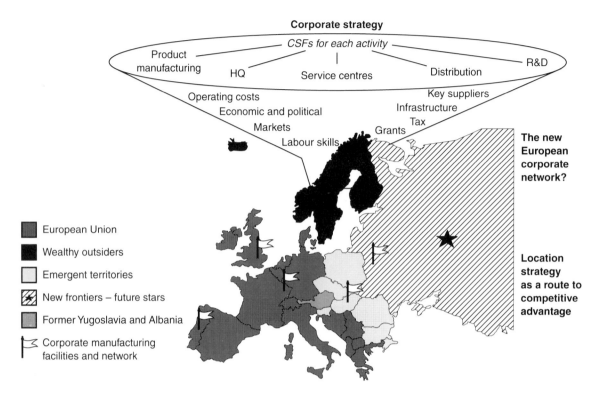

Figure 55.1 Europe: new diversity – new threats and opportunities

actual – with manufacturing locations established in Poland, back office functions in Ireland and headquarters in France, for example – companies are reexamining where each of their operations can be optimized and thus need to assess various locations on their own merits (see Figure 55.1).

The topicality of EU enlargement has only begun to underscore the need for companies to make full use of an integrated European economy. Whereas in the USA companies have long been used to selecting the best site for their various national operations, companies active in Europe are only just beginning to realize that the continent is no longer made up of nations, but of regions which have developed economic links and dependencies over decades, even centuries. The Benelux countries established full economic union as early as 1948. Alsace and the Ruhr valley have been the pole of economic convergence of France and Germany for well over a century. The crescent stretching from Milan to Valencia is fast developing into a growth zone with a strong high technology content.

The significance of these differentials has not been lost on regional economic development agencies, the most dynamic of which actively target specific sectors of the economy as potential investors.

The Côte d'Azur Development Agency, for example, actively seeks to attract health R&D operations, telecommunications companies and the financial functions of corporates. Grants and other financial incentives in most regions are subject to the company meeting the criteria which development agencies feel would bring the most benefit to their region. In effect, regions within Europe design and implement their own economic policy, in terms which are often much clearer than those of national governments.

So how do you choose the best location for your company's operations? As we mentioned above, the location decision process should be driven by the firm's strategy and flow from the goals which it seeks to achieve. An appropriate decision methodology needs to incorporate a variety of factors. The company or the function to be relocated must analyse in detail the variations in its cost profile which a change of location would bring about. For many companies, this would in all likelihood include analysis of differentials in labour, property and telecommunications costs. Other costs, such as transport, water, electricity, staff travel, etc, also can come into play depending on the nature of the operations to be relocated. Added to the operating cost profile of the selected operations, variations in tax treatment and financial incentives give a bottom-line indication of cost variations once the business fundamentals have been examined independently.

In addition to these cost differentials, companies then need to analyse the qualitative, non-financial factors which they consider to be vital to the success of their operations. As can be expected, these vary widely by region – ignoring these factors can mean a seemingly attractive business opportunity becomes a corporate nightmare. These factors typically include: proximity to suppliers or customers, working practices, productivity, unionization levels, regulatory constraints, quality of telecommunications or road infrastructure, etc. Once these qualitative factors and the cost differentials have been assessed, the decision to locate operations can be made objectively, in full knowledge that no stone has been left unturned.

Within Europe of the 1990s and the political events which are transforming it, a key question for many corporates must be the extent to which opportunities in CEFTA, and other former COMECON countries, should now be realized. Indicators of economic well-being have improved dramatically in CEFTA countries (see Table 55.1).

Concomitantly, the political risk of such countries is being regarded, for the most part, more

	1993	1994	1995	1996
Poland	3.8	5.0	5.8	5.3
Hungary	–0.9	2.0	1.4	2.4
Czech Republic	–0.9	2.6	4.1	4.6
Slovakia	–4.1	4.8	4.6	3.9

Source: Consensus Economics (October 1995)

Table 55.1

favourably. Many companies have made investments, some tentatively, in order to establish and develop their presence in the emerging markets of Central and Eastern Europe. Greater stability and trade agreements with the European Union, such as the Europe Agreements, now make significant manufacturing bases in countries such as Hungary, Poland, the Czech Republic and Slovakia a more tantalizing prospect. Average labour costs in these countries offer distinct advantages even compared to Portugal (see Figure 55.2), and access to the wealthy markets of Germany, Scandinavia and the Benelux countries is improving constantly. If European companies do not realize these opportunities, there is a danger that the benefits may be grasped by others.

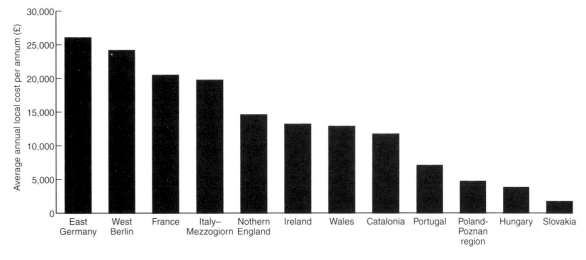

Source: Regional Development and Economic Offices

Figure 55.2 Average annual total cost of an assembly worker, including statutory and non-statutory wage and non-wage costs

56 The European HQ

John Siraut, Consultant, Ernst & Young's European Location Advisory Service (ELAS)

There are three main types of non-parent head-quarters: geographic, function and product. A large number of US companies have over the years established geographic headquarters to look after their operations in Europe. These often have a great deal of autonomy in deciding on investment and marketing matters across Europe. An increasing number of Japanese companies are also beginning to establish headquarters in Europe to oversee the expanding nature of their operations in Europe; Nissan has its in the Netherlands and Hitachi in the UK. By its very nature a European HQ is based in Europe. Well, in most cases; there are still some companies that have their European HQs in the USA.

European companies tend not to have a separate European HQ outside their home country although there are some exceptions, with British Petroleum and Pilkingtons both having European HQs in Brussels.

Other companies have followed a different line and have established product or function HQs. That is, an HQ will look after a particular product range or function such as marketing across the globe. In these cases Europe is in competition with other regions around the world to host the HQ. For example, AT&T's corded phone business has its headquarters in France while Hewlett Packard's marketing HQ for personal computers and peripherals is based in Singapore.

When it comes to choosing a European HQ, companies tend to have three options:

- co-locate the HQ with other functions such as manufacturing or R&D
- locate in a neutral location away from its main manufacturing base
- ignore both of the above and locate in the best location for an HQ.

The first option tends to be followed by smaller Japanese and US companies which may only have one manufacturing plant or service facility in Europe. In these circumstances it makes sense to co-locate operations and for this reason some of these, often small, HQs tend to be located in cities or areas which are not usually considered as European centres. For example, Nippon Silica Glass Europe is to establish its European HQ alongside its new manufacturing plant in County Durham. Some larger companies have also located their European HQs in the same country as their main manufacturing plant. Again in 1995, Samsung relocated its European HQ from Frankfurt to London; at the same time it announced a major new manufacturing plant in the UK.

As companies expand the number of their facilities in Europe, there is often intense internal competition between plants to attract new investment. If an HQ is located in a country with a major manufacturing operation, there is often a tendency for it to be staffed by local people who have a preference for supporting the local manufacturing plant. To overcome this problem and to ensure all national operations buy-in, there is a tendency to place a European HQ in a neutral location where there is a minimal manufacturing operation or which is seen as being a European rather than a national location. This is often to the advantage of countries such as Belgium (which promotes itself not as a country but as a European entity) and the Netherlands.

For the large company with operations throughout Europe, the key issue tends to be what is the best location for the HQ. In reality there are few cities that can seriously play the European HQ game. They are London, Paris, Brussels, Amsterdam/Rotterdam/The Hague, Zurich and Geneva. Germany without an obvious central city offers a more diverse choice with European HQs spread out between Munich, Hamburg, Dusseldorf and Frankfurt. While a number of German companies have moved their HQs to Berlin, the international community seems to be slower in following suit, although Sony is to relocate its European HQ to the city in 1999. Cities such as Vienna, Copenhagen, Madrid and Milan seem more successful in attracting sub-regional operations rather than full-blown HQs. In terms of numbers, Brussels, London and the three key Dutch cities between them account for around three-quarters of US European HQs. The remaining quarter is distributed, in descending order, between Switzerland, France and Germany.

An increasing phenomenon is that of companies reconsidering the location of their European HQs. The reasons they established an HQ in its original location are no longer valid. For example, many US companies set up their European HQs in Switzerland. Here was a country that was seen as a neutral European location with a well-established international image. However, over time and with the increasing importance of the European Union, Switzerland has been seen more as a peripheral location which is no longer at the heart of Europe in the way Belgium and the Netherlands have now become.

For those companies which have a genuine choice of location, the key factors that are taken into account include:

- proximity to key contacts, that is, ease of access to parent HQ, subsidiaries and business contacts whether customers, suppliers or partners;
- ability to attract and retain international high-flyers; most top jobs are recruited from a European if not a global workforce. So the HQ location has to be one to which people are prepared to move themselves and their families and feel comfortable there;
- ability to recruit highly professional local staff, especially bi- or even trilingual staff. For certain activities such as financial services where the HQ may require some specialist expertise, this can greatly reduce the number of location options available;
- expatriate tax regime. A number of countries have special expatriate schemes designed to attract international operations. While the UK has few special incentives it has a relatively low higher rate of tax;
- corporate tax regime. Again a number of countries have special benefits such as coordination centres aimed at attracting European HQs;
- labour costs and the cost of redundancy for senior staff. Cost factors tend to be less important in choosing a location for an HQ compared to a manufacturing site. However, a key problem is what you do if a senior placement does not work out and how much you have to pay to persuade a senior executive to leave the company. In some countries employment protection is such that it can be very expensive (many times the individual's annual salary) to make an executive redundant;
- quality and extent of international communications. In our global environment it is vitally important to be able to keep in touch with key contacts around the world. This applies to physical and electronic communications. So most HQs are situated within easy reach of the world's major international airports. In addition, companies invest heavily in telecommunication networks with quality of service rather than cost the overriding priority;
- property availability, especially well sited in relation to airport and prestigious sites;
- quality of life, especially for the expatriate workforce. If you cannot persuade your top executives to work in your chosen city then the company is often in considerable trouble. There is a wide range of issues to consider, such as the availability of international schools, cultural facilities, cost and ease of commuting from appropriate executive housing. In undertaking relocation studies for European HQs we often carry out surveys of key employees to ascertain what the personal requirements are and their views on prospective locations;
- quality and extent of business support facilities.

56

These include international banking, marketing and ease of doing business in that particular location.

London generally scores highly on all these points. There is a huge range of overseas companies, agencies and institutions based in the city. These range from the large number of international banks, representatives of most major overseas media organisations, as well as the international and European HQs of a vast number of companies. It is no surprise that two of the world's leading publications, *The Financial Times* and *The Economist* are based in London. All these factors help to create that international feel. One of London's advantages is that it is not a European city; it is a global city which has the world's business language as its native tongue.

Labour costs for locally employed staff tend to be lower than in most other major European cities and despite England's notorious reputation for learning foreign languages it is still easy to recruit bi-lingual staff, in part due to the large number of foreigners attracted to the city. Labour regulations are also far more relaxed than in many other European cities, making it easier to lay-off staff if necessary.

With regard to communications, London is almost without equal in Europe. Passengers can reach more European and world-wide destinations from London's main airports than from any other European city. With the liberalisation of tele-communications, companies in the city often have a choice of more than four service providers compared with just one state-owned monopoly elsewhere. As a result, international telecommunications costs are lower in London than any other European city and quality of service is generally higher.

Another factor helping to establish London as a global city is its outstanding reputation with regard to business support services. The City of London is the European and, in some cases, world leader in terms of financial markets, international banking and insurance. It has been advisers from UK consultancy firms, merchant banks and legal firms that have led the way in the privatisation and restructuring under way in Eastern Europe. London's marketing, advertising and PR agencies are all highly regarded throughout the continent. All these factors are important in portraying the image of a dynamic and cosmopolitan city where it is easy to do business.

London has begun to wake up to the fact that cities are in many respects like other products: they have to be marketed in the right way to the right people to ensure success. With the establishment of 'London First' to help promote London as a location for business and to assist companies considering establishing here, the city at last has a champion to ensure that it is properly represented and promoted to the world stage as one of Europe's leading locations for establishing a European HQ.

Environmental Risk in Europe

57

Stephen Tromans, Partner and Head of Environmental Law Department, Simmons & Simmons

Foreign private investment is a significant driving factor in growth in both developing and developed economies, and seems set to continue to be so. Such investment, by its nature, will often relate to industries or activities which carry high risks of environmental damage, or which bear a legacy of past environmental impairment. It is still the case that too few investors have a sufficient awareness of environmental risk, or of the strong tides running in favour of enhanced environmental liability regimes in Europe. The 1994 Dobris Assessment on the European Environment (the work of a task force including the EC, UNECE, OECD, UNEP and WHO) identified a number of major, intractable and growing problems, relating to air quality and health, water pollution, acidification of soils and water and the existence of old waste dumps. These are not problems which can be lightly dismissed.

A number of European countries (most notably Germany, Finland and Denmark) have adopted statutory systems to provide redress for environmental damage. The Lugano Convention of the Council of Europe on liability for environmental harm has attracted the support of a number of European countries. The European Commission and Parliament have been grappling with the issue throughout the 1990s, first in the context of a proposed directive on civil liability for damage caused by waste, and more recently in relation to the green paper on repairing environmental damage. The next step may well be a draft framework directive on the subject.

The truth is that even the best preventive systems cannot obviate all environmental damage, and that existing laws are increasingly being perceived as inadequate to ensure that such damage is rectified and that the costs of such rectification are internalized to the entity which causes it. As the House of Lords European Communities Committee found when it enquired into the issue of environmental liability in 1993, there will be growing pressure for more effective liability systems which, if not addressed at European level, may give rise to unacceptable distortions of competition. Politically, it must be questionable whether the present UK government's arguments on subsidiarity can withstand such pressure; even more so as the influence of new Scandinavian members of the Community is felt. It is also worth remembering that in general the liability regimes introduced so far have been the product of right- rather than left-wing governments, or indeed the possible left-wing/green coalitions now increasingly being mooted in Germany.

Investment in a country with non-existent or lax environmental controls is in many ways the most risky course of all. There can be no guarantee that future changes will not impose heavy liabilities to make good the consequences of past activity, or that environmental damage will not ensue from the normal course of loosely regulated operations, which

Who needs accurate air pollution measurements?

Measurements of air pollution are of little value unless they can be demonstrated to be accurate. If the measurements are also to be used for legal purposes, their accuracy needs to be validated. A cost effective method achieving confidence in the accuracy of measurements is to calibrate the instrumentation using standard gas mixtures.

For full details contact:
Peter Woods (ext 7095), Roger Partridge (ext 6783), or Arthur Davenport (ext 6828)
National Physical Laboratory, Teddington, Middlesex, TW11 0LW
Telephone: 0181-977 3222   Fax: 0181-943 6755

Standard gas mixtures are available for:

Carbon monoxide in nitrogen	10% to 1 ppm
Carbon dioxide in nitrogen	10% to 0.02%
Nitric oxide in nitogen	10% to 1 ppm
Propane in nitrogen or air	1% to 1 ppm
Methane in air	2% to 1000 ppm
n-Hexane in nitrogen	1000, 100 ppm
Multicomponent mixtures for exhaust emissions:	
CO, CO_2, C_3H_8 in N_2	6%, 15%, 2400 ppm
	3.5%, 14%, 2000 ppm
Multicomponent hydrocarbons in N_2 for air quality measurement	ppb-ppm levels

Standards of sulphur dioxide, nitrogen dioxide and methane at ambient concentrations and certain toxic gases including C_6H_6 and H_2S at occupational exposure levels will be available shortly.

will give rise to claims for compensation. One problem is that it may be difficult to assess the relative strength or weakness of regulatory controls in other jurisdictions. In some cases the law has developed rapidly; the Czech Republic, for instance, has enacted environmental law aggressively since independence. In other cases such law is lacking or, where it is in existence, may not be adequately enforced. For example, the Polish Environmental Protection Act has contained a requirement since 1980 for persons or organizations which cause soil degradation to restore the degraded land to 'a proper state' – an obligation backed by broad enforcement powers. But so far no industrial enterprise in Poland has been subjected to such liability. Where such broadly worded provisions exist, part of the problem lies in the lack of guidance on the degree of harm regarded as damage, or on the technical standards of remediation required.

Adequate knowledge of regulatory matters may require complex research of not only many different statutory sources, but also informal protocols, guidance notes and other non-statutory material, as well as an accurate feel for general regulatory attitudes. Clear policy itself may also be lacking – as a 1994

study by the Regional Environment Center for Central and Eastern Europe pointed out, inventories of problems are often still presented as policy!

Little wonder, then, that many investors and corporations are seeking alternatives to relying solely on compliance with applicable national legislation. One approach is to adopt the standards of the corporation's home country, applying these to all facilities, wherever located. This has the possible advantages of simplicity and consistency, but also many disadvantages. It ignores important and legitimate differences between countries in terms of geography, pre-existing levels of pollution, politics and culture, which will have shaped the legislative standards in the home country.

An alternative is to adopt relevant international standards from among the various instruments which have evolved, such as international codes of conduct, for example the UN Code of Conduct for Transnational Corporations. However, these may lack precision and add little beyond the basic requirement of compliance with applicable domestic law. Environmental management standards such as ISO 14000 may also be helpful in addressing man-

The Environmental Gas Standards Programme at The National Physical Laboratory

A research programme is underway at the National Physical Laboratory (NPL) which is part of DTI's commitment to provide and develop the UK's National Measurement System through the Valid Analytical Measurement initiative. It's objectives are: to provide government and industry with traceable standards of air pollution source emissions, occupational exposure and air quality, in order to meet UK and EC legislation and comply with national and international for requirements; to provide technical advice to industry and NAMAS laboratories in order to promote widespread takeup of validated internationally-accepted measurement methods; to ensure that UK standards and calibration procedures are consistent with those of other countries, particularly the EC.

Gas Concentration Standards: A national facility has been established where primary gas standards are prepared and maintained. Standards of different gaseous species with widely differing concentrations are produced in passivated containers using absolute gravimetric techniques. Their concentrations, which are expressed in absolute molar units, are traceable to the primary standard of mass. Rigorous quality assurance procedures ensure the accuracy of the standards.

Other gas mixtures are produced which are certified directly against the primary standards. These are then utilised as secondary standards and disseminated to industry, gas suppliers, governments bodies, etc. to provide the required measurement accuracy and traceability.

Gas Calibration Facilities: Calibration facilities are being developed to complement the work concerned with gas concentration standards. For example: A facility is being produced for calibrating instruments which are used to monitor gaseous species too reactive to be stored in containers (eg, HCI). The required concentrations are generated dynamically, and spectroscopic techniques are employed to measure their concentrations online. The gases are then directed into the instruments requiring calibration.

Quality Assurance of Gas Concentration Measurements: An effective way of demonstrating the accuracy and quality of measurements is to obtain accreditation through the NAMAS organisation. Assistance is given to laboratories seeking NAMAS accreditation in gas concentration methods. By this means commercial gas producers are preparing and disseminating an increasing range of traceable standards. One recent example is the Department of Transport's annual vehicle testing (MOT) programme.

International Collaborations: Collaborative activities are in progress with other laboratories in Europe and the USA, with the aim of determining the international uniformity of gas concentration measurements. For example:

(i) Collaborative research is carried out within an initiative know as EUROMET. EUROMET aims to coordinate work in national standards laboratories in European countries. The initiative on gas standards will bring greater experience to bear by developing different types of gas mixtures and quality assurance procedures in each laboratory. This will provide a greater range of internationally-validated standards to customers.

(ii) Intercomparisons have been carried out with the National Institute of Standards and Technology, USA. These demonstrated the uniformity of vehicle emission measurements in the two countries.

UK legislation and EC directives are placing increasing demands on industry and government to carry out valid environmental measurements, and a wider range of calibration standards and measurement methods will be required. If you require details on standards available, need new standards or better quality assurance procedures, or are interested in NAMAS accreditation, NPL, will be happy to advise.

agement systems, although they are not cheap to implement. Finally, it may be appropriate to adopt procedures followed by international monetary institutions such as the Development Banks, European Bank for Reconstruction and Development and the World Bank.

Such procedures can lessen the risk of ongoing activities giving rise to liability; what they do not address is the risk of contingent liabilities from past activities, perhaps triggered by some future change in law or enforcement policy. Such liabilities are not likely to be apparent on the balance sheet. Valuation methods used to date in Central and Eastern Europe have not taken account of environmental factors; indeed, reliable estimates for the impact generally of environmental issues on privatization in the area are difficult to come by. There may be undue concentration on pollution 'hotspots', often sensationally publicized. The main exception is the former East Germany, where a high-level political decision was made that the opening balances showing the assets and liabilities of state-owned enterprises (SOEs) should include environmental liabilities. To an extent this was made practicable by the existence of developed liability rules and standards in West Germany: the test was whether the SOE would be subject to

clean-up requirements if it were in West Germany.

While pre-privatization accounts may be deficient in not reflecting environmental costs, the privatized companies may adopt new accountancy systems which highlight environmental expenditure and liabilities more starkly.

Investors should therefore take steps themselves to understand what may be the driving forces which increase the risk of liability. These will differ depending on the country concerned. They may include domestic political pressure, membership or intended membership of the EU, privatization programmes, increased public participation, trade and financial pressures, institutional aid, and economic restructuring. All of these pressures are to be seen within the generally volatile context of economic and social change taking place in 'countries in transition', and the debate on environmental liability within Europe as a whole. To copy what is often the under-reaction of domestic purchasers or investors in the case of environmental risk in Central and Eastern Europe may be a serious mistake indeed.

Further information on the issues outlined in this chapter may be obtained from Stephen Tromans at Simmons & Simmons, 21 Wilson Street, London EC2M 2TX. Tel: 0171 628 2020; fax: 0171 628 2070.

Regenerating Derelict Land

58

Carl Hopkins, Nabarro Nathanson

Urban development and regeneration have progressed rapidly during recent years to become activities of considerable importance, and now account for a substantial proportion of public, private and voluntary sector investment in towns and cities. At national, continental and global levels, meeting the challenge of urban regeneration represents a fundamental element in the positive and purposeful management of post-industrial society. In addition, and increasingly recognized and accepted as the basis for future policy and action, the encouragement of urban regeneration is a vital component in attaining the goal of sustainable development. Irrespective of the particular circumstances of a nation or locality, north or south, developed or undeveloped, rich or poor, investment in urban regeneration can be seen to represent an important response to the tensions and troubles that are generated by economic, social, physical and environmental decay and neglect.

Members of the CBI widely appreciate both the contribution they can make and the commercial opportunities that the huge economic and social changes in Europe represent for them. We are familiar with the position in the UK where large tracts of industrial land became derelict in the late 1970s and early 1980s following the collapse of the ports and steel and coal industries. The government's response was to fund public initiatives to remove obstacles to investment and enable the private sector

to renew the local economy with job-creating development. Over the past 10 years considerable sums of public money have been spent and these have brought investment by the private sector.

The skills of CBI members as funders, investors, contractors and consultants are recognized widely across Europe. They have participated in the many major reconstruction contracts which have been awarded, usually using World Bank and European Bank for Reconstruction funds. Investments are on a gigantic scale and CBI members have been participating and will continue to do so.

There are as many strategies and styles of urban regeneration as there are regions, towns, cities and individual regeneration opportunities. Each individual unit of land or property, in an overall design for the regeneration of a neighbourhood or town, will make its particular contribution in a manner which reflects its origins, current condition, regeneration potential and resource base. Alongside each scheme, it is likely that there will be a number of common features, facilities and procedures, but even here the availability and implementation of such common elements will vary from place to place and over time. While urban development and regeneration are activities which can be seen in practice almost everywhere, they are distinguished by the individual nature of each scheme or project. At a conference arranged by the Town & Country Planning Association to discuss the Secretary of State's draft strategic

ADAS Land Restoration

Environmental issues are at the forefront when development is planned. Developers recognise that designing their project with environmental considerations built in from the start provides a cost effective method of obtaining planning permission. The Government is also extremely keen to see the remnant industrial sites, our so called derelict land, used in preference to green field sites.

Combining these two activities throws up major issues relating to risks, costs and suitability of afteruse that need careful evaluation. This is where ADAS, with its wealth of consultancy experience, research and laboratory services, knowledge and skills base, can provide a one stop service.

Since the 1940s ADAS has been involved in restoration and aftercare for British Coal. Currently we are restoring approx. 2000 hectares per year. Along with our work on colliery sites, disused lead and copper mines and landfill sites this has given us a unique capability to carry out audits, investigations and site assessments for a variety of beneficial afteruses. Our pioneering research work on vegetation management such as the development of wildflower meadows, translocation of hedges and heather regeneration have ensured restored sites quickly fit into the environment. Whether restoration is to built

development, sport and leisure such as golf, agriculture, woodland, conservation or amenity, ADAS can provide a comprehensive service to ensure a technically and cost effective solution.

ADAS has over 1500 consultants with some 50 specialisms available from its offices in England and Wales. Offices have also recently opened in Prague, Poland and Romania. Turnover in the past 2 years has been £76m. Our staff are experienced in working for individual businesses and for Government and its agencies at home and abroad. Where appropriate we can combine a range of technical expertise into teams matched to particular tasks. Our experience embraces the management of land, soil, water, air, vegetation, ecology, hydrology, landscape and building design, engineering, surveying, cartography, resource planning and meteorology together with a full range of biological sciences. All are supported by CAD and GIS systems.

ADAS is also experienced at networking, bringing together various potential sources of funds and contractors with relevant and complementary skills to develop collaborative ventures.

For total confidence in the complete service, you need look no further than your nearest ADAS office.

Contact David McDougall
Phone: +441623 846742 Fax: +441623 847424

Advertisement feature

guidance for London, the world competition faced by London was acknowledged. The conference recognized that within the UK we have a significant body of professional knowledge and skills to offer.

One of London's strengths is the critical mass of professional advisers which itself attracts inward investors who demand those services. The UK's consultants in the fields of engineering have been well regarded around the world for generations. There is a firm infrastructure on which to develop further the marketing of our professional skills to Europe in order to earn revenues for the UK and the businesses themselves, while undertaking work which is essential to the renewal of the European economy.

It is the complexity of urban regeneration which demands the skills that CBI members offer. The UK's urban regeneration programme has itself been difficult. But we recognize that the scale and complexity of the industrial decline in areas such as Poland have left devastated regions with no modern infrastructure and dreadful contamination.

At the time the Berlin Wall was removed there was a heightened awareness of the difficulties which Central and Eastern Europe faced. This resulted in many CBI members taking part in what has been described as the 'first wave' of private sector interest in the potential for growth and profits. There is now greater maturity at political and administrative level. Major infrastructure is under construction and the potential which was recognized a few years ago is now within a realistic timeframe. CBI members with skills, resources and experience in this field who are not already active in the area could review their business plans to see whether they can participate as the dust settles and more realistic opportunities emerge.

Ground-breaking
projects

From the Black Country
you can get to most of
Britain's major seaports inside
a single day's HGV drive.

MILES FROM THE SEA.
YET CLOSE
TO EVERY PORT.

BLACK COUNTRY
DEVELOPMENT CORPORATION

+44 (0)121-511 2000

Black Country Development Corporation,
Black Country House,
Rounds Green Road, Oldbury,
West Midlands B69 2DG.
Fax: +44 (0)121-544 5710 / +44 (0)121-552 0490.

What kind of companies invest

$6.680.000.000

in Wales?

The kind that reinvest

$4.167.000.000.

*Panasonic, Ford and L'Oreal are our kind
of companies. The kind that have moved
to Wales and then reinvested there.
Find out if yours is the kind of company
that could profit from a move
by calling WDA Customer Services.*

WALES

BEST BUSINESS CLIMATE IN EUROPE.
+44 1443 84 55 00.

WDA

WELSH
DEVELOPMENT
AGENCY

Wales – A Winning Location

Wales has one of the fastest growing economies in Britain and is one of Europe's most successful regions in attracting inward investment. Over 380 overseas parented operations have located in Wales, of which 150 are North American, around 170 European, and the remainder are from Japan, Asia Pacific and Australia. This successful programme of inward investment into Wales has been led by the Welsh Development Agency, the principal catalyst for industrial and economic regeneration in Wales.

Economic Diversification

In the past decade the Welsh economy has undergone a radical transformation. There has been a significant employment diversification with the decline of the traditional industries and the establishment of Wales as a centre of manufacturing; boasting strong automotive engineering, aerospace, and electronic sectors. It is not just manufacturing industries which are experiencing a resurgence, South East Wales, and Cardiff in particular, has firmly established itself as a centre for financial services which is expected to be a growth industry in the next few years. Top class international names including Chemical Bank, Dun and Bradstreet and Société Generale have all chosen to establish a major presence in Wales. Around 80 per cent of Cardiffs workforce are employed in the service industries and a recent forecast from the European Economic Research and Advisory Forum expects Cardiff to emerge as a major European financial and business services centre. Cardiff is also expected to be the fastest growing conurbation in the British Isles and the sixth fastest among Europe's largest cities, competing with Rome and Paris in terms of tourism and visitor spending.

Resilient Economy

The Welsh economy is not only more broad-based now but it is also proving far more resilient to the recessionary difficulties of the 1990s than the rest of the UK. Wales combines one of the highest levels of manufacturing productivity within the UK almost 7% above the UK average. Combined with the competitive wage levels, Wales is the lowest cost manufacturing region in the UK. Optimism among Welsh manufacturing businesses is buoyant and output is expected to continue to show strong positive growth. All the leading independent forecasting agencies expect Welsh GDP to grow strongly, at rates above the UK average until the end of the century.

Premier European Location

Both overseas and UK investors are recognising that by choosing to locate in Wales they are joining a successful economy and can reap the benefits of competitive costs, an adaptable and productive workforce, excellent industrial relations record and efficient road, air and rail communications. Since 1983 total inward investment announced in Wales from overseas parented companies has amounted to capital investment in excess of £6 billion. This amounts to 16% of the total inward investment projects into the UK, a remarkable achievement given that Wales has just 5% of the UK population. Wales' success is endorsed by the rate of expansion by companies that have already chosen to relocate there. Of the 131 development projects which attracted £920 million in the last financial year nearly half were from companies expanding their operations in Wales. Time and time again it is evident companies that come to Wales, stay in Wales and re-invest in Wales.

This enviable track record is the principal responsibility of the WDA and owes much to the approach called Team Wales. Team Wales aims to provide a one-stop solution for investors. It is an innovative approach that fosters close partnerships between the public and the private sector with all parties joining forces to form a professional team ready to help with any type of relocation plan. The aim is to identify the exact requirements of potential investors and then to provide it – be it land, buildings, planning permission, training programmes or advice on financial packages and labour.

Innovative Marketing

Maintaining this level of inward investment is a demanding task, especially as the competition for quality inward investment has increased, at a time when the global market for internationally mobile inward investment has declined. The Agency has had to be ever more responsive to the market place and to companies' needs and has adopted an aggressive and innovative marketing programme to spearhead its activities. A host of initiatives include in-flight video, the development of the CD-ROM as a presentation tool, and Network Wales - the all Wales information library – on the Internet.

Also, the Agency has been strengthening its overseas representations in its traditional markets of the US and Japan and, to take advantage of the strong economic growth rates of the whole of the Pacific rim area, the WDA has also expanded its representation in the developing markets of Australia, Taiwan, Hong Kong and South Korea. In addition, there are plans to extend its reach into Singapore Malaysia and Thailand. One of the first tangible successes of this initiative was the securing of Wales' first inward investment from Taiwan; Ringtel Electronics are setting up a £2.4 million plant in Gwent to produce connectors and cordage for the telecommunications industry at Cwmbran.

Supporting Indigenous Businesses

As well as being responsible for inward investment, an essential part of the Welsh Development Agency's work is in supporting indigenous businesses. Our Eurolink programme has helped to give companies in Wales vital support overseas and has forged alliances with key economic regions in Europe. Over 100 companies have been helped with technology transfer arrangements, joint marketing initiatives and joint product development. The success of the programme is such that it is being expanded worldwide and Global Link is now working to give Welsh companies the edge to compete in international markets.

Embracing technological change is one of the keys to a company's economic success and it was partly for this reason that 1995 was designated the Wales Year of Innovation and Technology. The year grew out of the Wales 2010 report produced by the Institute of Welsh Affairs and it had three objectives: firstly to raise awareness throughout Wales of the importance of technology and innovation; secondly to promote greater discussion and use of technology between business, academia and the education sector and thirdly to promote Wales' own innovative and technological activities and achievements. The WDA's Technology Transfer Group has spearheaded the Year of Innovation initiative and the team has been working with companies, research organisations and academic groups throughout Wales on a wide range of technology projects, some of which are part funded by the European Community or the Department of Trade and Industry. The team has been of particular help to small and medium sized enterprises with problem solving, analysis and product development. This compliments the WDA's Source Wales team which is active in creating links between academic establishments and industry to further the research, development and implementation of manufacturing and service initiatives.

Prosperous Region

Wales and the WDA are successfully meeting the challenges of a changing world economy and the country's diverse, broad-based economy is a testimony to its success as a world class investment location. Wales has the resources, communications, training, workforce, financial support and environment to provide international investors with a superb business climate. It will not be long before the prognosis of The Economist "The country of Wales is seen as having the potential to become one of Europe's most prosperous regions", is fulfilled.

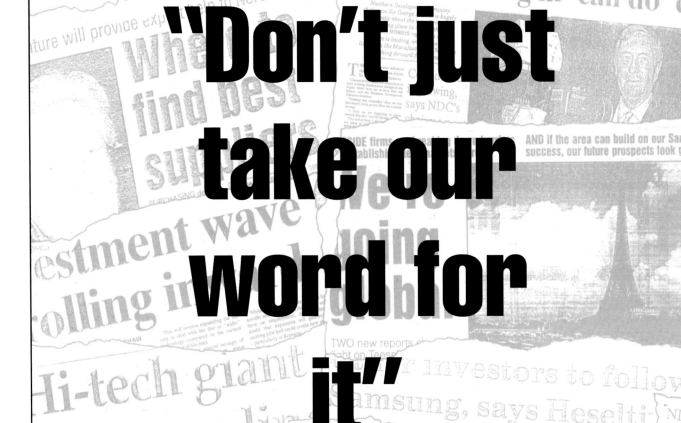

"Don't just take our word for it"

Since 1986, the Northern Development Company has attracted more than £5 billion worth of investment from leading global companies.
Understanding our customers' needs, paying attention to detail and working effectively with our partners in the North of England are the hallmarks of our success - but don't just take our word for it, find out for yourself by contacting us on (0191) 261 0026.

NORTHERN
Development
Company

Great North House, Sandyford Road, Newcastle upon Tyne NE1 8ND
Tel:(0191) 261 0026 Fax:(0191) 232 9069

The North of England – offering more to investors

Anyone who has taken an interest in the world of inward investment over the last 10 years cannot fail to have noted the outstanding run of success which the North of England has enjoyed.

Since Nissan's turn-key decision in 1984 to locate its prime European manufacturing facility on the site of the old Sunderland airport, the Region has emerged as a beacon for inward investment – particularly from the Far East – and is now home to more than 380 overseas companies.

The Northern Development Company (NDC) – the agency for economic development in the North of England – has been a significant player in helping to secure many of these and last year, co-ordinated the so-called "Winning Team" which persuaded Samsung Electronics to site a £450 million multi-product industrial complex on Teesside.

Earlier this year, NDC was voted one of the world's top ten Outstanding Development Groups of 1994 by Site Selection magazine – a leading global site location publication – which said: "Attention to detail is particularly crucial in today's competitive economic development environment and the Northern Development Company has refined it into a higher art form."

This followed on from awards in 1991, when NDC was voted Europe's Development Agency of the year (by Corporate Location magazine) and 1993, when Plant Location International named the North of England Europe's Best Region for investment in manufacturing industry.

After such a run of success it would be easy for complacency to set in, but at NDC's Newcastle headquarters, chief executive, Dr John Bridge, remains as determined as ever.

He said: "The accolades we have won are a well deserved reward for all the staff at NDC but we must not let success go to our heads. The competition for inward investment is getting fiercer by the day and if we are to maintain our success, we must set our standards even higher."

Within this intensively competitive environment, development agencies are constantly being forced to think of new and more innovative ways to attract companies. NDC's most recent initiative focuses on what suppliers in the Region have to offer and attempts to match the capabilities of the Region's supplier base with the purchasing requirements of inward investors.

This has a bonus effect of adding-value to an inward investment, through contracts secured by indigenous companies, but equally important, it makes the Region a more attractive place to prospective investors.

John Bridge explained: "A Region's ability to attract inward investment is heavily dependent on the capabilities of its supplier base. It follows that if we are to attract world class companies to the North of England then we must have a world class supplier base to service their demands."

NDC's supplier-chain-development programme works through a team of Business Development Managers who meet with large manufacturers, identify gaps in their supplier chains and transmit these to smaller Regional companies with the capability to fill it.

In the case of Samsung, NDC has designated two Business Development Managers to work with the project team and help them source construction, plant equipment and product suppliers from within the Region. This recently met with some success when Washington based, ARD, secured a £500,000 contract to become the Region's first component supplier to the Samsung Industrial Complex.

The development of a world class supplier base means that when NDC markets the North of England internationally it now has an additional string to its bow. As John Bridge said: "It is important to have things like a good labour force, available grants, high specification premises and good links to Europe. On top of this, we can now say to companies that the Region also possesses the type of SME's who can supply them components of world class standard."

Another factor which enables the North of England to offer more to investors is the existence of cultural facilities for inward investors. This isn't just a case of playing or golf or – as in the case of Samsung – going to watch Newcastle United, but actually creating a community support structure.

An example of this came recently when NDC assisted in the establishment of the Region's first Christian Church solely for Koreans. John Bridge explained: "NDC supported the establishment of the Korean church because we realise how important religion is to people in Korea where about 40 per cent of the population are regular church goers.

"Let's hope that the next Korean company that is considering Europe as a manufacturing base will look at the North of England and think – now that looks like a place where we will be made to feel at home."

The establishment of the Korean church and other cultural facilities like the Anglo-Japanese Society – for which NDC provides the secretariat – does reflect the existence of large numbers of overseas companies already in the Region and as competition for new investment grows these are increasingly valuable.

Re-investments now account for over half of inward investment into the UK and the Region has already experienced some of the benefits this can bring, with Nissan. The companies initial investment in 1984 was £50 million but subsequent re-investments mean that the total expenditure is now more than £1 billion, directly accounting for over 4,500 jobs.

In the case of Samsung, the fact that the company already had a successful facility manufacturing colour televisions at Billingham was cited as a significant factor in the decision to locate the complex at nearby Wynyard Park.

The Billingham operation not only gave the company first hand experience of the Region's plus points, it allowed them to develop a good working relationship with NDC and other economic development bodies in the Region.

In the case of Northern Development Company this went back to 1985 when they opened the talks which led to Samsung setting up in Billingham. The close links which NDC maintained after the investment – through its Aftercare programme – meant that the Region was well placed when Samsung came to decide where to locate its multi million pound complex.

John Bridge explained: "Keeping in touch with investors has always been important but now it is more so than ever. Although not technically an expansion, the experience of Samsung has shown the importance of maintaining good relations with all the companies that come to the Region."

To re-inforce this point, NDC recently expanded its Aftercare programme into an Investment Services unit which is solely responsible for meeting the future expansion and development needs of current investors.

Heading towards the next century, the competition will get even tougher and, as Dr Bridge admitted, development agencies will have to re-focus more of their efforts towards the service sector.

He said: "The service sector is becoming much more internationally mobile and in time it is something we will have to focus on. The internationalisation of credit card transactions and accounting procedures is taking place at a rapid rate and it is important that the Region secures its share of business from this."

The North of England has ventured into this area with some success and a number of back office and telesales operations have already located in the Region.

For the time being though, John Bridge is happy to keep the majority of NDC's work focused on the manufacturing sector.

He concluded: "Inward investment has had a revolutionary effect on the economy of the Northern region in terms of jobs created, the diversification of the industrial base and through encouraging companies to up-date their practices and methods of production.

"The challenge now is for NDC and all our Regional partners to capitalise on those achievements. Together we can build a world class future for the Region."

SCOTTISH ENTERPRISE
OUR ROLE IN LAND REGENERATION

ABOUT SCOTTISH ENTERPRISE

Scottish Enterprise is a Non-Departmental Public Body, established in 1991 through the merger of the Scottish  Development Agency and the Training Agency, to promote economic development, environmental improvement and training and skills in lowland Scotland. Responsible to the Secretary of State, our overall aim is to help business and to create jobs and prosperity for the people of Scotland. Our annual funding allocation is around £460 million and further funds are levered from the European Community and private sector partnerships.

The bulk of our expenditure and activities is delivered through a network of 13 Local Enterprise Companies (LECs) spread throughout our operational area. Scottish Enterprise National in Glasgow has a lead role in establishing the strategy and directing the activities of the Network.

OUR ROLE IN LAND REGENERATION

The emphasis of our environmental work is towards preparing and releasing land for industrial and commercial development, urban and rural regeneration aimed at revitalising key local areas, and optimising Scotland's tourism potential.

As the primary body in Scotland with the powers to treat vacant and derelict land, Scottish Enterprise provides best practice implementation reflecting international UK and European legislation.  We network with developers, lending institutions, legal and insurance companies to ensure development opportunities and economic benefits from land treatment. This comprehensive approach is targeted to give Scotland a competitive edge in the availability of development land and the recycling of brownfield sites.

We have a successful track record in providing development land with a quality of environment to meet the aspirations of new, inward investment and indigenous companies. During 1994/95 the Network renewed 805 hectares of land. A good example is in the Lanarkshire Enterprise Zone where contaminated land has been reclaimed, former mineral workings have been consolidated and site servicing provided. This effort has united public sector and European Commission finance, in preparation for private sector development.

BUILDING ON SCOTLAND'S EXPERTISE

For Europe: Scottish Enterprise wishes to build on the success of Scottish companies who have gained expertise in land regeneration - coal and mineral workings, dock lands, former defence and steelwork sites - and it is important that these skills are not lost to the benefit of Europe. We aim to provide a route through which Europe can benefit by these skills.

For the UK: At the UK level, we participate in a number of research projects aimed at developing knowledge and best practice throughout the UK - with the Department of Environment and the Construction, Industry, Research and Information Association. The projects include waste recycling, guidance on the buying and selling of contaminated land, decontamination technologies and case studies.

For Future Projects: We have been experimenting with alternative approaches to the traditionally expensive treatment of highly contaminated and heavily undermined sites. This has culminated in a sustainable demonstration project on a former steelworks site. The project involves the use of colliery waste and sewage sludge, fast growing trees to create short rotation coppice as a  renewable energy resource, and reed beds to absorb polluted surface water run-off. Scottish Universities are involved to help ascertain benefits of using trees as an aid to remediation. The end result will be an area of bio-mass and experimentation, community woodland, and leisure. If successful, it will prove that sites can be treated at minimal costs.

Scottish Enterprise

FOR FURTHER INFORMATION

Contact: Iain Hart, Scottish Enterprise, 120 Bothwell Street, Glasgow G2 7JP

Tel: 0141-248 2700 Fax: 0141-221 8457

Bulgaria: Choose the best to invest

Since 1990 Bulgaria has chosen the path of radical economic reforms and has been undergoing a peaceful transition to a democratic society and market economy. The end of 1994 witnessed the first signs of economic recovery and growth. Following four years of decline, GDP increased by 1.4 per cent in 1994 with estimates for 2.5 per cent growth in 1995.

The important cuts in government spending as well as the restrictive incomes policy allowed Bulgaria to make certain steps towards limiting the budget deficit to 5.9 per cent of GDP in 1994. The subsidies were reduced as a share value of expenditure from 43 per cent in 1989 to 2.9 per cent in 1994. Inflation, measured by CPI, was reduced from 338.5 per cent in 1991 to 17.6 per cent in the first 8 months of 1995. The exchange rate moved from 21.88 BGL/US$ in December 1991 to 68.15 BGL/US$ in September 1995, registering appreciation in real terms over the period.

At the beginning of the economic reforms the private sector accounted for 6.4 per cent of GDP, while at the end of 1994 it reached about 30 per cent. The government is committed to an irreversible process of encouraging the private sector's development.

Foreign investment has an important role and contribution to the transition. As of September 1995, the volume of foreign investment inflow totals $850m. About 4,000 companies with foreign participation were established mostly in manufacturing, transportation, trade and construction. The largest investors are Rover, Amylum, Willi Betz, Shell, etc. The foreign companies have been interested in the Bulgarian market for a long time but it seems as though they rediscovered Bulgaria not before the beginning of the economic reforms in 1990. After five years of political, economic and social changes, the Republic of Bulgaria now offers a friendly foreign investment environment. Along with the favourable legal framework including equal treatment of foreign and domestic investors, no limitations on the type, number and volume of foreign investment, there is a number of factors which attract foreign investors. Among them the most important are:
- stable political, legal and institutional environment for foreign investment;
- increasing domestic market of nearly 9m customers,
- strategic cross-road geographical position and established spring-board to the large markets of the CIS and the Middle East;
- strong technological infrastructure, inexpensive and highly skilled labour force;
- liberal foreign investment legislation and import-export regime;
- opportunity to use Bulgarian Brady bonds in the privatisation of state-owned enterprises, which can reduce their assets' value by up to 35 per cent;
- opportunity to participate in key infrastructural projects with international importance such as the construction of transportation corridors, oil and gas pipe lines, the modernisation of the telecommunications, the development of ecological production.

The institutional framework of foreign investment is simple and clear. To promote further investment in the country, the current government has established the Foreign Investment Agency, which is a "one-stop shop" institution for international business.

The main duties and services of the Agency are: to provide information on the legal framework, taxation, political and economic conditions for investment, concession, guarantees etc.; to direct foreign investors to the relevant state institutions; to supply analyses, reference books and publications concerning the general investment conditions in Bulgaria; to prepare analyses about the conditions and the interests of the foreign investors and to offer the best form of foreign investment; to select the most appropriate Bulgarian partners and companies; to provide full list of the state-owned companies' profiles opened for joint ventures and mutual cooperation and to disseminate information from the Geographical Information System – plots of lands and buildings for green-field investment.

Foreign investment promotion is one of the priorities in the governmental program. Attracting large investments in the key branches of the economy, speeding-up privatisation, improving the infrastructure, restructuring of the state sector and solving the foreign debt problem are issues of primary importance in the long-term strategy of economic reforms.

Foreign Investment Agency, Bulgaria
3, St. Sofia Str. 1000 Sofia, Bulgaria
Phone: +359 2 87 34 83
Fax: +359 2 88 55 17

PART

13

Travel and Conferences

When the searching has to stop . . .

Convenience, flexibility and expertise are your first considerations when selecting a venue.

Congratulations! You're looking at one now.

The Novotel London Hammersmith is anything but a "run of the mill" venue. This modern 3 star hotel is unique in linking spacious, high quality accommodation (635 en suite rooms) with excellent conference and exhibition facilities.

Located in Hammersmith, West London, minutes away from Knightsbridge, Theatreland and the heart of the City, we are only 9 miles from Heathrow Airport, with Hammersmith Underground just next door. The M4, M3 and M25 are only a short drive away from our 240 space car park.

We can confidently welcome every conceivable type of event. Fifteen separate conference rooms, including 3,000 square metres gross of dedicated exhibition space, can cater for 2 to 900 delegates for simultaneous conferences, exhibitions and banquets. A complete team of professional, experienced event managers and technical staff are constantly on hand to advise and assist from the initial planning stages through to the completion of your event.

Build up and breakdown of events is exceptionally smooth – drive-in loading bays are separately located from smart, comfortable visitor entrances.

Catering facilities are equally flexible. Whether your requirements are for our à la Carte restaurant or for a uniquely tailored, themed occasion, we can offer a variety of catering outlets for your individual use.

Impressed? There's more! Never a venue to rest on its laurels, Novotel London Hammersmith is also undergoing extensive refurbishment. Phases I and II have already been completed, namely all bedrooms and public areas. Phase III – all conferences and exhibition areas – are on line for completion of refurbishment by Autumn 1996.

If you'd like London as your location, you'll need Novotel for your event. Give us the chance to prove what an excellent choice you've made.

Call us today on 0181 741 1888.

We're waiting to welcome you . . .

Novotel
London Hammersmith Hotel
Hammersmith International Centre
1 Shortlands,
London W6 8DR

Tel: 0181 741 1888
Fax: 0181 748 2228
Telex: 934539

Where in London can you find 3000  square metres of conference and  exhibition space, full banqueting  facilities, 15 meeting rooms to cater from 2 to 900 delegates, 635  en-suite bedrooms  and parking for 240 cars..... all under one roof?

The Changing Face of Business Travel in Europe

60

Les Middleditch, Business Travel International

From domestic train journeys to long-haul flights, business travel is something nearly all of us participate in, but most people take it for granted and it is not viewed as a serious industry in its own right. This is surprising when you consider that business travel and entertainment expenditure in the UK alone last year was estimated to exceed £20 billion.

Spending on business travel has risen considerably over the past few years, especially as economies have pulled themselves out of recession across Europe: this increase looks set to continue. However, the change is more than one of volume alone: business travel is developing in many directions; our travel patterns are changing daily; the destinations we visit are changing; airlines are constantly adding new services and incentives to woo the business traveller. Underpinning these changes there have been dramatic advancements in technology which have helped with bookings, reservations, budget control and, importantly for most companies, the whole business of managing business travel.

A world of difference?

Business travel has probably changed more in the last year than in the last ten and I believe we are moving into our most exciting period yet. The walls have been 'coming down' both literally and metaphorically across Europe, with improved telecommunications and the information technology revolution increasing the ease of cross-border business. But rather than eradicating the need to travel as one might expect, these developments have actually stimulated more business, and despite the much heralded uses of techniques such as video-conferencing, it is our experience that clients still prefer to meet face to face to conduct their business.

Political developments will continue to have a strong impact on business travel in 1996. Since Sweden and Finland joined the EU at the end of 1994, for example, there has been a marked increase in trade into and out of the Nordic countries, with companies like Volvo and Erikkson assuming a previously unrecognized international status. If other countries join and if a common currency is introduced, further opportunities for business travel will undoubtedly follow.

During the 1980s in the UK we witnessed a considerable amount of business relocation, as companies moved out of expensive city centre locations to greenfield sites and out-of-town industrial estates. With improvements in travel and communications and the need to cut costs even further, we are now seeing companies moving plants and offices to other countries to capitalize on cheaper labour and other reduced overheads. The southern Mediterranean countries and Eastern Europe are particularly popular and indeed accessible from the major markets. As a result, we are also witnessing an increase in business travel to these markets.

Where East meets West

The single most significant growth area in Europe for UK and other European businesses has been Eastern Europe and the Former Soviet Union (FSU). And it's not just trade to Moscow and St Petersburg that is increasing: businessmen are finding that for the first time they have to actually visit contacts at farms in the Ukraine or oil fields in Kazakhstan, rather than deal through one central office in Moscow. As a consequence, existing airlines have expanded their routes and increased flights, and many new airlines now fly to the FSU. Cities like Almaty and Baku are increasingly recognized as major trade centres and have found their way onto the European business map.

Barriers to trade and travel in the FSU have come down but bureaucracy still holds a firm grip – and some would argue is getting worse. Travel to the FSU requires precise planning, set in motion at least a month before you wish to travel. Obtaining visas and a letter of support from a company in Russia, for example, is the only way of entering the country for business; with autonomy granted to each of the former republics, you do of course need separate visas for each of the new countries. Using a specialist business travel agency such as Worldmark, a joint venture company between British, Polish and Russian business travel agents, ensures that British business travellers to the FSU will get the most up-to-date information and advice, and indeed that all-important help from local experts on the ground.

Come fly away

If you have been a regular air traveller over the past few years you will already have noticed a great many changes as the airlines constantly compete, offering, for example, bigger seats, chauffeur services and new incentives. And if you are lucky enough to travel first class it would not have escaped your notice that this area of the plane on most airlines has also been shrinking, largely to accommodate the increase in demand for business-class seats. As the airlines compete for every piece of available business this trend is likely to continue, with only the larger, world-renowned airlines such as British Airways being able to sustain a viable first-class service. At the other end of the scale, and following the trend for 'no-frills' functional hotels, we are also likely to see the introduction of cheaper, no-frills airlines.

In 1997, deregulation will bring additional changes to air travel and airlines will need to use 1996 to gear up, consolidate their customer bases, sort their routes and ensure their service matches up to the competition. Further changes will also be afoot over the next few years if Heathrow is refused the development of Terminal Five. UK business travellers may be forced to start using Amsterdam or Frankfurt as a main European hub airport, adding time to some long-haul journeys.

Changes to airline schedules will make day commuting an increasing reality in Europe. This year we saw a move towards earlier and later flights, allowing business travellers to conduct their trips in one day and removing the need to stay overnight. Sometimes this saves costs, but the major benefit is to the individual who wants to minimize time away from home.

At the touch of a button

It has been suggested that in the foreseeable future all travellers will carry a Smart Card containing ticket, passport, boarding passes, company travel policy and a whole host of other relevant documents. While this is feasible, it will not happen in a widespread fashion in the near future as many countries are not in the position to adopt the technologies required. It is worth bearing in mind that progress on such issues is only really as quick as the slowest country to respond. There is very little point in having a Smart Card with advanced data capture, only to arrive in a less developed country that does not have the facilities to read that card!

That said, there are constant initiatives afoot to speed up the journey of the traveller: 'fast track' check-in has already been introduced and automated ticketing has been successfully trialed in some UK airports and rail terminals this year. If the growth in business traffic continues as expected, the additional pressure on the terminals, their staff and the airlines must mean that these approaches will surely become the norm for business travel across Europe.

As more and more business people travel, move into new markets and take advantage of the wide number of different options available to them, controlling travel can provide companies with a major headache. The combination of technology and a new breed of business travel consultants, such as those who work for Hogg Robinson BTI, Business Travel International's UK partner, is helping corporations large and small not only to manage their travel spending, but also to enforce travel policies onto their

What broadens the mind shouldn't narrow your margins.

How do you stop your company's business travel budget going all over the place? Talk to the people with the technology and experience to make every pound you spend go further. Benefiting from our expertise, over 6,000 British companies now keep travel costs under control without leaving quality or convenience behind. Call today for an information pack or contact Les Middleditch, Director of Sales on 01252 372000 (tel.) or 01252 371200 (fax.).

HOGG ROBINSON
Business Travel International

BUSINESS TRAVEL INTERNATIONAL

Hogg Robinson Business Travel International is wholly owned by Hogg Robinson p.l.c.

travellers. The agents can also use their knowledge and expertise to consolidate the buying power of their clients and use it to negotiate deals with airlines, hotel chains and car rental companies on their behalf.

Business travel typically represents the third most costly overhead, after staff and property, of most companies. It is hardly surprising, therefore, that professional travel partners are being employed increasingly to lead clients through this complex industry, help them keep one step ahead of the rapidly changing marketplace and obtain significant cost savings.

We're famous for our facilities

Opened in 1984, the purpose built Bournemouth International Centre offers first class facilities for conferences, exhibitions and entertainments.

With three main halls plus a variety of breakout rooms, catering areas, offices, loading and unloading areas, multi storey car park and leisure pool with full fitness suite facilties, the Internationally renowned BIC provides the conference organiser with a wide choice of accommodation for any event.

The BIC is located right on Bournemouth's seafront and is therefore very centrally situated for a wide range of hotels within a couple of minutes walk – indeed Bournemouth boasts 30,000 bedspaces within a five mile radius of the Centre.

Just three minutes walk through Bournemouth's magnificient gardens lies the Pavilion complex. Completely restored and refurbished to its' original 1940's splendour, it is a more traditional venue for conferences, entertainment and social occasions. The theatre seats a total of 1518 persons in a combination of fixed seating on a raked floor and an upper circle.

There is also an orchestra pit which can be raised to stage level forming a stage extension and a full theatrical stage with revolving centre, fly tower, 3 phase electricity and theatrical lighting and sound, making it an ideal venue for corporate presentations, product launches, conferences and entertainment.

As well as smaller conferences, the elegant Pavilion Ballroom is a beautiful setting for banquets, gala dinners, receptions and social functions of all kinds and is often used in conjunction with the facilities of the Bournemouth International Centre offering the conference organiser the widest choice of facilities.

The same management and caterers serve both municipal venues, making the complex the ideal choice for many major International organisations.

Bournemouth International Centre and Pavilion Complex

| | Meeting spaces | | | | Area | |
Style	Theatre style	Class-room	Banqueting style	Cocktail style	Sq. m grossing	Min ceiling height (metres)
B.I.C.						
Windsor Hall	3900	800	1200	3000	2000	7.0
Tregonwell Hall	1200	350	420	850	723	7.0
Tregonwell Bar	130	70	80	180	87	2.55
Purbeck Hall	1700	900	900	2000	1800	4.5
Purbeck Lounge	240	120	150	250	227	2.7
Purbeck Bar	70	40	60	140	171	2.38
Stour Room 1	50	25	30	50	42	2.46
Stour Room 2	50	25	30	50	47	2.46
Stour Rooms 1 & 2	120	70	60	100	89	2.46
Avon Room	55	30	35	80	48	2.49
President's Suite	40	20	20	60	40	2.45
Bourne Lounge	390	95	225	420	256	2.46
Solent Restaurant	n/a	n/a	130	250	187	2.46
Pavilion						
Theatre	1518	n/a	n/a	n/a	n/a	n/a
Ballroom	800	380	900	950	1053	2.9
Phoebe Lounges	n/a	n/a	n/a	80	78	2.56
Lucullus	120	60	120	180	150	2.5
Committee Room	50	24	36	60	43	2.6
Circle Bar	80	50	n/a	120	57	2.5

For years, we've been the Centre of much publicity.

In its first ten years the Bournemouth International Centre has rarely been out of the limelight, either because of the big name entertainments, or the big name conferences, that have been held here.

Both are a testimony to the superb range of facilities we can offer, which have had to satisfy equally the demands of Shirley Bassey and Margaret Thatcher, to name just two of the stars who have shone at Bournemouth.

The Centre comprises three main halls under the same roof. Between them they offer endless possibilities for events of up to 4,000 delegates.

It isn't just large numbers of people we can accommodate either. We have all the facilities you would expect at a first class purpose built centre. And of course, our team of helpful, experienced professionals are always available to lend a hand and make sure everything runs smoothly.

*Get the facts now – there's much much more to this unrivalled location. Please call Kevin Sheehan, Director on **01202 552122**, Dept. EBH, Bournemouth International Centre, Exeter Road, Bournemouth, BH2 5BH. Fax: 01202 299220.*

We're famous for our facilities

61 Turbulence Ahead for European Air Travellers

Tony Lucking, Air Transport Consultant

European air travellers have been looking forward to a golden age of competition and lower air fares, but the looming reality is ever more crowded airports, and fares soaring because of the 'scarcity value' of overcrowded terminals, and the restricted supply of landing and take-off slots at a growing number of airports. The ending of state subsidies is leading to the demise of unprofitable routes, which are often of value to business users. A September 1995 report from the UK Civil Aviation Authority (CAA) found that up to 25 per cent of the international routes from France and other countries had been closed down recently. It reported also that after April 1995, British Airways (BA) cut back sharply the competitive European services operated by its 'quasi subsidiaries' Deutsche BA and TAT in France, following losses totalling £171 million in the previous two years; and that British Midland, hitherto the leading price cutter, was seeking fare increases. Furthermore, the European Commission is considering a fuel tax, on the basis that railways are more environmentally friendly, notably for shorter journeys – although the airlines argue that the case was exaggerated, *inter alia* by basing it on the performance of an older aircraft (the Boeing 727), and failing to appreciate that surface journeys are 30 per cent longer on average. Britain is being pressed to impose VAT on travel from the end of 1996, but has responded that its Maastricht 'opt-out' applies. The resulting cutback in the volume of the

highly price-elastic leisure traffic would increase costs for all travellers.

Environmental lobbyists are opposing the development of airports throughout Europe. London's Heathrow airport is perhaps the worst affected by overcrowding and shortage of 'slots', although similar problems have arisen at Frankfurt and Düfsseldorf, and the airlines warn that numerous other airports will be 'full' by the year 2000 or shortly after.

Several European airports are in effect bond-financed public utilities, and obtain capital relatively cheaply: Amsterdam secures funds at 6 per cent, though there is pressure to increase this figure. At Heathrow, the high return demanded by private investors, in combination with the system of 'single till' regulation of operational charges, has caused a unique problem. Under the 1986 Act, the UK Civil Aviation Authority (CAA) and the Monopolies and Mergers Commission have permitted increases in these charges at much less than the rate of inflation, because of the large profits flowing from retail concessions, car parking, etc. In the year ended March 1995, these activities generated profits of £231 million, vs only £42 million from landing fees, passenger charges, etc. Yet most of the £2 billion capital at Heathrow is invested in operational assets, and it is now clear that the regulatory system has made further investment difficult to justify when there is strong competition for funds. A privatized BAA plc

ICC Berlin –
The European Meeting Point.

Messe Berlin GmbH
Messedamm 22 · D-14055 Berlin
Telefon 030/30 38-30 49 · Telefax 030/30 38-30 32

Internationales
Congress Centrum
Berlin

Your Partner in Organizing Meetings and Incentives

The Iceland Convention and Incentive Bureau (IC&IB) was established as a non-profit-making organization in 1992.

It was set up by leading members of the Icelandic travel industry along with leading hotels, conference centres and professional organizers.

The Iceland Convention and Incentive Bureau is a service company whose role is to market convention facilities and incentive possibilities in Iceland at an international level.

IC&IB provides its services free of charge. These include:

- Assistance with corporate meeting and conference preparations
- Information about meeting facilities, availability of accommodation and flights
- Suggestions for incentives, special events, spouse programmes and safaris
- Organization of inspection visits
- Information about suppliers of services for conferences and incentives
- Promotional material and bid support for conferences
- List of events

IC&IB is a small unit providing a realistic and personal service. Just one phone call or fax and you have made your Iceland connection.

Finding a Suitable Venue

As the world conference and incentive industry grows, so does the problem of finding a suitable venue in a new setting. Organizers might have to risk sacrificing facilities, technical standards or comforts for a real change of scenery – while simply swapping to a new hotel and meeting room in the same old metropolitan surroundings might turn a conference into a monotonous, routine affair.

In Iceland, we feel we can strike a healthy balance. Hotels, conference facilities, support services and modern comforts are on a par with the rest of Western Europe. What makes Iceland stand out as a venue is its unique natural beauty and pure environment, even in the capital. Dramatic volcano and glacier scenery begins right on Reykjavik's doorstep, within easy reach for conference delegates – and conversely, action-packed incentive trips are never far from the comforts of the city.

Iceland is just 2-3 hours by air from the European continent. A friendly country with an outstanding reputation for stability and personal safety.

Welcome to Iceland – for a real change.

Ársaell Hardarson, *Managing Director,*
Jóhanna Kristín Tómasdóttir
Tel.: +00 3545 626070
Fax: +00 3545 626073
Stephen Barnes
Sales & Marketing Manager
Tel.: 0171-387 5732   Fax: 0171-387 5711

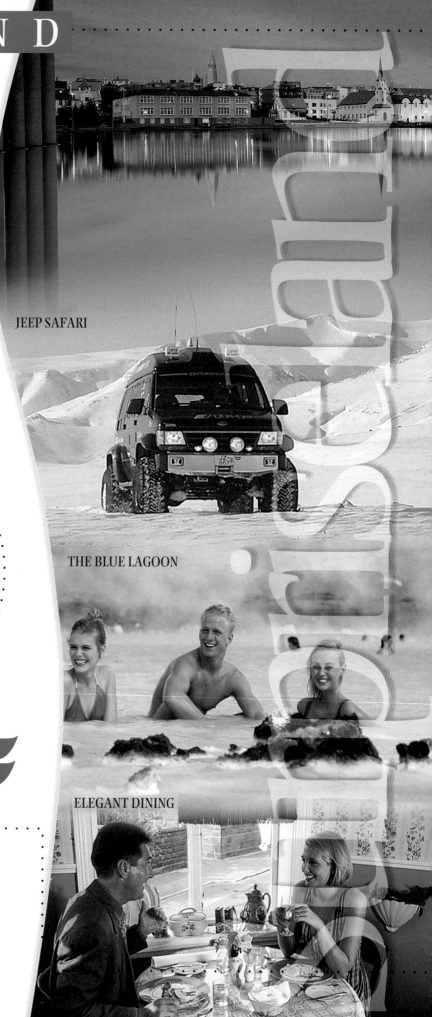

must consider whether its available capital can be more profitably employed in the USA, Australia or South Africa. Consequently, and assuming planning permission is granted, Terminal 5 will not be opened until 2003, even though BAA says that it is needed in 'about 1977 … to maintain service standards'. The financial imperative for the company is a large surge of customers on opening day! Yet current passenger numbers are running some 10 per cent in front of forecasts made only two–three years ago, adding to the congestion already encountered at the airport. Hence, there is an urgent need to revise the present regulatory system.

A further worrying aspect of airport capacity shortages is that all airlines nowadays are required to maximize profits, and long-haul services are much more profitable than those within Europe. So when there are restricted 'vacancies' on particular services, because a shortage of airport capacity forces the airline to use undersized aircraft, its yield control computer will 'cherry pick' the most profitable passengers. One of the conditions imposed on Air France by the Commission in authorizing the recent tranche of state aid was that it adopted computerized yield control, and a system purchased from American Airlines comes into use next year. A sophisticated system of this sort increases the average fare charged by 6–8 per cent, and the latest programs ('origin and destination' systems) examine the passenger's entire itinerary to maximize overall profitability. Thus, for example, an economy passenger Hamburg–London–New York who buys a ticket in Deutschmarks will yield nearly £400 more than two UK passengers purchasing respectively a £206 Club ticket for the European sector, plus an economy ticket London–New York at £422 – even though the latter is priced at nearly twice cost. As the UK CAA pointed out in a depressing report on European long-haul routes (November 1994), the fares charged by the four airlines on this route have converged at what was previously the highest level – a sad setback for those who hoped that a golden age of competition was in prospect; particularly when the USA is normally in the vanguard of anti-trust activity.

Among BA's evidence to the Heathrow Terminal 5 planning enquiry is a report by Coopers and Lybrand on the consequences for business users if the terminal is not built. Some services will have to move to less accessible airports, but the scarcity of terminal space is forecast to raise the average cost of

travel by between £78 and £87 per flight (ie double for a return trip). The airlines will be able to sell many more of the scarce seats at premium prices, and the yield control programs will exploit this situation to produce a 'famine' of Eurobudget and economy tickets. Currently, 57 per cent of business people flying BA purchase economy or cheaper tickets, but the airline's outstanding profit performance has been achieved to a considerable extent by its leadership in yield control. Although local European fares are often higher (in Deutschmarks, for example), BA's average 'take' is usually higher than that for other airlines, and Britons usually pay more than others. Indeed, some European airlines rarely charged their business passengers the published fare – although the Commission's recent actions on subsidy should end this happy situation!

Another worry is the wider lessons to be learnt from the withdrawal of numerous unprofitable long-haul services at UK regional airports. Although the aircraft were usually well filled, the airlines said that there were inadequate numbers of profitable business passengers, indicating that business passengers are required to cross-subsidise the leisure users. This deduction is confirmed by IATA cost committee data for the pre-recession year 1990–91, which showed

that there was a profit margin of 48 per cent on the Atlantic business class services, but a loss of 7.5 per cent in the rear cabin. Yet the economy fares are highly profitable, eg the £422 London–New York cited above: the problem is the volume and level of the discount fares.

This could be due to the airlines' need to sell off excess capacity arising from the recession. But it could also be due to one of the historic curses of competition in public passenger transport. From George Shillibeer's 1828 omnibuses onwards, 'head-on' competition has usually led successively to numerous operators on each route, excess capacity, subeconomic fares, bankruptcies, and finally cartelization or collusion. Is this why so many airlines have disappeared in the USA since deregulation? Is this what has happened on the Atlantic route, and is it what could happen in Europe? Or will the rapid advances in computerized yield control, and the resulting ability to segment the profitable 'on demand' traffic, enable the airlines to defeat this historic problem, while continuing rat-race competition in the rear of the aircraft? Whatever the answers, the airlines are moving on from the railway age of public services at public expense.

How do you stop your business committing a crime?

If you take an unauthorised photocopy of this publication, you may be guilty of a crime.

It is called theft.

The theft of copyright is just like stealing a magazine from a newsagent.

You can be caught, and you can be fined.

But take out a photocopying licence from the Copyright Licensing Agency and you have paid for the copyright, just as if you had paid for the magazine.

It's as simple as that. So take out a licence now.

Ring this number

If you want to take out a licence or tell us about unauthorised copying, please ring the
COPYWATCH HOTLINE: 0171 436 4242

Management Buy-Out of
Red Star Parcels Limited

from

British Railways Board

Equity provided by:

BZW Private Equity Limited

Debt provided by:

TSB Commercial Finance Limited

The undersigned advised the purchaser

_____

September 1995

**This announcement appears as a
matter of record only.**

KPMG Corporate Finance

City Jet

General advantages of Business Aviation

The most important advantages of general aviation are as follows:

• Direct flights to airports that are not or not directly served by the airlines • No "Check In"/"Check Out"/time delay • No long distances to reach the aircraft • no customs implications • No long distances to the terminal • Parking possibility only 50 meters from the aircraft • Minimizing of overnights at the destination • Possibility of pre- and post-conferences during the flight in quiet atmosphere • No need for change of aircraft for smaller destination airports • Personal service before departure and during the flight • Departure-time is determined by the passengers, not by the schedules of the airline • Luxurious interior equipment of the aircrafts • Quality catering, possibility of special requirements • High-level training of the staff

1992 – Foundation of City Jet

In 1992 Dr. Ernst C. Strobl founded one of the most solid companies of Business Aviation in Austria – CITY-JET Business Airline Vienna, which matches well; with his professional as a trader/businessman in the transport line of business. After two years of very intensive work CITY-JET may be considered one of the most versatile and financially strong enterprises. In the first two years CITY-JET started its operation with one Citation 550 until it became what CITY-JET represents today. CITY-JET is the number 1 for Business Aviation in Eastern Austria and shares 80% of the Austrian Business Aviation market with its West Austrian competitor TYROLEAN JET SERVICE.

Corporation structure

The majority of CITY-JET's shares is owned by Dr. Ernst Strobl, 10% of them by the DECSCO GmbH. The stock capital of the company equals approximately US$1,3 millions.

1994: ATS 45 millions turnover

After its start in 1992 CITY-JET's turnover in 1993 was already about ATS seven millions – this with four employees and one single own aircraft (Cit 550) only. In the first six months of 1994 the turnover increased to more than ATS 20 millions, the successful year of 1994 ended up with a total turnover of about ATS 45 millions and break even profit situation.

Personnel structure

At present CITY-JET employs 19 fixed employees five of which are captains, five more co-pilots as well as six administration employees and three technicians. Fifteen more staff members work for CITY-JET on working contracts as pilots, co-pilots or flight attendants.

7 aircraft operated and/or managed

The total of CITY-JET's fleet consists of 7 aircraft of various types held and operated or managed for private and/or corporate owners subject to different types of contracts.

4 Airtaxi jets

By now, CITY-JET's airtaxi charter fleet is composed of four modern business jets "Citation 500" "550" for 6 to 8 PAX, "Falcon 20" for 12 PAX and "British Aerospace HS 125/600/731" for 9 PAX. Other privately owned aircrafts are frequently chartered by CITY-JET in order to optimise their use of capacity. With its capacities up to 12 Pax CITY-JET operates the second biggest type-airfleet in Austria.

3 Aircraft managed

A foreign registered DASSAULT Falcon 50 is operate d under a aircraft management contract for the time it is used for the E uropean corporate business purposes of the owners.

The technical supervision for a LEAR 36 as well as an opera5tional contract supplies CITY-JET with small long-range jet capacity.

A FOKKER 27 MK 500 is being held on CITY-JET's registered and supplied with licences and technical and operational staff. Its operation is dedicated to Freight Charter Services.

1994: ATS 6 millions subcharter brokerage

Moreover, CITY-JET is the biggest broker in the fields of subcharter for long-distance flights. If required, CITY-JET charters additional aircraft owned by foreign aviation companies such as small jets for 5-8 PAX or Challengers for up to 16 PAX. In the year of 1994 CITY-JET passed on about 400 flight hours to third party contractors which equals a turnover of about ATS 8 millions.

The City-Jet fleet

On the base of official licences and register CITY-JET operates presently five aircraft of the following aircraft types (Falcon 50 and Lear 36 are registered privately):

Dassault Falcon 20

type: 2-engine middle-class business jet for short and middle distances

Range:	2,500 km
Country of production:	France
Passenger capacity:	9 to 12 PAX
Cabin size:	172 cm
Speed:	860 km/h

British Aerospace HS 125

type; 2-engine middle-class business jet for middle and long distances

Range:	24,200 km
Country of production:	Great Britain
Passenger capacity:	9 PAX
Cabin size:	172 cm
Speed:	840 km/h

Citation II/550

type: 2-engine extended small-class business jet for short and middle distances

Range:	2,500 km
Country of production:	USA
Passenger capacity:	8 PAX
Cabin size:	142 cm
Speed:	720 km/h

Citation I/500

type: 2-engine small-class business jet for short distances

Range:	1,900 km
Country of production:	USA
Passenger capacity:	5 to 6 PAX
Cabin size:	142 cm
Speed:	680 km/h

Fokker 27

type: 2-engine cargo jet-prop for short and middle distances

Range:	2,500 km
Country of production:	Netherlands
Cargo capacity:	1.7 tons
Cabin size:	192 cm
Speed:	420 km/h

1,200 business travellers 500,000 miles flown

In 1994 CITY-JET brought approximately 2,400 business travellers to about 70 different destination in Western and Eastern Europe, Africa, the Middle East and Asia. The fleet made about 500,00000 flight miles in the year of 1994 (approximately 120 to 180 flight hours per month) with a grade of reliability of 98.97% (only four delays caused by operational reasons occurred in 1994). In busy times up to eight aircraft are in action at the same time.

The turnover of single commissions ranges between ATS 30,000, – and ATS 1,6 millions per flight – dependent on the type of aircraft.

Partner companies

For technical concerns the co-operation with aircraft producers plays an important role. CITY-JET may name the following companies as its strategic partners; *Dassault Falcon Service, Le Bourget, Paris; Cessna Citation, Wichita, USA; British Aerospace, Raytheon Corporate jets, GB*

For the current technical maintenance CITU-JET has arrangements with the most important maintenance hangers/dockyards in Austria and abroad; *Vienna Aircraft Service, Vienna Schwechat; Austrian Airlines, Vienna Schwechat; Dassault Falcon Service, Le Bourget, Paris, France; Jet Aviation, Zurich/Basel, Switzerland; Dornier, Oberpfaffenhofen, Germany*

City-Jet sets new standards for business aviation

Quality – Exceptional emphasis is put upon the operational security. Particular customers' service and care is to be performed above average.

Own capital – An unusually high share of own capital for this line of business guarantees economical security, independence on credit organizations as well as solvency towards creditors.

Crew training – A contract with Flight Safety, one of the internationally most acknowledged training centers for pilots, guarantees outstanding training for all flight operation staff annually (pilots, technical engineers, dispatchers). With training investments of 1¹/₂ million Austrian Schilling every yet CITY-JET achieves a level of experience that is hardly reached by any other company in this business.

Maintenance – Due to the economical stability of CITY-JET maintenance is no domain to save money: for strategic considerations maintenance is always performed in time. All technical staff members attend courses regularly in order to stay up to date as far as maintenance know-how is concerned.

From June 1995 on CITY-JET will be licenced as JAR145 service station in Vienna and so will be able to perform own line maintenance, component change and a certain extent of repair for incoming third party customers.

Know how in the fields of transportation

With a 3-head managerial group: Dr. Strobl – transport economist, capital Lichtner-Hoyer – commercial director and responsible for legal concerns and Ing. Grunt – Flight-operational director 14,500 flight hours total) CITY-JET is able to offer most competent advice for both, charter customers and aircraft owners.

Official qualifications

Based on years of correct co-operation with the Austrian authorities for aviation CITY-JET's official licences are permanently checked to meet the European standards of aviation law.

Neutrality

Neither external political for financial factors have any influence upon the development strategy of CITY-JET. Due to the exclusion of any political or other ties of friendship, equal loyalty and neutrality to any customer can be guaranteed.

Price structure

The prices of CITY-JET are competitive in relation to its performance that is characterized by a big variety of accompanying services and special flexibility. A Business jet pays within a range of 1¹/₂ hours with a minimum of 5 PAX if compared to the airline rates.

Client structure

CITY-JET's clientele comprises a large variety of enterprises, artists, financially strong private persons from Austria and abroad as well as hospitals and representatives of the Austrian Federal Administration and Government.

Development of General Aviation in Austria

From 1980 to 1990 General Aviation –also called "Business Aviation" – developed as a relatively new segment of aviation and became an increasingly indispensable factor, especially for business travellers whose requirements such as free choice of schedule and destination could not be satisfyingly fulfilled by the big airlines.

A veritable boom in the eighties and the opening of Eastern Europe were the reasons for an uncontrolled and oversized offer. At the beginning of the nineties this led to a severe financial pressure for many companies that could no longer keep up the multitude of aircrafts due to their intensive maintenance and financial cost pressure.

In the past two years the resignment of a few important companies by bankruptcy and the reduction of the total offered airfleet by more than 12 aircrafts (weight classes C, D and F) general aviation underwent a fundamental change of offer-structure – and at the same time a loss of reputation.

The deficiency of services offered since 1992 as well as the expected positive economical development allowed the anticipation of some additional potential for general aviation.

Actual offer situation

At present, there are only two general aviation companies in Austria that dispose over more than three jets, namely Tyrolean Jet Service and City-Jet; others such as Air Med Grossmann Air Service, Air Salzburg, Comtel, Lauda, Almeta, LFS, Air Styria, Goldeck and Litag operate between one and three aircraft.

The offered performances of all general aviation companies are essentially similar; business flights within Europe and neighbouring countries. The quality of the services such as hired personnel, pilot's training, quality of maintenance and service organization, however, often differs significantly.

Most general aviation companies employ between one and five employees; additional staff – mainly pilots – are short-termly hired on base of contract of work. Only the bigger companies dispose over fixed employed staff for every aircraft, supplementary services and overhead organisation.

The actual companies' dimensions that vary greatly and are sometimes vaguely defined due to propaganda reasons can be checked at Austro Control (operators register) and at the Federal Ministry of Public Economy and Traffic (CAA).

Business Aviation in the European market

Especially in 1993 and 1994 the Austrian Business Aviation had to face new competition due to the changes within the European Union and to take a new orientation versus foreign competitors outside the country.

In order to achieve an optimise use of capacity and a Break Even economic situation foreign competitors have already occupied the whole of the European market. It is for that reason that the Austrian general aviation companies, too, should extend their activities on the entire European market.

Restricted capacities in Austria

Two factors made it possible for foreign competitors to serve customers in Austria directly: on the one hand the insufficient availability of bigger types of aircraft in Austria and on the oth er hand the cessation of a long-distance jet that has been operated until 1993. A s far as smaller aircrafts for 6 to 8 PAX are concerned, foreign competition, has increased in the meantime. In this respect the Austrian companies should provide a better and extended offer-potential in future.

Renovation of the Vienna General Aviation Center

The Vienna General Aviation Center is in more than a bad shape and hinders the business aviation companies represented in Vienna from a proper service. In order to be able to meet the requirements of the future a renovation and improvement of infra-structure of hangars and office space is absolutely indispensable.

Foreign Aviation companies with a representation in Austria

With a short time foreign aviation companies will have the possibility to establish themselves in Austria. Austrian Business Aviation companies will have one useful weapon against that development, namely to offer good prices and performance as well as solid service.

The future of Business Aviation

If one considers the over-occupation of the big airlines on the one hand the financial problems of some of them on the other hand, a stabilization of ticket prices is likely. Due to many inconveniences such as the overflow of the airports, journeys to the airline-places getting longer and longer and mass-dispatch, many companies and private persons regard private jets as the better alternative.

Air Partner

Nordic Travel Network was founded a couple of years ago, mainly because of 2 reasons:

– 1 –

Today, there is an oligopoly situation in the Swedish Travel market. Two International travel agencies (American Express and Hogg Robinson) controls 70% of the total commercial travel industry – hence to this, the Swedish market needs an independent strong alternative.

– 2 –

The owner of Nordic Travel Network have a very strong belief in Service concept – at its peak.

The travel industry has always been a low margin business, and that simply states that You cannot compete price-wise, and as a result of this statement, Nordic Travel Network have formed a group of companies, that fulfils many of the needs that a company can demand from a full service travel agency.

Nordic Travel Network is today concentrated in Stockholm, but will expand in Gothenburg and Malmö during this year.

NORDIC TRAVEL NETWORK
– A short presentation of the different companies –

N.T.N. Travel agency, Commercial
Five different locations, serves over 1,000 companies in the Stockholm area, with all common services like I.A.T.A. tickets, Hotels and Care Hire.
Company profiles, that also includes personal demands and personal vacation assistance.

N.T.N. operates with the global booking system Worldspan – a system that works in Windows.

During this fall, all the agencies will be able to work directly in the booking system and give all clients an alternative of using a competitive alternative to major airlines – AIR PARTNER. This is a calculation system, designed by AIR PARTNER, that vies an offer regarding destination, distance, flight time and price.

N.T.N. Travel agency, Private
Active Travel is a Tour Operator, specialising in Round the World Trips. As such, the agency does have very good agreements with all major Airlines and Hotels around the world, that of course helps the Network's clients in all ways.

All Nordic Travel Network's clients have access to the network's companies and partners, like, Ekvik.

Ekvik is a luxurious Conference Hotel, designed for top management groups. Thirty minutes from the heart of Stockholm, right at the waterfront of the fabulous archipelago, surrounded by the Baltic Sea is Ekvik located. The main aspect of the design is to adjust the nature to the building. Only natural material has been used, the light is always available.

Ekvik is more than a conference, it is a concept of its own. To really understand it, it must be experienced, to feel the material, understand the force, the water, the light and the silence.

Ekvik has 6 single rooms, 2 double rooms and 1 junior suite, 2 fully equipped conference rooms, 1 completely soundproof room protected against all interception. Dining rooms and meetings rooms, relaxation rooms *and last but not least*, 2 unique sauna as with a breathtaking view over the archipelago.

Furthermore, Ekvik is a member of Design Hotel International, a new group of designed Hotels worldwide, that offers clients a complete new, designed Hotel concept throughout the world.

Business Service Club. Client-related Helpdesk
Business Service Club is located in Stockholm, Gothenburg and Malmö since 1987. Through years of contracts and negotiations, B.S.C., can offer its clients advantages and prices that are extremely cost-effective. The service is free of charge – *one call* – all service, like • Tickets to events • Kick-off's and clients event of all sorts – small or big, near or far, budget or luxury – no problems! • Conferences or Hotels – always the best alternative • Night Clubs and Restaurants, B.S.C.'s V.I.P. card gives You many advantages.

Business Service Club, Incoming
B.S.C. have many years of experience in taking care of all kinds of groups, all in order to maximize the guests comfort and satisfactions.

Teaterbolaget
Three of the most interesting scenes in Stockholm's theatres, offers 3 different high quality shows – 1 International show at Berns "Hugo Berns Wonderful Universe."

Nordic Travel Network – +46 8 248 1200   Fax +46 8 7172086
Ekvik– +46 8 570 19230   Fax +46 857019270
Business Service Club – +46 8 702 0070   Fax +46 8 7021820

CHAPTER

62 Conferences and Exhibitions

Peter Cotterell, Managing Director, The Meetings Forum

The way that organizations view conferences and exhibitions has been substantially altered during the recession years, some would say to the advantage of those attending them.

In terms of conferences the two- or three-day residential presentation has given way to the one-day event. Delegate numbers have dropped sharply and state-of-the-art audiovisual extravaganzas have largely been replaced with interaction and syndicate work. Four- and five-star hotels are losing business to universities and dedicated management training centres.

Much of this change has simply been financially driven, rather than carefully considered strategy. What is emerging, however, is that the alterations have often improved the quality of the gatherings for the delegates. The shorter events have forced organizers to be more succinct and run tighter programmes. Lower numbers have allowed more U-shaped and boardroom-style layouts, encouraging more individual delegate involvement. This 'talking with' alternative to the theatre-style 'talking at' the delegates has enhanced the delegate experience and improved retention. And the enforced use of the lower cost academic venues has shown many formerly sceptical organizers that they can supply a very high standard of meetings facility, such as dedicated purpose-built lecture theatres, coupled with an atmosphere that positively encourages learning. Bedrooms and food,

once the two main reasons academic venues were shunned, have been substantially upgraded at many centres as they have begun to realise the financial potential of the market.

So what of the future for conferences? Bluntly, some don't have one. More than one organization has found that less time away means more work gets done, particularly as so many staff now operate alone with their personal computer. Some have found that cancelling the motivational sales conference has actually increased sales, by cutting the amount of time the salesforce is off the road. One Australian kitchenware company recorded an increase of over 4 per cent, and a saving of £60,000, when the four-day annual gathering was shelved.

For those conceiving, organizing and running conferences, there are some predictions that might prove helpful.

- Delegate involvement will increase. There will be more syndicate work, management games and teambuilding, less 'sit there and watch this'.
- The value of the right type of conference food, in terms of its effect on delegate retention, will become more widely recognized. The serving of alcohol will continue to diminish.
- The pressure of increased workload as the economy lifts will force more organizers to run events at weekends and during quiet business periods, such as the summer. More partners and even children will accompany delegates.

Travelling times will be cut by running events nearer to home.

▓ More commercial conferences will be run alongside exhibitions, where delegates may be easier to obtain.

▓ For small meetings videoconferencing will continue to find favour. For the larger event, it will continue to be an audiovisual novelty, except for those using large numbers of overseas speakers.

▓ More long residential events will be staged overseas as organizers discover that a week-long event can be run at a lower price, including travel costs, in destinations and resorts living off the tourist trade and relatively empty from November to March.

The exhibition market has also seen much change during the recession, some of which will undoubtedly improve things for exhibitors and visitors, if not the organizers and the venues.

The lack of business around has actually stopped many companies exhibiting altogether. Those that have continued to spend money on the medium have chosen to do so at fewer shows, and with smaller stands. The effect of this can perhaps be measured in the financial performance of one major organizer, Blenheim plc, whose share values have slipped from over £6 to just over £2 in the last three years. And, according to a recent analysis of exhibition/conference venues in the UK, over half are in financial difficulties.

Today's exhibitors are far more careful with their money and very few exhibit 'for PR' or 'to fly the flag', choosing instead to be more hard-nosed and exhibit for orders and sales leads, and to judge the event on its ability to generate both. The presentation now reflects this new order and the extravagant double-decker stands, lavish entertaining and decorative promotional girls have become the exception rather than the rule. Effort and budget now tend to be put into more serious areas such as stand staff training, staging live demonstrations, data capture and lead tracking after the show.

Visitors, too, have had to become more business like. The numbers actually attending trade events have dropped, as work load has increased and organizations have questioned the necessity for the number of staff previously attending. Hardly any now stay overnight, even for overseas events, and the distance that many are prepared to travel has been reduced.

So what of the future for exhibitions, both for exhibitors and visitors?

▓ More companies will find that running their own roadshows and attracting a small group of committed buyers is more effective than traditional exhibiting.

▓ As the restrictive 'gentlemen's agreements' between exhibition centres, organizers and hotels break down, more organizations will find the value of simply running a hospitality suite alongside a major exhibition.

▓ More organizers will recognize the above need and provide for it, rather than trying to prevent it gaining momentum.

▓ Exhibitions will become shorter – two days rather than three, and three rather than four.

▓ More exhibitors will evaluate their events on a cost-per-lead basis, and compare this with the figures achieved with advertising, direct mail and PR. Less exhibitors will fall for the silly 'Your competitors are there. Can you afford not to be?' ploy from organizers.

▓ More UK organizers and venues will realize that forcing exhibitors to use favoured and expensive contractors (to milk a commission), supplying awful food at high prices, and exploiting visitors with charges for car-parking and cloakroom services are the ultimate in short termism. More venues and organizers will work together to provide a visitor-friendly and exhibitor-friendly environment.

■ More organizers, aware that the industry has a well-deserved 'cowboy' image, will take steps to redress this. More will have their visitor figures independently audited and less will lie about their performance.

■ Visitors will become more demanding, request-

ing catalogues to study in advance of the exhibition, free travel to the event and better information about the exhibitors when they arrive.

■ More organizers will see the folly of arranging more than one event for the visitor to view, and of conferences that take buyers out of the exhibition area.

■ Those trade exhibitors showing their wares at whatever venue the Millennium Exhibition is staged at in 2001 will notice a sharp drop in business gained as visitors are lured away with yet another distraction.

CASTLE HOWARD, YORK

EVELYN WAUGH chose Castle Howard as the romantic setting for his novel "Brideshead Revisited' Granada chose it for their major television series.

This magnificent house was designed in 1699 by Sir John Vanburgh, with the aid of Nicholas Hawksmoor, for Charles Howard, 3rd Earl of Carlisle, and it is still lived in by the Howard family. It has rooms aglow with painting by Rubens, Gainsborough, Reynolds and Holbein; statuary from ancient Greece and Rome; furniture by Sheraton and Chippendale; exquisite porcelain and china.

There is a long tradition of warm hospitality and lavish entertaining at Castle Howard, and this continues in strength today in the form of Banquets, Receptions, Recitals, Wine Tastings, Clay Pigeon Shooting and Activity Days.

This magnificent house is the ideal backdrop for any occasion, contact the Promotions Manager for details and menus.

An evening at Castle Howard begins with a special tour of the House with an organist playing in the Chapel and musicians playing from the Gallery of the Great Hall during the Champagne Reception. Uniformed footmen are in the

background to guide your guests through the antique Passages and State Apartments into Dinner in the Long Gallery. Musicians play during dinner, and the evening could end with a surprise Firework Display on the North Lawns with music and marching by a Military Band.

Superb wines have always been offered at Castle Howard and our Promotions manager is a member of the elite Council of Judges, the Jurade of St. Emilion which pronounces on the classification of the wines of St. Emilion.

Location and parking

Castle Howard is situated in North Yorkshire 15 miles from York and 26 miles from Scarborough on the A64. It is easy to reach the main road from any direction. Nearest stations are Malton 6 miles and York 15 miles (London to York 2 hours). The nearest airport is Leeds/Bradford 40 miles. There is on site parking for 5,000 cars.

Castle Howard, York YO6 7BZ
Tel: (01653) 648444 Fax: (01653) 648462
Manager: Ian Martin
Conference contact: Judy Sladden

Battersea Park

Site and History

Battersea Park offers a unique combination of the natural, historical landscape of a 200 acre Victorian park and facilities to accommodate the most sophisticated conferences and corporate entertaining. Bordering on the Thames, Battersea Park has gardens, lakes, water features, and leisure facilities for both casual play and large-scale corporate competitions.

The park's tradition of hosting major events such as the Festival of Britain's Pleasure Gardens has left a number of prime show sites with water, electricity, drainage and vehicle access. The largest of these is the British Genius site, three acres of full-enclosed hard standing, which easily accommodates conference centres, exhibitions, cultural festivals, trade shows and other major events. The sites can easily be adapted to suit your needs with the expert help of our events team – whether it be a small product launch at the lakes

gallery, a reception on the Grand Vista overlooking the pools, fountains and clipped yews, a ball on the romantic riverside terraces or an international conference on the British Genius site.

To complement the outdoor sites is a lakeside Pump House recently converted into a gallery and function rooms. The award-winning architectural details and parkland views make it a popular venue for seminars, receptions and press launches.

Transport & Communications

Battersea Park is in the centre of London, at the heart of a good communications network for the rest of the country. It is well served by the motorway (A3, M3, A4) and trains, and hospitality buses are often arranged from Sloane Square and Victoria for large events. On site parking for 1000 cars is also available.

**Battersea Park
London SW11 4NJ
Tel 0171-924 7505
Fax 0181-871 7533**

Heathlands Hotels

Situated in Bournemouth and the New Forest, Heathlands Hotels are ideally placed in quiet locations, with easy access to the motorway networks and provide the perfect venue for meetings, conferences, training and team building exercises or just a chance to recharge your batteries on a leisure break.

The Bournemouth Heathlands Hotel has 115 en suite bedrooms, and extensive conference and banqueting for up to 270 delegates in a variety of 7 conference suites. New for 1995 is a purpose built Training Centre offering 1 main and 4 syndicate rooms all linked by CCTV with the advantage of a dedicated Business Centre which has up to date technology, including PC and access to the InterNet. Relaxation is provided by

an indoor health suite and outdoor heated swimming pool.

The New Forest Heathlands Hotel has 52 en suite bedrooms and includes 12 executive rooms, with whirlpool bath, and conference and banqueting for up to 200 delegates in a variety of 5 conference suites. Ideally placed just off J2 of the M27, makes it a first choice for meetings and conferences, and the 13 acres of grounds gives access for team-building exercises. Relaxation is provided by indoor health suite and 9 hole putting green together with 16th Century Vine Inn Pub.

Bournemouth Heathlands Hotel
Grove Road, East Cliff
Bournemouth BH1 3AY
Telephone: (01202) 553336

New Forest Heathlands Hotel
Romsey Road, Ower,
Southampton SO51 6ZJ
Telephone: (01703) 814333

Denmark

Dotted around the globe there are a number of countries which are a constant surprise to the first time visitor. The traveller, confident with a suitcase full of preconceived ideas and misconceptions, arrives only to find that the destination is nothing like what he or she expected.

Denmark is one such country.

Now everybody has heard of Denmark; it's a small country in Scandinavia. So perhaps there are fjords and reindeer, pretty girls and bitterly cold winters, lots of bacon and it's going to be expensive. Nothing much to see, not really worth making a detour. All wrong. Very wrong.

Yes, this is a small country – only about 16,630 square miles in all with a population of just over five million, about a quarter of whom are concentrated in and around the capital city, Copenhagen. No fjords, well a couple of large inlets but no mountains or hills to qualify them as fjords in the accepted sense; those reindeer which are around tend to spend their lives in the zoo or as exotic pets, and as for the bacon, well the Danes are not great bacon eaters and the best of it gets sent to the UK anyway Yes there are pretty girls, the winters are not that much colder than those in Britain and prices are about the same as they are in English Home Counties.

As for there being nothing much to see, this is where the visitor is confronted with the first big surprise. The truth is there is a lot to see in Denmark; its long and sometimes troubled history has left the country littered with castles, Medieval towns and often exotic country houses. Copenhagen itself, founded in the 12th Century, has the full range of palaces, grand theatres, historic buildings and scruffy Bohemian districts,which are the hallmark of all respectable European capitals. The surprising thing about Copenhagen is that, unlike London or Paris, all the interesting things to see are in a small concentrated area and literally within walking distance of each other. In fact this is an excellent city for strolling around since not only has a large part of its centre been turned into a pedestrian zone but Copenhagen is also probably the safest capital in Europe.

English is widely spoken; like the Dutch the Danes have recognised that few foreigners are going to be tempted to learn their language so virtually all of them are skilled in speaking not only English but often one or two other languages as well.

This being so, Copenhagen is almost certainly the best place in the world for an American visiting Europe for the first time to come to grips with European culture. Copenhagen has it all in one small compact area – royal palace complete with guardsmen with bearskins, some of Europe's most beautiful and exotic church spires, museums. art galleries, a weird Renaissance royal exchange building, lots of traditional shops and modern retail outlets and the Tivoli Gardens, the last remaining Victorian pleasure garden with restaurants and fun attractions to amuse young and old. And of course there are lots of pubs where the country's world-famous lagers can be enjoyed.

Outside of Copenhagen provincial Denmark has many attractive historic towns to visit including Roskilde, once the nation's capital, Odense, the birthplace of Hans Christian Andersen the fairy story writer, Ålborg, Århus and of course Helsingør, made famous by Shakespeare as the fictional home of the ill-fated Hamlet.

For the UK meetings planner, Denmark offers a wide range of extremely useful options and it is worth noting that, according to the Brussels-based Union of International Associations Copenhagen ranks amongst the ten most popular host cities for International congresses and as such is the most important conference destination in this part of Europe.

The city's main meetings facility is the Bella Center/ Copenhagen Congress Center which was designed to host both large and small events. Conveniently located just under four miles from Copenhagen's International airport at Kastrup, its largest meeting room can seat up to 4,000 delegates theatre style or 2,220 schoolroom style. In addition there are 16 other smaller rooms of varying capacities so the Bella can easily cope with a number of events at the same time, which it frequently does.

Copenhagen's second facility is the SAS Falconer Center, again purpose-build centre, which has a theatre style capacity of up to 2,150 theatre style. Two large modern hotels in the city, the 471 room Sheraton Copenhagen and the 542 room Radisson SAS Scandinavia both have large meetings facilities suitable for both association and corporate meetings. The Sheraton, near the city's central station, boasts a large ballroom which can handle 1,200 delegates theatre style while the Scandinavia, a little out of the city on the main highway leading to the airport, has a slightly larger ballroom capable of accommodating 1,500 theatre style delegates.

In the provinces, both Århus and Ålborg in Jutland and Odense in Funen, boast modern state of the art facilities. The largest room at the Aalborghallen in Alborg can seat 1,460 delegates theatre style, Musikethuset Århus, a splendidly designed all purpose concert hall, can seat over 1,470 delegates. In Odense the city's main facility, the Odense Conference Center, can take up to 3,000 delegates.

Denmark's own unique contribution to the meetings industry is Scandicon and there are two of these institutions in the country, one just outside Kolding in Jutland and the other a mile or two out of Helsingør north of Copenhagen. The Scandicons are devoted to providing peace and tranquility, relaxation and concentrated thought. Superbly designed in the Scandinavian style with all the modern technological facilities any corporate meetings planner would care for, the Scandicons provide probably the most effective venues for small high-powered meetings in Europe. Both nestle in the countryside seemingly away from it all, both are excellent venues for small groups concentrating on knotty problems.

Not that Denmark takes itself seriously all the time by any means and the country provides the UK – and for that matter, other West European countries – with an wonderful opportunity for short incentive breaks.

The Danes, in the main a jovial people who love to party, make excellent hosts and this reflected in the way all visitors are treated in the country. A tight network of very professional destination management companies can provide a wide range of theme party and activity options including Viking feasts, Hamlet evenings, both trips and even rides on veteran railway trains, all of which is only to be expected.

What is not expected, and which is hardly known outside the country, is that the Danes, like the British, have their fair share of cranks and a distinct sense of the ridiculous. The result is the country in general and Copenhagen in particular offer a wide range of the oddest things to do and see. For instance there is a royal musket club which restricts its membership to the high members of Danish society; even the Queen of Denmark is a member. Members have shields or targets at which they shoot bolts from huge old muskets. The club house, Sølyst, is a beautiful little mansion which can be used for parties, incentive groups can enjoy shooting at their own target shields whilst sipping Champagne.

Barsen is the city's old Royal Exchange, a deliciously exotic building with a twisted spire of three dragons and a wonderful place for a gala dinner. St Gertruds Kloster is, as its name suggests, an old priory, a veritable warren of a place which is now a restaurant lit not by electricity but by thousands of dripping candles. A superb place for a Medieval dinner right in the heart of Copenhagen. For groups the sommelier, another crank in the Danish mould, opens bottles of Champagne with a quick swipe of a cutless.

But that is not all. There is one other surprise in Denmark for the first time visitor and the incentive planner. The cuisine.

Everybody has heard of Danish open sandwiches and at their best they are a unique contribution to international cuisine; Danish pastries, sadly, are not really Danish but Austrian in origin. The skilful way the Danes have in preparing herring makes an open sandwich an absolutely delightful gastronomic experience.

What is less well-known is that the Danes are also masters of other forms of dishes and, surprisingly enough, Copenhagen in particular is the best place outside France to sample European haute cuisine at its very finest. From roast pork to fragrant salmon, from superb and delicate game to lusty puddings, Danish cuisine is an absolute delight. And, compared with the UK – and France – it is surprisingly inexpensive, too.

It's only part of the real surprise the first time visitor finds in Denmark. the point is that while everybody thinks the country is Scandinavian, it is really part of the Continental European mainland and manages to merge the culture of Scandinavia proper with that of the rest of Europe – especially at the dinner table.

A Scandinavian country with strong Continental influences or a part of Continental Europe with a dash of the Viking?

Come and decide for yourself!

Silversea Cruises

In the US, cruising has long been a popular leisure activity, both with the consumer and business markets. Now Europe is gradually catching on. More ships are being built, European ports are opening up to cruise ships and itineraries are becoming more adventurous.

Industry statistics from the Passenger Shipping Association (PSA) show that for the past eight years, the number of UK citizens taking a cruise has shown a steady increase. Passenger numbers have trebled in that time. Bob Duffet, chief executive of the PSARA predicts that 1995/1996 will show the biggest increase so far.

This rise is reflected in the corporate sector. Cruising is emerging into an increasingly sophisticated European Incentive and Conference market, as a viable and cost effective alternative to land-based incentives. As the concept becomes more attractive to conference and incentive buyers, so cruise lines are targeting their products more precisely to satisfy the demands of the business market.

Advantages of cruising for incentive buyers

Why cruising? The concept of a cruise retains a high perceived value for incentive winners and high achievers. The old expectation of rubbing shoulders with ancient aristocrats tottering around the deck is gradually fading; the average age on a Caribbean cruise is is now just 42. An incentive cruise continues to provide strong motivation.

For buyers, the ac'vantages of cruising are many. 'One stop shopping' saves time and hassle in budgeting and organisation. Few lines, such as Silversea Cruises, offer exclusive packages which specify fixed and variable costs right from the beginning. Packages always include food, accommodation, on-board entertainment and use of meeting facilities. With a luxury product such as Silversea Cruises, the final price per ad allows for, all port taxes, and extras such as drinks – both alcoholic and non alcoholic – throughout the ship, gratuities, corporate branding and special events on board.

Such an arrangement removes the need for endless individual negotiations with hotels and restaurants, and unexpected extras should not appear on the bottom line. In addition, groups are transported to a number of different destinations in a relatively short space of time, without having to undergo the tiring procedures of checking in and of airports and venues. In short, cruising is a timely multi-national experience.

Another bonus for buyers is that the final bill represents good value for money. "The perceived value of cruising is extremely high", comments Len Wilcock, Chairman of Worldspan International Plc, "but when it comes down to it, the costs are relatively moderate. Clients get lots of added value in a cruise: meeting space, transport and the cruise staff are effectively part of your team to assist with whatever is required to make the trip successful. I would say that cruising has proven to be excellent value for money". Len Wilcock has organised over 20 cruises.

Exclusive Charter

If your organisation can afford it, chartering is one of the best ways for incentive groups to make the most of a cruise.

As an incentive organiser, if you are in a position to charter a whole ship, it is easier to make your guests feel privileged. The group can contribute to making the decisions, down to which beaches are visited, rather than being just one part of a larger picture, in which a corporate group is at risk of losing its identity. When chartering a vessel the client is in control and can even have a say in the itinerary.

Smaller vessels are designed to meet the specific needs of single group charter. Generally speaking, this type of ship has one standard of accommodation throughout, all facing; a shallow draft which allows access to smaller, secluded beaches and ports, a restaurant or meeting space with enough capacity to accommodate all the passengers together.

The Silversea product

Silversea Cruises' two ships *Silver Wind* and *Silver Cloud* are excellent examples of the top end of the cruising product. The 16,800 ton ships are extremely spacious, carrying a maximum of 296 passengers although the ships would, in theory, have been able to carry up to 600 passengers comfortably therefore the available space per passengers on these ships is extremely generous. All of the suites are sea-facing; and all have twin beds or a queen size bed, walk-in wardrobe, a marbled bathroom and problems of 'first' and 'second' class cabins which sometimes cause problems within incentive groups, will never arise.

The ships both have a large multi-tiered show lounge that can comfortably accommodate up to 300 guests together. This is invaluable for conference presentations involving all passengers; the lounge is fully equipped with state-of-the-art audio visual equipment, and the stage is large enough to display cars or other large items for product launches. Evening entertainment can also be centred here and with exclusive use, the branding possibilities are enormous and almost infinite.

The ships each have two restaurants, giving buyers plenty of choice when planning evening activities. The five star restaurant is large enough to accommodate everyone together for dinner, and even features a smaller private dining area. This is particularly useful if organisers wish to maintain a cohesive group with no outside distractions, for example, for a gala dinner with speeches and presentations. For more informal dining, the Terrace Cafe, on-deck barbecues or even en-suite dining facilities can be utilised.

The 1995-1995 itineraries of the *Silver Cloud* and *Silver Wind* include the Baltic and European capitals; the Mediterranean; Canada and Colonial America; South America and the Amazon; the Caribbean; the Far East and Indian Ocean; the South Pacific and Africa.

Maarten Tromp,
Director of Incentive Sales and Charters,
can be reached on
(44) 0171-739 4029.

Silversea have perfected their craft.

Silversea Cruises are now established as a key player in the incentive market. The company's twin ships, Silver Cloud and Silver Wind are widely recognised as two of the world's finest cruise ships.

Their sleek Italian lines and elegant styling set them apart from other luxury vessels, making the ultimate statement in modern cruise ship design.

At 16,800 tons, the Silversea ships could comfortably accommodate over twice as many passengers but capacity has been deliberately limited to 296 passengers to allow that extra measure of spaciousness, comfort and personal service.

This unique combination makes Silver Cloud and Silver Wind the perfect ships for group charters, incentives, business conferences and new product presentations on a grand scale.

Our all-inclusive policy makes Silversea an even more attractive business proposition.

Everything is included in the price: All-suite accommodation including all meals, activities and on-board entertainment; complimentary alcoholic and non-alcoholic drinks; all services of our Business Centre and all gratuities.

Whatever your business needs, our worldwide cruise programme can be tailored to meet your specific group travel and incentive requirements.

Call Maarten Tromp on 0171 729 1929. He'll help you find true perfection.

All-suite accommodation, 75% with verandah.

The perfect conference centre-seating for over 300.

SILVERSEA
The ultimate incentive programme

THE SILVERSEA INCENTIVE

• Luxury suites, 75% with own private verandah. • A la carte dining in restaurant or in-suite. • 24 hour service
• No tipping policy. • Conference facilities for over 300 guests. • Two-deck multi-tiered show lounge with seating for 314.
• Full telecommunications and audio-visual facilities on board. • C.C.T.V with support broadcasting for special bulletins in-suite. • Special shore excursions can be arranged. • All-inclusive, highly competitive price. • No hidden extras.

Silversea 77/79 Great Eastern Street London EC2A 3HU. Tel 0171 729 1929. Fax 0171 739 7512

Barbican Centre

The Barbican Centre is Europe's largest Arts and Conference Centre situated in the heart of the City of London. An attractive venue for international conventions, it is unique in its ability to offer a broad range of business and entertainment facilities.

The Centre offers the impressive Barbican Hall with seating for over 2,000 delegates, two theatres, three air-conditioned presentation cinemas and numerous smaller conference suites, as well as 4,000 sq metres of exhibition space.

Entertainment facilities include the Barbican Theatre, London base of the Royal Shakespeare Company; the Barbican Hall, home of the London Symphony Orchestra; the Barbican Art Gallery, which holds exhibitions of important national and international artists; plus a varied programme of free foyer events throughout the year.

Uniquely, the Centre has a superb atrium style indoor Conservatory with adjacent terrace and function rooms plus three lakeside restaurants creating a cosmopolitan ambience which is welcomed by delegates from all over the world.

For more information, please contact the Sales Team. Tel: 0171-638 4141. Fax: 0171-638 7832.

The Heart of the City

Innovation, Quality & Customer Care

Innovation, Quality & Customer Care, are they just buzz words? *By Geoffrey Riesel, Chairman of Radio Taxicabs (London) Ltd, CBI, (London Region) Councillor*

Britain's business's, as member of the EU, cannot seriously ignore the importance of the tenets of *innovation, quality and customer care.*

This applies to every industry, be it manufacturing, service or business to business.

At the *CBI* we have been preaching this philosophy, and at *Radio Taxicabs (London) Ltd,* the practice has become reality.

A determination to innovate, convinced us yet again, to invest in the latest "super highway" computer despatch technology. Our goal became the resolve to become the market leader in new services, such as international taxi facilities, striving for fresh working practices ahead of the competition, not only being first, but at the same time, 99.9% right.

Absolute conviction in the theology of quality, ensured heavy investment in training and working practices commensurate with our recent award of BS EN ISO 9002, quality management standards. Consistent quality being essential.

Customer care, means just that. If European companies are to compete in the new world order of rising markets, then establishing customer need, and ensuring that need is satisfied without fail, has become an 'absolute' priority. Listening to the client is the first stage, determining never to make excuses is the second, reliability particularly in the province of services is vital.

Using this simple formula, Radio Taxis and their 2000 drivers, have grabbed increased market share since August 1993. A spectacular monthly growth averaging 27% in their corporate services business, has made them, suddenly, the 'rising star' of their industry.

Innovation, quality and customer care are they just buzz words? – definitely not! *For Radio Taxis, London, the leading licensed radio taxi network, they are the very key to success!*

Contact details –
Mountview House, Lennox Road,
London N4 3TX
Tel: 0171-281 4659
Fax: 0171-281 5709

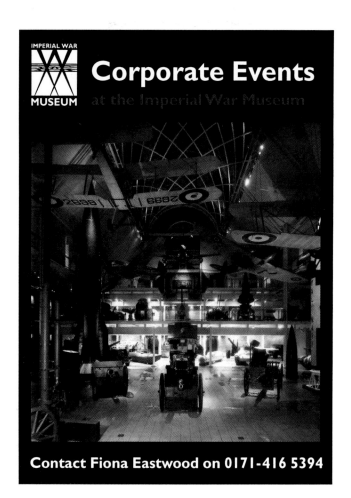

WESTMINSTER SOUND SYSTEMS

Leaders in simultaneous interpretation and specialised infra-red and hard wired audio-visual equipment for large and small conferences and factory tour groups. Among distinguished clients are The European Community; Western European Union; British Foreign and Commonwealth Office; World Bank; European Bank for Reconstruction and Development; International Wheat Council; International Coffee Growers' Association; American Express Euope; Wellcome Foundation; BBC; ICI; Lufthansa; Olivetti International; and many universities.

For free quotations and further information please contact:

Westminster Sound Systems
Wesminster House, Herschel Centre,
Church Street, Slough SL1 1PJ, UK.
Telephone: 01753 553325   Facsimile: 01753 553867
Freephone: 0800 592943

Westminster Sound Systems

According to a recent report from the EC, the only company they employ which is equipped with interpreters' booths for simultaneous interpretation conference work up to the EC standards, is Westminster Sound Systems. The company (which manages all of the audio systems in the Chambers of the Lords and Commons as well as their Select and Standing Committee rooms) can also cope with up to 20 languages and meetings of more than 1,000 delegates.

In addition to providing interpreters and state-of-the-art electronic equipment in many international locations as well as domestic ones, Westminster Sound Systems is familiar with top-level conferences (G7 – Heads of Governments, etc) and small groups. On occasion the small group interpretation work involves discreet, mobile tour systems which permit multi-lingual parties to inspect widespread working factories and processing plants.

Westminster is extremely helpful in guiding conference organisers through the maze of service possibilities and they also provide harassed planners a primer on do's and don'ts – a form of protection for all involved.

Their technicians are security vetted and this knowledge gives comfort to commercial enterprises who have concern over industrial secrets.

Asked what the commonest difficulties he encounters, Rob Wasmuth, General Manager, says many potential clients leave the ordering of audio services to the last minute and often they are unaware of their locations' technical problems and so need special guidance. But, he adds, that gives me an opportunity for bonding and often procures repeat orders.

Set in the heart of Maritime England, and with excellent road, rail and sea links, the University of Portsmouth is an ideal place to hold a conference, seminar, exhibition or training course.

The University has numerous halls, purpose built lecture theatres, and seminar or syndicate rooms to cater for every requirement, however specialised, and for up to 200 people.

During the summer, residential accommodation can be provided in either catered or self-catering halls.

Full, top quality catering services are available, providing anything from small, private lunches and buffets, to banquets for hundreds.

For further information, please contact: Central Reservations, Nuffield Centre, St. Michael's Road, Portsmouth, Hampshire PO1 2ED.

Telephone (01705) 8431178   Fax (01705) 843182

MEMBER

University of Portsmouth

A Centre of Excellence for University Teaching and Research

STEVEN FOULKES-MURRAY

BUSINESS TRAVEL - INCENTIVES - MEETINGS

TIME IS PRECIOUS, LET OUR INDEPENDENT STATUS ENSURE YOU GET THE QUALITY AND PERSONAL SERVICE REQUIRED IN TODAYS BUSINESS WORLD.

WE ARE DEDICATED TO PROVIDING THE HIGHEST STANDARDS TO EACH AND EVERY CLIENT

(TRAVEL TRUST ASSOCIATION No.T8205)

188 IVERSON ROAD, WEST HAMPSTEAD, LONDON NW6 2HL

TELEPHONE & FACSIMILE 0171 625 7452

STEVEN FOULKES-MURRAY

BUSINESS TRAVEL - INCENTIVES - MEETINGS

I am now currently networking with the Bury Travel Centre, together we can provide an all round business service, we are bonded through the Travel Trust Association (Number T8205).

Together we can offer the following services, business and leisure travel, hotel accomodation reservations, incentive ideas and implementation, venue finding and event management, and group travel.

We are also the representatives for Strata Safaris based in Kenya, offering a variety of golfing and activity holidays and incentives

Our independent status ensures that we provide impartial advice and a quality and personal service of the highest standards to all our clients.

WALES

When it's time to organise important business meetings and conferences away from the office or you need an inspired and innovative destination choice for your incentive or corporate hospitality event, there's one country you must consider. That country is Wales.

Easily accessible from all major gateways, Wales offers value for money with exceptional service and accommodation, extraordinary venues, first class events and a range of breathtaking incentive activities. From castles, historic houses and luxury country house hotels, to white water rafting, Celtic road safaris, panning for gold and cultural events, your clients will have a wealth of opportunities to experience.

The Business Travel Planner features quality venues and hotels, suggested itineraries and incentive and corporate hospitality opportunities, whilst the Business Travel Department based at the Wales Tourist Board's head office in Cardiff are able to offer advice and help with any aspect of your programme planning.

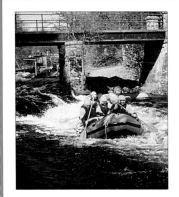

For more information, contact:
**Business Travel Department,
Wales Tourist Board,
Brunel House, 2 Fitzalan Road,
Cardiff CF2 1UY.
Tel: 01222 - 475202
Fax: 01222 - 475321**

FRESH INSPIRATION

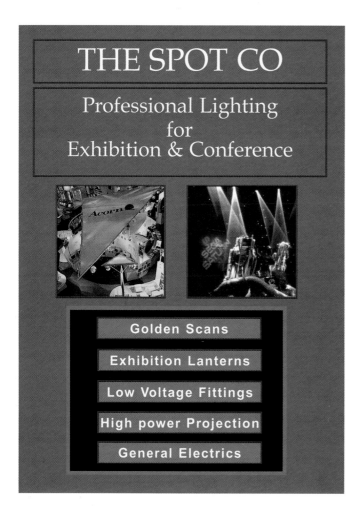

The Spot Company

Lighting Specialists for Exhibition & Conference.

The Spot Company was established in 1988 to fill a market desire for a newly available breed of lighting technology. Since that time we have developed an enviable reputation for high quality production work and a state of the art equipment range which is second to none.

Recently we have found that more and more of our corporate clients have been looking for different and more entertaining ways of projecting their image. To this end the themeing and branding of events has become particularly important.

The Spot Company is uniquely positioned to offer a variety of solutions to this problem, ranging from large scale projection down to more subtle Gobo options.

Prominent exhibition clients include Microsoft, Peugeot, BMW and Jaguar. They have already realised the full potential of incorporating special effects lighting into their conference and exhibition presentations.

The Spot Company offer a fast and reliable 24 hour technical and logistical helpline which offers reassuring support to our clients on all of their productions.

We are located at
53 Northfield Road, West
Ealing, London W13 9SY
Telephone at +44 181 566 5012
Fax at +44 181 566 5013

Hotels

Jonathan Langston, Director, BDO Hospitality Consulting

Western Europe

Signs that recession is gradually receding and turning to growth in the worldwide economies in 1994 had a considerable effect on the European hotel market, as increased tourist arrivals boosted occupancy levels, room yields and profits. Helped by a good summer, this improvement in the fortunes of hotels has continued well into 1995, with tourist arrivals up by 1 per cent compared with 1994.

Europe also continued to figure prominently in the high per capita spend market of the business traveller. In 1994, nine out of the top ten business destinations were European, with Riga, St Petersburg and Faro being the fastest growing business destinations worldwide. Since the United Kingdom was one of the first Western European economies to emerge from recession, the recent performance of hotels in London is perhaps a reasonable indicator for the rest of Europe's business centres. Average occupancies in 1994 were approximately 76 per cent, representing an increase on 1993 of almost 6 percentage points. However, this was not accompanied by similar growth in average room rates, as a result of continued discounting.

A similar pattern has also emerged from Spain where, overall, occupancies in 1994 increased, with resort-based properties having performed better than city centre hotels. These increases have, however, been at the expense of average room rates – a trend which appears to be widespread in the recovering economies of Western Europe. The difference in performance between resort-based properties and city centre properties is also indicative of other influences that have come to bear on countries in the European Union as a direct result of monetary policy emanating from Brussels. The currencies of Italy, Spain and the UK all became weaker against those of demand-generating countries, resulting in an increase in overseas tourists attracted by good value for money. At the same time these exchange rate movements made foreign travel for their respective nationals more expensive, leading to an increase in domestic tourist arrivals and spend. As arguments over a single currency continue to dominate the European agenda, it is likely that similarities will continue to reoccur, given the influence of exchange rate shifts on propensities to travel. This in turn will be influenced by future parliamentary elections in many EU countries and more importantly the outcome of the European Union's intergovernmental conference in 1996.

Outlook

Recent occurrences also illustrate the likely future trends for hotels in Western Europe. It is expected that the strategies of the major operators will increasingly be related to the lessons learnt from the recession and the consequent need to plan strategically in the face of wider, global competition. Inevitably, this will involve a greater degree of restructuring and the need to increase market share, either through geographical expansion or the creation of new markets. Developments such as the purchase of Scott's Hotels Ltd by Whitbread, thus acquiring the Marriott brand in the UK, confirms this expectation, as do the various acquisitions in Europe made by hotel groups based further afield. These include recent purchases by the Singapore based CDL group, and the Bangkok Lancaster Landmark Hotel Company which recently took over the former Regent Hotel in London.

It is expected that the budget-style hotel will continue to expand in some countries, accentuating the segmentation of the hotel market. It is envisaged also that this delineation in the supply of hotels will grow with more specific products appearing. This reflects the demographic changes (ageing population) and the more widespread price-sensitive mentality of the customer who became both more financially astute and conscious of the relation between price and product during the recession. As a result, hotels attached to hospitals, all-suite hotels and more integrated resorts can be expected.

The increasing role of up-to-date technology will also see its function increase. This will not only be in response to the need to manage yields more appropriately for better financial returns, but will also be determined by other factors. These include 'relationship marketing', acknowledging the growing significance of customer loyalty in a saturated European market and the need for better provision for the expanding female executive market. Women are expected to make up 50 per cent of all business guests at the turn of the century. More important is the role the Internet will play in the hotel market, cutting the tour operator cost to hotels. The importance of the above increases when seen in the light of Europe's decreasing share of world tourism and the efforts that will have to be made by hotel groups to retain and increase their customer bases.

Finally, it is hoped that the future role of tourism and therefore the fortunes of hotels will be further enhanced and recognized as an official EU activity when the Maastricht Treaty is revised in 1996. It is expected that such recognition will have a significant effect on the tourism industry in Europe and the financial and employment potential that exists.

Eastern Europe

The recent performance of hotels in Eastern Europe's major cities varies considerably, with Moscow recording the highest occupancy (70 per cent) and average room rate (US$210).

Other cities in Eastern Europe had an average rate of approximately US$110, with Bucharest coming in at US$93. The lowest average occupancy was recorded by Sofia at 49 per cent.

However, despite the considerable efforts that have been made by many governments in the former Eastern bloc, many countries still suffer from high rates of interest and inflation and the lack of a coherent strategy for the promotion of tourism. Moreover, the privatization of hotels has not only been haphazard but has not necessarily resulted in a better product, as many properties lack the required funds to invest and improve. Nevertheless, the considerable investment which occurred initially has now satisfied the demand for luxury hotels in many Central European cities, with investment and construction projects now focusing more on the Central Asian republics.

Outlook

Given that demand for certain categories of hotels has now been fulfilled, it is envisaged that the new wave of hotels in the former Eastern bloc are likely to be more relevant to their location, with new openings attempting to fulfil the demand for international standard mid-market properties. Other future developments however, will hinge for the most part on the political stability of the various countries in Eastern Europe, in order that investors can be content with future projects going ahead.

Other limiting factors also have to be removed. At present, these include isolation from potential markets due to poor communications, the general lack of efficient organization and infrastructure, and the continuation, in some areas, of two-tier pricing charging different rates to national and foreign visitors. It is essential that such barriers are removed in order for countries in Eastern Europe to be able to capitalize on their undoubtedly strong visitor potential.

APPENDIX

Prospects by Country

Austria

The Federation of Austrian Industrialists

Comparative advantages/ structural weaknesses

Internationally Austria is best known for its culture, music in particular, and for the beauty of its landscape. Indeed, on a per capita basis Austria is Europe's no. 1 in tourism, both as far as overnight stays and foreign exchange revenues from tourism are concerned.

What is much less known, however, even in Austria itself, is the fact that Austria is a highly industrialized country. Industry contributes some 30 per cent to GDP, somewhat less than in Germany, but more than the EU average. Over 50 per cent of industrial production is exported and the foreign exchange revenues stemming from manufacturing exports are about three times those earned by the tourist industry.

The typical Austrian manufacturing company is medium-sized and belongs to one of three groups: companies well-established in specialized niches, often with high market shares in Europe; companies operating as subcontractors to renowned international companies, eg the automotive industry; and companies operating in more traditional fields like paper and pulp, steel or textiles, but which in many instances are among the most efficient worldwide.

Austria is an attractive location for industrial operations, as illustrated by the presence of prestigious multinational corporations such as Philips, Sony, General Motors, Siemens, Chrysler, BMW and Alcatel. It offers a high degree of political, social and monetary stability, a well-trained and dedicated labour force, wage levels well below those in Germany, for instance, and one of the lowest burdens of business taxes in the Western industrial world. On the negative side of the balance sheet, industry in Austria is struggling with excessive bureaucratic and environmental regulation.

Economic indicators and prospects

It must be noted that economic fluctuations in the USA are three times as dramatic as in Austria, and in Germany they are two times as strong. The reason for this is the consistent economic policy to which the Federation of Austrian Industrialists has contributed a good deal. The result is stable private consumption, and even in economically weaker periods like that experienced in 1993 the setbacks are only moderate. In 1993 GDP declined by only 0.1 per cent (1992 + 1.8 per cent) and reached 2.7 per cent in 1994. For 1995 the Austrian economy is expected to grow by 2.4 per cent. Reasons for that seem to be improving real exports of goods (+ 6.3 per cent) and gross fixed capital formation (+ 3.5 per cent). For 1996 the gross national product is expected to grow by 2.1 per cent.

Moreover, the weakness of the labour market has been overcome; in 1994 employment was already 0.5 per cent above the previous year's value and is going to increase slightly (+ 0.3 per cent in 1995 and

1996). Manufacturing industry, on the other hand, employed some 4500 less at the beginning of 1995 than 1994. Another fall in industrial employment is expected in the course of 1995 in spite of increasing production. Therefore moderate productivity growth rates of around 2.3 per cent can be anticipated. Inflation (3 per cent in 1994) is going down very slowly (2.5 per cent for 1995 and 2.3 per cent for 1996). The previous year's current account deficit (ATS–22.3 billion) is expected to increase to ATS33.8 billion in 1995.

Money market interest rates decreased further to 5.0 per cent during 1994, whereas capital market rates went up in line with international rates.

Business confidence

Although the business survey conducted by the Federation of Austrian Industrialists in March 1995 showed fewer positive expectations than the previous survey, business confidence among federation members is rather strong: 43 per cent – compared to 46 per cent three months before – describe their orders in hand as satisfactory. While 47 per cent of firms indicated a good export order position, only 18 per cent complained about insufficient export orders. In December 1994 11 per cent of firms had complained about too few export orders. 28 per cent of enterprises describe their production activities as increasing, 66 per cent as stable and 7 per cent as decreasing.

A major reason for these positive results is certainly Austria's EU membership, which started on 1 January 1995. Nevertheless, one should not be too euphoric about these data, if looking at the 'hard figures' of 1994. Especially the large current account deficit (almost three times as high as 1993) should be kept in mind. Compared to Germany, where private consumption declined by 1 per cent in 1993 and experienced another fall in 1994, those branches in Austria which depend on private consumption were able to make profits in a year of recession. In 1994 private demand grew by 2.3 per cent, and about the same growth rate is expected for 1995. Concerning industrial investments, which suffered a decline of about 12 per cent during the recession in 1992/93, strong stimulation was recorded in 1994.

Recommendations for improving Europe's competitiveness

The Federation of Austrian Industrialists recommends that its member companies take advantage of Austria's EU membership. Especially companies operating in hitherto protected areas like the food industry, which had to adjust quickly to new competition from EU countries, will have to meet further challenges in the future. Yet it is also very important to conquer dynamic non-European markets, since Austria's position in Asia or in America is traditionally weak. Furthermore, the specialization in innovative products with high value added should continue.

Economic policy has to support the adjustment process by allowing more flexibility in working hours, increasing funds for R&D and promotion. In order to strengthen Europe's competitiveness, especially the legislative and fiscal environment within which SMEs operate, has to be improved. Therefore, administrative and legislative burdens on SMEs should be eased, through more effective impact assessments. Planning constraints should be reduced and environmental policy measures should be based on EU-wide action, rather than national initiatives.

External trade

Austria has definitely benefited from the breakdown of the Iron Curtain. Exports to Central and Eastern Europe have boomed since 1990 and account at present for more than 13 per cent of total exports. The trade balance with this region is in surplus in the order of 0.7 per cent of GDP. However, certain branches of industry have been confronted with increased low cost competition, making major restructurings inevitable.

Overall Austria's exports increased by 9.7 per cent after a 4.2 per cent decrease during 1993. Imports increased by 11.3 per cent in 1994 after a 4.9 per cent decrease in 1993. For 1995 goods exports are expected to rise by around 6 per cent. The strongest growth rates in 1994 could be observed for machinery, paper, non-ferrous metals, iron, steel and vehicles.

The vast majority of Austrian exports (62.9 per cent) is delivered to member countries of the European Union, with Germany being Austria's most important export market (share in exports 1994 of 38.1 per cent); 15.8 per cent of goods are sold overseas. Eastern and Central Europe is already the third most important region of Austrian exports. An increasing boom is recorded for Austria's exports to the Far East (+ 15 per cent), although the presence of Austrian enterprises could be stronger in this region.

Exports to the USA surged by 13 per cent after a steep increase in 1993, yet their share in Austrian exports is rather small. Imports grew by 11 per cent.

Concerning imported goods, two-thirds originate from Europe, whereas 19.6 per cent stem from overseas and 10.3 per cent are manufactured in Eastern and Central Europe.

Economists in Austria are slightly worried concerning the current account deficit, owing to the increase of imports but also to Austrian contributors to the EU. Austria currently does not fulfil two of the Maastricht criteria: the budget deficit amounts to 4.3 per cent and the public debt is about 64 per cent.

Priorities for the EU's Inter-governmental Conference

In preparation for the IGC in 1996 the Federation of Austrian Industrialists urges for an efficient and transparent European Union which could help ensure the competitiveness of European industry. As a consequence, the decision-making process should be simplified. Currently there are 23 different procedures depending on subject and involvement of the European Parliament. To improve the effectiveness in this field, majority voting should be expanded, but not as a general rule.

The Federation of Austrian Industrialists is in favour of the integration of Central and Eastern European countries as members of the EU in the near future, both for economic and political reasons. To get ready for this task preparations should begin as soon as possible. The *White Book* for the integration of these countries in this context is seen as a first step. Further considerations are necessary, especially in the field of the Common Agricultural Policy and the Regional Policy.

Conclusion

Since the disaster of the Second World War the Austrian economic history has been a success story and Austrian manufacturing industry has been the engine. Today Austria's per capita income is well above the EU average, resulting in a net contributing position to the EU budget. Both the transition of Central and Eastern Europe to market economy and EU membership are opening new opportunities for Austrian industry, but are also demanding additional efforts to take full advantage of them. Austrian industry is well on the way.

65 Belgium

Federation of Belgian Enterprises

Development and potential of the market

Belgium is a small open economy that has taken full benefit of its central position in Europe to become an export champion. Exports account for 70 per cent of GDP. By way of comparison, the average figure in the European Union is only 28 per cent, while Japanese and American exports only represent 10 per cent of their respective GDPs.

Belgium's main trading partners are Germany, France, The Netherlands, the UK, and Italy. These five countries account for 70 per cent of its exports. Belgium exports mainly machinery, transportation equipment, chemical products, metals, gems and electrical appliances.

Since 1990, closer linkage of the Belgian franc to the German mark has enabled Belgian interest rates to closely shadow German rates. Low inflation (currently below 2 per cent) and a large current account surplus (more than 5 per cent of GDP) guarantee the long-term viability of this exchange rate policy. In addition, the reduction of the state deficit from 13 per cent of GDP in the beginning of the 1980s to roughly 5 per cent in 1994 places Belgium close to fulfilling the Maastricht criteria and entering European monetary union with the first group of participating countries. The disappearance of exchange rate fluctuations between Belgium and its main commercial partners will intensify the trade relations with those countries and constitute thereby

an important factor of attraction for foreign investment.

In Belgium, companies can also benefit from one of Europe's most developed transport infrastructures. Belgium offers the most dense road network in Europe. Its 1600 kilometres of highways assure a swift link of all parts of the country with its neighbours and with its three main ports (Antwerp, Ghent and Zeebrugge). Thanks to one of the most developed rail networks in the world and almost 2000 kilometres of inland waterways, the maritime ports of Belgium hold excellent links with their hinterland.

Belgium has well-developed financial markets, on which the business sector can rely to finance its activities. Brussels is in the top 10 of the world's most important financial centres (according to the external assets criterion). Thanks to the implementation of a series of far-reaching reforms in recent years, Belgium has improved substantially the efficiency and competitiveness of its banking and financial markets, enabling them to face the increasing international competition.

One of the main comparative advantages of the Belgian economy is the quality of its labour force. Schools are free and offer a good level of qualification. Low university costs enable everyone to study; moreover, the quality of the teaching is high and does not noticeably differ from one university to another. Its universities attract many students from all over the EU and also from countries outside Europe.

The high productivity of Belgian labour tends to compensate for the cost of labour, which is increased by high levels of taxation and social contributions (the result of tax increases aiming at deficit reduction).

Economic prospects for 1995 and 1996

In common with other continental European countries, Belgium went through a recession in 1993. In 1994, GDP grew by 2.2 per cent. The main factors fostering economic recovery were the anticipated upturn of the European economy and the further development of growth in non-European areas. In 1994, the recovery was mainly export led, while domestic demand was still subdued: export volumes have grown by 8.1 per cent, while private consumption growth was very modest at 1.3 per cent, and industrial investment even decreased by 2 per cent. Economic growth is expected to gain strength in 1995 and 1996, as domestic demand (especially investment) will gradually take over from exports as the engine of economic activity.

The insecurity surrounding the reform of social security limits the recovery of private consumption. But thanks to high capacity utilization, investment should pick up strongly.

The export sector remains an important engine of economic activity, even if its growth is expected to slow down from 8.1 per cent in 1994 to 6.1 per cent in 1995. The current account surplus is expected to remain at record levels.

The Belgian Planning Bureau expects GDP growth to remain at 2.2 per cent in 1995 and 1996.

The weak domestic demand contributes also to the maintenance of a very low inflation rate. For 1995, an inflation figure close to 1.6 per cent is expected.

Level of business confidence

The business cycle indicator of the National Bank of Belgium grew during 1994, but in the first quarter of 1995 its trend progression has slowed down (while the gross indicator has even declined). This hesitation might indicate that, after its strong growth performance in 1994, the economy is heading now for a consolidation of activity at its present level. This slow down has been noted in all sectors covered by the survey, but it has been marked especially in com-

	1994	1995	1996
Private consumption	1.3	1.4	1.3
Public consumption	1.3	1.0	0.6
Gross capital formation	0.5	6.0	6.7
Export of goods and services	8.1	6.1	5.6
Import of goods and services	7.2	6.1	5.7
GDP	2.2	2.2	2.2
Inflation	2.4	1.6	2.2
Unemployment rate	12.9	12.9	12.7
Current balance (% GDP)	5.2	5.5	5.3
Public financing requirement (% GDP)	-5.3	-4.3	-3.0

Source: Planning Bureau

Table 65.1 Economic prospects

merce and construction, confirming the weakness of domestic demand.

A survey conducted between the member federations of FEB/VBO shows that basic industries (such as steel, non-ferrous metals, basic chemicals and metal transformers) experienced strong growth during 1994. These sectors benefited from good export performances, although their growth will probably be weaker this year as order-books are less filled. But sectors operating mainly on the domestic market and sectors feeling the competition from weak currency countries still do not experience a significant improvement.

Recommendations for improving European competitiveness

In order to promote competitiveness, European and national authorities need to do the following:

- Promote a stable macroeconomic environment. This implies the consolidation of public finances and the swift introduction of a single currency in the European Union. Exchange rate movements, which are not compatible with fundamental economic conditions, need to be avoided through closer cooperation between the G7 countries.
- Reduce significantly the cost of labour, especially by cutting employers' social contributions, but without increasing other production costs. This requires a far-reaching reform of social security systems, which have taken on unbearable proportions for European economies.
- Increase the flexibility of labour markets. This implies, for example, the reduction of hiring and

firing costs and more flexible working schedules. It requires also a revision of the wage formation process in order to bring wage increases in line with productivity growth and with the evolution of wages in competing countries.

- Revise regulations in a business-friendly way.
- Assure the full implementation of the agreements creating the World Trade Organization in order to guarantee free and fair international trade.

Priorities for the EU's Intergovernmental Conference

The Intergovernmental Conference must prepare the European Union for further enlargement and guarantee the efficient functioning of its institutions with more than 20 member states.

The completion of the internal market should not be compromised by hasty concessions to new candidates. Any temptation to revise the convergence criteria or the schedule of economic and monetary union should be resisted.

As for institutional matters, Belgian companies support the European Commission's right of initia-

tive. They also want a simplification of decision-making rules in order to increase the institution's efficiency.

In addition, the European Union should be brought closer to Europe's citizens through a reinforcement of certain obligations for consultation and transparency.

In order to maintain the credibility of the European Union, there should be a more stringent budget, which implies that fraud needs to be fought more efficiently and distortions of competition by the structural funds need to be avoided.

Conclusions

Belgium's economic policies focus increasingly on Europe. This is the consequence of a very high degree of economic integration with its neighbours. It is also the result of Belgium's willingness to deepen the internal market by the introduction of a single currency. This willingness expresses itself in the search for sound public finances and the revision of the wage formation process in order to adapt it to the requirements of monetary union.

In this way, Belgium strives to stay a front runner in the making of Europe.

Bulgaria

The Bulgarian Industrial Association

Development and potential of the Bulgarian market

Even though it is of a limited capacity (of only 8.5 million potential consumers), the national market should be considered primarily in terms of its significant unutilized potential, ensuing from the country's geographic location, the foreign trade orientation of the national economy, and the medium-term prospects and potential for growth in domestic consumption and investments.

The consumer market is characterized by an exceptionally high share of expenditure on food, which has continued so high for the whole time of reform (45 per cent in 1994, to 16–20 per cent for the developed countries, respectively). At the same time, in view of the expected stabilization of economic revival, a continuous, though small in volume, increase in expenditure on furniture, housing and services and a respective expansion of these market segments can be expected.

The market for investment goods remains dependent primarily on the progress of privatization, on the migration of private capital from services, trade and finance to industry and agriculture, and on the provision of financing for the large infrastructure projects envisaged.

Economic indicators and prospects

The last corrected data show an overall drop of GDP of about 24 per cent in the period 1989–93, while 1994 marks a growth of 1.4 per cent. Although modest, this growth is a proof of trends similar to the processes taking place in the economies of the Vishegrad Four (a Central European free trade agreement). Thus 1994 marked the end of the drastic downswing in GDP, typical for the whole period of transition to a market economy that began in 1989. This result was, however, achieved at the price of a considerable rate of inflation of about 122 per cent and a depreciation of the Bulgarian lev (from 33 to 66 levs to a US dollar at the end of 1993 and 1994 respectively). It is a widely accepted opinion that the major causes for this sudden and to a great extent unexpected shock are related to the necessity of a one-time adaptation of the economy to the negative effect of previous years that have been accumulating in privatization and the structural reform.

In the first half of 1995, an obvious stabilization was accomplished, finding its expression in inflation of 15.2 per cent (compared to 59.4 per cent for the same period of 1994), a practically unchanged exchange rate, increasing production and GDP (about 2 per cent), maintaining a comparatively low level of unemployment of 11 per cent relative to the preceding years. These are proofs of the beginning of changes to the better, which can be maintained only by decisive structural reforms, related primarily to the start of voucher privatization at the beginning of 1996 and the financial sanitization of the public sector.

The private sector's share of GDP is expected to reach 40 per cent (35 per cent in 1994) at the end of 1995, that is before the beginning of mass privatization. At the same time, there are a number of prerequisites for the target of 1.5 per cent of growth of GDP in 1995 to be exceeded (latest expectations for the rate of growth are envisaged at 2–2.5 per cent).

The first signs of revival are seen in construction, which is proof of the more lasting nature of economic revival. In July, for example, industrial production marked a 7 per cent growth in comparative prices against the same month of 1994. A number of enterprises and industries, like coal mining, ferrous and non-ferrous metallurgy, chemical industry, pulp and paper industry, glass and delftware contribute to this growth and to the increasing competitiveness, and something is seen which is particular symptomatic – a recovery of our markets for general machine engineering, one of the industries that suffered the severest drop in the reform period.

At the same time, it should be noted that a considerable part of the attained growth is accounted for by the increasing exports, and not by an increase of domestic consumption and investments. This is made possible by the stimulating effect of the domestic currency depreciation in 1994, the restrictive income policy, and the influence of the high interest rate level maintained until the middle of 1995 (the base interest rate was decreased from the record level of 72 per cent in September 1994 to about 34 per cent as of the beginning of August 1995).

The most significant tendencies in foreign trade in 1994 compared to 1993, which were generally preserved in 1995, are:

- almost unchanged exports to the former Soviet Union countries;
- increase by over 13 per cent in exports to Central and Eastern Europe;
- increasing exports to the EU by over 30 per cent, including exports to Germany (43 per cent), to Italy (31 per cent);
- shrinkage of imports in general;
- increase of imports from Macedonia (66 per cent); from Greece (23 per cent) and from Italy (13 per cent).

There was a record foreign trade surplus of US$304 million in the first half of 1995 (relative to US$152 million at the end of 1994). Quite surprisingly, in the second quarter Italy took first place, outpacing Macedonia and Germany, in the export of Bulgarian goods. In the first half of the year, 30.2 per cent of

Bulgarian exports were directed to the former Soviet Union countries and to Central and Eastern Europe, and 48 per cent to the OECD countries.

Considering the significant rise in 1994 exports, the following goods showed considerable competitiveness – cement, rolled steel sheets, urea, polyethylene, cotton fabrics, shoes. In relation to exports, there is a considerable increase primarily of electric household appliances, and further expansion of the market may be expected through a possible promotion of domestic consumption.

In the case of a positive development of negotiations with international financial institutions and a respective shortening of the country's debt servicing in 1996, considered as critical, as well as through a successful start of voucher privatization and speeding up of cash privatization, the national economy has considerable good prospects, both in terms of further expansion of exports and in reviving domestic consumption and investments. In the medium term, this would be facilitated by the start of a number of large-scale projects related to the common European structure, such as the realization of a new bridge on the Danube river, oil pipeline from the Black Sea Port of Bourgas to Alexandropulis, a railway link with the Republic of Macedonia. The law of securities, stock exchanges and investment companies recently passed by Parliament, and the forthcoming registration of a unified stock exchange through the consolidation of the existing stock exchanges provide the conditions for the revival of the stock exchange and its opening for portfolio investments by foreign and domestic investors. The adoption of the laws on corporate tax and income tax is expected to occur in 1997, thus stabilizing the taxation regime and the conditions for the operations of domestic and foreign investors.

Prevailing expectations and projects for 1996 envisage a growth of GDP between 2 per cent and 4 per cent inflation of 35–40 per cent not exceeding the level expected for 1995; a rise in the level of employment of 1–2 per cent; private sector's share in gross added value of 45–48 per cent.

Levels of business confidence

In comparison to 1994, a prevailing number of industrial managers note a general improvement of enterprises, based primarily on finding new and expanding existing external markets. As a result, more and more enterprises free themselves of accumulated stocks of ready products, in a situation of increased availability of orders and better utilization of production capacities. More than half of basic industrial products, monitored by national statistics, feature an increase of production, while industry provides over 90 per cent of commodity exports, and one-third of cash receipts come from sales on foreign markets.

Notwithstanding the continuing trade embargo against the former Yugoslavian countries and its impact on the Bulgarian economy, there are general expectations for a continuing improvement in the economic situation.

Recommendations for improving Europe's competitiveness

These are primarily in relation to:

■ seeking and implementing peaceful and mutually acceptable solutions to the conflicts existing on the Balkan peninsula and the consequent elimination of all related restrictions over business;

■ assisting integration and providing the conditions for acceptance of the Eastern European countries into the European Union in the foreseeable future;

■ expanding access to the Single European Market of competitive national products, like ferrous metals, chemicals, textiles, garments, agricultural produce, etc, and establishing free-trade zones between the countries of Central and Eastern Europe;

■ elimination of restrictions to the free movement of people (particularly for business trips) and capital;

■ acceleration in general and financial assistance for large-scale infrastructure projects, particularly for transport to integrate the Balkans with the countries of the EU and Central Europe;

■ cooperation in increasing access of small and medium-sized business to foreign credit lines and guarantees, joint investments, assisting foreign investments and the transfer of modern technologies.

67 Cyprus

The Cypriot Employers and Industrialists Federation

Development and potential

Cyprus, an island situated in the northeastern part of the Mediterranean, has a small, open economy based on the free enterprise system. This economy is relatively poor in natural resources and thus highly dependent on the import and export of goods and services. Since its independence in 1960, Cyprus's development has been internationally acknowledged as a success story in both the economic and social fields. Despite the acute political problems which emerged in 1974 when Turkey invaded the island occupying about 38 per cent of its territory, the economy quickly recovered owing to the concerted efforts of both the public and the private sector.

The island's strategic location and favourable climatic conditions are important comparative advantages for the Cypriot economy. Furthermore, advanced telecommunications and transport facilities, an educational standard among the highest in the world, excellent business relations with European countries and a generally favourable economic climate contributed to the rapid growth of the services sector and helped to establish Cyprus as a regional services centre. Considerable tax and other incentives have attracted a large number of offshore companies and foreign investors to Cyprus.

Cyprus's natural beauty and the excellent Mediterranean climatic conditions (with approximately 340 days of sunshine) make Cyprus an attractive holiday resort and hence tourism became one of the most dynamic sectors of the economy, with gross receipts averaging $1.5 billion per year.

One of the main structural weaknesses of the economy, which has been eroding the competitiveness of Cypriot products and damaging its industrial production for the past few years, is the relatively high production costs and in particular the per unit labour cost. High production costs, along with other external factors, led to the reduction in exports of the main manufacturing products such as clothing, footwear, travel goods and water pumps, produced mainly from small and medium-sized firms. Now efforts are made to upgrade these sectors and also to broaden the industrial base, thus offering more sophisticated products (eg pharmaceutical products managed in the last few years to penetrate even the most demanding markets).

Economic indicators and prospects for 1996

The economic situation and outlook improved markedly during 1994, following the subdued performance observed in 1993.

During 1994, the Cypriot economy exhibited a 5 per cent increase of GDP at constant prices, against a mere 1.7 per cent in 1993. This is mainly attributed to the strong rebound of the tourist sector which recorded a 17 per cent increase in gross receipts, as well as to the strengthening of domestic and foreign demand. Owing to the increase in domestic demand

and to other external factors, the inflation rate was maintained at relatively high levels (4.7 per cent), which is still higher than the average inflation rate that prevailed in the EU (3.1 per cent).

The upturn of economic activity helped maintain full employment conditions; unemployment reached 2.7 per cent as against 2.6 per cent during 1993.

In 1995, the economy is expected to continue to expand, with economic growth projected at about 4.3 to 4.6 per cent under the impetus of an expected expansion in both domestic and foreign demand. The more favourable international economic environment, and in particular the progressing economies of the EU (which constitute the predominant trade partner for Cyprus), provide the right setting for consolidating and strengthening the progress made in external demand for domestically produced goods but also for services. Tourism is expected to expand further with increasing tourist arrivals (around 3.2 per cent) and gross receipts. The inflation rate in 1995 will be reduced to less than 4 per cent. Uncertainty arises as to the implications of the GATT Treaty, which is to be fully implemented by January 1996 after its ratification by the Cyprus Parliament.

The prospects for 1966 and for the following few years will probably be favourable for the economy as a whole, in the sense that government's future policies are expected to be directed towards achieving more balanced growth in the economy with the adoption of the proper incentives. This will involve the upgrading of the tourist product, support for the proper restructuring of industry and the better promotion of the island as an international services centre.

Prospects generally for the coming years will be closely related to Cyprus's efforts to achieve full membership in the EU and thus harmonize its laws and practices to the *acquis communautaire*. The European Council reaffirmed on 6 March 1995 the suitability of Cyprus for accession and decided that accession negotiations 'will start on the basis of Commission proposals six months after the conclusion of the 1996 Conference'. Also, a 'structured dialogue' with the EU on various matters and at various levels was offered to Cyprus in June 1996.

Levels of Business Confidence

As a result of the strengthening of domestic and foreign demand, economic activity in the manufacturing sector during 1994 showed a turnaround following adverse performance recorded in 1993.

During 1994 manufacturing production expanded by 2.9 per cent in volume, in contrast to a decline of 9.5 per cent recorded in the previous year. The subgroups of paper products, food, beverages and tobacco exhibited the largest increases (7.2 and 5.4 per cent respectively). Increases were recorded in employment, productivity and investment expenditure.

According to a Business Opinion Survey conducted in the manufacturing sector in December 1994, entrepreneurs continue to be relatively optimistic about the prospects of their businesses in the near future; about a fifth of them anticipate an increase in production in 1995.

EU Intergovernmental Conference

Cyprus is a candidate for membership to the EU and according to the decision of the European Council negotiations will start six months after the IGC. Therefore its main concern is for the IGC to complete its business as soon as possible so that Cyprus's full membership is not delayed.

The OEB – Objectives and Services

The Employers and Industrialists Federation (OEB) is an organization of the Cyprus business community, through which the views and interests of the business community are conveyed to the government and the public at large, with the objective of defending and upholding the system of free enterprise.

The OEB's objectives are actively promoted through numerous activities and services offered to members and the business community in general. These include:

- representations to government, the House of Representatives, the trade unions and other competent bodies on economic, tax, fiscal and social matters;
- participation in numerous official tripartite and other committees where the views of the business community are put forward;
- informing the public about the views of the business community.

In addition, the OEB also provides members with specialized services in the areas of labour legislation, industrial and business issues, and furthering the development of Cyprus as a regional Services Centre.

68 The Czech Republic

The Confederation of Industry of the Czech Republic

Recent developments

In 1994 and 1995 the Czech economy continued its development in a consolidated, relatively stable economic environment.

Whereas GDP achieved in 1994 represented approximately 2.5 per cent, industrial production ceased falling.

Aggregated indicators suggest a differentiation of Czech industries into problematic and promising ones. The latter group includes mainly the paper industry, printing, glass, ceramics and china, wood processing, production of electrical and optical equipment, distribution of electricity, gas and water, production of rubber and plastic materials. The decline of industrial production was indicated in the following industrial branches: production of transport, leather making and processing, foodstuffs and pharmaceuticals.

Economic prospects

The inflation rate achieved in 1994 was approximately 10 per cent and a similar level has been forecast for 1995. In this relation the deregulation of limited prices which was realized in 1994 caused inflation to be a little higher and will still affect inflation development in 1995 and in the near future. The number of unemployed registered in the Czech Republic at the end of 1994 was 166,500. This represents a rate of 3.2 per cent. In 1995 the unemployment rate has even been declining a little.

In 1994, there was the end of the main phase of the privatization process, launched in 1991 with small-scale privatization in 1992. This phase meant the denationalization of the major part of the Czech economy and its principal sectors, both productive and non-productive. In this process nearly 80 per cent of the former state property was transferred to new owners and 57 per cent of the total value of state property became private. The rest of the state property in the economy is still foreseen as being privatized; however, the role of the state in several sectors of the economy will be maintained.

The investment rate as the share of fixed capital in GDP, in constant prices achieved in 1994, was 29 per cent, which is near the present level of investment in other European countries. Nevertheless, GDP in the Czech Republic has significantly reduced in the last several years and so the economy would need a higher rate of investment, especially in the production sphere. The greatest growth of investment was oriented to the banking sector, insurance companies and to selected industrial branches.

Foreign investments were focused mainly on the consumer industry, tobacco, transport equipment, building industry, banking and insurance. The amount of foreign investment has reached approximately US$ 3 billion since 1990. The stable increase of foreign investment was briefly broken in 1993 after the division of Czechoslovakia, but 1994 confirmed an increasing tendency again, as shown by Table 68.1.

New investments are expected in relation to the envisaged privatization projects of petrochemicals and telecommunications, as well as with further increase of Volkswagen's share in Škoda Mladé Boleslav.

1991	1992	1993	1994
523	1003	568	862

Table 68.1 Foreign investment (US$)

After a relatively positive evaluation of economic development, it should be emphasized that the Czech economy suffers from emerging macro-economic and structural weakness.

The cushion created by the strong depreciation of the currency in 1991, which significantly reduced production costs, especially labour costs, in Czech companies, seems to have been gradually exhausted. In most industrial sectors in 1994 average nominal wages grew more quickly than labour productivity. Labour productivity rose more rapidly than nominal wages only in the paper and printing industry, in coking coal, crude oil refining and the production of nuclear fuels and electrical and optical instruments. In the building industry the surplus of wages increases over labour productivity reached nearly 5 per cent.

Growth in production costs and price levels on the domestic market weakened the competitiveness of Czech products, which had an impact on the trade balance. Foreign trade in 1994 showed a deficit of US$ 436 million and development in 1995 has shown warning signs. The foreign trade deficit in just the first three months of 1995 was US$ 675 million; however, the current balance of payments has been showing better results with regard to non-trade accounts, especially tourism. The capital account has been recording a high surplus.

The trade deficit was mostly due to an almost twofold growth of imports over exports (13.3 and 6.9 per cent). The biggest trade deficit arose in trade with EFTA and OECD countries and with the former Soviet Union. In 1995 exports to the EU increased by about 3.2 per cent to April, whereas imports were about 45.3 per cent.

An absolute decline of 14.2 per cent was recorded in 1994 in trade with the second biggest trade partner, Slovakia.

As regards the commodity structure of foreign trade, the highest growth was recorded in animal and vegetable oils and fats, beverages and tobacco, raw materials (excluding fuels), chemicals and miscellaneous manufactured articles.

Machinery and transport equipment rose less than average. The share of machinery and transport in Czech exports shrank slightly from 27.7 to 26.1 per cent; however, an absolute increase was recorded.

The negative situation in the development of foreign trade could be partly caused by importing equipment utilized for modernization of the Czech economy, but as a whole it is a result of an insufficient export promotion policy and probably evidence of the slowly continuing process of restructuring of the Czech economy, especially industry, and of only slowly growing labour productivity.

The barriers obstructing faster export growth are at the same time barriers to the growth of GDP, which is mostly growing on account of increasing internal aggregate demand. This can hardly ensure long-term preconditions for stable powerful growth.

In this relation the entrepreneurial sphere represented by the Confederation of Industry calls for active pro-export policy, especially in engineering and investment exports. It calls also for active industrial policy which should help Czech industry to accelerate the restructuring process and to eliminate emerging difficulties. It refers especially to old burdens such as bad and uncollectable debts, that are proposed and required by industrialists to be compensated for by appropriate rapid tax deductions. The entrepreneurs also call for less restraint by the government towards standard measures of economic policy like anti-dumping laws or the promotion of high-tech investment imports.

The government's reserved approach to increasing and long-lasting difficulties in several industries, for example coal mining or transport, caused increasing social tension resulting in conflicts between trade unions and managements of companies, or even government with the dramatic situation on the Czech railways.

Another macroeconomic problem has been emerging with a rapid inflow of various forms of foreign capital investment which reached US$ 3 billion only in the first five months of 1995. Unfortunately, most of the investment is not productive direct investment, but short-term or non-productive portfolio investment using the interest rate difference in the Czech Republic in comparison with other countries, as shown by Table 68.2.

1993	1994	1995 (March)
13.95	9.26	10.38

Table 68.2 Interest rate PRIBOR 6 months

The central bank warns that the Czech economy ceases to be able to absorb such an inflow of foreign investment, and expresses its concerns about inflation developments. The potential measures that could be taken by the central bank to prevent the inflation pressures would on the one hand jeopardize the promising growth of the economy; on the other hand, they could with a further increase in interest rates attract increased inflow of foreign investment. Nevertheless, an increase of interest rates by the central bank of about 1 per cent in June 1995, combined with administrative measures such as an increase in obligatory minimum banking reserves and limiting an inflow of speculative capital by regulation of commitments of Czech banks in relation to foreign banks, convinces the entrepreneurial sphere of the Czech national bank's intention to combat inflation pressures resolutely.

Business Confidence

As regards the level of business confidence, the increasing interest of foreign partners in cooperation with Czech companies and in business activities in the country is an evidence of growing confidence.

Czech legislation enables foreign entrepreneurs to conduct business in the Czech Republic under the same conditions as apply to any Czech business. The Czech commercial code enables foreign investment without an upper limit. Foreign investment is guaranteed through bilateral inter-governmental agreements with more than 30 countries.

Foreign investors can take part in the activity of the Prague Stock Exchange. Another way of stock exchange trading is the RM System established during voucher privatization and referring to companies privatized by this means.

As regards the Czech currency, the Czech crown has been prepared for full convertibility which is

anticipated to be introduced in 1995. The steadily growing rating of the Czech National Bank provides a favourable condition for this process.

The business confidence of members of the Confederation of Industry is of course an individual matter. Nevertheless, member profiles comprising more than 1200 of the most important Czech industrial and transport companies and biggest joint ventures reveal that membership in the Confederation of Industry of the Czech Republic is a certain way of business confidence. Many members are famous exporters of complete plants and engineering equipment to the most demanding markets in the world.

Improving European competitiveness

It is very difficult to express any comments about improving European competitiveness when the Czech economy faces similar difficulties, arising from different reasons. Nevertheless, without improving economic competitiveness Europe would not be able to maintain its position in the world, achieve social progress or further objectives. It seems to be unavoidable to tackle the following problems:

- the slow increase of labour productivity in comparison to newly emerging economies;
- the quicker increase of labour costs in US dollar terms than in the USA or high performing economies in Asia;
- the lower profitability of capital invested in European companies than in Japan or the USA;
- the lower R&D expenditure and long time for commercializing new technologies;
- the slow structural change of European industry to high-tech and high-growth industries
- acceleration of the process of European monetary union and further economic integration in Europe.

These problems could become one of the most discussed at EU's inter-governmental conference in 1996. Czech priorities for this event will be accession of the country to the EU; further integration; an effective, coherent and transparent external trade policy in Europe; removal of barriers to foreign trade; and economic relations inside Europe. Emphasizing the role of socioeconomic actors in preparation and their participation and contribution to this conference would be appreciated.

Denmark

Confederation of Danish Industries

Development and potential

Denmark is a small, open trading country. It has a strong and healthy manufacturing base covering more than two-thirds of Danish exports of goods. And about 60 per cent of manufacturing production is exported.

Manufacturing industry consists of many small and medium-sized enterprises but only a few large firms. This has meant a tradition of subcontractors of great flexibility and adaptability combined with high quality and timely delivery. But Denmark also contains many of the world's leading companies in certain highly developed industrial subsectors. It has a stable labour market with one of the lowest rates of absenteeism in Western Europe, and a well-educated labour force.

Denmark has an inflation rate among Europe's lowest, one of the lowest public budget deficits, among the highest surpluses on current account and an unemployment rate around the European average.

However, there are some structural problems in the labour market and the social security benefit systems. Both public expenditure and tax pressure are higher than in most other European countries.

Economic indicators and economic prospects for 1995/96

Since mid-1993 the Danish economy has experienced a strong upturn. GDP growth peaked in 1994, reaching 4.4 per cent, the second highest in EU. Competitiveness deteriorated due to strengthening of the Danish krone. This and the lapse of temporary growth stimuli will lead to lower growth in 1995 and 1996. Thus, employment growth will slow down and the level of unemployment will be approximately 10.2 per cent in 1996, according to a forecast by the Confederation of Danish Industries in May 1995. The current account will be in surplus in 1996 at a level of 1.9 per cent of GDP, and inflation is expected to remain below 3 per cent.

Growth in private consumption in Denmark reached a total of 7.1 per cent in 1994, mainly due to falling interest rates but further stimulated by the fiscal policy of the Danish government, which was expansive in 1994 but is expected to become contractive in 1995 and 1996.

Exports of manufacturing goods increased at a rate of 9 per cent in 1994. This positive trend continued in the first half of 1995 owing to strong demand on export markets. The devaluation or depreciation of numerous currencies has decreased competitiveness for Danish exporters. This will lead to loss of market share abroad for Danish exporters. International growth will, however, imply an increase in manufacturing exports of 6 to 7 per cent in volume terms in 1995 and 1996.

High growth on domestic as well as foreign markets has led to increases in investment in 1994, particularly investment in machines and inventory.

This is expected to continue in 1995 and 1996.

Public consumption is influenced by the problems relating to the labour market reform put into effect on 1 January 1994. The reform seeks to create a more decentralized and flexible system, in which job training is adapted to the needs of the individual and the labour market. The reform did, however, face difficulties when it was put into effect. This led to a dramatic fall in the volume of public relief jobs, which led to a decrease in public consumption.

GDP growth peaked in the second quarter of 1994 with an annual rate of 6 per cent. Following this, growth has occurred at a more moderate rate. Over 1994 the growth in GDP was 4.4 per cent; this is expected to fall somewhat to approximately 3.6 per cent in 1995 and 2.6 per cent in 1996 (see Table 69.1).

The more moderate growth rates in the years to come are reflected in manufacturing production. The annual growth rate in 1994 of 8 per cent in volume terms will decrease to 5 per cent in 1995 and further decrease to 4 per cent in 1996. Because of this,

employment in manufacturing will grow at a slower rate. Employment in manufacturing has increased since the end of 1993 and is expected to do so for part of 1995 as well.

Despite rapid GDP growth in 1994 employment fell by 2500. A decrease in employment at such a growth rate comes about due to the new labour market reform, which has led to fewer people being activated in public employment schemes and many people being on paid leave schemes.

Adding the number of people on paid leave, the labour force increased markedly by 1.2 per cent in 1994. The simultaneous decrease in employment meant that the total of unemployed plus those on paid leave increased to 13.9 per cent of the labour force in 1994. For 1995 and 1996 a fall is anticipated in the total of unemployed and persons on leave, amounting to 13.1 and 12.3 per cent of the labour force respectively. The registered rate of unemployment was 12.1 per cent in 1994 and is expected to fall to 10.4 and 10.2 per cent in 1995 and 1996 respectively.

	1994	1994	1995	1996
	(DKK billion)	Percentage change in volume		
Private consumption	498.6	7.1	3.7	4.0
Public consumption	234.8	0.6	1.8	1.0
Gross fixed investment	138.6	3.6	5.5	1.2
Residential investments	28.0	8.9	4.5	3.5
Business investments	90.4	2.7	8.5	3.0
Special sectors[a]	29.0	−12.3	3.5	−10.0
Business cycle sensitive investment	61.4	12.5	11.0	9.0
Public investments	20.2	1.2	−8.0	−12.0
Change in inventories[b]	−2.5	0.6	0.6	0.0
Domestic demand	869.5	5.5	4.2	2.8
Exports of goods and services	324.5	6.9	5.5	4.5
Imports of goods and services	264.7	10.5	7.5	5.0
GDP at market prices	929.3	4.4	3.6	2.6
Current account (% of GDP)		2.4	2.1	1.9
Registered unemployment (% of labour force)		12.1	10.4	10.2
Unemployment plus leave (% of labour force)		13.9	13.1	12.3
Consumer prices (annual change, %)		2.0	2.4	2.7
Manufacturing production		8.0	5.0	4.0
Manufacturing exports		9.0	7.0	6.0
Manufacturing investments		14.0	10.0	8.0
Manufacturing employment ('000)[c]		356	370	373

Notes: (a) Investments in energy, ships, planes, and public enterprises.
(b) Real absolute change measured as percentage of GDP in the previous year.
(c) Employment in manufacturing enterprises with six employees or more.

Source: Confederation of Danish Industries 1 May 1995

Table 69.1 Supply and demand in the Danish economy

Weakening business confidence

Business indicators for manufacturing industry showed some moderation in the course of 1995, after the sharp turnaround in mid 1993 from weak and declining economic sentiment to expectations of new growth and fulfilment of expectations. A more moderate growth of manufacturing production in 1995 is thus seen, which should remove most risks of inflationary pressures.

In the first nine months of 1995 manufacturing production was up by 5.2 per cent compared to one year earlier, but growth was falling. The inflow of new orders also showed signs of slower growth. The stock of orders declined somewhat after reaching a record high at the end of 1st quarter 1995, being some 25 per cent higher than one year previously. Production is still showing most positive signs for export markets.

Recommendations for improving competitiveness

The most serious economic problem in Denmark is the lack of flexibility in the labour market. It has rather high minimum wages and a small wage differential. This is a barrier to employment, especially for people with the lowest qualifications.

In order to reduce structural unemployment it is imperative to reduce minimum wages. But this demands reform of the unemployment benefit system and the social security benefit systems concerning the level and duration of benefits. There should always be an economic incentive to seek employment, education or training rather than receive passive financial support from various social benefit systems.

In the longer term it is necessary to reduce the burden of the public sector and the tax pressure in order to leave more room for the self-financing of business activity.

There is a general need to strengthen adaptability in a rapidly changing economic environment with fast changes in technology, international trade, and consumer demands. More should therefore be done to encourage innovators and entrepreneurs to create business activity and to facilitate growth of small and medium-sized enterprises. This is true in Denmark as well as in Europe.

The EU Inter-governmental Conference

The following issues are regarded as the main priorities at the EU inter-governmental conference in 1996.

Enlargement of the Union with Eastern Europe would widen the internal market and secure political stability in Europe. To develop and enforce an effective internal market with 20 countries or more it will prove necessary to use qualified majority voting more generally, and it is important not to let subsidiarity be an excuse for creating barriers to the functioning of the internal market.

Economic and monetary union must be kept on track and implemented as soon as possible to reestablish European currency stability after the damaging turbulence on the currency markets since 1992. To ensure Danish companies reap the benefits of one single currency and correspondingly lower interest rates, the Confederation of Danish Industries will seek to persuade Danish politicians and voters that Denmark cannot afford to remain outside the third phase of EMU.

In the labour market and social dimension area, there is a need for a legislative pause in order to seek to exploit the advantages of voluntary agreements by collective bargaining on the national and European level, which has proven effective and contributed to labour market dynamism in Denmark.

Simplification of the legal and administrative procedures of the Union would add transparency and effectiveness to Union decision making, which is desirable in many areas.

More effort is also needed from the Union in the fight to remove distorting state subsidies throughout the world.

70 Finland

Confederation of Finnish Industry and Employers

The Finnish economy has recovered from the worst recession the country has ever experienced, and has now entered a robust cyclical upswing.

The devaluation and the subsequent floating of the Finnish markka, as well as zero wage increases during the recession together with fast growth in productivity, led to a sharp improvement in the price competitiveness of Finnish manufacturing industry in 1991–93. In 1993 competitiveness as measured by relative unit labour costs was over 40 per cent above its long-term average.

Lately price competitiveness has somewhat weakened, owing primarily to the substantial appreciation of the markka and the stronger rise in labour costs. Productivity has, on the other hand, continued to climb swiftly, and competitiveness remains good. Productivity in Finnish manufacturing has in fact risen by almost 11 per cent per year in 1992–94.

In spite of the recent recession the development of Finnish industry has been in many ways positive during the 10–15 years. Perhaps the most striking feature has been the success of high technology and especially information technology. R&D has increased probably faster than in any other industrial country, and is now on a level that can stand comparison internationally. One consequence has been that the share of high technology products in its exports has risen from 4 to 15 per cent in a decade. Finland intends to remain in the van-

guard of the development of information technology in future.

The infrastructure of Finnish society is good, some would say excellent. Partly in consequence of that, Finland – with many other countries – has lately had problems with public deficits and a growing state debt. At the end of 1994 the debt exceeded the limit of 60 per cent of GDP posed by the Maastricht Treaty, and the present coalition government intends substantially to curb state expenditure. The structural expenditure cuts are planned to be at least FIM20 billion, as compared to the present level. To achieve this, all budget items will be scrutinized, with the possible exception of education and research. Well-qualified labour and a high level of education for the whole nation will also be an important cornerstone of the Finnish economy in the future.

One drawback of the highly developed infrastructure and welfare society is the high level of taxation. Balancing of state finances will be carried out without increasing the overall tax rate, but the alleviation of the taxation of earned income obviously cannot start before 1996.

During the boom and overheated period of the latter part of the 1980s the foreign debt of the country increased alarmingly. The basic aim of economic policy since then has been to strengthen the export sector in order to achieve a surplus on the current account and to reverse the growth of foreign debt.

FINLAND — FIRST CLASS WITH FINANGLIA

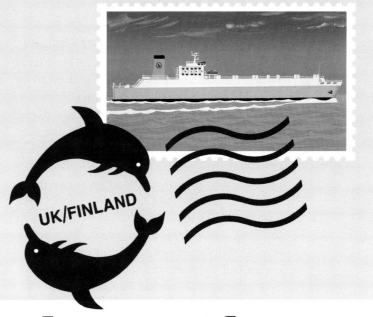

FOR
FINLAND
THINK
FINANGLIA

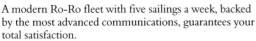

A modern Ro-Ro fleet with five sailings a week, backed by the most advanced communications, guarantees your total satisfaction.

With a containerised Door-to-Door service and the ability to take mobile and conventional cargoes Finanglia have the means of ensuring safe delivery — whatever you're shipping.

The Finanglia freightway means Finland the fast way.

FINANGLIA 📧

Finanglia Ferries Ltd.
Maritime House
18 Ensign Street, London E1 8JD
Tel 0171-481 0606
Fax 0171-488 4450 Telex 887002

▼ FINNCARRIERS

Finncarriers Oy Ab
Porkkalankatu 7
00180 Helsinki, Finland
Tel (00 3580) 134311
Fax (00 3580) 13431200 Telex 1001743

Economic indicators are positive: and future prospects good

The export-oriented growth strategy has proved successful, and the positive impact of increasing exports is now being felt in the overall economy. The gap between the export and domestic sectors is slowly lessening. Production growth accelerated last year, and at the same time the balance of the economy improved considerably.

Recent economic trends confirm the picture of robust and more broadly based growth in the Finnish economy. Total production increased in 1994 by almost 4 per cent, while in the first quarter of 1995 GDP rose by over 6 per cent. The positive development will continue during 1995 and 1996, growth being about 5 per cent, although capacity restraints will slow the economy down somewhat.

Exports have been buoyant, increasing lately at a rate of some 10 per cent in volume terms year on year. The recovery of domestic demand is evident in imports, which are rising now even more than exports. This trend will continue, as both private consumption and investment will rise briskly.

Inflation has been among the lowest in the EU; in 1994 around 1 per cent, and in the autumn of 1995 0.3 per cent. Recent pay settlements have, however, increased cost pressures, and at least a slight acceleration of inflation is to be expected. To avert the tightening of monetary policy it is essential to prevent further cost pressures. In this respect the role of the trade unions is central.

The trade and current accounts are running surpluses. In the first three-quarters of 1995 the current account surplus was almost FIM13 billion, which is well in line with the forecast of FIM15 billion for the year as a whole.

The main problems are still high unemployment and the large deficit of central government. Unemployment, which in 1994 reached 18.5 per cent, is now around 17 per cent and still declining. In 1995 employment will rise particularly in manufacturing industry. To halve the present unemployment in the next four years, which is the government's aim, more employment will be needed in private services too.

Business confidence remains high

The latest Business Trends Survey of the Confederation of Finnish Industry and Employers indi-

70

cates that steady improvement is continuing in industry. Industrial output grew in 1994 by almost 12 per cent and is still rising briskly. The most rapid phase of export and production growth might be over, however, as production capacity utilization is high and export companies have a lack of capacity. The level of orders is high and profitability continues to improve. The proper time for more investment has come.

According to the Confederation's Investment Survey, manufacturing industry investment increased in 1994 by 10 per cent, and will grow by up to 50 per cent in 1995. All manufacturing industry sectors will increase their investments in 1995, with the greatest increases being in the metal and engineering, forest and chemical industries.

The industrial confidence indicator calculated on the basis of the Business Trends Survey improved considerably since 1993 and remains positive. Recent trends and future prospects are especially good in the metal and engineering sector, especially in the electronics industry. In the forest industry, on the other hand, lack of production capacity is widespread, and already retards the growth of exports and production.

Improving Europe's competitiveness

Several carefully considered and well-founded programmes to improve Europe's competitiveness have been prepared during recent years. Now is the time to carry out these plans.

It is important to have competitiveness stated in the new Treaty as a clearly defined objective of the Union. This is necessary in order to create a more favourable operating environment for European companies and to use EU resources more effectively to strengthen the industrial sector in Europe. This would give important guidance for all Union activities, for instance in the fields of taxation, social policy, industrial policy and environmental policy.

The Intergovernmental Conference

It is of paramount importance to the whole Union that the 1996 inter-governmental conference is a success. The fewer issues the IGC attempts to tackle, the more likely it is to succeed. Therefore the conference should concentrate on a few issues, primarily how to prepare the Union for taking in new member states, and how to reform the Union by introducing greater clarity, transparency, openness, efficiency and democracy. The Treaty changes must gain understanding and wide support among EU citizens.

A strong, clear and businesslike approach to the reform of the Treaties is needed. Companies operating in Europe should spell out their own objectives for the future European Union. Companies need a European Union that has a complete, effectively implemented and monitored Single European Market, and economic and monetary union according to the Maastricht Treaty. Competitiveness is an overriding priority alongside other key objectives like economic and social cohesion. It is necessary to define clearly the competences of the EU and its member states respecting subsidiarity, combined with effective decision-making systems capable of protecting legitimate interests.

France

Confederation of French Industries and Services

France enjoys a strong position in world trade, with a significant EU trade surplus. The position is threatened by the rise in value of the franc, making French goods less competitive in world markets. Its current weaknesses lie in a high rate of unemployment and a large social security burden, both of which are currently being addressed by the government.

After the growth of GDP had slowed in 1994 it began to show an improvement in the first quarter of 1995 and INSEE forecast that GDP would increase by 3.1 per cent during the year as a whole. In the medium term, Rexecode anticipates that the French economy will engage in a cycle of moderate increase. GDP in 1996 is expected to be 2.6 per cent before returning to a rate of 2.3 per cent in subsequent periods.

Unemployment in France is relatively high, but improved in 1995 from 12 to 11.4 per cent. Job creation increased by 0.4 per cent during the second quarter of 1995, which included a recovery of employment in industry. However, the quality of jobs created was lower; many of them were part time or on fixed-term contracts. Rexecode forecasts that the improvement will continue for the rest of the decade, with the rate establishing itself at 10.7 per cent by the year 2000. This will lead to an increase in productivity, albeit at a moderate level of 1.5 per cent per annum.

The government is expected to take firm action in respect of social measures in order to put the social security accounts on a sound footing and to help meet the general government deficit target of 4 per cent of GDP by the end of 1996. A structural reform of the welfare, health and pension systems is anticipated in 1996. Expenditure on health rose by 7.2 per cent in the first half of 1995 and the government is turning its urgent attention to curbing this sharp rate of increase.

Wage and price inflation are continuing their gradual easing, making possible renewed market share gains. A public sector wage freeze will be implemented in 1996. Retail prices are expected to increase moderately at the rate of 2 per cent per annum in 1995, rising to 2.3 per cent in 1996. This will be compounded by the 2 per cent increase of VAT during the third quarter of 1995. Only a slight increase in the purchase of household goods is anticipated: 1.7 per cent in 1995 and 2.1 per cent in 1996. The rate of savings of households is expected to go back up to 13.9 per cent in 1995 (against 13.5 per cent in 1994) and stay there in 1996, while gross disposable income will increase by 2 per cent each year.

Rexecode anticipates that industrial investment should increase strongly in 1995 and 1996, falling back to a rate of approximately 3 per cent per annum by the beginning of 1997. This rapid increase in productive capacity is not, however, expected to be met by a corresponding interest in demand by the beginning of 1997, which may lead to there being a surplus in productive capacity. Interest rates, having been among the lowest in Europe in 1994, are now slightly increasing and assisting the expansion of productive capacity.

As to France's position in international trade, it is expected that exports will continue to progress at a sustained rate in 1995, slowing considerably in 1996. The cumulative surplus for the first half of 1995 was 40 per cent higher than in the same period in 1994. While France has maintained its trade surplus with Germany and the UK, it still has a deficit with the US and Japan. The appreciation in value of the franc will mean that France loses part of its share in world trade, which is likely to be compounded by a general decrease in world demand for French goods in 1996.

Levels of confidence

The confidence of business people is generally low. This was due in the first part of 1995 to the political and economic uncertainties during the presidential election period, and an unfavourable monetary outlook with rising interest rates and depreciation of foreign currencies. Latterly, the business community has been disappointed by the fiscal measures introduced by the June 1995 supplementary budget bill,

which included increasing VAT from 18.6 to 20.6 per cent and a surcharge of 10 per cent on both corporation tax and wealth tax.

This is to be contrasted with the INSEE consumer confidence survey which revealed that households were confident about their financial situation, but had become less optimistic about their standard of living. They generally expected an improvement in the labour market.

Recommendations for improving Europe's competitiveness

The Conseil National du Patronat Français (CNPF) has recommended that in order to improve Europe's competitiveness, member states should collectively adopt a prime objective of improving the competitiveness of the European Union as a whole, rather than approaching the question from a national standpoint. All new projects proposed by the Commission should be accompanied by an analysis of their effect on the competitiveness of the EU. Priority should be given to decreasing public spending throughout the EU and to reversing the trend in favour of increased taxation. No new provisions

	INSEE 1st quarter 1995 actual performance	Economy Ministry 1995	INSEE 1995	Rexecode 1995	1996
	Percentage change on a year earlier				
Goods and services Volume*					
private consumption	2.0	2.5	2.3	2.0	2.1
investment	5.0	5.9	6.0	4.9	.
outward business	6.4	9.3	8.3	7.2	
household residential		3.0	2.0	2.5	
government			4.8		
Exports	10.3	6.1	6.5	6.4	
Imports	6.4	7.0	6.3	6.5	
Total GDP	3.8	3.3	3.1	2.8	2.5
Marketed GDP					2.8
Consumer prices					
annual average		1.9	1.9		
end of year rate			2.5	2.2	2.0
Disposable income		2.4	2.6	1.8	
Saving rate		13.4	13.7	13.0	
Trade balance (fob/fob FF bn)		74	92	91	
Current account balance (FF bn)			71		
Unemployment rate (%)			11.6		

* For most estimates and forecasts, aggregates are compiled from the last quarterly accounts and volumes are at previous year prices, unless specified. Ministry of Economy: April 1995; INSEE: July 1995; Rexecode: June 1995.

Table 71.1 Economic indicators for 1995 and forecasts for 1996

should be introduced before the year 2000, such as the proposed European tax on CO_2 and energy. The impact of social costs should also be controlled by reforming member states' social security systems. A comprehensive study of the effect of social costs on European competitiveness should also be undertaken, and consideration given to developing alternative methods of financing social protection. The job market in Europe is currently too rigid and does not favour the creation of new jobs. More flexible terms of employment should be introduced in order to adapt to the changing needs of industry and individuals. Greater emphasis should be placed on education and training, and the commercial implications of competitiveness taught to young people.

Priorities for the EU's Inter-governmental Conference in 1996

CNPF has identified the following issues to be addressed in 1996:

Decisions to be taken in relation to current projects

- Adopt the 10th Directive on cross-border mergers.
- Strengthen industrial and intellectual property rights.
- Adopt the Directive on the secondment of personnel within the Community.
- Adopt the amendments to the Directives dealing with the taxation of parent and subsidiary companies, mergers, withholding tax on interest and rent, and offsetting losses of subsidiaries and branches.
- Improve the temporary VAT regime with a uniform system.
- Improve the harmonization of customs duties.
- Create trans-European networks, particularly in the fields of telecommunications, transport and energy.
- Strengthen the Commission's activity in the field of antidumpting/antisubvention.

Current proposals to be rejected

- Proposals for CO_2 tax.
- Proposals for the 5th Directive, which would inflict too strict a regime on company law.
- Proposal to harmonize law on compensation for environmental damage.
- Proposal to revise the system of most favoured nations.

New initiative proposed

- Appoint the Council as responsible for reducing public deductions.
- Begin a programme to last several years with a view to achieving a European legislative code.
- Ensure that every new project justifies its effects on competitiveness.
- Strengthen the multilateral surveillance of agreements of member states relating to the EMU.
- Negotiate a customs union framework with Central and Eastern European countries.

72 Germany

Federation of German Industries

Commercial prospects for 1995/96

After passing through its deepest recession in post-war history, the German economy is now in its second year of recovery. In the further course of 1995 this recovery will, however, prove less dynamic than had initially been indicated by business trends abroad and the framework created by economic policy.

Economic indicators and prospects

As the upswing gathered momentum in 1994, the western German economy continued to recover, supported by an improvement in general conditions as well as by a boost for demand from foreign markets. In addition, producers in western Germany had managed to improve their competitive position by adapting their cost structures and the patterns of goods and services offered.

	1993	1994	1995*
Western Germany			
Gross domestic product	−1.7	2.4	2.0
Unemployed ('000)	2271	2556	2560
Consumer prices	3.2	2.7	2.0
Eastern Germany			
Gross domestic product	5.8	8.5	6.5
Unemployed ('000)	1149	1142	1040
Consumer prices	8.4	3.7	2.0
Federal Republic of Germany			
Gross domestic product	−1.1	2.9	2.25
Unemployed ('000)	3420	3698	3600
Consumer prices	3.9	2.8	2.0
Balance on current account (DM bn)	−33.2	−34.2	−37.0
Government financing deficit (DM bn) (incl. Treuhand)	−143.2	−123.9	−109.5

* forecast

Source: Spring/Autumn 1995 Report by the Economic Research Institutes

Table 72.1 Economic key figures

In the new *Länder*, too, economic activity continued to expand briskly. With 9.2 per cent growth in their gross domestic product, they became Europe's no. 1 growth region in 1994. Yet account must be taken of the fact that direct stimuli to economic growth in eastern Germany have come from a broad range of incentive measures rather than from any inherent upward trend in economic activity. The transformation from a centrally planned economy into a social market economy has not yet been completed, and there can still be no talk of a broad, self-sustaining upswing. In fact, industry in the new *Länder* continues to be heavily dependent on western transfer payments.

Taken in isolation, business trends in both western and eastern Germany seem to indicate swift economic progress. Yet in 1995 this progress is being slowed by high wage agreements and a drastic appreciation of the German mark against the US dollar and some West European currencies. Should current exchange rate relations persist, a profit squeeze and deteriorating sales prospects must be anticipated for 1996.

Level of business confidence

Judging by the business climate index of the Munich-based IFO economic research institute, the appreciation of the German mark and wage agreements have clearly depressed the mood in the corporate sector (see Figure 72.1).

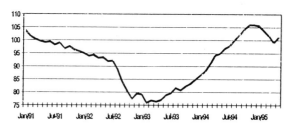

Source: IFO

Figure 72.1 Business climate

Nevertheless, production activity will probably continue to expand in the months ahead, owing to a large volume of orders still to be met. The extent to which cyclical effects will damp down future economic development will depend in no small measure on the degree of flexibility shown by business. Of decisive importance will be a major drive to increase Germany's strengths as an industrial location and to eliminate its weaknesses.

Comparative advantages and structural weaknesses of the German market

Owing to its political stability, Germany enjoys a good reputation in the international community as a politically and economically reliable partner. The comparatively high degree of industrial peace and a stable mark also seem to provide a sound and calculable basis for investment in Germany. What is equally important, investing and operating in Germany means benefiting from a well-qualified and motivated workforce and being close to the markets of Eastern Europe. This involves the chance of taking advantage of the international division of labour and opening up (future) sales markets.

In order to make Germany more attractive for both German and foreign investors, it will above all be necessary to remove the existing structural problems afflicting its economy. One such problem is the excessive cost burden borne by enterprises as a result of labour costs that are very high by international standards, and the high level of public debt. Thus, between 1989 and 1994, the public sector share of GDP in Germany rose from 45.8 per cent to over 50 per cent, compared with 36 and 32 per cent in the USA and Japan respectively.

Furthermore, the German welfare system can no longer be financed. Since 1970 social expenditure has continually been rising faster than investment. Today, more than one-third of GNP is eaten up by social welfare expenditure. In addition, there is the problem of overregulation in many sectors of the economy.

Recommendations for improving Germany's/Europe's competitiveness

Only by solving the structural problems and further improving the general conditions for industrial development will Germany be able to secure existing jobs and create new ones. For this to happen, politicians, the business community, the two sides of industry and society in general must reach agreement on a common line. This applies not only to Germany, but to the whole of Europe as well. What is needed is a medium-term strategy for growth, competitiveness and employment. Joint efforts by the member states and the European Union must be aimed at relieving the cost burden on enterprises, reducing the overall tax ratio, consolidating public budgets and encouraging privatization, debureaucratization and deregulation. Germany and Europe need more – not less – market competition.

Consequently, there should be no let-up in current fiscal policy efforts to cut expenditure with the aim of consolidating public budgets. At the same time, the burden of taxes and levies must steadily be eased. Only if the overall tax ratio is reduced can the urgently needed incentives for investment and individual performance be improved. This also calls for new priorities in public sector functions. Services that have so far been provided by public authorities should be entrusted to the private sector, wherever possible.

Pay increases must once again be related more closely to productivity gains. One can only distribute what has been earned. At the same time, enterprises must continue and step up their innovation efforts. The main thrust of whatever measures are taken must be to enhance economic growth, rather than distribute its results.

Priorities for the Inter-governmental Conference

Given the increasing economic interlocking within the European Economic Area, the German business community is anxious to see integration so far achieved in the EU put on a secure basis and further deepened. The overriding concern of all considerations and decisions must be to strengthen the global competitiveness of European industry.

This being said, the Intergovernmental Conference in 1996 should not aim too high. The participating states should above all refrain from any measures that might disrupt the common market and lead the Community to move backwards and degenerate into a mere free trade zone.

German industry's interest is in equal progress being achieved by all member states together. Multispeed progress and, above all, the 'opting-out' by individual member states in certain policy areas must not become an accepted practice in the further development of Europe. When enlarging the EU, care must be taken to ensure that the accession of new members will not compromise either the objectives of the Treaty or the *acquis communautaire*. Another requirement to be fulfilled before the EU is further enlarged is the adjustment of the existing institutions. The aim must be to maintain their ability to act and to make the decision-making process more efficient. Last but not least, the further development of the EU should be guided more consistently by the principles of proportionality and subsidiarity. Insufficient attention has so far been paid to the latter principle in particular.

In the final analysis, the main concern of the inter-governmental conference must be to improve the EU's ability to act with regard to its common foreign and security policy, as well as its domestic and legislative policy, to make the EU institutions more efficient, and to establish the institutional conditions for EU enlargement. Only in this way will it be possible to make Europe more competitive, secure existing jobs and create new ones. This is in the interests not only of German industry but of European society in general.

Greece

Federation of Greek Industry

Developments and potential of the Greek economy

The convergence plan implemented presently in Greece aims at stabilizing the Greek economy. The economy is currently on a virtuous circle with the recovery in economic activity assisting macro-economic adjustments and nominal convergence, which, in turn, reinforces investment and growth prospects. Financial and structural foundations, however, remain weak. At the heart of Greece's inability to profit from world economic growth is the rather intractable budgetary situation and unsustainable debt dynamics, which keep interest rates high and generate uncertainty. The sustainability of the favourable conjectural position of the economy in the months to come will depend on the scope and depth of the further fiscal consolidation required to implement the convergence programme and the implementation of long-awaited structural reforms to increase the growth potential of the economy. Delays in the big infrastructure projects and the uncertain pace of the privatization programme continue to affect prospects in the capital markets negatively.

Greece places high expectations on the 1994–9 Community Support Framework, which is expected to provide partial financing of projects of about 25 billion ECU over the period to 1999. However, unless there is strong private investment and growth, the Community's structural funds will not have a major impact on the economy.

On the other hand, there are some very positive developments for Greece. The countries of Central and Eastern Europe and the Balkan region compose the greater challenge for Greece since its entry to the European Union. Political changes in Eastern Europe are opening up a potential demand on which Greek companies are well placed to act. These markets will become a hinterland for Greece and offer the opportunity for internationalizing entrepreneurial activities.

Emerging markets in Eastern Europe are bound to affect the Greek business environment: first, through exports of Greek goods and services looking for a wider market; second, through increasing foreign direct investment in these countries; and third, through more foreign companies using Greece as a base to move into the Balkans and Eastern Europe. It is not just proximity that Greece has on its side in doing business with the Balkans. Historical and cultural ties are another strength which other Western countries will have trouble in matching. Greece's affinities with the Balkan countries hold great potential, but they require long-term strategies.

A research study undertaken by the Federation of Greek Industries (FGI) about developments of manufacturing exports during the first six months of 1995 shows that 27 per cent of Greek manufacturing companies export to Central and Eastern Europe, and 50 per cent of these companies increased their exports to this region by 30 per cent in comparison to the corresponding levels of the same six months in 1994.

A study by the European Commission *Trade and Foreign Investment in the Community Regions: The Impact of Economic Reform in Central and Eastern Europe* forecasts that if reforms in Eastern Europe succeed, Greek industrial production will increase annually by 10 per cent as a result of Greek business activities in those markets. In addition, a study by the Centre of Economic Policy Research of London forecasts an increase of Greek exports to the countries of Central and Eastern Europe of 2–5 times in comparison to the 1989 level. Another study by R. Porter and R. Faini, *European Union Trade with Eastern Europe*, argues that if the European Union expands eastwards, Greek exports to the Balkans will increase by 200 per cent compared to an import increase of only 91 per cent.

Main economic trends and indicators
Macroeconomic developments
After four years of continuous decline, manufacturing production in 1994 showed a mild increase of some 1.2 per cent. The recovery in industrial production continued in the first few months of 1995, although at a slower pace. The slowdown became pronounced in April. On average, however, production in the period January–April 1995 was higher than in the corresponding period of 1994 by 0.7 per cent. Overall, GDP growth in 1994–5 will fluctuate around 1 per cent, as agriculture and services, although strengthened with respect to 1993, are not expected to register significant advances in output.

Inflation and Unemployment
In the last few months, the markets saw the rate of inflation reaching the single-digit range for the first time in many years, with good prospects for further deceleration. Inflation has come down to 8.7 per cent at the end of August, supported by restrictive macroeconomic and incomes policies, as well as the pricing policies of public corporations. Unemployment, however, has been edging upwards, with overall unemployment surpassing 10 per cent of the labour force, as the pick-up in economic activity remains weak and restructuring in industry continues.

Balance of payments
As the recovery strengthens and the drachma exchange rate appreciates further in real terms,

import volume is expected to rise in 1995. Moreover, Greek export growth will rise substantially to meet the strong import demand in Greece's trading partners, although not commensurately, owing to competitiveness losses and the increasing difficulty of traditional Greek exports to penetrate world markets further. As a result, the trade balance deficit is expected to increase substantially in 1995. This marked deterioration is unlikely to be made up by the surplus on invisibles, due to weakening tourism receipts and despite the expected recovery in EU net transfers following the mediocre 1994 performance. Therefore, the current account deficit will widen from virtual balance in 1994 to about 1 per cent of GDP in 1995. In the capital account, despite the doubling of entrepreneurial capital inflows since 1994, net private capital inflows stagnated in dollar terms. This reflects a substantial outflow during March of 'other capital', which is mainly comprised of speculative short-term capital flows.

The 1995 budget
The 1995 budget reflects the full impact of the tax measures that were taken in spring 1994, followed by the Bank of Greece's outline of a monetary framework conducive to disinflation. Agreements have been reached by the social partners in recent years which limit wage adjustments to levels broadly consistent with the overall economic policy. Public revenue in the first few months of 1995 has been rising fast, exceeding expectations. The financing aspects of the central government deficit are also improving through the decline in the Treasury bill rates. Fiscal reforms and budgetary consolidation must proceed with rigour if a sustainable position is to be secured in the medium term.

Monetary policy
After successfully controlling liquidity in 1994 and steering interest rate differentials *vis-à-vis* the world market towards sustainable levels, monetary policy is called on to continue its anti-inflationary stance and support the government's goal of reducing inflation to 7 per cent by the end of 1995. The challenge for the Bank of Greece is to strike a balance between edging interest rates downwards, in order to support the recovery and reduce debt-servicing costs to the government, and pursuing its exchange rate objective of keeping the drachma sliding at no more than 3 per cent compared to the ECU, in the presence of

large capital inflows from abroad which tend to complicate the control of liquidity.

Business confidence among FGI members

Despite the slowdown of production, the general climate in manufacturing overall remains positive, indicating a possible improvement in production during summer 1995. The relevant index of industrial confidence has been constantly on an upward trend since the beginning of 1995. It appears, in general, that the positive trends that started in 1994 continue to exist, but that the recovery of industrial production is not poised for an acceleration as yet. Nevertheless, the picture emerging from IOBE's (Institute of Economic and Industrial Research) Business Trends Surveys indicates a generally positive climate. Having taken a dip in November 1994, the index of business prospects rose continuously in the following four months. There was a moderate fall in April 1995 to a level where the index stabilized by May 1995, despite which the index on average remains similar or higher than in the corresponding period of 1994. The persistence of positive business estimates and prospects for more than five months in a row leads to the conclusions that the reversal of the previously negative trend concerning industrial production that took place in 1994 will continue during 1995, and that the recent slowdown is probably temporary.

Recommendations for improving Europe's competitiveness

The FGI's vision for Europe is one with a high level of employment and steady growth in living standards. However, in order to achieve this vision, European firms will have to increase their competitiveness so as to be the engine of growth and development.

Action needs to be taken towards the following objectives:

■ a smaller and more efficient public sector;
■ reduction of labour costs (particularly non-wage costs), increasing the flexibility of labour markets and upgrading the skills and abilities of employees and the unemployed;
■ encouragement of continuous technological innovation and entrepreneurialism, particularly in SMEs;
■ creation of an open trading system and a cost-effective infrastructure, which can take advantage of the opportunities offered by chances in

the business environment as well as dealing with the threats posed by it;
■ establishment of a broader consensus to reflect the needs of the twenty-first century. Development of new forms of work organization, including closer partnerships throughout the value chain between firms, their suppliers and their customers, and between management, their employees and their representatives, and improvement of the level of management skills;
■ effective steps towards a common currency;
■ completion of trans-European networks.

Intergovernmental Conference

The IGC agenda is dominated by institutional questions, related to decision-making procedures, the division of powers between EU institutions, and the balance of competencies between EU and national bodies.

FGI believes that institutional reform should aim at making the EU efficient and manageable and the policy-making process effective and more transparent. The debate on institutional problems should target its efforts at finding an answer to the following question: 'How can the EU be widened and deepened while respecting the aim of economic and social cohesion between the member states?'

Within this context FGI does not support a multispeed Europe and Europe à la carte, because these models of integration will deepen the gap between the poor and the rich regions of the EU.

In addition, FGI:

■ is in favour of the enlargement of the EU, as long as it does not affect in a negative way the process of integration and respects the acquis communautaire;
■ feels that further enlargement would require the introduction of new structural policies which would counteract the negative consequences;
■ supports the position that countries which would like to enter the Union as full members should meet both political and economic criteria, as defined in the treaty;
■ believes that all member states should aim at participating in the third stage of EMU. To this end they must focus their efforts on implementing convergence programmes without any delay. A link between structural policies and convergence programmes might help to that direction;
■ believes that the criteria and procedures for a

member state to enter EMU have been well defined in the treaty. Therefore clarifications may be in order only concerning the procedures for a member state to enter the EMU *after* the initial dates (1997 or 1999) and their role in the decision making process;

- is in favour of the strict application of the provisions and rules of competition in the implementation of the policy. It notes the need for more transparent procedures in the implementation of the competition policy;
- supports the strengthening of the provisions dealing with the control of state aids;
- believes that the review of the EU budget should focus on solving the large gap between the EU's targets, as defined in the treaty, and the EU's economic means to implement its targets;
- stresses the importance of structural policies in the integration process;
- notes the importance of the social dialogue in the effective implementation of the structural programmes;
- believes that the participation of the social partners in all stages of formulation and implementation of the Community Support Frameworks can improve the results of structural policies;
- places high importance on social dialogue and supports the absolute necessity of social partners' participation in the formulation and implementation of social policy;
- believes that the framework agreements related to industrial relations can play an important role as long as further measures are taken at national level (according to the principle of subsidiarity). These agreements should be applied in each member state through agreements between social partners at national level. Should the Social Protocol be incorporated in the Treaty, all

member states of the EU must be engaged by social policy measures in the same way. Further enlargement of the treaty broadening workers' rights should not be considered;

- is not in favour of a further distinction between SMEs and very small companies;
- believes that the impact of EU legislative proposals on the international competitiveness of European companies must be mandated by the treaty, and must be appraised not only when the original proposal is put forward by the Commission but again when it is finally approved, if substantial amendments have been made in the process. The impact assessment must, where appropriate, be accompanied by a full cost/benefit analysis, in line with Declaration 18 of the EU Treaty;
- supports the introduction of a title for tourism in the treaty which will aim at making best use of the environment and preserving national identity, history and culture;
- is in favour of the introduction of a title for energy which will aim at the rational use of energy and at the increased coverage of energy needs by renewable sources of energy;
- supports a balanced approach concerning special trade agreements with the regions adjacent to the borders of the European Union (Eastern and Central Europe, Balkans and Mediterranean Countries);
- thinks that the IGC should examine whether the new treaty can mandate uniform implementation of EU regulations by the member countries, in particular concerning the functioning of the internal market;
- feels that security matters should form a part of the EU external policy. Bilateral problems of member states should be seen as aspects of European security as a whole.

Hungary

Chamber of Commerce and Industry, Budapest

The coalition government of the Hungarian Socialist Party and the Alliance of Free Liberals came to power in Hungary as a result of the second free elections after the fall of socialism, in June 1994. At that time widespread expectations were reflected in their overwhelming majority in parliament (74 per cent), and the patience with which the population and business accepted some harsh measures (eg an 8 per cent devaluation of HUF, the Hungarian currency, in August 1994, and price increases announced in energy and communication, an unavoidable new impetus to increasing inflation). Also, however contradictory it looked, for a relatively long period of time both population and business tolerated a seemingly inconsistent and less determined approach by the government to the handling of most of the delicate economic problems. It needs to be added that during the elections the socialists invited the leader of the most important trade union organization into their ranks as number two in the party hierarchy, and invested in a wide dialogue with many different lobby organizations, with a view to concluding a framework agreement rather quickly on the most important economic and social issues.

It became evident, however, that the first composition of the government was unable (or unwilling) to act according to the promises and expectations. As a result, towards the end of 1994 and beginning of 1995, some weeks after the forced departure of the president of the Hungarian National Bank (HNB)

and the sacking of the head of the state privatization, the minister of finance resigned too, allowing the prime minister to restructure the government and try to keep a closer control on its activities. The nomination of both the new head of HNB as well as the new minister of finance (Mr Gy. Surányi and Mr L. Bokros, respectively) satisfied the coalition partners and most of the business communities, although the new head of privatization seemed to be a compromise and the announcement of a drastic economic package by the minister of finance (12 March, 1995), particularly in relation to the welfare system, caused the resignation of two other ministers.

Ever since, and although some first impacts of the March economic package seem to have brought clear results, the internal contradictions of the government (more so inside the dominant socialist party) and of the way it handles the economic and social affairs are far from resolved, preventing a more smooth and well managed transition. In the summer of 1995, a long-lasting coalition crisis between the parties in the government (as yet not resolved) and consecutive decisions of the Constitutional Court, which forced the withdrawal of some of the key social elements of the March economic package, marked the political arena.

Real economy continued on the path started towards the end of 1993, with a modest average growth (GDP increase 2 per cent), more significant developments occurred in industry as a whole (over

74

	1994	1995 (forecast)
	% annual change	% annual change
GDP real growth	102	100–101
Industrial production	109.2	103–104
Construction	119.5	100
Agricultural production	102	100–102
Investments	111–112	101–103
Exports (US$)	120.1	120
Imports (US$)	116.1	110
Trade balance (deficit, US$ billion)	3.9	3
Balance of payments (deficit, US$ billion)	3.9	3
State budget (deficit, HUF billion)	237	250
Domestic savings (increase, HUF billion)	292	250–260
Domestic consumption (%)	101.3	96–97
Inflation (consumer prices, %)	118.8	129
Registered unemployment (thousands)	520	540

Source: Economic Research Institute (GKI Rt),Budapest (August 1995)

Table 74.1 Hungary – basic macroeconomic figures

9 per cent), especially in construction (close to 2 per cent) and telecommunications, while agriculture, food processing and tourism ended the year with relative success. All this was reflected in the level of investments, which also increased by 11–12 per cent in total. The modest increase in demand, especially for certain industrial products, pushed up the import level again, while the export performance of the economy still suffers from inherited shortages, therefore the foreign trade balance deteriorated sharply in 1994, causing a deficit of US$3.6 billion (reduced only by the net income from tourism, of around 0.5 billion). Foreign direct investments continue flowing in, almost unchanged in annual volume (around US$1.5 billion), but the current account of the balance of payments was far from satisfactory (at US$3.9 billion). Macroeconomic figures are detailed in Table 74.1.

Two positive issues in 1994 were undoubtedly the reduction of inflation in the consumer sector (under 19 per cent), together with a steady purchasing power for those on the payroll, while the number of registered unemployed was reduced to 520,000 (around 11 per cent). Another less satisfactory change was the insufficient progress of privatization, lasting deep into 1995: as a consequence the new government, in the summer of 1994, announced its acceleration and a new privatization law, but this promise could not be met until May 1995, and even after that there were restraints on many of the partners potentially involved. Hungarian firms are allowed, indeed stimulated, to borrow abroad (in consequence

of the very high domestic interest level and the shortages of the banking system for risk management), which adds to the already high level of the country's international debts. This contrasts with the consistent and cautious borrowing and bond issuing politics of the HNB, as a result of which Hungary succeeded in building up a convincing level of foreign exchange reserves, up to roughly US$8 billion at the end of 1994.

The underlying dynamism in the microeconomic environment still survives, however, and the March 1995 package put forward by the new minister of finance gave a new impetus to certain expectations, especially in the following aspects:

- An immediate devaluation of the currency by 9 per cent plus the introduction of a 'crawling peg' exchange rate policy for the current year as a whole (with consecutive monthly devaluations of 1.9 and 1.3 per cent for the first and second half respectively) gives the expected middle-term outlook, particularly as regards inflation and exchange rate issues (the same approach was announced recently for the first half of 1996, with around 1.2–1.3 per cent devaluations per month).

- The introduction, by 20 March, of an 8 per cent overall import surcharge (lasting until the middle of 1997) also encouraged most domestic producers, much afraid of the inflow of foreign products and critical of the very liberal import regime applied since the end of the 1980s (however, machinery and other imports with the purpose of investment are exempted from that measure).

■ Incentives and supplementary regimes and institutions for encouraging exports were also announced and introduced step by step – an approach and activity promised by the previous government and long expected by business (e.g. the extension of the mandate of the Hungarian EXIMBank, supplementary resources for the Hungarian Export Credit Guarantee System and EXIMBank, an increase in the support of production systems and foreign trade promotion resources, especially for the agricultural sector, etc).

■ A small (if only initial) reduction in the profit tax burden on companies which symbolized – and hopefully should continue to confirm later – the commitment of the government to developing a more entrepreneur-friendly regulatory environment. Other elements with similar impact were expected from more general social measures and proposals cited below.

To compensate for evident losses in the competitive advantages of Hungary compared to neighbouring countries, as well as to start to make the necessary corrections in the welfare systems financed by the central budget, but dangerously imbalanced for many years, drastic austerity measures were announced and some introduced: in the social, education, cultural and healthcare systems, the financial burden of which was not only inherited almost unchanged from the previous socialist regime, but extended because of unemployment and similar new social phenomena. These induced a further reduction in the standard of living (particularly pensioners, cultural workers, teachers and students) on the one hand and vehement reactions from certain groups and their representative organizations on the other. Many of these suggestions, however, although adopted by legislation in the Parliament at the end of May, continue being under revision by the Constitutional Court, on the initiative of different social lobbies (e.g. mothercare and family allowances, certain restrictions supposed to harm individual human rights or create discrimination between individuals), and discussions between the government and the disabled about implementation of the measures are not yet terminated.

Recent developments in the business sphere reflect the complexities deriving from these contradictions. On one hand, real economic growth is

expected to reach the 1 per cent level. The increase in industrial production is certainly slowing down (only construction, particularly house building, keeps on booming), but services (including commerce and transport, communication) seem to compensate for the loss in dynamism. Agriculture – in terms of volume production, particularly in basic food stuffs and maintaining the stock of animals – also keeps on the previous track, even if on a much lower level than traditionally. More evident however is that investments as a whole will not hold out (down to around 1–3 per cent increase only). Domestic demand (and with this, retail trade) suffers from the drastic cuts in real purchasing power (between 8 and 10 per cent), together with which the increase in domestic savings is expected to slow to around HUF 250 billion (HUF 292 billion in 1994). Inflation in consumer prices is at 28–30 per cent, and it is not expected to slow until the end of the year, and soundings among business show that order levels seem insufficient to keep up a high rate of activity.

Business expectations are consequently concentrated on the opportunities in foreign markets, hopefully supported by the business cycle in the Western European region (absorbing more than two-thirds of total Hungarian exports), and expecting more promising selling opportunities in the Central European Free Trade Association (CETRA) and CIS markets too (another one-fifth of the exports). Altogether, a 20 per cent export rise in current dollar terms is expected, while imports are only expected to grow by around 10 per cent. (The figures for the first 7–8 months in some sectors already confirm this last prognosis, e.g. individual car imports fell by 25–30 per cent.) Even so, the foreign trade balance would be in deficit by around US$3 billion. Tourism in 1995 will probably not be a success story, so it will bring in net revenue less than expected (by around US$0.3 billion).

One big question mark in the current business atmosphere concerns the deficit in the state budget and foreign debt. For the time being this deficit reaches almost 10 per cent of GDP, although without the accumulated debts and commitments (domestic and abroad) the deficit would remain in a practically manageable range, close to the Maastricht criteria. In addition to this burden, the 1995 budget foresees a HUF 150 billion income from the privatization alone, which most experts and institutions find exaggerated by around HUF 80–100 billion. Foreign debt commitments and domestic bonds, however, keep the interest rate high (normally at 30–33 per cent), and the lending capacities of the commercial bank sector very much limited, thus hindering the necessary financial stimulus for business to grow. It is in this connection that the necessary stabilization of the state and macroeconomic finances contrasts, both in monetary (credit) and financial conditions (first of all, taxation), with the need and expectation of business to expand and produce additional incomes. At the time of writing, the first signs of a slow downturn of interest levels are becoming obvious, as a consequence of the levelling off in the monthly figures in budget management, and a modest reduction in expectations for the annual trade and balance of payments deficits.

However, the Hungarian economy maintains its attraction to foreign investment, in taking over firms by privatization (notably, in 1995, electricity, energy production, the oil and gas industry and some commercial banks are to be privatized), or for new greenfield investments. The generous regulations for foreign investments, the supply of skilled and competitive labour, good market access for the products and services in a wide region outside Hungary, a dynamic development of the infrastructure of the country, convertibility of the Hungarian currency (expected to be announced for 1996) may all be counted as advantages. The inflow of FDIs (between US\$ billion 1.5 and 1.7 per year) confirms this

statement: at least 30 large multinationals are already engaged in investment and more than 23,000 joint ventures have been established in Hungary, with a total value of close to US\$10 billion, up to mid-1995.

One of the political priorities of the Hungarian government is to prepare the country to be integrated into the EU as a full member. The official application was presented in April 1994, and preparatory work started in the country, on government and business level alike. The adaptation to the Maastricht criteria, harmonization to the legal and administrative system of the EU, implementation of the EU white book on the internal market requirements, etc. are all reflected in recent activities of many of the authorities and business organizations. Expectations are that the EU Inter-governmental Conference will decide on an early start for negotiations with Hungary, probably together with other states, and the opportunities for getting involved in Community systems could be opened up as soon as possible. It should not be forgotten, however, that most businesses in Hungary still need a period of time to prepare for being able to work and survive under 'Euro-conditions', and while foreign-owned and joint (foreign–Hungarian) firms are mostly in favour of integration, thousands of entrepreneurs and firms would prefer to prolong this preparatory period.

Iceland

Federation of Icelandic Industries

Recovery

The Icelandic economy took a firm turn towards recovery in 1994. Economic growth significantly exceeded previous projections, led by a substantial increase in exports. A six-year period of stagnation, slow growth and slight recession thus finally ended. GDP growth was 2.8 per cent in 1994 and is expected to be 3.2 per cent in 1995, in line with the OECD average.

Successes

Economic policy has been successful on a number of fronts. There was a sizeable surplus on the current account in 1994, equating 2.0 per cent of GDP. A residue of 1 per cent is expected in 1995. The current account has thus been favourable for three consecutive years. The improvement is mainly owing to a sharp increase in exports, amounting to 10.2 per cent in 1994. This is explained by a considerable fish catch in distant waters, an increase in industrial production and advantageous conditions in foreign markets. Domestic stability and an agreeable operating environment for firms in sectors exposed to foreign competition also contributed positively.

The real exchange rate of the króna, which is an important indicator of the competitiveness of Icelandic industries, is currently at a historical low. The competitive position has been further strengthened by the lowering of taxes. A special turnover tax has been abandoned, and the income tax rate for businesses has been lowered from 45 to 33 per cent.

Inflation has been very low for the past few years. The cost of living index increased by 1.5 per cent in 1994 and is predicted to increase by 1.7 per cent in 1995. In the medium term, inflation is expected to remain low.

Interest rates came down considerably in autumn 1993 as a result of firm policy action taken by the government and the central bank. The easing of monetary policy was justified by the slack in the overall economy. Interest rate developments were also positive for domestic firms in the first half of 1994. In the latter half, however, and in the spring of 1995, interest rates rose somewhat owing to a slight increase in inflation expectations, stemming from the uncertainty in the labour market and higher interest rates in international capital markets. Uncertainty in public sector finances also added to the rise in interest rates. It is therefore considered to be of fundamental importance to ease the tension in the credit market and create space for the lowering of interest rates.

Because of these plausible developments in the operating environments for businesses, activity has increased in most sectors of the economy. This indicates that Icelandic firms are responsive and able to take advantage of improvements in the competitive position. Authorities should therefore be inspired to maintain a sound policy to strengthen the recovery.

75

Important tasks

In spite of the progress that has been made on a number of fronts, not all developments in the Icelandic economy are positive. As in many other OECD countries, public sector deficit and debt accumulation have been persistent problems in recent years. This has led to higher interest rates than would otherwise have prevailed. Business sector investment has therefore contracted, with the consequence of depressed economic activity.

The public sector deficit has both structural and cyclical components. An extended period of persistent deficit indicates a significant structural deficit. The cyclical deficit is explained by a fall in tax revenues, owing to the decline in national income, and also by an increase in expenditure on unemployment benefits and various labour market measures.

Notwithstanding the trouble with public finances, some results have been achieved in containing expenditure. It is, however, important to conduct a solid fiscal policy conducive to a firm balance in the financial market and further decline in interest rates.

Unemployment is likely to increase in 1995 to 5 per cent from 4.7 per cent in 1994. Although unemployment in Iceland is still low compared to international standards, it is considered to be a serious problem. One of the main aims of economic policy is therefore to reduce it.

Economic policy

After the parliamentary elections in April 1995, the Independence Party and the Progressive Party formed a coalition government. The government's policy declaration contains all the necessary ingredients for economic prosperity and sustainable growth. Heavy emphasis is placed on upholding price stability, a favourable real exchange rate of the króna and keeping domestic interest rates at a competitive level. In order to increase employment the government intends to promote innovation and new investments. It is also on the agenda to balance the budget during the next four years. The government's policy declaration therefore reflects understanding of the prerequisites of economic growth and improved living standards.

The primary objective of economic policy at present is thus to maintain stability and create room for lowering of interest rates. It is vital to preserve the improved position on the current account, the strong competitive position and low inflation. It is also of fundamental importance to prevent large fluctuations in the real exchange rate and, consequently, create more stability in the business environment. This will foster sustainable economic growth and create employment opportunities in the future.

The European issue

Iceland joined EFTA in 1970 and concluded a free-trade agreement with the European Community in 1972. In 1992, the EFTA countries and the EC signed an agreement to establish a free-trade zone, the European Economic Area (EEA). The treaty liberalizes the flow of goods, services, capital and labour in the area. The EEA agreement came into force on 1 January 1994. Owing to the large portion of external trade Iceland conducts with the EEA countries, it is of fundamental importance to strengthen ties with the area.

The new government does not intend to apply for membership of the European Union, although it has declared it as vital to strengthen the relationship with the EU. The Federation of Icelandic Industries, on the other hand, has expressed support for handing in an application. We are convinced that membership, given that certain requirements are met, will contribute positively to Iceland's economy and culture in the years to come.

Conclusion

The pillars of social welfare and economic prosperity, price stability, low interest rates, a strong competitive position, economic policy conducive to research and development, efficient infrastructure and political solidity must all be maintained and acknowledged. Neglect will harm competitiveness and discourage innovation and activity.

Ireland

Irish Business and Employers Confederation

Market size

Gross National Product (GNP) amounted to IR£33 billion in 1995. Over the past five years GNP growth has averaged just under 4 per cent per annum. Personal consumer expenditure amounted to IR£21 billion and has experienced an average annual real growth over the last five years of just over 3 per cent. The economy is extremely open, with exports of goods and services amounting to 72 per cent of GDP and imports of goods and services amounting to 58 per cent. GNP is about 12 per cent lower than GDP, the difference largely being accounted for by external debt servicing and profit repatriations to multinational corporations located in Ireland. As a result of bad economic policies at the end of the 1970s and early 1980s, Ireland built up a large debt which amounted to 125 per cent of GNP in 1987. This, however, has been reduced to under 90 per cent in 1995 and on current policies is expected to be under 70 per cent by 1999. Ireland has a young well-educated population, which has found favour with high technology industries, resulting in the location there of many leading electronics, computer and software companies. Despite rapid growth rates, unemployment remains high at 13.5 per cent in 1995, partly as a result of the rapidly expanding labour force because of demographic structure, increased female participation and a lower rate of emigration.

Economic indicators

Economic indicators so far in 1995 suggest another year of strong economic performance. In the first four months of 1995 manufacturing output was some 16 per cent above the same period of the previous year, and IBEC/ESRI survey data up to the middle of the year suggest a growth rate in manufacturing similar to the 12.8 per cent recorded in 1994. At present there is little to indicate that a growth in manufacturing of close to 10 per cent will not be recorded in 1996. GNP grew by 7 per cent in 1994 and is expected to record growth in 1995 of close to 6 per cent. Consumer spending is likely to grow by around 4.5 per cent in 1995, despite a disappointing growth in retail sales of only 2.2 per cent in the first five months of the year. However, sales are expected to pick up in the second half of the year as tax concessions granted in April start to take effect. Inflation picked up a little in May, recording an annual rate of 2.8 per cent, but fell back to 2.4 per cent in August. However, this increase was largely owing to an increase in interest rates affecting house mortgages, and the inflation rate for the year is expected to be 2.5 per cent. Given the modest 2.5 per cent per annum increase in wages negotiated in a three-year national wage agreement, which runs to 1996, inflation in 1996 should be no more than 3 per cent. External trade growth will remain strong and the current account

76

of the balance of payments surplus is expected to be around 6 per cent of GNP in 1995 and 1996.

Business confidence

Business confidence is close to an all-time high with order-books and production expectations close to peak levels. While sales on the home market have been relatively unimpressive, home sales expectations in the consumer goods sector have improved significantly. Expectations for export sales remain high. Some inflationary tendencies which were starting to show through at the end of 1994 and at the beginning of 1995 have abated, with manufacturers' selling prices expected to remain stable in the latter half of 1995.

Recommendations for improving Europe's competitiveness

There is an abundance of material which demonstrates clearly that the European economy has become a high cost, low growth and overregulated region by comparison to emerging economies across the globe. The Commission's White Paper, *Growth, Competitiveness, Employment*, the Commission's Communication of September 1994, *An Industrial Competitiveness Policy for the European Union*, and the UNICE report on competitiveness all focused on the key issue of competitiveness for business. EU governments, however, generally pay lip-service to the imperative of competitiveness. The Irish Business and Employers Confederation (IBEC) recommends that competitiveness should be written into the new treaty as an overriding principle and should be on a policy par with EMU and EU's social dimension. Thus if accepted it would be required that all new legislation emanating from the EU would seek to improve Europe's competitive deficit. The EU's Action Plan on industrial competitiveness dated 14 March 1995 must be implemented. The competitiveness advisory group set up by President Santer in February 1995 ought to consider the following:

- What can be done to improve Europe's export performance?
- What should the balance be between liberalization of public services and the need to safeguard social standards?
- What policy changes are needed to promote investment in intangible assets?
- What changes are required to improve the productivity of Europe's research programmes?
- What can be done to reduce the tax burden in Europe to the level in competitor economies?

Priorities for the Inter-governmental Conference

The IGC should be prepared over a much longer period than is currently envisaged. Europe needs a period of legislative consolidation and not a burst of new initiatives inspired by treaty changes. Public opinion must be convinced that whatever emerges from the next IGC is relevant and intelligible. Efforts should be concentrated on the implementation of the treaty.

There should be no further enlargement of the Union this side of the year 2000. As enlargement, however, is unavoidable, the IGC must find ways of reconciling the widening and the deepening of the Union.

EMU will have to be discussed and the 'rules of conduct' once a country becomes a member must be spelt out. The IGC should consider the issue of fiscal federalism.

The concept of competitiveness should be raised to a policy on a par with that of economic and social cohesion, and measures identified by the European Commission to implement its industrial competitiveness programme should be progressed. The uniform implementation of all outstanding internal market legislation should be guaranteed. An initiative on deregulation should be launched. The EU's competition policy should be reviewed.

Preparatory work should be put in train to facilitate the conclusion of a broadly based treaty between the EU and the USA.

Irish Business and Employers Confederation

The Irish Business and Employers Confederation (IBEC) is the independent voice of Ireland's business community, with a membership drawn from all sectors of commercial activity. IBEC promotes the development of Irish business at a national level and offers its expertise in a wide range of areas to members in order to protect their interests and keep themselves informed on issues affecting their business.

Italy

The Confederation of Italian Industry

Recent developments and forecasts

Recovery in economic activity in Italy, which had shown the first sign of an upturn in the last quarter of 1993, gathered pace in 1994 (Table 77.1). Export demand continued to grow, sustained by increase in world trade and depreciation of the lira, while domestic demand started to increase, in particular in household consumption. In the fourth quarter of 1994 domestic demand increased by 0.7 per cent

(annualized percentage change on previous period 3.8 per cent), industrial production by 1.6 per cent (annualized percentage change 6.9 per cent); while import growth (2.5 and 14.7 per cent respectively) was higher than export growth (0.1 and 10.3 per cent respectively). GDP expanded in 1994 at a sustained rate: 1.6 per cent (annualized change) in the second quarter, 3.8 per cent in the third, 2.7 per cent in the fourth.

In the first few months of 1995 production con-

	1994				1995			
	1st qtr	2nd qtr	3rd qtr	4th qtr	1st qtr	(b)	April	May
GDP (a)	0.4	1.0	1.3	0.0				
Domestic demand (a)	0.4	1.4	1.3	0.7				
Household consumption (a)	0.6	0.6	0.4	0.2				
Fixed capital investment (a)	0.5	0.9	−0.5	1.5				
Industrial production (a)	0.7	4.2	2.7	1.6	0.3	9.9	0.9	−1.0 (c)
Output prices (d)	1.2	1.1	1.0	1.9	2.7	6.8		
Consumer prices (e)	1.0	0.8	1.0	1.2	1.6	4.4	0.5	0.6
Wages (f)								
Total	0.8	0.3	0.6	0.3	1.8	2.7	0.2	
Industry	1.7	0.6	0.4	0.1	1.7	2.8	0.1	

Notes: (a) Seasonally adjusted data. (b) Percentage change over 1st quarter of 1994. (c) CSC survey estimates. (d) Manufactured products. (e) Cost of living index. (f) Contractual hourly rate.

Sources: Istat, Confindustria

Table 77.1 Main macroeconomic indicators (% changes over the previous period)

tinued to rise sharply. The first quarter industrial production index increased by 0.3 per cent over the previous quarter and by 9.9 per cent over the first quarter of 1994. According to Confindustria and IRS survey estimates, in April and May industrial production would have stabilized around first quarter levels: growth of the first five months over the same period of the previous year should have been around 8 per cent.

Gross fixed investment has shown very different behaviour in the two main components. Spending on construction has not yet shown signs of recovery, partially due to the reduction of public investment projects and the protracted recession in private residential building. Investments in machinery and equipment instead, which were depressed during 1993, benefited from the recovery in economic activity since the beginning of 1994. In the last quarter of 1994 investment growth was 2.4 per cent higher over one year and 1.5 per cent over the previous quarter. Recent surveys showed an acceleration of investment activity in the first months of 1995.

The household confidence indicator has strongly improved in the first three quarters of the previous year, decreasing afterwards, in particular in March 1995 following the lira crisis in the financial markets; in April and May it seems that household confidence has started again to rise back to the higher 1994 level.

Forecasts of the Italian economy for the next few years strongly depend on the increasing adjustment of public finances (Table 2). It is not only necessary to stabilize the debt/GDP ratio; it is also important how this result is achieved: cutting expenditures first of all. From this point of view the recent pension reform has been largely unsatisfactory; savings in fact have been delayed to the twenty-first century. Forecasts depend as well on wage increases being held within the Government's target inflation rate.

In this scenario domestic and foreign confidence would increase, the lira exchange rate could stabilize around 1.100 over the German mark by the end of 1995 and around 1.050 by the end of 1996; this would allow a decrease in the interest rate dif-

Turin

Turin is marked by the co-existence of two sometimes conflicting urban identities first, rooted in history, as a capital the second as an industrial city. In fact the first identity stems from the role Turin played the European history between 1559 and 1859: the capital of a small but expanding state (Savoy-Piedmont, later the Kingdom of Sardinia), at the intersection between French, Italy and Swiss cultural traditions, capable of exerting an influence on continental events outweighing it's limited size. Thanks to this background Turin became the first capital of unified Italy, and even when Rome superseded it, the city preserved to a large extent the urban and social structures created by such a role: a good system of higher education and cultural institutions, a population whose high degree of literacy was an exception in Italy – and on the physical side a wealth of aristocratic palaces and elegant public spaces, a network of road and railways connecting the city to Europe. The conditions proved beneficial for the rapid growth of an industrial system, earlier than elsewhere in Italy. But the city suffered from excessive success: the very growth of Turin as a manufacturing district tended to conceal and erode its capital roles. The huge inflow of non-skilled immigrants and the parallel growth of the physical city, that is the success story of 'fordist-Turin', left the smaller, fragile and sophisticated 'Turin-the-capital' very much in the background.

This former identity, however, never completely disappeared; Turin preserved the quality of a capital not only in terms of the built environment, but also under other respects. To make a few instances, Turin's newspaper, *"La Stampa"*, plays a respected national role; the University and the Polytechnic are among the nation's finest, and three of the five Nobel Prizes awarded to Italian scientists; after WW II went to Turin graduates; with 8% of the national population, Piedmont, the region around Turin accounts for 22% of the national R&D expenditure; finally, Turin is the seat of the registered offices and the research centre of the national telecommunication companies, and of the HQs of the largest Italian banking group, the first and third private groups, and three of the first ten insurance groups in Italy.

Reinterpreting Turin-the-capital was obviously a prime choice when fordist Turin started to face the typical problems of all industrial cities. Two main courses of action have been taken by the City administration: the first centres around internationalization, the second on the need for a higher urban quality.

Among the results achieved on the first line, there is an increasing attractiveness of the Turin region as a site for foreign investments, with a marked increase in 1994; but there is also the choice of Turin as the seat for two UN institutions, and for a major new EU body, the European Training Foundation. Obviously, this strategy could not work without an improved long-range accessibility: by 1998 Turin will be linked with motorway connections not only to all Italian cities but also to Geneva, Lausanne, Grenoble and Lyon, and before 2005 Nice, which all lie within a 300 km radius; while the Lyon-Turin-Milan high speed rail link should start its operations by the end of the decade, and the new airport with its rail connection to the city will be fully operational by 1996. A parallel process is the establishment of partnerships with other European cities; the traditional ties to Lyon and Geneva have been revamped, and Turin is a relevant actor in all the main Euro-networks. Finally, first among Italian cities, Turin will have from 1996 an agency devoted to the promotion of foreign investments. The new Lingotto Exhibition and Conference Centre, the most advanced in Italy, together with new logistic poles in the region, should also increase the role of Turin as a trading and exchange centre.

On the quality side, Turin is heavily investing on amenities. Together with the creation of new museums and the refurbishing of existing ones, there is an intensive program of requalification of historical buildings and public spaces, and rejuvenation of cultural institutions: about 100 million US$ per year are being spent in these fields. A crucial role in this process is played by the *'Piano Regolatore Generale'*, the master plan for the development of the physical city which Turin has defined in 1995. No other major Italian city has such an updated design for urban transformations: another Turinese advantage which investors should find especially attractive.

	1994	1995	1996	1997	1998
GDP	2.2	3.2	2.5	2.7	2.9
Domestic demand	1.9	2.8	2.7	2.8	2.9
Household consumption	1.6	1.7	2.0	2.5	2.9
Fixed investment	−0.1	6.9	5.2	4.4	4.3
Inventory investment (a)	0.8	0.4	0.3	0.2	0.1
Exports of goods and services	10.9	10.4	6.2	6.9	6.7
Imports of goods and services	9.8	9.1	6.9	7.1	6.7
GDP deflator	3.6	4.6	4.8	3.5	2.9
Household consumption deflator	4.7	5.7	4.4	3.7	3.1
Export prices	3.5	10.7	0.8	1.5	2.0
Import prices	3.9	14.7	−2.4	1.7	2.9

(a) Contribution to GDP growth

Table 77.2 Macroeconomic outlook in 1995–98 (% changes)

ferential over the German bank rate (at present over six per cent) with positive effects for servicing debt. GDP should grow by 3.2 per cent in 1995, by 2.5 per cent in the following year and by 2.8 per cent in 1997.

The effects of lira devaluation on Italian industry

Devaluation has spurred exports in 1994 and 1995, halting a negative trend for Italy in the main international markets. Italian exporting firms adopted an aggressive strategy – and reduced prices in foreign currencies – to increase penetration in foreign markets. Devaluation partially compensated for the effects of the 1991–93 recession (Figure 77.1); in 1994 production increased by 4.9 per cent, reaching a level close to the 1989 peak. Exports rose by 10.7 per cent in volume (+8.9 per cent in 1993), while export prices increased by 12.5 per cent (about half of the lira devaluation). Competitiveness measured on labour unit cost improved significantly (+25 per cent between the third quarter of 1992 and the fourth quarter of 1994); it reached a peak in the first few months of 1995.

Lira devaluation caused a sharp increase in imported input unit cost in the manufacturing sectors. This was partially compensated for by the acceleration of the unit cost of labour (+2.6 per cent in 1993, –2.5 per cent in 1994): total unit variable costs increased by 5.2 per cent in 1993 and by 1.8 per cent in 1994. Cost increases did not translate immediately to domestic output prices, which increased by 3.2 per cent in 1993 and by 3.7 per cent in 1994. Firms' mark-up on the domestic market reduced in 1993 and started to increase only in the second half of 1994;

total mark-up diminished slightly in 1993, and then recovered in 1994 (+14 per cent).

Europe's weaknesses and the decline in competitiveness

The decline in Europe's competitiveness is registered by several indicators: since 1980 European GDP per person has been growing more slowly than in the USA, and it is now 32 per cent lower. On the other hand, Japan GDP per capita reached the European level at the beginning of the 1980s and it is now 20 per cent higher. Also employment growth between 1980 and 1993 has been slower in Europe than in the USA and Japan (respectively, +0.4, +1, 8 and +1 per cent yearly average): the unemployment rate is now one and a half times higher than that of the USA.

There is not a single cause for this loss of competitiveness. Consequently the analysis needs to consider both micro- and macroeconomic aspects. Rigidity in the labour market, biases in market mechanisms, an unfavourable business environment (corporate taxation first of all, especially in Italy), low social mobility and unwarranted protectionism are some factors that limit Europe's growth potential. To correct this bias important reforms need to be introduced in several areas: public sector, labour market, training and education, infrastructure endowment, research and development, and small and medium-sized firms' activity.

To reduce the state presence in economy it is important to speed up the privatization process of all activities not strictly public (mail services, communications, energy, transports, banks, financial services). It is also necessary to rationalize transfer activity to families, in particular a reduction of the

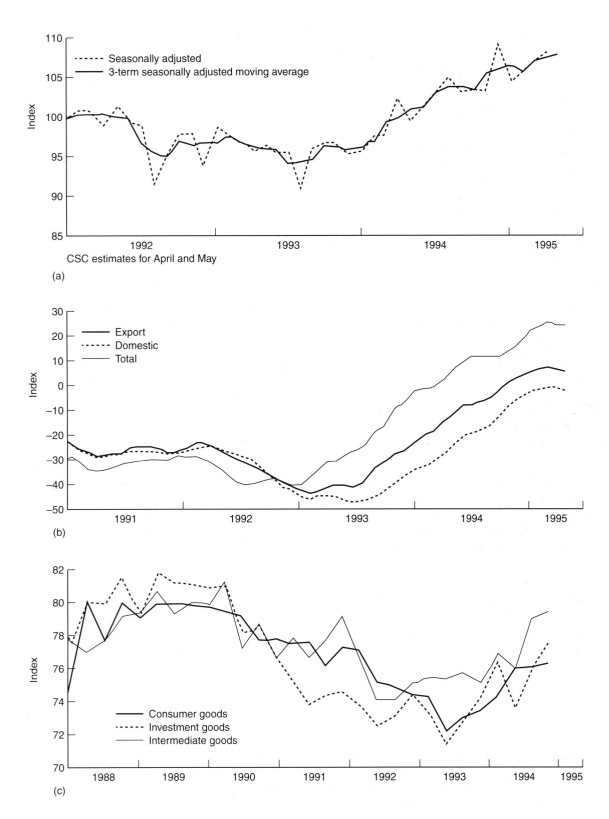

CSC estimates for April and May

(a)

(b)

(c)

Source: CSC, CSC estimates based on ISTAT and ISCO data

Figure 77.1 (a) Industrial production (indexes: 1990=100). (b) Orders (3-term seasonally adjusted moving averages of the difference between positive and negative answers to ISCO business surveys). (c) Plant utilization rate.

What does your company need to continue growing?

It needs to set its roots in fertile soil, in an economically strong region located within the growing heart of European development, where qualified human resources and an exceptional network of services are available at competitive costs.

Lombardia

Where

small

companies

grow

For further information:
Italian Trade Centre
37 Sackville Street London WIX 2DQ
tel. 0171-734.2412 - fax 0171-734.2516
Mr. Barry Walker

Export Intelligence in a Changing World

Many exporters will be familiar with Export Intelligence as the DTI service set up over 20 years ago to process export sales leads gathered in British embassies and other overseas posts for the benefit of British companies. Since the wholly owned Mercury subsidiary Prelink Limited took over and then retained the contract for providing Export Intelligence in the late '80s, both the service itself and the way it is marketed have been subject to change with substantial investments in technology and much enhanced information.

Independent research indicates that Export Intelligence generates significant additional business for UK exporters. This was estimated at some £400 million in 1993, including new and ongoing business resulting from Export Intelligence notices and more than doubled last year at £946 million. Export Intelligence customers are exceptionally diverse ranging from small companies that are predominantly exporters to major corporations and companies of all sizes, dipping their toes in the water for the first time.

At the present time Prelink is actively marketing partnership arrangements with Business Links and other organisations with incentives when such bodies encourage their members to become Prelink customers and new facilities for low frequency users. This means that newcomers to exporting and companies that previously used the service at second hand via their membership of trade associations or chambers of commerce can try low-cost entry and/or a much more timely service than was possible before.

The raw information that Prelink processes and distributes is gathered by commercial officers in over 200 British posts around the world. It includes sales leads given by overseas companies keen to buy British, details of overseas agents and distributors wanting to make new contacts, market trends, information about major pro-jects, and long and short dated calls to tender.

Historically the quality of information has varied according to local circumstances and business practices. However Prelink has been phoning in new guidelines on what is required over the last year with the result that the depth and consistency of intelligence received is being steadily upgraded to match current and future needs of exporters.

Customers began to see the benefits of this new quality control earlier in 1995 but it will be another six to nine months before the process is complete and the benefits have filtered through to the entire customer base of nearly 3,000 companies and business organisations.

Prelink receives information about 40,000 export opportunities each year, arriving by fax at a rate of up to 200 per working day. The processing they undergo is a matter of data inputting and matching against predefined product/service codes. Coding is a highly specialised task carried out by a team of 10 coders using specially developed software. The system include multi-level prioritisation of leads for more sensitive turnround and a unique integrated code search facility to ensure correct and consistent matching of information with customers' requirements.

Each company that joins Export Intelligence has a "profile' prepared which details the products and services offered against the codes and combines this information with the countries of interest and the types of intelligence wanted – for instance sales leads, agents and distributors seeking products to market, aid projects, tenders etc. The annual for fee ranges upwards from £250 plus VAT according to the diversity of products, types of information required and world regions of interest.

The result is that 500,000 Export Intelligence notices are distributed by fax and mail to Prelink's customers each year. As the market research suggests, the leads are extremely productive, however the diligence with which customer companies follow up the leads is as much a key to success as Prelink's ongoing process of upgrading the quality of leads.

Leads generally include information on how to respond whether in English or another language and often they advise a rapid faxed response to register interest and then a follow up with product specifications, price details and so forth.

The feedback received via British posts and from individual customers shows companies use the information to open up new markets and to build business in areas they have identified as being of prime importance.

Recent success stories include a wallpaper distributor delighted with new opportunities in Lithuania and eastern Europe generally, a business stationery company opening up new markets in the Caribbean to replace sales in Africa and numerous examples of engineering companies succeeding everywhere from Western Europe to Japan and the USA.

**For further information please contact
Trevor Fromant, General Manager,
Prelink Limited
Tel 0181-900 1313**

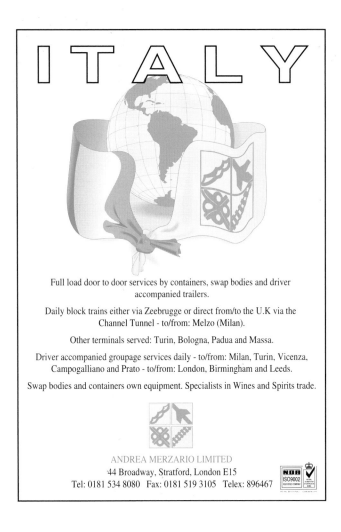
cost of the welfare system, with regard both to the health and social security systems. On the labour market it is crucial to increase actual flexibility through promoting agreements that reflect the economic conditions of the individual sectors. It is also important to provide incentives for geographical mobility to reduce the high unemployment imbalances observed around Europe. A way to increase

labour market flexibility is to improve links between the education system and industry. This could require revision of the present school programme and an increase in exchanges between industry and school staff. Finally, it is important to support the role of small and medium-sized firms, reducing fiscal pressure, improving the business environment, and facilitating access to capital markets.

Priorities for the Intergovernmental Conference

It is in the interests of firms themselves that the intergovernmental conference (IGC) takes place in the near future and concludes within a reasonable time, building up confidence in the Union and making it more efficient. More efficient institutions will improve firms' environment; firms will be able to better compete among them and in the outside world.

In particular it is relevant that Europe finds political leadership to decide quickly over crucial topics, as for example over the telecommunications business; to create a coordination mechanism among members in the energy sector; and in general terms to improve the decision process.

It is also important for Europe to develop its own foreign policy, acting as a political body towards other main countries, such as the USA and Japan. Finally, the Union should give an answer to the needs of the Eastern European countries. Enlargement to the East could allow an upgrading in efficiency of all European industry, and stimulate commerce and investment in an area with the highest potential in terms of growth.

Luxembourg

The Federation of Luxembourg Industries

Luxembourg, one of the smallest countries in the world (999 square miles and a population of about 400,000 people) as well as the smallest member of the EU, offers a wide range of advantages.

Luxembourg's central location in Europe, its proximity to the major European industrial and trade centres, its extensive network of international connections by road, rail, air and waterway, provides an excellent access to millions of consumers throughout Europe. The high level of education of its multi-lingual population (most people speak fluently German, French and English) as well as the social and political stability are other major assets. Although a third of Luxembourg's population are foreigners, racial conflicts are unknown.

Production costs still are competitive. Productivity is high and labour costs are generally lower than those of Germany, Belgium and The Netherlands. Private enterprise is encountered and there is a solid tradition of industrial peace and conciliation between the two sides of industry. Labour walkouts are extremely rare.

Compared to other countries of the EU, Luxembourg's competitiveness is somewhat hampered by the fact that automatic wage indexation still exists.

Economic activity during 1994

Luxembourg's economy highly depends on the economic activity of the other European countries. Nearly 90 per cent of its industrial production is exported. Because of the higher international demand, Luxembourg's business activity grew substantially in 1994. The excellent performance of Luxembourg's financial sector strengthened the positive development of GDP.

In 1994, gross domestic product (GDP) showed an increase of 4.1 per cent compared to 2.3 per cent in 1993. Private investment strongly increased partly due to the investment programmes in the steel industry and the communication sector.

Public consumption was buoyant (+2.1 per cent compared to 1993). Export of services was still very high and export of goods showed an upward trend, owing to the high demand of EU member states and overseas.

Employment

In 1994, domestic employment exceeded the threshold of 208,000 people, an increase of 2.5 per cent compared to 1993. By the end of 1994, 5500 people were unemployed, representing an unemployment rate of 3.0 per cent.

Consumer prices

The rate of inflation reached 2.2 per cent compared to 3.6 per cent in 1993. Among the EU countries, Luxembourg rated second in 1994, after being placed seventh in 1993 and fifth in 1992.

78

	1994	1995
GDP	4.1	3.0
Inflation	2.2	2.5
Unemployment	2.7	3.0

Table 78.1 1995 forecasts

Business confidence among industrial leaders

Production level	
Increase	33%
Stability	65%
Decrease	2%
Orders picked up	
Superior than normal	35%
Normal	61%
Lower than normal	4%
Level of stocks	
Superior than normal	13%
Normal	67%
Lower than normal	20%

Source: Inquiry of the National Service of Statistics

Table 78.2 Appreciation up to the end of the 1st quarter of 1995

Conclusion

To keep the industrial sector strong, it is necessary to improve companies' competitiveness. This can only be attained by an increase in productivity and the promotion of external trade. Therefore companies have to invest in new technologies, new marketing technologies, training, research and development, in order to raise productivity and to become more competitive.

The Federation of Luxembourg Industrialists

The Federation of Luxembourg Industrialists (FEDIL) was founded in 1918 as the representative professional association of Luxembourg's industry. FEDIL groups nearly all the small, medium-sized and large industries of the Grand Duchy, as well as a growing number of companies in the industrial services sector. About 400 companies and 13 professional associations are members of FEDIL today.

FEDIL's tasks consist in the safeguarding and defence of its members' professional interests and in the analysis of any social and economic matter concerning Luxembourg industry.

FEDIL assists and advises its members. These tasks cover each sector of social and economic life such as the right of establishment, investment aid, foreign trade, community legislation, innovation aid, labour legislation, collective agreements, social security, work and training.

FEDIL is constantly in touch with the authorities, economic circles, politicians and trade unions. Thus, the association is directly involved in the preparation of economic and social decisions, as it is represented in numerous deliberative bodies.

Malta

Malta Federation of Industry

The development of the Maltese economy

Following the publication of the Advice on Malta's application for full membership in the European Union, the government embarked on a very extensive programme of reform and change aimed at reviewing the entire regulatory and operational framework of the Maltese economy.

Events in 1995 have been dominated by the various measures introduced by the government to update the economic infrastructure in line with developments over the past few years and keeping in perspective Malta's insistence on early European Union membership. Among the more significant developments were the initial efforts to liberalize the monetary and financial sectors and the establishment of the Malta Financial Services Centre, together with the enactment by Parliament of legislation on banking, companies, trusts, tax management, investment services, professional secrecy, money laundering and insider dealing.

There was a further move by government which signalled its intention of moving closer to European Union membership when it decided on a virtual customs union by removing import duties on all industrial products of EU origin. A simultaneous measure to compensate for loss of revenue incurred was taken by the introduction of value-added tax (VAT) which took effect from 1 January 1995. This was intended to increase the proportion of indirect taxation in relation to direct forms. It was also seen as a move to further restrain the black economy and reduce evasion of income tax. Legislation was also implemented last year on consumer affairs and on competition to ensure fair trading practices and the protection of consumers. These measures will certainly have a bearing on the performance of local industry in the coming months, but it is as yet too early to draw any conclusions.

Emphasis on diversifying the Maltese markets

There has been a consistent effort in the past few years to build an efficient and effective economic base which would be inherently strong enough to adapt to changing circumstances. These policies have worked successfully and have helped Malta's economy to absorb the impact of the international recession. Currently, efforts are being made to ensure that the island would further improve the competitive edge of its economy. This now appears to depend heavily on how successful government will be in dampening inflationary trends partly expected after the introduction of VAT. Nevertheless, the economy has remained buoyant over 1994, with all sectors registering a positive growth and both the domestic and foreign components of GDP continuing to expand steadily.

The drive is still on to achieve higher export levels in an effort to overcome dependence by a

Appendix I

number of firms on a domestic market which has absolute limitations by virtue of its size. Positive results were recorded in 1994 as the level of domestic exports increased by 14.4 per cent over the comparable period of the previous year. Total consumption expenditure advanced by 7.1 per cent, of which private consumers' expenditure accounted for 4.9 per cent – in line with inflation figures. But government current expenditure, which increased by 13.8 per cent in 1994, is considered by the private sector to have now reached an alarming level which could be inviting higher inflation levels than those which the country has been accustomed to over the past decade.

In the meantime gross fixed capital formation advanced by 3.6 per cent during the first months of 1994. This was brought about by higher levels of investment in both construction and machinery. Meanwhile, the moderate recovery in the construction sector, which was itself partly due to the undertaking of a number of tourism-related projects, boosted the contribution of investment to growth.

The gainfully occupied population continued to rise, as new jobs were created in the construction sector, in tourist-related trades and private manufacturing firms. Data available at the Registrar of Partnerships shows that 69 new companies with non-resident equity participation were set up in 1994. Employment in the construction industry remained stable. Meanwhile, although the annual rate of inflation was unchanged from the 1993 rate, it followed a generally downward trend throughout most of the year.

Economic indicators for the first quarter of 1995 and prospects for 1996

Following several years of strong growth in the late 1980s and early 1990s, the Maltese economy is now entering a more sustainable phase. Brisk economic activity is expected in 1995, as the recovery in the economy of Malta's main trading partners (namely, Germany, Italy, the UK and France) gathers further momentum. The demand for exports of goods and services from Malta should in fact remain buoyant, with capacity utilization in export-oriented manufacturing firms rising to higher levels.

A number of large private and public sector projects should shortly come on stream. These include Malta Freeport Terminal Two. Progress should also be seen on the construction of approach

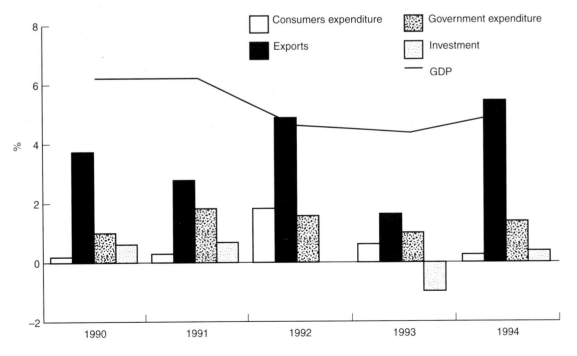

Source: Central Bank of Malta, Annual Report 1994

Figure 79.1 Contribution of demand components to DGP growth (net of imports)

roads and the buildings housing the San Raffaele Hospital, which will become Malta's second major public hospital. It is also expected that three five-star hotels now under construction will be functioning in late 1995 or early 1996. Other planned tourist-related projects possibly including the redevelopment of Manoel Island and Tigne should also register progress during 1995.

In the meantime, the tourism industry is expected to maintain the positive performance recorded in the previous years, both in terms of tourist arrivals and gross earnings from tourism. The opening of new air routes and good marketing strategies by the national airline, Air Malta, have already given satisfactory results in the tourist industry's bid to diversify its markets and obtain a better seasonal spread of tourist arrivals so as to avoid the capacity constraints usually encountered during the peak summer months.

The country's development in the manufacturing sector is further boosted by the activities of the Malta Development Corporation (MDC) which continues to organize promotional activities in several international business centres in order to attract foreign investment to Malta. The Corporation has also been appointed local representatives for the European Community Investment Partners (ECIP) programme. Together with the Malta Federation of Industry (FOI), the MDC has organized various business initiatives under the ECIP programme, offering considerable opportunities to local entrepreneurs for joint business collaboration with European partners.

Levels of business confidence

The Industry Trends Survey (first half 1995) conducted and published biannually by the Malta Federation of Industry (FOI), reveals that the mainly export-oriented industry is significantly more optimistic than it was six months previously. On the other hand, the main locally oriented section of industry is divided in its opinions with the smaller firms registering more optimism, while the larger firms are feeling less confident about the future.

The survey shows that the most important factors which are likely to limit capital expenditure over the next six months are uncertainty about demand and also the cost of finance. In the case of the mainly locally oriented sector, a further consideration is the inadequate net return on proposed investment, while export-oriented firms are mostly concerned with a shortage of internal finance.

The major negative finding of the Industry Trends Survey was in profitability. Respondents are forecasting a more negative situation than six months previously, in spite of the increased orders and increased prices for goods ordered. The main reason for this appears to be the increased costs of imported raw materials and of local production.

Competition in Europe

In view of Malta's aspirations to join the Single European Market, it is crucial that the competitive edge of Maltese enterprise is correctly identified. An essential element which gives Malta's enterprises a competitive edge in the global market is response time and quality standards. Tremendous advantages for Malta are found in its smallness, which makes it more easily adaptable to constant change. The increase in rhythm of change and the expansion of world trade present numerous niche market opportunities which allow space for Maltese entrepreneurs, willing to face the challenge of competition in the European market, the Mediterranean area and the Middle East.

Priorities for the Inter-governmental Conference

There is increasing awareness and interest in business circles in the inter-governmental conference (IGC) in 1996 at the end of which Malta will start the final round of negotiations for entry into the European Union. Besides, the IGC is being indicated as another major watershed for decisions that need to be taken on a number of important issues which are seen as the key to the future progress on the vision of a more united Europe. Maltese business is eager to see Malta belonging to a European Union where the Single Market operates better than it has done to date, where positive results are achieved towards a single European currency, a simpler decision-making process, which is not overbureaucratic and which respects the principle of subsidiarity. At the same time the Malta Federation of Industry, as the representative organization of Malta's industrial community, also expects to see the introduction of standard mechanisms and structures for consultation on issues which will affect industry. It is in this spirit that Malta's industrial community looks forward with eagerness towards a successful outcome of the IGC.

The FOI: reflecting the views of Malta's industry

Founded in 1946, the Malta Federation of Industry (FOI) is an independent, non-political organization which aims at influencing policies and legislation for the benefit of industry and is financed entirely by its membership. Its activities, objectives and services are directed towards the economic well-being of Malta by ensuring the successful development of a strongly competitive manufacturing and service industry. The FOI plays a very active role in safeguarding the interests of industry through its representation at national level on government boards and committees and by cultivating a mutual understanding with other employer bodies, government and unions. Through regular consultation among its member firms, the FOI is able to react appropriately to proposals affecting industry and guarantees a voice for its members at all levels.

The Netherlands 80

The Federation of Netherlands Industry

This time last week I was [?]

Development and potential of the Dutch economy

Despite its modest geographical size, the economic performance of The Netherlands is impressive. Of the 207 countries in the world, The Netherlands ranks 135th in terms of surface area; 55th in terms of population; 14th in terms of GDP; and 7th in terms of exports. With a GDP per head of US$21,400 (1994), it is one of the richest countries in the world.

The Dutch economy is characterized by a small but highly efficient agricultural sector, a broad industrial base, and a large service sector. The Netherlands is geographically extremely well located, at a point where three large rivers are flowing into the world's busiest sea. This has made the country one of the largest and most important centres of transport and distribution in the world, and has earned the name 'gateway to and from Europe'.

Macroeconomic indicators show the Dutch economy to be basically healthy. GDP growth is in line with EU and OECD averages, inflation and interest rates are low, the guilder is strong, and the current account shows a structural surplus. Economically, the country shares the same problems as the rest of Europe, notably with regard to public sector deficits and a structural weakness of the labour market, but generally The Netherlands has shown greater strength and stability in these areas than its competitors. The Netherlands is one of the few countries which has been able to reduce its public

deficit in recent years. Good industrial relations, sound fiscal and monetary government policies and an outstanding record on inflation all contribute to moderate wage developments. Unit labour costs increased only marginally over the past fifteen years. The Dutch guilder and the German mark are the only currencies which are still held within a fluctuation margin of 2.25 per cent, the narrow band of the 'old' Exchange Rate Mechanism (ERM).

Dutch competitiveness is consistently high. All international comparisons of competitiveness show The Netherlands to be among the top 10 countries in the world. The country ranks among the top countries with respect to the size of inward foreign direct investment. A large number of foreign enterprises have chosen The Netherlands as the location for their international distribution activities, head office or R&D activities.

The country has a well-developed network of physical infrastructure, as well as advanced and relatively cheap telecommunications facilities; it has an ample supply of skilled labour with a strong international orientation and the highest productivity in the world. Labour costs per hour are high, but owing to the very high labour productivity, unit labour costs are relatively low. Costs of capital are relatively low and investment capital is readily available. High quality offices are available at relatively low rents. The Dutch government does its utmost to improve the tax climate further. The country offers political stability and a stable macro-economic environment. Industrial disputes are few in number. Foreign investment and trade policies are liberal, the exchange rate is very stable and rates of return on capital are high.

Economic indicators for 1995 and prospects for 1996

Driven by a surge in exports, GDP grew in 1994 by nearly 2.5 per cent. Supported by a rapid increase of investment, economic growth will continue at a strong pace in 1995 and 1996. For 1995 a growth rate of 3.25 per cent is projected, while in 1996 growth is expected to level off slightly to 2.5 per cent.

The dynamic developments in world trade are expected to continue in 1995 and 1996, thereby laying a solid foundation for economic growth in The Netherlands. Exports will continue to be an important engine of economic growth in 1995, but production growth is getting more and more support from domestic demand, especially from business investment. In 1995 investment will increase by approximately 8 per cent, financed by a profitability which has been steadily rising since 1993. In 1996 this

will be followed by a more modest increase in investment of 4 per cent. Exclusive of investment in aeroplanes and the energy sector, however, an investment growth of around 8.5 per cent is foreseen.

With the usual lag, private consumption is responding to the cyclical upswing, albeit slowly in view of purchasing power developments. Inflation in The Netherlands is benefiting from the strong guilder. The slide in the dollar will lead to an effective appreciation of the guilder, but the effect on Dutch competitiveness will be limited, owing to the more moderate wage-cost developments in The Netherlands. In 1996 price competitiveness of Dutch exporters will be more than restored.

Contractual wages rose by only 1.8 per cent in 1994, almost a full percentage point below the inflation rate. A similar development is expected for 1995. For 1996 the average rise in contractual wages is projected to equal the inflation rate at 2.25 per cent. Increases in labour productivity exceed the wage increases. This explains the increasing rates of return on capital of enterprises in The Netherlands, to which must be added the positive results of the many successes of Dutch enterprises abroad.

	1992	1993	1994	1995	1996
International					
Relevant world trade	3.8	0.0	8.5	8.0	7.0
Guilder/US$ exchange rate (level)	1.76	1.86	1.82	1.65	1.7
Crude oil price (Brent, US$/barrel)	19.40	17.10	15.80	17.50	16.50
Wages and prices					
Real labour costs market sector	3.0	2.4	0.6	1.5	1.0
Consumer price index	3.2	2.6	2.7	1.75	2.25
Volume of expenditure and production					
Private consumption	2.5	0.7	1.9	2.25	1.75
Private investment (excl. housing)	−0.4	−2.7	0.5	8.0	4.0
Export of goods (excl. energy)	2.7	0.7	7.3	6.0	5.5
Import of goods	2.0	−0.6	6.1	6.0	4.5
Production by enterprises (excl. energy)	1.3	0.3	3.1	3.5	2.75
Gross domestic product	1.3	0.4	2.5	3.25	2.5
Labour market					
Employment growth ('000 full-time equivalents)	45	−7	−10	57	71
Unemployment rate (% of labour force)	6.7	7.7	8.7	8.6	8.5
Public sector					
Net lending general government (% GDP)	3.9	3.3	3.5	3.25	2.5
Other					
Labour productivity market sector (excl. mining)	0.1	0.2	3.6	2.75	1.5
Balance of payments on current account (bln. guilders)	13.1	18.9	22.5	24.5	25.5
Long-term interest rate (%, 10-year government bonds)	8.1	6.4	6.9	7.0	7.0

Source: Central Planning Bureau, April 1995

Table 80.1 Main economic indicators, 1992–96 (annual percentage changes, unless otherwise indicated)

The economic recovery, combined with moderate wage developments, leads to a greater demand for labour. However, the labour supply is also rapidly increasing. On balance, unemployment may start to decline this year to 7 per cent of the labour force.

For the rest of 1995 and 1996 prospects for non-inflationary growth of the Dutch economy are good. Helped by sound government policies, the public finances and the labour market are developing in a positive direction. For the medium term, the moderate wage and price developments are expected to continue. Real labour costs may even remain constant. The general government budget deficit is expected to be reduced structurally to a level well below the EMU maximum of 3 per cent.

Levels of business confidence

The latest survey by the Central Bureau of Statistics shows that business confidence, which has been rising since the beginning of 1993, is still improving. However, in the past few months, this rise is levelling off slightly. The same holds for the production index, while the order position has stabilized.

Recommendations for improving Europe's competitiveness

VNO-NCW fully endorses the report *Making Europe more competitive: towards world-class performance*, published by UNICE in 1993, as well as the consecutive reports by the European Round Table of Industrialists. The recommendations for improving Europe's competitiveness centre around the following issues:
- reducing the burden of the state;
- making the labour market more flexible;
- improving the infrastructure;
- increasing the level of inter-firm competition;
- promoting a better international trade system;
- improving technology and innovation;
- facilitating the growth of SMEs;
- stimulating the development of dynamic industrial clusters;
- encouraging investment;

- improving profitability;
- upgrading management practices.

VNO-NCW's priorities for the Inter-Governmental Conference in 1996
- VNO-NCW believes it is crucial for the EU not to readjust its convergence criteria; new EU members must accept these targets.
- An à la carte approach with respect to integration should be rejected.
- VNO-NCW advocates an increase in the efficiency and legitimacy of EU expenditure.
- VNO-NCW believes that the IGC should concentrate its efforts on ensuring that the EU is manageable, effective, efficient and transparent. The number of European Commissioners, for instance, should be such that decisive and coordinated action is still possible.
- Clear agreements are needed, especially in the area of taxation and social policy, about what competencies can be exercised at what level and by whom.
- The factors influencing the votes cast should not be confined to population size, but should also include economic criteria.
- If EU regulations are necessary in the area of social policy, they should apply to all member states.
- Regarding enlargement of the EU: as long as not all the conditions for entry can be met, a more gradual integration through ever increasing involvement should be preferred.
- In any case, before negotiations about admittance are concluded, it should be clear what agricultural, regional and structural policy reforms will be realized in order to prepare for the entry of new member states. Also the decision-making procedures should be such that decisive and coordinated action remains possible, while democratic decision making must be upheld.

Note
All information in this chapter was correct at the time of writing, June 1995.

81 Norway

The Confederation of Norwegian Business and Industry

Picking up speed

The Norwegian economy performed very well in 1994. The economy has been driven by increasing exports, strong private consumption and a boom in housing investment. Mainland gross domestic product (GDP), which excludes shipping and oil and gas production, has grown by 3.9 per cent in 1994, according to preliminary estimates. The growth of total GDP, including petroleum and shipping, is estimated at 5.1 per cent in 1994. Owing to strong export figures, particularly of petroleum products, the current account of the balance of payments will most likely show a surplus of NOK26 billion in 1994, compared to NOK17 billion in 1993. As the economy improves, the labour market has also been strengthened. Employment is expected to increase by 1.6 per cent in 1994, which equals 31,000 new jobs. That leaves the average unemployment rate in 1994 at 5.4 per cent; down from 6 per cent in 1993.

Recent economic indicators, as well as preliminary national account figures for the fourth quarter of 1994, point to a further upswing in domestic demand. However, the growth showed a somewhat more moderate tendency towards the end of 1994 compared to the first half of the year. Still, total real domestic demand was up 2.7 per cent in the third quarter of 1994 compared to a year earlier. Private consumption increased by 3.1 per cent in the fourth quarter, while public consumption hardly grew at all.

The picture of investment is rather mixed. While investment in fixed capital formation in the petroleum sector was down, investment in mainland Norway showed an overall increase of 9 per cent in the fourth quarter of 1994, compared to the same quarter of 1993. In particular, housing investment increased sharply and was up by almost 40 per cent in the third and fourth quarters of 1994.

According to quarterly national account figures, volume of total exports of goods and services increased by almost 8 per cent in the third quarter of 1994 compared to the third quarter of 1993. Exports of petroleum products, including both oil and natural gas, increased by 9 per cent. Exports of manufacturing products, especially cyclical products, increased even more sharply owing to the general recovery in international demand. Consumer prices rose by 1.8 per cent during the 12-month period ending in November 1994. Economic growth has started a slight upward pressure on prices, but still prices are increasing moderately. Consumer prices are estimated to have grown by 1.4 per cent from 1993 to 1994. The average wage increase is estimated to be close to 3 per cent. Preliminary figures indicate that manufacturing investment is now rising. After negative figures in the first two quarters of 1994, manufacturing investment rose by 7.4 per cent in the fourth quarter.

The Norwegian economy and the convergence criteria of the Maastricht Treaty

Even though Norway is not an EU member, the presently strong position of the Norwegian economy can be illustrated by how Norway meets the convergence criteria of the Maastricht-treaty.

Criterion 1: general government net borrowing

■ Should be less than 3 per cent of GDP.

■ General government net lending in Norway is projected to be 1.5 per cent of GDP in 1995.

Criterion 2: general government gross debt

■ Should be less than 60 per cent of GDP.

■ General government gross debt in Norway was equal to 48 per cent of GDP at the end of 1994. At the same time general government will have net financial assets of approximately 26 per cent of GDP if direct investments in state enterprises are capitalized.

Criterion 3: inflation rate

■ Observed over the last twelve months, this should not exceed the inflation rate in the three EU member countries with the lowest inflation rates by more than 1.5 percentage points.

■ Average inflation rate in Norway was 1.8 per cent in the 12-month period until March 1995 (as measured against the preceding 12-month period), against 1.8 per cent for the relevant EU member countries.

Criterion 4: nominal long-term interest rate of government bonds

■ Observed over the last 12 months, should not exceed that of the three EU member countries with the lowest inflation rates by more than 2 percentage points.

■ The average effective interest rate of government bonds over the 12 months until the end of March 1995 was 7.5 per cent, against an average of 8.0 per cent in the relevant EU member countries.

Criterion 5: currency

■ The currency should have been kept within the *normal fluctuation margins* provided for by the Exchange Rate Mechanism of the European Monetary System (EMS) for at least the last two years.

■ Norway is not an EMS member, and can therefore formally not fulfil this criterion. The currency was devalued in May 1986. From May 1986 until 10 December 1992 a fixed exchange rate was maintained, first towards a weighted average of the currencies of Norway's main trading partners, and from 22 October 1990 towards the ECU, with only small deviations (0 to minus 0.5 percentage points) from the established central value against the ECU. The currency has been floating since 10 December 1992. After an initial depreciation of approximately 3–4 per cent compared to the earlier central value against the ECU, the exchange rate has been relatively stable.

Economic prospects

While the economy in 1993 and 1994 was fuelled by quite a substantial increase in private consumption and housing investment, the growth impulses in 1995 will most likely come from the international upturn. However, one cannot expect such high growth rates in exports in 1995 as was the case especially in the second half of 1994.

Also private consumption growth is estimated to be more moderate in 1995 than in 1994. Mainland GDP is expected to grow by a rate of 2.6 per cent in 1995. Despite a rise in imports induced by the upturn both in exports and domestic demand, the current account surplus is expected to increase to a level of NOK36 billion in 1995, about 4.5 per cent of GDP.

In view of the relatively low interest rate level and the improved employment picture, the recovery of household spending is expected to continue through 1995. It is also important that households have come a long way in consolidating their financial position after the borrowing spree in the mid-1980s. But as fiscal policy tightens, private consumption should ease back to a more normal growth rate of some 2.5 per cent in 1995.

Oil investments accounted for a good third of Norwegian business investment in 1994, but will most likely decline in the years to come. Investments in the petroleum sector will to a higher degree be directed at maintenance rather than development of new fields of production. Reduction in investment in the petroleum sector could have a negative effect on GDP equivalent to some 1 per cent in 1995. Investments in mainland Norway, however, are expected to have a positive impact on production, partly as a result of continued growth in housing investment and the building of the new main airport.

A favourable trend in interest rates in the period ahead would most likely entail continued growth in household durable spending as well as residential investment. Also the rise in business investment will to some extent depend on the movement in interest rates in the coming period. It is thus essential that economic policy is geared towards stabilizing interest rates, preferably at a lower level.

A major uncertainty of the projections relates to the future cost development. The overall wage growth is estimated as 3 per cent in 1995. The long period of slack in the labour market may, however, have raised the level of structural unemployment. As a result, wage pressures could prove stronger than expected. This might affect competitiveness negatively and slow down economic growth.

Trends, competitiveness and business confidence in manufacturing industry

Manufacturing activity in Norway is closely related to the overall international business cycle and to investment on the Norwegian continental shelf. The production growth in 1993 and 1994 was to a considerable extent induced by the high investment level in the petroleum sector.

During the first quarter of 1994 demand gradually increased for most companies operating on the domestic market. In the last quarter of 1994 manufacturing activity picked up considerably and is currently to a large extent being positively influenced by the international upturn. Intermediate goods production, which include pulp and paper products, basic chemicals, plastic processing and various metal products, is largely influenced by the international business cycle. These intermediate goods account for 30 per cent of the value added in manufacturing and have a very high export share. In 1995, demand on the export markets is forecast to increase further, while reduction in petroleum investment and a tighter fiscal policy will most likely have a negative impact on production.

According to the production index, the combined production of manufacturing and energy products was up by 7.4 per cent in 1994 and 6.2 in January–March 1995 compared to the level in the same period the previous year. Manufacturing pro-

duction rose by 6.7 per cent last year and 8.2 per cent in the first quarter of 1995. In 1994 and the first quarter of 1995, all main manufacturing sectors showed an increase in production. Production of food, pulp and paper, chemicals, metals and non-metallic mineral products increased most sharply by 8–15 per cent in the first three months of 1995 from the same period last year.

Producer prices in manufacturing showed hardly any rise at all from 1991 to the beginning of the second quarter of 1994. In the major export sectors such as pulp, paper and metal industry, the prices then increased sharply as the major European countries started to move out of the recession.

Profitability developed favourably in 1994 owing to higher productivity as well as moderate wage increases. There has furthermore been a moderate increase in the costs of imported raw materials. Growing housing investment will also have a positive impact on the development in different branches of manufacturing, such as wood products, furniture and mineral products.

In the first months of 1995 managers in manufacturing have rather optimistic expectations. The number of industrialists planning to increase output during the coming months has risen and exceeds the number from the previous report.

At the same time, the levels of domestic and export order-books are good. The turbulence in the US dollar exchange market has apparently not yet had a strong impact on export.

The initial results of the investment survey of manufacturing industry point to a strong investment demand in 1995. After several years of low investment industrialists are now planning to increase investment by 30 per cent. A growth rate of this magnitude was last achieved in 1986. This development probably reflects the fact that the companies' competitive position has improved, and now it is time to augment capacity.

Norway has enjoyed a lower inflation rate than its trading partners during the last five years, and cost competitiveness has improved by about 11 per cent since 1988. The uncertainty attached to the projections above is partly related to the price and wage development in the years ahead, and the impact on interest rates of a stronger than expected nominal wage growth. The government has placed considerable emphasis on maintaining low price and wage inflation in order to strengthen the basis for production in the mainland economy.

Poland

Business Management and Finance, Warsaw

General characteristics of industry

1994 was another year of strong growth in GNP and industrial production in Poland. The transformation process of the economy was initiated in 1990 and was popularly named as the 'Balcerowicz Plan' after the then Minister of Finance, Dr Leszek Balcerowicz. In the first two years after the transformation Poland experienced a serious recession. The first positive results of the economic reform package were observed in 1992. Thereafter, growth in GNP and industrial production gained momentum. In 1994 GNP increased by 5 per cent and industrial production by 11 per cent. This growth is due to three main factors; export, investments and the development of the private sector. Polish industry is in the course of structural and ownership changes. The share of the private sector in industrial output is increasing, reaching 38 per cent in 1994. Production increase in the private sector reached 22 per cent in 1994, while the public sector recorded only a modest 6 per cent growth.

Sales in industrial enterprises (employing over 50 persons) are estimated in 1994 at about US$63 billion. Employment in large- and medium-sized industrial plants fell in 1994 by 2 per cent to about 3.3 million. With the high increase in production and reduced employment, per capita productivity increased by about 14 per cent in real terms. The real average net monthly salary was 2 per cent higher as compared with 1993. Net profit in large- and medium-sized enterprises was estimated in 1994 at almost US$1.5 billion, compared with a loss of US$900 million in 1993. In the first half of 1995 the profits of big enterprises (employing more than 50 persons for industry and more than 20 persons for other sectors) were still increasing and reached the highest level since the beginning of the economic reforms. The average net profit margin in the first five months was 2.5 per cent, 0.9 percentage points more than in 1994. In 1994, earnings before interest and tax (EBIT) increased by 75 per cent compared with 1993, and net cashflow improved by almost three times.

Dynamics of sales, production and prices

Categories (in current prices)	1993	1994	% change 1993/94
Output (PLN billion)	145.8	192.5	32.4
EBIT (PLN billion)	6.5	12.2	87.6

Source: NBP Information Bulletin

Table 82.1 Industrial production

The rate of growth of industrial production in Poland accelerated from 3.9 per cent in 1992 to 6.2 per cent in 1993 and 11.9 per cent in 1994. Sales of large- and medium-sized industrial enterprises increased in 1994 by almost 32 per cent (nominal) as compared with 1993.

A gradual decrease in the rate of inflation in industry is being observed. Increase in output prices in 1993 amounted to 31.9 per cent, ie 3.4 percentage points less than the cost of living index. In 1994 industrial prices increased by 25.3 per cent, though the prices of consumer goods and services rose by 32.2 per cent. The terms of trade index reached 101.8, ie price increases of exported products in 1994 was 1.8 per cent higher than the increase in import prices.

Labour market

The unemployment rate at the end of May 1995, at 14.7 per cent, reached the lowest level in 17 months and was 1.5 points lower than at the end of June 1994. The increase of the unemployment rate in June 1995 (to 15.1 per cent) is believed to be due to seasonal factors, including the inflow of graduates to the labour market. Compared to June 1994 the average employment level in enterprises rose by 1.7 per cent, with a 1.3 per cent rise in the manufacturing sector. The average gross monthly salary in enterprises was PLN 596 in the second quarter of 1994. It is estimated that employment in the entire national economy increased by 2 per cent in the first quarter of 1995 and by 1 per cent in the second quarter.

Domestic demand, foreign trade

One of the advantages of the Polish market (mentioned by many foreign experts) is its size and capacity. Poland's population of 40 million is the highest among Central and Eastern European countries, excluding the former USSR. The increase in domestic demand in 1994 was partly due to buoyant investment in the Polish economy. The total increase in investment expenditure in 1994 is estimated at 6 per cent. The highest increases were recorded in the machinery, services and transport sectors (14 per cent), while investments in buildings were much lower. Increase in consumption expenditure reached approximately 3 per cent in 1994.

The Polish economy is becoming increasingly involved in international trade. Exports increased by 25 per cent as compared with 1990. Goods turnover increased from US$33 billion in 1993 to US$39 billion in 1994. A negative trade balance continued for the fourth consecutive year. In 1994, exports grew more quickly than imports (24 per cent and 12 per cent respectively) and the trade deficit was reduced to

	1993	1994	% change 1993/94
Exports	13,585	16,950	24
Imports	15,878	17,786	12
Balance	–2,202	–836	

Source: NBP Information Bulletin

Table 82.2 Foreign trade of Poland in 1990–94 (US$ million)

US$836 million (see Table 82.2). However, there is substantial unrecorded 'over the border' trade which is estimated to yield a surplus of around US$2.6–3.0 billion.

The development of Polish exports, showing the highest growth rate since 1990 (which was an exceptional year as enterprises were forced to export due to lower domestic demand), was caused by a number of factors beneficial to Poland. Firstly, EU countries have significantly increased imports as a result of improvement of their economies, since the beginning of 1994. Secondly, Polish industry adjusted effectively to the fiercely competitive environment and took advantage of the appreciation of the mark against the dollar to increase sales significantly to countries in Western Europe. It is estimated that the volume of the export of goods and services (including purchases by non-residents) increased by 16 per cent in the first quarter of 1995 and 11 per cent in the second quarter of the year. At the same time, faster economic growth caused a rapid increase in imports, by 20 per cent in the first quarter and 10 per cent in the second quarter of the year.

According to this scenario, it is estimated that there will be a trade surplus of PLN 1.6 billion in the third quarter and a deficit of PLN 0.4 billion in the fourth quarter of 1995.

In 1994, major exports from Poland included: hard coal (US$1 billion); clothes, textiles and knitwear (US$1.8 billion); iron-smelting products (over US$1 billion); copper and alloys (US$600 million); passenger cars (US$500 million); ships (US$750 million) and furniture (over US$850 million). Main imported products included: crude oil (US$1.4 billion); pharmaceuticals (US$660 million) and plastic products (US$700 million).

Competitiveness

In 1994, Polish industry finally returned to profitability. It is estimated that this improvement was caused mainly by an increase in production and by the restructuring of debt. The law of 3 February 1993 on financial restructuring of enterprises and banks permitted a variety of arrangements between enterprises and their creditors. As a result, some debts were written down by banks, by the state budget and by other creditors; some were converted into equity, and others were rescheduled. One of the prerequisites of such debt restructuring was the submission of a recovery programme.

The depletion of industrial assets was halted – investment was almost twice as high as depreciation. One of the main factors contributing to the competitiveness of Polish enterprises is their highly qualified workforce and technical staff. With unit labour costs several times lower than industrialized nations, this remains one of the main strengths of Polish industry. This factor is also emphasized by many foreign experts. The share of salaries (gross remuneration and compulsory overheads for social security, which reached almost 50 per cent of gross salary) as a percentage of overall cost remains stable at around 22 per cent.

Forecasts for 1995

1995 is expected to see a continuation of the growth trends: GNP is expected to increase by another 5 per cent, while industrial production is set to grow at a somewhat slower rate of around 10 per cent. Inflation is expected to decrease. The planned target is 17 per cent (December to December), but will probably reach around 22 per cent. Increase in industrial production prices (year to year) will probably slightly exceed 20 per cent.

Real consumer demand is expected to continue at 1994 levels. Export and investment are expected to continue to fuel economic growth. Exports will increase, but at a pace lower than in 1994. Imports of capital goods and raw materials will grow, while those of consumer goods are expected to remain stable. An investment boom will continue, even though the ratio of investment to depreciation will decrease in 1995, mainly because of revaluation of fixed assets in the economy, which leads to higher depreciation charges.

Foreign investment

The government of Poland has often voiced its belief that foreign investment will play an important role in the modernization and realization of the activities of the respective economic sectors, above all in manu-

facturing industry, transportation, communication, banking and environmental protection. Most of the reforms introduced during recent years have made the business environment attractive for foreign investment. It is expected that the inflow of foreign capital and knowledge will lead to a modernization of production and services (above all technology and market structure), organization and management, and will contribute to the education of a Polish executive class.

By January 1995, almost 20,000 companies with foreign capital participation had been established in the country. Of these, approximately 5,000 were in the manufacturing sector and 6,500 were involved in trade. As at December 1994, US$4,400 million had been contributed in the form of foreign equity and loans, backed up with significant additional capital investment commitments in future years. Recorded foreign investment in Poland, including future commitments, amounted to an estimated US$9.5 billion in the year ending 31 December 1994; however, many opportunities still exist for foreign investors to address Poland's needs and exploit the business potential.

In the period since Poland's move to a market economy, a number of multinationals have made significant investments in Poland, either through equity participation in existing Polish companies or in 'green field' ventures. They include Alcatel, Asea Brown Boveri, AT&T, British Sugar, Coca Cola, CPC Foods, Curtis International, Epstein, Fiat, France Telecom, Gillette, Gerber, Henkel, Hewlett Packard, Ikea, International Paper Corporation, Levi Strauss, Lucchini Group, Marriott, Dr Oetker, PepsiCo, Peugeot, Philips, Pilkington, Procter & Gamble, RJ Reynolds, Siemens, Solco Basel, Thomson, Trust House Forte and Unilever.

Western businessmen still quote a number of negative factors influencing the inflow of foreign capital to Poland, such as political instability, the frequently changing legal and fiscal regulations (particularly in the area of customs duties and import taxes), the weak banking system, uncertainty concerning the issue of reprivatization, poor telecommunications, and the continuing high level of inflation. It should be noted, however, that most of the legislative reforms that have taken place in the last four years have made business conditions more attractive to investors. They have also speeded up the process of modernization and the removal of old bureaucratic barriers.

Incentives for international investors

Poland's almost 39 million inhabitants constitute a sizeable market which, for many products and services, remains largely untapped. The economy functions with significant surplus production capacity. Various types of facilities are in need of upgrading. Poland's location in Europe's geographical centre creates the possibility of easy access to the markets in Germany, the Commonwealth of Independent States and the other former members of COMECON.

Poland is rich in natural resources: coal, sulphur, salt, zinc, copper and wood, the prices of which are often substantially lower than in Western Europe. Industrial waste is not recycled to any great extent.

The zloty is convertible against foreign currencies. The prices of most goods and services have been deregulated and trade restrictions, including international commerce, have been removed. The association agreement with the European Union and preparation for future full membership of the organization, as well as Poland's membership in other international organizations, should lead to the lowering of the tariffs.

Government incentives and guarantees for foreign investors include the following:

- Full profit and dividend repatriation;
- Contributions 'in kind' to foreign-owned equity capital in the form of fixed assets are free of customs duty;
- Funds from the liquidation of a company or from the sale of shares may be repatriated;
- Foreign investors may obtain guarantees against losses resulting from nationalization;
- Bilateral treaties have been signed with several countries, including the UK, for the protection of investments, providing for fair treatment of all investments, and guaranteeing the investor's right to manage, obtain profits and utilize them;
- Double-taxation agreements have been signed between Poland and several countries, including the UK.

Certain additional guarantees may be obtained through negotiation with the central and local authorities.

The privatization of state enterprises makes it possible to acquire manufacturing facilities in a wide range of industries with established products and brand names. Many companies command a significant share of the domestic market for their products.

Privatization

The privatization programme is a key element in Poland's transition to a market economy and is an important feature in the government's economic policy. Privatization is therefore being undertaken on a very wide scale through a multi-method approach at all levels of state ownership including, not only the major industrial enterprises controlled by central government ministries and regional authorities, but also shops, local public services and housing.

The implementation of the Mass Privatization Programme, initially developed in 1991, will have started in the second part of 1995. According to this programme each Polish adult citizen will be able to buy, for a nominal amount, a voucher to the Mass Privatization Programme.

83 Portugal

Association of Portuguese Industries

The Portuguese economy in 1994

The main features relating to the Portuguese economy in 1994 were the beginning of a recovery in economic activity after the second quarter and the continued reduction in inflation to levels close to the European average. Gross domestic product grew approximately 1 per cent and inflation in December increased by 4 per cent compared with the same month in 1993.

The factors contributing to the deflationary trend were monetary and exchange rate policy, which aimed at defending the stability of the escudo after 1990, the slowing down of nominal wage increases and dull domestic demand over the previous two years. Nominal wages increased by 4.7 per cent in 1994 (three percentage points less than the previous year) and domestic demand increased by only 1.4 per cent (–2.5 per cent in 1993).

Private consumption in 1994 was at the same level as in 1993 and was the only component of domestic demand that has shown no signs of recovery in that year. However, the consumer confidence indicator showed some recovery by the end of the year.

The recovery of economic activity has been driven by exports of goods, which have shown a 14.3 per cent growth in volume in 1994 and, mainly after the second quarter, by the gross fixed capital formation (GFCF)

powered by investment from the state-owned companies and the administrative public sector.

Some delay in the recovery of the Portuguese economy occurred in relation to other European Union countries. This delay is a natural one, taking into account that Portugal is a small open economy and, consequently, highly dependent on foreign trade for achieving economic growth.

On the other hand, it is a healthy factor, from the point of view of controlling inflation, that such recovery has been driven by exports and investment, not by private consumption.

Prospects for 1995 and 1996

The March 1995 industrial production index recorded a variation of 2.9 per cent in manufacturing industry and 4.3 per cent for industry in general, in relation to the same month in 1994. There is a favourable evolution in all types of goods, particularly in investment and intermediate goods.

As to foreign trade, there was an increase in nominal terms of 16.9 per cent in exports and 13.2 per cent in imports in the first quarter of 1995, in relation to the same period in 1994.

Private consumption, on the other hand, is static and inflation maintains its downward trend (3.8 per cent in June 1995 in relation to June 1994).

The European Commission's forecasts for the Portuguese economy in 1995 and 1996 predict the growth percentage changes in real terms shown in Table 83.1.

Levels of business confidence

The confidence indicator for manufacturing industry in May 1995, although at a level higher than that recorded in the second half of 1994, has continued to decline from March as a consequence of the less favourable assessment regarding the evolution of demand.

The consumer confidence indicator showed

some stability from February to March 1995 and is higher than the average value in 1993 and 1994.

	1995	1996
GDP	3.0	3.2
Private consumption	1.4	2.0
Government consumption	0.9	1.0
GFCF	7.1	9.0
Exports	10.4	9.3
Imports	7.6	9.4

Table 83.1 Growth forecasts (% change in real terms)

	1991	1992	1993	1994
Real percentage change				
GDP	2.3	1.7	−1.2	1.0
Private consumption	5.2	4.6	−0.3	0.0
Government consumption	3.2	1.5	−1.5	1.4
GFCF (investment and stocks)	2.5	5.6	−7.6	4.2
Export (goods and services)	2.1	4.9	−0.8	9.4
Imports (goods and services)	6.4	11.6	−4.8	8.9
Wages	1.9	3.2	1.0	−0.7
Productivity	−0.7	0.8	0.9	1.1
As % of GDP				
Trade balance	−10.0	−9.8	−7.9	−7.6
Current account balance	−0.8	−0.1	1.0	−1.2
Public administration deficit	6.5	3.3	7.0	5.8
Direct gross public debt	69.3	61.4	66.6	69.6
Inflation (annual average)	11.4	8.9	6.5	5.2
Unemployment rate	4.1	4.1	5.5	6.8

Source: Banco de Portugal

Table 83.2 Main economic indicators (%)

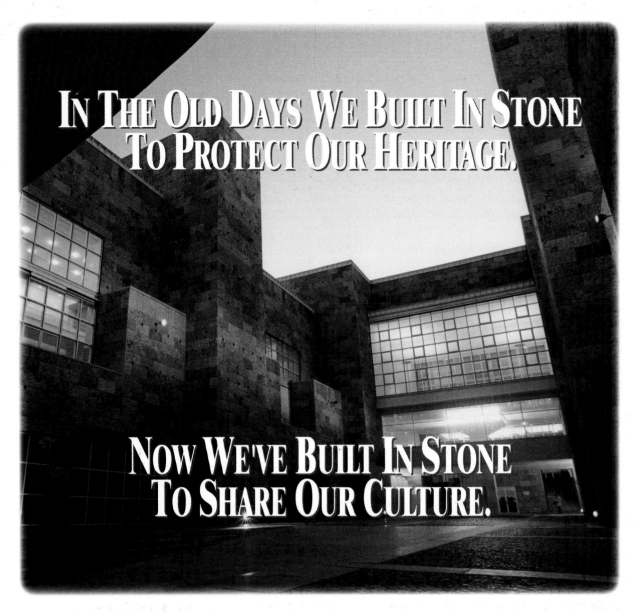

IN THE OLD DAYS WE BUILT IN STONE TO PROTECT OUR HERITAGE.

NOW WE'VE BUILT IN STONE TO SHARE OUR CULTURE.

In Lisbon, just a stone's throw from the Belém Tower, next to Jerónimos Monastery and the river Tagus, the Centro Cultural de Belém is the ideal local, with its open spaces it is just the right place to express and experience your innermost artistic creativity.

Go to concerts, operas, ballets and stage shows in the Performing Art Centre. Come and browse through exhibitions

of paintings, sculpture, photography and other works of art at the Exhibition Centre. Organise congresses and other business and vocational meetings in the Congress Centre. These are some of the many possibilities that the Centro Cultural de Belém offers you.

So, on your next visit to Lisbon don't forget to include culture in your programme and go to the Centro Cultural de Belém.

FUNDAÇÃO DAS DESCOBERTAS
CENTRO CULTURAL DE BELÉM

Praça do Império – 1400 Lisboa – Tel: (351-1) 301 96 06 / 362 27 72 – Fax: (351-1) 362 42 29

Romania

The Chamber of Commerce and Industry of Romania

Redesigning the market economy in Romania after more than 45 years of a command economy requires, like in other Eastern European countries, a painful but still necessary effort to introduce the essentials of this system.

European statistics drawn up at the beginning of the twentieth century ranked Romania among the first 20 European countries in terms of per capita industrial production, its economic development being comparable to that of Norway before the Second World War. At that time Romania was situated at the middle of the list of European countries. It fell towards the bottom of the list of European countries only owing to an inappropriate model of development during the communist experience. The decline accentuated between 1990–93, because of the radical changes incurred by several factors, such as the transition to a market system, the international crisis related to the dismantling of the Council of Mutual Economic Assistance (COMECON), world recession, wars and embargoes in Iraq and Yugoslavia.

At present, Romania is facing a great challenge: to identify its own pattern of economic development, with its specific driving forces, and to draw up its own coherent, long-term economic strategy. This model should exclude any isolation and be a highly interactive one, having as its main aim the acceleration of economic growth and development, so that the gaps that separate today's Romania from developed countries may be closed as soon as possible.

Setting up major economic goals for the longer term will allow better coordination of the transition process. Only a long-term economic strategy, tailoring all resources and external inputs and indicating the further legal and operative steps to be taken, will secure the takeoff of the economy.

Development and potential of the Romanian market

Economic performance in Romania is directly influenced by the comparative advantages enjoyed by the country, legal provisions and the current developments of economic reform.

Soon after 1989, many experts considered that, owing to their real comparative advantages, the Eastern European countries (or at least some of them) might rapidly change into new 'little mighty tigers'. Although the optimism of the early 1990s is yet to be demonstrated, the Eastern European countries do enjoy a number of economic and legal advantages. Romania seems to be a very good example in this respect as it combines a whole range of comparative advantages:

- a large domestic market of 23 million consumers, second only to Poland among Eastern European countries;
- a strategic geographical location at the crossroads of traditional commercial routes, which frees access to a larger market of more than 200 million customers;

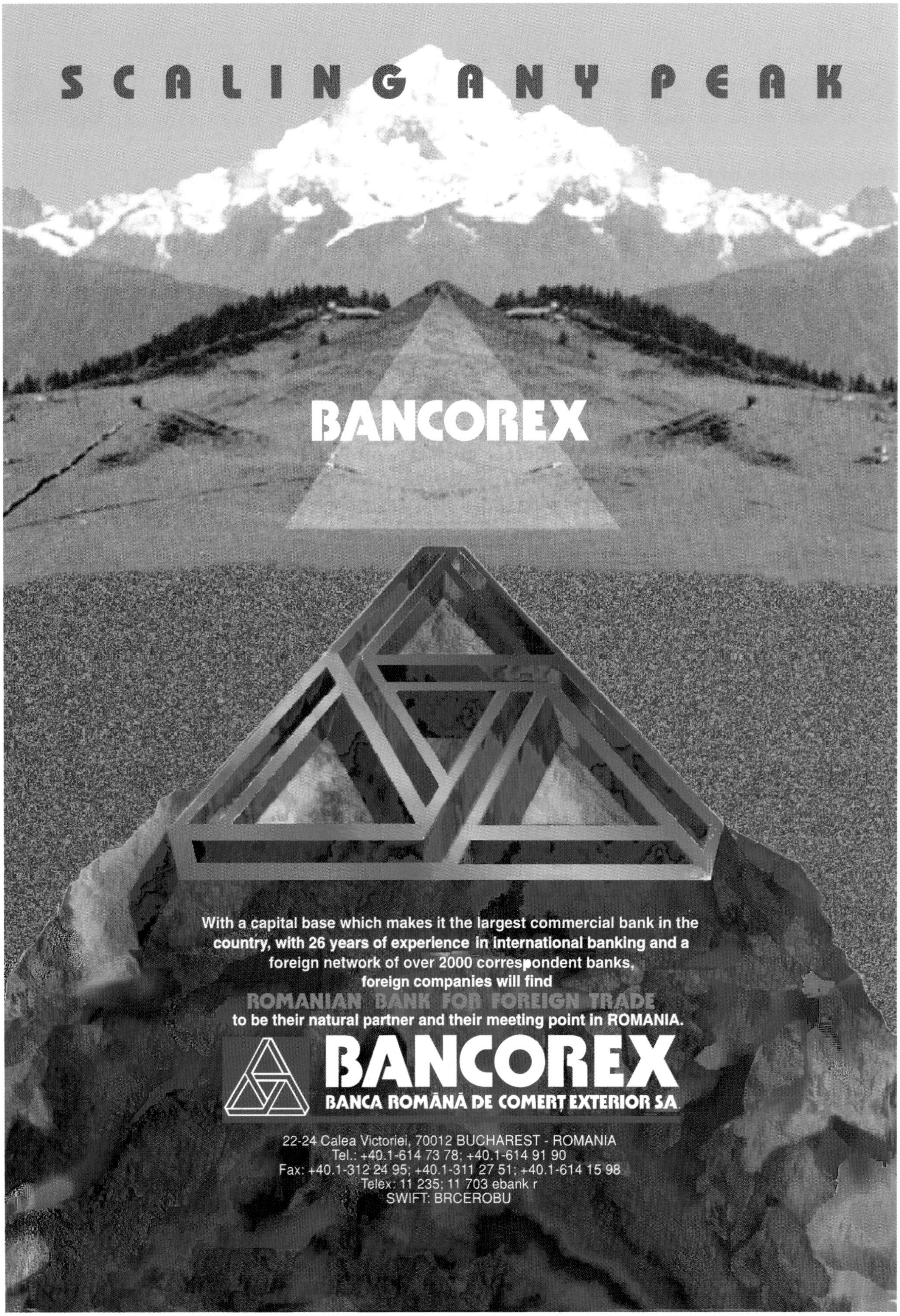
SCALING ANY PEAK
BANCOREX
With a capital base which makes it the largest commercial bank in the country, with 26 years of experience in international banking and a foreign network of over 2000 correspondent banks, foreign companies will find
ROMANIAN BANK FOR FOREIGN TRADE
to be their natural partner and their meeting point in ROMANIA.
BANCOREX
BANCA ROMÂNĂ DE COMERȚ EXTERIOR SA
22-24 Calea Victoriei, 70012 BUCHAREST - ROMANIA
Tel.: +40.1-614 73 78; +40.1-614 91 90
Fax: +40.1-312 24 95; +40.1-311 27 51; +40.1-614 15 98
Telex: 11 235; 11 703 ebank r
SWIFT: BRCEROBU

BANCA ROMANA DE COMERT EXTERIOR S.A.

22-24 Calea Victoriei, P.P. Box 6011, 70012 Bucharest, Romania. Tel: (+40) 1 614 7378; 614 9190. Fax: (+40) 1 614 1598. Telex: 11235; 11703 EBANK R
SWIFT:BRCEROBU
Commercial Universal Bank   Established July 1, 1968

Major Shareholders: State Ownership Fund (69.1%); Private Ownership Funds (29.6%); Bank's Employees (1.3%)
Major Subsidiaries: (Commercial Bank) Anglo-Romanian Bank Ltd, London (50%); Banca Italo-Romena, S.A. Milan (50%) (Commercial Bank); Banque Franco-Roumaine, S.A., Paris (50%) (Commercial Bank); Frankfurt Bukarest Bank, A.G., Frankfurt-Main (87%) (Commercial Bank); Misr-Romanian Bank, Cairo (19%)
Member: Romanian Bankers Association. **Hours:** 8-4. **Number of Employees:** 1,951. **4 City Branches & 17 Branches in Romania**

Kishinev Representative Office
Str. 31 August nr. 125, Hotel Codru 277004 Kishinev, Republic of Moldova. Tel: (0422) 23 7959; Fax: (0422) 23 7959

New York Representative Office
280 Park Avenue, West Building 16th floor, New York, New York 10017 USA. Tel: (212) 454-1404; Fax: (212) 454-1415

Moscow Representative Office
Moscow, 107078, 11 Masha Poryvaeva str., Russian Federation. Tel: (095) 204 7937; Fax: (095) 957 3898; Satellite: (7501) 204 2062

STATEMENT OF CONDITION, DECEMBER 31, 1994

ASSETS	LEI	U.S.D.	LIABILITIES	LEI	U.S.D.
Cash & Banks	828,669,000,000	464,054,640	Deposits	1,846,771,000,000	1,034,191,760
Investment	206,431,000,000	115,601,360	OtherLiabilities	1,150,953,000,000	644,533,680
Loans & Discounts	2,060,530,000,000	1,153,896,800	Capital	83,069,000,000	46,518,640
Other Assets	132,057,000,000	73,951,902	Surplus, Profits & Res	146,894,000,000	82,260,640
TOTAL	3,227,687,000,000	1,807,504,720	TOTAL	3,227,687,000,000	1,807,504,720

OFFICERS & DIRECTORS

Răzvan Liviu Temeșan	Chairman, President & Chief Executive Officer	Dan Stelian Mocanu	Managing Director/Operations	
Alexandru Ghiba	First Deputy Chairman & First Vice President	Radu Dumitru Ivanisin	Managing Director/ Correspondent Banks	
Marinel Burduja	Deputy Chairman & Vice President	Ecaterina Stefănoiu	Managing Director/ Foreign Trade Finance	
Filip Barbu	Deputy Chairman & Vice President	Ioan Gherasim Greu	Managing Director/ Credit Cards/Marketing	
Gheorghe Neagu	Deputy Chairman & Vice President			
Florin Ionescu	Secretary General	Corneliu Alexandru Enea	Managing Director/Equity Investments/Consulting	
Iulian Dumitru	Chief Economist/Managing Director	Răzvan Haritonovici	Managing Director/Mass Media Department	
Doina Marilena Epure	Managing Director/Strategy & Financial Management			

CORRESPONDENTS
Bank of New York, New York
Chemical Bank, New York
Credit Lyonnais, New York
Credisanstalt Bakverein, Vienna
Barclays Bank PLC, London
Lloyds Bank PLC, London
Deutsche Bank A.G., Frankfurt/Main
Union Bank of Switzerland, Zurich
Banca Commerciale Italiana, Milano
Credit Commercial de France, Paris

---

various maritime and river navigation facilities: Constanta is the largest port on the Black Sea, while the completion of the Rhine–Main–Danube Canal allows straight water access from the Black Sea to the North Sea, thus shortening the distance between Middle Eastern countries and Central Europe (Austria, Hungary, Czech Republic, Slovakia) by more than five days. Constanta will also be among the first free-trade zones to be established in Romania;

■ a wide range of natural resources, including fertile agricultural land, oil and natural gas, large deposits of coal and lignite, as well as mineral deposits, and significant tourist potential;

■ a diversified industrial structure, considered to be at a reasonable level of development and ranging from mining and machine building to consumer goods;

■ a skilled labour force, well trained in engineering and technology, at relatively low wages;

■ a new and friendly legal framework providing incentives for foreign investors and partners;

■ relatively low foreign debt compared to other Eastern European countries.

Another set of advantages which Romania can offer

are connected with the legal provisions and the current developments in economic reform:

■ a liberal and permissive trade policy, promoting free exchange, in keeping with GATT regulations;

■ a new customs tariff was adopted, based on the harmonized commodity description and coding system;

■ the liberalization of import and export of goods into/from Romania's customs territory;

■ a special law on free zones, according to which the first four entities are either already operating or preparing to start the activity;

■ Association Agreement with the European Communities, as well as the Agreement between the EFTA states and Romania;

■ the Romanian privatization programme, in which foreign investors are given the possibility of taking part at any stage of the process.

The liberty granted to private initiatives, as well as the process of restructuring the state-owned companies, have widely enlarged the sphere of economic agents in Romania. According to figures released by the National Trade Register Office of the Romanian Chamber of Commerce and Industry, by the end of

84

March 1995 in Romania 1046 autonomous regies (state enterprises), were registered as well as 447,921 trading companies with private capital and 6230 trading companies with public capital.

The private sector's contribution amounted to: 35 per cent of GDP (32 per cent in 1993); 69 per cent of retail sales (55 per cent in 1993); 30 per cent in foreign trade (27 per cent in 1993). In agriculture, private sector production amounted to 83 per cent of cereals, 69 per cent of sunflower, 74 per cent of sugar beet, 94 per cent of potatoes, 88 per cent of vegetables, 76 per cent of fruits. Over 18.5 per cent of the working labour force and 20 per cent of the total active population is employed in the private sector. The number of companies with private capital increased in 1994 to 422,000, up by 36.6 per cent as compared to 1993.

Economic indicators, end of first quarter 1995

Until now, Romania has achieved macroeconomic stability through its own economic programme, accepted and supported by the International Monetary Fund because of the comprehensiveness of its overall approach. And the results of the programme have been appreciated as very encouraging thus far. A new economic environment has been set up by rapidly decreasing inflation rates and by creating the opportunity to earn real, positive returns on savings in domestic currency. As a result, the growing confidence in the national currency enabled the authorities to liberalize substantially the foreign exchange system, while maintaining a relatively stable exchange rate. But since monetary and fiscal policy cannot sustain economic progress alone, Romania is now facing the challenge of implementing the structural reforms that will support financial measures.

According to a recent report by analysts at Nomura, the Japanese financial services group, quoted by the *Financial Times*: 'Romania, little noticed by the West, delivered last year probably the most impressive economic performance in Eastern Europe'.

Indeed, economic performance in 1994 has exceeded expectations: the GDP has increased by 3.4 per cent, thus confirming the positive change within the Romanian economy, which showed a growth of 1 per cent after four years of steep decline. Of even greater significance is that this growth was led by exports and investment: the improved trade perfor-

mance was due to an export surge of 23 per cent, while imports increased by only 5 per cent. The trade deficit was substantially lower than in 1994 (US$332 million). Investment increased by 15 per cent over 1993 and stood at 16 per cent of GDP.

The industrial sector increased by 3 per cent in 1994, while agriculture's contribution remained about the same (+0.2 per cent).

The profile of industrial production changed significantly from the previous year. Output of processing industries increased by 3.3 per cent, the best results being scored in the sectors of electrical apparatus (+55 per cent), leather and shoes (+12 per cent), food processing and drinks (+13 per cent). Mining activities, essentially stagnant during the previous two years, increased by 1.7 per cent, mainly due to metal production (+14.2 per cent) and coal (+2.8 per cent), while construction registered almost a 19 per cent increase. In 1994, exports stood for 18.6 per cent of total industrial production; in readymade clothes, exports accounted for 53 per cent, in furniture 52 per cent, metallurgy 32 per cent and textiles 22 per cent.

The strong increase in exports was owing to a more realistic foreign exchange policy and to the greater access on the EU market. Exports to the USA tripled, owing to the most favoured nation status extended in 1993. Out of total exports, 90 per cent were industrial goods, among which textiles, leather goods and readymade clothes, 24.3 per cent; metallurgical products, 17.6 per cent; machinery, 15.2 per cent; oil products, 11.5 per cent; and furniture, 10.2 per cent. Main destinations of Romanian exports were Germany, Switzerland and Italy, while imports came mainly from Germany, Russia and Italy and consisted mostly of energy (82–84 per cent). The reorientation of Romania's exports towards the EU was evident: exports to the EU amounted to 45.6 per cent of the total, compared to 39.3 per cent in 1993, while imports from the EU stood at 47 per cent, a 9.4 per cent increase over 1933.

One of the biggest successes in 1994 was the sharp reduction in inflation, from 195 to 61.7 per cent. Average gross salaries increased in real terms, reaching Lei 263,000 (a 96 per cent increase on 1993). Unemployment reached 11 per cent, while foreign debt increased to US$ 4.4 billion, which is still much lower than in other Eastern European countries.

In 1994, export volume showed a 22.6 per cent increase compared to the same period in 1993, while imports were 5.1 per cent higher than in the same

	1988	1989	1990	1991	1992	1993	1994	1995*
Exports	6.5	5.9	3.5	3.5	4.0	4.5	5.9	1.5
Imports	2.9	3.4	5.2	4.8	5.3	5.7	6.8	2.0

* first quarter

Source: National Bank Statistics

Table 84.1 Foreign trade evolution, 1988–93 (US$ billion)

period. According to Nomura, the strong export growth is likely to have resulted not only from favourable demand conditions in Western markets, but also from productivity improvements in Romanian industry.

Within the export structure, a significant share is held by textiles (18.5 per cent), common metals and metal articles (17.6 per cent), mineral products (11.9 per cent), chemical products (8.0 per cent). Textiles, footwear and furniture stood at 30.4 per cent of total exports in 1994, as compared to 27.5 per cent in 1993.

European Union countries enhanced their share of total Romanian exports from 39.3 per cent in 1993 to 45.6 per cent in 1994. Over three-quarters of this value was achieved with Germany, Italy and France. Following the applying of the most favoured nation clause, exports towards the USA tripled, being still low compared to the market potential.

In 1994, over 47 per cent of total imports also came from the member countries of the EU, a 9.4 per cent increase compared with 1993.

About a quarter of imports came from transitional economies in Central and Eastern Europe (3.1 per cent), while imports from Middle East countries decreased by 49.2 per cent as against 1993.

Foreign investment increased by 15.3 per cent in 1994 as compared to 1993. This positive evolution was largely owing to the friendly legal climate created in Romania in order to attract foreign investors.

After enforcing and updating the present legislation, 39,676 commercial companies with foreign capital participation were set up between 1990 and 17 April 1995, the capital of which amounts to US$ 1.35 billion.

As for the geographical distribution of foreign investments, the most important part comes from Western Europe (58 per cent), followed by Asia (17 per cent), North America (14 per cent) and the Middle East (7 per cent). In terms of the number of

commercial companies with foreign participation, the main flows of investment come from Western Europe (39 per cent), the Middle East (30 per cent), Asia (14 per cent), Eastern Europe (7 per cent) and North America (6 per cent).

Important partners in capital terms are South Korea (11.7 per cent), Germany (9.6 per cent) and the USA (8.9 per cent), while in number of companies set up in Romania the order is Germany, Italy and Turkey, with 5065, 4918 and 3788 companies respectively.

Recent statistical information shows that the recovery process started in the second half of 1994 has continued during the first quarter of 1995: industrial output increased by 10.2 per cent compared to the same period of 1994; exports showed a 22.5 per cent increase, while the import surge was even higher (40.4 per cent); the trade balance showed a US$291.8 million deficit. The inflation rate has marked its lowest level since price liberalization (1.5 per cent as compared to 6.4 per cent during the same period in 1994).

Considering all these elements and evolutions, the economic performance of the country may soon be placed on an upward trend and the encouraging signs already shown will be turned to better account in the not very distant future.

During his last visit to Bucharest, Maxwell Watson, IMF negotiator for Romania, underlined that Romania's economic performance in 1994 and the first few months of 1995 was assessed as 'very good' by international financial circles, especially with the inflation rate decrease and production growth. Moreover, at the end of his mission to Romania, the IMF representative for Romania, Joshua Greene, declared that 1994 was a very good year for Romania, taking into account the decrease in the inflation rate and the lower level of budget deficit, which accounted for only 2 per cent of GDP.

These positive signs of recovery seem to justify

84

the conclusions regarding the Romanian economy reached by the Vienna Institute for Higher Studies. Owing to the economic results achieved in 1994, experts from this institute consider Romania as 'a magnet for economic growth in the South East Europe'.

Prospects for 1995/1996

In spite of the positive economic results achieved during the last year and a half and the above-mentioned comparative advantages, Romania finds itself at a turning point of economic evolution; 1995 was acknowledged as the decisive year of the reform process. The completion of the legal framework with some other important laws for the operation of a market system in Romania, the setting up of other basic institutions of a market system (such as the stock exchange), as well as more visible results within the privatization process, will be essential to accelerating the reform process in the country.

Economic growth greater than the initial estimates is already envisaged; if the present features of savings policy are maintained, a 5 per cent economic growth rate is to be expected by the end of 1995. Recent estimates of the National Bank of Romania on economic growth for 1995 predict an even higher, perhaps 8 per cent, growth in GDP.

The European Bank for Reconstruction and Development's latest projections are slightly more cautious, with GDP forecast to grow by 3 per cent in 1995, and the inflation rate predicted to fall to 40 per cent by the end of the year.

However, each of the prognoses drawn up so far agrees on the importance that should be attached to resorting to important structural adjustment programmes in order to support the achievements already in place.

Privatization is fundamental to Romania's free market reforms, since the transfer of property to private ownership is one of the keys to economic restructuring and future growth.

The Romanian privatization programme was drawn up and is currently being updated to ensure that companies are privatized in the most appropriate way for their circumstances. Foreign investors can take part in this process and are welcome to buy shares or assets in any part of the privatization programme. In the meantime, foreign and Romanian investors are equally treated.

The legislation provides for:

■ free and equal distribution to the population of

30 per cent of state-owned capital (6300 commercial companies). The process was completed by distributing ownership certificates in five private ownership trust funds (POF) which had previously received 30 per cent of the equity of commercial companies;

■ sale of the 70 per cent interest in the commercial companies that are now under the administration of the State Ownership Trust Fund (SOF).

After enacting the law on privatization (Law no. 58/1991), subsequently completed by Law no. 114/1992, 15.5 million title deeds, called property vouchers, representing about 30 per cent of the social capital of the commercial companies likely to be privatized, have been distributed to Romanian citizens.

At its inception, the privatization programme included about 6700 companies, out of which 22 companies were privatized through the pilot programme carried out by the National Agency for Privatization and 1078 were privatized by the procedures unfolded through the POFs and SOF, starting with August 1993.

The recent law on accelerating the privatization process introduces some new elements:

■ In addition to the old property vouchers, an additional title deed was introduced: the nominal coupon. The voucher price has been set at 25,000 lei (about US$ 13), while the coupon is priced at 975,000 lei (about US$ 500). Benefiting from the coupons are only those who have not used their vouchers in the privatization process.

■ The proportion and volume of the social capital transferred freely has been modified from 30 to 60 per cent.

■ Only 3000 companies will be included in the mass privatization process.

After enacting the law on accelerating the privatization process, several steps will follow: approval of the list of companies to be privatized; setting up the list of citizens entitled to nominative coupons; distribution of coupons; subscription of bills of exchange and share certificates; selling procedures for 40 per cent of each of the commercial companies to be privatized; enacting other related laws (the law on transforming the POFs into investment funds and the law on the privatization of state-owned banks).

The privatization process is not limited to commercial companies, but also includes measures affecting housing, agricultural land and the banking sector.

For land privatization, Law no. 18/1991, was

considered the boldest of all measures of the same type adopted by Eastern European countries. By the end of 1991 the private sector represented nearly 80 per cent of the agricultural land and was responsible for the largest share of agricultural output (eg 83 per cent of cereals, 88 per cent of sugar beet, etc).

Besides the privatization process, a more comprehensive process of restructuring the Romanian economy is now under way, one of its main elements being industrial restructuring. This process is considered from two sides:

- improvement of managerial and technical skills in order to provide access to relevant international business information and create a modern business culture;
- upgrading of industrial processes and modernization of certain facilities for increasing production efficiency;
- therefore, sectoral restructuring strategies and economic policies were elaborated with a view to implementing the restructuring programmes at a microeconomic level.

According to these programmes, the investment activities required for upgrading the existing equip-ment and technology amount to US$ 7 billion for a 5–6 year period, out of which only 40 per cent can be covered from local resources.

The restructuring programme now includes 200 big companies (the so-called industrial giants), mainly selected from metallurgical, chemical and machine-building industries. From among these companies, 32 are to be restructured as a priority.

External trading environment

During the last five years, Romania's efforts have been directed towards introducing significant elements of economic reform: a liberal and permissive trade policy, promoting free exchange, in keeping with GATT regulations; a new customs tariff, based on the harmonized commodity description and coding system; the liberalization of import and export of goods into/from Romania's customs territory; the privatization programme, in which foreign investors are allowed and invited to participate.

The measures so far taken in this respect have started to bear fruit: 1993 brought about signature of the Association Agreement with the European Communities, as well as the Free Trade Agreement between the EFTA states and Romania, while most favoured nation status was restored to Romania by the USA in October 1994.

With effect from 1 May 1991, the EU has eliminated all quantitative export restrictions in Romanian goods and 120 customs tariffs formerly applied. These measures will complement the 'preferential treatment' already granted. According to a recent decision, the European Union will liberalize imports of industrial products, steel and textiles from Romania one year earlier. Liberalization has begun in 1995 for industrial products and will be in force in 1996 for steel and 1997 for textiles. In the meantime, Romania has to reform its subsidy system in order to comply with European standards.

Because of these steps, Romanian products now benefit from different forms of non-discriminatory or preferential treatment and can improve or regain access to the world market.

The law on free-trade zones was enacted with a view to enhancing both international exchanges and the proper use of national economic resources. According to this law, free-trade zones in Romania may be established in the maritime and river ports,

along the Danube–Black Sea Canal and other navigable canals, and in the territories neighbouring the frontier checkpoints.

The activities to be carried out in these areas include a wide range of operations: production, assembly, processing, storage, packaging, expertise, quality and quantity control, to transports, deliveries, stock exchange, financial and banking operations, services and other specific activities for free-trade zones. All these activities can be performed only subject to licences released by the administration of the respective free-trade zone.

The first zones of the kind to operate in Romania are: Sulina, Constanta – South Agigea, Galati and Braila – on the Danube river.

Priorities for EU integration

On 26 June 1995, Romania submitted its official request to join the EU, supported by a national strategy aimed at accelerating the country's integration with the EU.

At present, Romania is an associate member of the European Union, a full member of the European Council, and has very close economic cooperation

GALLUP: EASTERN EUROPE & CIS

The Most Comprehensive and Experienced Service in Eastern Europe and the CIS

* **Monthly Omnibus** in 18 countries – random sampling.

* **Qualitative Research** – rapid transcriptions, Video link.

* **Russian Media Monitor** – panel of 1000 respondents in European Russia reporting daily TV viewing in 15 minute segments.

* **Bulgarian Media Monitor** – panel of 600 respondents, reporting daily TV viewing.

* **Ukrainian Media Monitor** – launch date September 1993.

* **Adhoc research** using some of the best researchers in each of these countries. Affiliated to the Gallup International Network.

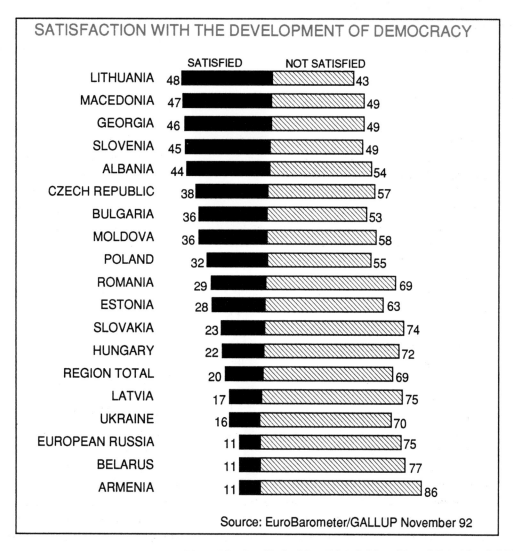

SATISFACTION WITH THE DEVELOPMENT OF DEMOCRACY

	SATISFIED	NOT SATISFIED
LITHUANIA	48	43
MACEDONIA	47	49
GEORGIA	46	49
SLOVENIA	45	49
ALBANIA	44	54
CZECH REPUBLIC	38	57
BULGARIA	36	53
MOLDOVA	36	58
POLAND	32	55
ROMANIA	29	69
ESTONIA	28	63
SLOVAKIA	23	74
HUNGARY	22	72
REGION TOTAL	20	69
LATVIA	17	75
UKRAINE	16	70
EUROPEAN RUSSIA	11	75
BELARUS	11	77
ARMENIA	11	86

Source: EuroBarometer/GALLUP November 92

Contact: Gordon Heald or Alan Hyde Tel. 071 794 0461 Fax 071 431 0252
Gallup Poll Ltd, Gallup House, 307 Finchley Road, London NW3 6EH

U.M.T.

We, **Uzinele Mecanice Timisoara,** are producing, improving and selling for over 35 years:

- Various types of **cranes** and **overhead travelling cranes** with lifting loads up to 600 t.
- **Truck mounted cranes** with 12.5 t; 18 t; 25 t; 40 t load.
- **Fork lift trucks** with 1.25 t; 1.6 t; 3.2 t lifting load.
- **Sideloaders** with 5 t lifting load.
- **Mining equipment:** drum shearers, mining supports, bucket-wheel excavators with 130 l/bucket; 470 l/bucket; 1400 l/bucket capacity.
- **Equipment for working in coal stores:** stackers, reclaimers, stacker-reclaimers.

We deliver technical gas: **oxygen, argon.**

Timisoara is connected to the international railway and road systems, being located at the following road distances from:

Amsterdam 1725 km
Athens 1324 km
Berlin 1222 km
Berne 1399 km
Bonn 1184 km
Brussels 1675 km
Budapest 257 km
Copenhagen 2143 km
Lisbon 3679 km
London 1993 km
Madrid 2992 km
Moscow 2466 km
Oslo 2694 km
Paris 1812 km
Prague 839 km
Rome 1472 km

U.M.T. products were exported to: Germany, France, Belgium, Poland, China, Egypt, India, Iraq, Turkey, Nigeria, Vietnam, Czech Republic, Slovakia, Bulgaria, Tunis, Syria, Switzerland.

WHEN YOU SAY BUSINESS
WE MEAN POWER

 UZINELE MECANICE TIMISOARA

ROMÂNIA- 1900 TIMISOARA
Str. Avram Imbroane Nr.9
Telefon +40 56 133970
Telefax +40 56 190204
Telex 71257

84

with EFTA countries. Understandably, the main and most challenging task is to join the EU and this step cannot be reached until and unless a dynamic pattern of economic development is inculcated in the economy. On the other hand, joining the 'club' of EU countries will surely create the necessary synergy for accelerating Romania's dynamic development.

In a world economy where interdependencies are becoming ever tighter, the Romanian Chamber of Commerce and Industry (CCIR) is widely promoting open contacts with countries all around the world. Special attention is given to the particular patterns of economic development pursued by the dynamic economies of the contemporary world.

As a Central European country, Romania is, of course, mainly interested in strengthening its economic and political relations with European countries and in joining the different forms of Euro-Atlantic structures. At the same time, it is aware of the fact that in order to facilitate and speed up the complete economic integration of Romania in the European Union, it has to develop and diversify its economic relations with countries all over the world and mainly with neighbouring countries. For instance, the summit of the Black Sea Economic Cooperation (BSEC) was recently held in Bucharest. Romania is actively participating and supporting this subregional cooperation, as a step to further integration with the EU. This is the only way to benefit fully from existing complementarities with countries worldwide and to gain more rapid access to European forms of economic integration.

Whatever the problems that might still confront the Romanian economy, the results achieved so far are generally considered as a success, and there is increasing evidence of interest and confidence of foreign investors and financial circles in the potential of the Romanian market.

Romania now enjoys a whole range of both comparative advantages and prerequisites that can recommend it as a reliable partner for companies and countries all over the world.

CCIR

Having assumed the role of helping building the necessary market-oriented mechanisms, the Chamber of Commerce and Industry of Romania (CCIR) strives to become an essential catalyst of economic development and progress, especially at the microeconomic level of companies.

Within this economic context, the CCIR actively supports the idea of drawing up a long-term economic strategy for the country, to which it tries to contribute by suggesting its own concept of the dynamic pattern of economic development on which Romania should decide.

The general policy of the CCIR is to expand business relations with countries all over the world. Regional and subregional collaboration, improving and strengthening traditional and natural links with neighbouring countries, is thus considered as a first step for turning to account the existing complementarities and for better preparing for further integration in European structures.

By all its activities, the CCIR is supporting the government of Romania in accelerating the transition process to a competitive market economy, mainly through privatization, and acts to place Romania on a track of dynamic development as soon as possible.

The Slovak Republic

85

The Federation of the Employers' Unions and Associations of the Slovak Republic

Slovakia is a nation whose positive economic indicators bode well for the future. Its own domestic market is showing rapid development and the country's location right in the heart of Europe puts it in a prime position to exploit a vast potential export market.

The macroeconomics regulations focused on stabilization were one, but not the only reason for the surprisingly favourable development of the Slovak economy in 1995. The effect of economic political measures focused on improvement in the foreign trade balance, promoted by revitalization in the world economy, was of primary importance and a turning point in the economic development from the expected stagnation to minor revitalization.

Strong exports and private sector growth are expected to fuel continued economic growth for Slovakia. GDP in 1995 after the first half grew by 6.1 per cent, with the forecast for 1995 growth at 6.4 per cent. GDP growth was particularly influenced by service sector development. Non-financial companies with 25 employees or more generated 63 per cent of total business profit volume.

The inflation rate decreased significantly in all measured price indices in comparison with the previous year. Consumer prices increased by 4.5 per cent to August 1995 compared to December 1994. This development meant Slovakia was the lowest inflation rate country among the transforming countries in 1995.

Services

The annual retail sale growth was 10 per cent and the annual transported goods volume growth was 12.1 per cent.

Investments market

The annual investment demand growth was 14.2 per cent. From the branch point of view, the highest volume of investments (22.1 per cent) was in industrial production, 10 per cent was in traffic, transport and communications, and 7.4 per cent in the financial sector.

Industry

In the first six months of 1995 industrial production continued to be dynamic with annual growth at 9.4 per cent. Growth in industrial production volume was 7.7 per cent.

There was higher growth in the transport of means of production (61.1 per cent), leather processing and leather goods production (21.6 per cent), rubber and plastics goods production (18.9 per cent); continued decline in food and drinks production (10.1 per cent) and in textile and clothing production (17.3 per cent).

Construction

The period of downward movement has ceased and revival has already begun. The annual growth rate is 4.5 per cent.

Agriculture

Sales volumes in agricultural production continued to decline. On the other hand, there was a positive trend in most farm animal reproduction parameters.

Foreign trade

The development of foreign trade in Slovakia represents one of the most important stabilizing and dynamizing components of its economic development. The turnover in foreign trade during the first eight months of 1995 increased by 21 per cent with a positive trade balance. Export volume (165.2 billion Slovak crowns) increased for this period by 22.2 per cent compared to the import volume (163.7 billion Slovak crowns) increase of 21.3 per cent. The forecast export volume for 1995 is for growth of 60 per cent in GDP share, accepting 4 per cent growth in GDP for 1995.

Slovakia is the only country in the Central European region whose trade balance with the European Union is positive. In foreign trade there is special emphasis on the export of products, an especially developed chemical industry sector, with industrial and agricultural chemicals and equipment for processing and production of pharmaceuticals and chemicals of good quality. The machine tools and tool industry, the wood processing industry, agricultural equipment industry as well as suppliers to the Slovakian automotive industry have strong potential.

From the selected items (to August), according to the customs register, most of the goods and materials exported were iron and steel (27.2 billion Slovak crowns), boilers, machines, tools, equipment and nuclear reactor components (12.9 billion Slovak crowns), chemicals (14.3 billion Slovak crowns), mineral fuels, mineral oils, and resin minerals and waxes (9.2 billion Slovak crowns), motor vehicles, tractors, motorbikes and their spare parts (7.8 billion Slovak crowns), plastic materials and goods made of plastic (9.2 billion Slovak crowns), products from iron and steel (7.2 billion Slovak crowns), furniture, cartons, paper (12.5 billion Slovak crowns).

The domestic market has been supplied, according to the customs register, by mineral fuels, mineral oils, and resin minerals and waxes (30 billion Slovak crowns), boilers, machines, tools, equipment and nuclear reactor components (25.7 billion Slovak crowns), electronic machines designed for picture and sound reproduction (10.6 billion Slovak crowns), chemicals (5.3 billion Slovak crowns), motor vehicles, tractors, motor bikes and their spare parts (8 billion Slovak crowns), plastic materials and goods made of plastic (5.7 billion Slovak crowns), products from iron and steel (5.4 billion Slovak crowns).

Foreign direct investment

To July 1995 approximately 7600 projects from 82 countries have created investment of US$582 million in Slovakia. Many blue-chip names such as Volkswagen, Siemens, Hoechst are in the list of investing companies whose presence is a testimony to the burgeoning Slovak economy and climate for investment.

Slovakia's position in the geographical centre of continental Europe means it is ideally placed to serve both Eastern and Western consumer markets. This factor has proved particularly pertinent in the case of its automotive components industry which is rapidly developing because of the ability to supply both existing markets in the West and the emerging markets in the East.

More importantly, perhaps, is the fact that it has good road, rail and water links, enabling the fast and efficient transportation of goods to those markets, including, of course, the countries of the European Union to which there is free entry for most products.

Slovakia has a highly skilled workforce, well-educated employees who are very receptive to new management techniques and Western-style practices. There are particular skills in precision engineering, in which there is a strong tradition in Slovakia, in the chemical, electronics, food processing, automotive industrial sectors and others.

Also important is the existence of a favourable taxation climate which includes the establishment of double taxation agreements, generous facilities for the importation of goods and components for further processing and use in production programmes, and the ability for companies to operate 100 per cent foreign ownership, if they wish, with full transfer of profits, after tax, in the convertible currency.

Industrial policy

Economic and industrial policy is focused on development of infrastructure systems in transportation, information technology, telecommunications, the energy sector, finance. Its strategic goals are stabilization of industrial branches, increases in efficiency, boost in exports and the competitiveness of production, reduction in energy consumption and claims on raw materials, increase of domestic raw materials use, greater value-added production and maintenance of a stable currency.

Priority is given to the following industries: chemical and pharmaceuticals, energy, wood processing and consumer goods, mechanical and electrical engineering. The government will stress active tourism promotion, the spa industry, health and rural tourism.

Forecast of economic development

- The state budget deficit will reach approximately 4 per cent of GDP.
- GDP growth will be 6 per cent.
- The inflation rate should be lower than 10 per cent.
- The unemployment rate should be approximately 13 per cent.
- The annual economical growth rate will be 6 per cent without significant inflation pressure.
- Foreign trade will still be a dynamic factor in GDP growth.
- Higher export levels as well as imports should be capable of generating sufficient foreign currency to ensure the necessary imports and currency stability.
- The technological reconstruction of production potential should be based on dynamic growth in gross fixed investments.

Federation of the Employers' Unions and Associations of the Slovak Republic

The Federation is the highest level representative of the employers and the entrepreneurs of the Slovak Republic. Based on the Federation Memorandum, the Federation:

1. Carries through and defends the interests of its members in tripartite negotiations with central organs of the state authority and with trade union organs in issues of economic and social policy and in issues which are the subjects of collective negotiations.
2. Signs agreements, including General Agreements and collective agreements of higher degree.
3. Represents members in tripartite initiatives, agreements and consulting organs.
4. Coordinates progress and puts forward the common interests of its members in relation to deputy corps and central organs of state relationships to international organizations of employers and the International Labour Organization.
5. Strives consequently for transformation of the Slovak economy into a free-market economy.
6. Supports legal, institutional and social consciousness transformations.

At present the Federation is a top level employers' representative which represents 29 members' unions and associations – about 70 per cent of all Slovak Republic employees. All other associations and unions of employers' entrepreneurs are based on the branch principle only and about 90 per cent of all are associated with the Federation.

86 Spain

The Confederation of Spanish Employers

At the end of the first part of 1995, the Spanish economy is consolidating the advances which had already taken place in the last months of the previous year, with a growth rate in Gross Domestic Product placed around 3 per cent. This increase in production has been based almost exclusively on internal demand, given that the positive contribution of the external sector of the past few years has been exhausted.

Within internal demand, investment has been the most dynamic variable factor, as it has shifted from a fall of 10.5 per cent in 1993 to reveal a real increase of 9 per cent in the first half of 1995. Wage restraint has contributed to this situation – the rate of increase in wages has gone from 6.8 per cent in 1993 to 4 per cent at present in terms of remuneration per wage earner – together with greater activity linked to the exportation of goods and services, a situation which has enabled a restructuring of the rather battered business enterprise results in the first four years of the 1990s. In this way, since the end of 1994 the profitability of assets has become equal to or higher than outside finance. This fact has made possible a total change of business investment in equipment which has become at this stage the main spur to internal demand, with a volume increase of 9 per cent in contrast to a fall close to 6 per cent in the same period of 1994. The other investment component, construction activity, has also revealed a significant uptrend in the first months of 1995, with an increase of 8.9 per cent.

One benefit of this investment growth has been a recovery in employment which, spurred by wage restraint, has reached an annual growth rate of 2.5 per cent. This growth in employment in relation to the growth in GDP has made it quite clear that one of the fruits of wage moderation is revealed in the amount of human resources per production unit, a fact which is very encouraging in a country like Spain with such an unfortunate record of unemployment.

This expansive phase of the Spanish economy, initiated by the positive contribution of the foreign sector and continued by means of an investment recovery, should continue based on a consolidation of a recovery of private consumption in harmony with the evolution of employment. However, this variable factor at the close of the first six-month period of 1995 denotes a certain slackening off in the recovery phase initiated in 1994. Thus, the latest indicators of consumer confidence, credit applications or car registrations, reveal that the advance has stagnated in the mid-term period of the year and a growth rate of slightly less than 2 per cent has been maintained since the end of 1994.

As has been shown by the Spanish experience in the second half of the 1980s, neither a slowing down of salary increases nor an increase in the proportion of temporary hiring contracts are factors which bring about a waning of consumption, but rather the climate of uncertainty which the consumer is aware of in the national sociopolitical panorama. Within this context, the propensity towards saving takes on greater relevance by the so-called precautionary effect and credit demand undergoes a withdrawal. This has been happening in Spain since spring 1995 and may bring about a requirement to carry out a downward revision of growth rates in GDP.

This upward trend in household savings enables the economy partially to compensate for the lack of saving initiatives in the public sector, whose debt requirements are very high, 6 per cent of GDP, and a reduction of the foreign deficit to reasonable levels, below 1 per cent of GDP. It is quite evident that the greatly desired consolidation of economic recovery in the near future without, at the same time, bringing about a deterioration of external accounts must, inevitably, entail a rebalancing of the public budget by means of restraint on expenditure.

The budgetary proposal which aims to bring the public deficit to a figure of 4.4 per cent in 1996 and 3 per cent in 1997 is a reasonable and necessary one, not only as a formal requirement of the European Union Treaty, but also as an urgent necessity to achieve an ordered financing of the Spanish economy, since the absorption of new saving by the public sector sets the private sector aside from the credit market, raises interest rates and prejudices investment and consumption, putting very serious limits on a real convergence with the EU.

On the other hand, once the inflationary tensions brought about by modification of direct fiscal measures, depreciation of the peseta and by the effects of adverse climatological conditions on food-stuff prices have been absorbed, restraint on unit labour costs and increasing market competitiveness are factors which have made possible a rate of price increases of around 4 per cent. It should not be particularly difficult to achieve nearer 3 per cent, towards convergence with the EU and taking as a departure point the supposition of a certain stability of the international prices of raw materials and the exchange rate, factors which may be envisaged as reasonably certain at the present time.

However, a failure by the markets to perceive a clear and decisive willingness to act on both fronts (that of an excessive budgetary imbalance and an inhibition which prevents the carrying out of the structural reforms which may contribute to the achievement of a less inflationary economic growth) is being penalized by greater financial burdens. Thus, taking as a point of reference the cost of long-term financing of the public debt, it is necessary to pay in

Spain some five points higher than the German figure. This is an abnormally high differential, above all if one takes into account the fact that the exchange rate is placed in a more realistic position in accordance with the fundamental bases of the Spanish economy.

It is thus necessary to assume that the struggle against the imbalances of the Spanish economy should come from more efficiency and without such negative collateral effects as those brought about by the exclusive use of monetary policy.

In the first place, the conviction should be conveyed that measures are going to be taken leading to a firm and decisive reduction in the structural public deficit. A cutback on current public expenditure, both in the field of consumption and that which may be achieved by a better control of the fraudulent use of social benefits, is still the main matter pending. Hope might be held out, perhaps, that the recovery may lessen the apparent seriousness of the budgetary imbalance, as was the case in the second half of the 1980s, by bringing about a greater tax return yield and a reduction of certain payments linked to economic cycles such as that of unemployment. At present, however, no less than 60 per cent of the public deficit, that is, close to 4 per cent of GDP, is not cyclical but rather structural and this demands specific measures to eradicate it, setting aside the economic circumstances, fundamentally on three fronts: public enterprises, the civil service and a revision of the blueprint which sustains the programmes of the so-called welfare state, while preserving public investment effort within the infrastructure of telecommunications, transport, hydraulic projects, etc., an indispensable element in order to be able to continue increasing the potential for balanced growth in the Spanish economy.

And secondly, the situation requires greater and swifter adaptation to demand in production, thus creating more propitious conditions for investment and employment in business enterprises by active fiscal and financial policies and an improvement in transparency and efficiency in the markets. This entails the necessity of introducing competitive elements in certain activities, particularly within the service sector, in line with the tendencies set down by the European Commission and the Spanish Competitive Defence Board, in fields such as transport, telecommunications, urban soil, and services and supplies depending on public administration.

We are undergoing a delicate and historically

THERE IS A PLACE IN EUROPE THAT OFFERS YOU MORE THAN 2,000 REASONS TO INVEST IN

CATALONIA
the motor of the Mediterranean's growing "Sun Belt", where more than 2,000 multi-nationals are successfully operating.

The Office of Foreign Investment (CIDEM), depending on the Department of Industry and Energy of the Autonomous Government of Catalonia, will help your company to discover the advantages of being in the heart of Europe's "Sun Belt".

Generalitat de Catalunya
Autonomous Government of Catalonia

BARCELONA Office
Tel.: 34-3-405 11 04
Fax: 34-3-419 88 23
Internet Code: HTTP://www.GENCAT.ES

NEW YORK Office
Tel.: 1-212-755 88 30
Fax: 1-212-755 88 37

TOKYO Office
Tel.: 81-33-222 15 71
Fax: 81-33-222 15 73

DÜSSELDORF Office
Tel.: 49-211-49 24 20
Fax: 49-211-492 42 42

important time in the process of European construction, in so far as the date envisaged by the Maastricht Treaty for access to the final phase of the EMU is approaching. The implications are enormous, both in the political and economic sphere, for all member countries and particularly for those who will be required to undertake a special effort of adapta-

tion and convergence, taking into account their more unstable departure point or their greater imbalances. For this reason, whether the pacesetters of the Spanish economy may be capable or not of adequate and convincing decision taking will determine its possibilities within the realm of development and social welfare in the near future.

Catalonia, the centre of Europe's new industrial growth region

As the European "Single Market" has rapidly moved from concept to reality, companies around the world are seeking the best location to serve the current and future needs of the European Union's more than 340 million consumers. Many of these are establishing production, distribution, or administrative operations in Catalonia, the Spanish region that the European Commission calls an integral part of Europe's "new centre of development".

This new "growth area", which includes parts of eastern Spain, southern Germany, northern Italy, and southern France, has positioned Catalonia, and its capital city of Barcelona, at the heart of a new industrial zone known as "Europe's Sun Belt".

Catalonia is not a newcomer to attracting foreign direct investment. Many of the more than 2,000 foreign-based firms already operating there have invested because of Catalonia's:

• Highly strategic location.

Within a radius of 1,200 miles, all of the countries of the European Union and North Africa can be reached easily from Catalonia. The region's transportation network, which includes nearly 7,000 miles of modern roads, some 1,000 miles of rails, international and domestic airports, and Mediterranean seaports with direct shipping lines to more than 100 countries, provides ready access to this expanding market of some 500 million people.

• Position as the leading industrial region in Spain.

Long the heartland of Spanish industry, Catalonia's annual industrial production level, providing 25 percent of Spain's industrial employment and 26 percent of the country's industrial gross domestic product, already makes it one of Europe's top five industrialised areas. The region's prospects for further growth are tremendous.

• One of the lowest tax rates in the European Union and record investment returns

The ability to profit from an investment in Catalonia is also high on the list of the region's competitive advantages. Foreign investors are attracted to Catalonia by one of the lowest tax rates in the European Union and a Spanish economy that has generated an average annual ROI of 19.3 percent for the past five years. This return is the highest of all the OECD countries.

• A quality work force and a commitment to maintaining high Labour standards

Foreign companies cite the quality, productivity and competitive cost of the Catalonian worker as key to success of their investment. The Government ensures the continued high quality of this work force through an educational system that includes more than 4,100 primary, secondary, vocational and university institutions. In addition Catalonia has a number of world-renowned management schools with links to international universities and to programs supported by the European Union.

• A favourable regulatory environment and a commitment to modern infrastructure

Catalonia's regulatory frameworks allow foreign investors to maintain 100 percent ownership of their ventures, and the right to repatriate invested capital, capital gains, dividends, and profits without restrictions or limitations.

Catalonia's "pro-business environment" is also reflected in public and private sector investments made in infrastructure to support the continued growth of a truly diversified economy.

• A unique Mediterranean quality of life.

The region has been a centre of European art and culture for hundreds of years. The region's quality of life goes beyond its artistic and cultural traditions.

A temperate climate and natural beauty that ranges from the snow-capped Pyrenees to miles of scenic Mediterranean coastline attract some 20 million tourists to Catalonia each year.

87 Sweden

Federation of Swedish Industries

Recent developments

After the worst depression since the 1930s, the Swedish economy bottomed out during 1993, and started to recover in 1994. The upswing has been driven by a sharp improvement in industry's international competitiveness, thanks to rapid productivity growth as well as the deprecation of the krona. Following a strong increase in exports, industrial production has risen by some 30 per cent since the beginning of 1993. Swedish exports increased by 28 per cent during 1993–94. This is an even faster growth rate than that following the 1982 devaluation, when exports rose by 21 per cent.

As a result of increased capacity utilization and improved profits, investment in industry increased by 27 per cent in 1994.

Recovery has to a large extent been limited to the export-oriented sectors and the situation is still weak in the domestic sectors. In particular, private consumption is held back by declining disposable income in the household sector and a high savings ratio owing to a high rate of unemployment and the necessary cuts in public spending. All in all, GDP grew by 2.2 per cent in 1994.

Economic prospects for 1995 and 1996

Looking at recent economic data it is clear that after two and a half years of unprecedented expansion, growth in the export sector is now slowing down.

This is partly due to slower growth in Europe and the USA. World trade, which grew by 10 per cent in 1994 – the fastest increase in two decades – is expected to decline considerably during 1995 and 1996. The slowdown is also explained by high capacity utilization in Swedish industry, limiting the short-term scope for further expansion. Thus exports, the major growth factor in the economy, are forecast to grow by 11 per cent in 1995 and 4–5 per cent in 1996, compared to close to 16 per cent in 1994. This also implies that destocking may take place, especially during 1995.

Given the high capacity utilization, investment plans for 1995 are very upbeat and fixed investments in manufacturing are expected to rise by 35 per cent in 1995 and by a further 20 per cent in 1996. The largest increases originate in the capital-intensive part of manufacturing industry and in companies with strong research activity. The engineering industry as a whole is investing at about the same level as during the previous peak year of 1989.

For the domestic sectors, a continued high rate of unemployment, a high real interest rate and the need for further cuts in public spending will keep private consumption low both in 1995 and 1996. Public consumption must be held back in order to reduce the budget deficit. All in all, GDP is forecast to grow by 2.9 per cent in 1995 and by 1.1 per cent in 1996.

Looking further ahead into 1997 and 1998, the rapid growth in business investments and the

Handelsbanken Markets

Nordic Specialists
in the
Global Markets

Svenska Handelsbanken

resulting increase in industrial capacity form a basis for continued industrial expansion and employment creation. Given its good international competitiveness, Swedish industry is well poised to take advantage of a new upswing in the international economy. Furthermore, by the end of 1996, unemployment will have decreased somewhat. This will strengthen private consumption, thus improving the weak domestic market. The prospects of a new growth phase are bright, especially for manufacturing industry.

There are two major risks to this optimistic forecast. The first one is the weak public finances. The budget deficit will be reduced during the coming years as the recovery continues and as the measures taken by the government gradually come into effect. However, despite improvements the government budget deficit will still be some 4 per cent of GDP in 1997, which makes the Swedish economy vulnerable to shocks. Further cuts in public spending should therefore be implemented. This would reduce interest rate differentials *vis-à-vis* Germany and thereby strengthen the recovery.

The other risk is increasing inflationary pressures. A short-term increase in the inflation rate to above the Central Banks target of 3 per cent during 1996 is probably inescapable following higher taxes and the rising PPI during 1994–95. What is of vital importance is to make sure that this is not transformed into a wage-inflationary spiral. However, given the cost-cutting measures, the rationalizations being implemented and the rapid productivity growth, there is a fairly good chance that inflation in Sweden will decline to an average European level in 1996. Another argument in favour of relatively low inflation is continued high unemployment. A stronger krona, following a reduction of budget deficits, would also reduce inflationary pressures.

Business confidence

Improved competitiveness, increased production and growing profits are reflected in a sharp increase in business confidence. The latest survey shows continued optimism. Almost one firm in two expects to increase production even further in the second half of 1995. The confidence indicator for the manufacturing industry is a historical peak.

Price expectations are still fairly restrained, with one firm in four expecting higher prices. However, this share increased somewhat during 1994, which is well in line with our forecast of somewhat increasing inflation during the course of 1996. Following the optimistic production forecast, some 20 per cent of companies expect to increase employment. Due to the lasting effects of productivity-raising rationalizations during the 1990–92 crisis, employment growth will remain lower than in the pre-crisis period.

Improving Europe's competitiveness

Sweden, as well as most European countries, has lagged behind US and Japan in terms of economic growth and market flexibility during the last decade. In order to improve long-term European competitiveness and increase the growth potential of Europe, major structural changes are needed.

First of all, the role of the state must be reduced. Short term, this implies cutting budget deficits by reducing public spending, thereby allowing for lower interest rates and more stable financial markets. In the long term, the high tax burden must be reduced, the social security system reformed and state monopolies exposed to private competition.

Secondly, labour market flexibility must increase. What is needed is, *inter alia*, a more decentralized wage-bargaining process, higher wage differentials and a widening of the gap between social benefits and net wage earnings. Furthermore, greater flexibility in terms of working time, work contracts, etc is also needed.

Thirdly, the quality of Sweden's and Europe's human capital must be improved. In order to compete successfully – and keep its position as a rich country – Sweden must rely on high-tech, high value-added products and processes, and compete with knowledge, not with low wages. An improved educational system is essential in order to create long-term competitiveness. This is also a prerequisite for a successful technology and innovation process. Reforms in the wage and tax system are also needed to increase incentives for education and retraining.

Priorities for the EU's Inter-governmental Conference

Swedish industry has stated three main priorities for the 1996 IGC. First of all, to improve the functioning of the internal market. Implementation and surveillance procedures must be strengthened. Secondly, to make the decision process within the EU more efficient and transparent. Thirdly, to open the EU to future new members from Eastern Europe.

Switzerland

Swiss Federation of Commerce and Industry

Development and potential of the Swiss market

Currently it is not easy to assess the state of health of the Swiss economy. There are some contradictory tendencies. On the one hand, Switzerland ranks among the most advanced economies of the world according to the world competitiveness report. Its per capita income is one of the highest and the Swiss franc one of the strongest currencies in the world. Regarding research and development Switzerland spends 2.8 per cent of GDP and ranks amongst the top nations. The same is true for the important current account surpluses. Finally, there is no country of comparable size with such an important number of world-class transnational companies.

On the other hand, public expenditure and public debt show a clearly increasing trend. Including social security, public expenditure is currently at some 45 per cent of GDP. As in other mature economies, demography reflects an ever-increasing number of elderly people with an important impact on social policy. In many sectors of industry, there remain overcapacities which have led since 1991 to a reduction of some 200,000 jobs. The industrial base is to a certain point eroding, a fact which obviously will also affect the service sector.

Thus, the overall picture of the Swiss economy shows both signs of strength and signs of weaknesses.

Economic indicators

According to recent surveys by the Swiss Federation of Commerce and Industry, the Swiss economy currently runs at a real growth rate of 1 to 2 per cent. The ongoing recovery seems to be stable, though without showing signs of acceleration. Industry's order intake and order books are moderately increasing. The main growth factor seems to be exports of goods and services. With the exception of investments, domestic demand is developing slowly. As is normal under such circumstances, the labour market takes more time to respond. Still, the number of unemployed people is decreasing and there are overall signs of a better future for job-seekers. Prices seem to be well under control. Interest rates are relatively low.

Levels of business confidence

The strong Swiss franc weighs heavily on a number of Swiss industrial sectors, mainly on those depending on exports. One of the consequences has been that a number of Swiss exporters have reduced their costs by importing more of the parts used in their final products from low cost countries. There is a constraint on doing even more to improve productivity in Switzerland. This means that investments have to be planned and executed rapidly. Even though the Swiss currency creates a number of problems, foreign demand seems to be all in all favourable for Swiss exporters. Swiss business depends to a high degree on the development of the advanced industrial economies. The current improvements in some of these large markets leave some space for optimism. This development is further underlined by the recent improvements in worldwide market access from finalizing the Uruguay Round and from the creation of the World Trade Organization.

Improving Europe's competitiveness

Switzerland's geographical situation in the middle of Europe implies that its economy depends very much on the overall development of European business. Therefore, Switzerland has a vital interest in a competitive European environment.

There are three main challenges to be taken into account in maintaining and improving European competitiveness:

- Europe should keep its doors wide open to outside competitors from North America, Asia, Eastern Europe and other parts of the world. It is this kind of global competition which forces European industry to keep their products at world class level. Nothing is more dangerous than closed markets, where industry can relax and neglect the outside development.
- Competition and access to markets within Europe have to be further improved. The internal market is already well advanced, but much has still to be done. This includes the full implementation across borders of the 'four freedoms' for goods, services, capital and persons. It is important that the factor markets can freely develop throughout Europe.
- Market economy rules have to be the base of the European economy. These rules only guarantee an efficient allocation of factors. They leave room for the individual economic actors. Government red tape has to be restricted to the absolute minimum (eg safety standards).

If all these three principles were to be thoroughly respected, the European economy would have a bright future.

United Kingdom 89

The Confederation of British Industry

Development and potential of the UK market

The continued constraint of domestic costs in the wake of sterling's devaluation has given the UK considerable advantages as a location from which to export. The domestic market is also expected to grow over 1995–6 as businesses spend significant amounts on the installation of new capacity, buildings and IT equipment. But consumer goods industries, especially those heavily dependent on activity in the housing market, will face weak demand conditions in the short term, unless the government makes generous tax cuts in the November 1995 Budget.

However, if the temptation to relax public borrowing can be resisted, then with a new framework for interest rate policy already in place, the prospect for a period of *sustained* growth will be encouraging – ultimately to the benefit of all sectors of the economy. The 1970s and 1980s, in contrast, were marked by periodic bouts of inflation-inducing consumer spending 'booms', followed by painful periods of recession.

Compared with other European economies, the UK has a flexible labour market, following 15 years of deregulation, declining trade union influence and decentralization of wage bargaining. Industrial relations have improved considerably since the 1970s, with the number of days lost through strikes now very modest. The UK is not bound by the European Social Chapter, although that would change if the present government were replaced in the next general election, due by mid-1997.

Inward investment has been significant during the last decade, and has had a knock-on effect on productivity as the more efficient practices of some foreign-owned manufacturers have been adopted by domestic producers. Both corporate and overall taxes are low by European standards. The country continues, however, to compare poorly in terms of educational achievement and skill levels, according to the OECD competitiveness rankings. And businesses remain concerned about inadequate road and rail systems. The government is aiming to place greater reliance on private finance in the provision of transport infrastructure, but it is not yet clear how much or how quickly this will improve the situation.

Main economic trends and indicators

Although the UK economy continues to grow strongly, there are some signs of weakness. Exports and private investment continue to grow strongly, while manufacturing output growth has started to abate. Those parts of the economy reliant on demand from overseas markets continue to thrive, while those nearer the consumer and the domestic market continue to falter. Consumer demand continues to be flat, with a depressed housing market and job insecurity, adding to the absence of the 'feel good factor' for consumers. If this recent trend continues,

Batley's *variety*

Batley's variety set to woo potential investors

Batley was once known throughout the country for its Variety Club, a top venue which was host to some of the largest stars in show business. Over the years the club has changed but now the town's City Challenge programme, is out to show that the town of Batley has lost none of its appeal and that it still has a variety of opportunities on offer.

Today, the town's big names are Fox's Biscuits, Skopos Design, Puma, Layezee Beds and Shackletons Furniture, just some of the many businesses who have recognised what Batley can offer.

Batley is well placed geographically for easy access to the main motorway networks, as well as having rail links and two regional airports within a short drive. The surrounding towns of Huddersfield, Dewsbury and Wakefield and the cities of Leeds, York and Sheffield all add to the dynamic appeal of the town.

Furthermore with the Yorkshire Dales and Bronte country on the doorstep, Batley makes an ideal place to live and work.

The town enjoys a healthy mix of manufacturing and services industry. Building on its former textile heritage, Batley's numerous mills are today the home to some of the new generation businesses including multimedia broadcasting, hi-tech electronics and computing. A new purpose built Technology Centre is tribute to the amount of interest the town is generating in these fields.

As one of the best funded places in Yorkshire, Batley is able to provide a range of grants, loans and other incentives to companies looking to relocate and create employment within the town. Wage subsidy schemes and comprehensive training packages make it easier for employers to recruit locally, whilst gaining well-qualified and experienced members of staff.

Home to Batley RLFC, a brand new tennis centre and numerous sports centres, Batley has a good reputation for its sporting achievements and facilities. Coupled with the town's equal commitment to the arts and entertainment, Batley boasts a thriving professional and amateur repertoire of theatre, drama and performance.

Museums, art galleries, public art, residents workshops, street theatre, festivals and meals are just a few examples of the variety of cultural activity that takes place within the town.

Batley Action, Chief Executive, Dr Tom Flanagan said: "Batley is a whole new show. We are spending £37.5 million of City Challenge money and something like £120 million of other monies over a five year period on a range of projects to regenerate the town. This means new roads, more housing, new business opportunities as well as a number of social, cultural and educational projects catering for the health and welfare of residents.

We are two years into programme and already major achievements have been realised. It is now time to let the rest of the country know what is happening.

We have launched a town guide and produced a video for businesses, we are starting a major trade press advertising campaign to spread the word about the variety of opportunities available in Batley."

Batley's City Challenge has a dedicated Business Support Team in place to handle enquiries about relocation as well as answering other business and training related queries. Anyone requiring further information should call on (01924) 422410.

then it may not be far off from the peak of UK base rates (which are currently at 6.75 per cent).

On a more positive note, inflationary pressures have, as yet, been muted. Although increases in manufacturers' imported raw material prices seen towards the end of last year have now begun to feed through to higher producer prices, inflationary pressure from this source has begun to abate. This, along with strong competitive pressure, bodes well for the future trend in retail price inflation.

Despite further significant economic growth so far this year, we still anticipate a slowdown over 1996–97. Growth in GDP is expected to average approximately 3.0 per cent over this period. Underlying retail price inflation – excluding mortgage interest payments – is anticipated to rise above the mid-point of the government's 1–4 per cent target range for much of 1995 and to a lesser extent in 1996. Inflation should fall from its peak of 3.1 per cent in the final quarter of 1995 to end 1996 at 2.8 per cent. With this in view, UK base rates are expected to peak and stabilize at 7.75 per cent by the final quarter of 1995.

Levels of business confidence among CBI members

Confederation of British Industry (CBI) survey evidence and official data in the first half of 1995 suggest that the growth of the UK economy has slowed. The strength of the export sector is offsetting the weakness in the domestic economy in 1995. The manufacturing sector experienced a buoyant period of growth in demand – certainly since the turn of the year – as indicated by January's and April's CBI Industrial Trends Survey. This has mainly been due to growing demand in key export markets, which has helped companies to maintain strong output growth based on healthy order books. Evidence of this growth can be seen by business optimism which has increased for 10 consecutive CBI surveys. Sterling's competitiveness has strengthened the position of UK manufacturing firms in overseas markets. This is reflected by optimism about export prospects for the year ahead, which remains the strongest reported since July 1973.

The slowdown in the growth of consumer spending in recent months has been attributed to many factors. The uneven pattern in retail sales has been blamed on poor weather conditions and partly on the tax measures announced in recent Budgets. However, perhaps more importantly, retailers have blamed poor sales growth on the lack of a 'feel good factor' which has especially hit sales of big ticket items, which may be owing to the lack of a revival in housing market activity. In 1996, modest tax reductions are likely to be implemented. These may favour the consumer, particularly if consumer demand shows signs of weakening during the course of 1995. Personal tax cuts would either counterbalance higher interest rates due to sterling's weakness or be funded by public spending cuts.

Improving Europe's competitiveness

The CBI supports the conclusions of UNICE's Competitiveness Report, published in 1994. That is, there is no single factor that affects European competitiveness and there are therefore a number of suitable policy changes at both European Union and member state levels which would improve Europe's competitiveness.

Important policy areas include creating a more stable and predictable macroeconomic environment, including a lower level of public expenditure and hence of taxation, reducing labour costs and in particular non-wage costs, increasing the flexibility of the labour market and upgrading employees' skills. Income support measures could be used to compensate for lower earnings in employment and lower benefits.

Continuous technological innovation, entrepreneurialism, particularly in SMEs, an adaptable workforce and strong competition between firms should be encouraged. An open trading system and a cost-effective infrastructure should also be developed. Policies should also focus on developing new forms of work organization – such as closer partnerships throughout the value chain between firms – and improved levels of management skills.

Implementing and building such policies will help improve European competitiveness, increasing growth rates across the Union, enhancing the standard of living and creating employment opportunities.

Priorities for the EU's Intergovernmental Conference

At the 1996 EU inter-governmental conference, the foundations for a cohesive structure on which Europe can work together are to be discussed. The debate must focus on certain key matters if the conference is to provide a clear way forward for Europe.

As various barriers to competition and trade still exist, effort must be made to overcome these obstacles so as to allow the Single Market to function properly. This will allow access to all markets for all private sector firms in the member states.

Enhanced employment opportunities have to be addressed. Encouraging member states to find creative approaches to the great social burden of unemployment will improve job opportunities and encourage the will to work. But the focus of the discussion should centre upon the flexibility of the EU's jobs market and allow local problems to be a matter for member states so as not to impair basic standards of social justice.

Despite many members having little chance to meet the convergence criteria, economic and monetary union should not be rejected. Businesses throughout Europe recognize the macroeconomic stability and long-term benefits that such a union would provide. The political and economic implications must be realistically assessed. Various other matters also require particular attention, such as further reform to the Common Agricultural Policy and a sensible look at environmental issues – both of which should be assessed while bearing in mind their implications for competitiveness and efficiency within the EU.

II Cost of Living in Western Europe

European Consortium of Management Consultants

BELGIUM   Belgian francs (BF)

Accommodation
Houses

Purchase price for 3/4 bedrooms, good area	12,095,000

Business

Average annual rent per square metre:

Office, including tax	8,035
Industrial, excluding tax	2,570

Clothes and personal care
Men – medium prices

Two-piece off-the-peg lounge suit (good quality)	12,156
1 pair all-leather town shoes (good quality)	3,242
1 polyester/cotton shirt	1,013
Haircut	608

Women – medium prices

Two-piece off-the-peg suit (good quality)	20,260
1 pair town shoes, leather uppers (good quality)	4,052
1 pair tights	1,013
Haircut and blow-dry	2,533

Consumer goods

All models are well-known makes, in the medium price bracket. All prices include tax:

Fridge-freezer	25,325
Electric cooker	22,286
Microwave oven	12,663
Washing machine	26,338
Vacuum cleaner	7,091
Portable television, 34 cm screen, colour	10,028
Videocassette recorder	12,156
Hairdryer	1,013

Entertainment

1 bottle Scotch whisky (well-known brand)	506
1 litre cheap wine	101
1 glass (25 cl) of lager	51
1 packet of 20 cigarettes	86
1 cinema ticket	223
1 theatre ticket	505–810
Average cost of an evening meal for four people in a fashionable restaurant, comprising one apéritif each, a three-course meal, two bottles of good wine and coffee, including tax and service charge	7,600
Average cost of a business lunch for four people comprising one apéritif each, a three-course meal, two bottles of medium-priced wine and coffee, including tax and service charge	6,078

Food

1 kg rump steak	363
1 kg chicken	127
6 fresh eggs	36
1 kg flour	38
1 kg sugar	46
1 kg butter	182
1 litre milk	30
1 litre olive oil	172
1 kg tomatoes	59

BELGIUM   Belgian francs (BF)

1 kg apples	51
2 kg potatoes	38
100 g jar instant coffee	71
0.5 kg tea	132

Transport

Renault Clio RN (1.2 petrol), plus delivery	410,872
Ford Mondeo GL (2.0 petrol), plus delivery	744,555
BMW 520i (petrol), plus delivery	1,207,500
1 litre of 4 star petrol	29
1 litre of unleaded petrol	27
Cost of car hire in city centre (Ford Escort 1.4LX for 1 week, unlimited mileage, including insurance and sales tax)	10,130
Minimum bus fare in city	35
Cost of two-zone travelcard for one week	223
Minimum taxi fare in capital city	122

DENMARK   Danish krone (DKr)

Accommodation
Houses

Purchase price for 3/4 bedrooms, good area	1,428000–2,550,000

Business

Average annual rent per square metre:

Office, including tax	612–1,224
Industrial, excluding tax	204–408

Clothes and personal care
Men – medium prices

Two-piece off-the-peg lounge suit (good quality)	2,160–3,060
1 pair all-leather town shoes (good quality)	714–1,428
1 polyester/cotton shirt	153–408
Haircut	102–204

Women – medium prices

Two-piece off-the-peg suit (good quality)	1,224–2,244
1 pair town shoes, leather uppers (good quality)	714–1,224
1 pair tights	31
Haircut and blow-dry	153–306

Consumer goods

All models are well-known makes, in the medium price bracket. All prices include tax:

Fridge-freezer	4,080–6,120
Electric cooker	4,080–6,120
Microwave oven	2,040–4,080
Washing machine	4,080–6,120
Vacuum cleaner	816–1,632
Television, 51 cm screen, colour	3,060–6,630
Portable television, 34 cm screen, colour	2,040–3,060
Videocassette recorder	2,040–5,100
Hairdryer	102–153

Entertainment

1 bottle Scotch whisky (well-known brand)	255
1 litre cheap wine	25–36
1 glass (25 cl) of lager	25
1 packet of 20 cigarettes	31
1 cinema ticket	41
1 theatre ticket	71
Average cost of an evening meal for four people in a fashionable restaurant, comprising one apéritif each, a three-course meal, two bottles of good wine and coffee, including tax and service charge	1,632–2,550
Average cost of a business lunch for four people comprising one apéritif each, a three-course meal, two bottles of medium-priced wine and coffee, including tax and service charge	1,020–2,040

Food

1 kg rump steak	112
1 kg chicken	36
6 fresh eggs	9
1 kg flour	8
1 kg sugar	22.5
1 kg butter	43
1 litre milk	7
1 litre olive oil	49
1 kg tomatoes	20.5
1 kg apples	16
2 kg potatoes	10
100 g jar instant coffee	49
0.5 kg tea	24

Transport

Renault Clio RN (1.2 petrol), plus delivery	142,800
Ford Mondeo GL (2.0 petrol), plus delivery	204,000
BMW 520i (petrol), plus delivery	459,000
1 litre of 4 star petrol	6
1 litre of unleaded petrol	5.5
Cost of car hire in city centre (Ford Escort 1.4LX for 1 week, unlimited mileage, including insurance and sales tax)	3,060–3,570
Minimum bus fare in city	6
Cost of two-zone travelcard for one week	123
Minimum taxi fare in capital city	20

FRANCE   French franc (FFr)

Accommodation
Houses

Purchase price for 3/4 bedrooms, good area	3,000,000
Apartment (100 m²)	2,000,000

Business
Average annual rent per square metre:

Office, including tax	2,500
Telephone, cost of national call per minute (peak period)	2.19
Telephone, cost of international call per minute (peak period) (Paris to USA)	5.95
First class domestic letter	2.80

Clothes and personal care
Men – medium prices

Two-piece off-the-peg lounge suit (good quality)	2,000–4,000
1 pair all-leather town shoes (good quality)	800
1 polyester/cotton shirt	250
Haircut	120

Women – medium prices

Two-piece off-the-peg suit (good quality)	1,500–3,500
1 pair town shoes, leather uppers (good quality)	500
1 pair tights	20–150
Haircut and blow-dry	200

Consumer goods
All models are well-known makes, in the medium price bracket. All prices include tax:

Fridge-freezer	3,400
Electric cooker	3,500
Microwave oven	1,500
Washing machine	4,000
Vacuum cleaner	1,500
Television, 51 cm screen, colour	2,300
Portable television, 34 cm screen, colour	1,700
Videocassette recorder	3,000
Hairdryer	120

Entertainment

1 bottle Scotch whisky (well-known brand)	130
1 litre cheap wine	14
1 glass (25 cl) of lager	10
1 packet of 20 cigarettes	17
1 cinema ticket	45
1 theatre ticket	150
1 compact disc	120
1 leading broadsheet newspaper	7

Average cost of an evening meal for four people in a fashionable restaurant, comprising one apéritif each, a three-course meal, two bottles of good wine and coffee, including tax and service charge — 1,500

Average cost of a business lunch for four people comprising one apéritif each, a three-course meal, two bottles of medium-priced wine and coffee, including tax and service charge — 800

Food

1 kg rump steak	130
1 kg chicken	20
6 fresh eggs	7
1 kg flour	6
1 kg sugar	8
1 kg butter	30
1 litre milk	4
1 litre olive oil	30
1 kg tomatoes	7
1 kg apples	11
2 kg potatoes	8
100 g jar instant coffee	17
0.5 kg tea	30

Transport

Renault Clio RN (1.2 petrol), plus delivery	68,000
Ford Mondeo GL (2.0 petrol), plus delivery	105,000
BMW 520i (petrol), plus delivery	152,000
1 litre of 4 star petrol	6.08
1 litre of unleaded petrol	5.85
Cost of car hire in city centre (Ford Escort 1.4LX for 1 week, unlimited mileage, including insurance and sales tax)	2,500
Minimum underground fare in city	7.5
Minimum bus fare in city	7.5
Cost of two-zone travelcard for one week	67
Minimum taxi fare in capital city	25

Utilities
Electricity (domestic)

Standing charge	150
Unit charge	0.70

Gas (domestic)

Commodity charge	0.58

GERMANY   Deutschmark (DM)

Accommodation
Houses

Purchase price for 3/4 bedrooms, good area	1,000,000

GERMANY   Deutschmark (DM)

Business

Average annual rent per square metre:

Office, including tax	360
Industrial, excluding tax	144
Telephone, cost of local call per minute (peak period)	0.23
Telephone, cost of long-distance call per minute (peak period)	0.69
First class domestic letter	1

Clothes and personal care

Men – medium prices

Two-piece off-the-peg lounge suit (good quality)	600
1 pair all-leather town shoes (good quality)	250
1 polyester/cotton shirt	80
Haircut	40

Women – medium prices

Two-piece off-the-peg suit (good quality)	500
1 pair town shoes, leather uppers (good quality)	270
1 pair tights	15
Haircut and blow-dry	100

Consumer goods

All models are well-known makes, in the medium price bracket. All prices include tax:

Fridge-freezer	1,400
Electric cooker	900
Microwave oven	500
Washing machine	1,400
Vacuum cleaner	400
Television, 51 cm screen, colour	900
Portable television, 34 cm screen, colour	500
Videocassette recorder	1,000
Hairdryer	75

Entertainment

1 bottle Scotch whisky (well-known brand)	38
1 litre cheap wine	6
1 glass (25 cl) of lager	4.80
1 packet of 20 cigarettes	4.85
1 cinema ticket	12
1 theatre ticket	60
1 compact disc	32
1 leading broadsheet newspaper	3
Average cost of an evening meal for four people in a fashionable restaurant, comprising one apéritif each, a three-course meal, two bottles of good wine and coffee, including tax and service charge	500
Average cost of a business lunch for four people comprising one apéritif each, a three-course meal, two bottles of medium-priced wine and coffee, including tax and service charge	600

Food

1 kg rump steak	35
1 kg chicken	7
6 fresh eggs	1.80
1 kg flour	2
1 kg sugar	1.80
1 kg butter	9.20
1 litre milk	1.10
1 litre olive oil	12
1 kg tomatoes	4
1 kg apples	3.50
2 kg potatoes	5
100 g jar instant coffee	6
0.5 kg tea	16

Transport

Renault Clio RN (1.2 petrol), plus delivery	18,190
Ford Mondeo GL (2.0 petrol), plus delivery	39,705
BMW 520i (petrol), plus delivery	52,800
1 litre of 4 star petrol	1.70
1 litre of unleaded petrol	1.57
Cost of car hire in city centre (Ford Escort 1.4LX for 1 week, unlimited mileage, including insurance and sales tax)	500
Minimum underground fare in city	2.90
Minimum bus fare in city	2.90
Cost of two-zone travelcard for one week	36.40
Minimum taxi fare in capital city	3.90

Utilities

Electricity (domestic)

Unit charge (Kw/hr)	0.30

Gas (domestic)

Unit charge (m^3)	0.92

GREECE   Drachma (Dr)

Accommodation

Houses

Purchase price for 3/4 bedrooms, good area	65,000,000

Business

Average annual rent per square metre:

Office, including tax	30,000
Industrial, excluding tax	10,000

GREECE   Drachma (Dr)

Clothes and personal care

Men – medium prices

Two-piece off-the-peg lounge suit (good quality)	87,000
1 pair all-leather town shoes (good quality)	20,000
1 polyester/cotton shirt	15,000
Haircut	3,800

Women – medium prices

Two-piece off-the-peg suit (good quality)	87,000
1 pair town shoes, leather uppers (good quality)	30,000
1 pair tights	1,000
Haircut and blow-dry	5,400

Consumer goods

All models are well-known makes, in the medium price bracket. All prices include tax:

Fridge-freezer	220,000
Electric cooker	130,000
Microwave oven	87,000
Washing machine	140,000
Vacuum cleaner	43,000
Television, 51 cm screen, colour	130,000
Portable television, 34 cm screen, colour	87,000
Videocassette recorder	110,000
Hairdryer	6,500

Entertainment

1 bottle Scotch whisky (well-known brand)	3,250
1 litre cheap wine	800
1 glass (25 cl) of lager	1,000
1 packet of 20 cigarettes	410
1 cinema ticket	1,300
1 theatre ticket	2,200
Average cost of an evening meal for four people in a fashionable restaurant, comprising one apéritif each, a three-course meal, two bottles of good wine and coffee, including tax and service charge	65,000
Average cost of a business lunch for four people comprising one apéritif each, a three-course meal, two bottles of medium-priced wine and coffee, including tax and service charge	43,000

Food

1 kg rump steak	2,400
1 kg chicken	750
6 fresh eggs	180
1 kg flour	240
1 kg sugar	270
1 kg butter	1,300
1 litre milk	280
1 litre olive oil	1,000
1 kg tomatoes	270
1 kg apples	325
2 kg potatoes	390
100 g jar instant coffee	660
0.5 kg tea	540

Transport

Renault Clio RN (1.2 petrol), plus delivery	3,570,000
Ford Mondeo GL (2.0 petrol), plus delivery	8,260,000
BMW 520i (petrol), plus delivery	13,300,000
1 litre of 4 star petrol	220
1 litre of unleaded petrol	210
Cost of car hire in city centre (Ford Escort 1.4LX for 1 week, unlimited mileage, including insurance and sales tax)	54,200
Minimum bus fare in city	80
Cost of two-zone travelcard for one week	980
Minimum taxi fare in capital city	330

IRELAND   Irish punt (IR£)

Accommodation

Houses

Purchase price for 3/4 bedrooms, good area	95,000

Business

Average annual rent per square metre:

Office, including tax	112
Industrial, excluding tax	39
Telephone, cost of local call per minute (peak period)	0.05
Telephone, cost of long-distance call per minute (peak period)	0.44
First class domestic letter	0.32

Clothes and personal care

Men – medium prices

Two-piece off-the-peg lounge suit (good quality)	259
1 pair all-leather town shoes (good quality)	40
1 polyester/cotton shirt	29
Haircut	10

Women – medium prices

Two-piece off-the-peg suit (good quality)	150
1 pair town shoes, leather uppers (good quality)	40
1 pair tights	1.50
Haircut and blow-dry	12.50

IRELAND   Irish punt (IR£)

Consumer goods
All models are well-known makes, in the medium price bracket. All prices include tax:

Fridge-freezer	479
Electric cooker	499
Microwave oven	139
Washing machine	400
Vacuum cleaner	140
Television, 51 cm screen, colour	399
Portable television, 34 cm screen, colour	199
Videocassette recorder	550
Hairdryer	20

Entertainment

1 bottle Scotch whisky (well-known brand)	11.99
1 litre cheap wine	3.99
1 glass (25 cl) of lager	1.40
1 packet of 20 cigarettes	2.80
1 cinema ticket	4.20
1 theatre ticket	8.00
1 compact disc	15
1 leading broadsheet newspaper	0.85
Average cost of an evening meal for four people in a fashionable restaurant, comprising one apéritif each, a three-course meal, two bottles of good wine and coffee, including tax and service charge	220
Average cost of a business lunch for four people comprising one apéritif each, a three-course meal, two bottles of medium-priced wine and coffee, including tax and service charge	80

Food

1 kg rump steak	7.79
1 kg chicken	2
6 fresh eggs	1.09
1 kg flour	0.85
1 kg sugar	0.88
1 kg butter	1.47
1 litre milk	0.60
1 litre olive oil	2.69
1 kg tomatoes	1.30
1 kg apples	1.23
2 kg potatoes	1.49
100 g jar instant coffee	2.40
0.5 kg tea	1.30

Transport

Renault Clio RN (1.2 petrol), plus delivery	10,070
Ford Mondeo GL (2.0 petrol), plus delivery	20,000
BMW 520i (petrol), plus delivery	30,000
1 litre of 4 star petrol	0.60
1 litre of unleaded petrol	0.58
Cost of car hire in city centre (Ford Escort 1.4LX for 1 week, unlimited mileage, including insurance and sales tax)	200
Minimum bus fare in city	0.55
Minimum taxi fare in capital city	2.50

Utilities
Electricity (domestic)

Standing charge	7.60
Unit charge	0.10

Gas (domestic)

Standing charge (per two-month period)	4.08

ITALY   Lire (L) ('000)

Accommodation
Houses

Purchase price for 3/4 bedrooms, good area (centre of city)	600,000–700,000

Business
Average annual rent per square metre:

Office, including tax	276–324
Industrial, excluding tax	240–276
Telephone, cost of local call per minute (peak period)	0.045
Telephone, cost of long-distance call per minute (peak period)	1–1.2
First class domestic letter	1

Clothes and personal care
Men – medium prices

Two-piece off-the-peg lounge suit (good quality)	600–700
1 pair all-leather town shoes (good quality)	250–320
1 polyester/cotton shirt	40–110
Haircut	30–50

Women – medium prices

Two-piece off-the-peg suit (good quality)	550–720
1 pair town shoes, leather uppers (good quality)	300–350
1 pair tights	3
Haircut and blow-dry	50–90

Consumer goods
All models are well-known makes, in the medium price bracket. All prices include tax:

Fridge-freezer	800–950
Electric cooker	700–800
Microwave oven	550–730

ITALY   Lire (L) ('000)

Washing machine	700–850
Vacuum cleaner	400–550
Television, 51 cm screen, colour	1,000–1,300
Portable television, 34 cm screen, colour	550–800
Videocassette recorder	750–1,100
Hairdryer	50–80

Entertainment

1 bottle Scotch whisky (well-known brand)	32
1 litre cheap wine	2
1 glass (25 cl) of lager	1.8
1 packet of 20 cigarettes	3
1 cinema ticket	10
1 theatre ticket	25–150
1 compact disc	20–35
1 leading broadsheet newspaper	1.5
Average cost of an evening meal for four people in a fashionable restaurant, comprising one apéritif each, a three-course meal, two bottles of good wine and coffee, including tax and service charge	400–500
Average cost of a business lunch for four people comprising one apéritif each, a three-course meal, two bottles of medium-priced wine and coffee, including tax and service charge	150–270

Food

1 kg rump steak	18
1 kg chicken	6
6 fresh eggs	2
1 kg flour	1.5
1 kg sugar	1
1 kg butter	4
1 litre milk	2
1 litre olive oil	4
1 kg tomatoes	2
1 kg apples	2.8
2 kg potatoes	3
100 g jar instant coffee	4.2
0.5 kg tea	5.5

Transport

Renault Clio RN (1.2 petrol), plus delivery	17,000
Ford Mondeo GL (2.0 petrol), plus delivery	35,000
BMW 520i (petrol), plus delivery	50,000
1 litre of 4 star petrol	1.3
1 litre of unleaded petrol	1.7
Cost of car hire in city centre (Ford Escort 1.4LX for 1 week, unlimited mileage, including insurance and sales tax)	400–470
Minimum underground fare in city	3
Minimum bus fare in city	2
Cost of two-zone travelcard for one week	30
Minimum taxi fare in capital city	6

Utilities

Electricity (domestic)

Standing charge	34
Unit charge	10

Gas (domestic)

Standing charge	6
Commodity charge	2.5

NETHERLANDS   Guilders (Dfl)

Accommodation

Houses

Purchase price for 3/4 bedrooms, good area	450,000

Business

Average annual rent per square metre:

Office, including tax	350
Industrial, excluding tax	125
Telephone, cost of local call per minute (peak period)	0.06
Telephone, cost of long-distance call per minute (peak period)	0.19
First class domestic letter	0.80

Clothes and personal care

Men – medium prices

Two-piece off-the-peg lounge suit (good quality)	700
1 pair all-leather town shoes (good quality)	125
1 polyester/cotton shirt	100
Haircut	30

Women – medium prices

Two-piece off-the-peg suit (good quality)	600
1 pair town shoes, leather uppers (good quality)	150
1 pair tights	4.25
Haircut and blow-dry	50

Consumer goods

All models are well-known makes, in the medium price bracket. All prices include tax:

Fridge-freezer	1,000
Electric cooker	779
Microwave oven	449
Washing machine	1,199
Vacuum cleaner	249
Television, 51 cm screen, colour	798
Portable television, 34 cm screen, colour	399

NETHERLANDS   Guilders (Dfl)

Videocassette recorder	499
Hairdryer	50

Entertainment

1 bottle Scotch whisky (well-known brand)	45
1 litre cheap wine	8.50
1 glass (25 cl) of lager	2.50
1 packet of 20 cigarettes	5
1 cinema ticket	12.50
1 theatre ticket	60
1 compact disc	39
1 leading broadsheet newspaper	2
Average cost of an evening meal for four people in a fashionable restaurant, comprising one apéritif each, a three-course meal, two bottles of good wine and coffee, including tax and service charge	450
Average cost of a business lunch for four people comprising one apéritif each, a three-course meal, two bottles of medium-priced wine and coffee, including tax and service charge	350

Food

1 kg rump steak	30
1 kg chicken	8.50
6 fresh eggs	1.24
1 kg flour	0.99
1 kg sugar	1.89
1 kg butter	5
1 litre milk	1.04
1 litre olive oil	10.69
1 kg tomatoes	1.58
1 kg apples	1.99
2 kg potatoes	1.49
100 g jar instant coffee	6.59
0.5 kg tea	5.70

Transport

Renault Clio RN (1.2 petrol), plus delivery	27,795
Ford Mondeo GL (2.0 petrol), plus delivery	46,865
BMW 520i (petrol), plus delivery	78,725
1 litre of 4 star petrol	2.04
1 litre of unleaded petrol	1.89
Cost of car hire in city centre (Ford Escort 1.4LX for 1 week, unlimited mileage, including insurance and sales tax)	815
Minimum underground fare in city	1.50
Minimum bus fare in city	1.50
Cost of two-zone travelcard for one week	38.75
Minimum taxi fare in capital city	5.60

Utilities

Electricity (domestic)

Unit charge	0.206

Gas (domestic)

Commodity charge	0.517

PORTUGAL   Portuguese Escudos (Esc)

Accommodation

Houses

Purchase price for 3/4 bedrooms, good area (centre of city)	64,000,000

Business

Average annual rent per square metre:	
Office, including tax	80,000
Industrial, excluding tax	200,000
Telephone, cost of local call per minute (peak period)	12.50
Telephone, cost of long-distance call per minute (peak period)	15.00

Clothes and personal care

Men – medium prices

Two-piece off-the-peg lounge suit (good quality)	80,000–150,000
1 pair all-leather town shoes (good quality)	14,000
1 polyester/cotton shirt	7,000
Haircut	500

Women – medium prices

Two-piece off-the-peg suit (good quality)	60,000
1 pair town shoes, leather uppers (good quality)	13,000
1 pair tights	1,500
Haircut and blow-dry	3,500

Consumer goods

All models are well-known makes, in the medium price bracket. All prices include tax:

Fridge-freezer	130,000
Electric cooker	140,000
Gas cooker	90,000
Microwave oven	100,000
Washing machine	120,000
Vacuum cleaner	80,000
Television, 51 cm screen, colour	70,000
Portable television, 34 cm screen, colour	50,000
Videocassette recorder	70,000
Hairdryer	2,000

PORTUGAL   Portuguese Escudos (Esc)

Entertainment

1 bottle Scotch whisky (well-known brand)	3,000
1 litre cheap wine	150
1 glass (25 cl) of lager	1,000
1 packet of 20 cigarettes	350
1 cinema ticket	600
1 theatre ticket	600
1 compact disc	3,500
1 leading broadsheet newspaper	500
Average cost of an evening meal for four people in a fashionable restaurant, comprising one apéritif each, a three-course meal, two bottles of good wine and coffee, including tax and service charge	40,000
Average cost of a business lunch for four people comprising one apéritif each, a three-course meal, two bottles of medium-priced wine and coffee, including tax and service charge	22,000

Food

1 kg rump steak	2,600
1 kg chicken	380
6 fresh eggs	150
1 kg flour	200
1 kg sugar	190
1 kg butter	960
1 litre milk	135
1 litre olive oil	800
1 kg tomatoes	220
1 kg apples	320
2 kg potatoes	85
100 g jar instant coffee	320
0.5 kg tea	2,800

Transport

Renault Clio RN (1.2 petrol), plus delivery	1,992,000
Ford Mondeo GL (2.0 petrol), plus delivery	6,830,000
BMW 520i (petrol), plus delivery	8,680,000
1 litre of 4 star petrol	155
1 litre of unleaded petrol	145
Cost of car hire in city centre (Ford Escort 1.4LX for 1 week, unlimited mileage, including insurance and sales tax)	48,000
Minimum underground fare in city	60
Minimum bus fare in city	150
Cost of two-zone travelcard for one week	2,350
Minimum taxi fare in capital city	250

Utilities

Electricity (domestic)

Standing charge	3,250
Unit charge	19

Gas (domestic)

Standing charge	593
Commodity charge	46

SPAIN   Pesetas (Pta)

Accommodation

Houses

Purchase price for 3/4 bedrooms, good area (new 180 m^2)	80,000,000

Business

Average annual rent per square metre:	
Office, including tax	20,000
Industrial, excluding tax	4,000
Telephone, cost of local call per minute (peak period)	1.90
Telephone, cost of long-distance call per minute (peak period)	140–255
First class domestic letter	30

Clothes and personal care

Men – medium prices

Two-piece off-the-peg lounge suit (good quality)	55,000
1 pair all-leather town shoes (good quality)	19,000
1 polyester/cotton shirt	7,500
Haircut	1,500

Women – medium prices

Two-piece off-the-peg suit (good quality)	70,000
1 pair town shoes, leather uppers (good quality)	17,000
1 pair tights	2,200
Haircut and blow-dry	7,500

Consumer goods

All models are well-known makes, in the medium price bracket. All prices include tax:

Fridge-freezer	130,000
Electric cooker	100,000
Gas cooker	40,000
Microwave oven	30,000
Washing machine	75,000
Vacuum cleaner	25,000
Television, 51 cm screen, colour	95,000
Portable television, 34 cm screen, colour	28,000
Videocassette recorder	40,000
Hairdryer	4,000

SPAIN   Pesetas (Pta)

Entertainment

1 bottle Scotch whisky (well-known brand)	1,500
1 litre cheap wine	250
1 glass (25 cl) of lager	65
1 packet of 20 cigarettes	200
1 cinema ticket	650
1 theatre ticket	2,000
1 compact disc	2,750
1 leading broadsheet newspaper	110
Average cost of an evening meal for four people in a fashionable restaurant, comprising one apéritif each, a three-course meal, two bottles of good wine and coffee, including tax and service charge	26,000
Average cost of a business lunch for four people comprising one apéritif each, a three-course meal, two bottles of medium-priced wine and coffee, including tax and service charge	22,000

Food

1 kg rump steak	1,450
1 kg chicken	425
6 fresh eggs	125
1 kg flour	112
1 kg sugar	157
1 kg butter	1,200
1 litre milk	96
1 litre olive oil	600
1 kg tomatoes	150
1 kg apples	215
2 kg potatoes	220
100 g jar instant coffee	429
0.5 kg tea	600

Transport

Renault Clio RN (1.2 petrol), plus delivery	1,810,000
Ford Mondeo GHIA (2.0 petrol), plus delivery	3,319,000
BMW 520i (petrol), plus delivery	5,068,000
1 litre of 4 star petrol	112
1 litre of unleaded petrol	111
Cost of car hire in city centre (Ford Escort 1.4LX for 1 week, unlimited mileage, including insurance and sales tax)	67,900
Minimum underground fare in city	125
Minimum bus fare in city	125
Cost of two-zone travelcard for one week	660
Minimum taxi fare in capital city	260

Utilities
Electricity (domestic)

Standing charge (per month)	4,230
Unit charge	16

Gas (domestic)

Standing charge (per month)	787
Commodity charge (per m^3)	56.70

SWEDEN   Swedish Krona (SKr)

Accommodation
Houses

Purchase price for 3/4 bedrooms, good area	1,127,000

Business

Average annual rent per square metre:	
Office, including tax	2,000
Industrial, excluding tax	800
Telephone, cost of local call per minute (peak period)	0.15
Telephone, cost of long-distance call per minute (peak period)	1
First class domestic letter	3.70

Clothes and personal care
Men – medium prices

Two-piece off-the-peg lounge suit (good quality)	5,995
1 pair all-leather town shoes (good quality)	1,395
1 polyester/cotton shirt	595
Haircut	170

Women – medium prices

Two-piece off-the-peg suit (good quality)	5,780
1 pair town shoes, leather uppers (good quality)	825
1 pair tights	35
Haircut and blow-dry	320

Consumer goods
All models are well-known makes, in the medium price bracket. All prices include tax:

Fridge-freezer	7,500
Electric cooker	8,000
Gas cooker	8,000
Microwave oven	2,200
Washing machine	6,000
Vacuum cleaner	2,700
Television, 51 cm screen, colour	4,144
Portable television, 34 cm screen, colour	2,462
Videocassette recorder	5,500
Hairdryer	278

Entertainment

1 bottle Scotch whisky (well-known brand)	417
1 litre cheap wine	52
1 glass (25 cl) of lager	33
1 packet of 20 cigarettes	31
1 cinema ticket	70
1 theatre ticket	160–400
1 compact disc	159

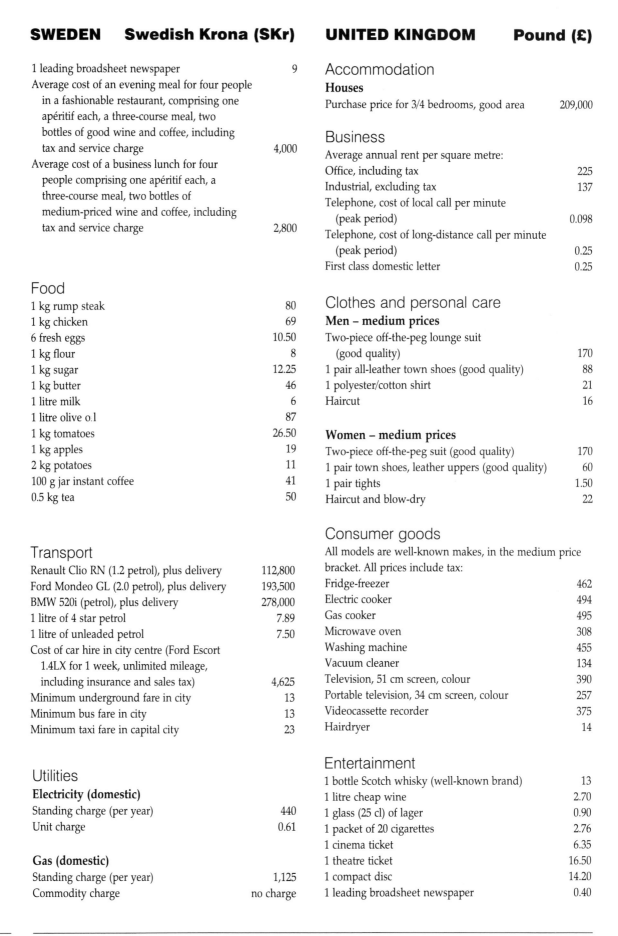

SWEDEN   Swedish Krona (SKr)

1 leading broadsheet newspaper	9
Average cost of an evening meal for four people in a fashionable restaurant, comprising one apéritif each, a three-course meal, two bottles of good wine and coffee, including tax and service charge	4,000
Average cost of a business lunch for four people comprising one apéritif each, a three-course meal, two bottles of medium-priced wine and coffee, including tax and service charge	2,800

Food

1 kg rump steak	80
1 kg chicken	69
6 fresh eggs	10.50
1 kg flour	8
1 kg sugar	12.25
1 kg butter	46
1 litre milk	6
1 litre olive o.l	87
1 kg tomatoes	26.50
1 kg apples	19
2 kg potatoes	11
100 g jar instant coffee	41
0.5 kg tea	50

Transport

Renault Clio RN (1.2 petrol), plus delivery	112,800
Ford Mondeo GL (2.0 petrol), plus delivery	193,500
BMW 520i (petrol), plus delivery	278,000
1 litre of 4 star petrol	7.89
1 litre of unleaded petrol	7.50
Cost of car hire in city centre (Ford Escort 1.4LX for 1 week, unlimited mileage, including insurance and sales tax)	4,625
Minimum underground fare in city	13
Minimum bus fare in city	13
Minimum taxi fare in capital city	23

Utilities

Electricity (domestic)

Standing charge (per year)	440
Unit charge	0.61

Gas (domestic)

Standing charge (per year)	1,125
Commodity charge	no charge

UNITED KINGDOM   Pound (£)

Accommodation

Houses

Purchase price for 3/4 bedrooms, good area	209,000

Business

Average annual rent per square metre:	
Office, including tax	225
Industrial, excluding tax	137
Telephone, cost of local call per minute (peak period)	0.098
Telephone, cost of long-distance call per minute (peak period)	0.25
First class domestic letter	0.25

Clothes and personal care

Men – medium prices

Two-piece off-the-peg lounge suit (good quality)	170
1 pair all-leather town shoes (good quality)	88
1 polyester/cotton shirt	21
Haircut	16

Women – medium prices

Two-piece off-the-peg suit (good quality)	170
1 pair town shoes, leather uppers (good quality)	60
1 pair tights	1.50
Haircut and blow-dry	22

Consumer goods

All models are well-known makes, in the medium price bracket. All prices include tax:

Fridge-freezer	462
Electric cooker	494
Gas cooker	495
Microwave oven	308
Washing machine	455
Vacuum cleaner	134
Television, 51 cm screen, colour	390
Portable television, 34 cm screen, colour	257
Videocassette recorder	375
Hairdryer	14

Entertainment

1 bottle Scotch whisky (well-known brand)	13
1 litre cheap wine	2.70
1 glass (25 cl) of lager	0.90
1 packet of 20 cigarettes	2.76
1 cinema ticket	6.35
1 theatre ticket	16.50
1 compact disc	14.20
1 leading broadsheet newspaper	0.40

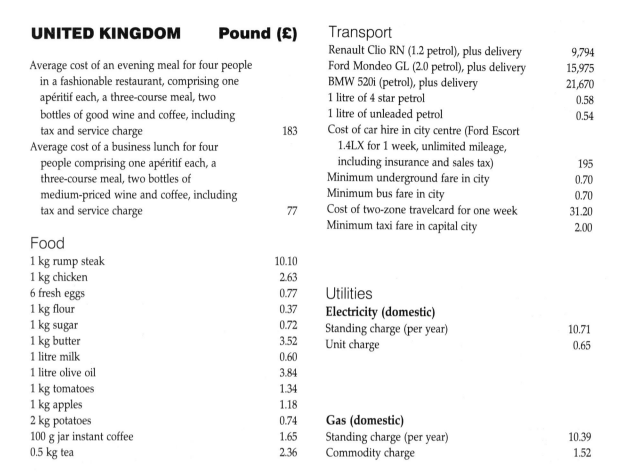

UNITED KINGDOM   Pound (£)

Average cost of an evening meal for four people
   in a fashionable restaurant, comprising one
   apéritif each, a three-course meal, two
   bottles of good wine and coffee, including
   tax and service charge   183
Average cost of a business lunch for four
   people comprising one apéritif each, a
   three-course meal, two bottles of
   medium-priced wine and coffee, including
   tax and service charge   77

Food

1 kg rump steak	10.10
1 kg chicken	2.63
6 fresh eggs	0.77
1 kg flour	0.37
1 kg sugar	0.72
1 kg butter	3.52
1 litre milk	0.60
1 litre olive oil	3.84
1 kg tomatoes	1.34
1 kg apples	1.18
2 kg potatoes	0.74
100 g jar instant coffee	1.65
0.5 kg tea	2.36

Transport

Renault Clio RN (1.2 petrol), plus delivery	9,794
Ford Mondeo GL (2.0 petrol), plus delivery	15,975
BMW 520i (petrol), plus delivery	21,670
1 litre of 4 star petrol	0.58
1 litre of unleaded petrol	0.54
Cost of car hire in city centre (Ford Escort 1.4LX for 1 week, unlimited mileage, including insurance and sales tax)	195
Minimum underground fare in city	0.70
Minimum bus fare in city	0.70
Cost of two-zone travelcard for one week	31.20
Minimum taxi fare in capital city	2.00

Utilities

Electricity (domestic)

Standing charge (per year)	10.71
Unit charge	0.65

Gas (domestic)

Standing charge (per year)	10.39
Commodity charge	1.52

III Contact List

Achilles Information
52 South Avenue
Abingdon
Oxfordshire OX1 1QR
United Kingdom
Tel: +44 (1235) 820813
Fax: +44 (1235) 821093
Contact: Colin Maund

The Adam Smith Institute
22 Albert Embankment
London SE1 7TE
United Kingdom
Tel: +44 (171) 735 6660
Fax: +44 (171) 793 0090
Contact: Peter Young

The Advertising Association
Abford House
15 Wilton Road
London W1V 1NJ
United Kingdom
Tel: +44 (171) 828 2771
Fax: +44 (171) 931 0376
Contact: Andrew Brown

Arthur Andersen
1 Surrey Street
London WC2R 2PS
United Kingdom
Tel: +44 (171) 438 3000
Fax: +44 (171) 831 1133
Contact: Robert Edwards, Helen Jones

Association of Portuguese Industry
Praca Das Industrias
1399 Lisboa Codex
Portugal
Tel: +351 (1) 362 0100
Fax: +351 (1) 363 9047
Contact: Rui Madaleno

Association of the Slovak Republic
Foreign Trade Entrepreneurs & Employers
Drienova 24, 82603 Bratislava
Slovak Republic
Tel: +42 (427) 233 356
Fax: +42 (427) 235 149
Contact: Parol Konstiak

Bank Austria
Bank of Austria House
32–36 City Road
London EC1Y 2BD
United Kingdom
Tel: +44 (171) 382 1000
Fax: +44 (171) 588 4560
Contact: F H Brittain

BDO Hospitality Consultants
8 Baker Street
London W1M 1DA
United Kingdom
Tel: +44 (171) 486 5191
Fax: +44 (171) 487 3686
Contact: Jonathan Langston

British Gas
100 Thames Valley Park Drive
Reading
Berkshire RG6 1PT
United Kingdom
Tel: +44 (1734) 292243
Fax: +44 (1734) 293066

British Telecom
BT Centre Room A353
81 Newgate Street
London EC1A 7AJ
United Kingdom
Tel: +44 (171) 356 5131
Fax: +44 (171) 356 6070
Contact: Mike Grabner

BSI Standards Information Centre
389 Chiswick High Road
London W4 4AL
United Kingdom
Tel: +44 (181) 885 7111
Fax: +44 (181) 995 7048
Contact: Anita Goodzeit

Bulgarian Industrial Association
16–20 Alabin Street
1000 Sofia
Bulgaria
Tel: +359 (2) 879 611
Fax: +359 (2) 872 604
Contact: Georgi Shivarov

Business Management & Finance SA
ul. Chnielna 132/134 00-805
Warsaw
Poland
Tel: +2 (656) 2222
Fax: +2 (656) 2223
Contact: Pawel Laszczyk

Catholic University of the Sacred Heart
26100 Cremona
Via Milano 24
Piacenza
Italy
Tel: +39 (372) 35972
Fax: +39 (372) 22560

Centre for Construction Market Information
26 Store Street
London WC1E 7BT
United Kingdom
Tel: +44 (171) 580 4949
Fax: +44 (171) 631 0329
Contact: Neil Martin

Collinson Grant Consultants Ltd
Colgran House
20 Worsley Road, Swinton
Manchester M27 5WW
United Kingdom
Tel: +44 (161) 793 9028/36
Fax: +44 (161) 794 0012
Contact: Simon Bates

Confederation of British Industry
Centre Point
103 New Oxford Street
London, WC1A 1DU
Tel: +44 (171) 379 7400
Fax: +44 (171) 240 1578

Confederation of Industry of the Czech Republic
Mrkulandska 7
113 61 Prague 1
Czech Republic
Tel: +42 (2) 2491 5679
Fax: +42 (2) 297 896
Contact: Oldrich Korner

Confederation of Danish Industries
HC Andersens Boulevard 18
DK–1787
Copenhagen V
Denmark
Tel: +45 3377 3377
Fax: +45 3377 3300

Confederation of Finnish Industries
Po Box 30
Fin-00131
Helsinki
Finland
Tel: +358 (0) 68681
Fax: +358 (0) 68682316
Contact: Johannes Koroma

**Confederation of French Industries
and Services**
31, Avenue Pierre 1er De Serbie 15/16
75784 Paris Cedex 16
France
Tel: +33 (1) 40 69 44 44
Fax: +33 (1) 47 23 47 32
Contact: Yves Monier

Confederation of Italian Industry
Confindustria
Viale dell'Astronomia, 30
001144 Rome
Italy
Tel: +39 (6) 59031
Fax: +39 (6) 5919615
Contact: Innocenzo Cipolletta

Confederation of Norwegian Business & Industry
5250 Majorstua
N-0303 Oslo
Norway
Tel: +47 (2) 296 5000
Fax: +41 (2) 296 5593
Contact: Karl Glad

Confederation of Norwegian Business & Industry
Rue Joseph ii, 40 – Bte. 7
B-1040 Bruxelles
Belgium
Tel: +32 (2) 285 05 60
Fax: +32 (2) 285 05 70
Contact: Gry Ulverud

Confederation of Spanish Employers
Diego de Leon, 50
28006 Madrid 6
Spain
Tel: +34 (1) 5639641
Fax: +34 (1) 5628023
Contact: Juan Jimenez Aguilar

Coopers & Lybrand
Plumtree Court
London EC4A 4HT
United Kingdom
Tel: +44 (171) 583 5000
Fax: +44 (171) 212 6366
Contact: G J Squires

Corporate Development Partners
36 Earls Court Square
London SW5 9DQ
United Kingdom
Tel: +44 (171) 370 6939
Fax: +44 (171) 835 2081
Contact: Tim Wood

Deutsche Bank Group
Taunusanlage 12
Frankfurt-Am-Main
D-60325
Germany
Tel: +49 (69) 910 33403
Fax: +49 (69) 910 33422
Contact: Norbert Walter

DTZ Debenham Thorpe
44 Brook Street
London W1A 4AG
United Kingdom
Tel: +44 (171) 408 1161
Fax: +44 (171) 491 4593
Contact: Nick Barnes

Electricity Association
30 Millbank
London SW1P 4RD
United Kingdom
Tel: +44 (171) 963 5700
Fax: +44 (171) 963 5959
Contact: Philip Daubeney

Cypriot Employers & Industrialists Federation
30 Grivas Dhigenis Av.
PO Box 1657
Nicosia
Cyprus
Tel: +357 (2) 445102
Fax: +357 (2) 459459

Edi
148 Buckingham Palace Road
London SW1 9TX
Tel: +44 (171) 824 8848
Fax: +44 (171) 824 8114

Ernst & Young
Becket House
1 Lambeth Palace Road
London SE1 7EU
United Kingdom
Tel: +44 (171) 928 2000
Fax: +44 (171) 928 1345
Contact: John Siraut

Euroconsultants
15 Braxted Park
London, SW16 3DW
United Kingdom
Tel/Fax: +44 (181) 764 40790
Contact: Gerry O'Brien

Eurocost
European Centre for Worldwide Cost of Living
   Comparisons
1 Rue Emile Bian
L-1235, Luxembourg
Tel: +352 40 48 06
Fax: +352 49 57 13
Contact: Steven Evans

European Association of Securities Dealers
Minervastraat 6, Box 2
B-1930 Zaventem
Belgium
Tel: +32 (2) 720 7870
Fax: +32 (2) 720 8306
Contact: Chris Pickles

European Consortium of Management Consultants
Colgran House, 20 Worsley Road, Swinton
Manchester M27 5WW
United Kingdom
Tel: +44 (161) 793 9028/36
Fax: +44 (161) 794 0012
Contact: Simon Bates

**European Interuniversity on Society and
Technology (ESST)**
Ecole Federale de Lausanne
Inr - 112, Epfl - Ecubiens
Ch - 10105 Lausanne, Switzerland
Tel: +41 21 693 71 91
Fax: +41 21 693 71 90
Contact: Derek Smith

European Venture Capital Association
Minverstaat 6, Box 6
1930 Zaventem
Belgium
Tel: +31 (2) 720 6010
Fax: +31 (2) 725 3036
Contact: Denis Mortier

Eurostat
Jean Monnet Building
Plateau du Kirchberg
L-2920
Luxembourg
Contact: Graham Ruddick

Federation of Austrian Industries
Haus der Industrie
A-1031 Vienna
Schwarzenbergplatz, 4
Austria
Tel: +43 (1) 711 350
Fax: +43 (1) 711 352507
Contact: Dr Franz Ceska

Federation of Belgian Companies
Rue Ravenstein 4
B-100 Bruxelles
Belgium
Tel: +32 (2) 5150811
Fax: +32 (2) 5150999
Contact: Tony Vandeputte

Federation of German Industries
Gustav-Heinmann-Ufer 84-88
50968 Cologne (Bayenthal)
Germany
Tel: +49 (221) 37 08 444
Fax: +49 (221) 37 08 790

Federation of Greek Industries
Xenofontos 5
105 57
Athens
Greece
Tel: +30(1)32 37325
Fax: +30(1)32 22929
Contact: G S Argyropoules

Federation of Icelandic Industries
Hallveigarstig 1
121 Reykjavik
Postholf 1450
Iceland
Tel: +354 (1) 27577
Fax: +354 (1) 25380
Contact: Sveinn Hannesson

Federation of Luxembourg Industries
7 rue Alcide de Gasperi
PO Box 1304
1013 Luxembourg
Tel: +352 435366
Fax: +352 432328
Contact: Lucien Jung

**The Federation of Netherlands
Industry (VNONCW)**
Postbus 93093
2509 AB The Hague
The Netherlands
Tel: +46 (8) 783 8000
Fax: +46 (8) 662 3211
Contact: Magnus Lemmel, Dr L. Doorn

Federation of Swedish Industries
Box 5501
S-114 85
Stockholm
Sweden
Tel: +46 (8) 783 8000
Fax: +46 (8) 662 3211
Contact: H Wessberg

**Federation of the Employers' Unions & Associations
of the Slovak Republic**
Drienova 24 826 03 Bratislava
The Slovak Republic
Tel: +42 (71) 379 7400
Fax: +42 (71) 240 1578
Contact: Jozef Horvath

Heronswood Associates
Maidstone Road
Pembury, Tunbridge Wells
Kent TN2 4DD
United Kingdom
Tel: +44 (1892) 822156
Fax: +44 (1892) 823611
Contact: Bruce Ballantine

Hogg Robinson BTI
Abbey House
282 Farnborough Road
Farnborough GU14 7NJ
United Kingdom
Tel: +44 (1252) 372 000
Fax: +44 (1252) 371 200
Contact: Les Middleditch

Hungarian Chamber of Commerce and Industry
1016 Budapest
Krisztina KRT 99
Hungary
Tel/Fax: +361 (156) 9000
Contact: Dr Gyorgy Farkas

IBM UK Ltd
PO Box 31
Birmingham Road
Warwick CV34 5JL
United Kingdom
Tel: +44 (1926) 464000
Fax: +44 (1926) 464620
Contact: Philip Hanson

Irish Business and Employers Federation
Confederation House
84–86 Lower Baggot Street
Dublin 2
Ireland
Tel: +353 (1) 660 1011
Fax: +353 (1) 660 1717
Contact: David Crougan

Jones Lang Wootton
22 Hanover Square
London W1A 2BN
United Kingdom
Tel: +44 (171) 493 6040
Fax: +44 (171) 408 0220
Contact: Simon M Trappes-Lomax

KPMG Management Consulting
PO Box 695
8 Salisbury Square
London EC4Y 8BB
United Kingdom
Tel: +44 (171) 236 8000
Fax: +44 (171) 248 6552
Contact: Charles Thomas, Vicky Pryce

Linguatel
13 City Forum
250 City Road
London EC1V 2I'U
United Kingdom
Tel: +44 (171) 762 6080
Fax: +44 (171) 762 6088
Contact: Faye Gregory

Linklaters & Paines
Rue de Luxembourg 47–51
B-1040 Brussels
Belgium
Tel: +32 (2) 513 7800
Fax: +32 (2) 513 2583
Contact: James Flynn

Lloyd's Register Quality Assurance Ltd
Irqa Ltd
Norfolk House, Wellesley Road
Croydon CR9 2DT
United Kingdom
Tel: +44 (181) 688 6882
Fax: +44 (181) 681 8146
Contact: Linda Campbell

London Business School
Sussex Place
Regents Park
London NW1 4SA
United Kingdom
Tel: +44 (171) 262 5050
Fax: +44 (171) 724 7875
Contact: Chris Voss

Maine Consulting Services
PO Box 73
Blackburn
Lancashire BB2 7BS
United Kingdom
Tel: +44 (1254) 693936
Fax: +44 (1254) 663774
Contact: David Murray

Malta Federation of Industry
Development House
St Anne Street
Floriana VLT 01
Malta
Tel: +356 234428
Fax: +356 240702
Contact: Edwin Calleja

Monks Partnership Ltd
The Mill House
Wendens Ambo, Saffron Walden
Essex CB11 4JX
United Kingdom
Tel: +44 (1799) 542222
Fax: +44 (1799) 541805
Contact: David Atkins

Moscow Narodny Bank Ltd
81 King William Street
London EC4P 4JS
United Kingdom
Tel: +44 (171) 623 2066
Fax: +44 (171) 283 4840
Contact: Paul Forrest

Nabarro Nathanson
50 Stratton Street
London W1X 6NX
United Kingdom
Tel: +44 (171) 493 9933
Fax: +44 (171) 629 7900
Contact: Carl Hopkins

National Economic Research Associates
15 Stratford Place
London W1N 9AF
United Kingdom
Tel: +44 (171) 629 6787
Fax: +44 (171) 408 0211
Contact: Graham Shuttleworth

National Power Plc
Trigonos
Windmill Hill Business Park
Whitehill Way, Swindon
Wiltshire SN5 6PB
United Kingdom
Tel: +44 (1793) 892925
Fax: +44 (1793) 892911

National Exhibition Association
29a Market Square
Biggleswade
Bedfordshire SG18 8AQ
United Kingdom
Tel: +44 (767) 316255
Fax: +44 (767) 316430
Contact: Peter Cotterell

Natwest Group
Ground Floor, 1-2 Broadgate
London EC2M 2AD
United Kingdom
Tel: +44 (171) 714 4400
Fax: +44 (171) 714 4374
Contact: David Kern, Howard Archer

**Nottinghamshire European Textiles and
Clothing Observatory**
Nottingham Trent University
Clifton Lane
Nottingham NG11 8NS
United Kingdom
Tel/Fax: +44 (602) 486610
Contact: Lynn Oxborrow

Oxford Institute of Retailing Management
Templeton College, Kennington
Oxford OX1 5NY
United Kingdom
Tel: +44 (1865) 735422
Fax: +44 (1865) 736374
Contact: Ross Davies

Prime Communications
3 Grosvenor Gardens
London SW1W 0BD
United Kingdom
Tel: +44 (171) 828 6988
Fax: +44 (171) 630 1929

Research International
6–7 Grosvenor Place
London SW1X 7SH
United Kingdom
Tel: +44 (171) 245 1940
Fax: +44 (171) 235 4170
Contact: Mia Bartonova

Romanian Chamber of Commerce and Industry
22 N Balcescu Boulevard
79 502 Bucharest
Romania
Tel: +40 (1) 615 4703
Fax: +40 (1) 312 3830
Contact: Dr A Ghibutu, President

Siddall & Company
16 Tideway Yard
Mortlake High Street
London SW4 8SN
Tel: +44 (181) 878 9144
Fax: +44 (181) 878 4438
Contact: David Blacklock

Siemens Plc
Siemens House
Oldbury, Bracknell
Berkshire RG12 8FZ
United Kingdom
Tel: +44 (1344) 396000
Fax: +44 (1344) 396133
Contact: Dr Heinrich Von Pierer

Simmons & Simmons
21 Wilson Street
London EC2M 2TQ
United Kingdom
Tel: +44 (171) 628 2020
Fax: +44 (171) 628 2070
Contact: Stephen Tromans

South Bank University
Euro-Managers Project
Mayfield Centre, 94 West Hill
London SE15 2UH
United Kingdom
Tel: +44 (171) 928 8989
Fax: +44 (171) 815 6799
Contact: Richard Warren

Spectrum Strategy Consultants Ltd
9 Chester Close
London SW1X 7BE
Tel: +44 (171) 235 0525
Fax: +44 (171) 235 3404

Swiss Federation of Commerce and Industry
Mainaustrasse 49, 690
8034 Zurich
Switzerland
Tel: +41 (1) 382 2323
Fax: +41 (1) 382 2332
Contact: Kurt Moser

Telia International Ltd
114a Cromwell Road
London SW7 4ES
United Kingdom
Tel: +44 (171) 416 0306
Fax: +44 (171) 416 0307
Contact: Paul Morgan

Thomas Cook
Commercial Foreign Exchange
45 Berkeley Street
London W1A 1EB
United Kingdom
Tel: +44 (171) 499 4000
Fax: +44 (171) 408 4507
Contact: Rachel Hoey

Touche Ross & Co
Stonecutter Court
1 Stonecutter Street
London, EC4A 4TR
United Kingdom
Tel: +44 (171) 936 3000
Fax: +44 (171) 583 1198
Contact: Rob Bailey, Kate Seekings, Graham Watson

Towers Perrin
Castlewood House
77–91 New Oxford Street
London WC1A 1PX
United Kingdom
Tel: +44 (171) 379 4411
Fax: +44 (171) 379 7478
Contact: Sylvie Riot

TNT Express
TNT Express House
Abeles Way, Allerstone
Warwickshire CV9 2RY
United Kingdom
Tel: +44 (1827) 303030
Fax: +44 (1827) 301301
Contact: James Wilson

UBS Ltd
100 Liverpool Street
London EC2M 2RH
United Kingdom
Tel: +44 (171) 901 3746
Fax: +44 (171) 901 1910
Contact: Mark Ebert

UNICE
Rue Joseph 11
40-Bte 4
1040 Brussels
Belgium
Tel: +32 (2) 237 6501
Fax: +32 (2) 231 1445
Contact: Zygmunt Tyszkiewicz

Unilever Plc
Unilever House
PO Box 68
Blackfriars
London EC4P 4BQ
United Kingdom
Tel: +44 (171) 822 5252
Fax: +44 (171) 822 5951/5898

Union Bank of Switzerland
Bahnhofstrasse 45
PO Box 8021
Zurich
Switzerland
Tel: +41 (1) 234 3275
Fax: +41 (1) 234 3925
Contact: Mark Ebert

Wavehill Consultants
Docklands Business Centre
10–16 Tiller Road
London E14 8PX
United Kingdom
Tel: +44 (171) 363 6131
Fax: +44 (171) 363 0036
Contact: Richard Brooks

WS Atkins International Ltd
Woodcote Grove
Ashley Road, Epsom
Surrey KT18 5DW
United Kingdom
Tel: +44 (372) 726140
Fax: +44 (372) 740055
Contact: David Howell

Index

Index of Advertisers